An Unappreciated Field of Endeavour

Dedicated to

450488 Sapper Arthur Stanley Hill Royal Engineers

Temporary Second Lieutenant Wilfred James Hill Duke of Cornwall's Light Infantry*

22270 Private Richard Hayden Brown South Wales Borderers

Three soldiers for whom logistics in the Great War were all too real

And in memory of my Father

PJX 762926 Able Seaman Clement Joseph Maginniss Royal Navy

1927-2007

* Died of Wounds on 17 September 1916 after action with the 6th Battalion at Flers-Courcelette on 15 September 1916.

An Unappreciated Field of Endeavour is not a comprehensive examination of British Expeditionary Force (BEF) logistics on the Western Front, nor indeed a short history. To achieve the former would involve several volumes and the latter would omit much fascinating detail. It does however bring a new and fresh perspective by analysing, in a series of engaging essays, the critical contribution of particular components of military and commercial logistics to the preparations and operations of the British and Empire Armies in the pre-war period and during the Great War on the Western Front, through the lens of specific elements and themes, each of which, cast penetrating light into dark corners of an important, yet mainly forgotten story.

The author explains how pre-war strategic, economic, political and defence dynamics constrained military logistic resilience but influenced the plans to rely upon commercial assets to support military and naval operations, before examining the role of the commercial railways and mercantile marine in the planning, preparation and execution of Defence mobilization and movement in the United Kingdom during Transition To War in 1914. The role of British railways in playing a defining part in a critical moment of European history is explored in depth as are the technical processes and managerial interfaces that enabled them. The contribution of British commercial and business leaders and managers to enhancing the combat capability of the BEF is examined through the lens of the increasing industrialization of logistic support to operations. In particular, the influence of commercial practice in improving military logistic efficiency and effectiveness, whilst also subtly changing military culture is matched to the dynamics and frictions of employing commercial logistic advisers in the operational environment of the Western Front.

Whilst, the exploits of the combat elements of the BEF in 1914 have been analysed in depth, the contribution of the logisticians who kept the BEF in the fight has effectively marched into the mists of time. *An Unappreciated Field of Endeavour* explores the success of the BEF's Quartermaster-General, Wully Robertson, in utilizing the skill of his logistic planners and soldiers to deliver the agile operational logistic capability that was the salvation of the BEF in 1914. Also examined, is the long forgotten but extraordinary logistic feat of deploying Indian Expeditionary Force A to France, through the mobilization and transportation of its soldiers across deserts and oceans before its complex logistic integration to the BEF in France. The solutions to the challenges in executing these operations by military and civilian logisticians from Britain, France and India, offer unusual insights into Coalition co-operation from three culturally diverse countries.

Rarely studied, logistic planning, resources and execution played a crucial role in the preparations for the Battle of the Somme. These important aspects are analysed to highlight a developing capability, through the process of 'logistic learning steps' of which, were of at least equal significance to those in the operational and tactical environments. The influence of the BEF's Wheeled Motor Transport (WMT) component upon the operational art on the Western Front is reviewed, including its impact upon the deployment and employment of armour, infantry, artillery and aviation. These were all affected by the expanding use of WMT, creating a requirement to improve its efficiency and effectiveness. Logistics were fundamental to the use of tanks in the Great War, an aspect comprehensively examined, to assess how transportation in particular, constrained the development of operational deployments. *An Unappreciated Field of Endeavour* also analyses how, in 1918, the BEF's logisticians were able to generate the capability to sustain All-Arms mobile three dimensional combat operations in a chemical warfare environment, whilst maintaining the momentum of the advance, having focused mainly upon supporting siege warfare for the previous four years.

The corporate memory of the commercial aspect is even more faded than the military one but it was an essential component of the British and Empire endeavours on the Western Front and is lucidly exposed. The combined military and commercial story has many facets: innovative people, constant training, emerging technology, developing doctrine, fresh ideas, new equipment, maturing experience, complex planning, increasing mechanization and relentless industry. This study draws these threads from the bobbins to weave a colourful pattern of achievement, whilst illustrating how logistics evolved to overcome complex challenges and in doing so, transformed operations, creating a Great War legacy that links to defence logistics in the 21st Century, particularly in the expanding arena of contractor support to operations.

Logistics however, do not swim alone in the military pond. At the operational level, the role of logistics is to develop, sustain and regenerate combat power to ensure that the tempo and effectiveness of the operations maintain momentum. Equally, logistics places constraints on strategy and tactics. On the Western Front, the BEF's enormous logistic capability was not an end in itself but a vital means to achieve the military aim, an observation as valid today as it was in 1918. Great War military logistics, not generally perceived to be racy, has, for far too long, held its light behind a bushel, its practitioners, from General to Private, long gone and the experiences they had and lessons they learnt, lying in dusty volumes in archives and libraries. *An Unappreciated Field of Endeavour* brings their important work to life, whilst assessing the significant aspects and identifying relevant lessons for military logistics in the 21st Century.

Clem Maginniss was born in Coventry and educated at Ratcliffe College Leicester and at the Royal Military Academy Sandhurst, and holds a Bachelor of Arts in Modern European History and International Relations from the University of Warwick. He served for 40 years in the Regular Army, the Territorial Army and the Army Reserve, first in the Royal Corps of Transport and then the Royal Logistic Corps. A graduate of the Army Staff College Camberley, he has held a range of fascinating National, NATO and United Nations appointments involving mobilization planning, railway operations, medical logistics, combat engineer support, tank transporting, officer training, flood relief, infrastructure development, estate management, humanitarian assistance and the Foreign Office. He has written extensively for the British Army Review and the Royal Logistic Corps Review on logistic history, doctrine, operations and equipment but *An Unappreciated Field of Endeavour* is his first book. His interests are Great and Second World War military and naval logistics, underwater exploration, ship-wreck research, defence archaeology, railway heritage, keeping fit and a range of outdoor pursuits. He lives in Norfolk with his wife Edwina.

An Unappreciated Field of Endeavour

Logistics and the British Expeditionary Force on the Western Front 1914-1918

Clem Maginniss

Helion & Company

Helion & Company Limited
Unit 8 Amherst Business Centre
Budbrooke Road
Warwick
CV34 5WE
England
Tel. 01926 499 619
Email: info@helion.co.uk
Website: www.helion.co.uk
Twitter: @helionbooks

Published by Helion & Company 2018. Reprinted in paperback 2020
Designed and typeset by Battlefield Design (www.battlefield-design.co.uk)
Cover designed by Paul Hewitt, Battlefield Design (www.battlefield-design.co.uk)

ISBN 978-1-913118-29-7

British Library Cataloguing-in-Publication Data.
A catalogue record for this book is available from the British Library.

Contents

List of Photographs

List of Maps & Diagrams

Plate Section

Diagrams

Maps

Map Symbols

Unit and Formation Map Symbols

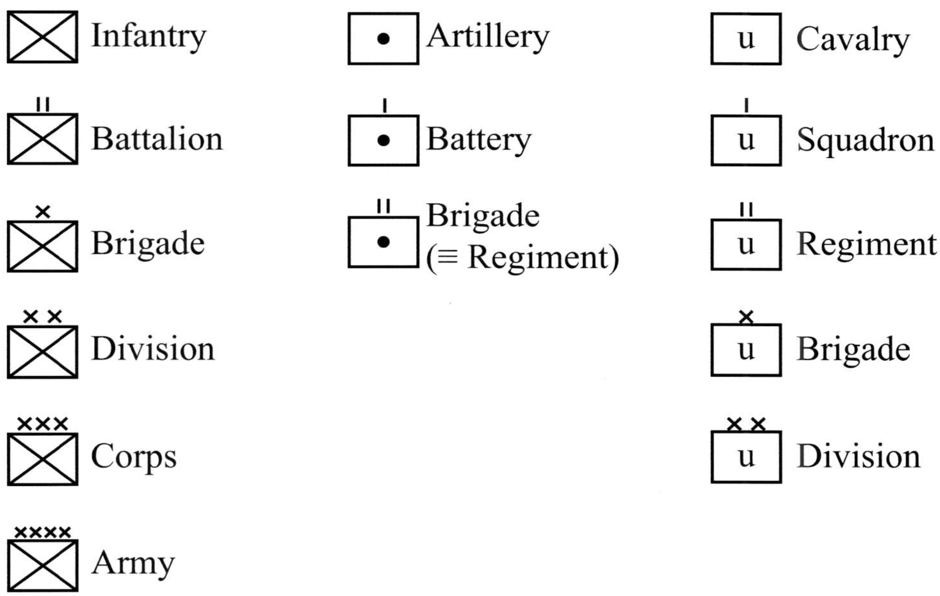

List of Tables

List of Abbreviations

AA	Anti-Aircraft (or Automobile Association)
AAA	Anti-Aircraft Artillery
AAM	Annual Army Manoeuvres
AA&QMG	Assistant Adjutant & Quartermaster-General
AAR	After Action Report
ADOS	Assistant Director Ordnance Services
ADRT	Assistant Director Railway Transport
AFV	Armoured Fighting Vehicle
AG	Adjutant General
AHQ	Army Headquarters
AMD	Army Medical Directorate
AMR	Army Motor Reserve
AOC	Army Ordnance Corps (or Auxiliary Omnibus Company)
AOD	Army Ordnance Department
AOO	Area of Operations
AOP	Auxiliary Omnibus Park
AOR	Area of Responsibility
APC	Armoured Personnel Carrier
AQMG	Assistant Quartermaster General
ARH	Ammunition Railhead
ARO	Army Routine Order
ARRV	Armoured Repair and Recovery Vehicle
ASC	Army Service Corps
ASD	Advanced Supply Depot
AT	Animal Transport
ATC	Annual Training Camp
ATR	Ambulance Train Railhead
BAC	Brigade Ammunition Column
BAD	Base Ammunition Depot
BAOR	British Army of the Rhine
BDA	Brechot-Desprez-Ameline (Medical Stretcher Frame)
BEF	British Expeditionary Force
BMTD	Base Mechanical Transport Depot
BSC	Brigade Supply Column
BSD	Base Supply Depot
CASEVAC	Casualty Evacuation
CCS	Casualty Clearing Station
CE	Combat Effectiveness
CF	Central Force

CGS	Chief of the General Staff
CHE	Container Handling Equipment
CID	Committee of Imperial Defence
CLC	Chinese Labour Corps
CO	Commanding Officer
COG	Centre of Gravity
COW	Coventry Ordnance Works
CPE	Collective Protective Equipment
CRE	Commander Royal Engineers
CSO	Contractor Support to Operations
CSS	Combat Service Support
CST	Combat Support Tanker
CW	Chemical Warfare
CWGC	Commonwealth War Graves Commission
DAA&QMG	Deputy Assistant Adjutant & Quartermaster-General
DAC	Divisional Ammunition Column
DADOS	Deputy Assistant Director Ordnance Services
DADMS	Deputy Assistant Director Medical Services
DAM	Delayed Action Mine
DCM	Distinguished Conduct Medal
DDGMS	Deputy Director General Medical Services
DDMS	Deputy Director Medical Services
DDOS	Deputy Director Ordnance Services
DDST	Deputy Director Supplied & Transport
DGMS	Director General Medical Services
DLK	*Deutsche Luftstreitkrafte*
DMO	Director Military Operations
DMS	Director Medical Services
DOAST	Desired Order of Arrival Staff Table
DOT	Direction of Travel
DQUAD	Destination, Demand, Distance and Duration.
DNI	Director Naval Intelligence
DR	Despatch Rider
DRP	Divisional Refilling Point
DSC	Divisional Supply Column
DSO	Distinguished Service Order
EAA	Elvedon Explosives Area
ECM	*En-cas mobile*
EF	Expeditionary Force
FPO	Field Post Office
FSD	Forward Supply Depot
FSR	Field Service Regulations
FV	Fighting Vehicle
GCR	Great Central Railway
GDP	Gross Domestic Product
GDS	Garrison Duty Station

GER	Great Eastern Railway
GF	Ground Forces
GHQ	General Headquarters
GM	Ground Manoeuvre
GMT	Greenwich Mean Time (ZULU time zone)
GNR	Great Northern Railway
GOC	General Officer Commanding
GPV	Gun Powder Van
GS	General Staff (or General Service)
GSE	Ground Support Equipment
GW	Gas Warfare
GWR	Great Western Railway
HD	Home Defence
HDF	Home Defence Forces
HDP	Home Defence Plan
HDS	Home Defence Station
HDU	Home Defence Unit
HE	High Explosive
HMLC	High Mobility Load Carrier
HMNB	His Majesty's Naval Base
HN	Host Nation
HNS	Host Nation Support
HOS	Head of Steel
HQ	Headquarters
HT	Horse Transport
IAB	Indian Administrative Base
ICE	Internal Combustion Engine
IED	Improvised Explosive Device
IEF	Indian Expeditionary Force
IFV	Infantry Fighting Vehicle
IGC	Inspector General Communications
IOD	Indian Ordnance Department
IOO	Inspecting Ordnance Officer
IWT	Inland Water Transport
KLI	Key Lesson (s) Identified
KLM	*Kaiserliche Marine* (German Imperial Navy)
KP	Key Point (s)
LBSCR	London Brighton & South Coast Railway
LF	Local Forces
LMG	Light Machine Gun
LMLC	Low Mobility Load Carrier
LMR	Longmoor Military Railway
LNWR	London & North Western Railway
LOC	Line of Communication
LRW	Locally Recruited Worker (s)
LS	Logistic Support

LSI	Large Scale Intervention
LSWR	London & South Western Railway
LXP	Logistic Exchange Point
MAC	Motor Ambulance Convoy
MBA	Main Base Area
MBT	Main Battle Tank
MC	Movement Control (or Military Cross)
MCO	Major Combat Operations
MEDEVAC	Medical Evacuation
MEDLOC	Mediterranean Line of Communication
MG	Machine Gun
MGC	Machine Gun Corps
MGNR	Midland & Great Northern Railway
MHE	Material Handling Equipment
MLO	Military Landing Officer
MM	Military Medal
MMG	Medium Machine Gun
MMLC	Medium Mobility Load Carrier
MOD	Ministry of Defence
MR	Midland Railway
MSR	Main Supply Route
MSWJR	Midland & South Western Junction Railway
MT	Mechanical Transport
MTC	Mechanical Transport Committee
MTF	Medical Treatment Facility
NATO	North Atlantic Treaty Organization
NDTO	Naval Divisional Transport Officer
NRN	National Rail Network
NTM	Notice To Move
OC	Officer Commanding
OOG	Out of Gauge
ORBAT	Order of Battle
OS	Ordnance Survey
PAT	Permanent Ambulance Train
PE	Peace Establishment
POL	Petroleum Oils & Lubricants
POW	Private Owner Wagon (or Prisoner of War)
PPE	Personal Protective Equipment
psc	Passed Staff College
PUP	Pick Up Point
PW	Permanent Way
QMAAC	Queen Mary's Army Auxiliary Corps
QMG	Quartermaster-General
RAF	Royal Air Force
RAMV	Reserves Accountability Mobility Visibility
RASC	Royal Army Service Corps

RCT	Royal Corps of Transport
RE	Royal Engineers
REC	Railway Executive Committee
RFC	Royal Flying Corps
RH	Railhead
RHA	Royal Horse Artillery
RHQ	Regimental Headquarters
RLC	Royal Logistic Corps
RMN	Rail Movement Number
RMS	Royal Mail Ship
RN	Royal Navy
RNAS	Royal Naval Air Service
RNOD	Royal Naval Ordnance Depot
RNVR	Royal Naval Volunteer Reserve
ROD	Railway Operating Division
ROO	Railhead Ordnance Officer
rpg	rounds per gun
RSD	Railhead Supply Detachment
RSMOI	Reception Staging Onward Movement & Integration
RSO	Railhead Supply Officer
RTC	Rail Tank Car
RTO	Railway Transport Officer
RWS	Ramp Wagon System
SAA	Small Arms Ammunition
SBR	Small Box Respirator
SECR	South Eastern & Chatham Railways
SEP	South East Ports
SFC	Single Fuel Concept
SITREP	Situation Report
SLOC	Sea Line of Communication
SMLE	Short Magazine Lee Enfield
SOP	Standard Operating Procedure
SPG	Self Propelled Gun
SPOD	Sea Port of Disembarkation
SPOE	Sea Port of Embarkation
SR	Special Reserve
SRD	Supply Reserve Depot
SRH	Supply Railhead
SS	Screw Steamer or Steam Ship
SSD	Supply Sub-Depot
STUFT	Ship Taken Up From Trade
TAT	Temporary Ambulance Train
TCL	Troop Carrying Lorry
TF	Territorial Force
TNA	The National Archives (UK)
TRH	Tank Railhead

TRW	Tank Ramp Wagon
TSI	*Train Sanitaire Improvise* (Improvised Ambulance Train)
TTF	Truck Tanker Fuel
TTW	Transition To War
UKOS	United Kingdom Ordnance Survey
UOR	Urgent Operational Requirement
WAAC	Women's Auxiliary Army Corps
WD	War Diary
WE	War Establishment
WF	With France (Plan) also Wilson-Foch (Plan)
WMT	Wheeled Motor Transport
WO	War Office
WOAT	War Office Ambulance Train

Nomenclature

Formations and Units. The nomenclature used in the *History of the Great War, Military Operations France and Belgium*, has been utilized throughout the work, except where contemporary document references are quoted and are different. Examples shown:

Army – spelled in full: Fourth Army

Corps – Roman numerals: III Corps

Division – number: 8th Division

Brigade (Cavalry & Infantry) – number: 25th Brigade

Brigade (Artillery, RFC or Tank) – Roman numerals: V Tank Brigade

Units (Cavalry & Infantry) – by number and title: 10th Hussars or 5th Norfolks

Units (Artillery Battery) – Roman numeral and title: XV (Howitzer) Battery

Units – (Engineer & Logistics) – number and title: 180 Mechanical Transport Company

RAF Squadron – by number and title: 218 (Bomber) Squadron

Nationality – assumed to be British unless noted: 1st (Australian) Division.

Formations. In the text, formations are described in full, for example 6th Division. In the tables and maps, symbology is used to create clarity. Army is thus shown as XXXX; Corps, XXX; Division, XX and Brigade, X

Ranks. During the Great War, hyphens were used in specific ranks, for example Brigadier-General.[1] This convention has been used in the work, except in reference to recent authors or where the contemporary document differs from it.

British Official History of the Great War. To improve clarity and to reduce the length of the text, the British Official History, History of the Great War, is abbreviated to BOH (British Official

1 The rank of Brigadier-General was abolished in the British Army in 1921, being replaced with the appointments of Colonel-Commandant and Colonel on the Staff, indicating the appointee was more a Senior Colonel and less a Junior General. Brigadier was created on 1 June 1928 to replace Colonel-Commandant and Colonel on the Staff but remained an appointment until 1 November 1947 when it became a rank.

History) in the Notes and Sources.

Ministry of Munitions. *The Official History of The Ministry of Munitions*, Volumes I-XII, HMSO, 1922; reprinted by Uckfield: Naval & Military Press, in 2008. Abbreviated to MOM in Notes and Sources.

Statistics of the Military Effort of the British Empire during the Great War, 1914-1920. This document, compiled by the War Office, was published by HMSO in 1922 and is abbreviated to MEBE in Notes and Sources.

Publication location. Official Publications that were not intended for public purchase or access are not ascribed a Place of Publication. These documents were almost exclusively published under the auspices of HMSO or the War Office.

Glossary

* Logistic terms imported from the French Army

Adjutant & Quartermaster-General. The overarching term, usually abbreviated to A&Q, used by the British Army in the Great War, to define those activities, which provided support to combat forces in the fields of administration and logistics. In the 21st Century these activities are described as Combat Service Support (CSS) and comprise Logistic Support, Equipment Support, Medical Support[1], Administrative Support and Logistic Engineering.

Advanced Base. An area within which, may be situated, the advanced depots of ammunition, supplies, animals and material, from which, issues are made to field units.

Air Interdiction. Air Interdiction (AI) is an air operation conducted to destroy, neutralize or delay the enemy's military potential, before it can be brought to bear effectively against friendly forces at such a distance from friendly forces, that detailed integration of each air mission with the fire and movement of friendly forces is not required.[2]

Battlefield Clearance. The removal of all military materiel, including enemy, from the field of battle, inclusive of human remains, munitions, fuel, vehicles, equipment and supplies.

Base. A place where the Line of Communication originates, Theatre materiel is held and where the principal business of supplying the forces in the field is located.

Broad Gauge Railway. A railway with a track gauge greater than 4 feet 8 ½ inches (1435mm). Used incorrectly, in some documents and publications, to refer to Standard Gauge.

Casualty Evacuation (CASEVAC). The movement of any person who is wounded, injured or sick to, from, or between Medical Treatment Facilities (MTF) without specialist medical control during transit.

Close Air Support. Close Air Support (CAS) is air action against hostile targets, which are in close proximity to friendly forces and which, require detailed integration of each air mission with the fire and movement of those forces. [3]

1 Health Service Support (HSS) is also a term that is used to describe this function, being defined as: a single, integrated system, consisting of all services performed, provided, or arranged to promote, improve, conserve, or restore the mental and physical well-being of personnel in the Army and, as directed, for other services, agencies, and organizations.

2 *Air Publication (AP) 3000, British Air Power Doctrine*, 3rd Edition, Directorate of Air Staff (UK MOD, 1999), p.3.13.2.

3 Ibid, p.3.13.1.

Combat Supplies. Combat Supplies are ammunition, POL and rations. Although the modern term Combat Supplies was not current in the British Army during the Great War, it neatly summarizes the items that were the most important in delivering direct military effect in the front-line. Ammunition included, in the Great War context, small arms and artillery ammunition, specialized infantry natures, chemical weapons and explosives. POL covered all liquids fuels, lubricants (oils and greases) and antifreeze. Rations included food for personnel and forage for animals, plus disinfectants and water purification chemicals.

Consist. The composition of a train, by wagon or coach, with the designation starting at the locomotive and ending at the brake van.

Courant* (stream). A continuous flow of empty trains to entraining stations, of loaded trains from them to the detraining stations, and of empty trains recovering to the entraining stations.

Cross-load. To transfer a consignment of materiel or material from one asset to another, within the same transportation mode.

Dump. A temporary storage area, usually in the open, for munitions, equipment, or supplies. A dump would have minimal security and possibly no dedicated technical manpower presence.

Economy Cost. *Measuring Worth UK* defines the Economy Cost of a project being measured using the relative share of the project as a percentage of the output of the economy. This measure indicates the opportunity cost in terms of the total output of the economy. The perspective is the importance of the item to society as a whole, and the measure is the most inclusive. This measure uses the share of Gross Domestic Product (GDP).

En-cas mobile.* (movable if necessary). A group of railway wagons, a barge, or other conveyance, kept permanently under load ready for immediate despatch on an emergency.

Equipment Support. Equipment Support (ES) includes the preparation and repair of equipment for battle and the repair and recovery of equipment battle casualties and failures. The ES staffs have a vital role in monitoring the serviceability of critical equipments in a formation to ensure that combat power is maintained.[4]

Equipment Support Management. A key component of ES is Equipment Support Management (ESM) which is the process of controlling the allocation, repair policy, refurbishment, redesign and replacement of, and re-supply of material for, equipment throughout its service life.[5]

Head of Steel. The furthest point on the Permanent Way (PW) to which, regular railway services could be conducted, although this point was not necessarily a railhead. Beyond the *Head of Steel* there might be another 10-12 miles of track under construction, which could support the operation of slow moving engineer trains loaded with railway material, ballast and water.

4 *Army Field Manual* (AFM) Vol. 1, *Combined Arms Operations*, Part 6, *Combat Service Support*, DGD&D 18/34/44, Army Code No 71344 (UK MOD, 1998), p.viii.

5 Ar*my Doctrine Publication* (ADP) Vol. 3, *Logistics*, DGD&D/18/34/63, Army Code No 71566 (UK MOD, 1996), p.xiii.

Labour Earnings. *Measuring Worth UK* defines Labour Earnings as the measure of the amount of income or wealth, relative to the earnings of an average worker.

Light Railway. There is no official international definition of a 'Light' Railway but it may be described as a one which is constructed to a lesser standard than that required for main or branch line operations; it may be broad, standard, or narrow gauge. Many documents, including those in War Office files of the period, refer to Narrow Gauge Railways (NGRs) as Light Railways, which, whilst not inaccurate, is not definitively correct. Confusingly, others call 60 centimetre gauge Light but not the Metre Gauge, which is referred to separately. Many of the Standard Gauge Railways (SGR) built for the BEF on the Western Front would be described as Light.[6]

Lines of Communication. The system of communication on land by rail, road and navigable waterways between the army and its base or bases, including the district through, which they pass, within allocated boundaries. There were also Sea Lines of Communication from the Home Bases of the United Kingdom and the Empire to the Theatres of Operations.

Lines of Support. Lines of Support are used to describe the boundaries of specific elements of logistic functions. Lines of Support was a term in use during the Great War appearing in various logistic publications and is a simple method of assigning capability to units and formations.

1st Line - organic to a unit.

2nd Line - organic to a brigade or division.

3rd Line - allocated to Corps or Army.

4th Line - provided by the Base. For the BEF, 4th Line was delivered in-Theatre and from the United Kingdom, although elements for the Indian Expeditionary Force A were supported from India.

Logistic Support. Transportation (sea, rail, air and road movement) Inland Water Transport (IWT) port operations supply, distribution, labour, food services and postal services.

Maintain. To take supply and repair action, in order to keep a force in a condition to conduct its mission.

Manoeuvre. The British Army describes 'Manoeuvre' as the employment of forces on the battlefield (using movement) in combination with fire or fire potential, to achieve a position of advantage in respect to the opposition in order to accomplish the mission.[7]

Material. Raw or semi-finished products required by the military forces in the field to conduct operations.

6 For a technical description and short history of Light Railways, see, *The Oxford Companion to British Railway History* (Oxford & New York: Oxford University Press, 1997), pp.263-265.

7 *Army Doctrine Publication* (ADP) Volume 1, *Operations*, HQDT/18/34/46, Army Code No 71565 (UK MOD, 1994), pp.3-17 to 3-19.

Materiel. From the French, materiel is a generic term applied to finished military products such as ammunition, equipment, stores, supplies and vehicles, although sometimes used to cover materials.

Mechanical Transport. Wheeled, tracked, or semi-tracked land vehicle utilised in a logistic context to move men and materiel to, on or from the battlefield and powered by the Internal Combustion Engine (ICE) either Spark Ignition (SI) or Compression Ignition (CI) fuelled by petroleum spirit or diesel oil respectively, or by steam (Steam Transport (ST)). Often abbreviated to MT, it does not include combat vehicles, such as tanks, Armoured Personnel Carriers (APC) or Self-Propelled Guns (SPG). Motor Transport (MT) included Wheeled or tracked or semi-tracked land logistic vehicle powered by the ICE but to provide specific clarification for wheeled vehicles, the term Wheeled Motor Transport (WMT) is used.

Medical Evacuation (MEDEVAC). The medically controlled process of moving any person, who is wounded, injured or sick to, from, or between Medical Treatment Facilities (MTF).

Narrow Gauge Railway. A railway with a track gauge of less than 4 feet 8 ½ inches (1435mm).

Navette** (shuttle). Applied to trains, which run backwards and forwards between two definite points with no alteration of the vehicles composing the train.

Permanent Way. Permanent Way (PW) is a 19th Century term, often abbreviated to PWay, which encapsulates all the guidance and support systems for the railway. This includes the rails, sleepers, ballast, blanketing and drainage. In the Victorian period, PW referred to the completed works, whilst the Temporary Way was the track laid to assist in the construction of the PW.

Railhead. A place on a railway, where transhipment to another mode of transport, usually WMT or HT, takes place. Sometimes specifically defined as the furthest point forward in military operations that materiel is delivered by rail. The *Field Service Pocket Book* of 1914 defines a railhead as a locality on the railway where ammunition and supplies are transferred to ammunition parks and supply columns.[8]

Rail Regulating Station. A place where railway trains are marshalled, and whence they are despatched to railheads.

Rame.* A group of coupled wagons, not necessarily of the same type, deemed either to be ready for movement or for future tasking. Also known as a Rake.

Refilling Point. A place where divisional ammunition columns and supply sections of divisional trains are refilled from ammunition parks and supply columns, respectively.

Rendezvous.* A place where supply columns or ammunition columns are met by representatives of the headquarters concerned, and directed to Refilling Points.

Reverse Logistics. Operations related to the reuse of products and materials, by moving them from their typical final destination of use for the purpose of capturing value or proper disposal.

8 General Staff, *Field Service Pocket Book*, War Office (London: HMSO, 1914), p.xi.

Rocade* (from castling in chess). Lateral movements of troops or other traffic behind the front to, distinguish them from movements to or from the front.

Roulement* (rolling or rumbling). The continuous flow of troop trains arising from the incessant movements of troops by rail for strategic concentrations or reliefs.

Set. Usually a complete train, including locomotive and wagons or coaching stock, or a mix of both, assembled to undertake a rail movement task. A 'Set' was usually associated with a recurring task.

Shipping Tonnage. Net Registered Tonnage (NRT) is the ship's cargo volume capacity, in register tons, one of which, is equivalent to a volume of 100 cubic feet (2.83m^3). It is calculated by subtracting non-revenue earning spaces such as the engine room and boiler spaces, fuel bunkers and crew quarters, from the ship's Gross Registered Tonnage (GRT). NRT is not a measure of the ship's weight or cargo. GRT is the measurement of the total internal volume of a vessel. Dead Weight Tonnage is the total weight of cargo stores and fuel carried by a vessel at her maximum permitted draught.[9]

Standard Gauge Railway (SGR). A railway which, had a track gauge of 4 feet 8 ½ inches (1435mm). In 2018, Standard Gauge is rated between 1432 mm and 1435mm to account for those SGRs, which have been reduced in gauge by 3 mm, to improve the ride of high-speed trains. In some documents and publications, SGR is described as Broad Gauge, which is technically incorrect but was a term used by some personnel in the BEF and appears in contemporary documents.

Supplies. Food, forage, fuel, light and disinfectants.

Sustain. Maintain the necessary levels of combat power for the duration required to achieve assigned objectives.

Theatre of Operations. The whole area of land or sea in which, fighting may be expected, or in which, the movements of troops and materiel are liable to interruption or interference by the enemy.

Track Gauge. The Track Gauge on a railway is the distance between the inside edges of the heads of the two rails, measured just below the running surface, the corners of which are rounded.

Train. (Other than the railway). Transport (usually HT) allotted to fighting units for the conveyance of their baggage, stores and supplies necessary for their subsistence.

Tranship. To transfer a consignment of materiel from one mode of transportation, to another.

Transportation. In the context of the Great War on the Western Front, transport by rail (SGR and NGR) Inland Water Transport (IWT) docks and the supporting movement control organizations.

Unit Echelons. Whilst the British Army is constantly reorganizing and re-equipping, the concept

9 See, *Dictionary of Nautical Words and Terms*, C W T Layton (Glasgow: Brown, Son & Ferguson, 1955).

of the unit echelon system has stood the test of time remarkably well, although the composition and nomenclature have varied over the years. The F Echelon contains the fighting forces, inclusive of personnel, weapons, vehicles and the allocated Combat Service Support (CSS), such as ES and Medical. A1, the first Administrative Echelon is designed to provide immediate CSS to fighting capability and usually includes reserves of Combat Supplies and some ES. A2, the second Administrative Echelon, contains technical stores and some ES and the Regimental Aid Post (RAP) may be in the battle-space. The B Echelon holds the non-urgent capabilities, such as clothing, stores, administrative staff; unit B Echelons were often grouped at brigade level. In the Great War on the Western Front, A1 and A2 is often identified as the 1st Line Regimental Transport and Trench Dumps, whilst the B Echelon is the Quartermaster's Store.

Denomination of Quantity

Most military logisticians will have suffered that sinking feeling when the Regimental Quartermaster discovers that someone has ordered ten pallets of Rolls, Toilet, White, 10, instead of ten packs of the said item. The British Army of the Great War had a bewildering array of Denomination of Quantity (D of Q)[1] a selection of which, is shown below:

Item	DofQ	Remarks
Ale	Butt	108 gallons
Ale	Hogshead	54 gallons
Ammunition, SAA, 0.303 inch	Box, 1000 rounds	Weight: 80 lb 8oz
Ammunition, SAA, Pistol, 0.455 inch	Box, 276 rounds	23 bundles of 12 rounds
Ammunition, 18 pdr, QF	Box, 4 rounds	
Blankets	Bale of 25	Weight: 112lb 8 oz
Boots	Case of 45	
Biscuits	Case, 50 rations	Weight: 70-75 lbs
Butter	Barrel	Weight: 224 lbs
Butter	Firkin	Weight: 56 lbs
Butter	Tub	Weight: 84 lbs
Coal	Sack	Weight: 224 lbs
Dressings, Field	Case of 500	
Flour	Sack	Weight: 280 lbs
Gunpowder	Barrel	Weight: 100 lbs
Kettles, Camp	Cradle of 5	
Mealies (Crushed)	Muid	Weight: 200 lbs
Mealies (Whole)	Muid	Weight: 196 lbs
Potatoes	Sack	Weight: 168 lbs
Raisons	Barrel	Weight: 112 lbs
Sheets, Ground	Case of 60	
Straw	Truss	Weight: 36 lbs
Tea	Chest	Weight: 84 lbs

1 Information extracted from the General Staff, *Field Service Pocket Book, 1914*, War Office (London: HMSO, 1914) and Army Council, *Army Service Corps*, Part II, *Supplies*, War Office (London: HMSO, 1909) (Reprinted 1914 with new Appx XII).

Logistics: Definitions and Applications

Logistics is a simple word but covers a most complex military subject. The Concise Oxford Dictionary,[1] defines logistics as the 'Art of moving & quartering troops & supplying and maintaining a fleet' and the Oxford Reference Dictionary, 'the art of supplying and organizing (orig military) services and equipment'.[2] Jomini described logistics as 'the practical art of moving armies', 'providing for the successive arrival of convoys and supplies' and 'establishing and organizing lines of supplies'.[3] The British Army has defined logistics as: 'The science of planning and carrying out the movement and maintenance of forces.[4] In its most comprehensive sense, logistics covers those aspects of military operations which, deal with:

> Design and development, acquisition, storage, transport, distribution, maintenance, evacuation and disposition of materiel.
>
> Transportation of personnel.
>
> Acquisition or construction, maintenance, operation and disposition of facilities.
>
> Acquisition or furnishing of services.
>
> Medical and health service support.

This definition of logistics encompasses the broad range of sustainment activity, from production to consumption, movement, deployment and withdrawal. It includes medical support and in a wider sense, the personnel services required to support the moral component of fighting power, thereby having a closer association to the term Administration,[5] which was the term in use in the British Army throughout most of the 20th Century until it became more closely associated with the processes of management. Since the 1990s, the British Army has utilized the term, Combat Service Support (CSS) to describe the key logistic functions[6] in combat:[7]

1 H W Fowler and F G Fowler (Eds.), *The Concise Oxford Dictionary of Current English*, Fifth Edition (Oxford: Clarendon Press, 1964).

2 Joyce M Hawkins (Ed.), *The Oxford Reference Dictionary* (Oxford: Clarendon Press, 1986).

3 A H Jomini, *The Art of War* (Philadelphia, 1873), p.225.

4 *Army Doctrine Publication* (ADP) Vol. 3, *Logistics*, DGD&D/18/34/63, Army Code No 71566 (UK MOD, 1996), p.ix. The definition is based upon a NATO one.

5 General Staff, *Field Service Regulations*, Part II, *Organization and Administration*, War Office (London: HMSO, 1909) and Administration in the Field, A26/GSTP/3351, Army Code No 71024 (UK MOD, 1975).

6 To enable commanders to judge the competency of logistic plans, the British Army has Five Principles of Logistics: Foresight, Economy, Simplicity, Co-operation and Flexibility. ADP, Vol. 3, pp.1-4 to 1-6.

7 *Army Field Manual* (AFM) Vol. 1, *Combined Arms Operations*, Part 6, *Combat Service Support*, DGD&D 18/34/44, Army Code No 71344 (UK MOD, 1998).

Logistic Support. Supply, distribution, transportation (road, rail, docks, Air Despatch (AD) Inland Water Transport (IWT) and Movement Control (MC)) Food Services, Labour Support and Postal & Courier (P&C). Delivered through the Royal Logistic Corps (RLC) formed in 1993 from the Royal Corps of Transport, the Royal Army Ordnance Corps (RAOC) the Army Catering Corps (ACC) the Royal Pioneer Corps (RPC) the Postal Section of the Royal Engineers (RE).

Equipment Support. Preparation and repair of equipment for battle and the recovery and repair of equipment battle casualties. Delivered through the Royal Electrical and Mechanical Engineers (REME) formed in 1942.

Medical Support.[8] Prevention of disease, treatment, evacuation, medical supply and veterinary services. Delivered through the Army Medical Services (AMS): Royal Army Medical Corps (RAMC) Queen Alexander's Royal Army Nursing Corps (QARANC) the Royal Army Dental Corps (RADC) and the Royal Army Veterinary Corps (RAVC).

Administrative Support. Mostly delivered through the Adjutant General's Corps (AGC) formed in 1992, and those staff from across the Army, serving in Headquarters. Provost Support, delivered by the Royal Military Police (RMP) seeks to prevent crime, restore and maintain order, control road routes, traffic, stragglers and refugee and process captured persons; Personnel Support includes the provision of reinforcements, tracking of casualties, care of the battlefield dead, legal, finance and soldiers' welfare.

Logistic Engineering. The provision and maintenance of essential infrastructure, including water supply, power, roads, railways, docks, hardened shelters, airfields, camps, hospitals and storage sites to an appropriate standard, in order that logistic activity can effectively and efficiently sustain the components of the deployed force. These tasks are delivered by the Royal Engineers, with the assistance, if required, of contractors.

There are of course overlaps and interfaces. Whilst the delivery of soldiers' mail is a Logistic Support activity, any failure of the system becomes a welfare issue for Administrative Support. A failure of Provost to control traffic on a route could require intervention from Equipment Support assets for recovery, repair by Logistic Engineering and in the meantime, a reduction in Logistic Support output. A current theme is the increasing use of contractors in the Logistic Support, Logistic Engineering and Equipment Support arenas, which is also a forgotten feature of the BEF's logistic activity on the Western Front and a critical one during the BEF's deployment from the United Kingdom to France in 1914. *An Unappreciated Field of Endeavour*, explores a number of themes in what is called in 2018, Logistic Support, which encompasses those functions delivered by the RLC. In 1914-18, the distribution of these functions was different. Combat Supplies (ammunition, petrol and rations) were an Army Service Corps (ASC) responsibility, whilst the storage of ammunition, MT and technical spares on the Line of Communication (LOC) were the prerogative of the Army Ordnance Corps (AOC) and Army Ordnance Department (AOD).[9] Pioneer Services were delivered by military and civilian labour and especially in the combat areas,

8 The term Health Service Support is increasingly used to cover the wider delivery tasks.

9 For a pre-war assessment of the responsibilities, tasks and development of the AOD and AOC, see Brigadier-General T Preston Battersby, 'The Army Ordnance Department and Corps', *The Army Review*, No2, Vol. 2 (April 1912), pp.428-443 and for a wider examination, Major-General A Forbes CB CMG, *A History of the Army Ordnance Services*, Vol. Two, *Modern History* (London: The Medici Society, 1929).

infantry battalions. Transportation, conducted by the RE, included rail operation and construction, Ports and Docks, IWT and MC; the RE were also responsible for Postal Services.

The other areas of Administration, to use the contemporary term of the time, appear in supporting roles. On the Western Front, Equipment Support capability was delivered partially in-house, especially in the technical corps and to a lesser extent by the artificers of the Royal Artillery, with the Tank and Machine Gun Corps responsible for spares and repairs of the early tanks. The AOC Engineering Branch was responsible for artillery equipment and other Arms and Services,[10] with the ASC assuming responsibility for the rapidly expanding task of heavy MT repair from the AOC is January 1915, an activity that widely involved French civilian garage facilities. Medical Support,[11] a very significant component of the BEF's logistic Diaspora, is one where transportation and emerging Motor Transport, had an especially important contribution to improving patient care outcomes and where failures, especially in evacuation planning or delivery, not only resulted in death or permanent disability to individuals but also a reduction in soldiers' morale and thus the capability of the BEF.

10 For details, see, Brigadier B B Kennedy CBE & Colonel J A Tatman, (Comps) *Craftsmen of the Army, The Story of the Royal Electrical and Mechanical Engineers*, Leo Cooper, 1970, pp.12-28.

11 For the official history of medical support on the Western Front, see, Major-General Sir W G Macpherson KCMG CB LLD, BOH, *Medical Services, General History*, Vol. II, *The Medical Services on the Western Front, and during operations in France and Belgium in 1914 and 1915* (London: HMSO, 1923) and Vol. III, *Medical Services during operations on the Western Front in 1916, 1917 and 1918; in Italy; and in Egypt and Palestine* (London: HMSO, 1924). For a recent assessment of capability, see, *The Medical War, British Military Medicine in the First World War*, Mark Harrison (Oxford: Oxford University Press, 2010). For Empire medical services see, Colonel A G Butler DSO VD, *The Official History of the Australian Army Medical Services in the War of 1914-1918*, Vol. II, *The Western Front* (Canberra: Australian War Memorial, 1940); Lieutenant-Colonel A D Carbery CBE; *New Zealand Medical Services in the Great War* (Auckland & Christchurch: Whitcomb & Tombs, 1924) and Sir Andrew MacPhail Kt OBE BA, *Official History of the Canadian Forces in the Great War 1914-1919*, The Medical Services (Ottawa: F A Acland for Canadian General Staff, 1925).

Notes on the Logistic System on the Western Front

Diagrams 1 and 2 show the main stages in the progress of materiel from the Sea Port of Disembarkation (SPOD) in France to units on the Western Front. There were two Lines of Communication (LOC) from the Channel Ports, North and South, which differed in their structure, organization and operations between port and Railhead (RH) plus the Mediterranean Line of Communication (MEDLOC) to Marseilles initiated to support Indian Expeditionary Force A. Base Depots were established near the Channel Ports where stocks arrived in bulk to be aggregated to wagon-loads and dispatched by rail to the Regulating Stations.

In 1914, Railway Regulating Stations (RRS) were established at Abbeville for the First Army and Rivière Neuve near Calais, for Second Army. When Third Army was formed in July 1915, Abbeville became its RRS and Boulogne developed for First Army. Romescamps was assigned to Fourth Army in February 1916. At the RRS, train-loads of commodities were organised into mixed quantities for each division, before being sent on by Standard Gauge Railway (SGR) to the Supply Railhead (SRH).[1] Each of these standard trains, known as Divisional Pack or Supply Trains consisting of 40 wagons, carried the daily non-ammunition requirements for two divisions and comprised the following:

30 x wagons: Rations, Forage and POL
2 x wagons: Coal & coke
4 x wagons: Ordnance stores & MT spares
2 x wagons: Mail & parcels
2 x Brake Vans

Experience confirmed that the maximum number of divisions that could be supplied through one RRS was 24 and thus the French system of one station per Army became the norm. SRHs were established at allocated sites, normally 10-15 miles behind the rear of the trench lines. At the SRH, the loads were collected by the Divisional Supply Column (DSC). The SRHs also sometimes stocked a reserve of various supply commodities, especially tinned rations, which provided a buffer if rail transportation was disrupted. These stocks were usually issued each month and replaced to ensure turnover and increasingly as the war progressed, were camouflaged from aerial observation and attack.

Stocks were loaded to Wheeled Motor Transport (WMT) controlled by the Divisional Supply Column for transport to Brigade Refilling Points, which were occasionally located with the RH, where stocks would be aggregated by the Army Service Corps (ASC) into dumps; one for each

1 The *Field Service Pocket Book* of 1914 defines a railhead as: a locality on the railway where ammunition and supplies are transferred to ammunition parks and supply columns.

supplied unit. 2nd Line Horse Transport (HT) from the Divisional Train, then moved the loads to the Unit Quartermaster, whose staff arranged distribution to companies as required using Regimental 1st Line HT. For units In the Line, stocks would be moved to the rear communication trenches by tramway or HT, and then to the forward troops by various ingenious load-handling systems or more likely, by labour parties from the unit.

There were of course, occasions when the doctrine and the procedures had to be amended. In 7th Division, in the period before the 1916 Somme offensive, a most interesting, if somewhat complex supply arrangement was in place. Materiel arrived by SGR, to a railhead, where it was transferred to 1st Line (unit) HT. The materiel was then taken to a Narrow Gauge Railway (NGR) railhead and transported to the advanced trenches, where it was transferred to a 60 cm Decauville railway, operated by manpower, for movement to the front trenches.[2]

2 TNA WO 95/454/1: HQ Fourth Army, DDST, WD, entry 2 April 1916.

Weights and Measures

The official Weights and Measures of the British Army of 1914-1918 were Imperial and not Metric, although in France, the logisticians were clearly often accounting in Metric, especially in the procurement of goods and services from French sources or if they were relaxing in an *estaminet*. Whilst logistics in the British Army of the 21st Century is almost entirely enacted in Metric, I have chosen to retain the historical Imperial because the contemporary publications and references use the system and referral to them requires no conversion. For those who prefer a Metric output, the following conversions may be used:

Pounds to Kilogrammes: x 0.453592

Tons to Tonnes: x 1.01605

Gallons to Litres: x 4.54609

Yards to Metres: x 0.914

Miles to Kilometres: x 1.60934

Acres to Hectares: x 0.405

Fahrenheit to Celsius: -32 then multiply by 5 then divide by 9.

A hundred-weight (cwt) was a common measure of the time and is 112 pounds. General Staff, *Field Service Pocket Book, 1914*, War Office (London: HMSO, 1914) has a section devoted to Weights & Measures; see pp.259-264.

Time is denoted within the 24 hour clock, for example 2000 (8 pm) although the BEF did not use this system until 1 October 1918. Greenwich Mean Time (GMT) is now described in the military as ZULU.

Foreword

The story of how the British Expeditionary Force's logisticians supplied and maintained what became the largest Army Britain has ever produced through four years of bloody conflict on the Western Front remains a neglected facet of that terrible war. As the title of this work wryly acknowledges, post conflict the workings of the military (and co-opted civilian) logistician is rarely the focus of either academic or public interest when reflecting on the Great War. Yet without the logisticians' dedicated labours an army will not long endure. It will either be defeated by an opponent or will dissolve from within. Neither fate befell the British Expeditionary Force.

The British Army of 1914 had an acute understanding of the importance of 'sound administration', to use the contemporary and all embracing term. Colonial campaigning had relentlessly reinforced this. Sustaining forces at reach across the globe often conducting highly mobile campaigns across vast areas in harsh environments schooled commanders and staff that the art of the possible was framed by what was logistically feasible. To keep British soldiers fit, healthy and confident in these conditions required high quality 'A and Q' support. Colonial wars ensured that in structural terms the Army gave due weight to its logistic capability and that a body of experienced practitioners developed. The Army Staff College at Camberley relentlessly reinforced this lesson.

The BEF deployed to France in August 1914 was some 150,000 strong. The mobile warfare of the opening weeks as the Army advanced, retreated and advanced again, demonstrated both the agility and the resilience of its logistic support. In desperate circumstances the logisticians delivered displaying both foresight and initiative. However the BEF was a minnow in a war of leviathans. Germany had mobilised 4 million men and had 2 million on the Western Front facing 2 million French soldiers. Kitchener on appointment as Britain's Secretary of State for War determined to increase the BEF from 6 divisions to 70. The scale of the challenge was unprecedented both in terms of the numbers required and the rate of expansion.

The easiest part, at least for the first 18 months, was finding enthusiastic manpower. There were a million volunteers by December 1914. The subsequent challenges were how to train them and equip them. With the regular army decisively engaged in Flanders, and suffering heavy losses, finding training staff and instructors who had experience of the conflict was an issue. To equip the army and produce the munitions commensurate with hugely revised consumption rates, industry had to be mobilised and re-tooled under an expanded central government bureaucracy. The munitions crisis of 1915 was the catalyst to establish the Ministry of Munitions under Lloyd George. It put the economy on a war footing. One illustration: in 1914 Britain produced 300 machine-guns, in 1918 120,000. The knock on effect of an impressive increase in output was that by 1916 the Army's logistic processes in France were struggling to cope and at risk of seizing up. The solution was the Geddes Mission and the co-opting of civilian expertise, pragmatically introducing commercial best practice.

The Geddes Mission illuminates the final and most intractable difficulty with the ambitious BEF expansion programme; how to grow sufficient competent commanders and expert staff to make optimum use of the Army being created. One lesson is that if expansion in wartime is envisaged the pre-war army needs to be structured to allow it. There was inevitably much learning on the job and a painful process it was too. The BEF did endure and in due course triumphed, alongside French and American allies. The Italian, French, Russian and German armies all reached breaking point at stages of the conflict, suffering widespread collapses in morale and discipline. No such fate befell the BEF. Its composure and resilience was notable. In 1918 it was the most effective of all the armies on the Western Front. How and why this came about continues to be an area of debate.

These thematic essays signpost some of the answers. Clem Maginniss has combined meticulous research with a lifetime of experience as a military logistician to produce an insightful and thought provoking work. I hope in this Centenary period it will broaden understanding of the BEF's achievements on the Western Front and prompt a renewed interest in the work of its logisticians.

Jacko Page
Lieutenant General
Late Parachute Regiment

Author's Note

One of the threads of this work is the value of accurate and timely information in planning and controlling military and commercial logistic operations. As Brigadier (Retired) Peter Foxton, military logistician and author,[1] often reminded his Team, "if you cannot measure it, you cannot manage it," although equally, Brigadier (Retired) Russell Beattie always prompted his staff not to waste time on attempting to "measure the immeasurable." Both of these early 21st Century senior military officers would certainly be favourably impressed by the level of detail their predecessors obtained and utilized to ensure the efficient and productive use of resources on the Western Front.

The advent of networked electronic Management Information Systems (MIS) has revolutionized the capability to deliver detailed real-time information, albeit with the constant threat of cyber disruption or deception, in a way that the logisticians of the British Expeditionary Force (BEF) in the Great War could never have dreamed of. In a practical sense, the 'Fog of War', has, to an extent, for logisticians, been lifted because there have been occasions in the past, when planners seemed to know more about the opposition's logistic capability than their own. There is now so much information available, not all of it timely or true, that whilst the fog has generally dispersed, the incoming 'Blizzard of Information' sometimes quickly reduces the visibility, bringing new challenges in dynamic environments.

The quest for accurate information to inform logistic operations in the BEF begins with the pioneering work of the North Eastern Railway (NER) in the late 19th and early 20th Centuries and was brought to fruition in the military environment by the introduction of commercial logistic experts to the BEF in 1915-1916. The culture it created, prompted the War Office, under the direction of the then Secretary of State for War, Lloyd George, to issue, from October 1916, a monthly *Abstract of Military Statistics*, which formed the basis for the comprehensive *Statistics of the Military Effort of the British Empire during the Great War*,[2] which remains, after nearly a century since it was published, an excellent tool for the military logistic historian. In this respect, the logisticians of the Great War sit with us as we research their failures, challenges and achievements. To clarify the references to the United Kingdom railways in the pre and Great War periods, readers may wish to have to hand, the indispensable, *Pre-Grouping Atlas and RCH Junction Diagrams*.[3]

Readers will note that there is some repetition in the footnotes. This is not an error but a consequence of each chapter standing on its own within the book.

On a personal note, the author would be pleased to receive, via the Publisher, any information relating to the soldiers in Photograph P8.1 including details of the Royal Engineer Company in which, they were serving.

1 P D Foxton, *Powering War: Modern Land Force Logistics* (London: Brassey's, 1994).
2 War Office, *Statistics of the Military Effort of the British Empire during the Great War, 1914-1920* (MEBE), (HMSO, 1922).
3 Philip Conolly (Intro), *Pre-Grouping Atlas and RCH Junction Diagrams* (Hersham: Ian Allan, 2014).

Preface

In the film '*Heartbreak Ridge*', Choozoo, the Company Sergeant Major of a Fighting Soldier, Marine Gunnery Sergeant Thomas Highway observed, with barely hidden sarcasm, to his Officer Commanding, Major Malcolm A Powers, that Supply and Logistics was 'an unappreciated field of endeavour'.[1] Equally, whilst his statement is true, it appears from an historical perspective, to have been much more carefully concealed than Gunny's cynicism because non-official publications on military logistics have, over the past century,[2] been rather sparse in comparison to other areas of soldierly activity.[3] General Archibald Wavell observed that:

> In most military books strategy and tactics are emphasized at the expense of the administrative factors........Bear in mind when you study military history or military events the importance of the administrative factor, because it is where most critics and many generals go wrong.[4]

The adage that 'amateurs study tactics but professionals study logistics'[5] is a view that certainly applies to British operations on the Western Front and one clearly held by Field Marshal Douglas Haig.[6] It is also true that whilst logistics may appear to be a rather dull element of

1 Clint Eastwood, '*Heartbreak Ridge*', Warner Brothers, 1986 (Running Time - 00:19:32). Everett McGill as Major Powers and Arlen Dean Snyder as CSM Choozoo.

2 Second World War logistics have received much better official coverage than the Great War. The United Kingdom 'Red Book' Series, *The Second World War, Army, 1939-1945*, published by the War Office for internal study in the late 1940s and early 1950s, has 13 volumes devoted to devoted to Logistics, Supply and Transport, whilst the *United States Army in World II* series published by the Department of the Army, Office of the Chief of Military History, allocated 14, with additional ones on Engineering and Medical Support.

3 Key general books from British and American authors in date order, include: Brevet Lieutenant-Colonel G C Shaw RAOC, *Supply in Modern War* (London: Faber & Faber, nd but 1938); Martin van Creveld, *Supplying War, Logistics from Wallenstein to Patton* (Cambridge: Cambridge University Press (CUP), 1977); Kenneth Macksey, *For Want of a Nail, The Impact of Logistics and Communications* (London: Brassey's, 1989); Major General (Retd) Julian Thompson, *The Lifeblood of War, Logistics in Armed Conflict* (London & Washington: Brassey's, 1991); Joseph Sinclair, *Arteries of War, A History of Military Transportation, Military Transportation from Alexander the Great to the Falklands-and beyond* (Shrewsbury, Airlife, 1992); John A Lynn, *Feeding Mars, Logistics in Western Warfare from the Middle Ages to the Present* (Colorado: Westview Press, 1993); P D Foxton, *Powering War: Modern Land Force Logistics* (London: Brassey's, 1994) and Thomas A Kane, *Military Logistics and Strategic Performance* (London & Portland Oregon: Frank Cass, 2001). Specific titles include: Duncan S Ballantine, *US Naval Logistics in the Second World War* (Princeton New Jersey: Princeton University Press, 1947); James A Huston, *Guns and Butter, Powder and Rice, US Army Logistics in the Korean War* (Selinsgrove: Susquehanna University Press, 1989); Phyllis A Zimmerman, *The Neck of the Bottle, George W Goethals and the Reorganization of the US Army Supply System, 1917-1918* (College Station: Texas A & M University Press, 1992); John Kennedy Ohl, *Supplying the Troops, General Somervell and American Logistics in WWII* (DeKalb: Northern Illinois University Press, 1994) and Major General Julian Thompson (Retd) (Ed.) *Gulf Logistics, Blackadder's War* (London & Washington: Brassey's, 1995).

4 'Generals and Generalship': *The Lees Knowles Lectures Delivered at Trinity College Cambridge in 1939*, Archibald Wavell (London: Macmillan, 1941), p.11.

5 General Omar Bradley, quoted in Terry C Pierce, 'Voodoo Logistics Sink', Triphibious Warfare, *Proceedings of the US Naval Institute*, Vol. 122, No 9, September 1996, p.74.

6 A key argument of *An Unappreciated Field of Endeavour* is that Field-Marshal Haig clearly comprehended the importance of logistics in winning the war on the Western Front and was prepared to take innovative and

operations,[7] they are absolutely critical to the effective prosecution of them, a point perceptively noted in 1899 by Colonel Charles Callwell, a British artillery officer: 'Supply and transport are intimately bound up with all military operations'.[8]

The BEF's strategy, operational art, tactics, politics and social aspects have been scrutinized in depth in the 100 years since the Armistice but little has been written on the logistic components of this vast force, which numbered 1,966,727 in November 1918.[9] Pre-1914 and post-1918, articles examining the role of logistics in the British Army in the Great War were a regular feature in professional military journals,[10] supported by the two logistic corps regimental histories from the Army Service Corps (ASC)[11] and Army Ordnance Corps (AOC).[12] Whilst the Royal Engineers (RE) history of the period was not published until 1952,[13] the Institute of the RE published, during the early 1920s, in several volumes, the comprehensive and detailed, *Work of RE in the European War, 1914-1919*,[14] covering a wide range of technical engineering logistic activity. Explicitly exploring the daily life of the logistic staff at divisional and corps level, *Behind The Lines, An Account of Administrative Staff-work in the British Army 1914-1918* was published in 1939,[15] whilst the sole and classic logistic Official History, *Transportation on the Western Front*, was published in 1937.[16]

controversial decisions to create the necessary effect.

7 During United Nations Peace Support Operations in Bosnia-Herzegovina in 1993, an infantry officer appointed as a Deputy Chief of Staff observed that planning Theatre refuelling was thoroughly boring. A logistic officer replied that it whilst it might be, it was nowhere near so boring as watching the grass grow under the tracks of a WARRIOR (a British Infantry Fighting Vehicle) because it had run out of diesel.

8 General Staff, *Small Wars, Their Principles and Practice*, Colonel C E Callwell, 3rd Edn, War Office (London: HMSO, 1906), p.58.

9 War Office, *Statistics of the Military Effort of the British Empire during the Great War, 1914-1920* (HMSO, 1922), p.62.

10 A small selection of the contributions included: Major H De Pree RFA, 'The Supply of Ammunition and Motor Transport', *Journal of the Royal United Service Institute (JRUSI)*, Vol. LVI (414), August 1912; Colonel P E F Hobbs CMG, 'The New System of Transport as carried out by the Blue Forces during Army Manoeuvres 1912', *The Army Review*, Vol. IV, No 2, April 1913; 'The Services of Maintenance in the Field: Some Object Lessons from the Army Exercise 1913', *The Army Review*, April 1914; 'Notes on the Entrainment of Troops To and From Manoeuvres', Captain J F C Fuller, *The Army Review*, July 1914; na, 'Sparking Plug, A Divisional Train of the Future', *Royal Army Service Corps Quarterly*, Vol. 8, April 1920; Brevet Major O W White DSO, Dorsetshire Regiment, 'The Abolition of Horse Transport in the Administrative Services', *JRUSI*, Vol. LXVI, February 1921; 'Land Transportation in the Late War', Colonel M G Taylor CMG DSO, *JRUSI*, Vol. LXVI, November 1921; H Cooper, 'An Outline of the French System of Mechanical Transport', *Royal Army Service Corps Quarterly*, Vol. 10, January 1922 and J Burnett-Stuart, 'The Progress of Mechanisation', *Army Quarterly*, Vol. XVI, April 1928.

11 Colonel R H Beadon CBE psc, *The Royal Army Service Corps, A History of Transport and Supply in the British Army*, Vol. II, (Cambridge: CUP, 1931). On 27 November 1918, His Majesty King George V conferred upon the Army Service Corps the prefix Royal, for its outstanding work in the war. The late Michael Young's splendid *Army Service Corps, 1902-1918* (London: Leo Cooper, 2000), has admirably supplemented the ASC regimental history. 'Ally Sloper's Cavalry' was the Corps' affectionate nickname after a cartoon character that appeared in the *Judy* magazine from 1867 and in books until 1916. Sloper was a cheeky, conniving, slippery hero, who enjoyed a drink. Less flattering nick-names, included 'Jam Stealers' and 'Underground Cavalry'.

12 Major-General A Forbes CB CMG, *A History of the Army Ordnance Services*, Vol. Three, *The Great War*, (London: Medici Society, 1929). The Royal prefix was conferred on 27 November 1918.

13 Major-General H L Pritchard (Ed.) *The History of the Corps of Royal Engineers*, Vol. V, *The Home Front, France, Flanders and Italy in the First World War* (Chatham: Institution of the Royal Engineers, 1952).

14 RE Institution, *Work of RE in the European War, 1914-19*, through W & J Mackay, 1920s. A series of comprehensive historical technical publications covering key logistic engineering capabilities encapsulating the RE operational experience on the Western Front.

15 Colonel W N Nicholson CMG DSO, *Behind the Lines, An Account of Administrative Staff-work in the British Army 1914-1918* (London: Jonathan Cape, 1939) concentrating on the personal element of logistic staff planning. *Behind the Lines* is a fascinating read; amusing, erudite, informative and definitely forthright. *The Army Quarterly*, Volume 38, stated that: 'Every officer, certainly every aspiring staff officer, should read this book'. 100 years on, one has to agree wholeheartedly with this statement. *Behind the Lines* was reprinted, with new historical notes, in 1989, by the Strong Oak Press and Tim Donovan Publishing (ISBN 1-871048-16-8).

16 Colonel A M Henniker CBE (Comp) BOH, *Transportation on the Western Front, 1914-1918* (London: HMSO,

Since then, with the notable exception of Ian Malcolm Brown's seminal *British Logistics on the Western Front*,[17] little material has appeared to examine the details of what should be a goldmine, although railway operations,[18] labour support,[19] operations in 1918[20] and sustaining the Soldier[21] have received niche attention. One forgotten gem, journalistic in style but illuminating nonetheless, is the contemporary, *The Business of War*,[22] in which its American author observed that the British logistic operation was 'the most remarkable business machine in the world'.[23] On the Centenary of the Great War Armistice, it seems therefore, apposite to repair some of the lacuna in the historiography and restore the logistics of the BEF on the Western Front to its rightful place, whilst embedding its lessons to the present.

An Unappreciated Field of Endeavour is not a comprehensive examination of BEF logistics on the Western Front, nor indeed a short history. To achieve the former would involve several volumes and the latter would omit much fascinating detail. It does however, bring a new and fresh perspective by analysing in a series of engaging essays, the critical contribution of particular components of military and commercial logistics to the operations of the British and Empire Armies during the Great War on the Western Front,[24] through the lens of specific elements and themes, each of which, cast penetrating light into dark corners of an important, yet mainly forgotten story.

An Unappreciated Field of Endeavour explains how pre-war strategic, economic, political and defence dynamics influenced the plans to rely upon commercial assets to support military and naval operations, before examining the role of the civil railways and mercantile marine in the planning, preparation and execution of Defence mobilization and movement in the United Kingdom during Transition To War in 1914. The influence of Royal Navy logistics is also examined to expose its role in enabling British sea power in Home Waters to ensure the safe arrival of the BEF to the Continent with its full combat power and logistic capability. The role of British railways in playing a defining part in a critical moment of European history is explored in depth, as are the technical processes and managerial interfaces that enabled them. The contribution of British commercial and business leaders and managers to enhancing the combat capability of the BEF is examined through the lens of the increasing industrialization of logistic support to operations. In particular, the influence of commercial practice in improving military logistic efficiency and effectiveness, whilst also subtly

1937), remains essential reading, covering the construction and operations of railways, roads, ports, docks and inland water transport and additionally, movement control. The Classic Text on the subject.

17 The seminal, Ian Malcolm Brown, *British Logistics on the Western Front, 1914-1919* (Westport Connecticut & London: Praeger, 1998), which is a comprehensive assessment of logistic strategy and policy.

18 Special War Transportation Number, *The Railway Gazette*, 21 September 1920. William A T Aves, *ROD, The Railway Operating Division on the Western Front on the Western Front, The Royal Engineers in France and Belgium, 1915-1919* (Donington: Shaun Tyas, 2009), is the illustrated work on railway operating within the BEF, whilst *Light Railways of the First World War, A History of Tactical Rail Communications on the British Fronts, 1914-1918*, W J K Davies BA AKC (Newton Abbot: David & Charles 1967), focuses on Narrow Gauge operations.

19 The ground-breaking John Starling & Ivor Lee, *No Labour, No Battle, Military Labour During the First World War* (Stroud: Spellmount, 2009) is a first class examination of the importance of logistic labour in the Great War.

20 Valuable work has been undertaken by Geoff Clarke, *Supplying The Battlefront: British Frontline Transport in Mobile Warfare 1918*, Unpublished MA dissertation (Birmingham: University of Birmingham, 2006) and Christopher Phillips, *A Modern Industrial Organization: A Case Study of Fourth Army during the battles of the Hundred Days*, Unpublished MA dissertation (Birmingham: University of Birmingham, 2009).

21 Alan Weeks, *Tea, Rum & Fags, Sustaining Tommy, 1914-1918* (Stroud: History Press, 2009) examines the Soldiers' experience of Western Front logistics; see also, John Ellis, *Eye Deep in Hell, The Western Front, 1914-1918* (London: Purnell Book Services, 1976), pp.124-140.

22 Issac F Marcosson, The *Business of War* (London: John Lane, The Bodley Head, 1918).

23 Ibid, p.17.

24 In 1942, Admiral Ernest J King, Commander-in-Chief United States Fleet and Chief of Naval Operations also grasped its significance, allegedly declaring: "I don't know what the hell this logistics is that Marshall is always talking about, but I want some of it!"

changing military culture, is matched to the dynamics and frictions of employing commercial logistic advisers in the operational environment of the Western Front.

Whilst, the exploits of the combat elements of the BEF in 1914 have been analysed in depth, the contribution of the logisticians who kept the BEF in the fight has effectively marched into the mists of time. *An Unappreciated Field of Endeavour* explores the success of the BEF's Quartermaster-General, Wully Robertson, in utilizing the skill of his logistic planners and soldiers to deliver the agile operational logistic capability that was the salvation of the BEF in 1914. Also examined, is the long forgotten but extraordinary logistic feat of deploying Indian Expeditionary Force A to France, through the mobilization and transportation of its soldiers across deserts and oceans before its complex logistic integration to the BEF in France. The solutions to the challenges in executing these operations by military and civilian logisticians from Britain, France and India, offer unusual insight into Coalition co-operation from three culturally diverse countries.

Rarely studied, logistic planning, resources and execution, played a crucial role in the preparations for the Battle of the Somme. These important aspects are analysed to highlight a developing capability, through the process of 'logistic learning steps' of which, were of at least equal significance to those in the operational and tactical environments. The influence of the BEF's Wheeled Motor Transport (WMT) component upon the operational art on the Western Front is reviewed, including its impact upon the deployment and employment of armour, infantry, artillery and aviation. These were all affected by the expanding use of WMT, creating a requirement to improve its efficiency and effectiveness. Logistics were fundamental to the use of tanks in the Great War, an aspect comprehensively examined, to assess how logistics and transportation in particular, constrained the development of operational deployments. *An Unappreciated Field of Endeavour* also analyses how, in 1918, the BEF's logisticians were able to generate the capability to sustain All-Arms mobile three dimensional combat operations in a chemical warfare environment, whilst maintaining the momentum of the advance, having focused mainly upon supporting siege warfare for the previous four years.

The corporate memory of the commercial aspect is even more faded than the military one but it was an essential component of the British and Empire endeavours on the Western Front and is lucidly exposed. The combined military and commercial story has many facets: innovative people, constant training, emerging technology, developing doctrine, fresh ideas, new equipment, maturing experience, complex planning, increasing mechanization and relentless industry. *An Unappreciated Field of Endeavour* draws these threads from the bobbins to weave a colourful pattern of achievement, whilst illustrating how logistics evolved to overcome complex challenges and in doing so, transformed operations, creating a Great War legacy that remains relevant to the British Army's logistics in the 21st Century,[25] especially in the expanding arena of contractor support to operations.

Logistics however, do not swim alone in the military pond. At the operational level, the role of logistics is to develop, sustain and regenerate combat power to ensure that the tempo and effectiveness of the operations maintains momentum. Equally logistics placed constraints on strategy and tactics, a critical point concisely summarized by a future field force QMG: 'Strategy and tactics are now tied hand and foot by administration'.[26] On the Western Front, the BEF's

25 See, William G T Tuttle, *Defense Logistics for the 21st Century*, Jr (Annapolis: Naval Institute Press, 2005).

26 Major (Temporary Lieutenant-Colonel) W G Lindsell DSO OBE MC psc RA, 'Administrative Lessons of the Great War', *JRUSI*, Vol. LXXI, February 1926, p.713. Lindsell was the author of the manual entitled *Military Organization and Administration* published in 1923 (Aldershot: Gale & Polden, 23rd Edition, 1941) which ran, in various editions, until the 1960s, which lucidly illustrates its resilience. He also wrote, *A & Q or Military Administration in War*, Third Edition (Aldershot: Gale & Polden, 1933). Lindsell held several senior QMG posts during the Second War World, including the BEF in France, Middle East and India.

enormous logistic capability was not an end in itself but a vital means to achieve the military aim, an observation as valid today as it was in 1918. Great War military logistics, not generally perceived to be racy, has, for far too long, held its light behind a bushel. Its practitioners, from General to Private are long gone and the experiences they recorded and the lessons they learnt, many still relevant in the 21st Century, lie in dusty volumes and files in archives and libraries. I trust that *An Unappreciated Field of Endeavour* brings their fascinating achievements to life.

Acknowledgements

I have many acknowledgements to all those who have laid the foundations over 50 years for this book. Foremost, I must thank my Mother and late Father and their parents, whose experiences of the First and Second World Wars were indelibly marked upon their lives and to Edith Woodward, my gracious Nan, whose life was similarly endowed and who not only bought me my first history book, *A Pageant of History*[1] but also persuaded me to read it. For all of them, the wars of the first half of the 20th Century were not a module of academic history study but a time of survival and heartache. My thanks are also due to, the legendary late Doc Orton, a Jewish refugee from Nazi Germany who was the Head of History at Ratcliffe College[2] in the late 1960s and early 1970s, whose energy and experience brought history alive in every one of his lessons;[3] to the late Lieutenant Colonel Bill Robinson, Contingent Commander of the Combined Cadet Force, whose leadership inspired me to seek an Army life and to the Professor of History, Volker Berghahn and the Lecturers at the University of Warwick in the mid 1970s, who offered such dynamic intellectual stimulation during three years of uplifting study.

I am indebted to the Trustees of the Royal Logistic Corps Museum at Deepcut and its archivist Gareth Mears for their constant support, including the most kind offer of photographs to assist in the illustration of this book and to the Senior Librarian, Andrew Orgill and his team at the Royal Military Academy Sandhurst, for their dedication in meeting my stream of requests for information. The staff of the Tank Museum at Bovington extended every courtesy and I am immensely grateful for the constructive assistance of that doyen of historical tank knowledge, David Fletcher MBE. My thanks are certainly due to the many staff at the Imperial War Museum and the National Archives at Kew who so efficiently deliver a wealth of research material to one's 'bird-box'; the operation is, in itself, a logistic marvel. My grateful thanks are also due to Hollie Barrett, whose scientific qualifications have been so well applied in the creation of the excellent maps and diagrams and her contribution to the cover graphics. I must thank the team at Helion, especially Duncan Rogers who took a risk with an unknown author and agreed to publish the work, who have turned the script on my hard-drive into a book on the shelf. I must also expressly thank Tom Donovan for his kind permission to reproduce a number of excellent photographs from his collection relating to Indian Expeditionary Force A.

I am also grateful for the support of the many officers and soldiers, all now retired, from different Arms and Services and the Royal Navy and Royal Air Force during my Army career, whose experiences have not only expanded my knowledge of military logistics but also encouraged me to keep the historical wheel turning. In particular, Lieutenant Colonel Alan Parker who inspired my interest in the Western Front though his outstanding battlefield tours, Brigadier Russell

1 na, *A Pageant of History, The Reigns of our Kings and Queens Famous People and Events in our History* (London: Collins, 1962).

2 Ratcliffe on the Wreake, Fosse Way, Leicester.

3 His impersonations of Adolf Hitler speaking at a Nazi rally were electrifying, made even more exciting if he stood on a desk or a table, none of which, ever appeared to be particularly stable.

Beattie, Brigadier Clive Elderton CBE, Colonel Jim Morrison CBE, Colonel Mike Crawshaw and Lieutenant Colonel Ian Hurley MBE. I must pay special thanks to Major Stephen Pope for not only his 40 years of Army comradeship but also his assistance with tank material, which has been invaluable, whilst his fascinating and comprehensive book, the *The First Tank Crews*,[4] encouraged me to write *An Unappreciated Field of Endeavour*. My grateful thanks are due to Lieutenant General Jacko Page CB OBE, late Parachute Regiment, who so kindly agreed to offer his thoughts on logistics from the perspective of a senior operational commander.

My greatest gratitude of debt though, is to my wife Edwina, who has, in addition to her demanding career, acted as sub-editor and proof reader, which she informs me has been a positive experience. Although a retired officer of the Queen Alexander's Royal Army Nursing Corps (Volunteers) she has proved herself to be a true logistician, who has sustained me day and night, morally and physically, whilst I have been head down researching and writing. She has done so much to ensure that our A&Q (Adjutant and Quartermaster-General) arrangements have never failed whilst I have been writing this book but her especial contribution has been, without doubt, the delivery, without fail, of outstanding Food Services and she has therefore, fully met the motto of the Royal Logistic Corps, *We Sustain*; thank you.

4 Stephen Pope, *The First Tank Crews, The Lives of the Tankmen Who Fought at the Battle of Flers-Courcelette*, 15 September 1916 (Solihull: Helion, 2016).

Introduction

Men without weapons and food, guns without ammunition, tanks without petrol, are useless encumbrances to an army in the field.[1]

In 1912, the Inspector of Army Ordnance Services, Brigadier-General Thomas Preston Battersby, reflecting upon the role and lot of the military logistician, wrote:

> It is a marked characteristic of human nature to take for granted - as part of the natural order of things - any incident which occurs with regularity, and is not interrupted by the unforeseen. We arrive in our London offices by the early morning express trains with unfailing punctuality (provided we are not fortunate enough to be dependent upon the tender mercies of the South Eastern and Chatham Railway)',[2] and which of us pauses to think of the labour and thought, the time charts and signalling problems involved in each apparently simple journey? Our letters are brought to our doors by the postman, and if he should be 10 minutes late we grumble; but who considers the vast complexity of the system which had to be evolved before it was possible to ensure that a letter posted anywhere in the civilized world should punctually reach its address?[3]

The logisticians of the British Expeditionary Force (BEF)[4] in the Great War faced several significant challenges. First and foremost, was the previous operational experience of the logistic services, which was, for the most part, based upon the colonial wars of the 19th Century, and whilst perhaps from the perspective of the 21st Century, logistics in these campaigns appear to have been of little importance to contemporary commanders, this was not always the case.[5] Mainly small in scale, Imperial operations provided officers and soldiers alike, plenty of opportunity for field service, not a little action, and a raft of lessons, not all of them relevant for every deployment in the future, in much the same way as Afghanistan has done in the early 21st Century. Logistics were not therefore, in any way irrelevant, with careful planning and execution in this arena being significant

1 Colonel W G Lindsell, *A&Q, or Administration in the Field* (Aldershot: Gale & Polden, 1933), p.7.

2 On a domestic note, it is comforting to know that some of the officers suffered from the same frustrations in their daily commute into Whitehall as their successors do in 2018.

3 Brigadier-General T Preston Battersby, 'The Army Ordnance Department and Corps', *The Army Review*, No 2, Vol. 2, April 1912, p.428.

4 The nomenclature British Expeditionary Force is an inaccurate and inadequate term to describe the deployment of so many troops from the British Empire. From the United Kingdom there were English, Scottish, Welsh and Irish troops, whilst the Empire provided units and labourers from Africa, Australia, Burma, Canada, China, India, Newfoundland, New Zealand and the West Indies. Arguably, 'British Empire Force' would have been a more accurate and appropriate description for the abbreviation BEF. In addition, GHQ BEF commanded, at some point during the operations in 1918, American, French and Portuguese formations and units.

5 For an example, see, General Staff, *Official History of the Operations in Somaliland, 1901-1904*, Vols I & II, War Office (London: HMSO, 1907). Vol. II is devoted almost entirely to logistics or what is now described in the British Army as Combat Service Support (CSS).

components in the success or failure of colonial campaigns, although the Boer War in South Africa 1899-1902 clearly demonstrated however, that some of these lessons were not fully applicable to significant force deployments, especially on the Continent of Europe.

Haldane's reorganization of the Army, in order to create a Regular expeditionary capability and the Territorial Force for Home Defence, was an essential step in preparing the Land Forces of the United Kingdom for a continental conflict.[6] A corollary of these developments was an increasing comprehension at many levels within the British Army of the importance of logistics in delivering military capability. One fundamental issue throughout the BEF's Western Front experience was the critical work of the Staff in planning, co-ordinating and delivering logistic capability at scale and one that went through various stages of failure and improvement during the Great War. There were structural and training challenges influencing the outcomes but there was no better teacher than hard practical experience, although the BEF's QMG in 1918,[7] also identified a cultural one: 'Bad Staff work mostly arises from not knowing the differences between an office and a trench'.[8]

Contrary to popular military belief, the Staff Courses at Camberley and Quetta contained significant logistic content[9] with 23 percent of the curriculum[10] devoted to A&Q[11] subjects,[12] whilst another feature of the immediate pre-Great War period was the number of logistic articles appearing in key defence publications outside of the logistic services, such the *Journal of the Royal United Service Institution* and *The Army Review*. Infantry and artillery officers, clearly demonstrating a healthy interest in logistics, wrote a significant number of these works, which suggests that the

6 For a description, see, Colonel John K Dunlop OBE MC TD. *The Development of the British Army, 1899-1914, From the Eve of the South African War to the Eve of the Great War, with Special Reference to the Territorial Force* (London: Methuen, 1938), pp.231-304. For analyses, see, Timothy Bowman & Mark Connelly, *The Edwardian Army, Recruiting, Training and Deploying the British Army* (Oxford: Oxford University Press (OUP), 2012), Spencer Jones, *From Boer War to World War, Tactical Reform of the British Army, 1902-1914* (Norman: University of Oklahoma Press, 2012) and Simon Batten, *Futile Exercise?, The British Army's Preparations for War 1902-1914* (Warwick: Helion, 2018). For the strategic aspects, see, John Gooch, *The Plans of War, The General Staff and British Military Strategy c1906-1916* (London: Routledge & Kegan Paul, 1974), pp.278-298.

7 Lieutenant-General Sir Travers Clarke GBE KCB KCMG took over as QMG in late 1917 having served for 18 months as the QMG in Salonika and four months as the Deputy Adjutant General in GHQ. At 46, he was certainly young for the post and according to Frank Fox, an officer on his Staff, was only a substantive Major; [Frank Fox] GSO, *GHQ, Montreuil-Sur-Mer* (London: Philip Allan & Co, 1920), p.226. Fox recorded, "T.C. had the ideal personality for a military leader. You were always dreadfully afraid of him and sincerely fond of him"; pp.227-228. Clarke's first wife, Mary Jordan died in 1918, although he remarried in 1921 to Irene Roe (nee Cross), the widow of an officer in his regiment, the Royal Inniskilling Fusiliers. From 1919-1923, he was QMG to the Forces.

8 Ibid, p.228.

9 In the period 1898-1903, 47% of the questions in the Army Staff College annual entrance exam were focused on A&Q subjects, whilst in 1898 and 1900 it was 57%. See Lt-Col H M E Brunker, *Notes on Organization and Equipment,* 6th Edn (London: William Clowes and Sons, 1909), pp.265-274.

10 Staff College Curriculum, 1912-1913 (Quetta), in Ian Malcolm Brown, *British Logistics on the Western Front, 1914-1919* (Westport Connecticut & London: Praeger, 1998) p.23.

11 The overarching term used by the British Army in the Great War, to define those activities, which provided support to combat forces in the fields of administration and logistics. In the 21st Century these activities are described as Combat Service Support (CSS) and comprise Logistic Support, Equipment Support, Medical Support, Administrative Support and Logistic Engineering.

12 In 1990, when the Commandant of the Army Staff College at Camberley, the then Major General Willie Rous OBE announced to the course that the revised logistic content had been doubled in length, a student, Captain Russell Beattie of the Royal Corps of Transport, had the courage to ask whether that meant there would be two periods of study instead of one. To raucous laughter from Directing Staff and students, Willie Rous, as ever, took the observation with good humour and the interjection clearly did the good Captain no long-term harm because he retired from the Army as a Brigadier. Major General Rous, late of the Coldstream Guards, promoted to Lieutenant General, was knighted and appointed in 1994 as Quartermaster-General to the Forces, retiring from the Army in 1996, when he became Chairman of Kingston Hospital. He died in 1999 from cancer and the Cancer Unit is named in his memory.

Officer Corps' had more interest in this field of endeavour than is generally recognized.[13]

One of the aspects of the colonial conflicts was the opportunity for logisticians to utilize their initiative, which in relatively small operations often produced effective results. It was, understandably, a process that became a central feature of early logistic operations on the Continent during 1914-1915 but one not adapted to resolve significant structural issues that developed on the Western Front and one, which created, by mid-1916, such serious concerns about the sustainability of the system, that senior commercial managers were introduced to the military logistic organization to generate efficiencies, streamline processes and improve outputs. The most significant change was the introduction of what the Americans describe as 'Big Logistics',[14] (Big L), which is the mobilization of industrial resources and production to support the defence requirement, which generated the need to create an effective interface with 'Small L' at Theatre military level, although as the very significant logistic operations of the BEF lucidly illustrate, the use of the word 'Small' is, in the BEF context, relative. On the Western Front, the key exposure of this critical task was the resolution of the 'Small L' transportation crisis in 1916 by the delivery of 'Big L' capability in, to use 21st Century Information Technology terms, 'hardware', such as locomotives, wagons, rails, workshops and operators and the 'software', in the form of commercial management.

In a wider sense, four fundamental issues confronted the British Army, the first being the dynamics of operations on the Western Front. The logistician of 1914 experienced in colonial operations was initially involved in supporting mobile warfare, then grasping all the intricacies and demands of siege operations before engaging in various types of mobile ones before supporting major offensive deployments involving infantry, artillery, tanks, chemical weapons and aircraft. As logisticians in 1914 discovered, it is probably impossible to ensure that the logistic systems and Order of Battle (ORBAT) meet precisely the requirement at the start of every operation or campaign. The key ability is to 'adopt, adapt and improve',[15] whilst ensuring the structures and systems that are in place can be altered and expanded to meet the need, a lesson that remains absolutely relevant to the British Army in the 21st Century.

The second challenge was one of scope and scale. Commanders and soldiers on the Western Front were confronting a military world that had few maps and the environment in which they were fighting was, for the most part, un-surveyed.[16] They were therefore, finding their way in a dark room, and not surprisingly, they collided with unseen or unexpected obstacles, which caused them to stumble and sometimes fall; that they did so is not surprising given the scale and dynamics of the task. Upon deployment to France in 1914, the BEF fielded six divisions rising at its peak to

13 Examples include, Brevet Major C N, Buchanan-Dunlop RA, 'Ammunition Supply', *Journal of the Royal United Service Institution* (JRUSI) Vol. LVII, January 1913, pp.87-92; Captain Sir T A A M Cuninghame Bart DSO, Rifle Brigade, 'The Supply of a Division in the Field with Special Reference to the use of Mechanical Transport', *JRUSI*, Vol. LVI, January 1912, pp.9-36; Major H De Pree RFA, 'The Supply of Ammunition and Motor Transport', *JRUSI*, Vol. LVI (414), August 1912, pp.1149-1164; Captain J F C Fuller, 'Notes on the Entrainment of Troops To and From Manoeuvres', *The Army Review*, Vol. VII, No 1, War Office, July 1914, pp.184-213 and Major (Temporary Lieutenant-Colonel) W G Lindsell DSO OBE MC psc RA W G, 'Administrative Lessons of the Great War', *JRUSI*, Vol. LXXI, February 1926, pp.712-719.

14 For a an analysis of United States 'Big L' during the Second World War, see, Alan Gropman (Ed.) *The Big L, American Logistics in World War II* (Washington DC: National Defense University Press, 1997).

15 I am indebted to my late Father, who was Chairman of Coventry Round Table, for this analysis. The motto was created from a speech by HRH Prince Edward, Prince of Wales made to the British Industries Fair in 1927, in which he stated that, 'The young business and professional people of this country must get together round the table, adopt methods that have proved so sound in the past, adapt them to the changing needs of the time and wherever possible improve them'.

16 For a comprehensive assessment of the British Army in the Great War, with a focus on the Western Front, see, Ian Beckett, Timothy Bowman & Mark Connelly (Eds.), *The British Army and the First World War*, Armies of the Great War (Cambridge: Cambridge University Press (CUP), 2017).

62 divisions, with the force consisting of over two million personnel.[17] This organization remains the largest single entity that the United Kingdom has ever created and logistic support was vital to its existence and operation. The BEF increased from a ration-strength of 269,711 in December 1914, to 601,498 in June 1915, 986,189 in December 1915 before reaching 1,343,457 on 1 June 1916, a five-fold increase in 18 months, with an average increase of 60,000 personnel per month.[18] Inevitably many of these personnel were inexperienced in their appointments, regardless of their rank or trade and this had a direct impact on the quality of the BEF's operational capabilities. In the same period, the largest logistic corps in the BEF, the Army Service Corps (ASC)[19], increased four-fold, rising from 54,055 in December 1914, to 140,585 in June 1916, 199,226 in December 1915 and then to 226,175 in June 1916.[20] The scale of the expansion was of course, not merely measured in terms of personnel. In the space of eight months during 1916, in addition to many other major projects, the BEF constructed along the Line of Communication (LOC) and then stocked, several expanding depots: six major ammunition sites,[21] one supply, two engineer stores locations and one for railway construction. Inevitably, quantity become more important than quality, and risks were taken, not all of them carefully calculated. In land transportation both in the United Kingdom and France, it was the Standard Gauge Railway (SGR) that was the defining capability, although Inland Water Transport (IWT) played an important, yet generally forgotten role, in supporting the BEF on the Continent.[22]

The third challenge was the nature of the war on the Western Front with the creation of the trench system in particular, generating a raft of challenges for the logisticians. Of especial note, was the demand for a range of new weapons,[23] such as trench mortars, hand grenades and gas munitions, all of which had to be procured, receipted, inspected, stored, maintained and issued. Given the scale of the need, this was no easy task. In addition, the trench war created a new and unexpected requirement for special stores: digging tools, ladders, water pumps, revetting, duck-boards, shoring timber, shuttering, water carriers, gum-boots, trench stretchers and many other items. Once issued, it was illogical to keep moving these stores with the unit, so many of these items were held not on

17 War Office, *Statistics of the Military Effort of the British Empire during the Great War, 1914-1920* (MEBE) (HMSO, 1922), p.64 (iii) Estimated Strengths of the Expeditionary Forces, France and Italy. The BEF's military strength peaked at 2,044,627 on 1 August 1917, although its highest total strength, inclusive of native labourers but exclusive of contractors, was 2,157,942 on 1 October 1917. MEBE, p.91, Table (i) (a) - Feeding Strength in France and Flanders, 7th December 1918 records 2,263,945 but this includes 189,622 Prisoners of War (POW). Colonel R H Beadon, CBE psc, *The Royal Army Service Corps, A History of Transport and Supply in the British Army*, Vol. II (Cambridge: CUP, 1931), p.145 notes 2,360,400 inclusive of POW. Whilst the figures may vary, the numbers lucidly indicate the scale of the logistic task.

18 MEBE, p.64 (iii) - Estimated Strengths of the Expeditionary Forces, France and Italy.

19 For a summary of ASC organization and tasks, see Brunker, *Notes on Organization and Equipment,* pp.96-104.

20 ASC figures extracted from MEBE, p.221, Strength of the Army Service Corps. The table title is Royal Army Service Corps, although the Corps did not receive its Royal prefix until 27 November 1918.

21 Ammunition in these sites was managed according to the classification of the day: Boxed, which included Small Arms Ammunition (SAA) 13 & 18 pdr rounds and 4.5 inch. Unboxed and heavy, for example 8 and 9.2 inch; trench munitions such as the Stokes mortar ammunition; Miscellaneous, such as pyrotechnics and demolition explosives, for example, gun-cotton and dynamite. Storage was by Group and Division; see, War Office, *Treatise on Ammunition*, 10th Edition (HMSO, 1915).

22 IWT is another aspect of BEF logistic capability that has had little light shed upon it and is the poorer for not having a prominent post-war history, in a companion volume to the comprehensive one exposing IWT operations in Mesopotamia; Lieutenant-Colonel L J Hill OBE (Comp) *The Inland Water Transport in Mesopotamia,* (London: Constable and Company, 1921). For a recent academic review, see, Christopher Phillips, 'Logistics and the BEF: The Development of Waterborne Transport on the Western Front, 1914-1916', *British Journal of Military History*, Vol. 2, No 2, 2016, pp.42-58.

23 For a detailed analysis of the requirement for trench weapons, see, Anthony Saunders, *Reinventing Warfare, 1914-18, Novel Munitions and Tactics of Trench Warfare*, Continuum Studies in Military History (London & New York: Continuum, 2012).

a Unit Equipment Table (UET) but as Trench and Village Stores,[24] an arrangement that required a different accounting system.[25] Given the enormous quantities involved, it was essential that this system operated effectively to make the best use of scarce resources. Other items, numbered in hundreds of thousands, included special gloves for handling barbed wire, ear-defenders for the Royal Artillery, black coveralls for night operations, white coveralls for snow conditions, body armour,[26] rifle breech covers and, a particularly attractive store, electric torches.[27] One rather less successful project driven by the General Staff, was the production and issue of hand-carts to haul Lewis guns and ammunition, which cost the taxpayer £500,000 in 1916 but produced no military effect.[28]

The fourth challenge was that of technology, which affected the logisticians as much, if not more so, than the tacticians. It introduced a wide range of new requirements for support; the aircraft and the tank are two examples and, whilst the equipments of the Great War were in no way comparable in complexity to those in the 21st Century, the introduction of these new military platforms created major challenges to the logistic system. How were they to be moved, stored, inspected, repaired and issued? How would ammunition and fuel be handled? How would 'Quality' be assured? Which organizations were best placed to undertake this new work? How would the interfaces with key agencies be effectively controlled? All these questions taxed the logisticians of the day just as similar ones do today but the Western Front was an environment in which major innovative weapon systems were deployed with remarkable rapidity, creating a process that the British Army describes in 2018, as 'Transforming in Contact'.

That the logisticians of the period surmounted these issues, albeit not perfectly, is testament to their tenacity, initiative and dedication. Technology also created new ways for the logisticians to deliver materiel and manage resources. Of particular note, was the emergence of the load carrying motor vehicle, which, whilst never replacing the horse or the railway during the Great War, created a new logistic capability that offered greatly enhanced flexibility to deliver material and move soldiers. There can be no finer example of the military embracing new and almost untried technology than the investment made in Wheeled Motor Transport (WMT) in the period 1914 to 1918. Inevitably, such capability came at a price. Personnel had to be trained to operate and repair these equipments, whilst fuel and spares had to procured and distributed. These were not easy tasks; training the trainer in order to provide the foundation for the expansion of this vast fleet was but one part of an immense challenge.

It is difficult, from the perspective of the 21st Century, with its almost instantaneous communications capability, to appreciate the enormous impact upon logistics that the telephone made during the Great War. It clearly had limitations, particularly during mobile operations but

24 Trench Stores included combat items such as sniper-scopes, rocket signals, mortars, ammunition, grenades and entrenching tools, although the Assistant Adjutant & Quartermaster-General (AA&QMG) of 17th (Northern) Division related that in one sector, a cow was included in the weekly returns. Village Stores generally included home-comforts, such as stoves, hurricane lamps, building tools and occasionally, china and glass. Colonel W N Nicholson CMG DSO, *Behind the Lines, An Account of Administrative Staff-work in the British Army, 1914-1918* (London: Jonathan Cape, 1939), p.202.

25 Major-General A Forbes, CB CMG, *A History of the Army Ordnance Services*, Vol. Three, *The Great War* (London: Medici Society, 1929), p.43.

26 For an examination of the development of body armour, see, Anthony Saunders, *Dominating the Enemy, War in the Trenches, 1914-1918*, (Stroud: Sutton Publishing, 2000), pp.24-59.

27 Forbes, *Army Ordnance Services*, p.43.

28 The intention was to issue the cart to units participating in the Battle of the Somme. The only lacuna in the plan was that the fully loaded cart was too heavy for the team to pull it across country; Ibid, pp.42-43. Forbes noted, 'This experiment cost half a million sterling and earned a mild reproof from the War Office'. If he is correct, then the economic cost, in 2016 prices, using GDP Economic Cost measurement, was £286.80 million.

it enabled logisticians, in a timely manner,[29] from their unit locations, to co-ordinate activities, discuss plans, order urgent stores and create the foundations for a remarkably robust basic tracking system, at least for critical items. The effective utilization of the system, now, as then, involved user ability and confidence, system reliability, unit access and process integration. The combination of tactics and technology also generated new combat environments. For example, German aerial and chemical (gas in the parlance of the day) warfare capabilities initiated adjustments in logistic operating procedures and the need to procure a raft of specialist equipment such as camouflage nets and respirators. In addition, the United Kingdom's decision to integrate chemical warfare to its military operations generated a significant requirement for the logisticians to store, inspect, issue and transport large quantities of noxious substances in cylinders and shells.

One aspect that is rarely mentioned is the influence of weather upon the logistics of the BEF. The changing seasons and the weather within them, affected not only the delivery of logistics but also the Army's requirements. Heavy snow could disrupt railway operations, significant rain might degrade the condition of the roads and gales the efficiency of maritime traffic.[30] The cold and the wet created the need for Internal Combustion Engine (ICE) anti-freeze products, foul-weather and specialist clothing, stoves and hard shelters, whilst the heat in the summer placed increased pressure on the provision and distribution of water, the requirement to control dust and more timely delivery of temperature sensitive products such as fresh meat. The weather thus influenced a whole range of logistic planning, provision and transport, all of which are equally relevant in the 21st Century.[31]

The Human Resource component posed equally demanding challenges on the logistic services as the expanding numbers of soldiers had to be equipped, clothed, fed, accommodated, cared for, transported and trained. Most recruits had not only to grasp the realities of soldiering but also had to learn new trades in an alien organization and then apply them in a demanding environment, often learning 'On the Job'. This was especially true of the logistic services and a factor that should be considered when assessing their performance during this period. These complex and inter-locking constraints were exacerbated by two issues, which the pre-1914 Army never had to contend with. The recruiting process, overwhelmed by the rush of volunteers, failed to ensure that civilian qualifications and experience were appropriately and effectively deployed within the Army. For instance, the employment of thousands of experienced railwaymen[32] from the numerous railway companies in the United Kingdom in infantry battalions, whilst the Army examined the best method of delivering trade training for those entering military railway units is an example of a major failure in this area.[33]

29 DDST HQ Fourth Army recorded the difficulties of travel on the Western Front on a journey of 20 miles: "Roads were in a shocking state owning to the frost and thaw, and it took me two hours to come from Doullens to Querrieu, though in part this was due to my not knowing the way and to the fact that the 51st Division were moving, and at times I was stopped for fifteen minutes to allow transport to pass." TNA WO 95/454/1: HQ Fourth Army, DDST, WD, entry 29 February 1916.

30 Winter gales were frequent in the English Channel causing delays to the loading, departures, voyages and discharge of ships as well as damage to and sometimes the loss of, vessels; Philip Eden, *Great British Weather Disasters* (London: Continuum, 2008), pp.220-226.

31 A key imperative during the Falklands campaign in 1982 was to complete the recapture of the Islands before the South Atlantic winter set in because of the significant challenges to force sustainment. During Operation GRANBY in 1991, the planners aimed to complete offensive operations in Iraq by late Spring to avoid the logistic burdens imposed in supporting forces in the heat of the summer.

32 *Railwaymen Died, St Paul's Cathedral Service in Memory of Railwaymen, Wednesday 14 May 1919*, Naval & Military Press reprint, nd. 65 railway companies lost 18,957 men from the 186,475 that served in the Armed Forces, a 10.16% fatality rate.

33 The War Office, to its credit, did not make the same mistake twice and there were much tighter controls of manpower skills in the Second World War. See, *The Second World War, 1939-1945, Army, Manpower Problems,*

There was also the impact upon LOC operations created by the losses sustained by the combat arms, particularly infantry officers. In order to replace these officers, LOC units were combed to supply suitable replacements. In many cases, highly experienced pre-war regular officers were posted to infantry battalions, leaving the detail of logistic activity to staff incapable of handling a growing task effectively. Whilst, the transfer of these officers provided a quick fix at the front, it created long-term fragility at the rear. Another issue was the reluctance within the pre-war Army to remove under-performing officers from their posts, a point clearly made in the Army Service Corps post-war history in reference to the Director of Transport in France, Major-General Boyce,[34] 'a strong and able organiser, who possessed that merit somewhat rare in the British Army of knowing when to dismiss subordinates, who, however agreeable in other respects, did not satisfy him professionally'.

The conditions of the Western Front created many challenges for logisticians but whilst examining them, it is useful to remember, as a bench mark, the current Principles of Logistics,[35] which are part of the British Army's operational planning: 'foresight, efficiency, simplicity, co-operation and flexibility', and although not described in this manner in the Great War, their importance was being slowly but steadily understood by the logisticians of the day. Through the application of a process of what is now called DQUAD: Destination, Demand, Distance and Duration,[36] planners were able to quantify, within working limits, future logistic requirements, in Time and Space. As the war progressed, strategic logistic forecasting became ever more important, seeking to create efficiencies at the highest level, whilst still enabling logisticians at the tactical level to engage in improvisation and innovation. Both are part of a fascinating story.

Major-General A J K Pigott CB CBE (Comp) (War Office, 1949) and *Personnel Selection*, Colonel B Ungerson CBE BSc (Comp) (War Office, 1953). See also, the Government perspective in, H M D Parker, *History of the Second World War, Manpower, A Study of War-time Policy and Administration* (London: HMSO, 1957).

34 Beadon, *Royal Army Service Corps*, p.86.

35 The Principles of Logistics are defined in *Army Doctrine Publication* (ADP) Vol. 3, *Logistics* (UK MOD, 1996), pp.1-4 to 1-6, paras 0108-0113 and *Army Field Manual* (AFM) Vol. 1, *The Fundamentals*, Pt 6, Combat Service Support (UK MOD, 1992), Chp 1, pp.1-3 to 1-5. See also, *The Royal Logistic Corps*, Vol. 1, Pam 1, *Logistic Support Doctrine* (UK MOD, 1997), p.1-2 and p 4-3.

36 For an explanation of the application of DQUAD, see, ADP Vol. 3, pp.2-3 to 2-5, paras 0207-0211. See also, *The Royal Logistic Corps*, Vol. 1, Pam 1, pp.3-4 to 3-5. A key point relating to Demand is not just the quantity but the timings, with requirements for a force of fixed size and composition being a mix of Steady State, for example rations; Cyclic, such as different clothing for changing seasons and Surge, for instance, ammunition and fuel for an offensive.

Part I

Perceptions and Plans

1

Sharpening the Sword

British military logistics on the Western Front in perspective

Setting the Scene

The forces at the disposal of the War Office in November 1918 totalled 98[1] British and Empire[2] divisions deployed across the globe in the main operational Theatres of the Western Front,[3] Egypt, Italy,[4] Mesopotamia,[5] Palestine,[6] Salonica[7] and Syria,[8] plus smaller task forces in places such as

1 War Office, *Statistics of the Military Effort of the British Empire during the Great War, 1914-1920* (MEBE) (HMSO, 1922), pp.27-28, Distribution of Divisions Abroad and At Home, December 1918. The figure of 98 includes three Territorial Force Divisions (43rd Wessex, 44th Home Counties and 45th Wessex) that were partly absorbed into other divisions in India, Mesopotamia and Egypt respectively.

2 In 1918, the British Empire consisted of Dominions, Colonies and Protectorates and by 1919, Mandated Territories assigned to Britain by the League of Nations. For an examination of the British Empire during the Great War, see, Robert Holland, 'The British Empire and the Great War, 1914-1918' in Judith M Brown PhD and Wm Roger Louis CBE D Litt FBA, (Eds.) *The Oxford History of the British Empire*, Vol. IV, *The Twentieth Century* (Oxford & New York: Oxford University Press (OUP), 1999), pp.114-137.

3 The British Official History (BOH) has extensive coverage of the operations on the Western Front, comprising 14 volumes on the operational aspects but only one on logistics focusing upon transportation, Colonel A M Henniker CBE (Comp), *Transportation on the Western Front, 1914-1918* (London: HMSO, 1937) and also held in the TNA in ZLIB 29/455 (Text) and 456 (Maps). Taking 33 years, the writing of the Official Histories was a task of significant scale and great complexity. For an assessment of the military Official Histories, see, Andrew Green, *Writing the Great War, Sir James Edmonds and the Official Histories, 1915-1919* (London & Portland Oregon: Frank Cass, 2003).

4 Brigadier-General Sir James E Edmonds CB CMG & Major-General H R Davies (Comps) BOH, *Military Operations, Italy, 1915-1919* (London: HMSO, 1949). See also, George Cassar, *The Forgotten Front, The British Campaign in Italy, 1917-1918* (London & Rio Grande: The Hambledon Press, 1998) and John Dillon, *Allies are a Tiresome Lot, The British Army in Italy in the First World War*, Wolverhampton Military Studies (Solihull: Helion, 2015).

5 Brigadier-General F J Moberly CB CSI DSO psc (Comp), BOH, *The Campaign in Mesopotamia, 1948-1918*, (London: HMSO) Vol. I, 1923, Vol. II, 1924, Vol. III, 1925, Vol. IV, 1927 and the *Critical Study of the Campaign in Mesopotamia up to April 1917*, Part 1, *Report*, compiled by Officers of the Staff College Quetta, October - November 1923 (Calcutta: Government of India Press, 1925). See also, A J Barker, *The Neglected War, Mesopotamia 1914-1918* (London: Faber and Faber, 1967) and Charles Townshend, *When God Made Hell, The British Invasion of Mesopotamia and the creation of Iraq*, 1914-1921 (London: Faber and Faber, 2010). For a contemporary review of immediate post-war operations, see, Lieutenant-General Sir Aylmer L Haldane GCMG KCB DSO, *The Insurrection in Mesopotamia, 1920* (Edinburgh & London: William Blackwood & Sons, 1922).

6 The BOH for Palestine also covers operations in Egypt and Syria; Lieutenant-General Sir George MacMunn KCB KCSI DSO psc & Captain Cyril Falls (Comps), BOH, *Military Operations, Egypt and Palestine* Vol. I, *From the Outbreak of War With Germany to June 1917* (London: HMSO, 1928) and Vol. II (in two parts) *From June 1917 to the End of the War*, Captain Cyril Falls (Comp), 1930 and also, *A Brief Record of the Advance of the Egyptian Expeditionary Force, July 1917 - October 1918*, compiled from Official Sources (London: HMSO, 1919). See, also, Colonel A P Wavell CMG MC, *The Palestine Campaigns* (London: Constable, 1928); Lieutenant-Colonel Clive Garsia DSO MC, *A Key to Victory, A Study in War Planning* (London: Eyre and Spottiswoode, 1940) and Yigal Sheffy, *British Military Intelligence in the Palestine Campaign, 1914-1918* (London & Portland Oregon: Frank Cass, 1998).

7 Salonica was called Macedonia in the official history; Captain Cyril Falls (Comp), BOH, *Military Operations, Macedonia* (London: HMSO) Vol. I, *From the Outbreak of War to the Spring of 1917*, 1933 and Vol. II, *From the Spring of 1917 to the End of the War*, 1935. See also, Alan Wakefield & Simon Moody, *Under the Devil's Eye, Britain's Forgotten Army at Salonika, 1915-1918* (Stroud: Sutton Publishing, 2004).

8 See, John D Grainger, *The Battle for Syria, 1918-1920* (Woodbridge: The Boydell Press, 2013).

East & West Africa,[9] Karun, Persia,[10] Northern Russia,[11] and three Indian Army Divisions at War Establishment on the North-West Frontier of India. In addition, there were the seven major Home Service Commands and Ireland,[12] whilst battalions and brigades manned colonial garrisons such as Burma, Cyprus, Gibraltar, the Falkland Islands, Hong Kong and West Indies, assisted by locally recruited units. The personnel manning these forces, in October 1918, inclusive of labour units (558,143) totalled 5,389,607[13] and of these 1,966,727,[14] were deployed in the British Expeditionary Force (BEF)[15] in Belgium and France. To support these formations across the Globe required a massive industrial and logistic effort, utilizing resources not only from the United Kingdom but also those of the Dominions, the Empire and the United States of America.

Some statistics provide a lucid illustration of the challenges confronting the BEF's logisticians. In October 1916, the front was relatively stable, yet the daily tonnage of materiel being delivered by rail to the BEF, amounted to nearly 40,000 tons, of which 11,000 was ammunition, and another 11,000 was stone for construction.[16] This huge quantity of materiel, was, for the most part, delivered to Standard Gauge Railway (SGR)[17] railheads,[18] whence it was transferred to units by Horse Transport (HT) Mechanical Transport (MT),[19] mainly Wheeled Motor Transport (WMT), and the Narrow

9 For operations in East Africa, see, Lieutenant-Colonel Charles Hordern (Comp) (from a draft by the late Major H Fitz M Stacke MC psc) BOH, *Military Operations, East Africa*, Vol. I, *August 1914 - September 1916* (London: HMSO, 1941). Vol. II was never published but draft chapters exist in the United Kingdom National Archives. See also, Ross Anderson *The Forgotten Front, The East African Campaign, 1914-1918* (Stroud: Tempest, 2004). For West Africa, see, Brigadier F J Moberly CB CSI DSO psc, *Military Operations, Togoland and the Cameroons, 1914-16* (London: HMSO, 1931) and Brigadier-General E Howard Gorges CB CBE DSO, *The Great War in West Africa* (London: Hutchinson, nd but 1930). See also, Edward Paice, *Tip and Run, The Untold Tragedy of the Great War in Africa* (London: Weidenfeld & Nicolson, 2007).

10 Brigadier-General F J Moberly CB CSI DSO psc (Comp), BOH, *Operations in Persia, 1914-1919* (London: HMSO, 1929). Compiled at the request of the Government of India, this document was classified CONFIDENTIAL and restricted to an edition of 500 copies at the direction of the India Office, which was concerned about political sensitivities within it. The Royal Military Academy Sandhurst Library is fortunate to hold a copy. A facsimile edition, with colour maps, was published in 1987 by HMSO, in conjunction with the Imperial War Museum.

11 In September 1919, there were 11,000 British troops based at Archangel and 5,000 at Murmansk; MEBE, p.24, Russia and Siberia. See, also, Clifford Kinvig, *Churchill's Crusade, The British Invasion of Russia, 1918-1920* (London & New York: Hambledon Continuum, 2006).

12 For post-war operations, see, Charles Townshend, *The British Campaign in Ireland, 1919-1921, The Development of Political and Military Policies*, Oxford Historical Monographs (Oxford: OUP, 1975) and William Sheehan, *A Hard Local War, The British Army and the Guerrilla War in Cork*, 1919-1921 (Stroud: Spellmount, 2011).

13 MEBE, pp.25-26, Formations at Home.

14 This total comprised: 1,859,246 military personnel, inclusive of 8,360 members of the RAF's Independent Air Force (IAF) and 107,481 civilian and native personnel and 17,180 women; MEBE p.62, Estimated Strength of the Expeditionary Forces, 1 November 1918.

15 The term 'British Expeditionary Force' is an inaccurate and inadequate term to describe the deployment of so many troops from the British Empire. From the United Kingdom there were English, Irish, Scottish and Welsh troops, whilst the Dominions, Colonies and Protectorates provided units and personnel from Africa, Australia, Canada, China, India, Newfoundland, New Zealand and the West Indies. Arguably, 'British Empire Force' would have been a more accurate and appropriate description for the abbreviation BEF. In addition, GHQ BEF commanded, at some point during the operations in 1918, American, French and Portuguese formations and units.

16 Henniker, BOH, *Transportation on the Western Front*, p.188.

17 A Standard Gauge Railway is defined as one with a track gauge of 4 feet 8 ½ Inches (1435mm). In 2018, Standard Gauge is rated between 1432mm and 1435mm to account for those SGRs, which have reduced their gauge by 3 mm, to improve the ride of high-speed trains. In some documents and publications, SGR is described as Broad Gauge, which is incorrect but is a term that frequently appears in contemporary material.

18 The *Field Service Pocket Book* of 1914 defines a railhead as: 'a locality on the railway where ammunition and supplies are transferred to ammunition parks and supply columns'; General Staff, *Field Service Pocket Book 1914* (FSPB 14), (London: HMSO, 1914), p.xi.

19 Mechanical Transport included wheeled, tracked, or semi-tracked land vehicle utilised in a logistic context to move men and materiel to, on or from the battlefield and powered by the Internal Combustion Engine (ICE) either Spark Ignition (SI) or Compression Ignition (CI) fuelled by petroleum spirit or diesel oil respectively, or by steam (Steam Transport (ST)). Often abbreviated to MT, it does not include combat vehicles, such as tanks, Armoured

Gauge Railway (NGR)[20] network but at some point, if not several, nearly every ton of it would be manually handled. Materiel support requirements for the BEF were remarkable in scope and size. During major offensive operations in September 1916, the daily requirement for each mile of front, excluding the road material to support the advance was a mighty 1,934 tons[21]. In the period 9 August 1914 to 10 November 1918, stocks amounting to 25,497,151 tons[22] were shipped to France, whilst additional stores, services and materials were procured in-theatre. Ammunition accounted for 5,253,338 tons of this total and its usage could on occasion be prolific.[23] From September 1914 to November 1918, the BEF fired 170.4 million artillery rounds,[24] and in one 24-hour period from

Personnel Carriers (APC) or Self-Propelled Guns (SPG). Motor Transport (MT) included Wheeled or tracked or semi-tracked land logistic vehicle powered by the ICE but to provide specific clarification for wheeled vehicles, the term Wheeled Motor Transport (WMT) is used.

20 A Narrow Gauge Railway is defined as one with a track gauge of less than 4 feet 8 ½ Inches (1435mm). For the technical definitions, and a short history of Narrow Gauge Railways, see, Jack Simmons & Gordon Biddle (Eds.) *Oxford Companion to British Railway History* (Oxford & New York: OUP, 1997), pp.337-338. For a short history of the British NGR, see, W J K Davies, *Light Railways of the First World War, A History of Tactical Rail Communications on the British Fronts 1914-1918* (Newton Abbot: David & Charles, 1967). For two excellent illustrated histories, see, Keith Taylorson, *Narrow Gauge at War* (Brighton: Plateway Press, 1987) and *Narrow Gauge at War*, Vol. 2 (Brighton: Plateway Press, 1996).

21 Henniker, BOH, *Transportation on the Western Front*, p.157. Lieutenant-Colonel H Osborne Mance in his comments on a lecture on 'Land Transportation in the Late War', by Colonel M G Taylor, Wednesday 5 October 1921, *Journal of the Royal United Services Institution (JRUSI)* Vol. LXVI (1921), p.715, suggests 2,200 tons but the difference may be the road construction materials. Mance admits that he is quoting "the figures from memory, but I think they are correct."

22 MEBE, p.485, Table 11 - Stores Shipped to France for the British Expeditionary Force from 9th August 1914 to 10th November 1918. Table 1 compiled from information in MEBE.

Table 1.1

Stores Tonnage Shipped to France for the BEF: 9 August 1914 - November 1918

Materiel	**Tons**	**Remarks**
Ammunition	5,253,338	
Canteen	269,317	Expeditionary Forces support
Coal	3,922,391	
Food	3,240,948	
Hay	2,460,301	
Mechanical Transport Stores	158,482	
Miscellaneous	539,398	
Ordnance	1,761,777	
Oats	2,978,301	
Petrol, Oils, Lubricants	758,614	
Railway Material	988,354	
Road Stone	761,540	
Royal Air Force Stores	123,570	
Royal Engineer Stores	1,369,894	
Tanks & Stores	68,167	
Timber	842,759	Royal Engineers & railways
Total	25,497,151	

MEBE, p.481, Table 5 - Approximate Cost of Gun Ammunition and Number of Rounds Expended by the British Armies in France from Noon, 28th September, to Noon, 29th September 1918.

23 As an average, shell manufacture was assessed to be £200 (£78,090 in 2016) per ton in 1918; Lieutenant-Colonel B A Hill DSO RAOC *Ordnance Duties* (London: HMSO, 1926), p.29. For details of the types and numbers of artillery munitions, see, MEBE, pp.434-435, Table (xii) - Ammunition sent to France.

24 MEBE, p.485, Table 12 - Approximate Expenditure of Ammunition in France during the War. This table refers

1200 hours on 28 to 1200 hours on 29 September 1918, the BEF fired 943,847 rounds.[25] The financial cost was just as prodigious; the 1918 value of the ammunition shipped to France was £1.05 Billion, which in 2016 prices is £409.90 Billion; thus, on average, the BEF's annual ammunition expenditure was approximately £95 Billion,[26] a scale of economic commitment, which is lucidly illustrated by the observation that the annual cost of BEF ammunition,[27] was 2.7 times the UK Defence budget in 2015-16,[28] and the highest daily expenditure was £3.871 million, which equates to £1.511 Billion at 2016 prices.[29] Given the scale and cost of these resources, the importance of audit and accountability became an increasing issue, with reconciliation between Issue and Receipt, becoming a key factor in ensuring resource control. One hidden aspect of this activity was the work undertaken by the General Headquarters (GHQ) Directorate of Supplies Investigation Department, which sought to drive down loss, theft, fraud and waste.[30]

The sustainability of the BEF on the Western Front was based on five factors, each of which played a critical part in ensuring the operational capability of Britain's deployed land and air components.[31] First, the industrial and economic production base of the United Kingdom, which combined with the output of the Empire and the United States, provided an enormous mass of materiel,[32] and the emerging criticality of 'Big Logistics' (Big L),[33] the mobilization of industrial resources and production to support the defence requirement underpinned by the interface with 'Small L' at Theatre level, was central to the BEF's developing war-fighting capability. Secondly, the capacity of the railway system in the United Kingdom to move troops, materiel and casualties to and from the Sea Ports of Embarkation (SPOE) and Disembarkation (SPOD).[34] Thirdly, the very

solely to artillery ammunition but includes 3 inch AAA. MEBE records that the BEF expended 170,385,295 artillery rounds.

25 MEBE, p.482, Table 5.

26 Lower in 1914-15, higher in 1917-18.

27 Of interest, is that the cost of consumables, for example ammunition, often exceeded by a significant margin, the expense of the capital equipment which, they were produced to support. For instance, the lifetime cost of an 18 pdr gun, carriage and limber was, in 1918, around £5,000 (£1,952,000 in 2016 prices) but the 10,000 rounds of ammunition it was expected to fire cost nearly £30,000 (in 2016, £11,710,000 - £1,171 per round); *Ordnance Duties*, p.29. 2016 prices based on the *Measuring Worth UK* Economic Cost measuring the comparison of its relative cost using the cost index of all output in the economy as a share of the Gross Domestic Product (GDP).

28 £35.10 Billion; *UK Defence in Numbers* (UK MOD, September 2016).

29 Based on the *Measuring Worth UK* Economic Cost.

30 Whilst initially focused on the Base Areas, the work of the Investigation Department extended to Armies. One of the key tasks was to ensure the efficiency of distribution, one successful example in July 1917, being the recovery of 199 loaded railway wagons that had disappeared from the tracking process whilst in transit; asset tracking remains equally important in 2018. See, Colonel R H Beadon, CBE psc, *The Royal Army Service Corps, A History of Transport and Supply in the British Army*, Vol. II (Cambridge: CUP, 1931), pp.101-102 and Issac F Marcosson, *The Business of War* (London: John Lane, The Bodley Head, 1918), p.118. The activities and effectiveness of the Investigation Department in delivering logistic capability in the BEF is worthy of academic study.

31 Royal Flying Corps until 1 April 1918 when the Royal Air Force was formed, although in practical terms, logistic operations remained extant. For the Official History of air operations, see, Walter Raleigh, BOH, *The War in the Air, Being the Story of The part played in the Great War by the Royal Air Force*, Vol. I (Oxford: Clarendon Press, 1922) and H A Jones, BOH, *The War in the Air, Being the Story of The part played in the Great War by the Royal Air Force*, Vols II-VI (Oxford: Clarendon Press, 1928-1937). For a resume, see *A Short History of the Royal Air Force*, Air Publication 125, Air Ministry, September 1929. The Royal Naval Air Service (RNAS) was also deployed on the continent.

32 Despite the massive industrial output of the United States, the logistic components of its Army were not prepared for operations on a strategic scale, and they faced similar initial problems to those of the BEF. For an analysis, see, Phyllis A Zimmerman, *The Neck of the Bottle, George W Goethals and the reorganization of the US Army Supply system 1917-1918* (College Station: Texas A&M University Press, 1992).

33 'Big L' is an American term, which neatly describes the activity. For an analysis of United States 'Big L' during the Second World War, see, Alan Gropman (Ed.) *The Big L, American Logistics in World War II* (Washington DC: National Defense University Press, 1997).

34 There was no official history of British railway operations in the United Kingdom during the Great War but Edwin A Pratt, *British Railways and the Great War, Organization, Efforts, Difficulties and Achievements*, Vols I & II (London:

significant resource of Britain's Mercantile Marine and the ability of the Royal Navy to reduce cargo and passenger shipping losses to a supportable minimum, which enabled materiel and personnel to be shipped from around the Globe to the Continent.[35] Fourthly, the ingenuity and dedication of the BEF's Theatre logisticians, military and civilian, who were able to efficiently integrate the deployed resources and Host Nation Support (HNS)[36] into a wide range of plans and effects, which included the movement of Indian Expeditionary Force A (IEFA) to France in late 1914 and the dispatch of two corps to Italy in late 1917.[37] Last but certainly not least, was the direction of this broad spectrum of activity, ranging from Command and Control, through to Co-ordination and Committee, through to key civilian supporting commercial processes.

Transforming in Contact

Of immense significance to this appraisal, is that the BEF was in 1918 and remains, the largest single co-ordinated entity in the history of the United Kingdom and from the logistic perspective, this makes it a most interesting area for study. Indeed, in commercial terms, the BEF was the largest and most powerful company within a global corporation,[38] with its vital logistic component headed by the Quartermaster-General (QMG).[39] The assets were co-ordinated on an international scale

Selwyn & Blount, 1921) may be considered to be so. For a short history, see, J A B Hamilton, *Britain's Railways in World War 1* (London: George Allen & Unwin Ltd, 1967).

35 In 1914, 44.4% of the World's tonnage of shipping was flagged to the United Kingdom, whilst the Dominions and Colonies contributed an additional 3.5%, which meant that Britain and the Empire controlled 47.9% of the World's shipping. In 1914, British flagged steam vessels totalled 12,602, with a Net Registered Tonnage (NRT) of 11,273,000, although only 3,747 were vessels greater than 1,000 tons, of which 3,675 were employed in trading, totalling 10,037,862 NRT. Of particular interest, is that 30% of the vessels accounted for 90% of the tonnage, reflecting Britain's economic need to drive costs down in her global trade. Investment was strong too, illustrated by the relative youth of the fleet; 68% of the ships had been constructed since 1900, 44% since 1905 and 20% since 1910. Sailing ships totalled 2,081. For details, see, *Annual Statement of the Navigation and Shipping of the United Kingdom for the Year 1913*, Command 7616 and Archibald Hurd, BOH, *The Merchant Navy*, Vol. I (London: John Murray, 1921), pp.85-94.

36 French AQ support to the BEF is another area requiring study. For an academic assessment of the wider issues, see the engaging Elizabeth Greenhalgh, *Victory through Coalition, Britain and France during the First World War* (Cambridge: Cambridge University Press (CUP), 2005).

37 The Mediterranean Line of Communication (MEDLOC) with the Sea Port of Debarkation (SPOD) at Marseilles was formed to support the move of IEFA but as it transpired, it retained logistic utility throughout the war for operations in Gallipoli, Egypt, Italy, Mesopotamia and Palestine. For a description of the movements aspects of the deployment to Italy, see, Henniker, *Transportation on the Western Front*, pp.297-302.

38 Of particular note in relation to this chapter, was the visit, oiled by the entry of the United States to the war, of the financial editor of the influential US *Saturday Evening Post*, Issac Frederick Marcosson, who was granted access to the Quartermaster-General to the Forces, Lieutenant-General John Cowans. As a result of his visit to logistic operations in the UK and on the Continent, he wrote a most illuminating book entitled, *The Business of War* covering the aspects of Big Logistics (Big L) in relation to the industrialized components of the British Army's support, with particular reference to the BEF's Small L. *The Business of War* is a fascinating read, and although rather journalistic in style with a liberal use of 'Americanisms' it is peppered with interesting logistic detail, which also brings to life the stories of a number of senior Great War military and commercial logisticians who have disappeared into the historical mist. The book has a signed photograph of Cowans, from a painting, opposite the title page, inscribed 'To I F Marcosson with great regards J S Cowans'. Issac Frederick Marcosson, *The Business of War* (London: John Lane, The Bodley Head, 1918).

39 General Sir John Stephen 'Jack' Cowans GCB GCMG (1862-1921) was commissioned into the Rifle Brigade in 1881 and died in 1921 as a result of complications arising from a kidney operation. He was the only member of the Army Council to remain in post throughout the Great War, serving as QMG between 1912 and 1919 and promoted the employment of uniformed women, particularly in the logistic services. His biographers summarized his contribution to the British Army during the Great War thus: 'No Quartermaster-General in history is even faintly comparable to him in achievement', Major Desmond Chapman-Huston & Major Owen Rutter, *General Sir John Cowans, GCB GCMB, The Quartermaster General of the Great War*, Vols I & II (London: Hutchinson, 1924), p.324. Sir Arthur Yapp, Director of the YMCA, described him as a 'genial autocrat'; Ibid, p. 250. Jack Cowans

from its Headquarters, the War Office,[40] in London, and the operations of its continentally based company, the BEF, were neatly summarized by Lord Northcliffe's comment that: "We have brought to France a considerable portion of industrial England."[41] In particular, the development of the concept of a seamless process entitled 'Factory to Fire-Trench' was a key component of BEF logistics delivery on the Western Front.[42] To function as an effective combat force, the BEF required not only a concomitant quality of command experience and ability at each level, which, arguably, until late 1916, did not exist[43] but also the personnel to control and direct what was a complex industrial and administrative operation involving nearly two million people.[44] The rapid expansion of its personnel was fundamental to its success and equally, many of its problems. Manpower in the BEF rose from 270,000 in December 1914 to 858,000 in August 1915,[45] a factor of 3.17 in 8 months. This was a remarkable rate of growth, which has rarely been achieved by any organization. In the 24 days between 1-24 August, 96,000 personnel joined the BEF and the expansion continued,[46] with its strength rising to 1.029 million in February 1916 and peaking at 2.044 million in August 1917.[47]

In addition to this incredible rate of expansion, the BEF suffered heavy casualties, learned different skills, employed new tactics, created its administrative and logistic base, tested emerging technology,[48] crafted its command systems, developed its Staff and formed training establishments for every conceivable activity. These were remarkable achievements but matched to the challenges the BEF faced, they were nothing less than extraordinary. Manpower and material were constant constraints and logistic commanders and staffs consistently reviewed organizations, procedures, processes and establishments to create more effective and efficient outputs to meet the BEF's operational needs but there were inevitably inherent risks.[49] Commanders and Staffs certainly faced

was a most interesting character and a very able administrator, whose industrious contribution to the British Army's capability during the Great War has, effectively, been forgotten; his time as QMG certainly deserves a modern study. See also, RHB, 'Sir John Cowans, The Greatest Quartermaster General', *Royal Army Service Corps Quarterly*, Vol. 13 (April 1925), pp.189-197 and for a short recent reappraisal of his life, particularly as QMG, see, Keith Grieves' examination in the *Oxford Dictionary of National Biography* (Oxford: OUP, 2004).

40 Marcosson remarked of the QMG, 'In a word, he is the Managing Director of one vast branch of the stupendous Business of War', *Business of War*, p.18.

41 The Transportation Mission to GHQ, 1916, *Look to Your Front, Studies in the First World War* by the British Commission for Military History, Spellmount, 1999, p.68. As an example, North Eastern Railway (NER) locomotives could be seen hauling London & South Western Railway (LSWR) wagons on rail previously laid on Midland Railway ballast; Marcosson, *Business of War*, p.276.

42 Marcosson in 1918 offered a description of the office occupied by the BEF's Director Transport, Brigadier-General Boyce, 'On a chart about three feet square, which hangs on the wall……..is a layout of the whole system from factory to field'; Marcosson, *The Business of War*, p.129.

43 See, Garry Sheffield & Dan Todman (Eds.) *Command and Control on the Western Front, The British Army's Experience, 1914-1918* (Staplehurst: Spellmount, 2004); Simon Robbins, *British Generalship on the Western Front, 1914-1918, Defeat into Victory* (London & Portland Oregon: Frank Cass, 2005) and Andy Simpson, *Directing Operations, British Corps Command on the Western Front, 1914-1918* (Stroud: Spellmount, 2006).

44 Marcosson observed of the QMG, 'Before him each morning is laid a sheet of paper less than a foot square on which is typed the feeding strength of all the British Armies - man and beast - in every theatre of war together with the precise quantity of food, fuel and forage available for them. On another sheet is a compact summary of all supplies contracted for or speeding on ships and trains towards the zones of distribution and consumption. At a glance therefore he can appraise the situation on which victory in the field stands or falls'; *Business of War*, p.17.

45 MEBE, p.64 (iii), Table (ii) - Estimated Strength of the Expeditionary Forces: France and Italy.

46 Compare this to Operation GRANBY, the largest British Land Force operational deployment since the Second World War, which totalled 40,000 personnel. Nigel Pearce, *The Shield and the Sabre, The Desert Rats in the Gulf, 1990-91* (London: HMSO, 1992).

47 MEBE, p.64 (iii), Table (ii) - Estimated Strength of the Expeditionary Forces: France and Italy.

48 For an assessment of the impact of technology upon the performance of the BEF, see, Tim Travers, *How the War Was Won, Command and Technology in the British Army, 1917-1918* (London & New York: Routledge, 1992).

49 For example, the implementation of direct cross-loading from Divisional Supply Column (DSC) Motor Transport (MT) to the Horse Transport (HT) of the Divisional Train reduced handling and the Operational Security (OPSEC) risks in having static dumps. Another economy was the creation of forward divisional railheads, thereby dispensing

enormous logistic challenges during this period, as they grappled with problems and resources beyond their experience and knowledge. A contemporary participant, GOC 4th Division,[50] was philosophical:

> I blame no particular General nor his Staff, each one was as bad, or I should say ignorant, as the other. We were dealing with much larger bodies that we had ever dealt with except on paper, the higher staff had no practice in command, and although they had been well trained in the theory of the writing and issue of orders, they failed in practice.[51]

It is therefore, surprising that so many aspects of the BEF's operations were eventually brought to a peak of finesse. In the round, the intellectual, structural and practical changes that enabled these activities to be successfully conducted were immense, and those who enacted them have never been given the credit they deserve.

Between 1890 and 1945, the Army underwent an enormous change in the manner in which, it conducted its operations and none more so than in the period 1914-1918, when it was transformed from what was in effect, mainly a colonial gendarmerie, to a continental war-fighting organization on a scale that the British Army had never experienced before nor indeed, has since.[52] 'Transforming in Contact', a key platform of recent British Army capability, is certainly not a new concept but in terms of size, scope, tactics, technology and logistics, the Great War, especially on the Western Front, is arguably the bench-mark by which all other developments in the British Army must be measured.[53] This transformation is well illustrated by an asymmetric action that took place near Mons in late August 1914 when soldiers of the 4th Divisional Ammunition Column (DAC) of the BEF equipped with 0.303 inch Short Magazine Lee Enfield (SMLE) rifles and driving motor lorries, engaged *Uhlan* Cavalry armed with lances. There were casualties on both sides, and whilst some the troops escaped with their vehicles, part of the DAC was captured. Fours years later, on the Western Front, in the autumn of 1918, the British Army, equipped with state of the art weapons, was conducting Combined Arms mobile warfare,[54] integrating infantry, tanks and artillery, without

with the MT of the DSC, with the Divisional Train drawing direct from the railhead, which also reduced the road traffic, with though an increased possibility of air or artillery attack on the fixed railheads. The risk of reducing the capability of the DSC, which followed, did not mature when mobile operations began in 1918 because in the winter of 1917-1918, another reorganization abolished Corps and Divisional Supply Columns, Ammunition Sub-Parks and Auxiliary Patrol Companies in order to pool the assets, by forming Divisional Mechanical Transport Companies, with a particular focus on producing a reserve to replace or reinforce railway movement in specific sectors if required. See, Beadon, *Royal Army Service Corps*, pp.126-128 and pp.138-139.

50 Major-General Sir Thomas D'Oyly 'Snowball' Snow. Snow graduated from the Army Staff College in 1893, later becoming General Officer Commanding (GOC) 4th and 27th Divisions before being appointed Commander VII Corps. He is Grandfather & Great-Grandfather respectively, of the broadcasters Peter and Dan Snow.

51 Extract from his private diary, published in 2011. See, Dan Snow & Mark Pottle, *The Confusion of Command, The Memoirs of Lieutenant-General Sir Thomas D'Oyly 'Snowball' Snow, 1914 –1918* (London: Frontline Books, 2011), p.5.

52 For assessments of the pre-Great War British Army, see, Spencer Jones, *From Boer War to World War, Tactical Reform of the British Army*, 1902-1914 (Norman: University of Oklahoma Press, 2012), Timothy Bowman & Mark Connelly, *The Edwardian Army, Recruiting, Training and Deploying the British Army* (Oxford: OUP, 2012) and Simon Batten, *Futile Exercise?, The British Army's Preparations for War 1902-1914* (Warwick: Helion, 2018).

53 For the wider context, see, Martin van Creveld, 'World I and the Revolution in Logistics', in Roger Chickering and Stig Forster (Eds.) *Great War, Total War, Combat and Mobilization on the Western Front, 1914-1918*, German Historical Institute (Washington DC: CUP, 2000), pp.57-72.

54 For recent assessments, see, J P Harris with Niall Barr *Amiens to the Armistice, The BEF in the Hundred Days Campaign, 8 August - 11 November 1918* (London & Washington, Brassey's, 1998); Jonathan Boff, *Winning and Losing on the Western Front, The British Third Army and the Defeat of Germany in 1918* (Cambridge: CUP, 2012) and Gary Sheffield & Peter Gray (Eds.), *Changing War, The British Army, the Hundred Days Campaign and the Birth of the Royal Air Force, 1918*, Birmingham War Studies (London: Bloomsbury, 2013).

the aid of computers, in a chemical environment, supported by Air Interdiction (AI),[55] Close Air Support (CAS)[56] and the delivery of supplies by air-drop.

Whilst not manoeuvre warfare in its late 20th or early 21st Century sense,[57] and sometimes lacking the close integration of the fighting components, which might have matured had the war continued,[58] the BEF was able to generate this impressive capability because its commanders, staff and soldiers seized the operational and tactical opportunities offered by the Internal Combustion Engine (ICE) not only for conducting mobile warfare but also to provide the expanding essential logistic requirement, whilst utilizing to effect, the proven technologies of the railways and Horse Transport (HT) to sustain, respectively, strategic and tactical logistic support. This integration of All-Arms was not however, the panacea for success because the Combined Arms solution did not, for various reasons, always work successfully[59] and it was then left to the resilience, courage and determination of the infantry soldier to carry the day.[60] What is clear though, is that the effective delivery of resources to the combat arms was critical to success on the field of battle; no infantryman, however brave, is continuously functional without weapons, ammunition, rations,[61] clothing, equipment, shelter, rest and medical care.[62]

Critical to the performance of the BEF was its logistic capability, itself expanding, developing and maturing, and an arena, which has had relatively little recent historical exposure.[63] The crucial role of military and commercial logistics in sustaining the operations of the BEF and enabling the victory of the British and Empire Armies on the Western Front, has for the most part, been

55 Air Interdiction (AI) is an air operation conducted to destroy, neutralize or delay the enemy's military potential, before it can be brought to bear effectively against friendly forces at such a distance from friendly forces, that detailed integration of each air mission with the fire and movement of friendly forces is not required. *Air Publication* (AP) *3000, British Air Power Doctrine*, 3rd Edition, Directorate of Air Staff (UK MOD, 1999), p.3.13.1.

56 Close Air Support (CAS) is air action against hostile targets, which are in close proximity to friendly forces and which, require detailed integration of each air mission with the fire and movement of those forces; AP 3000, p.3.13.2.

57 The British Army describes *Manoeuvre* as the employment of forces on the battlefield (using movement) in combination with fire or fire potential, to achieve a position of advantage in respect to the opposition in order to accomplish the mission. See, *Army Doctrine Publication (ADP)* Vol. 1, *Operations*, HQ DT/18/34/46, Army Code No 71565 (UK MOD, 1994), pp.3-17 to 3-19.

58 As a combined arms operation, the British Fourth Army attack at Amiens on 8 August 1918 bears comparison with any British Army battle since. For an assessment of the BEF's performance in 1918, see, Michael Crawshaw, 'The High Tide and the Turn', *British Army Review* No 145 UK MOD (Autumn 2008), pp.67-78.

59 Peter Simkins, *From the Somme to Victory, The British Army's experience on the Western Front, 1916-1918* (Barnsley: Pen & Sword, 2014), p.203.

60 Major-General Sir Arthur B Scott KCB DSO (Ed.) and P Middleton Brumwell MC CF (Comp), *History of the 12th (Eastern) Division in the Great War*, 1914-1918 (London: Nisbet & Co, 1923), pp.192-193. See also, Gary Sheffield, *Command and Morale, The British Army on the Western Front, 1914-1918* (Barnsley: Pen & Sword, 2014), pp.153-175.

61 The complex nature of the BEF's rations to support the British Army, the many different cultures from across the Empire and German Prisoners of War, is well described in Marcosson, *Business of War*, pp.81-88. As an example of the challenges, Colonel F M Wilson, Deputy Director Supplies & Transport (DDST) at HQ Fourth Army has left a particularly enlightening description of his difficulties in arranging the provision of potatoes; TNA WO 95/454/1, HQ Fourth Army, DDST, WD, entries, March & April 1916.

62 For the official history of medical support on the Western Front, see, Major-General Sir W G Macpherson KCMG CB LLD, BOH, *Medical Services General History* (London: HMSO) Vol. II, *The Medical Services on the Western Front, and during operations in France and Belgium in 1914 and 1915*, 1923 and Vol. III, *Medical Services during operations on the Western Front in 1916, 1917 and 1918; in Italy; and in Egypt and Palestine*, 1924. For an academic assessment of capability, see, Mark Harrison, *The Medical War, British Military Medicine in the First World War* (Oxford: OUP: 2010). For Empire medical services see, Colonel A G Butler DSO VD, *The Official History of the Australian Army Medical Services in the War of 1914-1918*, Vol. II, *The Western Front* (Canberra: Australian War Memorial, 1940); Lieutenant-Colonel A D Carbery CBE, *New Zealand Medical Services in the Great War* (Auckland & Christchurch: Whitcomb & Tombs, 1924) and Sir Andrew Macphail Kt OBE, *Official History of the Canadian Forces in the Great War 1914-1919, The Medical Services* (Ottawa: F A Acland for Canadian General Staff, 1925).

63 The notable exception is the seminal *British Logistics on the Western Front, 1914-1919*, Ian Malcolm Brown (Westport Connecticut & London: Praeger, 1998).

forgotten but it is fundamental to understanding how the BEF generated and delivered its combat capability.[64] In 1914, logistics was embedded in every area of existing military activity, although focusing on the infantry, cavalry and artillery but rapidly expanding to not only support the growth of existing capabilities but also developing to sustain air, armour, Anti-Aircraft Artillery (AAA)[65] and Gas Warfare (GW),[66] all new technologies with emerging logistic requirements[67] and challenges.[68] Supporting the offensive and defensive aspects of GW was but two of these new tasks, which introduced the need to procure, receive, store, account for, inspect,[69] repair, tranship, transport and issue a range of toxic munitions, which eventually involved developing different handling procedures to conventional ammunition.[70] As a corollary, logisticians also had to manage stocks of newly introduced GW Personal Protective Equipment (PPE) such as the Small Box Respirator (SBR),[71] in addition to Collective Protective Equipment (CPE) such as anti-gas curtains, warning alarms[72] and chemicals for neutralizing liquid chemical warfare agents. There was a particular responsibility to ensure that such equipment was serviceable upon issue; the consequences for soldiers' morale and BEF capability being all too clear if it was otherwise.

All of these outputs relied not only upon equipment but also trained personnel, capable of operating in coherent headquarters, units and formations, which, as the BEF expanded, were increasingly at a premium.[73] Historians of the BEF's Operational Art have identified a crucial

64 Most valuable work has been undertaken covering offensive operations in 1918 by Geoff Clarke, 'Supplying The Battlefront: British Frontline Transport in Mobile Warfare 1918', Unpublished MA dissertation (Birmingham: University of Birmingham, 2006); Christopher Phillips, 'A Modern Industrial Organization: A Case Study of Fourth Army during the battles of the Hundred Days', Unpublished MA dissertation (Birmingham: University of Birmingham, 2009) and Rob Thompson, 'Delivering the Goods, Operation Landovery Castle: A Logistical and Administrative Analysis of Canadian Corps Preparations for the Battle of Amiens 8-11 August 1918', in Gary Sheffield and Peter Gray (Eds.), *Changing War, The British Army, The Hundred Days Campaign and the Birth of the Royal Air Force, 1918*, Birmingham War Studies (London: Bloomsbury, 2013).

65 For an assessment of the development of British Anti-Aircraft Artillery in the Great War, see, Brigadier N W Routledge OBE TD, *History of the Royal Regiment of Artillery, Anti-Aircraft Artillery, 1914-55* (London & New York: Brassey's, 1986), pp.3-35.

66 Gas Warfare (GW) was the contemporary term for Chemical Warfare (CW). For an academic assessment of the BEF's GW capability, see, Albert Palazzo *Seeking Victory on the Western Front, The British Army and Chemical Warfare in World War 1* (Lincoln & London: University of Nebraska Press, 2000). Donald Richter, *Chemical Soldiers, British Gas Warfare in World War One* (Lawrence: University Press of Kansas, 1992), offers a tactical and regimental perspective. The classic text is L F Haber, *The Poisonous Cloud, Chemical Warfare in the First World War* (Oxford: Clarendon Press, 1986). Major-General C H Foulkes CB CMG DSO, *"Gas!" The Story of the Special Brigade* (Edinburgh & London: William Blackwood & Sons, 1934), is the contemporary account by the commander of the Special Brigade, with a style sometimes more 'Boys Own Paper' than professional military history, yet containing technical precision.

67 One of these requirements, was the increasing recognition in relation to materiel, especially as equipment and munitions became more complex, of the growing importance of what the British Army in 2018 describes as CADMID: Concept, Assessment, Development, Manufacture, In-Service and Disposal. The acronyms may be different but the processes and tasks were as relevant then as they are now.

68 For an excellent summary, see, Guy Hartcup, *The War of Invention, Scientific Developments, 1914-1918* (London: Brassey's, 1988).

69 The British Army in 2018 uses the acronym PRISMA to describe these tasks: Provision, Receipt, Issue, Store, Manage and Account.

70 Treatise on Ammunition, 10th Edition, War Office (HMSO, 1915) is the contemporary handbook for in-service ammunition in the Royal Navy and Army.

71 With the exception of improvised field protection, there were seven types of respirator on issue before the SBR, which became, with various modifications, the standard equipment from August 1916.

72 Strombus horns were issued on a synopsis of 20 per each mile of front. Football rattles were also issued, whilst units fabricated gong alarms from brass cartridge cases. Having been cleared from dusty lofts and attics, the latter items now often appear, sometimes in the original form, or adapted as trench art, at militaria and antique fairs, introducing a small forgotten element of Great War logistics to the 21st Century.

73 The DAA&QMG (Lieutenant-Colonel W M Nicholson) 17th (Northern) Division summarised the frustration, using salvage as the example: 'Required: a good salvage officer, and a very small staff'; Colonel W N Nicholson, CMG DSO, *Behind the Lines, An Account of Administrative Staff-work in the British Army, 1914-1918* (London:

tactical and operational learning curve[74] as the Expeditionary Force created its capability but the logistic learning process was equally significant.[75] Lieutenant-Colonel Walter Nicholson,[76] the Assistant Adjutant and Quartermaster-General (AA&QMG)[77] of 17th (Northern) Division summarized the process and the time required to effectively deliver it:

> During the next two years we learnt by real practical experience how to handle transport. This meant the combinations and permutations of first and second line wagons, pack transport, train, corps and army echelons, bus companies. It included light railways and broad gauge.[78] All these had to be brought into use to transport troops, ammunition, supplies and all the unforeseen requirements of war at the shortest possible notice in any direction; over roads that had been cratered, or in bad condition; roads that had to be traffic circuited and timed to avoid congestion and to allow of repairs.[79]

The BEF's logisticians also cast their nets into the French pond in the search for new ideas to improve capability. One concept, which the British Army quickly adopted was that of the *En-cas mobile* (ECM), literally 'movable if necessary', which was a mobile reserve of materiel, usually ammunition, held mainly on pre-positioned railway wagons[80] but also on WMT and occasionally barges, which were permanently loaded for despatch in an emergency.[81] Critical to the BEF's growing capability was the introduction of the Internal Combustion Engine (ICE) in nearly every field of military activity, which generated a very substantial need for a coherent Equipment Support (ES) system,[82] to sustain operations. Timely spares availability on a large

Jonathan Cape, 1939), p.205.

74 The 'learning curve' is increasingly being viewed as a series of steps, not all of them upward.

75 See, for example, *The Somme*, Robin Prior & Trevor Wilson (New Haven & London: Yale University Press, 2005); Simpson, *Directing Operations* and Boff, *Winning and Losing on the Western Front.*

76 Colonel Walter Norris Nicholson CMG DSO was commissioned into the Suffolk Regiment in 1900, commanding the 1st Battalion in the period 1924-1929, and was Colonel of the Regiment between 1939 and 1947. Much of his career was in A&Q appointments, including Deputy Assistant Adjutant and Quartermaster General (DAA&QMG) at the Cape of Good Hope in 1912, and then DAA&QMG of the Highland Division of the Territorial Force in 1914. He took over as Assistant Adjutant and Quartermaster General (AA&QMG) of 17th (Northern) Division in June 1916, and was promoted to Assistant Quartermaster General (AQMG) of XIII Corps in April 1918.

77 Equivalent to the Deputy Chief of Staff (DCOS) in a British division in 2018.

78 Nicholson is referring to NGR and SGR respectively.

79 Nicholson, *Behind the Lines*, p.213.

80 Whilst documents indicate that the British copied the French Army, a point reinforced by Major-General A Forbes, the pre-war FSR clearly articulates the conditions for forming the equivalent of ECM in the rail environment: 'This rule does not apply to such train loads of supplies or ammunition as the IGC may direct to be kept ready at certain stations for immediate despatch to the troops in case of necessity. The amount so retained will be strictly limited, and should not exceed one day's supplies for the force served'; FSR, Part II, *Organization and Administration*, War Office (London: HMSO, 1909), Chp VIII, Transport, Sect 63, para 6, p.95 and Major-General A Forbes, CB CMG, *A History of the Army Ordnance Services*, Vol. Three, *The Great War* (Medici Society, 1929), p.117. This may be a fine example of von Moltke's attribution that the British Army had the finest training pamphlets in the World but fortunately their officers never read them.

81 The concept was a feature of logistic planning to support 1st (British) Corps in West Germany until the last days of the Cold War. The Composite Maintenance Group (Reserve) (CMG (R)) was composed of trains loaded with ammunition, vehicles, rations and fuel, held in the Forward Maintenance Area (FMA) of the Rear Combat Zone (RCZ) awaiting call-forward to the Rear Corps Area (RCA); *Administration in the Field*, A26/GSTP/3351, Army Code No 71024 (UK MOD, 1975).

82 Equipment Support (ES) includes the preparation and repair of equipment for battle and the repair and recovery of equipment battle casualties and failures. The ES Staff play a vital role in monitoring the serviceability of critical equipments in a formation to ensure that combat power is maintained. *Army Field Manual (AFM)* Vol. 1, *Combined Arms Operations*, Part 6, *Combat Service Support*, DGD&D 18/34/44, Army Code No 71344 (UK MOD, 1998), p.viii. A key component of ES is Equipment Support Management (ESM) which is the process of controlling the allocation, repair policy, refurbishment, redesign and replacement of, and re-supply of, material for equipment

scale,[83] itself a new concept within the British Army, was critical to delivering this capability and it is of little surprise that senior logisticians within the BEF sought solutions from the commercial sector.[84] The rapid increase in the relatively new technology of Mechanical Transport, which became essential to the BEF's operations, was matched by the niche requirements of developing military aviation and armoured warfare. The ES for each of these elements was constantly evolving as new equipment and challenges appeared, including the provision of mobile workshops mounted on lorries and the employment of women in technical trades in Base facilities.

P1.1. The Wobbly Wheel: The provision of effective Equipment Support (ES) for a vast range of equipment, particularly transportation assets, was crucial to the BEF's capability. Whilst HT required the continuance of traditional skills and materials, the expansion of Mechanical Transport (MT), especially Wheeled Motor Transport (WMT), created an expanding requirement for the procurement, transport, storage, inspection, maintenance and issue of spares and the need for appropriate ES capabilities. (RLC Museum: AB/000783A)

The underpinning mechanical engineering required to sustain the railway also became a logistic military imperative as the BEF assumed responsibility from the French in late 1916 for the system in the British Area of Operations (AOO).[85] Whilst the technology was proven, the size and scope of

throughout its service life. *Army Doctrine Publication (ADP)* Vol. 3, *Logistics*, DGD&D/18/34/63, Army Code No 71566 (UK MOD, 1996).

83 This is in terms of range of items and quantity. Marcosson noted that the spares range for one type of American lorry consisted of 1,140 different parts ranging from a nut to an axle and that in one shed he visited at the Northern Base Mechanical Transport Depot, he viewed 44,00 pneumatic tyre covers, 40,000 inner tubes and 17,000 solid tyres; *Business of War*, p.136 and p.144. He also noted that the Northern Base Mechanical Transport Depot stocked 32,000 non-interchangeable spares totalling 1.7 million items, pp.137-138.

84 Marcosson recorded his impressions of the inventory control infrastructure at the Northern Base Mechanical Transport Depot: 'Go into its huge counting room - it looks precisely like the office of a great factory with its clicking typewriters, card indexes, ledger accounts, adding machines and other aids to business'; *Business of War*, p.134.

85 This task was the sole responsibility of the Royal Engineers, which ensured an integrated system of engineering and

the task required a rapid expansion of a limited capability,[86] the solution to which, was made more difficult by the recruitment, in late 1914 and 1915, of many semi-skilled and skilled staff[87] from the United Kingdom railway companies into, mainly, infantry regiments, rather than the Royal Engineers.[88] The importance of skilled railway mechanical engineering manpower to the UK's war effort in France had been clearly identified by the Railway Executive Committee in August 1914 but the outfall actions were ineffective in stemming the flow from the industry.[89] ES played a vital role in maintaining the outputs of transportation, aviation, logistic engineering and supply through a complex matrix of delivery but with the exception of various publications[90] on specific subject areas based upon Regimental or Corps responsibility, this important area awaits a coherent study.[91]

The operation of ammunition sites[92] and the widespread transportation of significant quantities

operating.

86 In 1914, there were only two regular (8 and 10) and three Special Reserve Railway Companies (One company Royal Anglesey RE and two companies Royal Monmouth RE). See, Colonel G H Addison (Comp) CMG DSO, *The Work of the Royal Engineers in the European War 1914-1918, Miscellaneous*, Royal Engineers Institute (Chatham: W & J Mackay, 1927).

87 This is another subject requiring academic study. Whilst the technical operating trades (drivers, firemen and signalmen) may not have reflected the emerging military requirement in the detail, the civil, mechanical and Signal & Telegraph (S&T) engineering staff were critical to any future development of a military railway capability. Equally relevant to the efficient operation of a busy railway, were personnel filling non-technical appointments, such as controllers, clerks, dispatchers, statisticians and tallymen. The creation of a 'railway instinct' within the future Railway Operating Division (ROD) relied on importing personnel who 'knew the business'. See, Lieutenant-Colonel E P Anderson DSO RE, 'The Railway Organization of an Army in War', *JRUSI*, Vol. LXXII, February - November 1927, pp.509-510.

88 By Saturday 15 August 1914, 27,600 railwaymen had either been mobilized as Regular Reservists or Territorials, or had left the railway to enlist in the Royal Navy or the Army. Of these, 61% were from only two companies; 9,265 were from the London & North Western Railway and 7,593 from the Great Western. In mid-September 1914, to stem the haemorrhage from the railways, the War Office directed Recruiting Officers not to accept volunteers from the companies unless the individual had a certificate of release from their employer. A steady flow of enlistments continued however, with approximately another 42,400 by January 1915 and the total number who joined the Colours by 11 November 1918 was 184,475, of which there were 21,522 deaths (Killed, Died of Wounds or Sickness) whilst on Active Service. Pratt, *British Railways* Vol. I, pp.348-378. Pratt notes that the death figure may not be accurate; the earlier memorial book states 186,475 enlistments and 18,957 deaths, *St Paul's Cathedral Service in Memory of Railwaymen, In Memory of the Railwaymen of Great Britain and Ireland who have Died in the Service of their Country during the War, 1914-1919*, Railway Companies Association, 1919.

89 'The railwayman who is really wanted for the Railway service is serving his Country just as thoroughly by remaining in that service as by joining the Forces'; TNA AN1, Railway Executive Committee, Minutes of Meeting, 28 August 1914.

90 The history of the BEF's Equipment Support (ES) operations is spread across many publications, with the best summary in Brigadier B B Kennedy CBE & Colonel J A Tatman, *Craftsmen of the Army, The Story of the Royal Electrical and Mechanical Engineers* (London: Leo Cooper, 1970), pp.13-29. The Royal Engineer activity is covered in the series, *Work of the RE in the European War of 1914-19,* Royal Engineers Institute (Chatham: W & J Mackay, 1924) and Major-General (Ed.) H L Pritchard, *The History of the Corps of Royal Engineers*, Vol. V, *The Home Front, France, Flanders and Italy in the First World War* (Chatham: The Institution of the Royal Engineers, 1952). The Army Service Corps ES contribution is embedded in Beadon, *Royal Army Service Corps*, and the Army Ordnance one, Forbes, *Army Ordnance Services*, whilst the Royal Flying Corps aspects appear in Raleigh, BOH, *The War in the Air,* Vol. I, and Jones, BOH, *War in the Air,* Vols II-VI. ES to tank operations is examined in David J Childs, *A Peripheral Weapon? The Production and Employment of British Tanks in the First World War* (Westport Connecticut & London: Greenwood Press, 1999), pp.93-108.

91 Equipment Support capability was delivered mainly in-house, especially in the technical corps, such as the RE, ASC and RFC and to a lesser extent by the artificers of the Royal Artillery and developing Tank Corps; the Army Ordnance Corps Engineering Branch was responsible for other Arms and Services. There was therefore, no single organization responsible of ES and progression of this issue had to wait until the Second World War, when the experience of the campaign in France and the Western Desert generated a series of reviews in relation to the delivery of ES capability culminating in the formation of the Royal Electrical and Mechanical Engineers (REME) in 1942. For a detailed explanation of the issues, see, Major-General Sir E Bertram Rowcroft KBE CB (Comp), *The Second World War, 1939-1945, Army, Royal Electrical and Mechanical Engineers*, Vol. I, *Organization and Operations* (War Office, 1951), pp.1-12 and Kennedy & Tatman, *Craftsmen of the Army*, pp.148-166.

92 In November 1918, there were six Theatre ammunition depots supporting the BEF, with a capacity of 331,500 tons, with the balance, a total of 168,500 tons, held in 10,000 ton sites operated by each Army and stocks held within

of explosive munitions across the BEF Theatre, whilst critical to capability, also introduced the potential for serious loss. Initially, storage and transport operations in the divisional areas were the most vulnerable to failure and the village of Wanquetin was destroyed and 25 people killed after handling procedures at the railhead were ignored.[93] The Base Ammunition Depots (BAD) became increasingly attractive targets for the *Deutsche Luftstreitkrafte* (DLK)[94], as it developed its AI capability,[95] and in the period 18-21 May 1918, the BEF suffered casualties of 25 soldiers killed and 86 wounded plus the loss 12,500 tons of ordnance, to air-delivered weapons. The Second Army lost 1,000 tons in a dump at Campagne on the night of 18-19 May, whilst in an attack on No 12 Ordnance Depot at Blargies on the night of 20-21 May 1918, air-delivered ordnance detonated 5-6,000 tons of ammunition out of the 27,000 tons in storage, also destroying two railway locomotives and 50 wagons.[96] Approximately 120 bombs were dropped, one of which, struck a shed containing 8 and 9.2 inch cartridges, and at one point during the attack, there were five major fires burning around the depot complex.[97] The DLK followed these successes by attacking No 20 Ordnance Depot at Saigneville on the night of 21-22 May 1918 and destroying another 5,600 tons of ammunition, out of the 40,000 tons in store.[98] The conflagration was such that the flames were visible from a distance of 40 miles, and the loss included the complete site stock of Small Arms Ammunition (SAA) amounting to 69 million rounds.[99]

corps and divisional ammunition dumps. In addition, two news sites were being constructed at Bourbourg and Conteville. See, Forbes, *Army Ordnance Services*, pp.130-131.

Table 1.2
BEF – Theatre Ammunition Sites: November 1918

Location	Capacity (Tons)	Remarks
Audruicq	44,000	Northern Area
Blargies (Nord & Sud)	64,500	Southern Area
Bourbourg	00,000	Under construction
Conteville	00,000	Under construction
Dannes	65,000	Northern Area
Rouxmesnil	49,000	Southern Area
Saigneville	60,000	Southern Area
Zeneghem	49,000	Northern Area
Total	331,500	

93 Assessed to be the preparation of 100 fuzes, a task, which was not permitted at railheads; training was also an issue; Forbes, *Army Ordnance Services*, p.143.

94 The German Air Force was not an independent organization but the air arm of the German Army, in the same way as the RFC in the British Army until the formation of the Royal Air Force. The *Deutsche Luftstreitkrafte* was formed in October 1916 from the *Fliegertruppen des deutschen Kaiserreiches*, the Imperial German Flying Corps. The German Imperial Air Service (GIAS) is often used in British sources as the term for the *Luftstreitkrafte* and its predecessor but neither German title translates thus. See, Peter Grey and Owen Thetford, *German Aircraft of the First World War*, 2nd Edn (London: Putnam, 1979), p.xxix.

95 For an examination of the Lessons Identified from *Luftstreitkraft* operations in this period, see, James S Corum, *The Luftwaffe, Creating the Operational Air War, 1918-1940* (Lawrence: University of Kansas Press, 1997), pp.37-40 and for a detailed description, E R Hooton, *War Over The Trenches, Air Power and the Western Front Campaigns*, 1916-1918 (Hersham: Midland Ian Allan, 2010), pp.196-227.

96 Forbes, *Army Ordnance Services*, pp.169-170.

97 For their efforts in fighting the fires and moving ammunition to safer locations, six Army Ordnance Corps personnel received awards for their gallantry. Captain Bailey and Lieutenant Corbett-Sullivan, the Military Cross; Lieutenant Johnson, a Bar to the MC; Sub-Conductor Harris, a Distinguished Conduct Medal; Sub-Conductor Bancroft and Staff Sergeant Jasper, a Military Medal; Ibid, p.170.

98 Ibid, p.171. Only six of the 52 sheds were struck and the updated design reduced the stock loss.

99 BOH, *War in the Air*, Vol. VI, pp.423-425.

Gas Guzzlers and Hay Burners

Operations on the Western Front consumed huge quantities of Petroleum, Oils and Lubricants (POL)[100] and the major advances, on a broad front in late 1918, compounded the demands of delivering the products. Petrol created the greatest problem because of the immense bulk involved, but the ever-increasing types and quantities of oils and lubricants required generated more challenges. In November 1918, the BEF had 57,051 Mechanical Transport (MT) vehicles[101] on charge, including 26,809 General Transport lorries,[102], 14,328 motor-cycles, 5,137 cars, 3,527 ambulances and 2,526 vans.[103] By February 1918, monthly BEF petrol consumption in France had risen to 8.75 million gallons: 8 million for ground operations, and 750,000 gallons of aviation spirit. By October, consumption had risen to 10.5 million gallons for ground fuel and 1.5 million for aviation spirit, a total of 12 million gallons per month totalling 41,441 tons.[104] This figure equates to 394,520 gallons per day,[105] and posed an increasing transport problem solved, at least partially, through innovative bulk refuelling systems, which included oil tanker deliveries of refined product to France,[106] the expansion of bulk tank storage and transport by pipeline. In addition, the BEF was allocated 180 Truck Tanker Fuel (TTF) vehicles, each with a capacity of 600 gallons, with a total lift of 108,000 gallons, and 150 Rail Tank Cars (RTC)[107] each with a capacity of 3,000 gallons and a total lift of 450,000. So in conjunction with cased petrol[108] moved by rail, road and barge, the logisticians were able keep pace with the requirement, although despite the bulk transport equipment, the distribution of petrol remained firmly wedded to the can, with only 15 percent being moved in bulk. Trials were run to test the suitability of the TTFs as kerbside refuellers but the results clearly highlighted a number of issues. The TTFs and most of the lorries had no off-road capability and as hard-standings were at a premium off the Main Supply Routes (MSRs) refuelling had to be conducted on the road. As the hand pumps delivered low flow-rates, fuel transfers were slow and refuelling convoys caused serious disruption to traffic. Whilst therefore, the concept was technically successful, the practical output was not,[109] so the can remained the solution for operational vehicle refuelling. The TTFs were however, utilized to deliver fuel forward to Refilling Points where special cans, reinforced for constant reuse were filled, thereby reducing the number of cans returning to the Base or being lost through damage. The expansion of strategic air operations created a different

100 Petroleum, Oils and Lubricants; the current British Army term is Fuels and Lubricants (F&L). One particular concern was the provision of the toxic substance methanol, which was used as anti-freeze. The engine coolant systems of the period were non-pressurised, which created constant evaporation of the methanol and thus a requirement to replenish it.

101 Exclusive of those vehicles transferred to the Royal Air Force upon its formation on 1 April 1918.

102 Approximately 86% of these lorries were rated 3 tons and the balance, 30 hundred-weight (cwt). See, MEBE, p.594, Table (i) - Mechanical Transport in France by Quarters.

103 MEBE, p.595, Table (ii) (a) - Monthly Census of Mechanical Transport in all Theatres.

104 These figures extracted from: MEBE, p.846, Supply, and Beadon, *Royal Army Service Corps*, p.443.

105 At 2017 pump prices, £5.46 pence per gallon, this is £1,908,379 per day.

106 For the wider issues relating to the delivery of petroleum products required by the United Kingdom, see, Mark Gibson, *Britain's Quest for Oil, The First World and the Peace Conferences* (Solihull: Helion, 2017), pp.48-70.

107 TNA MUN 4/203: Transport: 'Census & Control of rail tank wagons'. MEBE, p.847, Supply states 180 x RTC and 200 x TTF.

108 4 x 2 gallon cans were cased in a wooden box, the boxes as well as the cans requiring recycling because of the shortage of timber. There was also a four gallon can, which was a commercial expedient utilized to increase deliveries from the can filling plant at Portishead near Bristol. The can could not withstand the rigours of operational service, being described as 'flimsy' and was mostly used on the Continent for the carriage of paraffin oil being cased at two cans to the box. Beadon, *Royal Army Service Corps*, pp.441-442.

109 The bulk refuelling bowser, born prematurely during the Great War and so full of promise, made an important contribution to logistic operations but it had to wait another 50 years before the concept was fully integrated into British Army logistic doctrine.

problem. Whilst the eight-man crew of a Mark IV tank had little difficulty in handling the 30 cans required for a fill, it took 20 men the best part of eight hours to empty 700 cans of aviation spirit into the fuel tanks of a Handley-Page V/1500 bomber.[110] Engineers reduced this logistic task by building rail spurs to airfields, enabling bulk refuelling from RTCs to ground storage.

The transport of unit Combat Supplies[111] through the enemy's defensive zone was the subject of much discussion and innovation. The reasons were simple; not only was WMT and to a lesser extent HT, incapable of traversing the ground but they were vulnerable to the destructive effects of artillery. Unsurprisingly, the planners opted to use modified tanks and gun carriers as supply vehicles because they were armoured and tracked, so the two key challenges were immediately solved and the first use of supply tanks took place at Messines in June 1917.[112] The modified vehicles had though, many disadvantages and as the war ended, a small number of appropriately designed supply tanks were in production, based upon the Mark IX, an Armoured Personnel Carrier (APC).[113] The introduction of a tracked armoured logistic carrier did not however, resolve the three key issues inherent in its design: reliability, weight and fuel consumption.[114] Whilst some observers have attributed the failure to complete the mechanization of the BEF in late 1918 to an inbuilt aversion by commanders to the emerging technology, the reasons were more practical, not least those relating to movement, maintenance, POL and human endurance. For the era, tracked armour had very good cross-country capability but this was balanced by concerns over reliability, the position being reversed for WMT, with HT filling the mobility gap in many instances. Industrial capacity, particularly for tracked armour,[115] was also a major issue, although had the war extended into 1919, the fruits of the many contracts intended to significantly expand MT and WMT capability, and thereby replace a reducing supply of HT, would have been deployed to the Field, albeit with a concomitant increase in the requirement for liquid fuels.

Another innovative proposal was the Military Tractor Type A,[116] a soft-skinned tracked vehicle[117] capable of carrying 3 tons across country, at maximum speed of 10 mph. In his paper

110 Beadon, *Royal Army Service* Corps, pp.443-444. Munitions handling also became an increasing logistic issue with the introduction of aircraft such as the Handley Page O/400 capable of lifting a 1,650 lb bomb and the V/1500 a 3,360 lb weapon; Francis K Mason, *The British Bomber since 1914* (London: Putnam, 1994), pp.108-111.

111 Combat Supplies include ammunition, POL and rations.

112 Mark I and Mark II tanks were converted to the supply role, the work being undertaken at the Tank Corps Central Workshops. For a description of the operations of the Tank Supply Companies, see, Colonel J F C Fuller DSO, *Tanks in the Great War, 1914-1918* (London: John Murray, 1920), p.166-171.

113 The Mark IX was designed in 1916 as an Armoured Personnel Carrier (APC) but because of production difficulties only 36 vehicles were built, of which only two were complete before the Armistice, one of which was configured as an ambulance.

114 Tracked armour in the First World War was certainly spares-hungry and many of the items were heavy. Each sprocket wheel for example, weighed over 220 pounds and there was no Material Handling Equipment (MHE) that is taken for granted in the 21st Century. The Mk IX Supply Tank had a Combat Ready Maximum Authorised Mass (MAM) of 37 tons, inclusive of a logistic load of 10 tons. Fuel consumption was another constraint; the planning figure for the Mark IX was 2.4 gallons to the mile, although in certain terrain conditions, using the maximum consumption figure for the Mark IV, it could have been 12 gallons per mile. With a fuel capacity of 100 gallons, this meant, that at best, the range was 41 miles and at worst, eight. Refuelling was conducted by hand using two-gallon cans, a fill requiring 50 cans, thereby creating another logistic task. See, David Fletcher, *Landships, British Tanks in the First World War* (London: HMSO, 1984).

115 For the complex issues relating to tank production, see, Childs, *A Peripheral Weapon?* pp.31-89.

116 Designed by Colonel Henry Newton, serving in the Trench Warfare Department of the War Office, prototypes were constructed by his company, Newton Brothers of Derby, before a contract for 22,000 was let, mainly with three United States companies, Buick, Overland and Studebaker. Some machines had been delivered by November 1918, but with the war's conclusion, the contracts were cancelled. For more details of the equipment, and an illustration, see, David Fletcher, *British Military Transport 1829-1956* (London: TSO, 1998), pp.39-40.

117 Operation GRANBY 1990-91 created a not dis-similar issue and M548 tracked carriers had to be borrowed from the United States Army to enhance the mobility of unit stocks. The problem has not gone away; it is merely waiting to appear in another operation.

of May 1918,[118] Lieutenant-Colonel J F C Fuller[119] then General Staff Officer (GSO) 1 in Tank Corps HQ, was effusive in his assessment of the cross-country potential offered by the capabilities of the new equipments:[120]

> The network upon which strategy is woven is the system of communication which exists in the theatre of war. Hitherto this system has consisted of roads, railways, rivers and canals. Today the introduction of a cross country petrol driven machine, Tank or Tractor, has expanded this system to include at least 75% of the entire terrain of the theatre of war over & above communications as we at present know them. The possibility today of maintaining supply and moving weapons and munitions over open ground irrespective of roads and without the limiting factor of animal endurance introduces an entirely new problem in the history of war. At the present moment he who grasps the full meaning of this change, namely that the earth has become as easily traversable as the sea, multiplies his chances of victory to an almost unlimited degree.[121]

Petrol powered vehicles were not the only systems in use. In 1914, there were 876 HT vehicles in a division,[122] which despite a very considerable increase in WMT over the next four years, had reduced to only 822 by 1918. To draw these vehicles[123] and provide pack transport, there were, on 1 August 1918, 395,941[124] horses[125] and mules[126] in the BEF, each consuming an average of 22.2 pounds of forage[127] each day, the daily account being a staggering 3,924 tons.[128] Given that

118 'The Tactics of the Attack as Affected by the Speed and Circuit of the Medium D Tank dated 24 May 1918', which is examined in J P Harris, *Men, Ideas and Tanks, British Military Thought and Armoured Forces, 1903-1939* (Manchester: Manchester University Press, 1995), p.167.

119 Major-General John Frederick Charles Fuller CB CBE DSO (1878-1966) was an interesting yet controversial character. See, Anthony John Trythall, *"Boney" Fuller: Soldier, Strategist, and Writer* (New Brunswick: Rutgers University Press, 1977) and his theories, *J F C Fuller: Military Thinker, Brian Holden Reid* (New York: Palgrave Macmillan, 1987). See also, Harris, *Men, Ideas and Tanks*. Interestingly, Fuller is only mentioned once in the post-war Tank Corps history; Major Clough Williams-Ellis MC and A Williams-Ellis, *The Tank Corps* (London: Country Life, 1919), p.103.

120 Parts of Fuller's paper failed to recognize important Lessons Identified to the point that he acknowledged in his memoirs that parts of his paper were sensationalist; Major-General J F C Fuller CB CBE DSO, *Memoirs of an Unconventional Soldier* (London: Nicholson and Watson, 1935), p.322.

121 Quoted in Ibid, p.168. Unfortunately, Fuller, unlike Foot, failed to assess the logistic implications of his plans, which damaged his credibility. Whilst part of Fuller's vision was ultimately translated into fact and those armies which deployed their formations in tracked vehicles had much greater operational and tactical mobility, his perception that logistic support would be part of the same process, proved to be unfounded, although the US Army's initial logistic ground manoeuvre operations, reinforced by air and helicopter lift, in Iraq in 2003 were arguably very close to his concept. Despite this achievement, mechanized armies remain heavily dependent on wheeled logistic vehicles and rail networks.

122 Excluding gun carriages and limbers; FSPB 14, p.6.

123 HT whilst having limitations, still had a significant lift, much flexibility and good cross-country mobility and could often traffic roads impassable by WMT. The General Service (GS) Wagon Mark X introduced in 1905, could carry a wide variety of stores including single loads of: 108 x 18 pdr rounds, 66 x 4.5 inch, 200 x camp kettles, 600 x ground-sheets (cased), 640 x GS shovels, 350 x RE spades and 4 x hospital marquees. The detail of the types and quantities of other loads may be found in the FSPB 14, p.134.

124 MEBE, pp.400-401, Table (i) (a) - Remounts: Animals in All Theatres. The figure includes heavy draught horses, mules, officers' mounts and vehicle horses.

125 Horse total: 314,881, a reduction from 368,146 in August 1917 as a result of casualties and the transfer of horses to the American Expeditionary Force (AEF); MEBE, p.401. For an examination of the transfer of horses to the AEF, see, the seminal, Graham Winton, *Theirs Not to Reason Why, Horsing the British Army*, 1875-1925, Wolverhampton Military Studies (Solihull: Helion, 2013), pp.333-339.

126 Mule total: 81,060; MEBE, p.401.

127 Forage consisted of oats and hay. In barracks, heavy draught horses were allocated 15 lbs of oats per day, others between 10 and 12. Draught horses were rationed for 16 lbs of hay per day, the rest, 12 lbs. See, FSPB 14, p.169.

128 This figure is a calculation based upon the number of horses and mules multiplied by 22.2 lbs but is at variance with

Pl.2. Saddlery: With nearly 400,000 horses and mules on strength in August 1918, the provision and repair of equipment to support HT and AT remained a vital part of the BEF's logistic capability. (RLC Museum: AB/000783C)

the BEF's daily petroleum requirement in 1918 was 1,300 tons per day, and its coal consumption around 1,968 tons,[129] it is not surprising that many soldiers sarcastically described four-legged horse power as 'hay burners'. Yet, horses remained essential to the BEF's operational and logistic capability, so despite the increasing challenges in acquiring and transporting fodder,[130] the requirement remained, although acquisition and distribution constraints during the Hundred Days sometimes reduced the daily ration to below the average,[131] which itself, was not excessive

a QMG report in the Royal Corps of Transport (RCT) Archive (File No 1, B1 0754) which states an equivalent of 60,000 tons per month and thus 2,000 tons per day. MEBE, p.485, Table 11 - Stores Shipped to France for the British Expeditionary Force, 9 August 1914 - 10 November 1918, records 2,978,301 tons of oats and 2,460,301 tons of hay, totalling 5,438,602 tons, generating a daily average of 3,500 tons over 1554 days. Given there were reductions in the forage ration, fluctuations of animal numbers and inevitably forage losses, the figure of around 4,000 tons per day at peak seems a reasonable equivalent planning figure.

129 Coal was used widely throughout the BEF to deliver transportation capability: by early autumn 1918, the BEF was operating around 1,400 SGR and 360 NGR locomotives, 725 road steam lorries and 65 tractors. Coal was also used for infrastructure heating in fires, stoves and boilers, in hospitals and camps, producing hot water for washing, laundry and dis-infection. From 9 August 1914 to 10 November 1918, 3,933,391 tons of coal were shipped to France for the BEF; MEBE, p.485, Table 11 - Stores Shipped to France.

130 DDST Fourth Army noted that during a meeting at GHQ with the BEF's Director of Supplies, the latter had emphasised that, 'on no account are we permitted to buy hay in France'; TNA WO 95/454/1, HQ Fourth Army, DDST, WD, 29 February 1916. MEBE, p.845, Supply, notes that apart from hay from the UK, only a small additional amount was imported to France, from Algiers, for the BEF.

131 Colonel F M Wilson, DDST HQ Fourth Army, recorded that horses in the 9th Reserve Park had been receiving only 6 lbs of hay per day in February 1916 but despite being in the open in cold weather were in 'exceedingly good

for a horse undertaking hard work and inevitably increased sickness and reduced performance during the advance.[132]

The fundamental issues underpinning the dichotomy between MT and HT were articulated in a paper of 9 February 1918 by Major Stephen Foot[133] of the War Office Tank Directorate, entitled 'Petrol Versus Muscle'. Foot argued that by deploying tracked armoured logistic carriers at brigade level, major capability enhancements could be delivered, whilst significantly reducing the requirements for horses, forage and manpower. As an example, he estimated that 24 tracked carriers could replace 560 horses and mules utilized for logistic operations within a Field Artillery Brigade, thereby also creating a concomitant reduction in manpower from 320 to 72. Whilst the detail of manning, POL and forage can be debated, the kernel of his argument was sound, not least in relation to operational utilization. Tracked armoured logistic carriers could operate over ground and in tactical conditions that lorries and horses could not.[134] Tracked armoured logistic carriers were however, not the immediate and total solution. Tracks could never keep pace with lorries on the Main Supply Routes (MSR), whilst horses could still out-perform WMT in some terrain conditions, one example being initial diversions to avoid German bridge demolitions during the Hundred Days. HT regularly supported tank operations[135] and in late 1918, there were occasions when tanks were supplied solely by pack transport because there were no available supply tanks and WMT could not traverse the terrain or negotiate obstacles to reach the armour.[136]

Old Chestnuts and New Dimensions

The provision and distribution of POL products to the correct specification for ground and air equipments became an increasingly important task, with quality standards becoming especially important for the Royal Flying Corps (RFC).[137] Indeed, the substantial expansion of air capability[138]

condition'; TNA WO 95/454/1: HQ Fourth Army, DDST, WD, 6 March 1916.

132 For an analysis of this issue, see Winton, *Theirs Not to Reason Why*, pp.347-349.

133 Major Foot had worked in the oil industry before joining the Army. He served on the Western Front with II Tank Brigade, seeing action at Third Ypres and Amiens. Although Foot had a G Operations background, he was, unlike Fuller, clearly cognizant of the logistic implications of armour. He also believed that the German Spring Offensive had failed because the logistic plan was not sustainable; for further discussion of his role, see, Harris, *Men, Ideas and Tanks*, pp.159-194.

134 The experience of the British Army in the Second World War in the Western Desert, Italy and North West Europe clearly proved that the 4x4 truck could not effectively supply forward of A1, particularly when subjected to indirect fire. The solution was a tracked armoured logistic vehicle project that matured in the early-1960s as the FV431, which never entered service and was replaced by the FV 620, an adaptation of the commercially available un-armoured Alvis Stalwart, an amphibious 6x6 High Mobility Load Carrier (HMLC) developed for the oil industry. The Logistic Light Armoured System (LLAS) concept of 2008 was in, many respects, an acknowledgement of, and a solution to, a problem that has existed for nearly 100 years but has never been fully resolved. Whilst LLAS did not enter service, the introduction of protected logistic wheeled vehicles has created a partial solution.

135 TNA WO 95/112/2: 5th Tank Brigade, WD, '5th Tank Brigade, Preliminary Instructions No 1 dated 6 August 1918, Administrative Instructions' para 2 (b) Horse Transport.

136 15th Tank Battalion, WD dated 1 October 1918; Tank Museum.

137 For an examination of pre-war British military aviation, see, Raleigh, *BOH, The War in the Air*, Vol. I and Hugh Driver, *The Birth of British Military Aviation: Britain 1903-1914*, The Royal Historical Society (Woodbridge: The Boydell Press, 1997) and for details of the early aircraft, J M Bruce, *The Aeroplanes of the Royal Flying Corps Military Wing*, 2nd Edn (London: Putnam, 1992).

138 In November 1918, RAF strength on the Western Front, inclusive of the Independent Air Force (IAF) totalled 1,799 front line aircraft and 51,000 personnel in 99 squadrons, a considerable increase over the 66 aircraft and approximately 927 officers and men deployed by the RFC in four squadrons during August 1914. The figure of 927 is not definitive and calculated from subtracting the 109 officers who deployed to France from the 146 total in the RFC, matched by the percentage equivalent to the 1,097 Other Ranks (OR) on strength, thereby creating 818 ORs and a total of 927; figures extracted from Jones, BOH, *The War in the Air*, Vol. VI, Appendices XXVI and XXXV.

created a new requirement that demanded much more sophisticated and comprehensive support arrangements, which grew into the specialized area of aviation logistics, spawning a system that was clearly different to any previous military deployment.[139] Aviation logistics introduced three very important differences to past experience. First, there was the significant number of logistic personnel needed to sustain operations in the Field, which overturned the previous Combatant to Non-Combatant ratio,[140] figures indicative of future requirements as the equipment of war became more technical. As an example, on 1 November 1918, only 8 percent of RFC manpower[141] was classed as combatant, with the equivalent figure for the ground forces of the BEF being 65 percent.[142] Secondly, the numbers of line items within the RFC technical inventory expanded exponentially until by the Armistice it exceeded 50,000, a capability of such size and complexity that no single organization had previously achieved it.[143]

Thirdly, supporting the RFC created a new requirement for what is in the 21st Century, known as Reverse Logistics,[144] which has a much longer history than its promotion in 2018 would suggest.[145] Whilst nearly all of the ground force material in 1914 was uni-directional and consumable, the RFC led the way in recycling high value items, especially aero-engines and their key components,[146] a process which, slowly began to filter into other areas within the BEF as salvage,[147] reclamation,[148] reconditioning and re-issue of a variety of materiel[149] that eventually became vital to logistic sustainability.[150] Reverse Logistics matured into a critical component that reduced the Cross-

Based however, on the RFC percentage of the BEF of strength 160,000 being 0.59%, the figure is 944; see, MEBE, p.66, Table (iii) (a) - Comparative Strengths and Percentages of Arms and Branches.

139 For an excellent short analysis, see, Peter Dye, 'The Genesis of Modern Warfare: The Contribution of Aviation Logistics', in Gary Sheffield & Peter Grey (Eds.) *Changing War, The British Army, The Hundred Days Campaign and the Birth of the Royal Air Force, 1918*, Birmingham War Studies (London: Bloomsbury, 2013), pp.171-190 and his comprehensive and illuminating, *The Bridge to Air Power: Logistics Support for Royal Flying Corps Operations on the Western Front, 1914-18* (Annapolis: Naval Institute Press, 2015).

140 During the Great War, the Combatant arms were: Cavalry, Artillery, Engineers, Flying Corps, Infantry, Cyclist Corps and Tank Corps. Non-Combatant were: Service Corps, Medical Corps, Veterinary Corps, Ordnance Corps, Pay Corps and Labour Corps; MEBE, p.65, Table (iii) (a) - Comparative Strengths and Percentages of Arms and Branches, France.

141 Proportion of total strength categorised as aircrew (pilots, observers and air gunners). Monthly Return of Personnel of the Royal Air Force (Overseas) dated 1 November 1918; Air Historical Branch (Royal Air Force).

142 Rounded to 65% from 64.74%. Figure extracted from MEBE, p.66, Table (iii) (a) - Comparative Percentage Strengths of Arms and Branches France.

143 Dye, 'Genesis of Modern Warfare', pp.178-179.

144 Operations related to the reuse of products and materials, by moving them from their typical final destination of use for the purpose of capturing value or proper disposal. The issue of battlefield clearance is raised in the HQ 7th (Meerut) Division, DAA&QMG, WD, 5 May 1915: TNA WO 95/3932/2.

145 Casualty and medical evacuation is in a conceptual sense, a component of Reverse Logistics.

146 For a contemporary examination of the key aircraft sub-systems and components, see, War Office, *Technical Notes, R.F.C.* WO 43/FS/436 (London: HMSO, 1916).

147 Salvage also had a direct financial contribution. In the first six months of 1917, the estimated savings from the Paris Ordnance Depot totalled £961,716, which is £445,800,000 in 2016 values based on the *Measuring Worth UK* Economic Cost measuring the comparison of its relative share in terms of the total output of the economy; TNA WO 95/59: Director of Ordnance Services, WD, 11 November 1917. Salvage had two components. Battlefield Salvage involved weapons, ammunition, shell cases, clothing, equipment, vehicles and trench materials, whilst Normal Salvage consisted of logistic items such as packing cases, dunnage, fuel cans, blankets and accommodation stores. Marcosson, *Business of War*, p.175.

148 As an example of the wide-ranging reclamation activities, in the month of September 1918, Fourth Army reclaimed 1,057 pounds of solder from bully-beef tins and the like; TNA WO 95/445/5: HQ Fourth Army, 'Solder, September 1918'.

149 Inclusive of clothing, boots, personal carriage equipment, webbing and haversacks, weapons, vehicles spares and brass shell cases. The Paris Ordnance Salvage Depot employed nearly 4,000 French women and was focused on clothing salvage. Marcosson in *Business of War* offers an active contemporary description of its work, whilst Forbes, *Army Ordnance Services,* pp.100-115, provides a wider examination of the role of salvage.

150 This is another logistic subject that requires academic analysis. For a brief summary of its role and activity, see,

Channel shipping requirement, whilst battlefield clearance became an increasingly important task in supporting the re-use and recycling of materiel.[151] The AA&QMG 17th (Northern) Division, Lieutenant-Colonel W M Nicholson, recorded his thoughts of a visit to Le Harve in July 1917 describing one part of the Reverse Logistics process.

> In one place rose a mountain of ammunition boxes and shell cases, which German prisoners were busy loading on board ship. Further up the river many thousands of ammunition boxes lay in long lines. Ship succeeded ship, as fast as she could be loaded……..The disposal of other sorts of salvage, from cast-iron fragments to equipment, interested me particularly. Here, in some twenty sheds, 1200 French women under two British Ordnance officers were employed cleaning leather equipment, water bottles, rifles, bayonets; everything except clothing, which went to Rouen. The salvage came down from the battle area indescribably dirty, old and broken, and practically everything was made use of; empty cartridge cases found a purchaser in the French Government. Unfired S.A.A. had to be first cleaned then sent home for reboxing………At the time of my visit about sixty truck loads[152] a day came from the two armies this base served.[153]

Reverse Logistics were not however, free from controversy, with the theft of items from deceased officers personal kits in transit to the United Kingdom being a particularly sensitive issue, the prevention of which, took a considerable time and resources to resolve.[154]

The strides in the effectiveness and efficiency of operational military aviation were founded upon a growing excellence in logistics. From, in 1912, relying upon WMT for field mobility instead of the horse, through needing higher specification and quality POL, to being leading edge in Reverse Logistics, the RFC, created a more focused technical requirement in logistics, which has become the accepted norm in the 21st Century. Aviation also created new challenges to the dynamics of military logistic organization and the development of the Aircraft Park is an interesting example.[155] Originally a mobile field unit, its tasks expanded so rapidly that by mid-1915 it had acquired the permanency and immobility of a large factory, having imported industrial and retail processes. A Park was repairing aeroplanes, power-plants, wireless sets, weapons, cameras and a plethora of supporting items. In addition, it issued everything from nuts to planes, including lawn-movers for airfield grass cutting and special matches for igniting damaged aircraft that landed behind the German line.[156] Even in the static conditions appertaining at the time, it was quickly recognized that the Air Park could not effectively sustain future offensive operations, so the operational and logistic review that followed, created Army Air Parks for each RFC Brigade supporting an Army

Chapman-Huston & Rutter, *Quartermaster General of the Great War*, Vol. II, pp.190-196; *The Official History of The Ministry of Munitions*, Vol. VII, The Control of Materials (London: HMSO, 1922), pp.47-63 and for a personal view, GSO [Frank Fox] *GHQ, Montreuil-Sur-Mer* (London: Philip Allan & Co, 1920), pp.131-135. The detail of the salvage operations are remarkable, even extending to the collection of nails from roads to be not only recycled but also to reduce the frequency of lame horses, which of course, reduced logistic capability; Marcosson, *Business of War*, p.198.

151 Battlefield clearance is the removal of all military materiel, including enemy, from the field of battle, inclusive of human remains, munitions, fuel, vehicles, equipment and supplies.

152 Railway wagons.

153 Nicholson, *Behind the Lines*, pp.205-206.

154 Captain R Bonham-Smith, 'Railway Transport Arrangements in France', *JRUSI*, Vol. LXI (February 1916), pp.59-61.

155 In 1914, the Air Park was, within the Army, an almost unknown logistic capability, prompting the Landing Officer at Boulogne in France to wire GHQ BEF: 'An unnumbered unit without aeroplanes which calls itself an Aircraft Park has arrived. What are we to do with it?'. Raleigh, BOH, *The War in the Air*, Vol. I, pp.284-285.

156 Jones, BOH, *The War in the Air*, Vol. II, p.188.

P1.3. Reverse Logistics: Critical to developing logistic capability and sustaining the war economy. Reverse Logistics became big business by late 1916, recovering not only thousands of tons of material for re-use in some way but also reducing the requirement for and the expense of, industrial production. (RLC Museum: AB/000768B)

P1.4. The King of Logistics and the God of War: Standard Gauge Railway (SGR) moving heavy artillery. SGR was absolutely critical to the BEF's logistic and war-fighting capability. Having relied upon Host Nation Support until late 1916, the massive expansion of the BEF's military SGR capacity was a remarkable achievement, initially driven by commercial managers. (RLC Museum: AB/000783E)

and re-designated the static elements as Air Depots.[157]

Despite the rapidly expanding number of mechanically propelled road vehicles, the railway remained, throughout the war, the critical land transportation capability both in the United Kingdom and on the Western Front. Whilst the motor lorry had many advantages, especially for distribution of supplies forward of the railheads, for capacity, the Standard Gauge Railway (SGR) was King.[158] In addition, on the Western Front, most SGR assets were not within German artillery range but as the DLK developed its AI capability, their vulnerability to enemy action increased, although the availability of diversionary routes sustained operational resilience. At the beginning of 1915, the BEF's Railway Operating Division (ROD) had commenced operations with seven SGR locomotives loaned by the South Eastern & Chatham Railways (SECR) increasing to 59 locomotives and 675 personnel in December. By the Armistice in November 1918, the figures totalled 1,486 SGR locomotives[159] and 18,500[160] personnel[161] operating, constructing or supporting the SGR, assigned to 108 Operating Companies[162] and a plethora of survey, reconnaissance, telegraph, workshop and construction units.[163] As it transpired, the Army greatly underestimated the need for military railway units,[164] an emerging scenario created by a pre-war planning assumption accepting that the only meaningful solution upon initial deployment was to rely upon the French national railway system but as the BEF expanded during 1915 and 1916, it became increasingly clear that the BEF would need to expand its in-house railway capability, the delivery of which became a key output of the Geddes reforms in late 1916.[165] SGR played a defining role in the delivery of BEF capability in every area from railway artillery to medical evacuation but one forgotten niche

157 For more details, see, Ibid, pp.188-190.

158 The lift capacity of a train in the BEF, equated to approximately 150 motor lorries; see, Bonham-Smith, 'Railway Transport Arrangements in France', p.48.

159 TNA WO 107/69: Report Upon the Work of the Quartermaster-General's Branch of the Staff and Directorates Controlled, British Armies in France and Flanders, Major G E Pitt (DAQMG GHQ) (Comp) pp.16-17. MEBE, p.607, Military Railways, Material and Traffic, Table (i) - France, Progress of Transportation in France since January 1917, quotes an average of 1,398 SGR locomotives in traffic for November 1918 and 1,421 for December. The difference from the figures in TNA WO 107/69 may be the total strength against those available for operations.

160 Some sources quote 75,000 for the strength of the ROD. This figure approximates to the establishment of 74,950 of 1 June 1918 and includes all the personnel in Railway transportation, including SGR, NGR, ballast quarrying, relevant transportation headquarters staff, survey and labour. Strength on 1 June 1918 was 70,627; MEBE, p.600 (i) Military Railways, Table (iii) - Personnel: Establishment and Strength of Railway Personnel Employed in the Various Theatres.

161 TNA WO 107/69: Report Upon the Work of the Quartermaster-General's Branch of the Staff and Directorates Controlled, British Armies in France and Flanders, Major G E Pitt (DAQMG GHQ) (Comp) pp.16-17. MEBE, p.600 (i) Military Railways, Table (iii) - Personnel: Establishment and Strength of Railway Personnel Employed in the Various Theatres, quotes an Operating Personnel establishment of 15,744 and a strength of 14,224 for 1 June 1918, with a deficiency of 1,511.

162 On 1 August 1917 there were 105 Regular and three Special Reserve Companies, of which 48 were SGR Operating Companies; MEBE, p.165, Growth of the Royal Engineers.

163 For details of these units, see, General Staff, *Order of Battle of the British Armies in France*, GHQ, 11 November 1918, p.70. The total number of personnel employed on railway duties including construction, survey, quarrying, Narrow Gauge Railway (NGR) operations, workshops and stores and Headquarters on 1 June 1918 was 70,627 against an establishment of 74,950; MEBE, p.600 (i) Military Railways, Table (iii) – Personnel: All Theatres, Establishment and Strength of Railway Personnel Employed in the Various Theatres.

164 In 1914, the British Army had five railway units for operations and construction; three Regular and three Special Reserve. See, MEBE, p.165, Growth of the Royal Engineers.

165 Narrow Gauge Railways (NGR) were widely utilized in depots on the LOC and forward of SGR railheads in static conditions, especially in the period 1916-1917, when they played a significant role in delivering front-line logistic capability. Their importance to logistic output is gauged by the investment in them. On 1 June 1918, the establishment of NGR operating, construction and workshop companies was 17,589 personnel; the strength was 16,998. In November, NGR had 554 locomotives, operating over 752 miles of track and conveying, as a weekly average, 180,872 tons. MEBE, pp.606-607, Military Railways, Material and Traffic, Table (i) - France, Progress of Transportation in France since January 1917.

innovation was the attempt to create specialist care capability[166] for casualties with abdominal and thoracic injuries.[167]

Engineering a Solution

Contractor Support to Operations (CSO) is an expanding activity in the British Army in the early 21st Century and is an embedded component of Joint Expeditionary Force (JEF) capability within the concept of the Whole Force Approach (WFA). CSO is defined as the embedded or discretionary use of industry to deliver military capability through the provision of services in the Theatre of Operations.[168] Whilst apparently a new feature of military operations, the concept has a history and the activities of contractors on the Western Front, are of especial interest to maturing 21st Century capability.[169] The use of Paris taxis to transport French troops during the Battle of the Marne in September 1914 is well known; the transport, in 72 taxis, of thousands of picks and shovels, a generous donation from the French to the BEF, a long forgotten item of CSO history, as indeed is the use of French civilian labour to assist in the construction of the BEF's defence line near Le Cateau between Inchy South-East to Benin.[170] The non-discretionary nature of operations in France and Belgium generated imperatives for the British Army to introduce innovative logistical solutions to a multitude of military problems and the integration of contractors into what in the 21st Century is termed a Total Support Force (TSF) was one of them. The approach was generally dynamic and until mid-1916, focused upon tactical solutions, although these often had operational level results. CSO was not however, initiated as a result of experience on the Western Front in 1915 as the BEF expanded but was alive and well as it disembarked in France during August 1914. As operations developed, so did CSO, with an increasing focus on militarizing elements of it, especially in the arena of Labour Support, whilst railway operations were under-pinned by transferring some ex-civilian railwaymen to Royal Engineer units.

CSO was fundamental to engineer and logistic activity from the beginning of the BEF's deployment to France and without it, the BEF could not have delivered its operational capability in the manner in which it did, especially in relation to its expansion. Whilst the Command and Control of CSO in the engineering environment matured during operations, from the beginning,

166 To improve patient care outcomes, Deputy Director Medical Services (DDMS) III Corps, Colonel (later Major-General) Bruce Skinner, proposed to create specialist integrated care capability for casualties with abdominal and thoracic injuries based on railway assets. His idea focused on having the facility well forward to conduct early surgery but use the railway to evacuate the patients. Casualties would receive surgery in an operating car on a stationary train after which, they would be directly transferred to ward coaches for subsequent evacuation, thereby resolving the issue of the post-operative movement delay whilst the patient recovered in hospital before being evacuated. As the train had to be forward, protection was important, so a cutting near Albert was identified, which was no more than four miles from the front line. Logistic engineering was required to construct a loop-siding, protected accommodation in the embankment for the medical and nursing staff and ramps to give access to the train. DDMS III Corps 538/14 dated 29 March 1916 to DMS Fourth Army in TNA WO 95/447/1: DMS Fourth Army, March 1916.

167 For a recent medical assessment of the contemporary management of these injuries, see, Steven D Heys, 'Abdominal wounds: Evolution of management and establishment of surgical treatments', in Thomas Scotland & Steven Heys (Eds.) *War Surgery, 1914-1918* (Solihull: Helion, 2012), pp 178-211 and Steven D Heys 'Penetrating chest wounds and their management', pp.212-233.

168 The British Army defines CSO as consisting of three elements: Contractors in Deployed Operations (CONDO) Private Security Companies (PSC) and Sponsored Reserves (SR).

169 For an introduction to supply contracts of the period, see, *Army Service Corps,* Part II, *Supplies*, Army Council, War Office (London: HMSO, 1909), (Reprinted 1914 with new Appx XII) pp.215-219.

170 Brigadier-General Sir James E Edmonds CB CMG psc, BOH, *Military Operations, France and Belgium 1914*, Volume I, *Mons, The Retreat to the Seine, the Marne and the Aisne, August-October* 1914 (London: Macmillan, 1922), p.123.

GHQ directed CSO policy, whilst the control of contract execution was delegated to the relevant Commander Royal Engineers (CRE). This arrangement, ensuring that CSO was directed from the highest command authority, paid significant dividends in balancing resources, ensuring outputs, controlling finance and assuring quality control. The earliest BEF CSO output involved the use of French contractors, controlled by the HN, to construct the tented reception camp at Rouen in early August 1914, as part of the pre-war deployment plan. In late August, at Amiens, the Royal Engineers directed French contractors employed to support the establishment, using school buildings, of a General Hospital, the reconfiguration of a jute factory for a Veterinary Hospital, water distribution for a Remount Depot and the construction of a reinforcement camp for 6,000 personnel.[171] From this work, CSO grew to be an essential and prominent feature of engineer support throughout the war, of which there are many interesting examples.

Construction was a major element of CSO, with French companies initially conducting most of the work, although some of the labour output was of variable quality. By early 1915, British contractors deployed from the United Kingdom established permanent sites in the Main Base Areas (MBA) and increasingly became the major CSO construction player. The War Office supported both British and French CSO solutions but labour shortages in France by late 1916 created a clear decline in the ability of the latter to deliver capability. Both British and French companies however, were critical to the building, expansion or improvement of many key logistic facilities including depots, warehouses, camps, aerodromes, hospitals, bakeries, laundries, quarries, docks and railways. A cyclic annual task was the Winter Hutting Programme,[172] which delivered accommodation upgrades in preparation for austere conditions, in a wide range of capability areas, this work being mainly enacted through CSO. Another vital CSO task was the operation of the quarries, the output of which, in 1916, was approximately 1.06 million tons and crucial to the construction and maintenance of railways, roads and docks.[173]

Labouring Men and Women

Labour Support for the BEF was an enduring issue throughout the Great War on the Western Front in terms of its importance, availability, resilience and capability. Eric Geddes, as part of his transportation mission in Autumn 1916 observed that: 'Generally speaking today, the labour is wastefully used, due in my opinion to its total inexperience of the class of work it is doing and often to the inexperience of its officers. It may be unavoidable to use men withdrawn from the trenches for railhead and other labour work.[174] Whenever machinery can be substituted however, it should be used so that such fatigues can be reduced to a minimum'.[175] The challenge in constantly redirecting labour to different tasks and thereby, reducing its output efficiency,[176] is well illustrated

171 *Work of the Royal Engineers in the European War, 1914-19, Work under the Director of Works (France)* Institution of the Royal Engineers (Chatham: W & J Mackay, 1924), p.2.

172 For details of hut types and construction, see, Ibid, pp.169-179.

173 For a description of quarrying operations, see, Ibid, pp.207-216.

174 Of but many examples, a battalion history records that a working party of 100 was dispatched to a task which required only 50 men; Captain G K Rose MC, *The Story of The 2/4th Oxfordshire and Buckinghamshire Light Infantry* (Oxford: Blackwell, 1920), p.35.

175 Initial report from Geddes to Lloyd George in a Private and Confidential letter dated 15 September 1916; Sir William Guy Granet Papers held by the Modern Records Centre University of Warwick Library (MRCUWL) GB 152, MSS.191/3/3/9.

176 A working party might be involved in several different tasks on one day. The battalion history of the 2/4th Oxfordshire and Buckinghamshire Light Infantry recorded that one was involved in relaying duckboards, excavating submerged sleepers from a NGR, digging trenches for communication cables, filling sandbags and repositioning a pile of logs that had been dumped in the incorrect location; Rose, *The Story of The 2/4th.*

by the experiences of 127th Battalion Canadian Expeditionary Force, 2nd Battalion Canadian Railway Troops, which, in the period, 1917-1918 had attached to it, for labour support, elements of over 200 different units.[177] Initially, the BEF relied on its military manpower to deliver the majority of its labour needs but it quickly became obvious that this was not an effective utilization of precious assets, especially on the LOC. In addition, there were many tasks that required skilled tradesmen. The employment of civilian labour was certainly not a reaction to the deployment to France, as pre-war planning had identified, with the French, the need for the employment of civilians on the LOC, a process underpinned by British Army doctrine:[178]

> Commanders are responsible that the efficiency of the troops is not diminished by the employment of soldiers on work that can equally well be performed by civilians[179]............. Civilian labour will be hired or requisitioned for unloading and stacking supplies whenever possible. Military labour will not be used for this service if civilian is available, or unless military labour can be provided without interfering with the fighting efficiency of the troops.[180]

The direction given by *Field Service Regulations* (FSR) was however, much wider than a focus on Locally Recruited Workers (LRW) and allowed for the employment, often with a grant, pension or gratuity, of individuals or groups on a permanent basis from the United Kingdom or elsewhere, to execute specific tasks. Of additional interest, are the instructions regarding selection, skill testing, uniform, badges, Terms & Conditions of Employment, Pay & Promotion and the rules for the issue of personal weapons for protection.[181]

There was an insatiable appetite for labour to support operations on the Western Front and the War Office sought a variety of solutions outside that of military labour battalions, contractors or LRW,[182] particularly as the French civilian male labour pool declined because of military conscription and the friction created by wage differentials as the BEF paid a higher rate to obtain the personnel.[183] The BEF employed, within the LOC, French women in sanitary duties, laundries, workshops and ordnance depots but had to compete with recruitment from critical industries such as munitions and agriculture.[184] The key solution to the problem was the recruitment of foreign labour, either from within the UK, Europe or the Empire, which was controlled in a broad spectrum from individuals, through gangs, to semi-military and formed military units. Spanish labour was an embedded feature in French quarries and Belgian refugees manned a Road Maintenance Company and a Forestry Company, which was employed in port timber handling. On a larger scale, the War Office formed Labour Companies comprised of Russian immigrants in the UK and imported Italians, whilst also employing South African Native personnel, Fijians, Indians and West Indians in formed military companies and battalions.

177 Lieutenant-Colonel H M Jackson MBE ED, *The 127th Battalion CEF, 2nd Battalion, Canadian Railway Troops*, Industrial Shops for the Deaf, nd but 1957, pp.182-186.

178 FSR, Part II, Chp XVII, Civilians with an Army.

179 Ibid, p.179.

180 Ibid, p.82.

181 Ibid, p.180.

182 For a clear analysis, see the engaging and comprehensive, *No Labour, No Battle, Military Labour During the First World War*, John Starling and Ivor Lee (Stroud: Spellmount, 2009), pp.77-162.

183 TNA WO 95/34/4: GHQ QMG, WD, 3 May 1917.

184 Craig Gibson, *Behind the Front, British Soldiers and French Civilians, 1914-1918* (Cambridge: CUP, 2014), highlights the increasing friction between the British and French authorities as demands for civilian labour rose. In May 1917, the BEF employed 7,700 French citizens, rising to 15,000 in April 1918 and 20,000 in May and this despite French protests and British promises; see, pp.200-201.

Left: P1.5. Labour and More Labour: Military and Civilian labour from Base to the Fire-Trench was a critical component of logistics in the BEF. The insatiable demand for labour in the BEF drew in thousands of people from many different Nations across Europe and the British Empire, with the Chinese Labour Corps being especially significant. (RLC Museum: Postcard Collection)

Below: P1.6. The Lost Logisticians: The Indian and Chinese Cemetery at Ayette. Whilst the main British cemeteries receive a constant stream of visitors, the Indian and Chinese ones, containing the graves mainly of labouring logisticians, rarely have much footfall. (Author)

The largest single pool of fresh labour however, came from China and formed the Chinese Labour Corps (CLC).[185] The original driver for their recruitment was employment in railway Permanent Way (PW) construction and maintenance but this restriction was soon removed and the concept expanded into other areas. By early 1918, in addition to the manual labourers, there were approximately 4,800 skilled and semi-skilled tradesmen including bricklayers, tailors, boot-makers, automotive mechanics and railway wagon riveters, employed in companies delivering port construction, railway rolling stock maintenance, tank and MT repair and ordnance salvage. Managing this eclectic work force was certainly a complex task and deserves an individual study.[186] The key aspects are enduring: communication, culture, pay, Terms & Conditions and healthcare. Few of those selected to control these activities had received formal civilian labour training but many had some cultural experience, which was essential to effective management. Communication was constant issue; some officers spoke the relevant language but for the most part, interpreters were crucial to the business. Labour Officers were also particularly alert to the risk of relying upon LRW to support tactically mobile units, a problem that became endemic when operations gathered pace in August 1918.

P1.7. A Military Revolution: The integration of women, military and civilian, to the BEF's logistic capability, including employment in technical trades, was a key development in sustaining the Force and provided much needed reinforcement to release manpower from the Base for service within the Armies. (RLC Museum: 000768C)

185 In December 1918, the CLC comprised 87,713 personnel; MEBE, p.91, Table (i) (a) - Feeding Strength, France and Flanders, 7 December 1918.

186 Little has been published on this subject. For a contemporary personal account of service with the Chinese Labour Corps, see, Daryl Klein, *With The Chinks, In the Chinese Labour Corps* (London: John Lane, 1919) although the style may not be comfortable for a 21st Century readership.

Another area of innovation in the BEF logistic environment was the employment of women.[187] On 3 August 1918 there were 7,808 members of the Queen Mary's Army Auxiliary Corps (QMAAC)[188] serving in France, 31 of which were detached to the American Expeditionary Force.[189] Women were first officially employed with the Army, with the full support of the QMG at the War Office, for Home Service only, by the granting, on 3 August 1915, of special authority to the Women's Legion Cookery Section.[190] Employment of Women's Auxiliary Army Corps (WAAC) personnel in officers' messes and army formation HQs followed, before the Army Council authorized the formal engagement of the Women's Legion Motor Transport Section to serve with the ASC[191] and wear the cap-badge.[192] There appears to have been little resistance to the employment of women in France; the military pressures to find more manpower and the mass employment of women in the munitions and aircraft industries being significant drivers in this process.[193] The logistic services and in particular, the ASC and AOC were key employers of women in the BEF,[194] especially in areas, [195] which reflected many of the processes of industry and business,[196] whilst the RFC, as might be expected of a forward-leaning technically driven organization, had also identified opportunities to offer women an increasingly wide range of logistic trades, including aviation ES.[197] Although women had served

187 For an assessment of uniformed women's contribution to the Army, see, Diana Shaw, 'The Forgotten Army of Women: The Overseas Service of Queen Mary's Army Auxiliary Corps with the British Forces, 1917-1921', in Hugh Cecil & Peter H Liddle (Eds.) *Facing Armageddon, The First World War Experienced* (London: Leo Cooper, 1996), pp.365-379.

188 Initially called the Women's Army Auxiliary Corps (WAAC) it was re-titled Queen Mary's Army Auxiliary Corps on 9 April 1918 in appreciation of its services. After the formation of the Royal Air Force on 1 April 1918, and the establishment of the Women's Royal Air Force (WRAF) the Corps disbanded on 1 May 1920. Queen Mary was its first, and only, Commandant-in-Chief.

189 MEBE, p.93, Table (ii) - Number of Women Employed with the British Expeditionary Force in France, August 1918. In addition, there were 7,123 women employed by the RAMC as nursing sisters or support staff and another 1,094 operating in the same capacity for the organizations grouped under the British Red Cross. The various Welfare Societies (YMCA etc) employed 1,056 and Government Departments employed 99 Voluntary Aid Detachment (VAD) drivers. Total number of women employed in the BEF in August 1918 employed by official British organizations was 17,180.

190 Subsequently, employment was extended to undertake household duties in convalescent hospitals and to provide technical instructors in military schools of cookery; Army Council Instruction (ACI) 441 dated 26 February 1916.

191 ACI 221 dated 7 February 1916. The ASC was certainly progressive because the integration of women into the Army was, with the exception of the Army Medical Services, the Royal Army Chaplain's Department and the Ulster Defence Regiment (UDR) which had separate arrangements, not meaningfully achieved until the demise of the Women's Royal Army Corps (WRAC) in 1992.

192 When members were transferred to the WAAC, this issue created friction when it was proposed that these privileges would be withdrawn. See, Chapman-Huston & Rutter, *Quartermaster-General of the Great War*, Vol. II, pp.131-137.

193 There were understandably, concerns about the practical aspects of pay, administration, discipline and welfare but once the key decisions had been taken, events moved swiftly. On 13 March 1917, the first members, mostly ex-Women's Legion, were enrolled in the WAAC. ACI 537 dated 28 March 1917 authorized the deployment of WAAC members overseas and on 4 April 1917, the initial detachment sailed for France.

194 The WAAC's four sections, Cookery, Clerical, Mechanical and Miscellaneous, covered several trade areas within the logistic environment and women were employed in a variety of them. Tradition did not permit the King's Commission to be granted to women, so the senior officers were titled controllers and the juniors, administrators. NCO appointments were ascribed the term forewomen, whilst the ranks undertook trades, thus reinforcing the industrial nature of many logistic operations in the BEF.

195 Clerks, typists, cooks, driver-mechanics, suppliers, packers and postal. In addition, the ASC offered several technical trades to women. See, *Regulations for the Queen Mary's Auxiliary Corps*, War Office, 1918, pp.32-29.

196 Arthur Marwick, *Women at War, 1914-1918* (London: Fontana Paperbacks, 1977), pp.83-114.

197 On 4 March 1918, the RFC employed 8,403 women: 2,969 Clerks, 1,322 storewomen, 899 sail-makers, 263 fitters, 153 riggers, 436 MT drivers and 680 cooks; MEBE, p.505, RFC Women Employed. In October 1918, women comprised approximately 10% of personnel strength in the RAF, the War Establishment of 6th (Home Defence) Brigade RAF reflecting this, although the percentage for logistic trades was higher; Jones, *War in the Air*, Vol. VI, Appx XLV, Anti-Aircraft Defences in the United Kingdom, p.171.

in nursing and medical support roles within the BEF from start of the deployment, the decision to employ them more widely was in military terms almost revolutionary.[198] Whilst the engagement of uniformed women was less the product of a change in conventional attitudes and more driven by practical imperatives, Haig's support for the deployment of women in the BEF, and in many trades that had been the preserve of male soldiers, seems to belie the picture of a gruff and dour Field-Marshal, who, in the views of some historians, sought refuge from change and innovation.[199]

Conclusion

The Principles of Logistics in 1914 held good in 1918, although the scale and spectrum of the tasks and outputs changed dramatically over four years. In 1914, the QMG staff officers at GHQ BEF were directing the location of divisional railheads but in 1918, the QMG Branch was involved in staffing the 'Big Logistics' interface issues to support five armies.[200] The advent of aviation and armoured combat systems changed the historical uni-directional flow of materiel, creating the new feature of Reverse Logistics, whilst the expansion of WMT introduced greater flexibility in distribution, albeit with a concomitant increase in the requirement to procure, store and manage new inventories in fuel and spares. All of these new capabilities generated very significant training requirements, which in their turn were dependent upon a wide range of logistics. Despite the introduction of MT, the Horse remained an essential component of the logistic system until the end of the war, its terrain mobility far exceeding that of WMT.

The use of contractors, niche in 1914, expanded to become a crucial component of the BEF's logistic capability, whilst the employment of uniformed women lucidly demonstrated that the military imperative held more weight than societal attitudes. The importation of industrial processes to deliver 'Big Logistics' in the Theatre of Operations brought not only very significant improvements to resource management and military outputs but also the need to grasp the cultural adjustments that were vital to its success. At the tactical level, the logisticians in units and headquarters were constantly honing their skills by daily practise. It is true they sometimes failed,[201] especially as the BEF expanded when training and mentorship were both at a premium but by 1917, logistics in the BEF had become a crafted art; had it not been, the effect of the German offensive upon the BEF in March 1918 would probably have been catastrophic. That the BEF was then able to mount 96 consecutive days of offensive operations from August 1918 is testimony to the competence and resilience of its logistic planning, resources and soldiers.

198 Sadly, for the most part, their sacrifice has almost been forgotten. It is remembered though, in a post-war contemporary document, reprinted by The Naval & Military Press, entitled *British Women's Work During the Great War with a list of women who died on war service.* Whilst not on the Western Front, a particularly moving sight is at the Mikra British Cemetery near Kalamaria, Thessaloniki in Greece. In the North East corner, there are the graves of five nurses who lie together, one of whom held the Croix de Guerre with Palms, and one whose headstone is inscribed: 'A Nursing Sister of the Great War - Known Unto God'. It is impossible not to be moved.

199 See, Tim Travers, *The Killing Ground, The British Army, The Western Front and the Emergence of Modern Warfare, 1900-1918* (London: Allen & Unwin, 1987), p.111.

200 The populist historical perception is that the life of the staff was an easy military option, perhaps prompted by the Great War music-hall question: 'If Bread is the staff of life, what is the life of the staff?'. Answer: One big loaf'. The reality was very different. Fox recalled in *GHQ*, "I have seen a Staff officer faint at table from sheer pressure of work, and dozens of men, come fresh from regimental work, wilt away under the fierce pressure of work at GHQ." Given that Fox was an artillery officer who was twice wounded during actions on the Somme, the working conditions can hardly have been benign; GSO, *GHQ*, p.36.

201 'Bad mistakes were made by units, march discipline was indifferent, the overloading of lorries continued inexcusable'; Nicholson, *Behind the* Lines, p.213.

2

Of Vital Necessity

Reflections on United Kingdom defence mobilization and movements planning before the Great War

Planning Perspectives

Viewing 1912 from the 21st Century, it appears to be a year of stability but the reality is different.[1] Economic fragility, the Great Unrest, terrorist incidents,[2] industrial strife, international tensions and security concerns, all contributed to an interesting matrix of challenges for the government.[3] In particular, there was continuous debate about defence expenditure, funding priorities between the Navy and the Army, the possibility of compulsory military service and the potential military impact of Home Rule in Ireland, particularly as H H Asquith headed a minority Liberal government, which relied on Irish MPs for its majority.[4] Within government and financial circles, planning for war focused rather less on the naval and military dimensions and more on the economic and social ones.[5] As the events of the Boer War were assessed, there was conceptually, a view that the United Kingdom should not become involved in a land-based 'Continental Commitment' but rely upon the Royal Navy (RN) to blockade enemies and protect British maritime trade,[6] whilst enabling British industry to seize global market opportunities and supply allies with munitions and materiel.[7] From the defence perspective however, although planning started to mature, there were no certainties and in many respects, increasing uncertainties. The Admiralty considered that the naval building programme might be adversely affected by an economic downturn or the Liberal government's social welfare plans, whilst discussion continued about the Royal Navy's future deployment options.[8] The proposal to land the Army on the German coast in the event of a conflict with Germany had been rejected by the Cabinet in 1911[9] but the dialogue about economic warfare

1 Amongst other events in 1912: Titanic sinking, Suffragette Movement, Admundsen and Scott reached the South Pole, total eclipse of the sun in London, Anglo-French Naval Agreement, First Balkan War and Italian-Turkish War.

2 Whilst mostly airbrushed from history, the terrorist campaign conducted by the Women's Social and Political Union caused significant loss and damage, whilst also leading to public disorder; see, Simon Webb, *The Suffragette Bombers, Britain's Forgotten Terrorists* (Barnsley: Pen & Sword, 2014).

3 For an examination of these issues in a national context, see, David French, *British Economic and Strategic Planning 1905-1915* (London: George Allen & Unwin, 1982).

4 See, *The Army and the Curragh Incident, 1914*, Ian F W Beckett (Ed.), Army Records Society (London: The Bodley Head, 1986).

5 For an analysis of the political and welfare issues of the period, see, G R Searle, *A New England? Peace and War 1886-1918*, The New Oxford History of England (Oxford: Clarendon Press, 2004), pp.358-528.

6 For an academic analysis, see, Matthew S Seligmann, *The Royal Navy and the German Threat, 1901-1914, Admiralty Plans to Protect British Trade in a War Against Germany* (Oxford: Oxford University Press (OUP), 2012).

7 For an examination of these issues, see, Nicholas A Lambert, *Planning Armageddon, British Economic Warfare and the First World War* (Cambridge Massachusetts & London: Harvard University Press, 2012).

8 For a concise resume of the naval situation in which the Royal Nay was operating, see, Lawrence Sondhaus, *The Great War at Sea, A Naval History of the First World War* (Cambridge: Cambridge University Press (CUP), 2014), pp.8-61 and for a full analysis, see, Shawn T Grimes, *Strategy and War Planning in the British Navy, 1887-1918* (Woodbridge: The Boydell Press, 2012).

9 The proposal to land forces on the German coast, except perhaps as a diversionary raid, lacked intellectual rigour.

and its impact upon World Trade[10] or whether there would be the 'Big Clash' with the *Kaiserliche Marine* (KLM)[11] continued.[12] The War Office became increasingly Euro-centric in its operational thinking but there was no initial definitive: the BEF might deploy to France or Belgium, perhaps to Egypt or India[13] or be held in reserve in the United Kingdom. For all these reasons, the British came late to the mobilization planning process.[14]

The backdrop to Defence mobilization and movements planning is an interesting one because both the Royal Navy and the British Army were in transition.[15] In 1905 the Committee of Imperial Defence (CID)[16] was espousing the view that whilst elements of the Royal Navy and the British Army might be permanently allocated to overseas stations and garrisons, core components of British forces should, preferably, be concentrated in the United Kingdom, to enable deployments to be effected to defend the Empire.[17] The defence of the UK Base was not, in 1905, considered to be a primary Army task because the security of the Kingdom would be assured by the RN but the basing of a Ground Force expeditionary capability there, provided additional insurance, in addition to allowing the deployment of a structured force to Europe.[18] Many of the contemporary naval and military developments had a direct bearing upon the manner, in which, mobilization and movement would be enacted. Of particular note was the competition for transportation resources, which created the imperative for Naval and Army planning staffs to seek agreement on the priority of movement between the two Services. An Admiralty Memorandum of 1909 succinctly summarized the issue:

> My Lords fully recognize the necessity for ensuring the railway requirements of the two services do not conflict, but, at the same time they would be unable to assent to an arrangement by which an officer, not under their orders, would have ultimate control of supplies of vital necessity to the fleet, which is the principal safeguard of these Islands against invasion, and the movements of which must consequently take precedence even of the movements of troops. It is necessary therefore in their opinion, that a complete and definite

Placing aside the issues of sea control, the Germans would always be able to reinforce the landing areas faster than the British, with forces that would undoubtedly be larger.

10 For an examination of the interface between economics and strategy in the period, see, French, *British Economic and Strategic Planning.*

11 German Imperial Navy. For an examination of its development, see, Peter Padfield, *The Great Naval Race: Anglo-German Naval Rivalry 1900-1914* (London: Hart Davis, 1974); Holger H Herwig, *The Luxury Fleet* (London: Allen & Unwin, 1980) and Jan Ruger, *Great Naval Game, Britain and Germany in the Age of Empire* (Cambridge: CUP, 2007).

12 The Big Clash did occur, at Jutland, on 31 May 1916 and the number of publications on the subject certainly exceeds the numbers of ships that participated in the battle. Royal Navy Killed In Action (KIA) totalled 6,067 naval personnel, plus 30 civilians serving aboard ships; Admiralty, *Narrative of the Battle of Jutland* (London: HMSO, 1924), Appx C, p.95.

13 By 1911, the chances of an Expeditionary Force deployment to Egypt had receded, although protection of the Suez Canal from in-country unrest or Turkish incursions remained military tasks, which matured in August 1914.

14 For an assessment of British defence planning developments, see, Keith Neilson 'Great Britain', in Richard F Hamilton and Holger H Herwig (Eds.), *War Planning 1914* (Cambridge: CUP, 2010), pp.175-197.

15 For details of the Army in 1908, see Lt-Col H M E Brunker, *Notes on Organization and Equipment,* 6th Edn (London: William Clowes and Sons, 1909).

16 Arthur Balfour, then British Prime-Minister, established the Committee of Imperial Defence (CID) in 1904 as a result of the recommendations of the Elgin Committee. For an analysis of its work and an assessment of its outputs, see, Nicholas d'Ombrain, *War Machinery and High Policy, Defence administration in peacetime Britain, 1902-1914* (Oxford: OUP, 1973), pp.115-140. For a summary of the role of the CID, see, Brunker, Notes on Organization and Equipment, pp.11-12.

17 For an interesting geographic explanation of the challenges of defending the Empire, see, Captain D H Cole MBE FRGS, *Imperial Military Geography, Characteristics of the Empire in Relation to Defence* (London: Praed, 1924).

18 Brunker in 1909 wrote:' The governing idea of this force is that it should be small, professional, and fully trained, prepared to strike quickly at a distance, and mobile to the extent of the whole Empire'; Notes on Organization and Equipment, p.38.

> understanding should be reached on the question of priority, and arrangements made by the Director of Railways shall have standing instructions to treat the primary naval requirement as coming first in order of importance and urgency.[19]

The key naval change from the logistic perspective was the introduction of the Dreadnought, and with it, an increasing demand for coal, and the transport of larger and heavier gun barrels and shells. And yet, no sooner had one technical revolution in naval affairs been introduced, thinking was turning to other maritime options, such as submarines, fast cruisers and mining, whilst the growing number of smaller vessels such as destroyers,[20] were generating a concomitant increase in the complexities of logistic support.[21] For example, whilst coal remained the critical fuel for ships, experiments with oil-fired boilers were indicating a future need for the transportation and storage of liquid fuels, and the shortage of these logistic facilities and concerns about the security of supply, contributed to slowing the introduction of this technical advance.[22] The Army, meanwhile, was absorbing the lessons of the Boer War,[23] although the future need for very significant quantities of petroleum products,[24] to service the thousands of combat and logistic oil powered mechanical vehicles,[25] which were used during the Great War on the Western Front had yet to be identified. The requirement to create a coherent force structure to sustain Major Combat Operations[26] overseas was probably the most critical lesson of the South African War[27] and initially, the concept was to mount a six or seven division force to India[28] or Egypt.[29] From 1906 onwards however, the War Office became increasingly focused upon the possibility of a 'Continental Commitment'[30] and as a result

19 Admiralty MO 1259 dated 8 December 1909 in TNA WO 106/50: Naval Requirements for Railway Services.

20 Most destroyers constructed from 1905 onwards were oil-fired; TNA ADM 265/28: 'History of development of oil burning fuel in HM Service'.

21 For an examination of these interlocking issues, see, Nicholas A Lambert, *Sir John Fisher's Naval Revolution* (Columbia: University of South Carolina Press, 1999).

22 TNA ADM 265/29: Admiralty, Architectural and Engineering Works Department, 'Admiralty Committee on Use of Oil Fuel in Navy, Vol. 1, Interim Report' 1912, p.149.

23 Reform began while the army was still engaged in the Boer War in South Africa, arguably as early as the submission of the Army Estimates in February 1901 and gathered momentum in the next decade. The Elgin Commission of 1903 and the War Office (Reconstitution) Committee, usually known as the Esher Committee, of 1904, clearly articulated the challenging and complex demands of garrisoning the Empire and in particular India, the requirement of home defence and the possibility, turning into probability during Haldane's time, of war in Europe. Prompted by the experience of the Boer War, and operations in the Russo-Japanese conflict, the post of Commander-in-Chief was abolished and replaced by the Army Council, whilst a General Staff was constituted as a key component of military planning within the War Office. Training was revised, new equipment purchased and doctrine refined, culminating in the publication of *Field Service Regulations* 1909, supported by a series of operating, training and technical manuals.

24 The tonnage of Petroleum, Oils and Lubricants shipped to the BEF totalled 758,614; War Office, *Statistics of the Military Effort of the British Empire during the Great War, 1914-1920* (MEBE) (HMSO, 1922), p.485, Table 11 - Stores Shipped to France for the British Expeditionary Force from 9th August 1914, to 10th November 1918.

25 In November 1918, the British Expeditionary Force in France had, excluding assets allocated to the RAF, 55,473 WMT vehicles on the inventory; Ibid, p.595, Table (ii) (a) - Monthly Census of Mechanical Transport in All Theatres, November 1918.

26 In the context of the period, this meant at least two divisions.

27 For a contemporary assessment of the Lessons Identified, see, *Report of His Majesty's Commissioners Appointed to Inquire into the Military Preparations and Other Matters connected with the War in South Africa*, Command 1789 (London: HMSO, 1903).

28 For an examination of the imperatives to dispatch an expeditionary force to India, see, John Gooch, *The Plans of War, The General Staff and British Military Strategy c1906-1916* (London: Routledge & Kegan Paul, 1974), pp.198-237.

29 For an examination of the imperatives to dispatch an expeditionary force to Egypt, see, Ibid, pp.238-277.

30 For an excellent explanation of this re-orientation, see, Michael Howard, *The Continental Commitment, The Dilemma of British Defence Policy in the Era of Two World Wars* (London: Temple Smith, 1972), Chp 2. See, also, Gooch, *The Plans of War*, pp.278-298 and David Owen, *The Hidden Perspective, The Military Conversations, 1906-*

of these dynamics, the Army was restructured,[31] to create an expeditionary capability for overseas deployment, a Territorial Force (TF)[32] for Home Defence (HD)[33] and a UK Base supporting global garrison deployments and regeneration.[34]

Enter Sir Henry Wilson

Until 1910, the concept of a carefully planned mobilization and deployment lay in the planning syndicates at the Army Staff College in Camberley.[35] Much of this was driven by the Commandant, Colonel[36] Henry Wilson,[37] who was not only determined to provide a more meaningful challenge to the students[38] but also believed the role of the expeditionary capability had to be properly defined.[39] The outline plans for the mobilization of formations earmarked for imperial overseas service were measured in weeks rather than days, mainly because the imperatives for the movement to India or Egypt did not require a faster response and the lessons from South Africa indicated a measured deployment. Wilson,[40] through a series of processes, became an enthusiastic believer in providing an expeditionary force to support the French Army in the event of an invasion by

1914 (London: Haus Publishing, 2014).

31 In 1914 this comprised: BEF: seven divisions. TF: 14 divisions. Deployment of infantry battalions: UK: 83; India: 52; Overseas Garrisons: 22.

32 Consisting of 14 divisions, the Territorial Force (TF) was, after considerable opposition, formed on 1 April 1908, from the Volunteer and Yeomanry components of the Auxiliary Forces, with the Militia being disbanded, although on occasions, the complete strength of a Militia unit transferred to the Special Reserve; see, Colonel J K Dunlop OBE MC TD, *The Development of the British Army, 1899-1914, From the Eve of the South African War to the Eve of the Great War, with Special Reference to the Territorial Force* (London: Methuen, 1938), pp.266-290 and Peter Dennis, *The Territorial Army, 1907-1940*, The Royal Historical Society (Woodbridge: The Boydell Press, 1987), pp.4-37. For an examination of its structure, training, equipment, capability and tasks, see, K W Mitchinson, *England's Last Hope, The Territorial Force, 1908-1914* (Basingstoke & New York: Palgrave-Macmillan, 2008). See also, the first annual return of the TF, *The Annual Return of the Territorial Force for the Year 1908,* Command 4496 (London: HMSO, 1909). For a resume, see Brunker, *Notes on Organization and Equipment*, pp.198-208.

33 For a comprehensive description of the military plans and preparations for Home Defence, see, K W Mitchinson, *Defending Albion, Britain's Home Army, 1908-1919* (Basingstoke & New York: Palgrave-Macmillan, 2005).

34 For an explanation of the development of the British Army during this period, see, Dunlop, *Development of the British Army*. The narrative covers the Lessons Identified from the Boer War, the formation of the Expeditionary Force and the creation of the Territorial Force. For a recent academic analysis of the pre-Great War British Army, see, Spencer Jones, *From Boer War to World War, Tactical Reform of the British Army, 1902-1914* (Norman: University of Oklahoma Press, 2012) and Timothy Bowman & Mark Connelly, *The Edwardian Army, Recruiting, Training and Deploying the British Army* (Oxford: OUP, 2012).

35 Much of this chapter was written in Room 111 of the Former Army Staff College (FASC) located in the grounds of the Royal Military Academy Sandhurst. Whilst I was scribing, I was reminded of the many key figures involved in the planning and execution of the operations described, who once walked the corridors. Their guiding hand was almost tangible............

36 Acting Brigadier-General.

37 It is strange that an officer forever linked to such critical railway movement planning, should be commissioned into the Rifle Brigade. He graduated, as a Lieutenant, from the Army Staff College in 1893, with 30 other officers whose names are recorded on a somewhat aging and fading board on the first floor of FASC. A fellow graduate was T D'O Snow, later General Officer Commanding (GOC) 27 Division and Commander VII Corps and Grandfather & Great-Grandfather respectively, of the broadcasters Peter and Dan Snow.

38 There was a saying at the Army Staff College during Wilson's tenure as Commandant that there was no syndicate question to which, the answer was not six!

39 Wilson's appointment to the post is explored in, John Hussey, 'Appointing the Staff College Commandant, A Case of Trickery, Negligence or Due Consideration', *British Army Review*, No 114, UK MOD (December 1996), pp. 99-105.

40 For a recent assessment of Sir Henry's military career, see, Keith Jeffery, *A Political Soldier* (Oxford: OUP, 2008). For his involvement in BEF planning and his wider influence in supporting the concept, see pp. 64-105. His biography, Field Marshal Sir Henry Wilson: His Life and Diaries in two volumes written by Callwell was published in 1927 but Jeffery offers a much more balanced appraisal of his contribution. See also, Robin Neillands, *The Old Contemptibles, The British Expeditionary Force 1914* (London: John Murray, 2004), Chp 3, 'Wilson at the War Office'.

Germany,[41] which created the requirement for far leaner mobilization schedules. This fervour became more influential once he became Director Military Operations (DMO)[42] in 1910.[43] In essence, it was his direction that created the basis by which the BEF would be mobilized and moved, in accordance with a carefully crafted plan, to meet the mission. From this activity, flowed the structure, process, procedures and systems that enabled the plan to be initiated, controlled and completed. He exceeded his brief and authority in a number of areas, political, military and financial[44] but there is no doubt that had he not shaped the concept and driven it hard, the BEF would not have been deployed in the manner it was during August and September 1914.[45]

P2.1. Army Staff College Camberley: Training the Army's Brain. A small number of officers with the coveted psc, 'Passed Staff College', qualification were pivotal in developing the complex logistic mechanics of the Army's mobilization plans and particularly those for the BEF. (Author)

41 For the wider background, see, J McDermott 'The Revolution in British Military Thinking from the Boer War to the Moroccan Crisis', in Paul Kennedy (Ed.), *The War Plans of the Great Powers, 1880-1914* (London: George Allen & Unwin, 1979), pp.99-117.

42 For details of his Directorate and the officers within it, upon his arrival in post, see, C Newman Knight, *The War Office List and Administrative Directory for the British Army 1910* (London: HMSO, 1910), pp.46-48. The Military Operations Directorate had five main sections: Strategical and Colonial (MO 1) European (MO 2) Asiatic (MO 3) Geographical (MO 4) Miscellaneous (MO 5) and Medical (MO 6). Wilson reorganized MO 1-3 into three new sections: Expeditionary Force (inclusive of India and the Dominions), thereby including all the military forces of the Crown except the Territorial Force, which because it was committed to home defence was the responsibility of the Director of Military Training (DMT). The other two new sections were tasked, respectively, with examining the Dual Alliance (France and Russia) and the Triple Alliance (Germany, Austria and Italy). One key output from the branches of the Military Operations Directorate was the review and reissue of the comprehensive 'Handbook of' series on nearly every army in Europe.

43 Whilst Wilson drove the planning, the military conversations with the French were initiated in early 1906 by the Foreign Secretary, Sir Edward Grey, a fact he omitted to explain to Prime-Minister Herbert Asquith until 1911, three years after he had assumed the appointment. For an assessment of Grey's intervention in this area, see, Owen, *The Hidden Perspective*.

44 There were occasions, when, in presenting his views in support of an expeditionary force to support the French Army, his position appeared, more often than not, to be exposing the position of the French General Staff, rather than the view of the War Office.

45 On Thursday 22 June 1922, after returning home from unveiling a memorial at Liverpool Street Station to those members of the Great Eastern Railway Company who fell in the Great War, Field-Marshal Sir Henry Wilson was fatally shot outside his house in London, by two members of the Irish Republican Army, who were subsequently

The detailed development of the mobilization and movement plans was given impetus by the 114th Meeting[46] of the CID on Wednesday 23 August 1911[47] held in the shadow of the Agadir Crisis.[48] Chaired by the Prime-Minister, Herbert Asquith, it apparently resulted in the Army's strategic view on naval and military intervention on the Continent prevailing over that of the RN[49] and thus, Military Operations in the War Office, directed by Wilson planned to dispatch, if appropriate, a coherently structured expeditionary force to the Continent in support of the French[50] and not to engage in the naval options of landing troops on the German North Sea coast and islands,[51] a concept designed to draw German forces from the attack on France.[52] What the CID did not do, was to identify, discuss and action, the two key logical consequences from the decision, which were the requirement for a mass army and the creation of an industrial and logistic base to support it,[53] nor, given Wilson's focus on the despatch of the Expeditionary Force rather than the possible post-deployment scenarios, did the General Staff offer a considered military view on the outcome of the meeting based upon a formal strategic appraisal of the offensive operations embedded in the French Plan XVII.[54]

tried and executed. A plaque at the Station was added after his death, to commemorate his unveiling of the memorial on the morning of his murder. The inscription on the tablet reads 'To the Memory of Field Marshal Sir Henry Wilson Bart, GCB, DSO, MP Whose death occurred on Thursday 22 June 1922 within two hours of his unveiling the adjoining memorial'. He is also remembered by a plaque in the Central Reception Hall of the Former Army Staff College. For a description of the circumstances of his death and the outfall, see, Jeffery, *Field Marshal Sir Henry Wilson*, pp.281-298.

46 TNA CAB 38/19/49: Committee of Imperial Defence; Minutes of the 114th Meeting, 23 August 1911. This meeting, as Zara Steiner has observed, was, remarkably, the only occasion that the CID reviewed the wider aspects of British strategy before 1914; Zara S Steiner and Keith Neilson, *Britain and the Origins of the First World War*, 2nd Edition (New York: Palgrave, 2003).

47 For a discussion of the meeting, see, Geoffrey Miller, *The Millstone, British Naval Policy in the Mediterranean, 1900-1914, the Commitment to France and British Intervention in the War* (Kingston-upon-Hull: University of Hull Press, 1999), pp.166-177. This explores the performance of the First Sea Lord, Admiral Sir Arthur Wilson in relation to the more spirited one by Director Military Operations (DMO) Major-General Sir Henry Wilson.

48 See, M L Dockrill, 'British Policy during the Agadir Crisis', in F H Hinsley (Ed.) *British Foreign Policy under Sir Edward Grey* (Cambridge: CUP, 1977), pp.271-287.

49 For a recent analysis of the outcomes of the 114th CID Meeting and its influence on British military planning, see, Hew Strachan,'The British Army, Its General Staff, and the Continental Commitment, 1904-1914' in *The Schlieffen Plan, International Perspectives on the German Strategy for World War I*, Hans Ehlert, Michael Epkenhans & Gerhard P Cross (Eds.) (Kentucky: University Press of Kentucky, 2014), pp.293-317.

50 For a contemporary French published view of the possibility of British military involvement in Europe, see, Captaine d'Artillerie A De Tarle, Brevete Major d'Etat, 'The British Army and a Continental War' (translated by Colonel H Wylly CB) *Journal of the Royal United Service Institution (JRUSI)* Vol. LVII (March 1913), pp.384-401. De Tarle's post nominals of Brevete Major d'Etat, denote he was a graduate of the French Army Staff College.

51 For discussion of these plans, see, Grimes, *Strategy and War Planning in the British Navy*, pp.164-169.

52 It is remarkable that the First Sea Lord was still espousing these options in 1911 six years after DMO's staff had apprised their opposite numbers in the Admiralty, of their futility. Colonel Charles Callwell (author of *Small Wars, Their Principles and Practice*, 3rd Edn, War Office, 1906) wrote to Captain Ballard RN on 3 October 1905; 'It seems doubtful if 120,000 troops if they made a successful descent on the Baltic Coast would "contain" so many as 400,000 German regular troops and Landwehr.......the idea of any attack upon them by an army of 120,000 may be dismissed as impracticable. As long as this army remained in the United Kingdom it would constitute a certain menace to the German coasts. But it is probable that the most useful purpose to which it could be put would be to give support to the French Armies in the Field'. TNA WO 106/46: British Military Action in case of War with Germany, E2/5 dated 3 October 1905.

53 These two issues are eloquently examined by John Hussey in 'Without an Army, and Without any Preparation to Equip One, The Financial and Industrial Background to 1914', *British Army Review*, No 109, UK MOD, (April 1995), pp.76-84.

54 For an assessment of the French strategic offensive as a means of defence and the issues with Plan XVII, see, Jack Snyder, *The Ideology of the Offensive, Military Decision Making and the Disasters of 1914* (Ithaca & London: Cornell University Press, 1984), pp.41-56 and Stefan Schimdt, 'French Plan XVII' in *The Schlieffen Plan, International Perspectives on the German Strategy for World War I,* Hans Ehlert, Michael Epkenhans & Gerhard P Cross (Eds.) (Kentucky: University Press of Kentucky, 2014), pp.209-246.

A series of issues fell out from the CID meeting. A critical one, that placed additional demands on the Royal Navy, was that it would be responsible for securing the maritime battle-space in which, the proposed expeditionary force movement would take place.[55] Until this point, the Royal Navy had been focused upon command of Home Waters in order to prevent invasion,[56] the application of blockade to deny the KLM freedom of manoeuvre, restricting German merchant marine operations and finally, initiating measures to protect British sea trade.[57] The specific task of protecting an expeditionary force maritime movement[58] generated a requirement to re-allocate defensive and offensive assets afloat, and concomitantly adjust the structure and posture of the logistic lay-down.[59] It also meant that naval mobilization and deployment needed to be carefully co-ordinated with the Army, a process that created much closer co-operation between the Admiralty and the War Office. Another key factor was the decision to deploy the force on the left flank of the French Army, in conformity with Host Nation (HN) planning in anticipation of an encounter battle, following a German attack[60] that was deduced to be most likely through Belgium, South of the River Meuse.[61] The decision, a result of much staff work by the Wilson's Military Operations team in the War Office, resulted in the refinement of the planning, particularly with regard to Time and Space, two critical elements upon which the deployment was focused. One hidden feature however, now long forgotten, is that from the first War Office involvement with the Foreign Office in 1906 and the subsequent staff conversations with the French,[62] the DMO of the day,[63] highlighted the absolute importance of logistics in any expeditionary force deployment to the Continent.

55 For an examination of the Anglo-French naval relationship, see, Samuel R Williamson Jr, *The Politics of Grand Strategy, Britain and France Prepare for War, 1904-1914* (Cambridge Massachusetts: Harvard University Press, 1969).

56 The spectre of German invasion in this period was fuelled in the public arena by the publication of various novels purporting to expose the truth behind the myth; William Le Queux was the most prolific author of the genre. Of note were: William Le Queux, *The Invasion of 1910* (London: Everett & Company, 1906) and *Spies of the Kaiser, Plotting the Downfall of England* (London: Hurst & Blackett, 1909). The most famous book however, is Erskine Childers, *The Riddle of the Sands, A Record of Secret Service* (London: Smith Elder & Co, 1903). During the Great War, Childers served in the Royal Naval Air Service (RNAS) and was awarded the DSC and a MID but became involved in the campaign for Irish independence and was executed in 1922. For a fascinating assessment, see, Maldwin Drummond, *The Riddle* (London: Nautical Books, 1985).

57 For background, see Sir Julian Corbett, BOH, *Naval Operations*, Vol. I, *To the Battle of the Falklands, December 1914* (London: Longmans, Green & Co, 1920), pp.18-22 and Arthur J Marder, *From The Dreadnought To Scapa Flow*, Vol. I, *The Road to War, 1904-1914* (London: OUP, 1961), pp.344-358.

58 The protection arrangements were innovative. Anglo-French surface forces, supported by air reconnaissance, submarines and destroyers, were to blockade the Eastern and Western ends of the English Channel to prevent German ships from reaching the shipping routes and a Life Saving Patrol was established along the shipping routes; TNA ADM 116/1043B: RN War Plans.

59 Given the complexity of these issues, it was fortunate that the Admiralty War Staff was established in 1912. For an assessment of its contribution, see, Nicholas Black, *The British Naval Staff in the First World War* (Woodbridge: The Boydell Press, 2009).

60 The British were generally well informed about German equipment, training and doctrine. For a general overview of British military intelligence of the period, see, Thomas G Fergusson, *British Military Intelligence, The Development of a Modern Intelligence Organization* (London: Arms & Armour Press, 1989), Chps X & XI. For more detail, see, Matthew S Seligmann, *Spies in Uniform, British Military & Naval Intelligence on the Eve of the First World War* (Oxford: OUP, 2006) and Matthew S Seligmann (Ed.), *Naval Intelligence from Germany, The Reports of the British Naval Attaches in Berlin, 1906-1914* (Aldershot: Ashgate (for the Naval Records Society), 2007). See also, General Staff, *Report on Foreign Manoeuvres*, 1912, War Office, 1913, pp.49-56.

61 See, Terence Zuber, *Inventing the Schlieffen Plan, German War Planning, 1871-1914* (Oxford: OUP, 2002). For an examination of the logistic aspects, see, Martin van Creveld, *Supplying War, Logistics from Wallenstein to Patton* (Cambridge: CUP, 1978), Chp 4, The Wheel that Broke.

62 See, Owen, *The Hidden Perspective*, pp.27-81 and Williamson, *The Politics of Grand Strategy*, pp.89-114.

63 Major-General James Moncrieff Grierson. As a Lieutenant-General, Grierson was Commander II Corps in the BEF but died of a heart aneurysm at 0700 on Monday 17 August 1914 whilst travelling on a train near Amiens. His body was repatriated and he is buried in the Glasgow Necropolis. For a resume of his military life, see, Mark Connelly, 'Lieutenant-General Sir James Grierson' in *Stemming The Tide, Officers and Leadership in the British Expeditionary Force 1914*, Spencer Jones (Ed.), Wolverhampton Military Studies (Solihull: Helion, 2013), pp.133-150.

> There are a great many points which we must settle before we can make our plans for the despatch of a force to either join the French or Belgian armies.......there are arrangements to be made as to the utilisation of railways, harbours, billets, transport, and supplies, which would be quite different in a friendly country from those we should have to make 'on our own' in a hostile country, and these greatly influence our establishments and consequently the numbers we can put into the field.[64]

A further issue in the planning process was the prevention of invasion, which was a sensitive issue that was constantly being revisited by the CID, the Admiralty and the War Office. Whilst all three parties accepted that the RN could defeat a major landing,[65] there were several issues that rarely rested, not least the Admiralty's reassessment of the threat. In 1908, the Admiralty had given an absolute guarantee that it would detect and intercept such a force but as a result of naval exercises in the period 1910-1912, downgraded this capability to a 'reasonable expectation' that it could.[66] The possibility that raiding parties might avoid detection and in so doing, have a serious affect on naval and maritime operational capability,[67] public confidence and the Nation's morale by seizing or sabotaging key facilities,[68] generated a view in Military Operations in the War Office that two divisions should be retained in the United Kingdom until the CID was satisfied that the TF[69] could defeat any incursion.[70] The blocking of commercial harbours was a significant concern, actions, which, if successful, would not only interfere with trade but also more importantly, the timely deployment of any expeditionary force to the Continent, especially if the Germans, perhaps using a proxy, sank merchant ships in harbours before war was declared.[71] German raiding and special operations were not however, the only concerns. Unrest in Ireland and the possibility of civil disorder on the Mainland were powerful, if not over-riding arguments for the retention of regular forces because political and military imperatives dictated that the TF should not be used to suppress

64 Major-General J M Grierson to Lord Sanderson, FO 371 dated 11 January 1906 in *British Documents on the Origins of the War, 1898-1914*, Vol. III, *The Testing of the Entente, 1904-1906* (London: HMSO, 1938), pp.172-173. In the letter, he claims to have only a chance meeting with Major Huguet the French Military Attache, whilst out riding in Rotten Row in Hyde Park December 1905. Williamson in *The Politics of Grand Strategy* provides evidence that his statement as to chance and dates were disingenuous, see, p.65 and fn 16.

65 The CID had been convinced in 1904 that an invasion force would require at least 70,000 troops in 200 ships, which would then be subjected to attrition by the Royal Navy before it landed; TNA CAB 3/1/20A1: Committee of Imperial Defence, Home Defence Memoranda dated 23 February 1904.

66 TNA CAB 37/115/24: Admiralty Notes, Problems of Overseas Attack, Appx XXII dated 25 June 1913.

67 One concern was the sabotage of the drainage systems of the Lincolnshire Fens. See, correspondence May - June 1910 in TNA WO 32/7087: Coastal Flooding as a Means of Defence in Fen County. The Royal Navy, in response to the perceived shortage of coastal artillery on the Tyne, Humber and at Harwich, assigned submarines to those areas; TNA ADM 116/3107: Organization of East Coast Defences, August 1913.

68 These included coastal defence batteries, naval logistic facilities, for example dockyards, magazines and jetties, commercial ports, communications facilities such as wireless, cable and telegraph stations, water treatment plants and railway infrastructure. See, Brigadier-General R M B F Kelly CB DSO, 'Coast Defence', *The Army Review*, Vol. VI, No 2 , War Office (April 1914), pp.521-523.

69 One of the concerns about the capability of the TF was the age profile of its 188,785 soldiers. In 1908, 10% of the TF strength was under 18 and 21.8% under 19, whilst men over 50 only comprised 0.3%; *Annual Return of the Territorial Force for the Year 1908*, p.106, Table 9.

70 TNA CAB 3/2: Home Defence A Series, Papers 41-80, Volume 2 (SECRET) - Attack on the British Isles from Overseas, Standing Sub-Committee of the CID dated 15 April 1914. This was the view that the Invasion Committee of 1908 had taken and one that was espoused at the 114th Meeting of the CID on 23 August 1911, although the Director of Military Training, Major-General Sir Archibald Murray, responsible for Home Defence, stated that the mobilized Territorial Force was capable of repelling raids; Lord Hankey, *The Supreme Command, 1914-1918* (London: George Allen & Unwin, 1961), Vol. One, p.82.

71 TNA CAB 3/2/56: Fixed Defence of Ports on the West Coast, 'Measures to Prevent the Blocking of Commercial Harbours, May 1913' and TNA CAB 3/2/66: Committee of Imperial Defence, Home Defence Memoranda, 'Blocking of Commercial Harbours, February 1914'.

either, unless there was no alternative. Clearly, the retention, or otherwise, of the regular divisions, would have a considerable impact upon the rail and shipping movement plans.

The Home Defence Plan (HDP),[72] which started to mature in 1911,[73] under-pinned the growing concerns of the CID that the UK Home Base had to be secured with Land and Naval forces.[74] Whilst forward defence remained a naval responsibility, a Land based backstop was deemed to be increasingly essential. This consisted of two components: Local Forces (LF) and the Central Force (CF) each composed mainly of TF and Reserve units. LF included forces in forts and garrisons,[75] supported by four TF divisions,[76] to secure Vital and Key Points. LF were to delay and attrite German forces, whilst the RN interdicted their maritime supply lines, thereby creating the conditions for the CF to defeat the enemy in the field.[77] The CF was the manoeuvre element and its mission was to counterstroke German incursions through mobility. Thus only one formation from its ORBAT, 1st London Brigade of 1st London Division was reassigned to a specific, although absolutely vital, static defence task, which was to protect the railway infrastructure, mainly of the London & South Western Railway (LSWR) between London, Aldershot, Salisbury and Southampton, an asset that

72 The first examination of the role of the Home Army in securing the Home Base was conducted in 1908 by the War Office General Staff, led by Brigadier-General A J Murray, Director Military Training, 1907-1912; TNA WO 33/462: 'Appreciation of the Situation in the in the Event of Hostilities with a European Maritime Power, 1 September 1908'. Murray was later Inspector of Infantry (1912-1914) and then Chief of the General Staff (CGS) in GHQ BEF in 1914. For an analysis of his career as a senior officer, see, J M Bourne, 'Major-General Sir Archibald Murray, Chief of Staff, GHQ', in Jones (Ed.), *Stemming The Tide*, pp.51-69.

73 By 1914, the HDP had evolved into one of detail of Troops To Task but equally, had sufficient flexibility, to integrate Regular forces that might not deploy to the Continent. TNA WO 33/694: Central Forces Scheme, August 1914 and TNA WO 33/692: Distribution of Home Defence Forces, August 1914.

74 For a contemporary perspective by the National Service League on the requirements for Home Defence, see, Colonel A Keene DSO, 'Our Requirements for Home Defence', *The Army Review*, Vol. III, No 1, War Office (July 1912).

75 For a history of coast defence, see, Ian V Hogg, *Coast Defences of England and Wales, 1856-1956* (Newton Abbot: David & Charles, 1974) and for archaeological details of the period, Catrina Appleby, Wayne Cocroft and John Schofield (Eds.) *The Home Front in Britain, 1914-18, An Archaeological Handbook* (York: Council for British Archaeology, 2015), pp.87-100. For the Order of Battle (ORBAT) and locations of the UK Coast Artillery in April 1918, see, General Sir Martin Farndale KCB, *History of the Royal Regiment of Artillery, The Forgotten Fronts and the Home Base, 1914-18* (Woolwich: The Royal Artillery Institution, 1988), Annex 4.

76 The LF TF divisions were initially deployed as follows:

Table 2.1
Local Force – Territorial Force Divisions

Division	Location & Task
Northumbrian	Tyne defences
Lowland	Scottish coastal defences
Welsh	Welsh Borders then Northampton
East Anglian	East Anglia local defence

77 LF included land Coast Defence formations, most of which comprised TF reinforced with Regular Reservists. See, Kelly, 'Coast Defence', pp.508-531; he raises a series of pertinent points relating to Land and Maritime joint co-operation in coastal defence operations, including whether capability might be better served by the Royal Navy commanding the battle-space including the shore-based artillery, rather than the assigned arrangements. Whilst apparently a revolutionary proposal, this was an evolutionary process, which included for example, the Royal Navy assuming responsibility for submarine mining from the Royal Engineers. For example, Fort Blockhouse at Gosport, originally a coastal defence facility, became a naval shore station, HMS *Dolphin*, becoming the home of the Royal Navy's Submarine Service between 1904 and 1999, although somewhat bizarrely as the Defence wheel turns, the submarines have departed and the Army is once more the significant occupant of this historic site.

was critical to the deployment of the BEF.[78] The CF was organized into three corps,[79] although the nomenclature of the time assigned them as armies, totalling ten light divisions consisting of 195,000 personnel and 60,000 horses.[80] To support these forces, a wealth of logistic preparations were required, which were embedded in the plan, including the movement requirements,[81] hourly capacity of railway stations, accommodation for personnel and horses, infrastructure for conversion to medical and veterinary facilities, route allocations plus water, food, gas and electricity availability in the assembly areas. The HDP also recognized the need to retain regular units to handle civil unrest, which remained a Government concern until the public attitude to the war became clear. The two aspects that created the greatest concerns were potential industrial disorder, specifically in the coalfields and the possibility of civil dislocation in the capital, particularly if the KLM successfully blockaded the Port of London. Government planning focused upon the deployment of regular forces for these tasks because of the sensitivity about the use of TF units to support the civil authorities.

A Rum Task

The naval mobilization issues were different to those of the Army.[82] In particular, there was no requirement to mobilize, assemble and move large units from one part of the United Kingdom to another. The first two tasks, recalling sailors from leave and courses and re-calling reservists were achieved by the use of scheduled rail services and needed no additional resources. RN mobilization focused on people rather than major units, including the crews of small vessels, such as trawlers and

78 TNA WO 33/694: Central Forces Scheme, August 1914 and TNA WO 33/692: Distribution of Home Defence Forces, August 1914.

79 The CF ORBAT in August 1914 is shown below:

Table 2.2
Central Force ORBAT – August 1914

1st Army (HQ Bedford)	2nd Army (HQ Aldershot)	3rd Army (HQ Luton)
	East and West Lancashire Divisions until deployed to Ireland	
Highland Division	1st London Division	2nd London Division
West Riding Division*	Home Counties Division	North Midland Division
1 x Mounted Brigade	Wessex Division *	South Midland Division
2 x Cyclist Battalions	2 x Mounted Brigades	2 x Mounted Divisions
	3 x Cyclist Battalions	1 x Cyclist Battalion
	4th and 6th Divisions if not deployed with the BEF	

*If allocated.

80 TNA WO 33/694: Central Forces Scheme, August 1914; TNA WO 33/692: Distribution of Home Defence Forces, August 1914 and TNA WO 153/115: Distribution of Home Forces, 31 August 1914.

81 The plan required in the period Mobilization plus 13-16 days, 241 trains from Scotland and the Midlands to East Anglia and 70 trains from Wiltshire to Aldershot, with an additional 105 trains to move two TF divisions (East and West Lancashire) and a mounted brigade to the ports of Heysham, Holyhead and Liverpool, for the short-sea crossing to Ireland. In August 1914, whilst the East Lancashire Division's battalion advance parties for horse purchase and billeting travelled to Ireland, the divisional deployments were cancelled and the parties recalled. TNA WO 95/4594: WD, 1/7th Battalion Lancashire Fusiliers, 1 August 1914 - 30 April 1915 and TNA WO 95/4595: WD, 1/5th Battalion East Lancashire Regiment, 1 August 1914 - 31 May 1915. 42nd (East Lancashire) Division deployed to Egypt and then Gallipoli before serving in France. 55th (West Lancashire) Division was held in the UK, its infantry units reinforcing the BEF until it was disbanded and the remaining capability transferred to what became 57th (West Lancashire) Division. 55th Division was reformed in France in 1916, with many of its original units returning to the fold.

82 Documents appertaining to naval rail requirements are held in TNA WO 106/50.

drifters requisitioned for naval service; many of these men lived in or near the port of registration. There were however, logistic issues,[83] which taxed the minds of staff in the Admiralty. First, was coal for ships. Pre-war, colliers delivered nearly all the Fleet's requirements from ports in South Wales to UK naval bases but Admiralty planners recognized that KLM operations in the North Sea and possibly in the English Channel, might disrupt this vital activity and arrangements were made to partially switch to a rail alternative, although this decision was not taken without careful consideration. A King Edward VII Class Pre-Dreadnought had a bunker capacity of 2,200 tons of coal[84] and the Dreadnought Iron Duke, 3,250.[85] Most rail coal wagons varied in capacity from 8-12 tons, so, with an average of 10 tons,[86] 325 wagons were required to fill the Iron Duke's bunkers from empty.[87]

In January 1912, the Admiralty estimated that it would need approximately 50 coal trains per day to move coal from South Wales to the Humber, Tyne and Forth ports, plus 30,000 filled wagons to act as a mobile reserve,[88] which would require the initial transfer of 3,000 empty,[89] bottom-hopper coal wagons from the Tyne area to the South Wales coalfields,[90] and an average of 120 trains per day each way within the UK to sustain the naval fuel and stores requirement.[91]

During the Great War, the railways transported nearly 5,452,400 million tons of coal for the Grand Fleet in 13,631 trains between 27 August 1914 and 31 December 1918. Nearly 90 percent of this coal came from collieries situated in the Aberdare and Rhondda districts of South Wales. The wagons were marshalled at Pontypool Road on the Great Western Railway (GWR) from the various companies serving the coalfields, although it was necessary to invest in additional infrastructure to support the operation. The GWR worked the traffic to Warrington for movement to Carlisle by the London & North West Railway (LNWR) and thence to its destinations in Scotland via the Caledonian, Glasgow & South Western or North British railway companies.[92] Two other routes to Scotland[93] were used whilst coal was also dispatched to His Majesty's Naval Bases (HMNB) at

83 The details relating to capital ships have been extracted from Dr Oscar Parkes OBE AINA, *British Battleships, A History of Design, Construction and Armament* (London: Seeley Service, 1957). This massive tome took 31 years to write, 1925-1956.

84 Ibid, p.426.

85 Ibid, p.545.

86 For details, see, R J Essery, D P Rowland & W O Steel, *British Goods Wagons, From 1887 to the Present Day* (Newton Abbot: Charles, 1970), pp.112-114. There were some higher capacity wagons on the Network, which were usually allocated to bulk movement tasks such as coal exports and power generation. The North Eastern Railway (NER) had hopper wagons of 20 ton capacity plus and trialled wagons of 40. The Lancashire & Yorkshire Railway (L&Y) also had a 20 tonner but this vehicle type was usually allocated to the transport of locomotive coal.

87 In 1913, Britain produced 287 million tons of coal. Accounting for some internal colliery use, local distribution by road and some movement by canal, the railways were moving approximately 600,000 - 650,000 tons per day. For an analysis of coal distribution, see, Va Nee L Van Vleck, 'Delivering Coal by Road and Rail in Britain: The Efficiency of the "Silly Little Bobtailed" Coal Wagons', *The Journal of Economic History*, Vol. 57 (March, 1997), pp.139-160.

88 TNA CAB 17/30: Internal Distribution of Supplies in time of War.

89 In August 1914, the Admiralty hired 4,000 wagons rising to 16,000 at some points during the war, nearly all hires being transacted through one agency. See, Edwin A Pratt, *British Railways and the Great War, Organization, Efforts, Difficulties and Achievement*, Vol. I (London: Selwyn & Blount, 1921), p.489.

90 TNA WO 106/50: Naval Requirements for Railway Services.

91 Ibid.

92 For details of the railway companies, see, The Railway Gazette, *The Railway Year Book for 1913, The Whitaker of the Railway Service*, (London: The Railway Publishing Company, 1913).

93 Pontypool Road to Cardiff on the Great Western and thence to Gloucester to join the Midland Railway for movement North or via the Brecon & Merthyr Railway to Talyllyn, then onto the Cambrian Railways to Gobowen, for the GWR to haul to Chester and then Warrington. Traffic on the Cambrian Railways was particularly difficult to work because the line was mainly single track with plenty of testing gradients. See, R W Kidner, *The Mid-Wales Railway*, Oakwood Library of Railway History, No 79, 2nd Edition (Usk: The Oakwood Press, 2003).

Dover, Harwich,[94] Immingham, Plymouth, Portsmouth and the Tyne. Grangemouth[95] became the main railhead for Grand Fleet coal because the Highland Railway (HR) and its terminus at Thurso, were not capable of handling all the naval traffic.[96]

Coaling ship was a manpower intensive task, which was filthy, slow and unhealthy, so the Admiralty had been cautiously examining an alternative, and from 1912, the *Arethusa* Class cruisers were constructed with oil-fired boilers.[97] In August 1914, although some capital ships used oil as an auxiliary fuel[98], there were no purely oil-fired battleships in service but the five Queen Elizabeth class battleships in construction were to be so.[99] From the logistic perspective, the expanding use of oil was a leap of faith because whilst petroleum was slowly being embedded into the economic base in the United Kingdom by 1914,[100] naval storage facilities required expansion,[101] whilst 93 percent of the products were imported.[102] These supplies, including those from British concessions in the Middle East,[103] were by no means assured,[104] and the key issue was not total production from oilfields but the UK's access to the exportable surplus.[105]

94 Coal for HMNB Harwich was mainly received from Yorkshire coalfields; Pratt, *British Railways and the Great War,* Vol. I p.489.

95 Journey time from Pontypool Road to Grangemouth was usually just shy of 48 hours, with the numbers of coal trains sometimes being 19 per day carrying a total of 7,600 tons; Ibid, p.491.

96 An interesting aside was the proposal to construct the Mid-Scotland Ship Canal linking the Forth with the Clyde to enable the movement of the largest battleships of the Royal Navy from the North Sea to the Atlantic without having to transit Pentland Firth. This project, which was initially commercially driven, conceptually matched the Kiel Canal and was on a scale to rival the Suez or Panama Canals. The estimated cost in 2016 values was in excess of £15 Billion, which is about the same as London's Cross-Rail system. The strategic imperatives however, persuaded the Government to spend defence funds building ships rather than infrastructure.

97 TNA ADM 265/28: TNA ADM 265/28: 'History of development of oil burning fuel in HM Service'.

98 The King Edward VII class carried 380 tons except for HMS *New Zealand*, and the Iron Duke class 1,600 tons, 550 tons of which was held as a reserve. The oil was burnt, by spraying it at high-pressure, onto the hot coals; Parkes, *British Battleships*, p.425, p.432 and p.545.

99 HMS *Queen Elizabeth*, commissioned in December 1914, had a capacity of 3,400 tons but also carried 100 tons of coal for domestic use, so the Single Fuel Concept (SFC) had not quite been delivered; Ibid, p.562. The keel of HMS *Queen Elizabeth* was laid down on Monday 21 October 1912, ten days before that of the first US oil-fired battleship, the USS Nevada.

100 By 1901, Anglo-American had 500 x Rail Tank Cars (RTC) in the United Kingdom, rising to 2,444 in 1918. By 1914, there were 117 Private Sidings on the railways for the delivery of petroleum products and over 1,000 distribution outlets, from which, these products were delivered by road, mainly using HT. For a fascinating insight into the history and distribution of petroleum products in the United Kingdom, see, Alan Coppin, *Oil on the Rails, The Story of an Industry and its Influence on Britain's Railways and its Rail Tank Wagons* (The Historical Model Railway Society, 1999).

101 There was a civilian storage facility for 40,000 tons of bunker oil at Thameshaven and the depot at Purfleet had a capacity of 10,000 for petroleum products; Ibid, p.37.

102 UK oil import proportions in 1913 were 62.3% USA, 11.6% Romania, 7.7% Russia, 7.7% Dutch East Indies, 4.1% Mexico and 6.5% Other; Mark Gibson, *Britain's Quest for Oil, The First World and the Peace Conferences* (Solihull: Helion, 2017), Table 4.1, UK oil imports 1913, p.91, sourced from, TNA CAB 24/59, G.T 5267, Slade p.1.

103 For an assessment of the issues relating to the supply of oil to the Royal Navy, see, Geoffrey Miller, *Straits, British policy towards the Ottoman Empire and the origins of the Dardanelles Campaign* (Kingston-upon-Hull: University of Hull Press, 1997), Part Three, Oil and Gibson, *Britain's Quest for* Oil, pp.21-47.

104 In 1913, the UK domestic oil production was 289,684 tons, contributing to a British Empire total of 1,541,434, of which India produced 1,110,211. The Empire thus produced 2.79% of the World's oil against the 64.0% from the USA. Persian production was only 243,621 tons. Figures extracted from Mark Gibson, *Britain's Quest for Oil,* Appx 1, World oil production, 1913-20, sourced from Marian Kent, *Oil and Empire, British Policy and Mesopotamian Oil 1900-1920,* (London: Macmillan, 1976), Appx VIII.

105 This pertinent point was raised by Admiral Sir Edmond Slade, as head of the expedition to Persia for the Anglo-Persian Oil Company, October 1913 - February 1914.

P2.2. Black Gold: despite the potential of oil as a fuel for transportation in 1914, coal was critical to powering the railways and ships so vital to the projection of British defence assets in 1914. Whilst during the Great War, the Royal Navy and the Army increasingly relied on petroleum products to power ships and lorries, the mercantile marine and the railways remained firmly wedded to coal. (Author)

P2.3. Liquid Gold: commercial logisticians were quick to expand bulk transportation capability by rail before 1914. In 1901, Anglo-American had 500 x Rail Tank Cars (RTC) in the United Kingdom, rising to 2,444 in 1918,[106] whilst by 1914, there were 117 Private Sidings on the railways for the delivery of petroleum products.[107] (Author)

106 Coppin, *Oil on the Rails*, p.49.
107 Ibid, pp.115-121, Appx 1 - Geographical Distribution of Oil Company Private Sidings.

Munitions were another key element in preparing the Royal Navy for war. Capital ship main armament projectile weight rose from 850 pounds[108] for the 12 inch guns mounted on the King Edward VII Class to 1,920 pounds[109] for the 15 inch guns,[110] mounted on the Queen Elizabeth class. Propellant charge[111] weights were 307 and 428 pounds[112] respectively. These munitions had to be safely stored and appropriately inspected to ensure they were fit for operational use, particularly in respect of cordite[113] and as the Royal Navy expanded, the Admiralty enhanced its munitions storage infrastructure,[114] which was served by Standard[115] or Narrow Gauge[116] railways, to move its growing inventory of shells, propellants, pyrotechnics, mines and torpedoes.[117] Whilst the Admiralty used ammunition ships for inter-port transfers on the South coast, the move of the Grand Fleet to Scapa Flow, created serious concerns about their vulnerability, especially to submarine attack and stocks were therefore, planned to be moved by rail to Inverness.[118]

The massive guns that fired such large rounds also had to be moved from the factory to the naval dockyards. Several railways[119] built special vehicles, called gun-sets, each with a capacity of 160 tons to move them. For smaller guns, the companies used armour plate trucks, boiler wagons, surplus tender frames and bolster wagons. One of the key manufacturers of naval guns in the United Kingdom was the Coventry Ordnance Works (COW).[120] Located at Foleshill in the

108 *Treatise on Ammunition*, 10th Edition, War Office (HMSO, 1915), p.224.

109 Ibid, p.225.

110 Filled shell weights are nominal. Each shell type has a Higher and Lower quality control limit. Projectiles not meeting the specification values were rejected.

111 In 1914, the sole supplier of naval propellant was the Royal Gunpowder Factory (RGPF) Waltham Abbey and to ensure security of supply, the Admiralty had its own facility, Royal Naval Cordite Factory (RNCF) constructed at Holton Heath in Dorset. A dedicated railway connected it Rocklea Jetty in Poole Harbour. One of the by-products was nitre cake, which was shipped to Hull for the manufacture of the domestic cleaner, Harpic. For details see, Wayne D Cocroft *Dangerous Energy, The Archaeology of Gunpowder and Military Explosives Manufacture* (Swindon: English Heritage, 2000), pp.159-163 and M R Bowditch and L Hayward, *A Pictorial Record of the Royal Naval Cordite Factory, Holton Heath* (Caversham: Finial Publishing, 1996).

112 Parkes, *British Battleships*, p.564. A London Class pre-dreadnought carried 132.6 tons of cordite and 294.5 tons of projectiles; TNA ADM 116/1370: HMS Bulwark Explosion and Loss.

113 During the Great War, the Royal Navy lost four ships through cordite explosions; CB 1515, *The Technical History and Index*, Vol. 2, Part 24, Storage and Handling of Explosives in Warships, Admiralty, October 1919 and Chp V, Explosion in Warships during the War. For cordite storage testing and its relationship to the loss of HMS *Bulwark*, see, David Evans, *Arming The Fleet, The Development of the Royal Ordnance Yards, 1770-1945* (Gosport: English Heritage, 2006), pp.140-144. For the story of three of the losses, HMS *Bulwark* (moored on the River Medway, 26 November 1914) HMS *Natal* (at anchor, Cromarty, 30 December 1915) and HMS *Vanguard* (at anchor, Scapa Flow, 9 July 1917), see, A Cecil Hampshire, *They Called it Accident* (London: William Kimber & Co, 1960). HMS *Glatton* was lost at anchor at Dover on 16 September 1918. The nature of RN losses at Jutland caused by the improper handling of cordite have been analysed through the lens of underwater survey conducted by Innes McCartney; see, *Jutland 1916, The Archaeology of a Naval Battlefield* (London: Bloomsbury, 2016).

114 The three key sites were: Bull Point at Plymouth, Priddy's Hard at Gosport, with new magazines at Bedenham and the Upnor, Lodge Hill and Chattenden complexes in Kent. The War Office also used some of the storage.

115 A railway which, had a track gauge of 4' 8 ½ inches (1435mm). In 2018, Standard Gauge is rated between 1432mm and 1435mm to account for those SGRs, which have reduced their gauge by 3 mm, to improve the ride of high-speed trains.

116 A railway with a track gauge of less than 4' 8 ½ inches (1435mm).

117 For an historical survey, see, Evans, *Arming The Fleet*, pp.145-185.

118 Ammunition sidings and a branch line to the Harbour were constructed in May 1915, with ammunition ships transporting the stocks to Scapa Flow. Construction of the branch by the Highland Railway, assisted by 100 men of the Royal Engineers, took ten days; H A Vallance, *The Highland Railway, The History of the Railways of the Scottish Highlands*, Vol. 2, 4th Edn (Newton Abbot: David & Charles, 1985), pp.101.

119 Caledonian, Great Central, London & North Western, Midland and North Eastern. The Great Western used converted girder wagons.

120 The company was established in 1905 by a consortium of British shipbuilding firms, John Brown, Cammell, Laird and Co and Fairfield, in order to compete with the duopoly of Vickers and Armstrong-Whitworth. The author's maternal Grandmother lived near the COW, of which the Naval Gun Shop and some railway lines were extant in 2017. See, *Coventry Canal Conservation Area Appraisal*, English Heritage, 4 July 2012, p.36; accessed through www.

North East of Coventry, it was as far from the sea as it is possible to get in the United Kingdom, so the railways[121] were a critical component within the supply chain for the delivery of naval combat capability. The transport of naval propellers was resolved by the use of special trolley wagons used by industry to support merchant ship construction and repair.[122]

All the major naval ports were served by rail and although not all of the Royal Naval Ordnance Depots (RNOD)[123] constructed in the 19th Century were connected to the National Railway Network (NRN) some being served solely by sea, many of them had an internal Narrow Gauge Railway (NGR) system. The first RNOD to be rail-served was the new site at Lodge Hill in Kent, which was part of the Medway Development Scheme[124] and new depots such as RNOD Crombie on the River Forth, which opened in 1915 to serve His Majesty's Naval Base Rosyth.[125] Of little initial importance in pre-war planning were the Highland Railway[126] and Great North of Scotland Railway,[127] both of which became key contributors to naval logistics once the Grand Fleet began to use Scapa Flow as an operational base.[128] The changing footprint of naval port expansion was certainly enabled by the railway, with in particular, greater agility in supporting submarine and mining operations and the Grand Fleet at Scapa Flow, Cromarty and Invergordon, when its main manning bases were in the South of England.[129]

Green Issues

By 1912, the War Office had defined its mobilization and movement requirements in terms of size and sequence. Before mobilization movement could commence however, it was essential that the relevant 'Logistic Enablers'[130] were positioned at the correct time because the personnel executing

coventry.gov.uk on 28 February 2017.

121 The COW was initially connected to the National Rail Network (NRN) in 1905 by a line to the Foleshill Railway. In 1914, it received another connection via the Three Spires Junction loop.

122 For illustrations, see, Essery, Rowland & Steel, *British Goods Wagons*, pp.112-114.

123 Including Bull Point in Devon and Marchwood and Tipner Point in Hampshire; Priddy's Hard received a retrospective connection. By 1914, Marchwood was mainly being used for the storage of munitions awaiting disposal; Evans, *Arming The Fleet*, p.185.

124 Lodge Hill was served by the South Eastern & Chatham Railways via exchange sidings at Sharnal Street to the Chattendon Naval Tramway. RNOD Chattendon and Upnor were served by NGR; Ibid, pp.180-181. For an orientation of the SR and NGR serving naval and commercial facilities on the River Medway, see, Richard Harman & Gerry Nichols, *Atlas of the Southern Railway* (Addlestone: Ian Allan, 2016), Map 76.

125 RNOD Crombie and HMNB Rosyth were both served by the North British Railway (NBR), the former via the Charleston Branch; Philip W Conolly (Introduction), *Pre-Grouping Atlas and RCH Junction Diagrams* (Hersham: Ian Allan, 2014), p.109.

126 For a summary of wartime operations, see, Pratt, *British Railways and the Great* War, Vol. II, pp.940-960 and Vallance, *The Highland Railway*, pp.100-107.

127 For a summary of wartime operations, see, Pratt, *British Railways and the Great War*, Vol. II, pp.919-921; Sir Malcolm Barclay-Harvey KCMG, *A History of the Great North of Scotland Railway*, 2nd Edn (London: The Locomotive Publishing Company, 1949), pp.215-221 and H A Vallance, *The Great North of Scotland Railway, The History of the Railways of the Scottish Highlands*, Vol. 3, 2nd Edn (Newton Abbot: David & Charles, 1989), pp.139-141.

128 For an explanation of the railways' role, see, Pratt, *British Railways and the Great War*, Vol. I, Chp XXXIII.

129 This was facilitated through the Euston-Thurso Naval Special and its supporting connections to and from key naval bases and ports such as Dover, Chatham, Harwich, Milford Haven, Portsmouth and Plymouth. The Euston-Thurso route was 717 miles, with the Northbound train departing Euston at 1800 and arriving Thurso at 1530 the next day, with a journey time of 21 hours 30 minutes. The Southbound train departed at 1145, arriving Euston at 1005 the next day, after a timetabled run of 22 hours and 20 minutes. For details of the operation, see, Pratt, *British Railways and the Great War*, Vol. I, pp.507-514.

130 The term 'Logistic Enablers', although of recent vintage, aptly describes the arrangements of the period. The key enablers were: Railway Transport Officers (RTO), Military Landing Officers (MLO), Naval Divisional Transport Officers (NDTO) and the support staff for these key appointments.

P2.4. Supporting the Grand Fleet: the rusting metals of the Charleston Branch of the North British Railway looking towards Royal Naval Ordnance Depot (RNOD) Crombie in 2006. Connecting the RNODs to the National Rail Network (NBR) created much logistic flexibility for the Royal Navy. (Author)

the rail movement plans were critical to its success. The first part of the mobilization process[131] involved the return of Regular sailors and soldiers from courses and leave, and for the Army, units to barracks from training. The movement of individuals utilized scheduled rail services on a warrant. Local re-deployments were a unit responsibility, usually conducted by road but the plan could not define the details for units deployed outside the garrison area that required a rail move. The location, numbers and size of units were known once the annual exercise and training programme was confirmed but the constant dynamics made it impossible for a detailed movement plan to be created for every scenario. The key to delivering this part of the mobilization process was to scope the worst case and hot-plan through the commercial transportation system. This problem also applied to the TF, the units of which might be on Annual Training Camp (ATC) during the mobilization, although as most of these were held in the summer, activation outside this period would require fewer resources. The next phase would involve the movement, by rail, of reservists from their hometowns, to Regimental Depots, and once processed and equipped, to their allocated units.

Once unit mobilization was complete, Regular units assigned to the BEF were to march to a nominated railhead to embark for the departure port, although in some instances, units appropriately located, would move directly to the docks. Concurrently, units, mostly from the TF, detailed for

131 For a summary of the Army's mobilization processes, see Lt-Col H M E Brunker, *Notes on Organization and Equipment*, 6th Edn (London: William Clowes and Sons, 1909), pp.162-167.

HD would be moving to their War Stations. Whilst some were involved in local defence, others had to be moved by rail, potentially supported by selected Regular units and Special Reserve (SR) battalions generated from Regimental Depot resources. From the War Office perspective, the deployment of expeditionary units within a tight timeframe to meet the operational imperative was the Main Effort and required the greatest planning; the HD elements were more flexible. Beyond this point, the War Office expected a dynamic planning process to deliver the capability. There might be the requirement to move Regular units returning from abroad, dispatch additional Regular units to the BEF, move territorial divisions to overseas stations,[132] re-deploy HD units and move casualties from UK ports to hospitals.

Platforms and Plans

The legislation that enabled Defence control and utilization of the railways in TTW and War was enshrined in the Regulation of the Forces Act 1871 and the National Defence Act 1888.[133] The 1871 Act granted authority for the government to take control of all or part of the railway system, whilst the latter directed that naval and military traffic was to have precedence whenever an Order for the Embodiment of the Militia was in force.[134] One of the key aspects of the mobilization plan was secrecy. The United Kingdom had no alliance with France but the manner in which, the deployment plans were crafted, were carefully honed to meet the French mobilization scheme. Whilst this made excellent military sense, politically it suggested a much closer tie than had been agreed by the Cabinet, a process made more sensitive because the Government strategy had not been exposed to Parliamentary scrutiny. DMO was understandably keen therefore, to ensure that for internal reasons, the mobilization plan and its supporting components were kept secret. Parliament and most members of the Cabinet were not sighted on the detailed developing political involvement with France and specifically the scope and depth of the United Kingdom's potential military commitment to a Continental conflict. Discussions and plans were therefore, tightly controlled to prevent un-informed disclosure and debate. Indeed, such was the sensitivity of them, that most of the typing was conducted by the Staff Officers and not the clerks, which speaks volumes for the clerical industry, if not the skill, of the former.

The effectiveness of BEF's deployment relied greatly upon the enemy being surprised by its appearance on the battlefield, so it was important to ensure its proposed arrival in time and space remained unknown to them, whilst also offering the British and French, opportunities for deception. In addition, it was also critical that the Germans remained ignorant of the movement arrangements, particularly the shipping plan, knowledge of which would have enabled them to plan and execute counter-measures. Despite concerns about domestic sabotage, the UK rail operation was the most robust aspect of the plan. Security was certainly effective because the Germans were

132 The East Lancashire Division deployed to Egypt in September 1914; Major A F Becke (Comp), BOH, *Order of Battle, Divisions,* Part 2 A, *The Territorial Force Mounted Divisions and The 1st-Line Territorial Force Divisions (42nd-56th)* (London: HMSO, 1936) pp.35-41. The Wessex Division, with the exception of the staffs of the infantry brigades, the ammunition columns of the artillery brigades, the Royal Engineers, the Royal Army Medical Corps and the Hampshire Heavy Battery, RGA, deployed to India in October 1914; Ibid, pp.43-48.

133 See, TNA WO 32/5289 and 32/5290: Defence of the Realm Acts, for powers possessed by the Government under the National Defence Act, 1888, and Regulation of the Forces Act, 1871.

134 There were three additional Acts relating to Defence operations. The Regulation of Railways Act 1844 required companies to provide conveyance for the transport of troops at fares not exceeding a scale given in the Act, with maximum fares also prescribed in regard to public baggage, stores and ammunition, with exceptions for gun-powder and explosives; the 1867 Act extended all these provisions to the Army Reserve. The Cheap Trains Act 1883 amended the law relating to Railway Passenger Duty and the conveyance by rail, of the Queen's forces.

unaware that the BEF was taking to the field,[135] until units were arriving in France,[136] although this happenstance should in no way suggest that German intelligence collection was an amateur operation.[137] The cloak of secrecy was so effective that even the Quartermaster-General, Sir John Cowans,[138] some of whose key staff were involved in the planning, was not fully apprised of the detailed elements of the plan, until mid-July 1914.[139]

A significant aspect of the war planning scenarios was the potential for the naval situation in the North Sea to prevent sustainable commerce to and from the East Coast ports. Of particular importance was the possible interruption to shipping using the Port of London, which was vital in sustaining the life of the City and its fast-growing environs. In September 1908, the Director of Naval Intelligence (DNI)[140] raised concerns about the KLM blockading East Coast ports, although unbeknown to him, KLM planners had, in 1897, abandoned plans to attack shipping in the Thames Estuary[141] and there had been no appetite to revive them.[142] For politicians and senior civil servants, the widespread transportation and dock strikes of 1911,[143] had given some idea of the impact that such disruption could cause and plans were put in hand to assess whether London could be supplied by directing shipping to Western ports and then moving merchandise by rail.[144] The results were not especially encouraging, especially with respect to port flexibility and, with other more soluble issues at hand, the matter was placed in the pending tray.

135 1st Battalion Northumberland Fusiliers entraining at Portsmouth for Southampton noted the 'Woking' destination boards on the coaches. Whether this was an attempt at deceiving potential spies or that the London & South Western Railway did not remove them having completed the previous passenger task is unknown. See, Brigadier H R Sandilands CMG DSO, *The Fifth in the Great War: A History of the 1st & 2nd Northumberland Fusiliers, 1914-1918* (Edinburgh & London: G W Grigg & Son, 1938) and John Mason Sneddon, *The Devil's Carnival, The First Hundred Days of Armageddon, 1st Battalion Northumberland Fusiliers, August - December 1914* (Brighton: Reveille Press, 2012), p.43.

136 For a description see, Andrew Christopher, *Defence of the Realm, The Authorised History of MI5* (London: Allen Lane, 2009), pp.29-52 and Thomas Boghardt, *Spies of the Kaiser, German Covert Operations in Great Britain during the First World War Era* (Basingstoke & New York: Palgrave Macmillan, 2004). For details of individual operations, see, the fascinating internal departmental history, Nigel West (Ed.), *MI5 in the Great War* (London: Biteback Publishing, 2014).

137 'As for the German spies, they were undoubtedly well-briefed, professionally managed and often quite colourful'; West, *MI5 in the Great War*, p.xi.

138 Sir John had a family background in railways, including the famous family firm, Cowans & Sheldon, which manufactured railway cranes. For the only biography, see, Major Desmond Chapman-Huston & Major Owen Rutter *General Sir John Cowans, GCB GCMG, The Quartermaster-General of the Great War*, Vols I & II (London: Hutchinson, 1924).

139 After his briefing on the highly sensitive With-France plan, Sir John spent the last weekend of peace in 1914, attending a country house-party at Highclere House, the filming location of the ITV Series, '*Downton Abbey*'.

140 Captain then Rear Admiral and later Admiral, Sir Edmond John Warre Slade KCIE KCVO held the post 1907-1909. Slade was to play an important role in delivering naval and military logistic capability as Chair of the Admiralty and War Office Inter-departmental Committee on Transport for the Expeditionary Force in the period 1913-1914 and as head of the expedition to Persia for the Anglo-Persian Oil Company, October 1913 - February 1914.

141 The Germans revived the concept during the Second World War using aerially delivered magnetic mines. Some must still lie on the sea-bed; one was found by divers in Swanage Bay in 2009 and destroyed, complete with 'Larry the Lobster' who had made the casing its home and refused to leave, by a Royal Navy Explosive Ordnance Disposal (EOD) Team. The concept of attacking the commercial maritime capability of London became reality on 7 September 1940 when the *Luftwaffe* commenced a focused series of attacks on Docklands.

142 See, P M Kennedy, 'The Development of German Naval Operational Plans against England, 1896-1914', *English Historical Review*, Vol. 89 (1974), pp.51-55.

143 For a social analysis, see, Juliet Nicolson, *The Perfect Summer, England 1911* (London: John Murray, 2006).

144 See, TNA WO 32/5289 and 32/5290: Defence of the Realm Acts, for powers possessed by the Government under the National Defence Act, 1888, and Regulation of the Forces Act, 1871, to secure the distribution of essential supplies, including food, by rail. See also, the 'Report of the Standing Sub-Committee of the Committee of Imperial Defence on the Internal Distribution of Supplies in Time of War' (SECRET 152B) dated 12 June 1912 in TNA WO 32/5290.

Conclusion

Initially confined to a small number of senior officers, the expansion of the work, including the requirement to generate detailed movement plans, led to wider military and civilian involvement, although very few people had visibility of the complete plan, interactions being conducted on the basis of 'need to know'. Another important feature of the planning process was co-ordination not only between the Armed Services but also with various civilian agencies and companies. For the military, such activity was initially novel; for the civilians, it was in some respects, an extension of their commercial task. Of critical significance was the ability of the commercial railway and shipping sectors to deliver operational and logistic capability within the United Kingdom, whilst also projecting it to Continental Europe. In the 21st Century, there is an on-going debate about the military-civil logistic balance but in 1912, the role of the commercial sector in enabling the projection of military power was becoming well established, although with reservations by some officers in the military planning environment.

The process was slowly refined, taking three years to mature with the detailed mobilization and movement plans not being issued until early 1914, whilst some of the shipping issues were not resolved until May. In the intervening period, the planners grappled with a whole series of problems that repay study. First and foremost, was the need to develop the appropriate structures and mature the close working relationships across the plethora of organizations that were responsible for delivering the outputs. These included the Admiralty, War Office, Board of Trade, the railways, shipping companies and port authorities. Despite the complexity of the interfaces, there were many positive aspects of the process that were conducive to success. The shared experience of deploying armed forces to South Africa to fight in the Boer War (1899-1902) generated a comprehension of the scale of the potential mobilization, if not the timescale. Frequent deployment and recovery of units, naval and military, to and from far-flung parts of the Empire provided practise of administrative and movement tasks by staff and enablers, whilst integrating railway and shipping companies to the Defence culture. Secondly, the need to define the Defence mobilization requirement was clearly understood by all parties but it took strong leadership to secure success because political, defence, intelligence, economic, social and technological issues all contributed to the debate and influenced the outcome but it was the logistic capability of the commercial sector which delivered the forces to the operational ground and supported their presence upon it.

3

Quite a False Impression

The role of commercial logistic capability in the planning of Defence mobilization and movement in the United Kingdom before the Great War

Introduction

In July and August 1914, the Royal Navy (RN) and the British Army[1] prepared for war as the crisis in Europe reached a defining moment.[2] Reservists were mobilized, Territorial units[3] re-called from camp, the Royal Navy sailed to its war stations in preparation for operations against the *Kaiserliche Marine* (KLM),[4] whilst the War Office deployed the British Expeditionary Force (BEF) to France and Home Defence Units (HDU) in the United Kingdom. The mobilization, movement and field deployment was a masterpiece of military and civilian planning,[5] and execution, conducted in immense secrecy,[6] which was the culmination of three years intense analysis, staffing, exercising and training.[7] The General Officer Commanding (GOC) of 4th Division,[8] observed, 'Nothing could have been better done than the arrangements for entraining and embarkation and the whole thing was a great triumph for the Quartermaster-General'.[9] Most of these activities, critical though

1 For a broad analysis of the British Army, Regular and Territorial, in 1914, see, Charles Messenger, *Call To Arms, The British Army 1914-18* (London: Weidenfeld & Nicolson, 2005), pp.15-93 and in more detail for the Regular Army, Timothy Bowman & and Mark Connelly, *The Edwardian Army, Recruiting, Training and Deploying the British Army* (Oxford: Oxford University Press, 2012) and for the Territorial Force, K W Mitchinson, *England's Last Hope, The Territorial Force, 1908-1914* (Basingstoke & New York: Palgrave-Macmillan, 2008). For the tactical aspects, see, Spencer Jones, *From Boer War to World War, Tactical Reform of the British Army, 1902-1914* (Norman: University of Oklahoma Press, 2012) and Simon Batten, *Futile Exercise? The British Army's Preparations for War 1902-1914*, (Warwick: Helion, 2018).

2 For a concise insight of Britain's move from peace to war in July and August 1914, see, Trevor Wilson, *The Myriad Faces of War, Britain and the Great War, 1914-1918* (Cambridge: Polity Press, 1986), pp.7-40. For a comprehensive analysis of European events, see, T G Otte, *July Crisis, The World's Descent into War, Summer 1914* (Cambridge: Cambridge University Press (CUP), 2014).

3 For a comprehensive contemporary survey of the Territorial Force, see, *The Annual Return of the Territorial Force for the Year 1908*, Command 4496 (London: HMSO, 1909) and Walter Richards, *His Majesty's Territorial Army* (London: Virtue & Co, 1909) (Four volumes).

4 For a summary of Royal Navy mobilization and deployment, see Sir Julian S Corbett, BOH, *Naval Operations*, Vol. I, *To the Battle of the Falklands December 1914* (London: Longmans, Green & Co, 1920), pp.18-30.

5 For an assessment of the military and civilian plans of the European Powers, see the two key books on the subject: Paul M Kennedy, *War Plans of the Great Powers 1880-1914* (London: Allen & Unwin, 1979 and Richard F Hamilton and Holger H Herwig (Eds.) *War Planning 1914* (Cambridge: CUP, 2010).

6 Such was the sensitivity of the movement information, most of the typing was undertaken by the officers, the clerical staff not being granted access to the secret papers.

7 For a broader strategic examination from the British perspective, see, John Gooch, *The Plans of War, The General Staff and British Military Strategy c1906-1916* (London: Routledge & Kegan Paul, 1974). For a European assessment, see, Kennedy, *War Plans*.

8 Major-General Sir Thomas D'Oyly 'Snowball' Snow in his private diary, published, with notes, in 2011. Snow graduated from the Army Staff College in 1893, later becoming General Officer Commanding (GOC) 4th and 27th Divisions before being appointed Commander VII Corps. He was Grandfather & Great-Grandfather respectively, of the broadcasters Peter and Dan Snow.

9 Dan Snow and Mark Pottle, *The Confusion of Command, The Memoirs of Lieutenant-General Sir Thomas D'Oyly 'Snowball' Snow, 1914-1918* (London: Frontline Books, 2011).

they were to arguably the most important deployment of the British Army in its history,[10] have received relatively little attention in recent years, perhaps reflecting the space allocated to it in the Official History of the Great War.[11] Indeed, it appears such a model of logistic efficiency that there would little of value to learn by analysing it.[12] General Sir Percy Radcliffe,[13] in 1914 GSO2 MO1 (a) in the Directorate of Military Operations,[14] which was responsible for the BEF's deployment planning, was keen to ensure the post-1918 generation clearly understood the importance of the meticulous logistic arrangements, without which, the fighting-power of the BEF could not have been brought to bear on the German Army in a timely manner:

> Certain passages in the Official History appear likely to give quite a false impression of the extent and thoroughness, which had been made by the British Naval and Military authorities for the embarkation of the Expeditionary Force and its concentration in the theatre of operations.........It would be a very bad thing indeed if the idea should be allowed to gain ground that the movement of a large force from its place of mobilization in the United Kingdom to the ports of embarkation - its transport by sea, its disembarkation at the French ports and movement thence by rail to the concentration area, all within a period of 14 days, could be improvised on the spur of the moment.[15]

General Radcliffe's view has certainly survived the test of time because there has been remarkably little written on the subject and what has been, has focused upon the dispatch of the BEF to France and not the detailed planning and preparation that enabled it.[16] There were however, other

10 The plan for the deployment of the BEF to France, the 'With-France Scheme' is understood to have comprised approximately 70 individual documents, some of which were in excess of a 100 pages. The SECRET Expeditionary Force Railway Timetables of 45 pages of printed A2 are held in TNA WO 106/49B/3, the SECRET Disembarkation Tables (A1732) in TNA WO 106/49B/7, the SECRET (A1647) Detrainment and Billeting Tables (A1647) in TNA WO 106/49B/5 and the CONFIDENTIAL Remount Statement (A1729) are but four examples of these incredibly detailed documents. A note from an officer in Staff Duties at the War Office in April 1937, highlights the frustration in not being able to identify all of them: 'After 23 years the search for the scheme as a whole seems a doubtful project to pursue after midnight'; TNA WO 106/49A/2: Outline of Wilson-Foch Scheme.

11 Brigadier-General Sir James E Edmonds CB CMG psc (Comp) BOH, *Military Operations, France and Belgium*, 1914, Vol. I, *Mons, The Retreat to the Seine, the Marne and the Aisne, August-October* 1914 (London: Macmillan & Co, 1922).

12 The biographers of the Quartermaster-General summarized the operation thus: 'The Movements of the Expeditionary Force was the most perfectly worked-out and complex piece of Staff-work ever carried out by the British Army. Amongst other elements of perfection it had extraordinary flexibility, which was just as well, as in the very beginning its elasticity was to be subjected to a most searching test'. Major Desmond Chapman-Huston & Major Owen Rutter, *General Sir John Cowans, GCB GCMB, The Quartermaster General of the Great War*, Vols I & II (London: Hutchinson, 1924), Vol. I, p.274.

13 Remarkably, General Radcliffe was a Troop Commander in G Battery during the Boer War at the same time as an ancestor of the author. Corporal Whitcroft was killed near *Goedelegen* on Monday 21 October 1901 as a result of an exploding breech. He is remembered on the Royal Artillery Boer War Memorial at the junction of Horse Guards Parade and the Mall on the North East corner of St James' Park. See, Major H M Dawson, *The Story of G Troop Royal Horse Artillery* (Woolwich: Royal Artillery, 1919), p.82.

14 For details of the Directorates and Branches in the War Office, see, C Newman Knight BA, *The War Office List and Administrative Directory 1910* (London: HMSO, 1910). Interestingly, despite *The War Office List* being an official document containing the outline appointment details of military officers and civil servants employed in the War Office, it was an open publication, priced at five Shillings (£23.42 in 2016 based on the Retail Price Index) and the first 11 pages contained commercial advertisements headed as the 'War Office List Advertiser'.

15 With France, The WF Plan & The Genesis of the Western Front, General Sir Percy Radcliffe KCB KCMG CB DSO, in TNA WO 106/49A/1. There is continuing debate about the abbreviation WF, which according to General Radcliffe's account is 'With-France', whilst nearly all the files appertaining to the deployment are entitled 'Wilson-Foch'. Given Wilson's propensity for personal association, With-France is much more likely to be the official title but as he did in so many aspects of his military career, Henry Wilson has stamped his personal mark on our archival records.

16 The most recent and comprehensive is Chp 4, Mobilization, Transport and Logistics, 1911-1914 in Robin Neillands,

significant naval and military activities, which involved considerable logistic input to service them that ran concurrently with, or sequentially to, the deployment of the BEF,[17] which were integral to the defence of the United Kingdom and the Empire. These included the completion of naval mobilization and subsequent deployments,[18] the complex and significant task in concentrating and deploying regular, territorial and reserve units within the UK for Home Defence (HD)[19] and the dispatch of land and maritime forces to protect the Empire. The story is a fascinating one, which offers a most interesting insight into staff planning, logistic support and movement processes before the Great War. Over 100 years have passed since these plans matured and it is timely to re-assess their contribution to British military history.

The aim of this chapter is to analyse the role of the commercial logistic capability and especially the railways,[20] in pre-war planning for the mobilization and movement of the Royal Navy and the British Army during Transition To War (TTW) in 1914. Whilst railway movement planning and operations[21] are central to the story,[22] there are many other important aspects,[23] which will be exposed: the political dimension, maritime trading, shipping acquisition,

The Old Contemptibles (London: John Murray, 2004). See also, *The Report of the Committee on the Lessons of the Great War*, A3629, War Office, 1932, originally published as CONFIDENTIAL; TNA WO 32/3116: Training, Lessons of the 1914-1918 War.

17 One small but illustrative point of the plan's complexity is shown by the table below, outlining the movements of the five battalions assigned to the LOC Defence Troops.

Table 3.1
Movements of LOC Battalions

Battalion	Home Station	SPOE UK	SDOD France
1st Devonshire*	Jersey		Le Havre
1st Royal Welch Fusiliers	Portland		Rouen
1st Cameronians (Scottish Rifles)	Glasgow	Southampton	Le Harve
1st Middlesex	Woolwich		Le Harve
2nd Argyll & Sutherland Highlanders	Fort George		Boulogne

*1st Battalion the Devonshire Regiment remained with the LOC when the other four battalions formed 19th Infantry Brigade on 22 August 1914.

18 For a brief illustrated resume of the railways contribution in 1914, see, Alan Earnshaw, *Britain's Railways at War* (Penryn: Atlantic, 1995), pp.13-27 and for an overview of mobilization movements, J A B Hamilton, *Britain's Railways in World War I* (London: George, Allen & Unwin, 1967), pp.31-36.

19 For a contemporary review, see, Colonel A Keene DSO, 'Our Requirements for Home Defence', *The Army Review*, Vol. III, No 1, War Office (July 1912), pp.1-18.

20 There was little input from Inland Water Transport (IWT). Road transport, in the form of motor, steam and horse, played a limited but quite important local role. The railways were therefore, the critical strategic system. For details of the railway companies, see, The Railway Gazette, *The Railway Year Book for 1913, The Whitaker of the Railway Service* (London: The Railway Publishing Company, 1913).

21 This analysis does not cover the maritime and IWT component of railway operations in 1914. Many of the major companies owned or operated sea-going vessels and canals, neither of which will be examined; the port and dock operations will be mentioned as part of the rail activity. The railways, in August 1914, owned or operated 170 sea-going vessels, of which 85 were requisitioned, hired or bought for Government Service during the Great War; 37 of which were acquired in 1914. The Germans interned four ships; the Great Central Railway (GCR) owned three and the fourth, the Lancashire & Yorkshire Railway's SS *Dearne*, was sunk later in the war; The GCR was therefore, the first British organization to suffer a war loss and before hostilities commenced. See, A J Mulley, *Railway Ships at War, For the King's Service* (Easingwold: Pendragon, 2008), pp.9-55.

22 'It is impossible to over-estimate the importance of railways when considered as a factor in modern warfare, and it is hardly too much to state that success or failure in military operations, at any rate in civilised countries, depends now to a very large extent on the efficiency of the arrangements for the transport by railways of the armies engaged, and of their baggage, stores, and supplies'; Lieutenant-Colonel, Sir George Findlay, 'On the Use of Railways in the United Kingdom for the Conveyance of Troops', *United Service Magazine*, Vol. CXXVII (April 1892), p.37.

23 Merchant shipping was fundamental to the UK's defence capability and critical to Britain's projection of military power. The planning and execution of the naval and maritime aspects of the BEF's deployment is a fascinating

coalition planning, Joint Service co-ordination[24] and the interface with civilian authorities; all of these tasks are as vital today as they were a Century ago. In terms of resources, the Army required the greatest slice of the cake, whilst the deployment of the BEF was the most complex and time-sensitive element of all the rail movement plans. The composition of this chapter will reflect these issues but it is also important to balance the exposure of Main Effort, with a series of other significant defence activities that were crucial to naval and Home Defence (HD) operations, in securing the Empire, the Sea Lines of Communication and subsequent support to the BEF: reinforcement, casualty evacuation and Reverse Logistics.[25] The critical thread though, is the risk that senior Admiralty and War Office planners were prepared to take in relying entirely on the civil sector to deliver the Defence movement outputs, an aspect crucial to the British capability. Whilst the shipping component required a detailed study to create the confidence that it was sufficiently resilient for purpose, the equally long relationship with the railways was cemented in during the 1909 Annual Army Manoeuvres (AAM) by a particularly professional performance by the Great Western Railway (GWR) in moving at short notice, 15,055 men, 2,682 horses, 615 Horse Transport (HT) vehicles and 25 guns in 64 trains in three days, 40 of which ran on one day, from 11 stations,[26] with almost no lead-time pre-planning.[27]

Problems and Processes

By 1912, the mobilization and movement planners had been directed to execute three key tasks. First and foremost, to complete, within 12 days of mobilization, the move of the BEF, consisting of up to seven Divisions[28] and supporting units, from Garrison locations in the United

subject that requires further study.

24 See, for example, the CONFIDENTIAL *Manual of Combined Naval and Military Operations* (A1674) War Office, 2 September 1913.

25 Operations related to the reuse of products and materials, by moving them from their typical final destination of use for the purpose of capturing value or proper disposal. In the Great War, it was the Royal Flying Corps (RFC) that pioneered Reverse Logistics, particularly with regard to refurbishing high value sub-systems such as aero-engines. The concept spread across the Army under the term Salvage, involving everything from brass cartridge cases through horseshoes to clothing.

26 'The military authorities and the Army contractors expressed their pleasure at the manner in which the work was performed by the Company's staff, and we were gratified to be able to add our testimony to the excellent behaviour of the troops whilst on the railway'; 'The Transport of an Army', *Great Western Railway Magazine*, Vol. 21, November 1909, p.257.

27 Planning between the War Office and the GWR commenced on Tuesday 21 September at a Joint HQ at Faringdon Station in Oxfordshire. The first trains ran the next day, with 40 running on Thursday 23 September; 'The Transport of an Army', p.257. The Faringdon-Uffington line closed to passengers on 31 December 1951 and to freight in 1964; G Daniels and L Dench, *Passengers No More* (Shepperton: Ian Allan, 1964), p.43. The Station building is extant (UK OS GRID SU 287951) but there is nothing that offers a direct reminder of its role in the defence of the United Kingdom.

28 Details of the trains required for a divisional move in the United Kingdom are shown in the table below:

Table 3.2

BEF – WE Divisional Establishment Summary v UK Train Lift

Resource	Infantry Division+	Cavalry Division*
Personnel	18,073	11,553
Horses	5,592	12,897
Guns	76	30
Horse Transport Vehicles	1192	671
Cars	9	28
Motor-cycles	9	21
Bicycles	275	506
Trains	85	95

+ 3 x Infantry Brigades * 5 x Cavalry Brigades

Kingdom, to the BEF Concentration Area in France.[29] The planning figures were assumed to be approximately 166,000 personnel and 60,000 horses, although in the event, the initial deployment movement numbers were slightly less than the estimated figures because the initial execution involved four not six infantry divisions.[30] The second task was to deploy HDU to United Kingdom War Stations and the third one, to deliver support to naval operations. To execute this work, the operational planners in the Admiralty[31] and the War Office[32] had to agree an outline phased plan,[33]

29 General Staff, *Field Service Regulations* (FSR) *Part I, Operations*, War Office (London: HMSO, 1909) (reprinted, with amendments, 1912) summarized the task: 'The process by which an army is brought into the theatre of operations is called the strategical concentration. This effected by sea, by rail, by water or by road, or by a combination of these means. In the case of operations conducted outside Great Britain, the concentration must be begun by sea, whilst it may be necessary to complete either by rail, water or road'; Chp III, Movements By Land and Sea, Sect 22, The Strategical concentration, p. 44. Even with the 1914 amendments though, the FSR was out of date because the WF Plan included the deployment of elements of the RFC by air.

30 Based upon a six infantry division deployment, the May 1913 strengths are shown in the table. Figures extracted from TNA WO 106/49A/1: History of the Growth of the Wilson-Foch Scheme, Appx 1 and TNA WO 33/606: Expeditionary Force Tables, November 1912.

Table 3.3

BEF Six Division Deployment – May 1913

Officers: 5,748	Horse Transport Vehicles: 7,199
Other Ranks: 160,146	Motor Transport Vehicles: 1,185
Nurses: 759	Motor-cars: 187
Horses: 60,368	Motor-cycles: 179
Guns: 492	Bicycles: 2493
Machine Guns: 190	Total All Ranks: 165,894

31 The Admiralty also appointed a Liaison Officer, Lieutenant Peile RN to MO 1 (a) to co-ordinate the shipping requirement; note in TNA WO 106/49A/1: Growth of the Wilson-Foch Scheme. Peile appears as a Commander RN in the 1918 Navy List as the Captain of the sloop, HMS *Rinaldo*; *The Navy List for October 1918*, corrected to 18th September 1918 (London: HMSO, 1918), p.896.

32 The War Office Team was based on Military Operations 1 and consisted of the officers shown below, with their appointments. The * indicates the star rank each officer achieved: * Brigadier-General; ** Major-General; *** Lieutenant-General; **** General.

Colonel Harper psc*** - General Staff Officer (GSO) 1 MO1
Colonel The Honourable Alan Richard Montagu-Stuart-Wortley*** psc - Assistant Director of Movements QMG (Quartermaster General) 2
Major Cameron** - GSO 2 MO1 (a) vice Major Gorton* psc - GSO 2 MO1 (a)
Major Johnson* - GSO 2 MO1 (a)
Major Radcliffe**** - GSO 2 MO1 (a)
Major Tarver** - Deputy Assistant Director (DAD) Supplies QMG 6
Captain Mance* - Staff Captain Railways QMG 2
Captain Ommanney psc (KIA 1914) - GSO 3 MO1 (a)

33 Table 3.4

Mobilization and Movements – Outline Plan

Activity	Remarks
Mobilization Day (M-day)	Essential to synchronize with the French M-Day
Recall Regulars from Leave and Courses	Scheduled rail services
Return Regular units to Garrison Duty Stations	Special Trains
Return Territorial Force (TF) units to Garrison Duty Stations	Special Trains
Recall Regular Reservists to Regimental Depots	Scheduled and Special rail services
Mobilize Regular & TF units	In barracks. Arrival of Regular Reservists critical
Dispatch Regular Reservists to units	Scheduled rail services
Deploy BEF units to Sea Port of Embarkation (SPOE)	Deployment Trains
Deploy HDU to HD Stations	Deployment Trains
Dispatch BEF units from UK ports	Interface with French railways essential

to allow the Staff[34] to progress the detailed movements schedules.[35] Whilst the logisticians of the period did not use the current British military term DQUAD: Destination-Distance-Demand-Duration,[36] it is clear from the manner in which, they approached the challenge in quantifying the requirement that these concepts were embedded in their thinking.[37] They understood their business, took risks because they had too and were masters of detail.[38]

From the Army perspective, the key enabling process was the mobilization of units, with the priority focusing upon those allocated to the BEF.[39] Mobilization was staged over six days, allowing a phased movement flow.[40] The first units to mobilize were logistic enablers,[41] with Railway Transport Officers (RTO) and their staffs the priority. Infantry units located outside their country of origin within the UK completed mobilization by 2359 on Mobilization Day (M)+4 to allow an extra travel day for the reservists. Cavalry units were tasked to complete by 2359 on M+5 and artillery on M+6, thereby providing additional time to requisition the horses to bring units and Headquarters (HQ) to War Establishment (WE).

34 It is of significance that 50% of the members of the War Office Planning Team were Staff College graduates; the drafting and crafting of the mobilization plans was clearly a complex issue that required sharp minds. Such officers were in much demand because of the small numbers in the pool. All of the officers made Star (*) rank, with the exception of Captain Rupert Ommanney RE, who was Killed In Action, aged 36 on Saturday 31 October 1914. He was attached to HQ 2nd Division, when a German shell struck the building in which the HQ was based; he is buried in the Ypres Town Cemetery Extension in Grave III AA 6.

35 The initial creative tension between the Admiralty and the War Office concerning this issue is well described in a letter (MO 1259 dated 8 December 1909) from the former to the latter in TNA WO 106/50.

36 *Army Doctrine Publication (ADP)* Vol. 3, *Logistics*, DGD&D/18/34/63, Army Code No 71566 (UK MOD, 1996), pp.2-3 to 2-5.

37 Note the three QMG officers in the MO team. Despite their crucial contribution, the QMG, Sir John Cowans, was not party to the full detail of their involvement, although he must have been sighted on some of their work because he is recorded as having chaired a meeting of Command Assistant Quartermaster-Generals (AQMG) on the subject of railway arrangements upon mobilization on Friday 31 January 1913; TNA WO 106/50: Military Mobilisation Railway Programme. A note in TNA WO 106/49A/2: Wilson-Foch Scheme, Revision of Programme, suggests he received a full briefing sometime in July 1914. In addition to the officers detailed to MO, QMG 2 and after 1912, QMG 3, staffed routine railway issues.

38 For example, the A1585, Expeditionary Force Table (EFT) a 36 page SECRET A5 document lists every unit allocated to the EF, listing Peace Station, mobilization details (location, equipment and role) and its operational task; TNA WO 33/106: EFT November 1912. A note in the file suggests that the SO2 MO1 (a) Major Cameron compiled it.

39 The BEF ORBAT in outline was: GHQ, Army Troops, I Corps (1st & 2nd Divisions) II Corps (3rd & 5th Divisions) III Corps (4th & 6th Divisions) Cavalry Division (5 x Brigades) and Line of Communication Troops. For more details, see, Edmonds, BOH, *France and Belgium*, 1914, Vol. I, Appx 1, pp.471-487. For the detail of the divisional ORBATs, see, Major A F Becke MA (Comp), BOH, *Order of Battle of Divisions*, Part I, *The Regular British Divisions* (London: HMSO, 1935). For Unit War Establishments (WE) see, TNA WO 106/49/8: Expeditionary Force Tables.

40 The Mobilization Summary is extracted from TNA WO 106/49A/8: Mobilization dates by Commands.

M Day
M+2: Logistic Enablers
M+3: English Infantry Units in England
M+4: English & Scottish Infantry in Ireland
: Scottish & Irish Infantry in England
: Motor Transport
M+5: Cavalry Units
M+6: Artillery Units

41 The BEF's A&Q at 3rd Line (Corps and Army level) and 4th Line (Base) was comprehensive, including: 7 x Divisional Ammunition Parks, 7 x Divisional Supply Columns, 1 x Base Mechanical Transport Depot, 1 x Base Horse Transport Depot, 1 x Base Remount Depot, 12 x General Hospitals, 6 x Clearing Hospitals, 3 x Hospital Ships and a number of supporting assets: 8 x Railway Supply Detachments, 8 x Railway Supply Detachments, 6 x Field Bakeries, 15 x Veterinary Sections, 11 x Sanitary Sections 6 x Medical Stores Depots, 11 x Sanitary Sections and 1 x Aircraft Park. Edmonds, BOH, *France and Belgium* 1914, Vol. I, Appx 1, pp.483-484.

The movement of the six infantry divisions was, from a conceptual planning perspective, relatively simple, the only complication being the formations located in Ireland. The 5th Division movement was easily resolved because the units were planned to load in the Irish ports of Belfast, Cork and Queenstown and sail to France.[42] The 6th Division however, had one brigade in England and two in Ireland.[43] The Irish based formations had to be railed to Irish ports, execute a sea crossing to the Mainland and then rail to the divisional concentration area between Cambridge and Newmarket.[44] The mobilization of the Royal Navy was much less complex because its mobile combat capability was platform based, with ships supported by established naval bases, although as operational concepts matured the timely delivery of more flexible logistics became increasingly important. The War Office had a different problem with formations located across the UK and units spread even more widely,[45] with the Highlands of Scotland being an especial

42 Becke, BOH, *Divisions*, Part 1, p.70.
43 16th Brigade was based at Fermoy and 17th at Cork, with supporting units in several other locations. 18th Brigade in Northern Command had units in Litchfield, Sheffield and York. 24th Heavy Artillery Battery was located in Eastern Command at Woolwich. Ibid, p.78.
44 Ibid, p.78.
45 The locations of UK formations in August 1914 are shown in the table below. For details of the Orders of Battle, see, Becke, BOH, *Divisions*, Part 1 and Major A F Becke (Comp) *Order of Battle of Divisions*, Part 2A, *The Territorial Force Mounted Divisions and The 1st Line Territorial Force Divisions (42th-56th)* (London: HMSO, 1936).

Table 3.5

UK Formations – August 1914 Garrison Locations

Formation	Location	Remarks
1st Infantry XX	Aldershot	BEF
2nd Infantry XX	Aldershot	BEF: 4 X at London and Windsor
3rd Infantry XX	Bulford, Ludgershall, Tidworth & Woolwich	BEF
4th Infantry XX	Colchester, Dover, Shorncliffe & Woolwich	BEF
5th Infantry XX	Belfast, Curragh, Dublin, Kildare & Londonderry	BEF
6th Infantry XX	16 X (Fermoy) & 17 X (Cork) Limerick & Woolwich	BEF: 18 X - Lichfield, Sheffield & York
7th Infantry XX	Lyndhurst Hampshire	Assembly commenced 31 August 1914
8th Infantry XX	Baddesley Common - Southampton	Assembly commenced September 1914
1st Cavalry X	Aldershot	Allocated to 1st Cavalry XX (BEF)
2nd Cavalry X	Tidworth	Allocated to 1st Cavalry XX (BEF)
3rd Cavalry X	Curragh, Dublin & Newbridge	Allocated to 1st Cavalry XX (BEF)
4th Cavalry X	Canterbury, London & Shorncliffe	Allocated to 1st Cavalry XX (BEF)
5th Cavalry X	Various	Independent X (BEF)
1st Mounted XX	Bury St Edmunds, Diss and Ipswich	Formed mid-August 1914
2nd Mounted XX		Formed early September 1914
1st London (TF) XX	London - North, East & South East	XX HQ - New Broad Street
2nd London (TF) XX	London - South East & South West	XX HQ - Chelsea
Home Counties (TF) XX	Kent, London & Sussex	XX HQ - Hounslow
Wessex (TF) XX	Cornwall, Devon, Dorset, Hampshire & Somerset	XX HQ - Exeter
North Midland (TF) XX	North Midland counties	XX HQ - Lichfield
South Midland (TF) XX	Gloucestershire, Warwickshire & Worcestershire	XX HQ - Warwick
East Anglian (TF) XX	East & West Anglia and East Midlands	XX HQ - Warley
East Lancashire (TF) XX	Based on Cotton & Colliery Towns	XX HQ - Manchester
West Lancashire (TF) XX	X HQs - Lancaster & Liverpool	XX HQ - Liverpool
West Riding (TF) XX	X HQs - Sheffield, Skipton & York	XX HQ - York
Northumbrian (TF) XX	Durham, Northumberland and Yorkshire (North & East)	XX HQ - Richmond
Highland (TF) XX	X HQs - Aberdeen, Inverness & Stirling	XX HQ - Perth
Lowland (TF) XX	South of Line - Firth of Forth to Loch Lomond	XX HQ - Glasgow
Welsh (TF) XX	Cheshire, Marches & Wales	XX HQ - Shrewsbury

challenge.[46] Having secured an outline plan, the Staff then tackled the myriad of problems, which needed to be solved before the desired outcome could be delivered. In this, the planners were fortunate that the capacity and flexibility of the UK railway system far exceeded the military requirement for TTW, and, with the exception of naval guns and propellers, all service equipment was in gauge for rail movement; in planning the complex Army moves, this was of particular import.

There were several issues that required resolution, with 'Just In Time' logistics, so prominent in the 21st Century, being of particular prominence to meet strategic imperatives. The French railways had to execute the mobilization and deployment of French Forces and it was critical that the BEF conformed to the French movement plan. At the strategic level, this meant that British mobilization had to be synchronized with the French, whilst at the tactical one, unit train loads in the UK had to parallel those in France; the former was controlled by the politicians, the latter by the planners. Within the operational arena, UK trains had to arrive at South coast ports to meet shipping, with sailings planned to arrive in France to meet rail departures designed to reduce to a minimum, waiting times in transit facilities.[47] There were therefore, thorough planning sessions with the French,[48] to identify significant differentials and similarities, one key aspect being that to move a British infantry battalion required two trains in the UK but only one in France.[49] The UK rail movement plan was thus designed to feed formed units to French ports in a manner that they would arrive ready for onward movement.[50] In addition, whilst there was flexibility in wagon space in the UK, the French Standard trains[51] did not permit additional men and equipment[52] so proposals to increase BEF unit War Establishments (WE) were not only closely scrutinized by planning officers in the War Office but also generated much Staff effort if they were to be enacted.[53]

46 TNA WO 33/661: Mobilisation - Scottish Command Scheme, Railway and Steamship Programmes, January 1914, which contains nine appendices.

47 Inevitably, plans did not always mature correctly. 1st Royal Welch Fusiliers departed from Dorchester in two trains on 10 August 1914 for Southampton. HQ, A and B Companies marched from the railhead to the dock to embark on a 'wretched Irish pig-boat, the Glengariffe, in which they sailed', whilst C and D Companies had to wait until 13 August to embark on a ship, in the meantime living in very basic transit facilities, with the constant noise of ships and railways around them. Major C H Dudley Ward, DSO MC (Comp), Regimental Records of the Royal Welch Fusiliers, Vol. III, 1914-1918, France (London: Forster Groom, 1928), p.23.

48 One such technical meeting was held on Friday 27 September 1912 at the French Embassy between Commandant Barbier and two representatives from the War Office (Military Operations) Major Cameron and Captain Ommanney, to discuss rail transport arrangements, with a particular emphasis on Command, Control, Communications, Co-ordination and Resource Management (C4RM) and Standard Operating Procedures (SOP). Whilst these are modern terms, they aptly describe the subjects. As a result of this meeting, Commandant Barbier issued a note on Sunday 29 September 1912, 'Railway Concentration Movement of the British Army'; TNA WO 106/49B/6/7. There was a meeting in Paris in October 1913 to discuss details on a range of issues, the notes of which, are in TNA WO 106/49A/1: History of the Growth of the Wilson-Foch Scheme.

49 French military trains were longer and heavier, which resulted in increased loading times and slower speeds but required half the number of train paths.

50 TNA WO 106/49B/6: French Railway Arrangements, contain a blank Tableaux (Table) D which was the form the French Army used for all its rail mobilization movement details and an outline Rail Movement Table for the BEF dated September 1912, plus a colour graphic plan for BEF rail schedules on the 11th day of movement.

51 Units moved in two types of fixed train consists; '*Train Combattant*' for infantry, artillery and cavalry units and '*Train Parcs*' with additional wagons for MT and HT vehicles to move ammunition columns and divisional trains; TNA WO 95/3915/1: HQ 3rd (Lahore) Division, AQMG, WD, entries, 1-20 October 1914.

52 Spears in *Liaison 1914*, reinforces this point in an observation of the 'carefully prepared French railway scheme'. 'No change, no alternation is possible during mobilisation. Improvisation when dealing with nearly three million men and the movements of 4,278 trains, as the French had to do, is out of the question'; Brigadier-General E L Spears CB CBE MC *Liaison 1914, A Narrative of the Great Retreat* (London: William Heinemann, 1930), p.35.

53 The effective date for the introduction of the 1914 Edition of the Railway Mobilisation Time Tables (RMTT) was delayed from 1 February to 1 April 1914 because of significant changes to the structure of the cavalry division and the replacement within the BEF, of light draught horses with heavy. The issues in changing establishments are lucidly demonstrated by the complexity of the Movement Plans, the SECRET Detrainment and Billeting Tables

Whilst unit suggestions were usually opposed unless there were equivalent compensating options, the War Office had to grapple with the impact of the Army re-equipment programme.[54] Mechanical Transport (MT),[55] consisting mainly of Wheeled Motor Transport (WMT), was slowly replacing Horse Transport (HT) or being introduced as additional capability, whilst the artillery was receiving new 13, 18 and 60 pdr guns. These projects generated the need to amend manpower and equipment establishments and adjust the requirements for fuel and forage and concomitantly the allocation of wagon space; all of this work combined to keep the planners on their toes. Another concern was the speed of train loading;[56] failure to keep to the allocated timings would clearly adversely affect the carefully crafted timetables,[57] and there was much less flexibility in the French schedules than in the UK.[58] Whilst there were no guarantees that units would deliver in this area, the experiences of rail movement during the AAM in 1912-1913 gave good reason for optimism.[59] From this perspective, the timely execution of rail movements would, partially at least, be in the hands of unit Commanding Officers and Rail Transport Officers (RTO).

Commercial Capability

Railway infrastructure was another major issue that the War Office took a great interest in because late 19th and early 20th Century main line additions created enhanced flexibility and capacity for Defence. The Midland & South Western Junction Railway (M&SWJR)[60] was mainly single line with passing loops connecting Cheltenham to Andover. Commercially an impecunious company, it gave much improved military and naval transportation access to Southampton from the Midlands and garrisons on Salisbury Plain.[61] The Great Central Railway's (GCR) extension opened in 1899 from Nottingham to London[62] was built to the continental Berne Gauge, had only one public level

(A1647) being but one example; Copy No 11 is held in TNA WO 106/49B/5: Expeditionary Force to France, Detrainment and Billeting Table D.

54 Apart from the amendment of the movement tables, 60 Mobilization Stores Tables required compilation; TNA WO 106/49A/2: Wilson-Foch Scheme, Revision of Programme.

55 Mechanical Transport (MT) was a wheeled, tracked, or semi-tracked land vehicle utilised in a logistic context to move men and materiel to, on or from the battlefield and powered by the Internal Combustion Engine (ICE) either Spark Ignition (SI) or Compression Ignition (CI) fuelled by petroleum spirit or diesel oil respectively, or by steam (Steam Transport (ST)). Often abbreviated to MT, it does not include combat vehicles, such as tanks, Armoured Personnel Carriers (APC) or Self-Propelled Guns (SPG). Motor Transport (MT) included Wheeled or tracked or semi-tracked land logistic vehicle powered by the ICE but to provide specific clarification for wheeled vehicles, the term Wheeled Motor Transport (WMT) is used.

56 The importance of entraining and detraining of units to the success of the operation was clearly articulated by FSR: 'Rapidity in entraining and detraining is imperative'; General Staff, *Field Service Regulations*, Part II, *Organization and Administration*, War Office (London: HMSO, 1909), Amdts 1914, Chp VIII, Railway Transport, p.95.

57 The railway companies, at the behest of the War Office provided ramps in specific locations to enable units to practise rail loading; TNA WO 106/49A/1: History of the Growth of the Wilson-Foch Scheme. Also noted was a French entrainment exercise at Douai and Valenciennes on Saturday 24 January 1914 relating to possible British deployment.

58 The planning length for troop train platforms in the UK was 250 yards, whilst portable ramps were entrained to enable the loading and unloading of horses if no suitable infrastructure was available. Lt-Col H M E Brunker, *Notes on Organization and Equipment*, 6th Edn (London: William Clowes and Sons, 1909), p.137.

59 Captain J F C Fuller, 'Notes on the Entrainment of Troops To and From Manoeuvres', *The Army Review*, Vol. VII, No 1, War Office (July 1914), pp.184-213.

60 This railway closed in 1963, except for the line from Andover to Ludgershall, which serves the Ministry of Defence (MOD) railhead for the Salisbury Plain Training Area (SPTA). For an operating history, see, David Bartholomew, *The Midland & South Western Junction Railway*, Vol. I (Upper Bucklebury: Wild Swan Publications, 1982).

61 Ludgershall and Tidworth. The London & South Western Railway (LSWR) served Bulford and Larkhill. See, Richard Harman & Gerry Nichols, *Atlas of the Southern Railway* (Addlestone: Ian Allan, 2016), Map 25.

62 Despite its futuristic features, most of the line closed in 1966. An eight mile section of the GCR between Loughborough and Leicester has been preserved and is the only double tracked heritage railway in the UK that

crossing,[63] and was the physical exposition of the vision of the Channel Tunnel.[64] In particular, the link between the GCR at Woodford & Hinton,[65] to the Great Western Railway (GWR) at Banbury enabled transit from North East England to Southampton via Salisbury Plain. The GWR Direct Line from Birmingham to London, involving 18 miles of high specification construction between Aynho and Ashendon Junction, which opened in 1910, created more main-line capacity.[66] Despite these improvements, the coal trains for the Royal Navy from the South Wales coalfields to naval bases in the North of England and Scotland,[67] were usually run on lines in Wales and the West of England,[68] to Carlisle, rather than laterally across the country to the East Coast mainline routes.

In 1912, the railway companies, whilst not involved in main-line construction projects, were still making improvements to the system. The Cambrian Railway invested in additional loops and platforms to speed the entraining and detraining units conducting exercises in Wales, facilities which made a positive contribution to the deployment in 1914.[69] The London & South Western Railway (LSWR) was central to the major enhancements to the rail infrastructure to and within the major Sea Port of Embarkation (SPOE) of Southampton, whilst at an operational level, improvements to the speed of the BEF's movement plan in the UK was predicated upon on several key improvements on the National Rail Network (NRN). The Great Northern Railway (GNR) commenced the

replicates a main-line of the period. The railway scenes in the film '*Enigma*' (BVI, 2001) were shot on the heritage GCR.

63 This is at Beighton, on the Western edge of the Rother Valley Country Park to the South-East of Sheffield and remarkably, the crossing remains operational in 2017.

64 For a detailed survey of Channel Tunnel issues between 1850-1945, see, Keith Wilson, *Channel Tunnel Visions, 1850-1945, Dreams and Nightmares* (London & Rio Grande: The Hambledon Press, 1994). For 1945 onwards, see, Terry Gourvish & Mike Anson, *The Official History of the Channel Tunnel* (London: Routledge, 2006). See also, *Channel Tunnel, Full Details of the Present Scheme* - Military, Engineering, Financial, W Turner Perkins (Ed.) Channel Tunnel Company Ltd, December 1913. For an action novel based on the Channel Tunnel in 1911, on a theme much in keeping with contemporary spy novelists, see Joe Poyer, *Tunnel War* (London: Michael Joseph, 1980).

65 To understand the importance and complexity of the links and junctions, see, *Official Railway Junction Diagrams*, (London: Railway Clearing House, 1915).

66 This created a direct line from Banbury to Princes Risborough. For details of the planning, construction and operation, see, John Norris, Gerry Beale & John Lewis, *Edwardian Enterprise, GWR 1900-1910* (Didcot: Wild Swan Publications, 1987), pp.37-59.

67 During the Great War, the railways transported nearly 5,452,400 million tons of coal for the Grand Fleet in 13,631 trains between 27 August 1914 and 31 December 1918 and nearly 90% of the coal came from collieries situated in the Aberdare and Rhondda districts of South Wales. The first Grand Fleet train, loaded with 400 tons of coal, departed Pontypool Road for its 375 mile trip to Grangemouth on 27 August 1914; despite an average speed of only 8 mph, the Admiralty was highly satisfied with the service. Bizarrely, as coal travelled North East from Wales, stocks were being moved South East from Yorkshire to the destroyer base at Harwich; Edwin A Pratt, *British Railways and the Great War, Organization, Efforts, Difficulties and Achievements*, Vol. I (London: Selwyn & Blount, 1921), pp.488-496.

68 The wagons were marshalled at Pontypool Road on the Great Western Railway (GWR) from the various companies serving the coalfields, although it was necessary to invest in additional infrastructure to support the operation. The GWR worked the traffic to Warrington for movement to Carlisle by the London & North West Railway (LNWR) and thence to its destinations in Scotland via the Caledonian (CR), Glasgow & South Western (G&SWR) or North British Railway (NBR) companies. The two alternative routes were Pontypool Road to Cardiff on the Great Western and thence to Gloucester to join the Midland Railway (MR) for movement North or via the Brecon & Merthyr Railway to Talyllyn, then onto the Cambrian Railways to Gobowen, for the GWR to haul to Chester and then Warrington. Traffic on the Cambrian Railways was particularly difficult to work because the line was mainly single track, with plenty of testing gradients. See, W Kidner, *The Mid-Wales Railway*, R, Oakwood Library of Railway History, No 79, 2nd Edition (Usk: The Oakwood Press, 2003).

69 These projects included doubling the 4.5 miles between Newtown and Moat Line Junction, extending platforms at Cemmes Road and the down platform at Borth, and an enhanced crossing capability at Llanfihangel; these works, costing £20,000 were complete in time for the 1912 AAM, which at 2016 values is approximately £16.80M based upon the *Measuring Worth UK* Economic Project Cost. See, Rex Christiansen & R W Miller, *The Cambrian Railways*, Vol. II, 1889-1968 (Newton Abbot: David & Charles, 1968), pp.59-60.

construction of the Cuffley to Langley Junction Loop in August 1912, which, although commercially driven, had military applications. The project ceased shortly after the outbreak of war but resumed in 1917, opening for goods traffic on 4 March 1918.[70] The London & North Western Railway (LNWR) opened the Coventry Goods Avoiding Line,[71] on 16 August 1914, creating additional access to the important Coventry Ordnance Works (COW)[72]. The Northern Railway Junction Scheme was another commercial concept that had military applications, the QMG,[73] Sir John Cowans declaring to the Parliamentary Select Committee in 1913:

> The proposed line would be a great advantage in time of emergency if it was constructed in its entirety. The Army Council felt that it would provide important routes between the South of England and East Anglia and the North. At present trains had to come from Aldershot to Clapham Junction by the South-Western line, and there be broken up and sent over congested City lines on to the Great Northern. By the proposed line military trains could be handled without dividing them and be transferred to the Great Northern or Great Eastern without being sent over the congested City lines.[74]

Simply described as the railway equivalent of the North-Western section of the M25,[75] it would have linked the main routes to the North and East to those running West and South West; it was rejected, by the House of Commons, in 1914.[76] The one major infrastructure project that could have had a major impact upon the deployment of the BEF was the Channel Tunnel.[77] This came

70 This was a significant undertaking. Although a single line, it was approximately 15 miles long, from Cuffley via Hertford to Langley Junction, with a connection to the main line south of Stevenage and included the 2,684 yards of the Ponsbourne Tunnel between Cuffley and Bayford.

71 This is another railway track-bed that has disappeared beneath black tar.

72 The company was established in 1905 by a consortium of British shipbuilding firms, John Brown, Cammell, Laird and Co and Fairfield, in order to compete with the duopoly of Vickers and Armstrong-Whitworth. The author's maternal Grandmother lived near the COW, of which the Naval Gun Shop and some railway lines were extant in 2017. See, *Coventry Canal Conservation Area Appraisal*, English Heritage, 4 July 2012, p.36; accessed through www.coventry.gov.uk on 28 February 2017.

73 General Sir John Stephen 'Jack' Cowans GCB GCMG (1862-1921) was commissioned into the Rifle Brigade in 1881 and died in 1921 as a result of complications arising from a kidney operation. He was the only member of the Army Council to remain in post throughout the Great War, serving as QMG between 1912 and 1919 and promoted the employment of uniformed women, particularly in the logistic services. His biographers summarized his contribution to the British Army during the Great War thus: 'No Quartermaster-General in history is even faintly comparable to him in achievement', Chapman-Huston & Rutter, *Quartermaster General of the Great War*, Vol. II, p.324.

74 Edwin A Pratt, *The Rise of Rail-power in War and Conquest, 1833-1914*, (London: P S King & Son, 1915), p.204.

75 The proposed route ran 17.75 miles from the London & South Western Railway (L&SWR) at Brentford on the West of London, to Wood Green in the North on the Great Northern Railway (GNR) passing through Acton, Wembley Park, Hampstead and Finchley, with connections to the Great Central, Metropolitan and District Railways. The idea had initially been floated in 1910 as the Greater London Railway (GLR) with a route of 57 miles, with an extension to Tilbury. Charles Klapper, *London's Lost Railways* (London: Routledge & Kegan Paul, 1976), pp.67-68.

76 Objections included the adverse effect, initially upon the Hampstead Garden Suburb, and when the proposed route was altered, upon the desirable residential district of Finchley. Damaging the environment of the rich and influential was as equally objectionable in 1913, as it had become in 2013. There was also a suggestion that the military advantages stated by the Army Council were part of a deception to support the promoters of the scheme, and by implication, that senior officers were, if only by default, not playing with a straight bat. The proposal was therefore, rejected by the House of Commons by a majority of 77; Pratt, *The Rise of Rail-power*, p.204.

77 There were many opponents of the Channel Tunnel project. Military opponents debated its vulnerability to enemy action, commercial opponents its adverse impact upon cross-channel shipping and political opponents, its influence on Britain's increasing role in Europe. The presentational aspects, like the issues, are timeless; TNA CAB 17/25: Committee of Imperial Defence - Correspondence and Memoranda, Home Defence, Channel Tunnel, contains a superb coloured linen-backed diagram of the proposed route of the Channel Tunnel link in Kent, bound in a dark

close to approval before the Great War, military objections having usually been to the fore in supporting rejection,[78] although from a Defence transportation perspective, a Channel Tunnel[79] certainly had much to commend it.[80] First, it would have enabled a quicker deployment of the BEF to France or allowed a decrease in requisitioned shipping and naval escorts; the General Staff estimated a reduction of 48 hours to move six divisions.[81] Secondly, it would have limited the opportunity for interference from the Germans and obviated the effects of adverse weather. Thirdly, it would have greatly simplified logistic support to the BEF. Sir Henry Wilson summarized the dilemma of supporting Forward Defence on the Continent against Home Defence on the island of Great Britain

> If we are going to take part in European wars, the more tunnels we have the better. If not, then the fewer we have the better.[82]

In addition to the problems directly relating to railway operations, there were a series of issues that were capable of disrupting the emerging plans. Top of the list was the possibility of industrial unrest, which based on the experiences of 1911, suggested serious potential for interruption to Defence plans. Few people in 1912 could have anticipated the positive response to the outbreak of war in August 1914 and Defence planners spent much time in examining mitigating options. If the railway workers went on strike however, all the carefully crafted plans to support the Royal Navy, deploy the BEF to France and execute the HDP would come to nought.

Reservists and Horses were two other issues that were unknowns.[83] Regular Reservists were critical to British defence capability in 1914, filling the ranks of the RN and army units, regular and reserve, upon mobilization.[84] Apart from individuals deliberately avoiding further military

blue leather case with a gold-block title.

78 Field-Marshal Sir John French wrote in his appointment as Chief of the General Staff (CIGS) 'that the military objections to the project are on the whole of insufficient weight to justify us in placing an embargo on a scheme which may possibly prove of vast economic advantage to the Nation at large'. Memorandum nd but October 1913, in TNA WO 32/5300: Channel Tunnel.

79 The Chief of the Imperial General Staff (CIGS), signed a memorandum on the Channel Tunnel to the Committee for Imperial Defence (CID) dated 9 July 1914, which summarized many of the points which had been highlighted in previous correspondence; see, CAB 38/28/34. See also, TNA WO 32/5300: Channel Tunnel, input from the General Staff and the South Eastern & Chatham Railways (SECR).

80 'The only aspect of the Channel Tunnel which invites attention is its utility for the despatch and maintenance of an expeditionary force in support of France against Germany. In such a contingency the tunnel would be of great value, but I agree with the General Staff in doubting whether the contingency is sufficiently probable, and our *entente* with France sufficiently permanent, to justify the construction of a tunnel for this reason alone'; TNA CAB /3/2/74A: 'Comment by Field-Marshal Lord Nicholson GCB dated 19 May 1914'.

81 A supporting Memorandum by the War Office General Staff noted, 'The Channel Tunnel would enable a reduction of 48 hours in the transportation of a six division EF; even an acceleration of 24 hours in the concentration of the EF may have an important bearing on the course of the campaign'. The imprint of Sir Henry Wilson as DMO seems firmly stamped on this note and yet given the gravity of what was to occur three months later, his concern over the importance of time is certainly prescient; War Office, General Staff Memorandum in TNA CAB /3/2/74A.

82 Sir Henry Wilson, Diary, 3 March 1914. A document in TNA WO 32/5300: Channel Tunnel, has two further versions of this observation; they are, presumably, General Staff drafts but may have been written by Wilson. 'In short, from a purely military point of view, if our troops are to become engaged in a European war fighting alongside the French, the more tunnels we possess between this country and France the better, if, on the other hand, no such operations are in contemplation then: a. we want no tunnels at all; b. we shall be far better off without any tunnels at all'; nd but possibly, March 1914.

83 For a comprehensive examination of procurement, control, issue, role and care of horses in the British Army in 1914, including remounts, requisitioning and veterinary, see, the seminal, Graham Winton, *Theirs Not to Reason Why, Horsing the British Army, 1875-1925*, Wolverhampton Military Studies Series (Solihull: Helion, 2013).

84 The Commanding Officer of the Warwickshire Yeomanry, although a Territorial Force unit, clearly had absolutely

service, there were a number of factors, which might reduce the numbers reporting for duty: sickness, employment pressure, family issues and administrative failure by the authorities.[85] In some Regular Army units, 60 percent of the personnel on the WE were reservists, which offers a guide to level of concern to the authorities should individuals fail to report for duty. The Army was reliant upon the requisitioning of horses from commercial, public and individual sources, requiring an additional 135,000 to support mobilization of the Regular Army and TF.[86] For horses and soldiers, there were mature plans for their mobilization[87] but no practical experience to identify emerging serious potential failures,[88] whilst the Staff had no benchmark to judge how effective or efficient the result would be. A poor response from either reservists or the equine community would certainly disrupt unit mobilization and concomitantly, rail schedules, although the direction from the War Office was that trains would run to the timetable regardless of unit status.[89]

Of particular note, was the shape and size of the proposed Land component commitment to Continental Europe, which was, in the light of developing Home Defence contingency planning, constantly reviewed. Whatever the agreed maximum, there always remained the requirement to retain at short notice, some units to contain German raiding parties and control civil unrest, whilst providing forces to ensure order in Ireland and provide manpower for industrial intervention. Matched against what was a finely honed movements plan, these requirements created some interesting challenges for the planners, which, in the event, matured. A brief survey of these is instructive. M-Day, the first day of mobilization provided the bench-mark from which, plans were developed forward and back but from the railway transportation perspective, provided a challenge because no one knew which day of the week it would be, nor when in the year. The first scenario meant rolling stock positioning could not be assured, particularly on Sundays and Bank Holidays and the second offered infinite variations on the location of units, which could easily create a complex movements sub-set. The planners concluded however, that the capacity of the railways was such, that despite these disruptive possibilities, the network would be more than able to handle the mobilization tasks, although there were scenarios that taxed specific components of

no intention of being found wanting in this respect: 'Every member of the Regiment must have in his possession a copy of *Instructions on Receipt of Orders to Mobilise*, and Officers Commanding Squadrons are responsible that all ranks in their squadrons are thoroughly conversant with them'; *Standing Orders of the Warwickshire Yeomanry*, The Regiment (Warwick: Hugh Rees Ltd, 1912), Part IV, Squadron Organisation and Administration, Sect X, Para 5, p.48.

85 An additional unknown was the numbers of reservists reporting for duty who would be unfit for military service, temporarily or permanently because of illness or injury.

86 The horse PE for units of the BEF was 19,000; 36,000 additional horses were required for WE. The TF needed another 81,000 and the balance of 18,000, for reserve units and Remount Depots. The Army's Remount Mobilization Statement (A1729) which was classified as CONFIDENTIAL upon publication, was a complex statistical document of 103 pages listing the additional horses by type and quantity, required upon mobilization for every unit in every Command in the United Kingdom and the numbers and type, which were authorised to be held by each unit on the Peace and War Establishments; TNA WO 106/49B/8: Remount Statement, 1914-15. For an examination of this subject, see, Brigadier-General T R F Bate CMG, 'Horse Mobilisation', *Journal of the Royal United Service Institution* (JRUSI) Vol. LXVII (465) (February 1922), pp.16-23.

87 TNA WO 32/9133: 'Revised railway arrangements for transport of horses to Aldershot on mobilization'.

88 The War Office Staff Officers probably did not envisage the loss of two chargers from the Queen's Own Oxfordshire Hussars at Churn Camping Ground on 31 August 1914, when Lieutenant Adrian Keith-Falconer's second servant drove the picketing pegs in so lightly, the horses walked off at daybreak and, according to the Regimental History, were 'never to be seen again'; Adrian Keith-Falconer, *The Oxfordshire Hussars in the Great War* (London: John Murray, 1927), p.21. In addition, at Newbury Racecourse, the 1st South Midland Brigade, consisting of the Gloucestershire, Warwickshire and Worcestershire Yeomanry regiments and the Warwick Royal Horse Artillery (RHA) suffered a significant stampede resulting in serious injury to many horses; The Honourable H A Adderley (Comp), *The Warwickshire Yeomanry in the Great War* (Warwick: W H Smith & Son, 1922), p.8.

89 Note in TNA WO 106/49A/2: Revision of Programme.

the system to the limit. Whilst interference with civilian traffic on the day was generally relatively minor, the railways had to plan carefully to ensure this outcome. In the event, naval mobilization was partially complete before the Army commenced its process, which was certainly beneficial because it transpired that a full naval mobilization would have clashed with the Bank Holiday and movement for TF Annual Training Camps.

Another matter was the criticality of shipping. In 1914, 44.4% of the World's tonnage of shipping was flagged to the United Kingdom[90] but the key question was whether sufficient ships of the right type could be acquired to meet the timeframe. Of especial concern, was shipping for horses.[91] To gauge the scope of this issue, the Admiralty and the Board of Trade (BOT) conducted, during 1912, a meticulous 12 month census,[92] of the daily shipping movements of every port in the United Kingdom, which gave a comprehensive understanding of the potential availability on any day, of the types of ships[93] that would be required to move the BEF to France and support naval operations from the UK Base, whilst concurrently, port information from the United Kingdom and France was collated by the Admiralty.[94] In February 1913, a reconnaissance of French Channel Ports was conducted by Admiralty and War Office officers, supported by two highly respected shipping consultants, resulting in the Royden and Fletcher Report being published in May 1913.[95]

90 The Dominions and Colonies contributed an additional 3.5%, which meant that Britain and the Empire controlled 47.9% of the World's shipping. In 1914, British flagged steam vessels totalled 12,602. For details, see, *Annual Statement of the Navigation and Shipping of the United Kingdom for the Year 1913*, Command 7616 (London: HMSO, 1913) and Archibald Hurd, BOH, *The Merchant Navy*, Vol. I (London: John Murray, 1921), pp.85-94.

91 Once the necessary ships had been identified, the War Office had to procure, purchase and store the fittings to enable the transportation of horses. The funding and purchase of these items remained confidential. In 1914, animal management was an embedded culture in the British Army; for details of maritime horse transportation, see, Major A G Todd, Army Veterinary Corps, 'The Management of Horses on Board Ship', *The Army Review*, Vol. VII, No 4, War Office (October 1914), pp.413-425.

92 The Shipping Census was absolutely critical to generating, through statistical analysis, a high level of confidence that the appropriate shipping would be available within the prescribed timeframe to complete cross-Channel transportation of the BEF. The complexity of the task is demonstrated by the summary of the 373 planned sailings 9-27 August 1914 in TNA ADM 116/1331: Expeditionary Force Arrangements.

Table 3.6

BEF Planned Sailings from UK Ports – August 1914

Port	Sailings
Avonmouth	42
Belfast	6
Channel Islands	2
Cork	9
Dublin	25
Glasgow	3
Liverpool	20
Newhaven	106
Queenstown	4
Southampton	156
Total	373

93 Suitable ships were assigned to one of four categories: Class 1 - Personnel; Class 2 - Horse Transport; Class 3 - Mechanical Transport and Class 4 - Supplies & Ordnance.

94 In the United Kingdom, there was a bonus, in that many of the major ports were owned or operated by railway companies, which generated an effective synergy as well as delivering clearer lines of control.

95 The reconnaissance was conducted by Commander Aylmer (Admiralty) Captain Ommanney (War Office) and the shipping consultants T Royden and E L Fletcher. Le Harve was selected as the Main Base Area (MBA) port with

With a wealth of information to hand, the planners were able to assess capacity, warehousing, quays, cranes, rail links, communications, ships' draughts and tides that allowed decisions to be made about which ports should be used for the deployment of the BEF,[96] and the equally important naval support. This complex work was co-ordinated by the Slade Committee,[97] and included the requirements for procurement of charts, wireless, visual signalling equipment, the provision of pilots, sailing orders, Masters' instructions, frozen-meat ships, lighters, launches, tugs, brows, horse-stalls,[98] gangways, portable derricks, slings and spreaders, berthing, coaling and river passages.[99] In addition, there were supporting administrative, contractual and financial issues that required resolution, for example, charter agreements, requisitioning procedures, compensation policy, pension liabilities, control of cash accounts, insurance[100] and the commissioning of Mercantile officers into the Royal Naval Reserve.[101]

As a result of this meticulous research, War Office pre-war planning work had identified potential issues that might not be resolved within the mobilization planning timeframes. One key aspect was to ensure that units were loaded to ships in a manner that retained administrative integrity during the short-sea crossing to France and ensured combat capability was not

Rouen as the Subsidiary Base Area (SBA). Calais was not selected as a SPOD; the sea routes to the port being considered to be vulnerable to attack by German submarines and light craft. Boulogne was to be utilized only during the concentration period to accelerate the force build-up, and, of particular note, most of the Royal Flying Corps (RFC) deployment was to be conducted through the Temporary Base Area (TBA).

96 The ports selected for the BEF are shown in Table 3.7:

Table 3.7
BEF Deployment & Reception Ports

United Kingdom	Remarks
Avonmouth	POL & MT
Belfast	5 XX
Cork	6 XX
Dublin	5 XX & 3 Cavalry X
Glasgow	Short Sea Route – Belfast
Liverpool	Short Sea Route – Dublin plus MT & frozen meat
Newhaven	Ammunition & Stores
Queenstown	6 XX
Southampton	Main Sea Port of Embarkation (SPOE)
France	
Boulogne	Temporary Base Area for Ammunition, Medical Stores and RFC
Le Harve	Main Base Area
St Nazaire & Nantes	6 XX & New Main Base Area
Rouen	Subsidiary Base Area

97 The Inter-Departmental Committee on Shipping was commonly known as the Slade Committee. Chaired by Admiral Sir Edmond John Warre Slade, it consisted of Admiralty and War Office representatives and met twice weekly. Its first meeting was on Thursday 6 March 1913 and the last (probably) Monday 9 June 1914. The minutes are in TNA ADM 1331, 1332, and 1333; see also, TNA WO 106/49/B2. The War Office representatives were Colonel E M Perceval, Assistant Director of Movements (QMG 2) and Colonel G M Harper (MO 1).

98 The provision and fitting of horse-stalls was critical to the plan but the appropriate ships had to be available for the installation and the accessories directed to the relevant port. IDC 27, nd but probably April 1914 in TNA WO 106/49B/2: Interdepartmental Conference, Slade Committee.

99 TNA ADM 116/1331: Expeditionary Force Arrangements.

100 The Charter Agreement, Clause II, states that Shipping Owners shall provide and pay for the ship's insurance but does not mention what risks are to be insured against; Ibid.

101 Ibid.

compromised during debarkation, although there was an acceptance that compromises might have to be made, especially in relation to the use of ships fitted for the transport of animals: 'In some cases, Transports fitted for horses will convey troops on early voyages. Where this is so, the troops will utilize the unoccupied horse stalls as required'.[102] Detailed planning could not of course, eliminate every potential failure as GOC 4th Division noted: 'The only hitch was the vessel allotted to the H.Q. Staff of the Division was so light, and therefore so high out of the water, that the cranes on the jetties were not high enough, or the chains long enough, to be able to load her.[103] The stores earmarked for that ship had to go on another which caused some confusion'.[104] Major Temple Willcox of the 3rd (King's Own) Hussars,[105] recorded the Regiment's negative experiences of its embarkation at Southampton:

> Our recollections of her [the SS City of Lucknow] are not of the best. There was no covered accommodation for the men, the holds were full of cargo and on their hatches were placed the vehicles. The sanitary arrangements, we were to discover on the voyage, were totally inadequate, and nothing had been prepared for the conveyance of horses. The only method of getting the horses on board was by slinging - two or three gangways would have been so simple! A valuable charger of the Colonel nearly came to grief in the operation. On board the horses were tied about the main deck round the hatches.[106]

Southampton was selected to be the Main SPOE, which placed its owner, the LSWR,[107] as the key railway company supporting the deployment. Its importance is clearly illustrated by the table below, which summarizes the 130,177 personnel and key materiel exported through it, 9-31 August 1914 having been delivered by 711 special trains.[108] Of note, is that between 2212 on Friday 21 August and 1812 on Saturday 22, 73 trains arrived, at a rate of one every 16 minutes and moving 12 percent of the personnel in the deployed BEF.[109]

102 Instructions for Divisional Naval Transport Officer Southampton, shown at Para 38 of IDC 27, nd but probably April 1914, in TNA WO 106/49B/2: Interdepartmental Conference (Slade Committee).

103 Presumably the ship was loading on a High Water Spring tide and had light ballast.

104 Snow & Pottle, *Confusion of Command*, p.12.

105 Lieutenant-Colonel A A Kennedy commanded the Regiment from 2 April 1913 to 13 April 1915 before commanding the 7th Cavalry Brigade, 4th Cavalry Division, 75th and 230th Infantry Brigades, and after the war, he was appointed the as the British Military Governor of Cologne. Walter Willcox commanded the Regiment 15 April 1915 - 2 April 1921.

106 Everard Wyrall, *The History of the King's Regiment (Liverpool) 1914-1919*, Vol. I, 1914-1915 (London: Edward Arnold, 1928), p.3.

107 The LSWR was also known as England's 'Military Line' because of its support to the many army facilities in the South of England but primarily the garrisons at Aldershot, Bisley, Bulford, Bordon, Larkhill and Woolmer, with a link via the MSWJR to Ludgershall and Tidworth; see, Harman & Nichols, *Atlas of the Southern Railway*, Map 25.

108 Involving 1,422 train movements in and out of the SPOE.

109 TNA WO 106/49B/4 contains a neatly scribed handwritten SECRET Staff Table for Southampton Port export arrivals, with rail traffic in blue and listing: Train Number, Time of Arrival, Departing Station, Army Division allocation, Unit, Passengers, Vehicles, Artillery pieces, Stores Tonnage and Telegraph Codes. The table also lists, in red, road arrivals, an often forgotten component of the deployment plan.

Table 3.8
Southampton – Military Exports
9-31 August 1914

Officers: 5,006 Other Ranks: 125,171	Horses: 38,805 Wagons: 1,574	Guns: 344 Motor Vehicles: 277	Motor & bicycles: 1,802 Stores: 6,528 tonnes

The advent of military aviation created new requirements, not least in the method of movement. For the first time in the British Army's history, equipment and personnel left the shores of the United Kingdom on an operational deployment, other than by sea, self-deploying to the Theatre of War.[110] Unlike most of the BEF, the Sea Port of Disembarkation (SPOD) for the Royal Flying Corps (RFC) was Boulogne instead of Le Harve. For such a relatively small element of the BEF's Order of Battle (ORBAT),[111] the movement arrangements were quite complex as the table below illustrates:[112]

Table 3.9
Movement of RFC Component to France – August 1914[113]

Sub-Unit	Location	SPOE	Remarks
HQ RFC	Farnborough	Southampton	
2 Squadron	Montrose	Glasgow	Aircraft flown to Farnborough then Dover.
3 Squadron	Netheravon	Southampton	One aircraft crashed after take off and the two crew members killed.
4 Squadron	Eastchurch	Southampton	
5 Squadron	Gosport	Southampton	
Air Park	Farnborough	Avonmouth	Four aircraft in cases to Avonmouth by rail. Eight flown to Dover.

110 Self-deployment had its own issues. Several aircraft were involved in accidents, with 3 Squadron RFC suffering the loss of Second-Lieutenant R R Skene and Mechanic R K Barlow after taking off from Netheravon Airfield, whilst Lieutenant R M Vaughan of the Royal Inniskilling Fusiliers, spent a week under French arrest, having forced landed near Boulogne. See, Walter Raleigh, BOH, *The War in the Air, Being the Story of The part played in the Great War by the Royal Air Force*, Vol. I (Oxford: Clarendon Press, 1922), pp.286-287.

111 66 aircraft and approximately 927 officers and men in four squadrons and an Air Park. The figure of 975 is not definitive and calculated from subtracting the 109 officers who deployed to France from the 146 total in the RFC, matched by the percentage equivalent to the 1,097 Other Ranks (OR) on strength, thereby creating 818 ORs and a total of 927. Figures extracted from H A Jones, BOH, *The War in the Air*, Vol. VI (Oxford: Clarendon Press, 1937), Appx XXVI and XXXV. Based however, on the RFC percentage of the BEF of strength 160,000 being 0.59%, the figure is 944; see, War Officer, *Statistics of the Military Effort of the British Empire during the Great War, 1914-1920* (MEBE), (HMSO, 1922), p.66.

112 Of interest, is that only one pilot in the deployed RFC component was a Corps badged logistician, Lieutenant Reynell Henry Verney, Army Service Corps (ASC), serving with the Air Park. Verney was a TF officer in the Warwickshire 4th South Midland (Howitzer) Brigade Royal Field Artillery before commissioning into the ASC as a regular officer in 1910. Promoting in the Equipment Support discipline in the RFC, he transferred to the RAF post-war, where, as Director Technical Development in the rank of Air Commodore, he played a crucial role in RAF aircraft design in the period 1934-1938 being awarded the OBE in 1919 and the CBE 1937. For his contribution in this arena, see, Colin Sinnott, *The RAF and Aircraft Design 1929-1939, Air Staff Operational Requirements* (London & Portland, Oregon: Frank Cass, 2001).

113 Compiled from information in Raleigh, BOH, *The War in the Air*, Vol. I, pp.283-287.

Most of the BEF's horses, HT vehicles, motor-cycles plus most of the baggage, ammunition and stores were moved by rail to the key SPOEs of Southampton and Newhaven, whilst the WMT travelled by road to Avonmouth and Liverpool,[114] a mostly forgotten component of the BEF's deployment plan. Some of these vehicles were requisitioned motor-cars and vans collated at Regent's Park Barracks in London and driven to Southampton, highlighting another aspect of commercial logistics supporting military capability.[115] Reliance on the commercial sector to provision the movement multipliers reinforced the importance of ensuring efficient financial and contractual arrangements were in place;[116] so whilst officers in the Admiralty and War Office laboured to produce the movement tables, Civil Servants honed the contracts with companies and accounted for the funding to pay them.[117]

Rail Plans

As the Admiralty and the War Office Staff were refining their plans, the railway companies were examining how to deliver the necessary effect.[118] One of the fundamental components was the requirement to 'through-run' trains from one company area to another, which, to be effective, required meticulous planning by the civil engineering and operating departments. In 1914, goods wagons moved between companies supported by a comprehensive, if not always efficient, manual tracking and audit system.[119] Practicality dictated an open system because it was much easier to move the wagons across the network that it was to tranship the goods, with the concomitant delays, loss and cost;[120] that approximately 43.5 percent of the goods wagons on the National Rail Network (NRN) were Private Owner Wagons (POW) reinforced this process, although there were many problems created by their design, construction, maintenance and control.[121]

114 Given the condition of British roads and the reliability of WMT in 1914, this solution imported additional risk to the BEF's capability.

115 One of these vans was allocated to 5 Squadron RFC, which used it as the ammunition lorry. Painted a brilliant scarlet, with the legend 'The World's Appetiser' on the sides emblazoned in gold, it belonged to Elizabeth Lazenby & Son, sauce soup, and pickle manufacturers of London. During the withdrawal from Mons, the pilots of 5 Squadron were thus able to identify from the air, their transport. See, BOH, *The War in the Air*, Vol. I, p.287 and *Whitaker's Red Book or Who's Who in Business 1914* (London: J Whitaker & Sons, 1914).

116 For details, see, Pratt, *British Railways and the Great War*, Vol. I, pp.98-108.

117 The 1910 War Office List has 11 pages devoted to finance, audits and contracts. See, Knight, *War Office List*, pp.87-96; the additional page is 93A.

118 One of the forgotten aspects of the interface between the War Office and the principal railway companies is that the General Managers were members of the influential Engineer & Railway Staff Corps RE, holding the rank of Lieutenant Colonel; see, Knight, *War Office List*, p.71, War Railway Council, Railway Members. In addition, the Chief Traffic Officers of the London & South Western Railway, South Eastern & Chatham Railways, London & Brighton & South Coast Railway, Great Central Railway and Great Northern Railway had, in May 1909, been granted commissions in the rank of Major; see, Major (Retd) C E C Townsend TD, *All Rank and No File, A History of the Engineer and Railway Staff Corps RE*, 1865-1965 (London: The Engineer and Railway Staff Corps RE (TAVR) 1965), p.41. Guests at the Engineer and Railway Staff Corps 1913 Annual Dinner included nearly all the military members of the Army Council, with General Sir John French (CIGS) heading the list. Major-General John Cowans, the QMG, was also dining with one of his junior staff officers, Captain H O Mance, Staff Captain (Railways) in QMG 2 who was a member of the War Office Expeditionary Force Planning Team; Ibid, p.42.

119 The organization that controlled this operation was the Railway Clearing House (RCH). The RCH was established in 1842 to improve commercial efficiency and operational effectiveness, becoming involved in finance, wagon design and maintenance, operating standards, signalling and a host of other issues. Whilst not directly engaged in military planning before the Great War, the RCH's work in integrating the operations of the many companies delivered the coherence that was necessary to ensure the relevant support to the Defence requirement. For the story of this largely forgotten but nonetheless significant element of British railway operations, see, Phillip Bagwell, *The Railway Clearing House in the British Economy 1842-1922* (London: George Allen & Unwin, 1968).

120 Initially goods had been trans-shipped from the wagons of one company to those of another; the result was chaos.

121 One control mechanism is demurrage, which is, in the railway context, the payment of financial compensation for

Much of the initial naval traffic was either coal or Out Of Gauge (OOG) tasks that the railways undertook daily, so the in-place systems were effective. The War Office requirement was much more complex because of the combined passenger and goods movement.[122] Apart from specific expresses and specials, passenger stock and locomotives did not usually travel across company boundaries, the railways having deduced it was much easier for the passenger to conduct self-transhipment. To meet the need of the War Office, 'through-running', often with a mixed train, was essential. To reduce the complexities, a series of Standard Train consists were created based on the various types of unit.[123] This solution reduced stock requirements, improved efficiency and minimized niche requests. There were few limitations to passenger stock movement but the allocation of steam motive power needed careful planning. Selected locomotives needed the tractive effort to haul the Standard Trains through the specified sections, whilst remaining within the operating envelope. This meant that the various civil engineering departments had to confirm and approve axle loading, gradient, curvature and loading gauge. A key component of efficient operating was 'balanced working', which sought to return stock through planned cyclic loops, thereby regenerating resilient lift capacity. Whilst effective, it was also vulnerable to disruptions and short notice change, although the railways had sufficient reserve stock to cover unexpected demand.

Once the technical issues had been resolved, the operating department continued the process. Hours were spent on creating the train paths,[124] a process conducted by experienced staff using comprehensive and detailed train-graphs.[125] Crew rosters and locomotive exchanges had to be planned and crew pilots integrated for travel over foreign[126] rails because footplate staff from one company were not route cleared for another. Whilst time consuming, these tasks had precedent. Most of the Scottish traffic to and from England involved several railway companies,[127] using interface arrangements to support 'through-running' for express services and there was long-term of experience of joint-running and specials. There was also the question of rail logistics, the effective execution of which, whilst embedded in daily operations was critical to capability. The consumption of coal, lubricants and water depended upon the locomotive type, train weight, speeds, gradients and track curvature but for planning purposes the War Office used worst-case figures averaged from

undue detention of a wagon, and was introduced as an inter-company transaction by the Railway Clearing House in 1842. For the most part, whilst the concept was sound, this was one area of commercial practice that failed to create the desired efficiency on the railways because the allowances were too generous to prevent companies using the wagons from other companies as temporary storage facilities; Bagwell, *The Railway Clearing House*.

122 A planning tool was *The Clearing House Official Handbook of Railway Stations* (London: The Railway Clearing House, 1912), a document of 700 pages, which listed the outline infrastructure and capability of every railway station and nearly every siding and private siding, in the United Kingdom, comprising approximately 41,500 entries. Needless to say, it was not published annually; the first was in 1904, the second in 1912 and the third in 1925.

123 For details, see, General Staff, *Field Service Pocket Book 1914* (FSPB 14), War Office (London: HMSO, 1914), p.140.

124 The railway companies were not paid to conduct this work and initially there was considerable resistance to delivering it, although eventually, the War Office Finance Branch agreed that small gratuities could be paid to certain members of railway companies who had spent excessively long hours in the preparation of the time-tables. The War Office was certainly keenly aware of this issue and was careful to manage the staffing flow to avoid periods when the railways timetabling teams were busy creating civilian programmes. MO1 noted on 9 December 1912: 'The main trouble is that we have under our present arrangements, to depend upon the railway companies to do the work which they have no legal obligation to complete and which they do not consider so important as we do'; TNA WO 106/50: Military Mobilization Railway Programmes.

125 Pratt recorded that such was the pressure on key individuals, that 'In one instance, at least, the early death of an especially talented time-table expert was directly attributed to the strenuous and exhausting toil which the work in question had involved'; Pratt, *British Railways and the Great War*, Vol. I, p.16.

126 A contemporary term, for the lines of other railway companies within the United Kingdom.

127 Notably, the London & North Western with the Caledonian, and the Great Northern and North Eastern, with the North British.

an eight-wheeled coupled tender goods locomotive[128]. This used approximately 100 pounds of coal and 70 gallons of water per train mile;[129] thus a return trip from Inverness to Southampton Western Docks[130] required 53.8 tons of coal and 377.7 tons (84,420 gallons) of water.

To direct these complex operations, a comprehensive command and control system was established with links at each appropriate level, between the railway companies and Defence; it was a meeting of minds because the two organizations had similar processes, systems and cultures. Given the numbers of railway companies, a simple but effective system was devised. The LSWR was selected as the lead or 'Secretary Railway',[131] to represent the all the companies involved[132] at meetings with the lead Defence agency, the War Office. Within each Army Command, the railway company with the most engagement in the movement acted as the lead for the others, interfacing with the military HQ and the LSWR.

Upon mobilization, the principal companies created rail military movement sections to plan and control Defence movements.[133] Admiralty interests were represented at National level through the War Office and locally through the Army Command HQ. The whole process was overseen by the Railway Executive Committee (REC),[134] which delivered the strategic coherency so vital to success. The REC issued policy, although the appointed personalities within it had a strong grip on the operational realities. Detailed military plans and instructions were issued by the War Office, which

128 Although 0-6-0 freight locomotives were the most common in the United Kingdom, examples include the Great Western Railway (GWR) 2800 Class, introduced in 1903, a 2-8-0 heavy long-distance freight locomotive weighing 118.65 tons, tendering 6 tons of coal and 3,500 gallons of water and the North Eastern Railway (NER) 0-8-0 Q6 Class, introduced in 1913, which weighed 110 tons with tender and carried 5.5 tons of coal and 4,125 gallons of water. The most famous was the Great Central Railway (GCR) Class 8K, introduced in 1911, which was the design used by the Ministry of Munitions for the Railway Operating Division's 2-8-0 locomotive. It had an operating weight of 121.5 tons, tendering 6 tons of coal and 4,000 gallons of water. One is preserved, by the National Railway Museum, in the United Kingdom, which was GCR No 102, and latterly 63601 in British Railways service, which runs on the heritage Great Central Railway and appeared in the film *Enigma*. For details of period locomotives, see, H C Casserley (Ed.) *The Observer's Book of Railway Locomotives of Britain* (London: Frederick Warne & Co, 1955) and O S Nock, *British Locomotives of the 20th Century*, Vol. I, 1900-1930 (Wellingborough: Patrick Stephens, 1983).

129 See, General Staff, Summary of Working Tables for Tender Engines in *Railway Manual (War)*, War Office (HMSO, 1911) (reprinted with amendments 1914) pp.27-29.

130 Based on a distance of 602 miles 69 chains for a single journey and rounded to 1,206 miles for a return.

131 In 21st Century terminology, the LSWR was the Prime Contractor.

132 The representatives of the LSWR were integrated at the War Office senior staff planning level, with the lead senior officers being briefed through the Railway Executive Committee (REC) as well as through the company management. As an example, the LSWR planners attended a conference held at the War Office on Tuesday 9 December 1913. Agenda items on this occasion included the potential change of date for the 1914 Expeditionary Force Tables (EFT) from February to April, watering and feeding for horses on delayed trains, discussions on the tabulation format of the EFT and the size and strength of the paper upon which it was to be printed; TNA WO 106/50: Military Mobilisation Railway Programmes.

133 Three companies, the London and North Western, Great Western and LSWR created Military Departments pre-war, with the first two devoting the staff exclusively to military traffic; Pratt, *British Railways and the Great War*, Vol. I, p.123.

134 The REC was established, after much debate because some railway company boards were not originally in favour, in November 1912. Chaired by the President of the Board of Trade, most meetings convened under the Vice-Chair, a nominated railway representative, initially Sir Frank Ree (LNWR) who was succeeded, upon his death, by H A Walker, of the LSWR, a wise choice, professionally and operationally. The 10 leading companies were represented by their General Managers, with representation from the Admiralty, War Office, Chief Inspecting Officer of Railways and Engineer and Railway Staff Corps; the London Brighton & South Coast Railway (LBSCR) joined in August 1914. Whilst focused on policy, during the mobilization and deployment period, it met four times a day. The HQ was in the LNWR office in Parliament Street Westminster; the REC had, upon formation, a secretarial and support staff of six. The REC had two forebears; the Army Railway Council formed in 1896, which became the War Railway Council in 1903 to include the Admiralty. For details of REC operations, see, Pratt, *British Railways and the Great War*, Vol. I, pp.40-48 and 82-97. The Communications Board, chaired by the QMG and consisting of representatives from the railways and several key government departments, including the Admiralty and the War Office, supported the tasks of the REC.

were converted into a wealth of operating railway detail by the relevant company staffs;[135] train paths, routing, stock allocation, locomotive watering and coaling. From this information, the War Office generated unit deployment and entrainment tables,[136] which were issued to Commands.[137] The information in these documents matched those produced by the railway companies, so a Railway Transport Office (RTO) in an Army Command should, at least in theory, be able to converse in the same language as his opposite number in the relevant railway company.

In 1911, the process by which, the periodical revisions of the plan were conducted changed, which resulted in amendments being reviewed at HQ Commands and the War Office. The War Office therefore, adjusted its organization in December 1912, placing greater emphasis on delivering mobilization rail planning by the QMG 2 staff branch and transferring responsibility for routine rail matters to QMG 3,[138] although by 1914, the annual revision had reached the point where the previous one had not been completed before the next one started.[139] In addition, plans were developed to train RTOs for deployment in the UK to support Home Commands and for an expanded team to be attached to the BEF.[140] Communications were essential to executing the movement plan and extensive improvements were made to Private Wire speech capacity between the railway companies,[141] War Office and the Admiralty, a system that supplemented the existing capability, which included telegraph and telephones. At a strategic level, the *Field Service Regulations* (FSR) recognized the importance and complexity of railway systems in supporting military operations, whilst exposing the factors for effectiveness or failure:

> A railway system is a highly sensitive machine dislocated by unskilled treatment; it is at the same time an organism most vital to the maintenance of an army............ the convenience

135 The Expeditionary Force Railway Timetables of 45 pages of printed A2 are held in TNA WO 106/49B/3: 'Expeditionary Force Railway Timetables'. The details include the train number, Division, Brigade, particulars of traffic, collection and delivery stations, train consists and the lead railway company. The Serial Tables, which provide the foundation for the railway timetables, are beautifully scribed in light blue ink on the A2 printed form and held in TNA WO 106/49B/4: 'Expeditionary Force to France, Serial Tables, Southampton'. There is also a note appertaining to the provision of gangways, horse-brows, MT slings and portable derricks for off-loading ships in France.

136 The key documents were: 'Entrainment and Movement to Areas of Concentration' in TNA WO 106/49A/6. 'Mobilization Appointments', A1590 dated April 1914 - Part I Expeditionary Force, held in TNA WO 106/49A/9. This document was classified SECRET (indeed, it still is according to the front cover) and detailed all the staff appointments for every HQ from Army to brigade, Bases, Depots, Ports and Rest Camps, with details of the appointment, nominating HQ, reporting place and timings. 'Instructions for the Entrainment of the BEF' are small pamphlets (A6) classified CONFIDENTIAL and cover Instructions for the Entrainment and Embarkation (Short Voyage) for Units of the Expeditionary Force in Great Britain and another for Ireland. Documents are in TNA WO 106/49B/1: 'Expeditionary Force to France, Instruction for Entrainment and Embarkation (Short Voyage) for Units of the Expeditionary Forces'.

137 Command BEF railway mobilization documents are held in the TNA. Southern Command (WO 33/657) Scottish Command (WO 33/661) and Eastern Command (WO 33/676 (Horses), 679 (Reservists) and 684 (General)).

138 QMG 2 and QMG 3 reported to the Director of Movements and Quartering, through an Assistant Director Movements and Railway Transport Subdivision; see, Knight, *War Office* List, pp.62-63. Given the task list and the establishment of QMG 3, which comprised a Grade 3 and two clerks, it was almost certainly a busy staff appointment.

139 Pratt noted, 'Under the Command system, in fact, the mobilisation programme, which had hitherto been a relatively small matter, assumed very large proportions, the tables to be prepared and the mass of details to be dealt with involving an amount of labour greatly in excess of what had previously been necessary'; Pratt, *British Railways and the Great War*, p.16.

140 The Railway Transport Establishment (RTE) consisting of six Deputy Assistant Directors (DADs) and 24 Railway Transport Officers (RTOs). For details, see, 'The Railway Transport Establishment of the Original Expeditionary Force, World War One', Movement Control Historical Society, MCHS 0076, *Movement Control Association*, 2005.

141 Private Wire circuits were One-2-One telephone connections.

of individual bodies of troops must be subordinated to the working of the line as a whole.[142]

Conclusion

Commercial capability and in particular, the railways, played a crucial role in pre-war Defence planning. The carefully crafted mobilization plans matured by the War Office and under-pinned by the UK railways, had to be integrated with a complex shipping matrix and across the English Channel, the French railway military movement schedules. The railways were also essential to the mobilization of the TF and the deployment of the wider round of HD assets. The Royal Navy also relied heavily on rail movement for mobilization and sustainment, although fortuitously, in the event, many of the initial moves were completed before the Army mobilized. The flexibility of the railways did, however, enable the Royal Navy to adjust its logistic posture as it developed its plans to protect the maritime element of the BEF's deployment to France.

The detailed staffing processes that delivered UK defence capability in 1914, was from the British perspective, the foundation-stone of future systems. For the first time in British military operations, forces were deployed, using processes involving concepts, systems and structures that are readily understood today. It defined British military rail planning during the Great War, the deployment of the BEF to France in 1939, and its successors to the end of the British Army of the Rhine (BAOR); Movement Instruction (MI 45) the rail movement plan supporting BAOR in TTW during the Cold War, was a direct descendant of the War Office Command Railway Movement Tables of 1914. Whilst the use of the commercial sector to deliver military capability was not new, its close integration to a series of specific military plans certainly was. What is remarkable is that whilst there were no meaningful available alternatives, the senior officers in the Admiralty and the War Office not only had the confidence to rely on the railway and shipping companies but also were content, after much debate, to bring key commercial directors into what was an extremely sensitive military planning arena. The General Staff summarized the risk: 'The LSWR co-ordinates the work of the Home Railways. As they themselves have prepared the programme, we take it for granted that they will be able to work it on mobilization'.[143]

In addition, the finance and contracts issues were fundamental to success and deserve further study. The processes and procedures that were used to develop the plans have an unexpected similarity today: identification of the aim, studies, analysis, collation, planning, reassessment, revision, publication and distribution. Apart from the 21st Century access to technological tools, our forebears would be surprisingly comfortable in today's environment: consultants, contractors, civil servants, and committees; perhaps not quite so much has changed as one might believe. What is clear though, is that our logistic predecessors were remarkably adept at planning and making things happen.

142 FSR, Part II, Amdts 1914, Chp VIII, Railway Transport, p.95.

143 General Staff Memorandum, 1914 in TNA WO 106/49A/2: Expeditionary Force to France, i, 'Factors affecting plan of movement and Staff work'.

4

Riding the Rails

The railways of the United Kingdom and their role in the deployment of the British Army in 1914

Introduction

The role of commercial logistic capability in supporting Defence mobilization and deployment planning in the period before the Great War matured in late July and August 1914, when the tasks embedded in the plans were enacted and the military risks taken in relying upon the civilian transportation systems were tested. The aim of this chapter is to examine how the railways executed the plans to deploy the British Expeditionary Force (BEF) to France and the Territorial Force (TF) to Home Defence Stations (HDS) in the United Kingdom (UK) and the subsequent improvisation to support to the BEF, including reinforcement, casualty evacuation and Reverse Logistics.[1] In addition to the mobilization and deployment plans, the chapter also explores the practical railway movement experience the Army gained in the pre-war period,[2] which was a product of deployment to and recovery from, annual training exercises.

Surprisingly, military railway units played little part in supporting the mobilization. In 1912, the Royal Engineers had three regular railway companies (8, 10 and 53) and three Special Reserve companies,[3] so in August 1914 military railway involvement was focused upon the preparation of this niche capability for potential service and not delivering rail movement in support of Defence mobilization. In the UK, with the exception of the Woolmer Instructional Military Railway (WIMR)[4] and the civilian staffed Admiralty and War Office sidings, the commercial railways

1 Operations related to the reuse of products and materials, by moving them from their typical final destination of use for the purpose of capturing value or proper disposal. In the Great War, it was the Royal Flying Corps (RFC) that pioneered Reverse Logistics, particularly with regard to refurbishing high value sub-systems such as aero-engines. The concept spread across the Army under the term Salvage, involving everything from brass cartridge cases to horseshoes and clothing.

2 Whilst the use of British railways to move the British Expeditionary Force (BEF) to the Sea Ports of Embarkation (SPOE) appears to be an obvious solution, there had been considerable debate in the early 1890s as to whether the railways were capable of delivering short notice capability, initiated by Colonel J S Rothwell, Professor of Administration at the Army Staff College; see, Colonel J S Rothwell, 'The Conveyance of Troops by Railway', *Royal United Service Magazine*, Vol. CXXVII (December 1891), pp.215-221. His views were swiftly countered by arguments exposed in, Lieutenant-Colonel, Sir George Findlay, 'On the Use of Railways in the United Kingdom for the Conveyance of Troops', *United Service Magazine*, Vol. CXXVII (April 1892), pp.37-49.

3 53 Company was disbanded in 1912, so, in 1914, there were two regular (8 and 10) and three Special Reserve Railway Companies (One company Royal Anglesey RE and two companies Royal Monmouth RE). For pre-war details of railway units, see, Colonel G H Addison (Comp) CMG DSO, *The Work of the Royal Engineers in the European War 1914-1918, Miscellaneous*, Royal (Chatham: Engineers Institute, 1927), p.30 and Major-General H L Pritchard (Ed.) *The History of the Corps of Royal Engineers*, Vol. V (Chatham: Institute of the Royal Engineers, 1952), pp.116-122.

4 Better known as the Longmoor Military Railway (LMR), the official title of the railway until 1935 was the Woolmer Instructional Railway (WIMR), although informally, the 'Will It Move Railway' was a common tag of the period. The WIMR delivered military railway training, which focused upon survey, construction and maintenance rather than operating.

conducted all the key railway mobilization operations. As the French had stated that there would be little or no requirement for British military railway capability on the Continent, only 8 Company Royal Engineers (RE)[5] was dispatched to France, whilst the others prepared to operate the WIMR[6] and stand ready for overseas service and Home Defence (HD) tasks. It was a light start to a war that would require, by 1918, over four hundred RE railway companies. The Engineer and Railway Staff Corps[7] retained its crucial advisory role, with selected senior operating and engineering managers in the railways serving in it as commissioned officers.[8]

Practise Makes Perfect

There was never a full pre-war mobilization exercise, which practised the various components of the plans but from the railway and unit perspectives, the practical applications of rail movement were tested regularly. There was a movement and embarkation exercise 24-25 January 1912 involving, from Aldershot, a cavalry regiment and artillery battery representing combat units and for A&Q, an ammunition column and field ambulance, all at War Establishment (WE).[9] The London & South Western Railway (LSWR) despatched 14 trains from Aldershot to Southampton and the units then embarked upon the SS *Minneapolis*.[10] The exercise cost £3,507 inclusive of £967 for rail movement, which equates in 2016 to the not insignificant sums of £2.952M and £0.814M respectively.[11] There was also a Staff Ride undertaken at Southampton Docks in June 1913 to detail 8th Day Mobilization Working followed by a Staff College student tour to prepare selected personnel to be Assistant Embarkation Staff Officers. Trials in loading Mechanical Transport (MT)[12] were conducted at Avonmouth Port near Bristol,[13] whilst the 2nd Division in Aldershot conducted an internal mobilization exercise in July 1914 using soldiers from the 1st Division acting as Regular

5 Documents appertaining to 8 Company are held in TNA WO 95/4052/8 and 10 Company, WO 95/4052/11.

6 For a history of the LMR in the period, see, D W Ronald & R J Carter, *The Longmoor Military Railway* (Newton Abbot: David & Charles, 1974) and Colonel David Ronald & Mike Christensen OBE, *The Longmoor Military Railway, A New History*, Vol. One: *1903-1939*, (Lydney: Lightmoor Press, 2012). Far removed from the drama of war, the LMR was the setting for all the railway scenes shot for the film, '*The Great Saint Trinian's Train Robbery*' (British Lion Films & Columbia Pictures, 1966). The scenes give a splendid feel of the LMR before its demise in 1969. Longmoor Camp and the surrounding training areas, remain in use as a Defence Training Facility.

7 For a history, see, C E C Townsend, *All Rank And No File, A History of the Engineer and Railway Staff Corps*, 1865-1965 (London: Engineer and Railway Staff Corps, 1965).

8 One of the forgotten aspects of the interface between the War Office and the principal railway companies is that the General Managers were members of the influential Engineer & Railway Staff Corps RE, holding the rank of Lieutenant Colonel; see, C Newman Knight, *The War Office List and Administrative Directory 1910* (London: HMSO, 1910) p.71, 'War Railway Council, Railway Members'. In addition, the Chief Traffic Officers of the London & South Western Railway (LSWR), South Eastern & Chatham Railways (SECR), London & Brighton & South Coast Railway (LBSCR), Great Central Railway (GCR), and Great Northern Railway (GNR), had, in May 1909, been granted commissions in the rank of Major.

9 TNA WO 106/50 (WE1): Embarkation and Ports of Embarkation.

10 The SS *Minneapolis* was sunk by submarine torpedo on Thursday 23 March 1916, 195 nautical miles North East of Malta with 12 lives lost; *Navy Losses and Merchant Shipping (Losses)* (London: HMSO, 1919).

11 Based on the *Measuring Worth UK* Economic Cost measuring the comparison of its relative cost using the cost index of all output in the economy as a share of the Gross Domestic Product (GDP).

12 Wheeled, tracked, or semi-tracked land vehicle utilised in a logistic context to move men and materiel to, on or from the battlefield and powered by the Internal Combustion Engine (ICE) either Spark Ignition (SI) or Compression Ignition (CI) fuelled by petroleum spirit or diesel oil respectively, or by steam (Steam Transport (ST)). Often abbreviated to MT, it does not include combat vehicles, such as tanks, Armoured Personnel Carriers (APC) or Self-Propelled Guns (SPG). Motor Transport (MT) included Wheeled or tracked or semi-tracked land logistic vehicle powered by the ICE but to provide specific clarification for wheeled vehicles, the term Wheeled Motor Transport (WMT) is used.

13 Avonmouth Port was served by the Great Western Railway; Philip W Conolly, (Introduction) *Pre-Grouping Atlas and RCH Junction Diagrams* (Hersham: Ian Allan, 2014).

Reservists in order to practice unit reception and preparation drills. Unit moves in the United Kingdom, except local administrative or tactical ones, were conducted by rail, which created plenty of opportunity for units to exercise their skills, the Staff to co-ordinate planning requirements and the railways to meet the military; a wide range of directives, instructions, pamphlets and handbooks supported these practical activities.[14] The importance of entraining and detraining of units to the success of the operation was clearly articulated by *Field Service Regulations* of 1909: 'Rapidity in entraining and detraining is imperative'.[15]

The location of the Royal Navy (RN) and the Army in the United Kingdom inevitably meant some railway companies were more involved with Defence than others. The LSWR served His Majesty's Naval Bases (HMNB) Devonport and Portsmouth and the major army garrisons at Aldershot, Bordon, Bulford and Larkhill, whilst the South Eastern & Chatham Railways (SECR) served Woolwich Arsenal and Dockyard. The Great Eastern Railway (GER) served HMNB Harwich and Colchester Garrison but other railways had little regular defence traffic, although the significant manoeuvres and Territorial Force (TF) Annual Training Camps (ATC) often created high levels of activity for short periods. In 1912, the Annual Army Manoeuvres (AAM)[16] were held in East Anglia and involved approximately 50,000 troops organized into Red and Blue Forces,[17] each comprising a cavalry division, two infantry divisions, army troops, two aeroplane flights, and an airship.[18] 200 military trains, consisting of 4,000 coaches and wagons, most of which, were handled by the GER,[19] were required to support the exercise. What is remarkable though, is that the railways in East Anglia were able to sustain this major military exercise in mid-September, after the very damaging floods, especially in Norfolk during 26-27 August, which left Norwich without rail and road communications for nearly three days, over 40 bridges destroyed, telegraph communications disrupted, crops and eco-system of the Broads severely damaged and thousands of acres of Norfolk under water, in some places to a depth of 13 feet.[20] In 1913, the AAM were held in the area of the South Midlands and Northern Home Counties[21] and, whilst smaller in the numbers

14 These included: *Railway Manual (War)* 120 Mobn 264 (War Office, 1911), Amended, 1914. General Staff, *Field Service Pocket Book* 1908 & 1914, (FSPB 14) War Office (London: HMSO, 1914), pp 138-155. FSR, Part I, *Operations*, Chp III, Movements by Rail, pp.59-63 and Sea, pp.64-67 and Part II, *Organization and Administration*, Chp VIII, Railway Transport, pp.91-96. *King's Regulations and Orders for the Army 1912*, War Office (London: HMSO, 1914), pp.281-289, paras 1417-1487.

15 FSR, Part II, Chp VIII, Transport, p.95.

16 For an excellent survey and analysis of the pre-war AAM in the UK, see, Simon Batten, *Futile Exercise? The British Army's Preparations for War 1902-1914*, (Warwick: Helion, 2018).

17 The forces of an imaginary country, Red, had crossed the frontier dividing Red from Britain, Blue, between Wells-next-the-Sea and Hunstanton. Blue ordered general mobilisation and its prime goal was to prevent Red forces entering London. For the logistic aspects see, Colonel P E F Hobbs CMG, 'The New System of Transport as carried out by the Blue Forces during Army Manoeuvres 1912', *The Army Review*, Vol. IV, No 2, War Office (April 1913), pp.412-430.

18 Each Force was based on a Corps. A regular division provided the Red cavalry, whilst the Blue cavalry division consisted of two brigades comprising the Household Cavalry, Scots Greys, Yeomanry, and Cyclists. Red infantry consisted of 1st and 2nd Infantry Divisions from Aldershot, whilst Blue comprised the 3rd Infantry Division (Southern Command) and 4th Infantry Division (Eastern Command) supported by battalions of the TF. Ibid.

19 H J Prytherch, 'The Great Eastern Railway and the Army Manoeuvres in East Anglia - 1912', *Great Eastern Railway Magazine*, November 1912, pp.356-359.

20 The torrential rain lasted for over 30 hours, depositing an average fall of 4.92 inches across the County, totalling 150,000 million gallons of water. Brundall, five miles to the East of Norwich City Centre, recorded 8.1 inches and such was the event that some areas, especially to the East of Norwich, remained under water until the late Spring of 1913. In these respects, the floods of Summer 2007 and others are in no way 'unprecedented' in the manner that politicians and the media are constantly reminding us, a matter that lucidly illustrates the abuse of historical context. Philip Eden, *Great British Weather Disasters* (London: Continuum, 2008), pp.91-100.

21 The Ordnance Survey published, in conjunction with the War Office, maps, scaled at 2 miles to 1 inch of the relevant exercise areas, showing the boundaries for the AAM and the Out of Bounds for Troops Areas. Price Two Shillings, which in 2016 money, using the Retail Price Index is £8.87, comparing favourably with the 2016

of troops, involved the deployment of 38,000 personnel, 8,000 horses, 100 guns and 1,400 HT and MT vehicles.[22]

The AAM schedules, whilst not as intense nor as complex as those for mobilization, were an excellent chance to practise rail movement on a large scale. In particular, the exercises created a wide range of opportunities that enabled essential training to be conducted to ensure the successful execution of a full mobilization by integrating at different levels of responsibility, railway companies, Command HQs, Railway Transport staff and units. The 1913 AAM directly involved nine out of the 11 principal railway companies and encompassed locations ranging from Glasgow to Plymouth, Dover to Holyhead and Colchester to Dublin. Approximately 8,000 railway employees supported the AAM and the trains travelled over 3,000 miles of routes. TF units, which nearly always deployed to the ATC by rail, had regular, if infrequent, opportunities to practise their movement drills. None of these peacetime moves replicated the full aspects of mobilization even at unit level, a problem, which was especially acute for the TF. Units on the AAM usually deployed from barracks with fewer personnel than the Peace Establishment (PE) whilst the War Establishment (WE) might be twice the size of the PE, with the balance being comprised of reservists. The disparity was greater with animals because the PE for horses was small in comparison to WE, and additional animals were procured from the civilian sector to support the exercises.[23] This additional training scale was not acquired from the garrison but was provided at the place of detrainment. This saved money on movement because the additional horses did not require rail transport to the exercise area, and it reduced hire and forage costs but there was one clear disadvantage; unit railhead drills for mobilization entrainment were not the same in scope,[24] or procedure,[25] although from the movement perspective, even exercises based on PE (-) could be significant. One of the 1912 AAM railheads, Bartlow Junction,[26] 18 miles South East of Cambridge, was a village station but handled, in 58 hours, 17 trains, which moved 6,000 personnel, 300 horses, 200 horse drawn vehicles and 150 bicycles.[27]

Artillery movement was an important component of these exercises, although they did not replicate the ammunition out-loads that were crucial to the mobilization plans; ammunition was though, moved by rail and road transport to support artillery camps. In 1912, the total Unit Shell Allowance at Okehampton in Devon for the 21 batteries of 18 pdr, 60 pdr and 4.5 inch, planned to fire there, totalled 8,740 rounds of shrapnel, High Explosive and practice,[28] which presented no logistic challenge but did offer some practise in handling procedures[29]. Ammunition loading and

Landranger Map at £8.99. See, *Ordnance Survey, England & Wales, Army Exercise Map, 1913, Southern Sheet.*

22 For the logistic aspects, see, Colonel E E Carter CMG MVO, 'The Services of Maintenance in the Field: Some Object Lessons from the Army Exercise 1913', *The Army Review*, Vol. VI, No 2, War Office (April 1914), pp.473-489.

23 To create more complexity, TF soldiers serving in the Yeomanry, of which there were 56 regiments, could bring their own horse.

24 In particular, during exercises, the Quartermaster staff spent much time in conducting the Handover and Takeover of horses, whilst the layout of the unit waiting areas at the railhead had to be adjusted to enact these procedures.

25 The loading of horses in UK was also different to the procedure adopted in France. In the UK horses were positioned transversely across the wagon, whilst in France, they were loaded longitudinally from the end, with heads facing towards the centre of the wagon; Captain R Bonham-Smith, 'Transport Arrangements in France', *Journal of the Royal United Service Institution* (JRUSI), Vol. LXI (February 1916), p.50.

26 Bartlow Junction, operated by the Great Eastern Railway (GER) in 1912, closed in 1967. Many of the buildings remain, having been converted for residential or commercial use. Viewing it in 2016, it is difficult to believe that almost two brigades were moved from its platforms and loading docks. An Advanced Supply Depot (ASD) was also deployed in the grounds of Althorp Park, 6.5 miles North-West of Northampton, which was connected to the National Rail Network (NRN) by a siding specifically constructed for the period of the AAM.

27 Captain J F C Fuller, 'Notes on the Entrainment of Troops To and From Manoeuvres', *The Army Review*, Vol. VII, No 1, War Office (July 1914), p.188. J F C Fuller was a student at the Army Staff College when he wrote this article so the meticulous attention to detail was no doubt prompted by his educational experience there.

28 'Okehampton Artillery Camp Historical Appraisal', Wessex Archaeology, Defence Estates, 2002.

29 Artillery units of the Territorial Force were restricted, during this period, through financial constraints, from firing

unloading was a labour intensive activity in an era before Material Handling Equipment (MHE) and insufficient manpower at a railhead could easily cause significant disruption. In 1912, regulations for the storage and transport of explosives were governed by the Explosives Act 1875,[30] and were just as important as they are today.[31] Indeed, given that the explosives[32] were less stable 100 years ago, more so.[33] The provision of specialist Gun Powder Vans (GPV) internally sheathed with copper for the rail transportation of sensitive explosives, which included dry guncotton, picric acid and gunpowder, unless in an approved metal container, was a critical task during the deployment period and because there were insufficient to complete the out-load from depots to ports within the timeframe, the Armed Services and the railways were granted dispensation to use appropriately modified closed vans.[34] Amatol, wet guncotton, cordite and cordite cartridges could be moved in locked standard vans, whilst shell, boxed Small Arms Ammunition (SAA) and fixed ammunition could travel in sheeted open wagons, although closed wagons, especially for SAA, were preferred.[35]

Artillery pieces were the largest single items of army equipment that the railways had to move in this period and it was a subject that required special attention by the planners and more than one 'Shoulder to the Wheel' in units. The significance of rail movement is well illustrated by the numbers of contemporary articles that were published in military journals in the period before the war. Of especial note, is the article entitled *Notes on the Entrainment of Troops To and From Manoeuvres* by a Captain J F C Fuller of the Oxfordshire and Buckinghamshire Light Infantry.[36] This offers an excellent analysis of the practical application of railhead operations at unit level and contains a wealth of detail and useful tips. Its focus upon the technical aspects of military rail movement is indeed a far cry from his strategic concepts of mechanized warfare, which were only four years in the future.[37] Major A M Henniker, Royal Engineers, also made an important contribution through his lively article, *Troop Movements by Rail in the United Kingdom*,[38] which focused upon the interface with the railway companies.

annually, with a rotation on alternate years. 1/1 Warwickshire Battery RHA (TF), Royal Artillery Historical Society Autumn Meeting, 22 October 2008 at Larkhill.

30 For an explanation, see, Wayne D Cocroft, *Dangerous Energy, The Archaeology of Gunpowder and Military Explosives Manufacture* (Swindon: English Heritage, 2000), pp.97-102.

31 The Army utilized Army Form General (AFG) 996 to authorize the movement of explosive stores and AFG 980 for other dangerous goods. War Office, *King's Regulations and Orders for the Army 1912*, (London: HMSO, 1914), para 1471.

32 See, *Manual of Field Engineering 1911*, General Staff, War Office (London: HMSO, 1911), pp.84-103. In accordance with the regulations, no explosives, except Small Arms Ammunition (SAA) and small quantities of pyrotechnics, could be carried on passenger trains and there could only be five wagons carrying explosives in a freight train. Upon mobilization, the Government granted dispensations for the carriage of government explosives in order to expedite operations.

33 As an example, there were serious explosions at the Ardeer Nobel Factory in Scotland in 1913 and 1914, resulting in the deaths of 7 and 8 employees respectively; TNA CAB 37/132/17: Ardeer Explosion.

34 All iron and steel had to be covered with leather, cloth or lead sheets; David Evans, *Arming The Fleet, The Development of the Royal Ordnance Yards, 1770-1945* (Gosport: English Heritage, 2006), p.190.

35 During the Great War there were minor incidents and several serious ones involving munitions travelling by rail in the UK. The most dramatic, was the incident on the London to Brighton line of the London Brighton & South Coast Railway (LBSCR), in which three ammunition trains collided in Redstone Tunnel near Redhill in Surrey, with, miraculously, no explosion or loss of life. Edwin A Pratt, *British Railways and the Great War, Organization, Efforts, Difficulties and Achievements*, Vol. I (London: Selwyn & Blount, 1921), pp.466-474.

36 Fuller, 'Notes on the Entrainment of Troops', pp.184-213.

37 For an examination of his life, see, Anthony John Trythall *"Boney" Fuller: Soldier, Strategist, and Writer* (New Brunswick: Nautical & Aviation Publishing Company of America, 1989) and his theories, Brian Holden Reid, *J F C Fuller: Military Thinker* (New York: Palgrave Macmillan, 1990). See also, J P Harris, *Men, Ideas and Tanks, British Military Thought and Armoured Forces, 1903-1939* (Manchester: Manchester University Press, 1995).

38 Major A M Henniker RE, 'Troop Movements by Rail in the United Kingdom', *The Army Review*, Vol. VI, No 2, War Office (April 1914), pp.490-497. Colonel Henniker CBE as he became, was the Deputy Assistant Director (DAD) of Railways in the BEF and is the author of the comprehensive BOH, *Transportation on the Western Front, 1914-1918* (London: HMSO, 1937).

P4.1. Gun Powder Van; A shortage of these vans to meet mobilization requirements required dispensation from the Board of Trade to move ammunition and explosives in modified wagons. (Author & Jim Graham).

To War

As the count down to war began, the first elements of the Army assigned to operational tasks were not regulars but TF.[39] Special Service Sections (SSS) of the cyclist battalions and those of several infantry battalions were ordered to deploy on Tuesday 28 July 1914. 200 soldiers of 5th Black Watch (TF) left their camp at Crieff[40] in Perthshire Scotland, by rail, to commence digging defences around the River Tay estuary, whilst the SSS of 5th Green Howards and 5th Durham Light Infantry, departed from their summer ATC near Deganwy in North Wales on Monday 27 July to move into defensive positions at Scarborough and Hartlepool respectively. A critical initial task in early August 1914, executed by 1st London Division, was to detach the 1st London Brigade comprising four Royal Fusilier battalions to guard Key Points (KPs) on the London & South Western Railway (LSWR)

39 Naval reservists were mobilized on 2 August 1914 and began to travel to naval barracks by scheduled trains and 239 specials. A considerable number of naval reservists lived in naval and sea-ports; for these personnel, mobilization involved a walk or a tram ride.

40 Crieff was a station on the Perth to Balquhidder line of the Caledonian Railway. Crieff Station closed in 1964 as result of 'The Reshaping of British Railways Study' conducted by Doctor Beeching, although with the exception of Comrie, the other stations closed in 1951; the track was removed in the late 1960s. British Railways Board, *The Reshaping of British Railways,* (London: HMSO, 1963), p.123. Crieff was one of many stations that were crucial to the mobilization and deployment plan in 1914 but have long since been erased from the railway map; G Daniels & L Dench, *Passengers No More* (Shepperton: Ian Allan, 1964), provides a comprehensive summary.

network between London, Aldershot, Salisbury and Southampton.[41] 1st London Brigade was railing to summer ATC at Perham Down and Wareham on Sunday 2 August; the units were recalled to their drill halls before deployment by rail to railway security duties on 3 August.[42] These duties were not without considerable hazard; in the period August - December 1914, fourteen soldiers were killed after being struck by trains and another two in firearms incidents,[43] whilst another lost his life before full mobilization had commenced whilst on guard duty at Rochester on 30 July 1914,[44] perhaps being the first British soldier to lose his life as the result of the preparations for the coming conflict. Across the country, HD battalions, usually the 3rd Special Reserve (SR) and TF units were being mobilized, organized and deployed and often redeployed, to War Stations, usually KPs. Rail was fundamental to these operations, creating a flexibility that perhaps sometimes caused confusion rather than order but was nonetheless a quantum leap forward in military HD capability. As an example, the 3rd (SR) Battalion the Devonshire Regiment, having mobilized in Exeter, was dispatched by train to Fort Renney in Plymouth to complete task organization[45] to secure KPs in dispersed locations: the Severn Railway Tunnel, Southampton Docks, Marchwood Naval Magazine, Lloyds Signal Station at the Lizard and the Sennen Cove Cable Station. The Devonshire TF 4th, 5th and 6th Battalions were railed to the Salisbury Plain Training Area (SPTA) before concentrating at Newton Abbot in Devon for deployment on the North East Coast between Northumberland and Scarborough.[46]

Mobilizing and moving TF units and reservists in Scotland, especially those in the Highlands and Islands was a particular challenge, with a requirement to integrate inter-island and mainland sea crossings with the inter-connecting rail services.[47] Two peculiarities of the Army's recruiting and deployment systems generated many extended and complex rail movements for reservists. Contrary to popular belief, the County regimental systems did not create locally recruited units. The Duke of Cornwall's Light Infantry for example, recruited, in the period 1883-1900, only 12.1 per cent of its soldiers from within county boundaries,[48] which meant that in 1914 the majority of its reservists travelled, for mobilization, from London and the Midlands, to the regimental depot at Bodmin. From there, men allocated to the 1st Battalion, had to move by rail and sea to Ireland to join the unit, which was based at the Curragh before the battalion deployed

41 1st London Brigade of 1st London Division, was a formation assigned to the Central Force (CF) 2nd Army, and was the only formation specifically allocated to a non-mobile task; TNA WO 33/694: Central Forces Scheme, August 1914 and TNA WO 33/692: Distribution of Home Defence Forces, August 1914. The infrastructure of the London & South Western Railway (LSWR) between London, Aldershot, Salisbury and Southampton was critical to the deployment of the BEF.

42 Adrian Gray in *South Eastern and Chatham Railways, A Marriage of Convenience* (Midhurst: Middleton Press, 1998), records three security incidents on SECR metals during the deployment. One on Sunday 9 August, in which windows of a troop train were broken through small arms fire and another shooting at Graveney on Saturday 15 August. On Thursday 24 September, an attempt was made to derail a Boat Train at Grove Park by fastening an iron chair to the rail but a policeman identified the sabotage and a derailment was prevented; see pp.161-162.

43 Documents appertaining to the legal authority for the military, navy and police guarding railways to challenge and fire upon people are in TNA WO 32/13745. A sad incident relating to the death of a deaf man aged 27, James Edward Carroll in Aldershot, at the railway under-bridge in Church Lane East, on Thursday 20 August 1914 having been shot by a Territorial Force sentry, Private William Calfe of the 1st London Infantry Brigade, exposes that soldiers were not the only casualties.

44 Gray, *South Eastern and Chatham Railways*, p.210.

45 'Task Organization' is the arrangement of a unit to most effectively meet a specific mission, ensuring that each grouping has sufficient resources to complete its allocated tasks. Whilst not in 1914 use, this 21st Century term aptly describes the activity.

46 C T Atkinson, *The Devonshire Regiment, 1914-1918* (Exeter: Eland Brothers, 1926), pp.1-7.

47 TNA WO 33/661: Mobilisation - Scottish Command Scheme, Railway and Steamship Programmes, January 1914, which contains nine appendices.

48 In this period, the Royal Warwickshire Regiment was the most successful (72.3%) and the Cameron Highlanders the least (9.6%). For an excellent analysis, see David French, *Military Identities, The Regimental System, the British Army and the British People c1870-2000* (Oxford: Oxford University Press (OUP), 2005), pp.31-60.

P4.2. Railway Motive Power was critical to BEF deployment and sustainment. The WF Plan required through running to meet the schedules so it was critical that allocated locomotives could run upon different railway company metals. A Class 27 locomotive, of the Lancashire & Yorkshire Railway, a type introduced in 1889, still steaming on the North Norfolk Railway in 2011. (Author)

to France. Other Army Reservists had equally bizarre journeys. A Scottish soldier who lived in Plymouth having completed his Colour Service, travelled by rail to his Regimental Depot in Aberdeen. After his mobilization, he was issued a rail warrant to join his unit, 1st Battalion Gordon Highlanders,[49] stationed in Plymouth. Bizarrely, French and German reservists were also travelling on the railways, heading to Dover, Folkestone and Queenborough, courtesy of the South Eastern & Chatham Railways (SECR).

Chuffing and Juggling

Despite the reduced requirement for trains to support the RN because of the naval mobilization exercise in mid-July, after which, some reservists had remained on duty, the railway companies raised their concerns to the War Office about a full mobilization occurring on the Bank Holiday and requested that the second phase of TF ATC movements be deferred. Surprisingly, the Secretary

49 For details of the 1914 locations of all regular infantry and cavalry units, see, E A James OBE TD, *British Regiments, 1914-1918* (London: Samson Books, 1978) and Chris Kempton, *Locations of Regiments and Battalions of the British Army, 1 August 1914 and 1 September 1939* (Milton Keynes: Military Press, 2000).

of State refused,[50] which meant that many units were deploying to ATC when the mobilization order called them back to drill halls, causing the chaos predicted by the railway planners. A world away from the detailed minutiae of military planning and political wavering, it was therefore, the operating expertise of the commercial railway companies, with their ability to run short-notice special trains, and thereby recover these units, which was the first hot-planning contribution to mobilization.[51] The London & North Western Railway (LNWR) ran 76 specials and the LSWR, 48. Relative to capability, the Cambrian Railways (CR),[52] operating a mostly single line system,[53] executed the most impressive lift, moving 2,500 troops of an infantry brigade training at Llanidloes[54] in Central Wales to locations on the North East coast of England using eight specials within 10 hours of being given a Notice To Move (NTM) on Thursday 31 July 1914.[55] On Sunday 3 August, the Cambrian was also tasked with moving 9,000 Welsh Territorial soldiers from their camps at Aberystwyth (5,000) and Portmadoc (4,000) to their home billets in North and South Wales. This move was executed on Monday 4 August with 26 special trains in the middle of the Bank Holiday period;[56] a fine performance.

The first Expeditionary Force Train was X101 arriving North Camp & South Farnborough near Aldershot on M+1 at 0823 and departing at 0940. Travelling on SECR metals to via Redhill, it was scheduled to arrive at Newhaven at 1240.[57] The load was No 1 and 14 Unit Supply Depots, which were key logistic enablers for the movement of ammunition. X1905, the last planned train, on M+19, was Chatham (Main Line) to Southampton Docks conveying No 12 Stationary Hospital, departing 0730 and arriving 1305. The SECR were therefore, by one of those strange coincidences in the planning arena, responsible for both the first and the last trains shown in the schedule.[58] It is regrettable but understandable that most of the post-war divisional and regimental histories shed little light upon mobilization and the subsequent movement.[59] Three examples though, give

50 Whilst the evidence is not clear on this matter, it is probable that the Secretary of State, H H Asquith, who was also the Prime Minister, was either distracted by the gravity of wider events or was reluctant to offer the political impression of full army mobilization whilst the British Government was still making international attempts to prevent the outbreak of war.

51 The hot-planning capability of the railways had been noted by the planning staffs in War Office as a result of experience from the 1909 AAM, during which, the Great Western Railway (GWR) had proved particularly adept in meeting short-notice requirements; 'The Transport of an Army', *Great Western Railway Magazine*, Vol. XXI (November 1909), p.257.

52 The Cambrian Railways were not a shining example of an efficiently run commercial operation; the company went bankrupt twice. See, Rex Christiansen & R W Miller, *The Cambrian Railways*, Vols 1 & 2 (Newton Abbot: David & Charles, 1967 & nd but 1968).

53 Traffic on the Cambrian Railways was particularly difficult to work because the line was mainly single track with plenty of testing gradients. See, R W Kidner, *The Mid-Wales Railway*, Oakwood Library of Railway History, No 79, 2nd Edn (Usk: The Oakwood Press, 2003).

54 The track-bed of the railway that once transported soldiers to war has been buried under the tarmac of the A470. The impressive station building has though, been renovated and is used commercially.

55 Pratt, *British Railways and the Great War*, Vol. I, p.110.

56 Ibid, p.110.

57 The movement of the X101 offers an excellent example of the planning required. It travelled from North Camp to Ash Junction on SECR metals, then on LSWR tracks via Guildford to Shalford Junction to rejoin the SECR to Redhill Junction, from where it ran on LBSCR rails via Lewes to the Harbour Station at Newhaven. TNA WO 106/49B/3: Expeditionary Force Railway Timetables.

58 TNA WO 106/49B/3: Expeditionary Force Railway Timetables. Given the SECR's reputation for commuter train punctuality, one wonders whether the rail planning officers thought this was a wise decision. The Inspector of Army Ordnances Services observed, 'We arrive in our London offices by the early morning express trains with unfailing punctuality (provided we are not fortunate enough to be dependent upon the tender mercies of the South Eastern and Chatham Railway)'; Brigadier-General T Preston Battersby, 'The Army Ordnance Department and Corps', *The Army Review*, No 2, Vol. 2 (April 1912), p.428.

59 See, Lieutenant-Colonel Walter Temple Willcox CMG, *The 3rd (King's Own) Hussars in the Great War (1914-1919)* (London: John Murray, 1925), p.2: 'The details of mobilization may be of interest to a few, but in the interests of

P4.3. Llanidloes Station: a rural Welsh station, critical to mobilization in 1914 in 2011. The railway, which was so vital to the deployment plan now buried under black tar. (Author).

a flavour of the time. The 1st Battalion the King's Regiment marched from Talavera Barracks in Aldershot,[60] the leading company departing at 0600 on Sunday 12 August to arrive at Farnborough Station at approximately 0700. The departure of the battalion from station was a low-key affair, the regimental history recording that it was bade farewell by two or three porters, a few officers' wives and a sleepy paperboy.[61] The first of two trains left at 0800, arriving at Southampton docks at 0930.[62] The 1st Gloucesters had a similar experience:

> In the early hours of 12th August, the 1st Gloucesters without bands playing or any of the flag waving usually associated with the departure of troops to take part in an overseas war, paraded and marched to Bordon Station where they boarded two trains, the first of which arrived at Southampton at 5 am and the second at 6.30 am.[63]

The 1st Duke of Cornwall's Light Infantry entraining at the Curragh Siding in County Kildare with other units of 14th Infantry Brigade on Thursday 13 August had a different experience:

> The ladies of the Regiment bid the Battalion farewell and displayed typically British fortitude under the circumstances which were most trying. On reaching Dublin the troop train did not stop at the City Station but carried the Cornwalls into the Docks, alongside the vessel on

the many we will skip it'.

60 Talavera Barracks, constructed in the period 1856-1859 and demolished in 1959, formed part of Wellington Lines. In 2018, Talavera Park Married Quarters occupies the site.

61 Everard Wyrall, *The History of the King's Regiment (Liverpool) 1914-1919,* Vol. I, *1914-1915* (London: Edward Arnold, 1928), p.4.

62 Ibid, p.4. This was a relatively simple journey, the trains running from Farnborough to Southampton Docks via Winchester solely on LSWR metals.

63 Everard Wyrall, *The Gloucestershire Regiment in the War, 1914-1918* (London: Methuen, 1931), p.4.

> which they were to embark. Only authorised persons were allowed inside the dock gates to witness the departure of the troops, but enthusiastic crowds occupied the windows of every house overlooking the docks.[64]

In contrast to the public transit of personnel, the movement of munitions and supplies was more discreet. Ammunition for the BEF's Theatre Reserve was out-loaded from the Royal Arsenal at Woolwich to Newhaven and for the Ammunition Parks from Aldershot,[65] Hilsea and Tilbury to Southampton.[66] Ordnance stores were out-loaded from Weedon, clothing from Pimlico, 290,500 gallons of petroleum spirit[67] from civilian storage, to Avonmouth and 16,000 tons of supplies from the Supply Reserve Depot (SRD) at Woolwich to garrisons and Newhaven, and 24,000 tons from contractors to the same locations.[68] Another issue was the requirement to transport horse fodder. For the BEF, the daily requirement was 614 tons and for the TF, 904 tons,[69] although it was the bulk rather than the weight, which generated the logistic challenge. The initial out-load from Aldershot consisted of 1400 tons of War Office compressed hay followed by contracted stocks. For the most part, during mobilization, fodder was provided at key points along the route, so the amount of forage carried by the unit did not necessarily reflect the journey times. The most complex component during the deployment period was providing fodder and water for the TF infantry divisions[70] and mounted brigades, a problem made more challenging by the interesting and sometimes dynamic, itineraries that some of them had.

Artillery[71] and its associated ammunition both of which were critical to the Combat Effectiveness (CE) of the Expeditionary Force and Home Defence Forces,[72] was a very significant logistic movement issue as Table 4.1 illustrates, showing the types and weights of the guns[73] in field unit service, the weights of the projectiles[74] and the numbers of

64 Everard Wyrall, *The History of the Duke of Cornwall's Light Infantry, 1914-1919* (London: Methuen & Co, 1932), p.5.

65 The depot at Aldershot stored the ammunition for No 1 and No 2 Divisional Ammunitions Parks (DAP). Hilsea stored munitions for 3 & 6 DAPs plus Army Troops and the Cavalry Division. Tilbury stored ammunition for No 4 and 5 DAPs; TNA WO 106/49A/2: Revision of 1914 Programme.

66 The out-load of stocks for the Ammunition Parks took place on the 6th Day of Mobilization (DOM); the MT vehicles travelled separately; TNA WO 106/49A/2: Revision of 1914 Programme.

67 275,000 gallons were MT spirit and 15,500 for aviation. Anglo-American was contracted to supply 200,000 gallons of MT spirit and the aviation fuel; Carlea, Capel & Leonard, 25,000 gallons with in 48 hours of the order and 25,000 within four days, whilst the Gas Lighting Improvement Company had contracted to an immediate delivery of 25,000. Figures extracted from a draft document on petroleum planning dated 2 January 1913 in TNA WO 106/49A/1: Expeditionary Force, History of the Growth of the Scheme.

68 TNA WO 106/49A/2: Expeditionary Force to France, Sect x, Supplies. Petroleum spirit was shipped as follows: 75% in 50 gallon barrels and 25% in 2 gallon tins.

69 Forage consisted of oats and hay. In camp, heavy draught horses were allocated 15 lbs of oats per day, others between 10 and 12. Draught horses were rationed for 16 lbs of hay per day, the rest, 12 lbs. See, FSPB 14, p.169.

70 For details of ORBATs, see, Major A F Becke (Comp), BOH, *Order of Battle, Divisions*, Part 2A, *The Territorial Force Mounted Divisions and The 1st-Line Territorial Force Divisions (42th-56th)* (London: HMSO, 1936).

71 These units were defined as Royal Horse Artillery (RHA) supporting cavalry units and Royal Field Artillery (RFA) for other formations. Guns of the coastal artillery, manned by the Royal Garrison Artillery (RGA) are not shown but ammunition and charges for them were moved by rail to specified railheads and thence by Mechanical Transport (MT) or Horse Transport (HT) to the fortified batteries. Six siege batteries RGA with 6 inch howitzers, were deployed to France and Belgium by October 1914 plus a detachment from 7 Siege Battery RGA, to man the sole 9.2 inch howitzer; TNA WO 95/4052/11: 10 Company (No 2 Railway) RE, WD.

72 The 15 pdrs were of two types. The QF equipped TF artillery units supporting cavalry brigades and the BLC, TF artillery units in infantry divisions. The guns required different ammunition, creating an additional logistic burden.

73 For technical details of these guns, see, Hogg, *Allied Artillery of World War One*. For ammunition details, see, *Treatise on Ammunition*, War Office, 1915 (10th Edition). This publication was Joint Service and encompassed all navy and army munitions.

74 Weights and dimensions extracted from *Treatise on Ammunition*, Table No 19, Shell BL, BLC, QF and QFC Shrapnel, pp.186-191.

guns[75] and shells, likely to be moved in the initial mobilization period, which included out-loads for the BEF and Home Defence[76]. The 18 pdr ammunition,[77] was by a clear margin, the most numerically significant.[78] The specialist heavy artillery of the 9.2 inch howitzer had yet to enter general service,[79] although the railways were to play a key role its urgent operational deployment.[80]

Table 4.1
Field Unit Artillery – 1914[81]

Piece	Weight*	Population	Projectile*	Quantity	Remarks
13 pdr	1014	30	12.50 lb / 76.2 mm	30,000	Through Newhaven to France
15 pdr QF	1031	56	18.50 lb / 76.2 mm	14,784	TF - UK HD
15 pdr BLC	1441	512	14.00 lb/ 76.2 mm	135,168	TF - UK HD
18 pdr	1369	318	14.00 lb/ 84 mm	318,000	Through Newhaven to France
60 pdr	4484	24	60.00 lb/ 127 mm	12,000	Through Newhaven to France
4.5 inch (How)	1369	108	35.00 lb/ 114 mm	86,400	Through Newhaven to France
4.7 inch	3830	56	45.00 lb/ 119 mm	7,840	TF - UK HD
5 inch (How)	1216	32	50.00 lb /127 mm	4,000	TF - UK HD
6 inch (How)	3704	24	100.25 lb/ 152 mm	12,000	Through Newhaven to France
9.2 inch (How)	15286	1	380.00 lb/ 234 mm	Not Known	In reserve

* Weight in Imperial Pounds; calibre in mm

75 Unit War Establishment. War Maintenance Reserve (WMR) figures are in addition. For example, 45 x 4.5 inch Howitzers were in WMR in 1914.

76 The Home Defence scales of ammunition are based on 50% of BEF holdings. The quantities for initial movement are also proportionally as well as mathematically less because UK Base holdings remained in the depot, whilst the BEF Base ammunition had to be shipped to France. QMG 10/2812 in TNA WO 106/49A/2 notes the proposal to retain in the UK, 50% of the ammunition, explosives and stores allocated to the BEF. Ammunition reserves in UK depots for BEF guns were therefore, probably as follows: 13 pdr (27,000 - 900 rpg) 18 pdr (159,000 - 500 rpg) 4.5 inch (43,200 - 400 rpg) and 60 pdr (12,000 - 500 rpg). Weapon population calculated from divisional ORBATs at 6 x guns per battery for BEF units and 4 x guns per battery for HD, except for the 60 pdr and 6 inch howitzer at four per battery.

77 The in-Theatre 1,000 rounds per gun (rpg) was distributed thus: 24 in limbers, 152 in battery transport, 76 in the Brigade Ammunition Column and 126 in the Divisional Ammunition Column, totalling 378. The balance of 622 was held in ASC Ammunition Parks and AOC Theatre ammunition depots.

78 Whilst 318,000 appears to be a considerable quantity, 5,372,000 rounds of 18 pdr were fired in the period 8 August - 6 September 1918. See, War Office, *Statistics of the Military Effort of the British Empire during the Great War 1914-1920* (MEBE) (HMSO, 1922), p.481, Table 4 - Ammunition Expenditure in France.

79 Secondary sources are at variance in relation to the numbers of 9.2 inch howitzers available in August 1914. Most state that none were in service. Ian V Hogg in *Allied Artillery of World War One* (Marlborough: Crowood Press, 1998) suggests that the Royal Artillery was completing trials on a prototype and that several others were at different stages of manufacture at the Coventry Ordnance Works.

80 The WD of 10 Company (No 2 Railway) clarifies that a detachment, commanded by Lieutenant Wellesley, from 10 Company RE, deployed to Ostend sailing from the Woolwich Arsenal Wharf on the SS *Pentwyn* on Monday 5 October 1914 to support 7 Siege Battery Royal Garrison Artillery. 10 Company commenced the construction of one mile of SGR Permanent Way for a 9.2 inch railway mounted gun and assisted in the railway aspects of its firing, before recovering to the UK arriving Avonmouth on Saturday 24 October via Le Harve on the SS *Cheniston*. TNA WO 95/4052/11: 10 Company (No 2 Railway) RE, WD.

81 The information in this table has been compiled from several primary and secondary sources and correlate with the figures shown in the Mowatt Modified Reserve Tables. The sources include: *The Annual Return of the Territorial Force for the Year 1908*, Command 4496 (London: HMSO, 1909); FSPB 14, BOH, *Ministry of Munitions*, Vol. I, *Industrial Mobilization 1914-15* (HMSO, 1922); Major A F Becke (Comp) BOH, *Order of Battle, Divisions*, Part 1 - *The Regular British Divisions* (London: HMSO, 1935); Becke, BOH, *Order of Battle, Divisions*, Part 2 A; General Sir Martin Farndale KCB, *History of the Royal Regiment of Artillery, Western Front 1914-18* (Woolwich: Royal Artillery Institution, 1986).

Whilst the BEF was moving to the Channel embarkation ports, Home Defence Force (HDF) units,[82] mostly from the Territorial Force, were being railed to their concentration areas.[83] The movement of the TF was a complex task because of its peacetime footprint. Excluding Headquarters companies, each of the 14 TF infantry divisions had between 70 and 80 sub-units, often based in as many or more locations. In actuality, the difficulties were compounded because when mobilization was declared, seven of the divisions were either at, or entraining for, ATC. The movement planners, whilst adept at their task and having foreseen the worst-case scenario, were restricted in their ability to generate dynamic flexibility not only by the geographic dispersion but also because of the communications of the day; that they achieved what they did is a credit to their dedication and industry. Then, just to tax the operations staff a little more, the War Office decided to form, from the TF Mounted Brigades,[84] two mounted divisions. The 1st Mounted Division, with its brigades[85] from Eastern England and counties from Nottinghamshire in the North to Berkshire in the South concentrated initially around Bury Saint Edmunds, Diss and Ipswich before redeploying to Newbury in late August. The 2nd Mounted Division was formed on 2 September and assembled around Churn before being deployed in November as a reserve in defence of the North and East Norfolk coast. The 1914 plan also involved the East and West Lancashire Divisions[86] deploying to Ireland. Whilst the East Lancashire Division's battalion advance parties for horse purchase and billeting travelled to Ireland, the divisional deployments were cancelled and the parties recalled.[87] The table below clearly illustrates the complexity of the TF movement plan.

Table 4.2

TF Divisions – Outline Movement Plan[88]

Formation	Location on Mobilization	Movement
1st Mounted Division	Garrison Duty Station (GDS)	HDS – Norfolk/Suffolk-Newbury
2nd Mounted Division	Garrison Duty Station	HDS – Churn – Norfolk
1st London (TF)	Annual Training Camp (ATC)	GDS – Home Defence Stations (HDS) – 1st X to Malta
2nd London (TF)	Salisbury Plain Training Area	GDS – HDS (St Albans)
Home Counties (TF)	Garrison Duty Station	GDS – HDS – India (via Southampton)
Wessex (TF)	Salisbury Plain Training Area	HDS – GDS – India (via Southampton)

82 The distribution of Home Forces on 31 August 1914 is listed in TNA WO 153/115: Distribution of Home Forces, 31 August 1914.

83 Command Home Defence railway plans are held in the TNA WO 33/654: Western Command and WO 33/670: Irish Command.

84 There were 14 mounted brigades, each of three yeomanry regiments, based on a geographical foot-print. In addition, there were another 14 regiments, one assigned to each TF infantry division. For details, see, *The Annual Return of the Territorial Force for the Year 1908*.

85 Eastern, 1st South Midland, 2nd South Midland and Nottinghamshire & Derbyshire.

86 42nd (East Lancashire) Division deployed to Egypt and then Gallipoli before serving in France; Becke, BOH, *Order of Battle of Divisions*, Part 2A, pp.35-41. 55th (West Lancashire) Division was held in the UK, its infantry units reinforcing the BEF until it was disbanded and the remaining capability transferred to what became 57th (West Lancashire) Division. 55th Division was reformed in France in 1916, many of its original units returning to the fold; Ibid, pp.133-139.

87 TNA WO 95/4594: 1/7th Battalion Lancashire Fusiliers, WD, 1 August 1914 - 30 April 1915 and TNA WO 95/459: 1/5 th Battalion East Lancashire Regiment, WD, 1 August 1914 - 31 May 1915.

88 Table compiled from information in *The Annual Return of the Territorial Force for the Year 1908* and Becke, BOH, *Order of Battle, Divisions*, Part 2A.

North Midland (TF)	Garrison Duty Station	HDS (Luton)
South Midland (TF)	Garrison Duty Station	HDS (Chelmsford)
East Anglian (TF)	Annual Training Camp	GDS – HDS (Chelmsford) – Norfolk
East Lancashire (TF)	Garrison Duty Station	Ireland (CX). Egypt (via Southampton)
West Lancashire (TF)	Annual Training Camp	GDS – Ireland (CX) -HDS
West Riding (TF)	Annual Training Camp	GDS – HDS
Northumbrian (TF)	Annual Training Camp	GDS – HDS (Tyne Defences)
Highland (TF)	Garrison Duty Station	HDS (Bedford)
Lowland (TF)	Garrison Duty Station	HDS (Scottish Defence – East Coast)
Welsh (TF)	Garrison Duty Station	HDS (Northampton)

Some units had the misfortune to be directed from one task and thus location, to another. Few however, were as well travelled as the 2nd Battalion Lancashire Fusiliers, a unit in 12th Infantry Brigade. The battalion's travels were generated by the decision to retain the 4th Infantry Division, of which 12th Brigade was a component, for Home Defence operations.[89] The table below, clearly summarizes, how trying this period was for units, although it does not show the marching required to and from railway stations for local billeting.

Table 4.3

2nd Battalion Lancashire Fusiliers – Movements in mid-August 1914[90]

Date	Movement	From	To	Remarks
Saturday 8	Rail	Dover	Cromer	
Tuesday 11	Rail	Cromer	Norwich	
Thursday 13	March	Norwich	Costessy	5 miles
Monday 17	March	Costessy	Norwich	5 miles
Monday 17	Rail	Norwich	North Wembley	
Friday 21	Rail	North Wembley	Southampton	
Saturday 22	Rail	Southampton	Boulogne	SS *Saturnia*

The frequent relocations of the TF Queen's Own Oxfordshire Hussars (QOOH) of the 2nd South Midland Mounted Brigade, provides an excellent example of the dynamic movement tasks the railways companies were expected to deliver. The three Sabre Squadrons deployed to Reading from their Home Stations during Tuesday 11 - Wednesday 12 August 1914. A Squadron from Oxford and C Squadron from Henley-upon-Thames marched by road, whilst D Squadron travelled

89 There is an interesting historical development to this deployment. According to the papers, published in 2011, of the GOC 4th Division, Major-General Snow, the movement of 12th Brigade to Cromer was ordered by Winston Churchill, the First Lord of the Admiralty. It appears that Mrs Churchill was playing golf at Sheringham and commented to her husband that she had seen no troops. Snow is scathing on the deployment, noting its military uselessness and its adverse affect upon training and resources. See, Dan Snow & Mark Pottle, *The Confusion of Command, The Memoirs of Lieutenant-General Sir Thomas D'Oyly 'Snowball' Snow, 1914 -1918* (London: Frontline Books, 2011), p.11 & p.52.

90 Details compiled from Major-General J C Latter CBE MC, *The History of the Lancashire Fusiliers, 1914-1918*, Vol. I (Aldershot: Gale & Polden, 1949), p.6.

by train from Banbury. On Saturday 15 August, QOOH entrained for Bury Saint Edmunds in Suffolk before road marching to Thetford in Norfolk on Thursday 20. On Thursday 27 August, the QOOH travelled North to East Dereham before moving to Blickling in North Norfolk the next day.[91] Warned for Egypt, with preparations required for a rail move to Southampton, an order then cancelled, the QOOH marched to Cromer on Saturday 29, entraining in three trains for Churn Camping Ground five miles South of Didcot on Sunday 30, a journey which took eight hours via Norwich, Cambridge, Bletchley and Oxford.[92]

The speed of entrainment, well practised on AAM, was critical during mobilization movement. Delays to loading quickly created interruptions to schedules, dislocation of train paths, disruption to shipping and an adverse impact upon stock re-circulation. The pressures to avoid delays were constant but even in good weather in daylight there was little room for error; during darkness, loading was much more complex, particularly when significant numbers of horses were involved. The demands of a night load, especially with many requisitioned horses unused to rail travel,[93] are well illustrated by the experiences of D Squadron QOOH loading at Banbury Station:

> But any feelings of sentiment or romance were quickly dispelled on reaching the station, where a scene of much bustle and activity took place. The process of entraining some 150 horses, all quite unused to such adventure, in the dark and in the rather inadequate sidings not constructed to deal with such large numbers, occupied nearly two hours and entailed a good deal of shouting by officers and sergeants and much perspiration by the men.[94]

Subsequent Operations

Once the movement of the BEF and HDF was underway, the railways focused their attention on the subsequent tasks,[95] not all of which had been planned in much detail. One that had was the contribution to medical evacuation in the UK and the railways' workshops were busily engaged in converting rolling stock to create military and naval ambulance trains.[96] The War Office maintained one permanent train in peacetime for operations in the UK.[97] Known officially as

91 Inevitably accidents were a feature of these moves. Entering East Dereham through the hamlet of Toftwood, the black mare hauling a ration cart bolted downhill and the cart overturned resulting in the spare horse-shoes, nails and rations being spread across the road; Adrian Keith-Falconer, *The Oxfordshire Hussars in the Great War* (London: John Murray, 1927), p.20.

92 Ibid, pp.19-21. The rumour of Russian troops transiting through UK to France may have been reinforced by this move, created by the soldiers removing their tunics because of the heat of the August day and travelling in their white under-shirts. This journey required the troop trains to travel across the metals of the Great Eastern Railway (GER) the London & North Western Railway (LNWR) and the Great Western Railway (GWR).

93 Long distance travel was a particular concern especially in the summer with watering and ventilation two key issues. The regimental histories of units located in Scotland recorded the loss of horses during the journey to Southampton, including an incident in which, a horse carcass was removed from the rail wagon and left on the platform of Newcastle Station. 1st Battalion, Cameronians (Scottish Rifles) was particularly unfortunate in this respect, having several dead animals on arrival at Southampton, allegedly caused by the low internal height of the cattle wagons that were allocated but watering and ventilation may have also have influenced this outcome.

94 Keith-Falconer, *Oxfordshire Hussars*, pp.18-19.

95 One hidden task was the provision of military manpower. By 15 August 1914, 27,600 railway staff had been mobilized (TF and Reserves) or volunteered for military service. In mid-September, the War Office directed recruiting offices not to accept railwaymen unless they had a certificate of release from their company. See, Pratt, *British Railways and the Great War*, Vol. I, pp.348-378.

96 For a history of ambulance train operations in the British Armed Forces, see, John H Plumridge, *Hospital Ships and Ambulance Trains* (London: Seeley Service, 1975).

97 The Army, through 79 Railway Squadron RCT/RLC and the Army Medical Services (AMS) Ambulance Train Group (V) maintained an ambulance train capability in Germany until the demise of the British Army of the Rhine (BAOR). In 2010, some of the stock was slowly rusting away in a siding at Montzen, near Aachen. The UK based

the War Office Ambulance Train (WOAT)[98] and informally as the 'Netley Coaches',[99] it operated between Southampton Docks and the Netley Military Hospital[100] and could transport 75 stretcher cases but was reinforced in August 1914 with LSWR passenger coaches for sitting patients. Working to specifications and drawings agreed with the staff of the Director General Army Medical Services (DGAMS), seven companies also produced 12 ambulance trains,[101] each approximately 350 feet in length and weighing 250 tons. Capable of transporting 100 stretcher cases in five ward coaches, the trains also had the following carriages: pharmacy, including a treatment room, offices and medical stores, kitchen-diner, staff accommodation and a stores wagon. Two passenger coaches were provided for sitting casualties; supporting equipment, was provided by the War Office, from its Ambulance Train Mobilization Store. These 'company' trains retained their liveries but had the Red Cross on the roofs and sides. All the trains were ready for operations by the end of August, a tribute to the planners, engineers and craftsmen.[102]

Unforeseen by the military planners was the continuation of the holiday trade in the UK and to Europe.[103] Whilst ammunition was being out-loaded through the port of Newhaven, and the Germans marched across Belgium and into France, on the East Anglian coast of England, near Lowestoft, amongst various incidents, Territorial soldiers were hastily digging trenches but close by, children were constructing sandcastles on the beach, whilst a pleasure steamer plied its trade through a convoy of Royal Navy minesweepers.[104] Little wonder that the GOC 4th Division, responsible for anti-invasion operations in the area noted that Peace and War were 'curiously mixed' and recorded his frustration that 'The War Office knew little of what was required, the entire General Staff having vanished on mobilisation, the exact moment when they were most required'.[105] The LBSCR continued to issue rail and ferry tickets to Italy, Spain, Switzerland and France, except for the *Nord* and *Est* railway areas, but also issued a directive banning Germans, Austrians and Hungarians from travelling on the Newhaven-Dieppe route although because passports were not required, it could not be enforced.[106] Despite its commitment to mobilization and deployment, the LSWR maintained its rail and sea services to Le Harve and the Channel Islands. Another unforeseen requirement was to entrain at the South East Ports (SEP) American, Belgian and British refugees fleeing from the Continent. Much work was also conducted to support maturing anti-invasion planning. Critical to this, was the definition of Evacuation Areas, mainly on the East Coast. Railway company operating managers began to study service suspension, infrastructure denial, evacuation of locomotives and stock, and the provision of armoured trains.

capability was conceptually much as it was in 1914, with British Rail contracted to convert stock.

98 No 1 Naval Ambulance Train comprised vehicles from the LNWR; the consist was a guards van for stores, seven compartment corridor coaches, two cot coaches, day coach, three cot coaches, stores coach, kitchen diner, family saloon and rear guards van. The cot coaches were converted from parcels vans, using equipment funded and provided by the Admiralty. 574 feet in length, its planned capacity was 120 cot cases and 72 sitting but the maximum it carried in 1914 on a move, was 363 patients.

99 The War Office coaches were fitted with the Westinghouse air-braking system, an advanced feature for the period.

100 For details, see, J R Fairman, *Netley Hospital and its Railways* (Southampton) Kingfisher Railway Productions, 1984.

101 GCR (2) GER (1) GWR (2) LNWR (3) MR (2) L&Y (1) and LSWR (1).

102 The first live ambulance train move, with WOAT, was conducted, from Southampton to Netley, on Monday 24 August 1914, only 48 hours after first contact, near Obourg, between the 4th Dragoon Guards and the German Army. The first company train, from the GCR, ran the route on Friday 28 August with 62 lying and 125 sitting casualties.

103 Despite the war, the German language signs at Charing Cross remained in place at Charing Cross Station until August 1916; Gray, *South Eastern and Chatham Railways*, p.162.

104 Snow & Pottle, *Confusion of Command*, p.9.

105 Ibid, pp.9-12.

106 This is not an isolated incident in military history. In 1993, as the war raged in Bosnia, Eastern European tourists mingled with United Nations soldiers deploying through Split Airport.

Concurrently, assessments of the transportation requirements to support the evacuation of the civil population and hospitals, military and civilian, were put in hand. This work matured with a major anti-invasion exercise in November 1914 focused upon the North Norfolk coast. Military deployment, although not fully executed, required 840 trains with planning for hundreds more to support civilian evacuation. The two key companies involved, the Great Eastern Railway and the Midland & Great Northern Railway (M&GNR)[107] did well to deliver this capability, which also involved closing the railway system on Tuesday 17 November between Norwich, Cromer and Sheringham to prevent German use of the facilities.[108] In the meantime, trains were run to deploy, via Southampton, the East Lancashire Division (-) to Egypt on 10 September, the Wessex Division (-) to India on 9 October and the Home Counties Division (-) also to India, on 30 October. Ammunition flowed by rail from industry to depots and thence to the ports, whilst drafts of soldiers travelled to France from regimental depots across the United Kingdom. As if these tasks placed insufficient demands upon the railways, units, equipment and individuals were returning from abroad to be reorganized in the UK, and an increasing flow of damaged materiel from France arrived for repair as the importance of a Reverse Logistics chain became clear.

Conclusion

The railways of the United Kingdom played a fundamental and critical role in mobilizing, deploying and supplying British Army both in France and within the UK during August and September 1914. Of critical significance, was the delivery of the BEF to the Sea Ports of Embarkation within the allocated planning times, a process that ensured it was able to take its place in the Line, in France and Belgium. The Secretary of State for War was clear about the contribution of the railways: "I have to remark that.........the railway companies, in the all-important matter of transport facilities have more than justified the complete confidence reposed in them by the War Office, all grades of railway services having laboured with untiring energy and patience."[109]

The scope, size and timeframe of the BEF's planned deployment in 1914 was far greater than the Armed Services had experience of and the effective delivery of the mobilization and deployment was a tribute to the meticulous planning conducted by military and civilian logisticians. The contribution, in 1914, of the railways and railwaymen of Britain undoubtedly changed the course of events in France, and possibly, the outcome of the Great War and thus the future of Europe. Whilst it may be over a century since these momentous events occurred, the industry, diligence, skill and intelligence of the people who were involved in this complex operation are still marvels to behold.

107 Wags called it the 'Muddle & Go Nowhere Railway'. Given the paucity of railways and a not particularly resilient road system in the region in 2018, it is a shame it has gone.

108 The railway from Norwich to Sheringham via Cromer remains operational as part of the National Railway Network (NRN). The section from Sheringham to Holt through Weybourne has been preserved and runs for 5.25 miles as the North Norfolk Railway (NNR) often known as the Poppy Line. Travelling on these metals in the 21st Century it is difficult to imagine the dramatic events that unfolded.

109 Lord Kitchener, House of Lords, 25 August 1914.

Part II

Finding A Way

5

Muddling Through

Wully Robertson, agile operational logistics and the salvation of the British Expeditionary Force in 1914

100 Years on

In the late summer and early autumn of 1914, the British Expeditionary Force (BEF)[1] was engaged in a brutal fight[2] in the fields and villages of Belgium and Northern France.[3] On Monday 7 September, as the BEF advanced across the Grand Morin,[4] the BEF's Commander-in-Chief, Field Marshal Sir John French, wrote in his despatch of the positive work undertaken by his Quartermaster General (QMG): 'Major-General Sir William Robertson[5] has met what appeared to be an almost insuperable difficulties with his characteristic energy, skill and determination; and it is largely owing to his exertions that the hardships and sufferings of the troops - inseparable from such operations - were not much greater'.[6] At face value, these words were indeed high praise but they failed to give the QMG the true accolades he and his logisticians deserved. On the same day, Wully Robertson wrote to his counterpart at the War Office, General John Cowans,[7] in a rather different vein on

1 For an explanation of the BEF's organization, see, Major A F Becke (Comp) BOH, *Order of Battle of Divisions*, Part I, *The Regular British Divisions* (London: HMSO, 1935). For a description of the strategic construct of which the BEF was a part, see, John Gooch, *The Plans of War, The General Staff and British Military Strategy c1900-1916* (London: Routledge & Kegan Paul, 1974).

2 The many regimental histories give an excellent description of the fighting at battalion level. At the divisional level, there is much less choice; of the 12 British divisions deployed as part of the BEF in 1914, only the 2nd, 5th, 7th, and 8th have post Great War histories, although a recent addition is Grahame P Kingston, *History of the 4th (British) Infantry Division: 1914-1919* (London: London Press, 2018).

3 For a detailed description of operations, see, Brigadier-General Sir James E Edmonds CB CMG psc, BOH, *Military Operations, France and Belgium 1914*, Vol. I, *Mons, The Retreat to the Seine, the Marne and the Aisne, August - October* 1914 (London: Macmillan, 1922). David Escoli, *The Mons Star, The British Expeditionary Force 1914*, (London: Harrap, 1981) offers a broad view. For more recent and detailed assessments, see, Robin Neillands, *The Old Contemptibles, The British Expeditionary Force 1914* (London: John Murray, 2004) and Allan Mallinson, 1914, *Fight the Good Fight, Britain, The Army & the Coming of the First World War* (London: Bantam Press, 2013). Also, Adrian Gilbert *The Challenge of Battle, The Real Story of the British Army in 1914* (Oxford: Osprey, 2013) and Peter Hart, *Fire and Movement, The British Expeditionary Force and the Campaign of 1914* (Oxford: Oxford University Press (OUP) 2015). For a revisionist and controversial view of the BEF, see, Terence Zuber, *The Mons Myth, A Reassessment of the Battle*, Terence Zuber (Stroud: The History Press, 2010). For a penetrating review of the senior military actors, see the engaging Spencer Jones (Ed.) *Stemming The Tide, Officers and Leadership in the British Expeditionary Force 1914*, Wolverhampton Military Series, (Solihull: Helion, 2013).

4 The Grand Morin is the left tributary of the River Marne and flows for 73 miles from its source near the village of Lachy to the Marne at Esbly, flowing West through the towns of Esternay, La Ferte-Gaucher, Coulommiers and Crecy-la-Chapelle.

5 He wrote an autobiography, entitled, perhaps unsurprisingly, *From Private to Field-Marshal* (London: Constable, 1921).

6 Sir John French Despatch, dated 7 September 1914, in John Grehan and Martin Mace (Comp), *Despatches from the Western Front, 1914-1916* (Barnsley: Pen & Sword, 2013), p.7.

7 For a biography, see, Major Desmond Chapman-Huston & Major Owen Rutter *General Sir John Cowans, GCB*

a rather more pressing matter: "We have no railway of our own but are entirely in the hands of the French authorities. They are more or less off their heads and the railways hereabouts are in a state of chaos, however, we shall no doubt muddle through."[8] This situation was described in less emotional terms by a contemporary railway staff officer, who also the noted that the experience was particularly challenging because in recent Imperial operations the British usually had direct influence, if not control of the Colonial Government railway capability.

> In France we are dependent upon transport by railways (some owned by the State, others by private companies) which are the property of an allied nation, over which, consequently, we have no direct control, and which are staffed by French officials who rarely have any knowledge of the English language. The difficulties of the situation are obvious, and they have only been overcome by the exercise of considerable tact by both sides, and the great - and, to many people, unsuspected - talent of the French nation for organization.[9]

There was though, some cause for optimism; not only was the BEF advancing on a three corps front after days of tiring withdrawal,[10] involving approximately 200 miles of marching but also the left flank of III Corps rested on Crecy, which no doubted lifted many an English spirit.[11] Whilst from the logistic perspective,[12] the immediate danger of the BEF being cut off from its Line of Communication (LOC)[13] had passed, the threat had not disappeared and the QMG was keenly aware of the requirement for the BEF not only to conform to French operational tempo[14] but also for its logisticians to replenish an army now on the advance after such a demanding retirement. It would be no easy task but Wully Robertson was not a man to be overwhelmed by a challenge; indeed, he was the epitome of that old cliché, 'when the going gets tough, the tough get going'. The Man and the Moment had met.

As the senior logistician within the General Headquarters (GHQ) of the BEF, Robertson was faced with a demanding scale of logistic challenges,[15] such that all pre-war organizational assumptions were on trial. Creative thinking and decisive actions would be critical for the survival of the BEF and its logisticians were not found wanting. It was indeed fortunate that it was in Robertson's character to view his appointment as requiring him to focus on ensuring that important

GCMG, *The Quartermaster-General of the Great War* (London: Hutchinson, 1924) (Two volumes).

8 Letter from Robertson to Cowans dated 7 September 1914; TNA WO 107/13: QMG and IGC Correspondence, Stores and Equipment, 1 September - 31 December 1914.

9 Captain R Bonham-Smith, 'Railway Transport Arrangements in France', *Journal of the Royal United Service Institution, (JRUSI)* Vol. LXI (February 1916), p.48. This arrangement though, was clearly explained in General Staff, *Field Service Regulations* (FSR) Part II, *Organization and Administration*, War Office (London: HMSO, 1909) (reprinted, with amendments to October, 1914) Chp VIII, Transport, Sect 60, Technical Railway Personnel, p.92.

10 For an engaging reflective review of the withdrawal, see, the late Richard Holmes, *Riding the Retreat, Mons to the Marne 1914 Revisited* (London: Jonathan Cape, 1995).

11 For a detailed description of operations from a British perspective from Mons to the Aisne, see, Edmonds, BOH, *France and Belgium 1914*, Vol. I, pp.75-95; Antony Bird, *Gentlemen, We Will Stand and Fight, Le Cateau, 1914* (Marlborough: Crowood Press, 2008) and Jerry Murland, *Retreat and Rearguard 1914, The BEF's Actions from Mons to the Marne* (Barnsley: Pen & Sword, 2011).

12 For a brief summary of the logistic issues relating to the early part of this period, see, Roger G Miller, 'The Logistics of the British Expeditionary Force, 4 August to 5 September 1914', *Journal of Military Affairs*, XLIII (3) October 1979, pp.133-138.

13 For a resume of the LOC roles, units and responsibilities, see Lt-Col H M E Brunker, *Notes on Organization and Equipment*, 6th Edn (London: William Clowes and Sons, 1909), pp.232-241.

14 The British Army describes 'tempo as the rhythm or rate of activity on operations, relative to the enemy'; *Army Doctrine Publication (ADP)* Vol. 1, *Operations*, HQDT/18/34/46, Army Code No 71565 (UK MOD, 1994), pp.2-9 to 2-10.

15 This article examines logistics at the operational level. Logistics at division and below deserves its own study, especially for the cavalry divisions, the operations of which, posed specific challenges to the logisticians.

tasks were not left undone rather than focusing on enacting them.[16] To add to the challenge, the General Staff (GS)[17] component of GHQ did not operate coherently,[18] placing additional pressures upon the QMG and the Adjutant General (AG).[19] As an example, the Sub-Chief of Staff, Major-General Henry Wilson, clearly in a flap, telegraphed, informally on Thursday 27 August 1914 to the General-Officer-Commanding (GOC) 4th Division: 'From Henry to Snowball:[20] 'Throw overboard all ammunition and impediments not absolutely required, and load up your lame ducks on all transport, horse and mechanical, and hustle along'.[21] To compound the problem, GHQ issued Operation Order 9 the same day, which included the following instructions at Paragraph 6: 'All ammunition on wagons not absolutely required and other impedimenta will be unloaded and officers and men carried to the full capacity of all transport, both horse and mechanical'.[22]

These orders were to have an adverse affect upon the delivery of logistic support, although whatever Robertson thought of them, he made no record in his autobiography; presumably it was not fit to print. It does however, indicate that the GHQ Operations element was not administratively fully competent,[23] and GHQ was most fortunate in having a QMG who was. Robertson's note to General Cowans, and given the trying circumstances he could be forgiven for it, was a strange mixture of over and understatement, combined with a balance of pessimism and optimism but oddly, in effect, all correct in fact. The Host Nation (HN) controlled and operated the BEF's key artery of transportation, and the rail operations on it,[24] so critical to the BEF's logistics, had been severely disrupted.[25] Whether the French were indeed 'off their heads',[26] or more likely, attempting to prioritise the French Army's logistic requirements over the BEF's within an operational environment that was clearly not delivering to plan, remains open to discussion but his concern is obvious. He and his logisticians however, did much more than 'muddle through';[27] they kept the BEF in the line and in the fight, thereby sustaining French morale and ensuring their forces in the field continued to erode German offensive capability. It was an amazing feat but one

16 Robertson, *Private to Field-Marshal*, p.200.

17 In a 1914 Headquarters, the General Staff element, responsible for Operations, was termed G. The AG's Branch, abbreviated to 'A' was responsible for people, including discipline, morale, military law, personnel, casualties, reinforcements and the medical and sanitary services, whilst the Quartermaster-General's staff focused on logistics, Q. In 2020, British Army terminology assigns General Staff branches in a different way: G (Operations) is G2 (Intelligence & Security) G3 (Operations) G5 (Plans) G6 (Command Information) and G7 (Training). A (Adjutant-General) is G1 (Personnel) G8 (Finance and Resources) and G9 (Civil-Military) whilst Q (Quartermaster) is G4 (Logistics & Infrastructure).

18 For an assessment of the BEF's command issues, see, Nikolas Gardner *Trial By Fire, Command and the British Expeditionary Force in 1914* (Westport Connecticut & London: Praeger, 2013) and for discussion of the internal GHQ issues, pp.33-71.

19 Major-General Sir C F N Macready KCB; bizarrely, the Deputy Adjutant-General was the same rank.

20 Major-General T D'Oyly Snow, later GOC 27th Division and VII Corps Commander, and Grandfather & Great-Grandfather respectively, of the broadcasters Peter and Dan Snow. Wilson and Snow were contemporaries at the Army Staff College Camberley, graduating in 1893.

21 Brigadier-General E L Spears CB CBE MC, *Liaison 1914, A Narrative of the Great Retreat* (London: William Heinemann, 1930), p.254.

22 Edmonds, BOH, *France and Belgium 1914*, Vol. I, p.521.

23 Some observers have suggested this was caused by the failure of the Army Staff College to study A&Q. Malcolm Brown's work however, indicates that at least by 1912, the time allocated to intelligence, training and operations (G2/G3/G7) at 38.6% was matched by 23% for Administration and Quartermaster (A&Q) (G1/G4/G8). See, the seminal, Ian Malcolm Brown, *British Logistics on the Western Front, 1914-1919* (Westport Connecticut & London: Praeger, 1998), p.23.

24 For an explanation of the French railway organization, see, Edwin A Pratt, *The Rise of Rail-power in War and Conquest, 1833-1914*, (London: P S King & Son, 1915), pp.149-174.

25 GHQ, QMG, WD entry of 3 September 1914 noted that: 'much confusion and delay prevails on all railways in the neighbourhood of PARIS and the running of all trains cannot be depended upon' and the issue is raised again on 5 September; TNA WO 95/27/1.

26 Letter from Robertson to Cowans dated 7 September 1914; TNA WO 107/13.

27 Ibid.

that has sadly been forgotten over the passage of a Century.[28] Indeed, it is remarkable that despite his achievements and those of his logisticians, he should only receive one passing mention in the official narrative of the campaign.[29] It is therefore, the aim of this chapter to assess his contribution to operations, which enabled the logisticians of the BEF to ensure not only its survival but also its expansion and transformation and to reflect upon some of the Lessons Identified. The story is a fascinating one, offering a varied insight into the role of doctrine, the friction of command, the complexities of maturing staff planning processes, interaction with a coalition partner and the developing dynamics of logistics of Army in the Field under immense operational pressure.

Wully Roberston

Sir William Robertson is unique in the history of the British Army, as he was in 1918 and still is, the only person in the British Army who enlisted as a Private Soldier, to reach the rank of Field-Marshal. Born in 1860 in the village of Welbourn, Lincolnshire, he left school at 13 and was in domestic service as a footman before enlisting as a Trooper in the 16th Lancers in 1877. His abilities, dedication, industry and skills brought swift promotion in the ranks, culminating in a rare event for the time, success in the officers' entrance exams and a commission, in 1888, in the 3rd Dragoons.[30] He would have almost certainly been commissioned earlier but for his wish to remain in the Cavalry, which created a particular financial challenge, these problems being resolved by an offer of a commission with a regiment in India where pay was higher and the cost of living lower. Focused upon his professional development, the now Captain Robertson learned six languages,[31] won the prize for Best Officer-at-Arms in 1894, was and awarded the Distinguished Service Order (DSO) for gallantry in the 1895 Chitral Expedition.[32] He was selected, having been nominated by the Commander-in-Chief India, for a place at the Army Staff College, for 1897-1898, the first ex-ranker to so do, achieving second place in his year and qualifying as an interpreter in French.

His appointment as the BEF's QMG[33] came by quite by chance because in 1914 he was serving as the Director of Military Training (DMT). As Robertson recorded:

28 The most recent academic assessment is Brown, *British Logistics on the Western Front*, pp.41-73.

29 Edmonds, BOH, *France and Belgium* 1914, Vol. I, p.286. His two biographies dwell little on this period, focusing upon his time in the War Office; see, Victor Bonham-Carter, *Soldier True, The Life and Times of Field-Marshal Sir William Robertson* (London: Frederick Muller, 1963) and David R Woodward, *Field-Marshal Sir William Robertson: Chief of the Imperial General Staff in the Great War* (Westport Connecticut & London: Praeger, 1998). For the most recent assessment of his work in the BEF as QMG, see, John Spencer, 'The Big Brain in the Army, Sir William Robertson as Quartermaster-General', in Spencer Jones (Ed.) *Stemming The Tide*, pp.89-107.

30 The London Gazette, No 35832, 26 June 1888, p.3498.

31 Gurkhali, Hindi, Pashto, Persian, Punjabi and Urdu.

32 Whilst engaged on a reconnaissance patrol in support of the Chitral Relief Force, during the Siege of Malakand in April 1895, Robertson, who was suffering from dysentery, was attacked and wounded by his two native guides, one armed with a shotgun and the other, known as 'Kazi', with Robertson's sword. Fortunately the pellets missed and Robertson punched the swordsman to the ground before driving off his assailants with revolver fire. 'Kazi' was wounded before being later captured, tried by Courts-Martial and executed. Robertson attributed the Kazi's failure to hit him from 10 yards with both barrels from a 12 bore as: 'the direct intervention of Providence', whilst reflecting that "A "mention in despatches" and the award of the Distinguished Service Order, then a rather rare decoration, tended to alleviate, but did not entirely dispel, the mortification I felt at not having put up more of a finished fight and accounted for both of my assailants. I was chaffed a good deal at the time for having been cut about with my own sword, and for not acting up to the standard displayed at the Rawal Pindi assault-at-arms. I deserved to be chaffed"; Robertson, *Private to Field-Marshal*, pp.76-77.

33 His immediate staff were: Colonel Dawkins (Assistant Quartermaster-General (AQMG)) Major Jebb (Bedfordshire Regiment) and Captain Percival DSO ASC as Deputy Assistant Quartermaster-Generals (DAQMG) and Captain Woodruffe RHA as ADC. Robertson was particularly fortunate to have Percival on his team because as a member of the War Office QMG 5 Transports and Remounts Directorate, he was a key player in the reorganization of field transport system before becoming an instructor at the Staff College; Ibid, p.201.

> As the Director of Military Training became, in war, Chief General Staff Officer of the Home Defence Force, there seemed to be no chance when war broke out of my going to France. At the last moment however, Grierson.....was given the command of the Second Army Corps, and Murray, originally intended to be the Quartermaster-General of the Force, was selected to succeed him [as BEF CGS]. The appointment of Quartermaster General thus became vacant and Douglas [CIGS] was good enough to give it to me.[34]

Given Murray's faltering performance[35] as BEF CGS, the product of several factors, including his physical health, it was providential that there was such happenstance. Whilst Robertson was not a career logistician, he certainly had plenty of relevant practical experience. As a cavalryman he had a thorough grounding in horse-mastership at a time when Horse Transport (HT) was a critical component of logistic operations and a clear comprehension of HT support, itself a complex activity and if improperly managed, a fragile area. In 1890, he was supervising an 11,000 acre Indian Government grass farm at Rawalpindi, which was a crucial element of the forage supply chain and in 1891 was the Railway Transport Officer at Hasan Abdal during operations on the North West Frontier, whilst his Intelligence appointment in 1892 brought him into close contact with the field activities of the QMG's staff. Post Staff College, he was involved in operational planning in the War Office before deploying to South Africa for intelligence duties. In the period 1907-1908, he was in a premier logistic appointment: Assistant Quartermaster General (AQMG) in Aldershot Command, which was the peacetime organization that, upon mobilization, formed I Corps.[36] In this post, he was responsible for overseeing the planning and execution of operational A&Q.[37]

Doctrinally Pure?

The A&Q arrangements for the BEF were a product of recent operations and exercises, including the North-West Frontier of India, the British experience of the South African War (1899-1902)[38] a flavour from the Russo-Japanese conflict[39] and lessons from the Army Annual Manoeuvres (AAM)[40]

34 Ibid, pp.195-196.

35 The most recent and undoubtedly balanced account is 'Major-General Sir Archibald Murray, Chief of Staff, GHQ' by J M Bourne, in *Stemming The Tide*, pp.51-69. See also, Simon Robbins, *British Generalship on the Western Front, Defeat into Victory* (London & Portland Oregon: Frank Cass, 2005), pp.116-117. Major A F Becke (Comp) BOH, *Order of Battle*, Part 4, *The Army Council, GHQs, Armies and Corps, 1914-191* (London: HMSO, 1945), p.11 and Edmonds, BOH, *France and Belgium, 1914*, Vol. I, p.471, state he held the Temporary or Acting rank of Lieutenant-General whilst CGS BEF.

36 I Corps comprised 1st Division of 1st (Guards) and 2nd and 3rd Infantry Brigades, each of four battalions and 2nd Division of 4th (Guards) 5th and 6th Infantry Brigades, also each of four battalions. The brigades were supported by Divisional Troops, comprising Mounted Troops (Cavalry and Cyclists) Artillery with 13 batteries, two engineer Field Companies and a Signal Company. Logistic units comprised five ammunition columns (one Divisional, three Brigade and one Heavy Battery) one Divisional Train ASC and for medical support, three Field Ambulances. Edmonds, BOH, *France and Belgium 1914*, Vol. I, pp.473-476.

37 Adjutant & Quartermaster-General, the overarching term, usually abbreviated to A&Q, used by the British Army in the Great War, to define those activities, which provided support to combat forces in the fields of administration and logistics. In the 21st Century these activities are described as Combat Service Support (CSS) and comprise Logistic Support, Equipment Support, Medical Support, Administrative Support and Logistic Engineering.

38 One lesson, sadly ignored after much debate, was the decision in 1908 to confirm that officers would be issued with swords instead of rifles; see, Army Council Minutes in TNA WO 163/13.

39 A particular issue was the expenditure by the Japanese of artillery ammunition, with rates of up to 80 rounds per gun per day. See, Historical Committee of the Committee of Imperial Defence, *Official History of the Russo-Japanese War*, Part II, *From the Battle of the Ya-Lu to Liao-Yang Exclusive*, General Staff (London: HMSO, 1908), Appx F.

40 Cogent logistic papers explaining the Lessons Identified from the AAMs of 1912 and 1913 were published. See, Colonel P E F Hobbs CMG, 'The New System of Transport as carried out by the Blue Forces during Army Manoeuvres, 1912', *The Army Review*, Vol. VI, War Office (April 1913), pp.716-730 and Colonel E E Carter CMG

in the United Kingdom.[41] Also key, was the appointment of a Chief of the Imperial General Staff (CIGS) and the supporting General Staff, which was constituted as a key component of military planning within the War Office[42] and as a consequence, A&Q was underpinned by the creation of the AG's Department responsible for manpower and manning, through the Directorates of Organization, Personal Services, and Medical Services[43] and a QMG's Department[44] supporting the Soldier with equipment and supplies through Directorates for Transport & Remounts, Movements & Quartering, Supplies & Clothing and Equipment & Ordnance Stores.[45]

As concepts were tested in exercises and new equipment entered service, logistic unit organizations, formation procedures and doctrinal publications matured. Of particular note, was the publication, in 1909, of the two volumes of *Field Service Regulations* (FSR).[46] Part I (Operations) was the G (Operations) component, with Chapter 3 devoted entirely to Movements.[47] Part 2 (Organization & Administration) was the underpinning doctrinal document for A (Administration) and Q (Quartermaster).[48] The FSR was a very significant publication, which not only provided the foundation for the effective development of embedded A&Q to the Expeditionary Force but also complimented a series of supporting specialist publications.[49] Whether FSR constituted doctrine in the 21st Century sense remains an interesting debate[50] but one of its key tenets was its under-pinning of the fifth Principle of Logistics,[51] Flexibility. This is of particular significance because the FSR was not Euro-centric, being written as a fundamental document upon which an expeditionary force would base its operations and logistics, wherever it deployed. Robertson clearly understood its relevance in relation to the forthcoming deployment

MVO, 'The Services of Maintenance in the Field; Some Object Lessons from the Army Exercise, 1913', *The Army Review*, Vol. VI, War Office (April 1914), pp.473-489. Also, Major A M Henniker RE, 'Troop Movements by Rail in the United Kingdom', *The Army Review*, Vol. VI, War Office (April 1914), pp. 490-497 and Captain J F C Fuller, 'Notes on the Entrainment of Troops To and From Manoeuvres', *The Army Review*, Vol. VII, War Office (July 1914), pp.184-213.

41 For an excellent survey and analysis of the pre-war AAM in the UK, see, Simon Batten, *Futile Exercise? The British Army's Preparations for War 1902-1914* (Warwick: Helion, 2018).

42 For details of the Directorates and Branches in the War Office, see, C Newman Knight BA, *The War Office List and Administrative Directory 1910* (London: HMSO, 1910). Interestingly, despite *The War Office List* being an official document containing the outline appointment details of military officers and civil servants employed in the War Office, it was an open publication, priced at five shillings (£23.05 in 2015 based on the Retail Price Index) and the first 11 pages contained commercial advertisements headed as the War Office List Advertiser.

43 Knight, *War Office List*, pp.54-61. In 2018, 'Personal' Services is now entitled 'Personnel' Services.

44 The duties of the AG and QMG Branches in the Field are described in FSR, Part II, Chp III, Function of Forces in the Field, The Staff, Sects 16-19, pp.40-42 and Administrative Services and Departments, pp.44-48.

45 For details of the twelve QMG Branches, the roles and responsibilities and the staff officers assigned to them in 1910, see, Knight, *War Office List*, pp.62-71.

46 General Staff, *Field Service Regulations*, Part I, *Operations*, War Office (London: HMSO, 1909) (Reprinted, with amendments, 1912) and Part II, *Organization and Administration*, (London: HMSO, 1909) (Reprinted, with amendments, 1914).

47 It is instructive that Movements, a Q (Quartermaster) function is inextricably linked in the two documents by appearing in both, demonstrating its critical role to G (Operations).

48 Now G4 (Logistics & Infrastructure).

49 For example, Army Council, *Army Service Corps Training*, Part I (London: HMSO, 1909) (Reprinted, 1915 with amendments) and Part II, *Supplies* (London: HMSO, 1909) (Reprinted, 1914 with new Appx XII) and General Staff, *The Field Service Pocket Book*, War Office (London: HMSO, 1908) (New edn, 1914), which was packed with useful logistic information.

50 For an analysis, see, Spencer Jones, *From Boer War to World War, Tactical Reform of the British Army, 1902-1914* (Norman: Oklahoma Press, 2013) and Timothy Bowman & Mark Connelly, *The Edwardian Army, Recruiting, Training and Deploying the British Army* (Oxford: OUP, 2012), pp.64-105.

51 The Principles being: Foresight, Economy, Simplicity, Co-operation and Flexibility; *Army Doctrine Publication* (ADP), Vol. 3, Army Code No 71566, DGD&D/18/34/63 (UK MOD, 1996), p.1-6.

to France, instructing, at the BEF QMG's[52] Directors pre-deployment meeting,[53] that the system of supply was to be elastic, maintenance in the field was to be decentralized to the greatest extent and subordinates were to accept responsibility for actions on the ground, points he reinforced in his autobiography: 'It was necessary that the Quartermaster-General's staff should examine the situation from every point of view, and introduce such elasticity into the supply arrangements as would promptly afford the Commander-in-Chief the greatest possible choice of action'.[54] These cultures had all the hallmarks of 21st Century Mission Command,[55] seeking to maximize the opportunities for the 'Man on the Spot' to seize the initiative.

Whilst the principle of Flexibility was embedded in this approach, the management of logistic co-operation with a Host Nation whose transportation planning was centralized was a pertinent issue raised, pre-war, by Lieutenant-Colonel Forbes[56] of the Army Ordnance Department (AOD) in a report to the War Office, after attending the French Army manoeuvres in 1913:

> It will be seen that a great contrast exists between the system of supply of stores to the French army and our own system. The French plan is designed to meet a campaign on a large scale in a highly civilized country with the best of rail and road communications. Ours, on the other hand, is based upon our experience of warfare in less civilized countries where everything has to be got from a remote oversea [sic] base.[57]

Whilst clearly not explicit, the FSR focused upon British National operations, which given the importance of the forthcoming partnership was a key limitation, particularly in the logistic environment. Like the French Army, the British had no recent experience of coalition operations[58] and despite the close co-operation created by the planning staffs there was much practical friction on the ground[59] during the deployment because the participants had never practised together.[60]

The BEFs logistic structure was predicated on three In-Theatre Bases facilities supplied mainly

52 The pace of his appointment and deployment to this important appointment is of note: "Within forty-eight hours, I once again left the War Office, and then joined the headquarters of the Expeditionary Force then mobilising at the Metropole Hotel in Northumberland Avenue;" Robertson, *Private to Field-Marshal*, p.196. The War Office requisitioned the Metropole during the Second World War before purchasing it. Sold by the Ministry of Defence in 2007, the building has been refurbished and is now the Corinthia Hotel.

53 Held in his office in Horse Guards on Saturday 8 August 1914 at 1100. For details, see the GHQ, QMG War Diary (Q/CR/2099) in TNA WO 95/27, Part 1. The AQMG, Colonel Dawkins and supporting staff embarked at Southampton Berth 43 on the SS *Comrie Castle* Tuesday 111000 August 1914 arriving Le Harve on Wednesday 121600. The QMG sailed from Dover on HMS *Sentinel* arriving at Boulogne on Friday 141300 August 1914.

54 Robertson, *Private to Field-Marshal*, p.205.

55 Mission Command is a style of command, which promotes decentralized control, freedom of action and initiative. Its under-pinning principles are: 'Unity of Effort, Decentralization, Trust, Mutual Understanding and Timely and Effective Decision Making'. For their application in the Mission Command environment, see, *Army Doctrine Publication* (ADP) Vol. 2, *Command*, HQDT/18/34/51, Army Code No 71564 (UK MOD, 1995), pp.2-4 to 2-10.

56 After the Great War, during which he was promoted to Major-General, Forbes was the author of the *A History of the Army Ordnance Services*, Vol. Three, *The Great War* (London: Medici Society, 1929).

57 Forbes, *Army Ordnance Services*, p.3.

58 In the 12 major wars in which Great Britain was involved in the period 1688-1945, 10 were in coalition but by 1914, the Nation was out of practice, with the previous coalition being with the French and the Ottoman Empires, supported by the Kingdom of Sardinia, against the Russians in the Crimea, in the period 1853-1856.

59 Host Nation Support (HNS) was a key component of the BEF's operational capability, a factor clearly comprehended by the planning staffs and articulated in a raft of instructions. Unfortunately, the mechanisms by which, it was enacted, had not been jointly exercised by the British and French practitioners.

60 The War Office was well informed of French A&Q organization and arrangements. See, General Staff, *Report on Foreign Manoeuvres* in 1912, CONFIDENTIAL (War Office, 1913), pp.33-46 and General Staff, *Handbook of the French Army*, 1914, War Office (HMSO, 1914).

through a Sea Line of Communication (SLOC) with Sea Ports of Disembarkation (SPOD) at Boulogne, Le Harve[61] and Rouen. Le Harve was the Main Base Area (MBA) supported by Boulogne as a Temporary Base Area (TBA) and Rouen as specific Subsidiary Base Areas (SBA). The TBA was used for medical stores and ammunition,[62] a conflicting combination, in order to prime the LOC in France, and the SBA for Mechanical, mainly Wheeled Motor Transport (WMT).[63] The operation was enabled by considerable material and service provision, mainly by contractors[64] through Host Nation Support (HNS)[65] delivering supplies by rail[66] along a LOC via a Rail Regulating Station (RRS) to nominated railheads. Stocks were collected by a Supply Column equipped with WMT, which delivered to a Divisional Refilling Point (DRP) for collection by the HT of the Divisional Train.[67] The BEF's logistic emphasis was at divisional and army level, with no assets permanently assigned to corps and only the Brigade Ammunition Columns (BAC) to brigades.[68] In addition, there were specific capabilities allocated to move artillery ammunition, which were under the control of the Royal Artillery (RA) and not the ASC but which were a

61 At both SPODs, the French provided a *Commission de Port*, responsible for ships entry, disembarkation of troops, accommodation, emergency rations and animal forage. At Le Harve and Rouen, a Naval Divisional Transport Officer (NDTO) and a Military Landing Officer (MLO) represented the interests of the United Kingdom. These personnel reported to the British Principal Landing Officer, Rear-Admiral Edward Shortland; TNA WO 106/49A2: Revision of the 1914 Programme. For the duties of the MLO, see, FSR, Part II, Chp III, Functions of the Forces in the Field, Sect 13, pp.36-37.

62 Boulogne was used to in-load divisional and unit ammunition, with Theatre reserves being dispatched to Le Harve and Rouen. Boulogne was also the Sea Port of Disembarkation SPO for Royal Flying Corps' personnel, MT and supporting initial deployment stocks of POL and rations. Some of the BEF's medical stores, including the *Brechot-Desprez-Ameline* (BDA) frames for ambulance trains, were also planned for distribution through Boulogne, after which, the TBA was to close.

63 Wheeled, tracked, or semi-tracked land vehicle utilised in a logistic context to move men and materiel to, on or from the battlefield and powered by the Internal Combustion Engine (ICE) either Spark Ignition (SI) or Compression Ignition (CI) fuelled by petroleum spirit or diesel oil respectively, or by steam (Steam Transport (ST)). Often abbreviated to MT, it does not include combat vehicles, such as tanks, Armoured Personnel Carriers (APC) or Self-Propelled Guns (SPG). Motor Transport (MT) included Wheeled or tracked or semi-tracked land logistic vehicle powered by the ICE but to provide specific clarification for wheeled vehicles, the term Wheeled Motor Transport (WMT) is used.

64 French contractors constructed the tented reception camp at Rouen in early August 1914, as part of the pre-war deployment plan. In late August, at Amiens, the Royal Engineers directed French contractors employed to support the establishment, using school buildings, of a General Hospital, the reconfiguration of a jute factory for a Veterinary Hospital, water distribution for a Remount Depot and the construction of a reinforcement camp for 6,000 personnel. Institution of the Royal Engineers, *Work of the Royal Engineers in the European War, 1914-19*, Work under the Director of Works (France) (Chatham: W & J Mackay, 1924), p.2.

65 Initial HNS was considerable and included the provision of reception camps, storage facilities, preparation of detraining stations, all rail movement, local transport, working parties and interpreters. In addition, 100,000 gallons of petroleum was to be delivered to the BEF by M+7 plus 150,000 rations per day and forage for 45,000 horses in the period M+7 to M+10 delivered by Daily Supply Trains (*Train de Vivres Quotidiens*) and one Reserve Train (*Vivres de Reserve*). See French Support for Supply, SECRET Note No 4 dated 19 July 1913 in TNA 106/49A/1: History of the Growth of the Wilson-Foch Scheme.

66 All rail movement was the responsibility of the French railways, directed by the railway regulating authority, *Commission Regulatrice*, the section responsible for British movement, being W.

67 The French Army had a similar system. See, *Report on Foreign Manoeuvres* in 1912, pp.41-42, although the observer noted that 'the general idea in France is that mechanical transport may be used for anything', indicating the British system was more proscriptive.

68 A Brigade Ammunition Column (BAC) was integral to the Royal Field Artillery brigade, which though described thus, was a Regimental organization comprising three batteries and the BAC. Although badged to the Royal Artillery, the BAC was a logistic unit established to hold a mobile reserve of Small Arms Ammunition (SAA) for an infantry or cavalry brigade and to transport 18 pdr gun ammunition to the artillery batteries, or 13 pdr in a cavalry brigade. For an explanation of its operations, see, FSR, Part I, Chp XII, Ammunition Supply, Sect 160, pp.218-220.

fundamental component of the supply chain.[69] The delivery of Combat Supplies[70] in the field was an ASC[71] responsibility, whilst the storage of ammunition, weapons, technical items and MT spares in the LOC was the prerogative of the Army Ordnance Department (AOD) and Army Ordnance Corps (AOC)[72] under the direction of a Director of Ordnance Services.[73] The ASC was also partially responsible for the road transport components of the medical evacuation chain and the provision of Labour Companies. The Royal Engineers (RE) were responsible for Postal Services and Transportation, which included rail operation and construction, Ports and Docks, Inland Water Transport (IWT) and Movement Control (MC).[74] In the combat areas, Labour was provided by units but on the LOC, Locally Recruited Workers (LRW) were employed, which brought its own challenges.[75] Whilst there was a key reliance on individual Regular Reservists to man the BEF, there were no logistic Territorial Force (TF) units assigned to the Order of Battle (ORBAT)[76] with the exception of a component of the Category C Special Reserve,[77] allocated to reinforce Army Service Corps Reserve Parks.[78]

69 At divisional level, the Divisional Ammunition Column (DAC) provided divisional reserves for the brigade artillery and the divisional 4.5 inch howitzer brigade and the Heavy Battery Ammunition Column (HBAC) supporting the 60 pdr battery plus SAA for All Arms and natures specific to the infantry. For the operations of the DAC, see, FSR, Part I, Chp XII, Ammunition Supply, Sect 159, pp.217-218.

70 Ammunition, petrol, forage, rations and water.

71 For the ASC aspects of the period, see, Michael Young, *Army Service Corps, 1902-1918* (London: Leo Cooper, 2000), pp.5-70 and Colonel R H Beadon CBE psc, *The Royal Army Service Corps, A History of Transport and Supply in the British Army*, Vol. II (Cambridge: Cambridge University Press (CUP) 1931).

72 For AOC aspects, see, Forbes, *Army Ordnance Services*, pp.3-34 and for a pre-war assessment of the responsibilities, tasks and development of the AOD and AOC, see, Brigadier-General T Preston Battersby, 'The Army Ordnance Department and Corps', *The Army Review*, No 2, Vol. 2 (April 1912), pp.428-443.

73 The Director of Ordnance Services, in the rank of Brigadier-General, had very broad responsibilities. These were defined as: 'the provision, storage, and distribution of the following to the best advantage - arms, ammunition of all kinds, personal and camp equipment, vehicles, harness and saddlery, signalling stores, guns of all natures and their appurtenances, entrenching and other tools, barracks and hospital stores, bridging material, telegraph stores, miscellaneous stores, clothing and stationery' and of course keeping most of these items in repair. Ibid, p.442.

74 See, Colonel A M Henniker CBE (Comp) BOH, *Transportation on the Western Front, 1914-1918* (London: HMSO, 1937), pp.1-38 and Major-General H L Pritchard (Ed.), *The History of the Corps of Royal Engineers*, Vol. V, *The Home Front, France, Flanders and Italy in the First World War* (Chatham: The Institution of the Royal Engineers, 1952), pp.153-174.

75 John Starling and Ivor Lee, *No Labour, No Battle, Military Labour During The First World War* (Stroud: Spellmount, 2009), pp.77-80.

76 The Special Reserve also provided Combat Arm capability in the form of three mounted squadrons assigned as Army Troops, which were A and C Squadrons of the North Irish Horse (NIH) and B Squadron, South Irish Horse. A half squadron from NIH reported to HQ 4th Division on Tuesday 25 August 1914 but lost contact with it and fought with 3rd Division at Caudry on 26 August, returning to 4th Division on Friday 28 August, this becoming the first component of the British Army's formed Volunteer Reserve to engage in combat in the Great War. Edmonds, BOH, *France and Belgium* 1914, Vol. I, p.148.

77 This component was the 'Wolds Wagoners', formed in 1913 with 400 volunteers from farm-labourers and tenant-farmers by Colonel Mark Sykes, 6th Baronet, Sledmere, Yorkshire. Most of the volunteers did little military training but were accepted because of their horse-wagon driving skills and the unit numbered 1,000 by August 1914. Most of them were allocated to the six ASC Reserve Parks deploying with the BEF, and thus had the honour of being the first Volunteer soldiers to serve on operations with the BEF; another 200 were posted to Royal Engineer bridging trains in Ireland. See, Graham Winton, *Theirs Not To Reason Why, Horsing the British Army 1875-1925*, Wolverhampton Military Studies (Solihull: Helion, 2013), pp.261-262 and for a detailed description of operations on the Continent, "Contact", 'Yorkshire Waggoners with the ASC', *Journal of the Royal Army Service Corps* (November 1935), pp.497-508. There is variation in the spelling, which is either, Wagoner and Waggoner; although the former is correct. During the Great War, Sykes was appointed by Kitchener to the de Bunsen Committee advising the Cabinet on Middle Eastern Affairs and was the British signatory to the secret 1916 Anglo-French Sykes-Picot Agreement partitioning the Ottoman Empire. He died of Spanish Flu in the *Hotel Le Lotti* Paris on 16 February 1919, aged 39, whilst attending the peace negotiations and is buried, despite having been a Roman Catholic, in the Anglican churchyard of Saint Mary's Sledmere; the family continue to occupy Sledmere House, which is also the home to the Wagoners Museum.

78 The term 'Park' is confusing because it was not a stationary unit operating a depot or dump but a mobile HT

Left: P5.1. Gone but not forgotten: Wolds Wagoners Memorial at Sledmere East Yorkshire. In comparison to 2018, when the British Army relies considerably upon logistic skills from the Volunteer Reserves to reinforce significant overseas deployments, the BEF had only one unit from the Special Reserve. (Author)

Below: P5.2. The Wolds Wagoners was the only logistic Volunteer unit to participate in the BEF's Great Retreat. Memorial detail showing the Wagoners re-supplying the BEF, whilst fending off German attack. (Author)

The land LOC, often presumed to be a transportation tube, was a multi-spectrum operation,[79] encompassing the A&Q matrix, being in effect, a logistic division, delivering many of the functions at Corps and Theatre level.[80] The table below summarizes the array and indeed complexity of this capability, the control of which was undertaken by the Inspector General of Communications (IGC) a Two Star or Three Star[81] officer[82] who reported directly to the Commander-in-Chief at General Headquarters (GHQ).

Table 5.1

BEF Line of Communication Units – December 1914[83]

Transport & Supply		**Ordnance**
6 x Divisional Ammunition Parks	2 x Advanced Remount Depots	8 x Ordnance Companies
1 x Cavalry Ammunition Park	**Engineers**	**Veterinary**
1 x Cavalry Brigade Ammunition Park	Railway Transport Establishment*	11 x Mobile Veterinary Sections
6 x Divisional Supply Columns	2 x Railway Companies	8 x Veterinary Sections
1 x Cavalry Supply Column	1 x Works Company	**Pay**
1 x Cavalry Brigade Supply Column	2 x Fortress Companies	1 x Base Army Pay Unit
1 x Army Troops Supply Column	1 x Printing Company	**Postal**
1 x Base Mechanical Transport Depot	**Medical**	1 x Base Post Office
1 x Advanced Base Mechanical Transport Depot	6 x Clearing Hospitals	1 x Advanced Base Post Office
	12 x Stationary Hospitals	2 x Stationary Post Offices
1 x Base Horse Transport Depot	12 x General Hospitals	**Provost**
1 x Advanced Horse Transport Depot	6 x Ambulance Trains	1 x Field Prison Unit
6 x Reserve Parks	3 x Hospital Ships	**Bases**
6 x Field Butcheries	3 x Advanced Base Medical Stores Depots	3 x Infantry Bases
8 x Bakery Sections		
6 x Field Bakeries	3 x Base Medical Stores Depots	**Air**
8 x Railway Supply Detachments	2 x Sanitary Sections	1 x Aircraft Park
1 x Central Requisition Office	11 x Sanitary Squads	**Defence**
1 x Branch Requisition Office		1 x Infantry Battalion

* For details of the duties of the Railway Transport Establishment, see, FSR, Part II, Chp VIII, Transport, Sect 62, pp.93-94.

organization established to carry 'on wheels' two days iron rations with groceries, and two days of oats for one division, plus one-sixth, of a cavalry division and one-sixth of the total strength of units forming Army Troops. Groceries included tea, sugar, tinned milk, bacon, jam and cheese. The Reserve Park was a Line of Communication (LOC) unit and provided a mobile reserve of supplies in the event of the supply chain from the Base being disrupted.

79 Originally there were five battalions upon deployment but four were formed into 19th Infantry Brigade on 22 August 1914; Edmonds, BOH, *France and Belgium* 1914, Vol. I, p.483.

80 The Field Prison was located at Le Harve; TNA WO 106/49A/2: Revision of 1914 Programme.

81 Two Star rank in the Army is Major-General and Three Star, Lieutenant-General.

82 There appears to be confusion as to rank. F S Robb, the initial IGC and R C Maxwell who replaced him on 19 September 1914, were both Major-Generals and Robertson only referred to him by that rank, although Becke, BOH, *Order of Battle*, Part 4, p.16 states he was a Lieutenant-General. Maxwell is recorded as being a Temporary Lieutenant-General in contemporary IGC documents; see also, Supplement to the *London Gazette* dated 18 February 1915, which notes both officers holding this rank.

83 Table compiled from information in Edmonds, BOH, *France and Belgium* 1914, Vol. I, Appx 1, pp.483-484.

The IGC commanded what would be described today as an Enabling Command and was responsible for Reception Staging Onward Movement (RSOM)[84] and sustainment whilst GHQ was responsible for Integration.[85] This appeared to be a logical and practical arrangement, which relieved GHQ of the administrative, yet nonetheless important, tasks but created a number of anomalies, one of which was confusion as to status. IGC was a commander,[86] not a staff officer and he reported directly to the C-in-C[87] but was tasked by the AG and QMG and another officer, who commanded the LOC Defence Troops. A further complication was the location of many of the Directors working for the AG and QMG, who were positioned in the Base and who thus worked to IGC instead of the AG and QMG. As a result of these complications, IGC effectively became the fourth senior staff officer within the GHQ structure but without any formal recognition.[88] In the short-term, IGC chose to informally subordinate his operational direction to the key logistic staff officer, the QMG and it was indeed fortunate that Major-General Robb had a sound personal and professional relationship with Robertson.[89]

It was clear however, that the situation that led to such an arrangement would need review, particularly because of the fundamental unresolved doctrinal issue under-pinning whether material would be pushed forward by the IGC or pulled forward under the direction of GHQ.[90] An additional complication was that whilst FSR clearly made the C-in-C responsible for the success or failure of his Command, his responsibilities did not extend to A&Q unless he chose to exercise them.[91] Unsurprisingly, the General Staff (GS) tended to avoid A&Q matters unless a crisis emerged and even then, there was an understandable tendency to remain disengaged for fear of assuming responsibility for any perceived impending disaster. As a corollary, GHQ became less coherent than its organization might suggest.

The BEF thus deployed to France with a A&Q command capability that organizationally, was not as effective as it could have been, although fortuitously the performance of the practitioners offset this limitation. Operations in France certainly confirmed Robertson's view that GHQ required greater control over IGC activities in support of divisions and as a result, GHQ directed the location of the divisional railheads and all logistic operations immediately forward of them not controlled by divisions, on the basis that not only was GHQ more capable of reading the tactical battle but also it enabled IGC to focus on delivering the LOC outputs. Equally though, GHQ does not appear to have gripped some operational decisions, particularly in relation to the specific

84 RSOMI is a modern term describing the process by which a force is received into Theatre, is initially administered, issued with additional equipment, conducts specific training, receives operational munitions and then concentrates for battle.

85 The military scenario in August 1914 precluded for the most part, the delivery of effective Integration. Units detrained in the Concentration Area with the expectation that operations would commence almost immediately; TNA WO 92/25: GHQ, AG, WD and WO 95/27: GHQ, QMG, WD, both August 1914.

86 IGC commanded all LOC units exclusive of Defence Troops and was responsible for the control and co-ordination of all traffic on the LOC up to and including the Rendezvous Points or locations fixed by GHQ; FSR, Part II, Chp III, Functions of the Forces in the Field, Sect 11, para 1.

87 Instructions for the Inspector General of Communications (A1770) were classified SECRET; a copy is held in TNA ADM 116/1324, Appx K-10. Instructions for Base Commandants at Ports B, C and R (A1771) are at Appx K-1.

88 Neither Edmonds, BOH, *France and Belgium*, 1914, Vol. I, nor Becke, BOH, *Order of Battle*, Part 4, mentions the post of IGC, either in GHQ or in the LOC ORBATs.

89 That the system as articulated in FSR had failed upon first contact with the enemy is clearly illustrated by Entry 502 in IGC, WD of November 1914; TNA WO 95/22.

90 For an assessment of the wider issues within GHQ, see, Dan Todman, 'The Grand Lamasery revisited: General Headquarters on the Western Front', in Gary Sheffield and Dan Todman (Ed.) *Command and Control on the Western Front, The British Army's Experience 1914-18* (Staplehurst: Spellmount, 2004), pp.39-70.

91 'It is a principle of war organization that the C-in-C is relieved of direct responsibility for the conduct of the business of providing the requirements of the forces in the field, unless he sees fit to interpose'; FSR, Part II, Chp III, Functions of the Forces in the Field, Sect 8, para 2.

locations of future Main and Subsidiary Base Areas, which arguably should have been a GHQ call, although this may have been the result of disrupted communications and Robertson's preference for Major-General Robb the IGC to exercise Mission Command[92] within the LOC, especially as GHQ had assumed authority for controlling the railhead locations.

To France

The mobilization, movement and field deployment[93] of the BEF to France was a masterpiece of military and civilian planning,[94] and execution, which was the culmination of three years intense analysis, staffing, exercising and training.[95] The effectiveness of the With France (WF)[96] Plan[97] produced by the War Office General and Logistic staffs,[98] under the tutelage of the Director of Military Operations (DMO) Brigadier-General Henry Wilson,[99] certainly enabled the BEF to arrive in France in sound order, although inevitably units had varied experiences.[100] Nonetheless, it imparted a very positive momentum to the operation, whilst demonstrating the effectiveness of the

92 One aspect that stands out from the GHQ QMG War Diary is the number of entries requesting clarification or decisions on what arguably should have been, as the Theatre HQ, GHQ QMG responsibilities. For example, on Monday 31 August 1914, HQ IGC is requested to confirm whether Saint Nazaire has been selected to be the new Main Base Area and on Sunday 6 September, whether HQ IGC has any information on the arrival of 8th Division. Whilst the latter may be a result of disrupted communications with the War Office, the former was appropriately a GHQ decision; TNA WO 95/27/1: GHQ, QMG, WD, August - September 1914.

93 Whilst the complex machinery of war started to turn across the United Kingdom, in Coventry, Special Constable Edgar Palmer, the author's maternal grandfather, was faced with a rather different challenge. On foot patrol, he discovered a dead horse at the end of Vecqueray Street, which was partially obstructing the public highway. Allegedly, because the senior constable summoned to assist was unable to spell 'Vecqueray' for the duty report, they engaged members of the public to drag the carcass a few feet into Lower Ford Street, thus solving this potentially embarrassing administrative problem. Horses, alive and dead, and ingenious solutions, were all to be crucial hallmarks of logistic operations in 1914.

94 For an assessment of British military and civilian plans, see, Keith Wilson, 'Great Britain' in Richard F Hamilton and Holger H Herwig (Eds.) in *War Planning 1914* (Cambridge: CUP, 2010), pp.175-197.

95 The underpinning work is, 'The WF Plan and the Genesis of the Western Front, A Previously Unpublished Account' by General Sir Percy Radcliffe KCB KCMG CB DSO, in *Stand To! The Journal of the Western Front Association,* No 10, Spring 1984, pp.6-13. For a brief illustrated resume of the railways contribution in 1914, see, Alan Earnshaw, *Britain's Railways at* War (Penryn: Atlantic, 1995), pp.13-27 and for an overview of mobilization movements, J A B Hamilton, *Britain's Railways in World War I* (London: George, Allen & Unwin), 1967, pp.31-36.

96 There is continuing debate about the abbreviation WF, which according to General Radcliffe's account is 'With-France', whilst all the files appertaining to the deployment are entitled Wilson-Foch. Given Wilson's propensity for personal association, With-France is much more likely to be the official title but as he did in so many aspects of his military career, Henry Wilson has stamped his personal mark on our archival records.

97 The WF Plan was comprehensive, comprising approximately 70 detailed documents, with those that are known to exist being held mostly in the TNA WO 106/49 series. The key components were: Entrainment and Movement to Areas of Concentration (WO 106/49A/6) Mobilization Appointments (A1590 dated April 1914 - Part I, Expeditionary Force) held in WO 106/49A/9. This document was classified SECRET (indeed it still is according to the front cover) and detailed all the staff appointments for every HQ from Army to Brigade, Bases, Depots, Ports and Rest Camps, with details of the appointment, nominating HQ, reporting place and timings. The Disembarkation Tables 1914 (A1732) document is the critical movement plan matching sea moves by units to the French Table D railway plan, which is in TNA WO 106/49B/7.

98 For a description of the WF Plan and its development, see, Radcliffe, 'With France'; TNA WO 106/49A/1.

99 For a recent assessment of Sir Henry's military career, see, Keith Jeffery, *Field Marshal Sir Henry Wilson, A Political Soldier*, (Oxford: OUP, 2008). For his involvement in BEF planning and his wider influence in supporting the concept, see pp.64-105.

100 Mobilization and rail movement to the ports generally received very favourable comment but the sea movement rather less so. The regimental history of The 3rd (King's Own) Hussars noted of their ship, the *SS City of Lucknow*, 'Our recollections of her are not the best. There was no covered accommodation for the men ....the sanitary arrangements, we were to discover on the voyage, were totally inadequate, and nothing had been prepared for the conveyance of horses'; Lieutenant-Colonel AW T Willcox CMG, *The 3rd (King's Own) Hussars in the Great War, 1914-1919* (London: John Murray, 1925), p.3.

logistic planners and services. Unit deployment was especially slick but some of the weaknesses in the logistic aspects soon emerged and occasionally led to embarrassing failure and adverse impacts upon the soldiers. At the tactical level, logistic co-ordination, so very important when the plan unravelled was often easily disrupted by the language barrier. Rail Transport Officers (RTO) critical to the movement plan were not assigned to the most appropriate levels of French railway command, a factor compounded by misunderstandings of French railway Standard Operating Procedures (SOP) particularly in relation to loading and unloading.[101]

Operationally, the formation of the Advanced Base at Amiens[102] demonstrated a failure of intellectual rigour by logistic commanders. Apart from utilizing critical manpower and complicating stock control, it added no value in defensive operations immediately forward of the BEF's Concentration Area nor provided a meaningful intermediate base to support a substantial advance. The selected site offered no expansion capability, always a significant aspect of base development and was vulnerable to German offensive operations.[103] Medical evacuation was a critical area in which the logisticians were involved, although in this instance, the War Office planners dealt GHQ BEF a poor hand because it was the one area where the WF Plan was weak, despite the intervention of the War Office Army Medical Directorate (AMD).[104] Medical evacuation at 2nd Line partially relied on ASC transport returning to DRPs, an arrangement which was doctrinally embedded.[105] Whilst an interesting approach to efficient asset utilization, it was not conducive to patient care or indeed, to the effective distribution of Combat Supplies. The shortage of motor ambulances in the first months of the war certainly diminished the recovery chances of the wounded and led to questions in the House of Commons.[106] Indeed the failure was so great, the provision of appropriate ambulances became an Urgent Operational Requirement (UOR) with GHQ issuing a directive that Motor Ambulance Convoys (MAC) each of 50 ambulances, were to be established for each Army Corps to provide a more coherent response to this critical requirement.[107] Another

101 Given the level of detail in the Expeditionary Force Mounting Instructions, it seem surprising that this was an issue; TNA WO 106/49A/7: 'Instructions for 1st and 2nd Army Commanders and Officers of Advanced Parties and Railway Transport Establishment'. In addition, the Planning Team in the War Office was briefed on a French entrainment exercise at Douai and Valenciennes on Saturday 24 January 1914 relating to potential British deployment movements; TNA WO 106/49A/1: History of the Growth of the Wilson-Foch Scheme.

102 The concept was recommended by the QMG Staff at GHQ; TNA WO 95/27/1: GHQ, QMG, WD, 21 August 1914. Fortunately, very few stocks were accumulated otherwise they would probably have been lost during the withdrawal.

103 Major-General Forbes is especially critical of this failure; *Army Ordnance Services*, p.8.

104 Sect XI, Medical Service, in TNA WO 106/49A/2, articulates the shortfalls, many of which, were awaiting financial approval to create resolution. These included the *Brechot-Desprez-Ameline* (BDA) frames for ambulance trains, stretchers, additional hospital bed capacity and issues relating to the movement of stretchers on MT. For a detailed description of the complexities of medical evacuation in the BEF, see, Major-General Sir W G Macpherson KCMG CB LLD, BOH, *Medical Services, General History*, Vol. II, *The Medical Services on the Western Front, and during the Operations in France and Belgium in 1914 and 1915* (London: HMSO, 1923), pp.171-341.

105 Lieutenant-Colonel C H Burtchaell, 'The Wounded in War'. *The Army Review*, Vol. II, No 2, War Office (April 1912), pp 417-427, offers a concise contemporary description of the doctrinal arrangements. In Diagram 1, HT of the Divisional Train and Supply Column MT, assisted and 'local means of conveyance' are shown as supporting the movement of casualties from the Dressing Station to the Ambulance Train Railhead (ATR). Burtchaell was the Assistant Director-Director, Army Medical Service.

106 Similar issues relating to Ground Manoeuvre (GM) medical evacuation arose during the early 21st Century conflicts in Iraq and Afghanistan. For an examination of the historical and technical aspects of recent military ambulance development, see, Lieutenant Colonel C H Maginniss BA RLC, 'One Four Bravo, An analysis of the imperatives for the design of military ambulances supporting ground force operations in the 21st Century', *British Army Review*, No 150, UK MOD (Winter, 2010/2011), pp.73-81. In this respect, Burtchaell highlights the importance of effective First Aid, as relevant now, as then: 'Many years ago a distinguished German surgeon said that "the fate of the wounded rests in the hands of the one who applies the first field dressing';" 'The Wounded in War', p.426.

107 By 1 October 1914, the BEF had received 58 of the 88 initially requested; TNA WO 107/13: QMG and Correspondence, IGC Stores and Equipment, 1 September - 31 December 1914. For a critical analysis of medical evacuation during this period and its logistic implications, see, Mark Harrison, *The Medical War, British Military*

component, which was not effective in the medical evacuation plan, was the provision of *Train Sanitaire Improvise* (TSI). The capability of these improvised ambulance trains,[108] comprised of box-trucks, with the appropriate stretcher and equipment fits,[109] was clinically fragile because of the poor ride of the wagons and further compromised by the failure to co-ordinate the timely assembly of the *Brechot-Desprez-Ammeline* (BDA) frames, rolling stock and stretchers.[110] Essential supporting ordnance stores were also unavailable, although the AOC resolved many of the basic equipment deficiencies through local purchase and manufacture.

The Great Retreat

There was however, one fundamental and potentially fatal flaw in the operational plan and that was the assumption that should the BEF withdraw, it would do so along a secure LOC based upon the Channel Port of Le Harve. Whilst this concept was entirely logical and in keeping with the doctrine of the day, the reality was very different because the plan took no account of the possibility that the BEF would almost certainly be subject to French strategic and operational direction, which in the case of withdrawal, might compromise the logistic arrangements for the BEF's support. Why this arrangement was never effectively challenged in the planning phase is impossible to confirm from the documentary evidence but it had been raised at the Committee of Imperial Defence in 1911.[111] It is possible that the staff effort was so focused upon the effective delivery of the deployment that sustainment was a secondary consideration, or equally likely, that the General Staff, its experience founded upon National operations, assumed the BEF would operate independently. Examination of the WF Plan[112] certainly reveals no suggestion of creating a contingency re-basing option by holding stocks in the UK ready for deployment to another Channel Port, which given Britain's immense maritime capability would have been a robust solution. Perhaps withdrawal was deemed unlikely, or if it occurred, that it would reflect the logistic needs of the BEF.

Actuality however, did not accord with pre-war planning because the BEF, in order to conform to French operational orders,[113] withdrew South, to the East of Paris,[114] instead of South-West to the North-West of the City. GHQ considered three Courses of Action: pulling out of the line to re-deploy to the original LOC, withdrawing to Le Harve for evacuation to the United Kingdom if necessary; operating a lateral LOC to Le Harve, or creating a new LOC. The QMG summarized the problem: 'It was necessary that the Quartermaster-General's staff should........ be prepared to meet any and every reasonable contingency, for no matter how skilful the plans of the Commander-in-Chief might be, they would almost certainly fail in execution if the troops were not properly fed,

Medicine in the First World War (Oxford: OUP, 2010), pp.16-26.

108 For a description of the development of ambulance train evacuation operations in the period, see, Macpherson, BOH, *Medical Services,* Vol. II, in each of the campaign sections.

109 In the 1913-14 War Office Estimates, £4,000 (£3.226M in 2016, using the *Measuring Worth* Economic Cost valuation as a share of the output of the economy based upon the share of Gross Domestic Product (GDP)) had been funded to purchase 1,100 frames for six trains; TNA WO 106/49A/2: Revision of Programme, 1914.

110 Note in TNA WO 106/49A/1: History of the Growth of the Wilson-Foch Scheme. According to the GHQ AG War Diary, in early September 1914, one or two trains per day were deemed sufficient. By 14 October, the War Diary indicates there were eight available; TNA WO 92/25: GHQ, AG, WD, September and October 1914.

111 114th Meeting of the Committee of Imperial Defence (CID) on Wednesday 23 August 1911; TNA CAB 38/19/49: Committee of Imperial Defence, Minutes of the 114th Meeting, 23 August 1911 and Hankey, *The Supreme Command,* Vol. One), p.80.

112 TNA WO106/49A/2: Wilson-Foch Scheme, Expeditionary Force to France, Sect X, Supplies.

113 For a comprehensive account, from a British perspective, of the operations of the French Fifth Army in August and September 1914, see, Spears, *Liaison 1914.*

114 TNA WO 95/27/1: GHQ, QMG, WD, 31 August 1914.

quartered and kept supplied with ammunition'.[115] Withdrawing from the line was considered as a serious option[116] but the Secretary of State for War made it absolutely clear that the political and military consequences were so great that it was impossible to adopt.[117] Operating a lateral LOC was possible, although it would be at grave risk from disruption by the enemy, whilst also conflicting with French logistic operations.[118] Creating a new LOC appeared to be logistically impossible in the timescale[119] with the available resources but it was the one that the QMG viewed as the only one that could keep the BEF in the line[120] and in the fight.[121] It was though, a bold decision and one that a lesser man might have been reluctant to take, although one fully supported by FSR.[122] Robertson was however, an individual of foresight, initiative and courage under-pinned by his knowledge of German operational thinking. Of his action, he wrote: "There are not many other instances in military history I imagine, if any, of measures having being taken before the first battle of a campaign to change the base of an army which has been deliberately selected after long and careful consideration. It was fortunate they were taken on this occasion……"[123]

On Saturday 22 August 1914,[124] as Robertson's order initiated Base relocation contingency planning,[125] the 4th Division began landing at Le Harve[126] and conducting its RSOM through the LOC, whilst the IGC logisticians were issuing bicycles to the new formed Divisional Cyclist Companies, and to infantry battalions, mobile field kitchens, which were not held by units when the BEF commenced the deployment to France. In addition, ad-hoc logistic units[127] were also

115 Robertson, *Private to Field-Marshal*, p.205.

116 It appears that Kitchener learned of French's proposal to leave the line to refit from Major-General Robb who was Inspector General of Communications; TNA WO 33/713: Telegrams. It is possible that Robb believed a monumental disaster was on the horizon, which compelled him to act but it is certainly unusual for a Two Star officer under command of a Field-Marshal, to communicate directly with the Secretary of State for War. For an assessment of this incident, see, George H Cassar, *Kitchener's War, British Strategy from 1914-1916* (Washington DC: Brassey's, 2004), pp.88-89.

117 Outcome of the meeting of Field-Marshal Kitchener and the Commander-in-Chief BEF, Sir John French, in the British Embassy in Paris on Tuesday 1 September 1914. Kitchener's telegram to the Cabinet, confirming the direction that he had given, is in TNA WO 159/6: Private Office Papers of Lord Kitchener. See also, Richard Holmes, *The Little Field-Marshal* (London: Jonathan Cape, 1981), pp.232-234.

118 There is an oblique reference to this option in TNA WO 95/27/1: GHQ, QMG, WD, 3 September 1914, based upon the original decision to re-orientate the LOC to support the BEF to the North-West and West of Paris.

119 The GHQ QMG War Diary records that the time to re-orientate and re-organize the LOC would be three weeks and that any future change would require three weeks warning to ensure an efficient transition; TNA WO 95/27/1: WD, 3 September 1914.

120 Having created the new LOC, there was also the option of the BEF withdrawing from the line behind the River Seine to refit and then be assigned the role of Strategic Reserve.

121 There is though, one strange co-incidence relating to the situation the QMG was grappling with. As Director Military Training (DMT) Robertson was responsible for crafting the AAMs, which were normally conducted at Corps level and provided plenty of opportunity to practice logistic operations on a large scale, particularly deployment and re-supply of rations and forage. For 1914, Robertson had intended to exercise a scenario in which Friendly Forces would withdraw under attack from a much larger Enemy Force attempting to envelope it, in order to practice retirement along the LOC.

122 'The selection of the base or bases, and the general direction of the L of C are determined by the plan of operations'; FSR, Part II, p.49, Chp IV, General Principles of Maintenance of The Forces in the Field, The Strategical Concentration, Sect 24, Preliminary Arrangements.

123 Robertson, *Private to Field-Marshal*, p.206.

124 The GHQ QMG WD notes growing concerns about the use of railways and the forwarding of supplies in the direction of Valenciennes on Friday 21 August; TNA WO 95/27/1.

125 GHQ QMG WD of 28 August states that a reconnaissance of the Loire ports (Saint Nazaire and Nantes) was in progress by staff from HQ IGC; TNA WO 95/21/1.

126 Even as the 4th Division was disembarking, it was clear that there might have to be adjustments to the pre-war deployment plans, with Robertson writing to Robb, the IGC, 'Information requested as to how much latitude as regards the time and zone of detrainment of 4th Div could be given'. TNA WO 95/27/1: GHQ, QMG, WD, 23 August 1914.

127 For a personal account of the formation and operations of 19th Brigade Train ASC, see, Alfred Clifton-Shelton, *On the Road from Mons, With an Army Service Corps Train, By its Commander* (London: Hurst and Blackett, 1916).

forming to support new combat formations, one of which was 19th Infantry Brigade created from assets within LOC Defence Troops.[128] Remarkably, despite the many challenges, this fundamental readjustment of logistic posture was achieved, although far from perfect in execution,[129] because the concomitant dislocation created chaos for inventory control and distribution.[130] The QMG summarized the situation:

> Even when the move had been completed, many days, and in some cases weeks, elapsed before the required articles became available. In the hurry and confusion attending the evacuation of the original bases, the ships had been loaded on no system except that of getting out of the place as rapidly as possible…….different kinds of stores were inextricably mixed; machine guns were on one ship and their tripods on another, while the articles wanted first, were, as often as not, at the bottom of the ship, below sacks of oats and bales of hay, and therefore were the last that could be got out. Moreover, the establishment of a new base, even at a good port, is a matter which demands considerable time and previous preparation.[131]

The worst case Coalition strategic scenario, in which the BEF would leave the line and withdraw along the original but collapsing LOC and require evacuation from Le Harve, was thus avoided by a logistic solution, albeit, by creating a significant reduction in its efficiency. Whilst Kitchener's meeting with Sir John French has always been seen as a defining moment in shaping the next stage of the BEF's campaign, the re-orientation of the LOC had commenced before it took place and in effect fixed the BEF to staying in the line supported by its new LOC. The evidence indicates that Sir John French did not clearly comprehend the logistic re-posturing that was underway nor that the option to relocate the MBA to La Rochelle[132] rather than the ports of Saint Nazaire or Nantes on the River Loire, to accommodate the BEF's withdrawal to the line of the River Seine to the East of Paris, would create yet more disruption to the logistic support to the BEF.[133]

While re-orientating the LOC might have appeared to be the only option at GHQ, it created what seemed to be an insurmountable task for HQ IGC and the Base staffs, although no doubt the colonial operational experience of many personnel would have provided a leavening of optimism in the detail, if perhaps not the scope of the task, as from the tactical and logistic perspectives,

128 19th Infantry Brigade comprised 2nd Royal Welch Fusiliers, 1st Scottish Rifles, 1st Middlesex, and 2nd Argyll & Scottish Highlanders. A&Q units included 19th Brigade Ammunition Column, Field Ambulance and ASC Train. See, Becke, BOH, *Order of Battle of Divisions*, Part I, p.75.

129 One of the casualties of this outcome was the unfair dismissal of the Director Ordnance Services, Brigadier-General Perry, who later became Director of Supplies in Mesopotamia and then Director-General of the newly formed Indian Army Ordnance Corps. Robb, the IGC, was also removed from post, to be replaced by Maxwell. Given that the BEF remained in the field as a coherent fighting Army and continued to be sustained by the logisticians despite the challenges, it is probable that personal frictions within the Command Chain played a part in their removal.

130 Forbes noted, 'The stores, loaded in this haphazard way, were in hopeless confusion. There were cases of service dress caps, parts of guns and machine guns, bales of horse-rugs and blankets, ammunition, tentage, signalling gear, etc. - much in broken packages-mingled with forage, medical, veterinary, and other goods…….to sort out this chaos was a lengthy and tedious operation, accompanied by a considerable amount of looting'; *Army Ordnance Services*, p.15.

131 Robertson, *Private to Field-Marshal*, p.209.

132 GHQ QMG WD, 29 August 1914, noting the correspondence between the War Office and the C-in-C regarding the changes to Base to posts on the French Atlantic coast; TNA WO 95/27/1.

133 Interestingly, the GHQ QMG WD is silent on communications with C-in-C on the implementation of the LOC until Thursday 3 September, when the record states 'Letter addressed by QMG to CGS pointing out that a new L of C was in process of being established on the assumption that the army would fall back by NW side of Paris. Owing to decision to fall back on [the manuscript is not clear but it is possibly, S Line, presumably referring to the Seine] L of C selected was not so suitable'; TNA WO 95/27/1. One can only assume that CGS did brief the C-in-C on this critical issue.

the European conflict was emerging as a very different one to the Boer War of 1899-1902.[134] In summary, the Amiens Advanced Base,[135] MBA Le Harve, TBA Boulogne[136] and SBA Rouen had to be cleared of all materiel,[137] remounts[138] and personnel,[139] and relocated at Saint Nazaire and Nantes,[140] with the rail LOC re-orientated from these ports to the Rail Regulating Station at Le Mans.[141] To achieve this, British shipping[142] had to be re-tasked from sustainment to redeployment and the French were requested to move stocks by rail,[143] from Le Harve to the forming MBA.[144]

The priority of loading was SAA,[145] artillery ammunition,[146] artillery pieces, engineer stores, vehicles and clothing[147] but the bizarre result of this order was that the most important items were often placed in the bottom holds of ships, which of course, adversely affected the establishment and operation of the new base, a clear example of the priority being focused upon recovery rather than redeployment. Whilst this major relocation was being enacted, the IGC was also expected

134 For an analysis of the tactical aspects for infantry, artillery and cavalry, see, Jones, *From Boer War to World War*, pp.71-206. The logistic aspects require study.

135 Robb, the IGC had suggested to Robertson, that in the event of Le Harve being abandoned, Creil should replace Amiens as the Advanced Base; TNA WO 95/27/1: GHQ, QMG, WD, 23 August 1914.

136 Boulogne was evacuated by sea on Wednesday 26 August 1914. The withdrawal from the site was a relatively easy task because closure was planned once its TBA tasks were complete.

137 There is variance in the published documents as to the tonnage of material out-loaded from Le Harve. The BOH states 60,000 tons, whilst *Army Ordnance Services*, notes that the Le Harve Base had 20,000 tons; Edmonds, BOH, *France and Belgium 1914*, Vol. I, p.287 and *Army Ordnance Services*, p.14. It is possible that the figure of 60,000 relates to the tonnage in-loaded to St Nazaire, which included stocks from Le Harve, Rouen and the United Kingdom.

138 Remounts were an especial and critical component of the BEF's logistic and operational capability. For a detailed review of remount mobilization and operations in the period, see the outstanding study by Graham Winton, *Theirs Not To Reason Why*, pp.259-257. Approximately 7,000 horses were moved during the Base re-location operation.

139 The Official History states 20,000; Edmonds, BOH, *France and Belgium 1914*, Vol. I, p.287.

140 St Nazaire was the preferred port, partly because it was at the entrance to the River Loire but there was no site suitable for a base depot, so Nantes was selected, although the area offered little capability for expansion, so stocks and stores had to be located on both sides of the river; Forbes, *Army Ordnance Services*, p.14 and TNA WO 106/50: 'Areas required for depots at Bases'. The location of both ports on the Atlantic Coast of France immediately introduced logistic inefficiencies to the BEF's operations because of the increased voyage times from and to ports on the coast South of England.

141 Le Mans was never a Main Base Area, although the *Direction de l'Arriere*, the Directorate of French GHQ responsible for Supply and Maintenance, granted authority on 2 September 1914 for it to be a Temporary Advanced Base; TNA WO 95/3949: IGC WD, August 1914.

142 The successful delivery of this task was a product of the Royal Navy's control of the English Channel; had this not been the case, the outcome would probably have been different. In this respect, British sea power played a critical, if forgotten, role. See, Sir Julian Corbett, BOH, *Naval Operations*, Vol. I, *To the Battle of the Falklands December 1914* (London: Longmans, Green and Co, 1920), pp.72-82 and pp. 92-98.

143 Some of the stocks from Le Harve and Rouen were moved by rail to Nantes or forward to divisions but rail was also used to transfer material within Nantes. The SS *Inventor*, a 10,000 ton liner, could only dock at Nantes on the top of a Spring tide and then only on the port side of the River Loire, which meant that most of the material had to be railed to the opposite bank; Forbes, *Army Ordnance Services*, p.15.

144 Le Harve was cleared by Saturday 5 September, just as the Corps elements of the BEF were ending their withdrawal.

145 The priority for ammunition was SAA; it is possible that the Base logisticians had quickly learned of the high consumption of SAA at Mons.

146 One lesson that was identified from this urgent removal of ammunition was the need to store munitions in or near the port areas, and as a consequence, the BEF took enormous risks in storage. Initially, in August 1914, quantities of Small Arms Ammunition (SAA) and small amounts of artillery rounds and charges were stored in the port areas at Boulogne and Rouen, sometimes in sheds with other ordnance stores, a practice, which continued as more ammunition arrived. At Rouen by early 1916, 20,000 tons of munitions were stored in the port area and had an explosion occurred, the port and the town would have been very seriously damaged; Forbes, *Army Ordnance Services*, pp.123-124.

147 The importance of the replacement of soldiers' clothing is summarized by a soldier of the BEF remembering: 'what equipment we had was torn; instead of boots we had puttees, rags, old shoes, field boots - anything and everything wrapped around our feet. Our hats were the same, women's hats, peasants' hats, any old covering, while our trousers were mostly ribbons. The officers were in a similar condition'. Corporal Bernard John Denore, 'The Retreat from Mons' in C B Purdom (Ed.), *Everyman at War: Sixty Personal Narratives of the War* (London: J M Dent, 1930), p.8.

to deliver support to the BEF whilst it was withdrawing.[148] Effectively therefore, divisions had to rely upon 1st and 2nd Line materiel[149] until the new LOC was established,[150] although some of the stocks from the closing Bases were sent forward to divisions as part of the re-deployment plan, with roadside dumps being established along the withdrawal routes.[151]

Advance to the Aisne

The advance to the River Aisne[152] posed a very different set of logistic problems to the Great Retreat, with the BEF requiring personnel and equipment to deliver re-constitution in the line, Combat Supplies to keep in the fight and most significantly, the transportation capability to deliver the assets, which was predicated upon rail movement from the Base to railheads and thence by WMT to refill the divisional dumps. To add yet more complexity, on Thursday 9 September, advance elements of 6th Division arrived at St Nazaire to RSOM through the new LOC.[153] The challenge, as the QMG staff quickly discovered, was the significant damage the rail LOC had suffered North of the River Marne during the Great Retreat.[154] This was compounded by the dislocation to rail services supporting the BEF by the dynamic strategic scenario, a situation lucidly foreseen in FSR which recognized the importance and complexity of railway systems in supporting military operations, whilst exposing the factors for effectiveness or failure: 'A railway system is a highly sensitive machine dislocated by unskilled treatment; it is at the same time an organism most vital to the maintenance of an army............ the convenience of individual bodies of troops must be subordinated to the working of the line as a whole'.[155]

The BEF was thus in a quandary. It was critical to conform to French operational plans but the BEF was obviously a second priority in the rehabilitation of the railway capability and GHQ clearly recognized that the plan to rely solely upon HNS railway support in the combat area had been a significant mistake,[156] especially as there were no plans agreed with the French to utilize

148 One key issue adversely affecting distribution from RPs and sometimes railheads, was the movements of refugees. The QMG recorded: 'Distribution was further hampered by the endless stream of refugees fleeing before the advancing enemy, and it was not until steps had been taken to shepherd them into batches, under proper supervision, that either troops or transport could move along the road with some semblance of regularity'; Robertson, *Private to Field-Marshal*, pp.210-211.

149 1st Line related to materiel held with units and 2nd Line, stocks held by divisions.

150 Interestingly, John Lucy, a Regular Private in 2nd Royal Irish Rifles (7th Infantry Brigade, 3rd Division) in his excellent autobiography, which covers his 1914 experiences in detail, makes only passing mention of supply shortages at section level, which given the intensity of the fighting his battalion was engaged in, probably indicates that the logistic system maintained distribution of Combat Supplies from 2nd Line stocks. See, J F Lucy, *There's a Devil in the* Drum (London: Faber & Faber, 1938). Supplying rations during the advance to the Aisne was more difficult. Frank Richards, a reservist in 2nd Battalion, The Royal Welch Fusiliers, recorded: 'Our rations were very scarce at this time. Bread, we never saw; a man's daily rations were four army biscuits, a pound tin of bully beef and a small portion of tea and sugar'; Frank Richards DCM MM, *Old Soldiers Never Die* (London: Faber & Faber, 1933), p.27.

151 Lucy's description of a dump, at Caudry, is particularly illuminating: 'we passed a huge dump of army rations on the way there; bags of bread and sugar, tea chests, tinned milk, and piles of carcasses of sheep - the food of a whole division it seemed'. See, Lucy, *There's a Devil in the Drum*, p.128. Robertson was particularly irritated by the loss of considerable quantities of bacon because there were no date stamps on the boxes and the rations were condemned as inedible; see, Letter Robertson to Cowans dated 22 October 1914 in TNA WO 107/13: QMG and IGC Correspondence, Stores and Equipment, 1 September - 31 December 1914.

152 The River Aisne flows for 221 miles from its source in Champagne-Ardenne to the River Oise.

153 TNA WO 95/27/1: GHQ, QMG, WD, 9 September 1914.

154 Similar problems occurred on the rail LOC during the advance of the Hundred Days in 1918.

155 FSR, Part II, p.95.

156 Similar issues emerged during BEF operations in France 1939-1940. On this occasion though, the Army deployed 24 specialist companies to support survey, construction, stores, operating, maintenance and signalling and were primed to take over agreed sections of the rail LOC once ground combat began. See, Lieutenant Colonel (Retired) C H Maginniss,

the deployed RE Railway Company to assist in repairing key rail infrastructure.[157] In addition, there were occasions, often for sound operating reasons, when the HN dictated the location and timings of British railheads, a matter which created considerable frustration within the QMG's Branch. It was fortunate therefore, that in 1912, the War Office had authorised the replacement of two echelons of HT with one of WMT, a decision, which promoted much discussion about the potential effects upon distribution in the field.[158] Not only did this give greater flexibility to the supply of ammunition,[159] especially for artillery,[160] it also offered the opportunity to route, through the military supply chain, fresh bread and meat that in the past could only be provided to units from local sources. At the same time, the requirement for forage was reduced, the supply and distribution of which, was a very significant task in the BEF.[161]

The BEF had had a surprisingly large contingent of motor lorries, 1,468 being dispatched by the end of September 1914,[162] although most of them were impressed from the commercial sector. Robertson rapidly seized on the opportunities created by this new and expanding Theatre capability directing that WMT be used to bridge the gap between railhead and divisional dumps and refilling

'Tracks Across France, The role of railway operations in supporting the British Expeditionary Force in France in 1939-1940', *Royal Logistic Corps Review*, Regimental Association of the Royal Logistic Corps (2013), pp.66-71.

157 No 8 Company (No 1 Railway Company) arrived at Le Harve on Saturday 15 August 1914 on the SS *Caledonia*; TNA WO 95/4052/8, 8 Company RE, WD. Agreement with the French authorities as to its employment to repair railways in the combat area along the BEF's original LOC was not resolved until Thursday 17 September. It commenced its first task, repairs to the bridge at Pont de Metz on the Amiens-Rouen line, on Sunday 20 September. For details of its employment or rather unemployment, in the intervening period, in published material, see, Henniker, BOH, *Transportation on the Western Front*, pp.53-57. Two RE Special Reserve (SR) railway companies arrived in November 1914.

158 See, 'The Supply of a Division in the Field with special reference to the use of Mechanical Transport', Captain Sir T A A M Cunninghame Bart, DSO, Rifle Brigade, *JRUSI*, Vol. LVI (January 1912), pp.9-36 and Lieutenant-Colonel E E Carter CMG MVO psc ASC, 'The New Transport System: its Principles and their Application', psc ASC, *Journal of the Army Service Corps* (May 1912), pp.671-707. Interestingly, Major-General Robb, the future IGC was in the Chair for the post-presentation discussion.

159 Major De Pree of the Royal Field Artillery (RFA) was both effusive and as it transpired, prescient, in his praise for what he viewed as a step-change in British Army logistics: 'War Establishments published with Army Orders in February 1912 have sanctioned the conversion of the old divisional ammunition column into a divisional ammunition park, the transport of which is to be motor lorries. The first step has thus been taken in what will probably revolutionize the supply of ammunition in European war'. Major H De Pree RFA, 'The Supply of Ammunition and Motor Transport', *JRUSI*, LVI (414), (August 1912), pp.1149-1164.

160 Of particular note, is his calculation relating to the importance of the motor lorry in delivering artillery ammunition at a rate of 432 rounds per gun per day (rpgpd) for 13 and 18 pdrs, 256 rpgpd for field howitzers and 280 for the 60 pdr. Given the stocks held in July 1914, this equated to the following Days of Supply (DOS) at Intense Rates: 4.4 for the 13 pdr and 3.5 for the 18 pdr; Ibid. See also, *History of the Ministry of Munitions* (MOM) Vol. I, *Industrial Mobilisation*, Part I, *Munitions Supply*, 1914-15 (HMSO, 1922), p.87.

161 For more details, see, Winton, *Theirs Not To Reason Why*, pp.190-212.

162 The initial MT deployment is in Sect IX of the WF Plan held in TNA WO 106/49A/2. See also, TNA WO 107/18: New Armies, 'Mechanical Transport Statement and Returns - MT with the EF dated 2 October 1914'. The table below, showing the average monthly petroleum issues for September to December 1914, illustrates the significant motor vehicle activity in France during the period of mobility:

Table 5.2
BEF: Average Monthly Petroleum Issues
September – December 1914*

Depot	Monthly Issues (gallons)+
Le Harve	338,091
Rouen	222,011
Total	560,102#

* Extracted from Beadon, *Royal Army Service Corps*, p.87.
+ The Unit of Measure in the period was the Imperial Gallon.
# As at the 2017 average price of £5.46 Sterling per gallon, this equates to £3,058,156.

points. Writing to Cowans, he concisely explained the interim solution, whilst demonstrating his frustrations about the logistic failure that was at this point, out of his control:

> Mechanical Transport is daily becoming of increasing importance because of broken railways........the French are by way of doing the work but they are not very business like and spend half the day talking. At the present moment the Troops are 40 miles in front of our available railway and there is no immediate prospect of obtaining a more forward railhead. This will show you our difficulty, and the need of ample Mechanical Transport.[163]

Almost in an instant, WMT had come of military operational age,[164] becoming, at this juncture, so important to the BEF that the QMG was voicing grave concerns over its sustainability:

> These pave roads knock them all to pieces, and the undisciplined drivers rattle the lorries along far too quickly.[165] I am trying to make a few sharp examples of these gentlemen ....but we have been so hustled in more ways than one, that it is a miracle, I think, our condition is at good as it is. We are getting through a terrible lot of them, I fear, and during our rearward movement of the last fortnight the Germans have got a good many of them.[166]

Implicit in his statement were many considerations relevant today; driver training, the pressure of operational imperatives, maintenance and the provision of spares; Robertson was to be deeply involved in all of these issues before the end of 1914. The greatest difficulty though and the one the QMG had the least influence over in a dynamic tactical environment, was the delivery of supplies forward of the Refilling Points (RP).[167]

Holding The Line

The advance to and battle of, the River Aisne,[168] marked a watershed in BEF mobile operational logistics. Having marched up to 250 miles in the withdrawal[169] and then approximately another 125 miles at an equivalent daily pace in the advance,[170] the BEF fought a fourth major engagement

163 Letter Robertson to Cowans dated 11 September 1914; TNA WO 107/13: QMG and IGC Correspondence, Stores and Equipment, 1 September - 31 December 1914.

164 For a summary of the development of MT in the period 1900-1914, see, Beadon, *Royal Army Service Corps*, pp.24-45.

165 Robertson's comment remains absolutely pertinent to British Army operations in the 21st Century and lucidly demonstrates that Senior officers in 1914 were alert to the fine balance of sustaining operational logistic capability, the timely delivery of tactical combat support and the contribution of safe operating practice as a force multiplier.

166 Letter Robertson to Cowans dated 7 September 1914; TNA WO 107/13: QMG and IGC Correspondence, Stores and Equipment, 1 September - 31 December 1914.

167 Note from Major-General Robb (IGC): 'Robertson, who is far more in touch with the troops than myself, says he cannot even fix rendezvous and refilling points for them, every time he has tried he has failed'; TNA WO 79/63: Private Papers of Sir A J Murray.

168 See, Edmonds, BOH, *France and Belgium 1914*, Vol. I, p.358-453. For a recent analysis, see, Jerry Murland, *Battle on the Aisne 1914, The BEF and the Birth of the Western Front* (Barnsley: Pen & Sword, 2012).

169 Between 20 August and 5 September 1914, 2nd Division marched the furthest on 250 Statute miles and 4th Division the least, with 151.5. The distances are those marched on roads and do not include additional miles for tactical positioning. The average daily distance for 2nd Division, which had no rest day, was 16.6 miles. See, the 'Length of Marches' Table in Edmonds, BOH, *France and Belgium* 1914, Vol. I, p.542.

170 The hardship of the long march upon the infantry soldiers was a feature of the campaign. An extract from a regimental history explaining the retreat from Mons is testimony to the trial: 'As the sun rose higher in the skies their discomfort increased. They had no food and very little water. When the periodical halt took place near a well there was rush to fill water bottles, but only a few succeeded before the time was up to move again.......The heat

P5.3. Coming of operational age; Load carrying WMT played a crucial part in sustaining the BEF's war-fighting capability. (RLC Museum: MT Collection)

in the Aisne and by the end of September, the British casualties totalled 29,598.[171] There were two critical logistic outfalls from the initial 40 days of combat operations. The first was confidence in the logistic achievement. The logisticians had kept the BEF in the line and in the fight, despite changing the carefully prepared Base and LOC structure, whilst also ensuring the onward movement of two infantry divisions and weathering the rail crisis. The second issue was the growing recognition that not only was the BEF's A&Q effort effectively spent for the immediate future but also there were a series of emerging problems that required effective solutions if the BEF was to successfully expand and develop resilient logistic capability. From the command and planning perspective, what is fascinating, is the content of the QMG and IGC War Diaries. Initially focused upon Theatre logistic issues, as operations on the Aisne declined, activities became driven by the detail, whilst the resolution of old problems and emerging challenges began to overtake the immediate operational imperatives; the BEF's logisticians needed to take stock, practically and intellectually.[172]

The most urgent task was to replenish stocks and re-constitute units with a wide range of equipment. Robertson in his usual manner, pressed on with a package of initiatives to progress this work including a programme of salvage and re-cycling to collect rifles, entrenching tools,

at midday was sweltering. Between 4 and 5 pm a heavy thunderstorm burst and in a few minutes everyone was drenched to the skin. At last, about 6 pm, Inchy was sighted and the hungry foot-sore soldiers entered the village fit to drop. No one, however was permitted to undress, so that whatever rest was possible had to be taken in wet clothes. The village was bare of food'; Major-General C R Simpson CB, *The History of the Lincolnshire Regiment, 1914-1918* (London: The Medici Society, 1931), pp.16-17.

171 Killed In Action (KIA) Died of Wounds (DOW) Died of Disease and Non Battle Injuries (DNBI) Wounded, Missing and Prisoner; deaths totalled 4,099; War Office, *Statistics of the Military Effort of the British Empire during the Great War* (MEBE) War Office (HMSO, 1922), p.249.

172 An examination of the key logistic aspects of the campaign through the perspective of DQUAD (Destination, Demand, Distance, Duration) is instructive and merits further study.

bayonets, packs, great-coats[173] and saddlery,[174] whilst pursuing the acquisition, through the War Office, of an additional 220 Field Kitchens and the staffing of an Urgent Operational Requirement for winter clothing and defence stores. Initially, the bureaucracy of the financial process that under-pinned the pre-war Ordnance system stifled action, and a very frustrated Robertson had to intervene to bring a relaxation of Treasury rules,[175] although the experience of the South African War had demonstrated to the Army Council the importance of appropriate controls on materiel,[176] an issue that quickly re-emerged as the BEF expanded.[177]

Ammunition, particularly for the artillery, was of especial concern because the Mowatt Reserve, upon which all munitions reserve stocks had been based,[178] was greatly depleted and industry was not keeping pace with demand.[179] In this respect, the Aisne had been a hard logistic lesson, with the unexpected utilization of 60 pdr, 4.5 and 6 inch shell,[180] all of which were deemed essential to counter German artillery and defences in the topography of the Aisne area,[181] whilst the depletion of 13 and 18 pdr rounds exacerbated the challenges the QMG had in managing dwindling in-Theatre stocks. The request for replenishment and the pressing need for new munitions,[182] such as grenades and mortars, were passed to the Master-General of the Ordnance at the War Office and the provision of munitions soon became significant government business but in the short term all the QMG could do was to attempt, with Major-General Royal Artillery, to husband the stocks on hand.[183] The withdrawal and replacement of Webley Mark IV pistol ammunition, driven by

173 The deficit of personal equipment was a considerable irritation because some of the losses were self-inflicted by the GHQ Encumbrance Order of 27 August 1914. On 2 October 1914, deficiencies were 20,000 packs and 20,000 bayonets and a GHQ letter of 22 October 1914 noted a loss of 22,000 great-coats, some of which were recovered after being dumped by reinforcing units; TNA WO 107/13: QMG and IGC Correspondence, Stores and Equipment, 1 September - 31 December 1914.

174 Saddles, bridles, bits, reins, sword frog and rifle buckets; note dated 2 October 1914 in TNA WO 107/13: IGC Stores and Equipment. The arrival of two Indian Cavalry divisions in late 1914 exacerbated this problem.

175 Robertson wrote of the Director Ordnance Services, Brigadier-General Perry: 'The senior ordnance officer at G.H.Q. was at first terribly perplexed to know what to do, for, owing to the strict financial control exercised over the smallest details, and which had its origins in the Treasury, his professional capacity was mainly estimated by the way in which he kept his accounts and produced innumerable "vouchers" for the action he took'. Perry was removed from post in October 1914, which from the perspective of his technical competence was grossly unfair but Robertson, under pressure to deliver, was undoubtedly frustrated by the intransigency of officers who failed to comprehend the change in the dynamics. Robertson, *Private to Field-Marshal*, pp.208-209. Perry's replacement, Brigadier-General H D E Parsons, was clearly more attuned to GHQ requirements, remaining in post until June 1918, whilst also being promoted to Major-General and knighted.

176 The Inspector of Army Ordnance Services, Brigadier-General T Preston Battersby had noted in 1912 the importance of gripping the control of materiel, writing, 'an Ordnance officer will now be attached to the headquarters of each division who, besides performing other duties, found most necessary by the experiences of the South African War, will constitute a check upon extravagance and waste of stores'; Battersby, 'The Army Ordnance Department and Corps', p.442. The war on waste eventually became a key tenet of logistic activity in the BEF.

177 The creative tension between the demands of logistic control and supporting combat were certainly comprehended by the pre-war Inspector of Army Ordnance Services, who recorded: 'Of course, innumerable conundrums, for the solution of which no "precedent" exists, will turn up on active service.......and the ultimate success of the departmental arrangements will depend solely upon the men who carry them out'; Ibid, pp.442-443.

178 The rapidly expanding need for different types of ammunition is clearly illustrated in the comprehensive War Office Handbook on the subject: *Treatise on Ammunition* (10th Edition) War Office, 1915.

179 For an excellent analysis of the economic construct, which was the precursor to this problem, see, David French, *British Economic and Strategic Planning, 1905-1915* (London: George Allen & Unwin, 1982) and John Hussey, 'Without an Army, and Without any Preparation to Equip One', *British Army Review*, No 109, UK MOD (April 1995), pp.76-84. See also, BOH, MOM, Vol. I, Part I, pp.7-92.

180 The failure to deliver the correct fuses with the shells compounded this issue. Note dated 17 September 1914 in TNA WO 107/13: QMG and IGC Correspondence, Stores and Equipment, 1 September - 31 December 1914.

181 TNA WO 107/13; Letter Robertson to Cowans dated 17 September 1914.

182 For an examination of the weapons and tactics, see, Anthony Saunders, *Reinventing Warfare 1914-18, Novel Munitions and Tactics of Trench Warfare* (London & New York: Continuum, 2012).

183 See, the SECRET Statement of Ammunition on the L of C DTG 250800 September 1914, which summarizes the

concerns related to the Geneva Convention, was another matter requiring the QMG's attention. The bullet had a flat nose,[184] resembling that of the proscribed expanding hollow bullet and German and Neutral media circulated stories of their use. The War Office firmly informed Robertson that the rounds were legal but when troops were exposed to rumours that the Germans were shooting prisoners found in possession of them and the possibility that the Germans might retaliate with similar rounds, the War Office withdrew the stocks and replaced them with a conical bullet.[185]

The arrival of the Indian Expeditionary Force A (IEFA),[186] commencing on Saturday 26 September, of two infantry and two cavalry divisions, whilst introducing fresh operational capability also brought new logistic responsibilities to ensure that the Indian Corps had, where possible, systems and equipment compatible with the BEF and commensurate with operations on the Western Front. These including the creation of a new LOC from the SPOD at Marseilles,[187] specific rations, special equipment, weapon provision,[188] additional clothing requirements and planning around different divisional logistic establishments,[189] as well as the QMG having to personally intervene to arrange the movement of an Indian prince's horse. Religion and caste were important factors in personal supply items, especially rations and cooking equipment, which Ordnance officers with no experience of the Indian Army found a particular challenge.[190] Less taxing in the detail but more so in quantity, was planning the arrival of 8th[191] and 27th[192] Infantry Divisions in the period October

ammunition stocks in France, up to and including the railheads but exclusive of munitions held by divisions. SAA 477 rounds per rifle and 14,000 per machine gun. Artillery in rounds per gun (rpg): 13 pdr (449) 18 pdr (290) 60 pdr (177) 4.5 inch (206) and 6 inch (90); TNA WO 95/3949: IGC, WD.

184 *Treatise on Ammunition* (10th Edition) War Office, 1915, p.536, states that the Mark IV and V bullet has 'a flat head'. For details of the issued Webley & Scott pistol ammunition, see, pp.536-538 and Plates CXII and CXIII.

185 This matter was rapidly expedited, as the first mention in the QMG WD is dated 2 September and by 4 September, the War Office had dispatched 250,000 rounds of conical ammunition to France, whilst on 5 September, HQ IGC proposed that GHQ issue an order prohibiting the use of 'illegal ammunition'. From the legal perspective, the War Office had declared the flat-nose round in accordance with the Geneva Convention, so the use of this term may relate to internal regulation, although this is not expressly stated; TNA WO 95/29/1: GHQ, QMG, WD, September 1914.

186 For the ORBAT, see, Brigadier-General Sir James E Edmonds CB CMG (Comp) BOH, *France and Belgium* 1914, Vol. II, *Antwerp, La Bassee, Armentieres, Messines and Ypres, October-November 1914* (London: Macmillan, 1929), pp.481-486. For details of the operations of the Indian Corps, see, Lieutenant-Colonel J W B Merewether CIE and the Right Honourable Sir Frederick Smith Bart, *The Indian Corps in France* (London: John Murray, 1919) and Gordon Corrigan *Sepoys in the Trenches, The Indian Corps on the Western Front 1914-1915* (Staplehurst: Spellmount, 1999). For the most recent critical analysis, see, George Morton-Jack, *The Indian Army on the Western Front, India's Expeditionary Force to France and Belgium in the First World War* (Cambridge: CUP, 2014).

187 On Sunday 23 August, Telegram 691, from Field-Marshal Kitchener, the Secretary of State for War, to the Commander-in-Chief (C-in-C) BEF, Field-Marshal French, noted that the Indian Corps would disembark in Marseilles. Given the subsequent work by the staffs of QMG and IGC to resolve the details of the Port of Entry, this may have been an assumption by Kitchener that the French would agree to any request. GHQ, QMG, WD, 23 August 1914. Robertson was apprised of the outline plans for the arrival of IEFA on 28 August 1914; TNA WO 95/27/1, GHQ, QMG, WD, 28 August.

188 TNA WO 95/3932/1: HQ 7th (Meerut) Division, AQMG, WD, entries 13-16 October 1914 and Marseilles Disembarkation Orders, Sect 2 and Appx 1, 'Instructions re Arms, Ammunition and Clothing'; TNA WO 95/3932/2: HQ 7th (Meerut) Division, AQMG, November 1914, Appx 2.

189 TNA WO 95/3932/1: HQ 7th (Meerut) Division, QMG, 'Some Points of Difference Between the Home and Indian Organization and Procedure'; nd but probably late September 1914.

190 TNA WO 95/74: GHQ, Director of Supplies, WD, 3 November 1914. The Director of Supplies commented: "The feeding of the Indians is becoming very difficult........As far as I can see in a very short time we shall have at least half a dozen different classes of rations for Indians."

191 For a resume of the formation, mobilization, ORBAT and deployment of 8th Division, see, Becke, BOH, *Order of Battle of Divisions*, Part I, pp.89-94, *The Eighth Division in War, 1914-1918,* Lieutenant-Colonel J H Boraston CB OBE and Captain Cyril E O Bax (London: The Medici Society, 1926) and Alun Thomas, *Unfailing Gallantry, 8th (Regular) Division in the Great War 1914-1919*, University of Wolverhampton Military Studies (Solihull: Helion, 2017), pp.25-38.

192 For a resume of the formation, mobilization, ORBAT and deployment of 27th Division, see, Becke, BOH, *Order*

to December 1914, the slow trickle of Territorial Force (TF) units[193] sent as reinforcements, and, rather more of a problem, integrating the 3rd Cavalry and the 7th Infantry Divisions,[194] to the BEF after they had completed covering the evacuation of Antwerp. The decision to re-deploy the BEF to Flanders, whilst generating short-term pain in the logistic arena enabled the re-establishment of the original Base Areas, whilst also reconstituting the shorter SLOC and LOC. By Sunday 27 September, ten trains per day were clearing stocks from Saint Nazaire to Le Harve[195] and, as time was less critical than during the hurried re-deployment of early September during which, many lessons had been learnt, the reconstituted bases were in-loaded with a mix of material despatched from the Home Base and stocks held in France.[196]

Policy issues also began to tax the logistic staff. In particular, the relationship between the QMG and IGC required clarification and refinement, whilst work to refine logistic command interfaces with the HN was clearly important and indeed in some areas urgent; continuing fragility, especially in the vital realm of railway operations,[197] certainly could not be sustained.[198] The introduction of the MACs and new ambulance trains required a required a review of the logistic interfaces with the staff of Director Medical Services,[199] whilst the future expansion and utilization of WMT was obviously an important task, with training in the United Kingdom an essential foundation. The supporting development of fuel and lubricant procurement, storage and distribution and the re-orientation of maintenance and repair systems, were all vital to sustain a growing logistic capability based upon the Internal Combustion Engine (ICE). Logistic support to the Royal Flying Corps (RFC),[200]

of Battle of Divisions, Part I, pp.97-102. There was no post-war divisional history of the 27th.

193 By 31 December 1914, the following units had arrived in France: seven Yeomanry Regiments, six RE Special Reserve (RE) and eight TF Companies, and 23 infantry battalions; these units were often deficient in equipment; Edmonds, BOH, *France and Belgium 1914*, Vol. II, pp.486-488.

194 For a resume of the formation, mobilization, ORBAT and deployment of 7th Division, see, Becke, BOH, *Order of Battle of Divisions*, Part I, pp.81-86 and C T Atkinson, *The Seventh Division 1914-1918* (London: John Murray, 1927), pp.1-18.

195 GHQ, QMG, WD, 27 September 1914; TNA WO 95/27/1.

196 Note dated 2 October 1914 stating that supplies for 200,000 men and 70,000 horses would be dispatched to France to initiate the establishment of new bases; TNA WO 107/13: IGC Stores and Equipment.

197 For details of the Command and Control arrangements in this area, see, Henniker, BOH, *Transportation on the Western Front*, pp.39-81 and the CONFIDENTIAL 'Report upon Rail Transport arrangements of the British Army on the Continent' by Brigadier-General Sir E P C Girouard in TNA WO 32/5144. Girouard's review of the BEF's railway structures had much merit but he caused friction in GHQ and HQ IGC when he stepped, perhaps understandably in the circumstances, outside his Terms of Reference, drawing a stinging rebuke from Maxwell, the IGC: "In my opinion it would have been well if Sir P Girouard had restricted himself to what he was told to do. He has far exceeded his instructions. He was not told to produce a scheme for uprooting organizations deliberately laid down after deep deliberation;" Letter Maxwell to Cowans through Robertson, dated 17 October 1914 in TNA WO 32/5144.

198 Whilst Girouard certainly upset Maxwell and Robertson, he was an experienced railway engineer and operator, whose principles generated success in many transportation arenas. His report exposed a whole series of issues that matured later as the BEF expanded but as Chapman-Huston and Rutter observe in Cowan's biography, the issue was rather less the report's content and rather more that neither the IGC nor the QMG were ready for change, combined with their distrust of interference from the War Office. See, Chapman-Huston & Rutter, *Quartermaster General of the Great War*, Vol. II, p.102. There may also have been some antipathy because Girouard was a 'Kitchener Man' and a wish to have a period of stability after the changes and reversion on the LOC.

199 For a detailed description of the BEF's medical services and the role of logistic capability in delivering them; see, Macpherson, BOH, *Medical Services*, Vol. II, pp.171-341.

200 For a critical assessment of operational air developments in 1914, see, Eric Ash, *Sir Frederick Sykes and the Air Revolution 1912-1918* (London & Portland Oregon: Frank Cass, 1999), pp.50-65. For an excellent expose of the role of RFC logistics, see, Peter Dye, 'The Genesis of Modern Warfare, The Contribution of Aviation Logistics', in Gary Sheffield and Peter Gray (Eds.) *Changing War, The British Army, The Hundred Days Campaign and the Birth of the Royal Air Force, 1918*, Birmingham War Studies (London: Bloomsbury, 2013), pp.171-189 and his comprehensive and illuminating, *The Bridge to Air Power: Logistics Support for Royal Flying Corps Operations on the Western Front, 1914-18* (Annapolis: Naval Institute Press, 2015).

a small consideration in 1914, had, during encounter operations, demonstrated the importance of mobility of the ground support services and the criticality of effectively supporting this new military capability. Remounts remained a significant concern, as enemy action, withdrawal and advance and the dislocation of LOC had not only caused losses, injury and illness but also disrupted supply, training and veterinary services.[201] Reverse Logistics grew in significance as brass shell cases and a host of other equipment was salvaged for refurbishment or reuse. The co-ordination of the railhead-Supply Column interface also required resolution to ensure the efficient delivery of post and parcels, the failure of which had caused a significant backlog throughout the LOC to UK.[202] There was certainly more than enough work to keep a large HQ of 21st Century logistic Staff Officers busy for months!

Conclusion

The Principles of Logistics were as valid in 1914 as they are now and it was propitious that the BEF had a QMG who not only had foresight but the confidence, as the principal logistic staff officer, to make decisions and give clear direction. That he had the support of the Commander-in-Chief, Sir John French and the respect of the AG and IGC, clearly suggests a man of stature, competence and ability, although he was not infallible. Without these relationships, it is difficult to see how the vital logistic decisions could have been effectively executed. Whilst Robertson was a master of regulation and procedure, he clearly believed the rules must guide rather than constrain creativity, support to operational capability being the key imperative. Sir Maurice Hankey, Secretary to Lloyd George's War Cabinet lucidly summarized his persona: 'His greatest quality, transcending his great powers of work, his mastery of principle, his organizing capacity, and his judgement of men was "character". He was a dominating personality. He knew what he wanted, and he nearly always got his way'.[203]

Robertson, the BEF and the Nation were undeniably fortunate that the War Office had opted to introduce a WMT echelon to the logistic chain in 1912 and so effectively delivered the capability, mainly through impressments of vehicles from the commercial sector. Had this not been the case, Robertson's options would have been greatly limited, although the French may then have been forced to devote the relevant resources to repairing the British rail LOC in order to enable the BEF to conform with French operational plans. As it transpired, this particular failure in HNS prompted GHQ to take a much firmer stance in requesting British control of components of the BEF's LOC, although Robertson was sufficiently wise to comprehend the sensitivities of French commanders and scarcity of British resources to replace HN capacity.

The seven division ORBAT of the initial BEF enabled Robertson to extemporize solutions to the logistic challenges that emerged during operations in the summer and autumn of 1914 but as the force expanded it became obvious that a more structured approach would be required, although it took another two years before the industrial lay-down of BEF Theatre logistics had begun to mature. Robertson's decision to re-orientate the LOC and the ability of his logisticians at every rank to ensure the BEF stayed in the line and in the fight, undoubtedly changed the course of events in France, and possibly, the outcome of the Great War and thus the future of Europe.

201 For an explanation of the issues, see, Winton, *Theirs Not to Reason Why*, pp.281-297.
202 Note dated 2 October 1914 in TNA WO 107/13: QMG and IGC Correspondence, Stores and Equipment, 1 September - 31 December 1914.
203 Hankey, *Supreme Command*, Vol. I, pp.445-446.

6

Meerut to Marseilles

The forgotten but extraordinary logistic feat of deploying Indian Expeditionary Force A to France: August - December 1914

Introduction

In August and September 2014, commemorations were held in the United Kingdom, Belgium and France to remember the deployment, in the summer and autumn of 1914, of the British Expeditionary Force (BEF)[1] to the Continent.[2] Perhaps unsurprisingly, the logistic aspects of these early operations, although critical at the time, have been largely, if not completely, forgotten but none more so than the hidden feat that brought Indian Expeditionary Force A (IEFA) 7,000 miles from the hills and plains of India to the fields and villages of France and Belgium.[3] Remarkably, this collective amnesia started almost as soon as the Great War had ended, with key senior officers making only passing reference, in their books,[4] to the deployment, which, by 1918, had involved nearly 159,356 personnel and 51,776 animals.[5] Whether this was borne of the institutional antipathy towards the Indian Army by some within in its British counterpart,[6] or because the components of IEFA[7] were integrated to the BEF and, unlike the Australian and Canadian Corps,

1 For an explanation of the BEF's organization, see, Major A F Becke (Comp), BOH, *Order of Battle of Divisions*, Part I, *The Regular British Divisions* (London: HMSO, 1935). For a description of the strategic construct of which the BEF was a part, see, John Gooch, *The Plans of War, The General Staff and British Military Strategy c1900-1916* (London: Routledge & Kegan Paul, 1974).

2 There was no IEFA Official History. The Secretary of State for War, Lord Kitchener, appointed Sir Fredrick Smith to the Staff of the IEFA to record its operations but when Sir Fredrick joined the coalition government in late spring 1915, the War Office selected Lieutenant-Colonel J W B Merewether of the Indian Army to succeed him. Their book, *The Indian Corps in France* (London: John Murray) was published in December 1917 under the authority of the India Office and ran to a Second Edition in January 1919 with additional tactical details, which were omitted earlier for reasons of security. The book devotes about five pages to the deployment from India but offers little of logistic significance.

3 There are very brief resumes in: Colonel R H Beadon CBE psc, *The Royal Army Service Corps, A History of Transport and Supply in the British Army*, Vol. II (Cambridge: Cambridge University Press (CUP), 1931), p.121 and Major-General A Forbes CB CMG, *A History of the Army Ordnance Services*, Vol. Three, *The Great War* (London: Medici Society, 1929), pp.32-34.

4 The BEF's QMG (then Major-General) Wully Robertson places a one word mention in his autobiography, *From Private to Field-Marshal* (London: Constable, 1921), p.217, whilst the biographer of the Army's QMG, General Sir John Cowans, noted: 'On October 19 the first Indian troops reached the Flanders Front and thus began those complications regarding variety in Supplies which were to haunt the QMG's Department throughout the war'; see, Major Desmond Chapman-Huston and Major Owen Rutter, *General Sir John Cowans, GCB GCMG, The Quartermaster-General of the Great War* (London: Hutchinson, 1924), Vol. II, pp.46-47.

5 Figures from War Office, *Statistics of the Military Effort of the British Empire during the Great War, 1914-1920* (MEBE) (HMSO, 1922), pp.777-779, India's Military Contribution to the War.

6 'A Hazardous Experiment: Command and the Indian Corps in the First Battle of Ypres' in Nicolas Gardner, *Trial By Fire, Command and the British Expeditionary Force 1914* (Westport Connecticut & London; Praeger, 2003), p.183.

7 Published literature on the IEFA is limited. The IEFA's original commander, General James Willcocks wrote a personal account, *With the Indians in France* (London: Constable, 1920) and apart from the many post-war

never fought as a comprehensive doctrinally pure national Three Star formation,[8] is an area for research. What is not in doubt, however, is that at a critical period of the war, IEFA[9] provided a significant reinforcement to the BEF, constituting 14.8 percent of the force in December 1914,[10] although when the decision was taken in August to send IEFA to France, the importance of its military, political and social contribution was not foreseen.

The deployment had many complexities. First, it was not the only Indian Expeditionary Force to be dispatched from the Indian Sub-Continent, which initiated some difficult decisions, particularly in relation to priorities of movement and supply.[11] Secondly, whilst significant internal military planning had been undertaken for overseas expeditions, the India Office had not approved this activity, so the Indian Army was structured and equipped for operations on the North-West Frontier, and to assist in the provision of Internal Security.[12] Thirdly, the Indian Army was not logistically prepared to deliver effective overseas expeditionary capability;[13] this resulted, upon mobilization, in divisional combat reorganizations and the requirement for additional logistic resources, neither of which solved the doctrinal incompatibilities.[14] Fourthly, IEFA was initially destined for Egypt to protect the Suez Canal from Turkish incursions; the redirection to France, whilst clearly perceived in Whitehall as critical to the British Empire war effort, generated a significant additional mission for the BEF's fully committed planners and logisticians in order to deliver the vital Reception,

regimental histories and the unofficial Official History, Smith & Merewether, *The Indian Corps in France*, the story of IEFA was laid to rest until Gordon Corrigan wrote a most enlightening book *Sepoys in the Trenches, The Indian Corps on the Western Front 1914-15* (Staplehurst: Spellmount, 1999). By far the most academically extensive and intellectually expansive analysis, and the most recent, is George Moreton-Jack, *The Indian Army on the Western Front, India's Expeditionary Force to France and Belgium in the First World War* (Cambridge: CUP, 2014), which does full justice to the subject, except for logistics. Shrabani Basu, *For King and Another Country, Indian Soldiers in the Western Front, 1914-1918* (London: Bloomsbury, 2015), beautifully integrates the personal stories of Indian officers and soldiers to the military and social history of the Indian Army in the United Kingdom and France. Chris Kempton, *Duty & Fidelity, The Indian Army 1914-1921*, Three Volumes (Milton Keynes, Military Press, 2009), is impressive in covering the operational history, structure and nomenclature of all divisions, brigades and regiments. Simon Doherty & Tom Donovan, *The Indian Corps on the Western Front: A Handbook and Battlefield Guide* (Brighton: Tom Donovan Editions, 2014), is most illuminating, containing a clear structured resume of the many different IEFA facets and a selection of excellent photographs. Kaushik Roy (Ed.) *The Indian Army in the Two World Wars* (Leiden: Brill, 2011) offers a wider perspective whilst 'Across the Black Waters', in David Olusoga, *The World's War* (London: Head Zeus, 2014), places the pertinent cultural aspects of the deployment within the global context of colonial soldiers fighting in a Great Power conflict.

8 A corps, normally consisting of two, three or four divisions, with supporting additional capability, including artillery, engineer, transport, supply and medical assets.

9 For the ORBAT, see, F W Perry (Comp) BOH, *Order of Battle of Divisions*, Part 5B, *Indian Army Divisions* (Newport: Ray Westlake Military Books, 1993) and Brigadier-General Sir James E Edmonds CB CMG psc (Comp), BOH, *Military Operations, France and Belgium 1914*, Vol. II, *Antwerp, La Bassee, Armentieres, Messines and Ypres, October-November 1914* (London: Macmillan, 1929), pp.481-486.

10 Based upon information in MEBE, p.64 (iii), Table (ii) - Estimated Strength of the Expeditionary Forces, France and Italy. The British Army in India component totalled 15,357 personnel and the Indian contingent, 24,572.

11 These were: IEFA to France, B and C to East Africa, D to Mesopotamia, E and F to Egypt and G to Gallipoli.

12 Lord Kitchener's reorganization of 1903-04 not only restructured the Indian Army but confirmed that its Mission was to defend the North-West Frontier against an aggressive enemy. The maintenance of Internal Security was a Supporting Task, in that it released the Field Army to execute its functions.

13 For a summary of the organization of the Indian Army, see, Lt-Col H M E Brunker, *Notes on Organization and Equipment*, 6th Edn (London: William Clowes and Sons, 1909), pp.209-218.

14 For an examination of the pre-war reorganization of the Indian Command QMG's Department and the Administrative Services, see, Major-General Sir George MacMunn KCB KCSI DSO, 'The Quartermaster-General's Department and the Administrative Services in India from the Mutiny to the Present Time', *The Journal of the Royal United Service Institution (JRUSI)*, Vol. LXX (February 1924), pp.107-111. The revised QMG pre-war responsibilities were:

Staging, Onward Movement and Integration (RSOMI) process.[15] That India Command and GHQ BEF achieved these tasks, across three continents and with the telegraph as the primary means of communication was, and remains, a remarkable feat. Whilst the deployment had more than a few imperfections, frustrations and failures, its success was not only a tribute to the planners and logisticians but also to the power of the Royal Navy and Mercantile Marine, and the French who, as the receiving Host Nation (HN) were able to allocate the relevant assets at the right time to enable the operation to be completed.

Concepts and Plans

Neither the British nor Indian Governments had, pre-war, authorised planning for an IEF to deploy to France in support of the Home Army.[16] This situation did not however, prevent the General Staff in Army Headquarters (AHQ)[17] of India Command from engaging in a secret project entitled NATHI[18] in the period 1910-1911. Driven by the Chief of the Indian General Staff, Lieutenant-General Sir Douglas Haig, the project aim was to create plans for the despatch of two forces, one to France, via Egypt, to fight the Germans and the other, through the port of Basra to Mesopotamia for operations against the Ottomans. NATHI generated instructions, schedules and timetables for the 3rd (Lahore), 6th (Poona) and 7th (Meerut) Divisions[19] plus four cavalry brigades, to be mobilized and entrained for despatch from Karachi and Bombay. Such activity was a classic case of Mission Creep, which although initiated at the highest command level, was in direct contravention of government direction for the Indian General Staff to work solely upon matters related to sub-

Table 6.1
GHQ India: Pre-War QMG Responsibilities

Directorate	QMG	Responsibility
Movements & Quartering	1	Movements - Routine
	2	Movements - Operations
	3	Quartering
	4	Cantonment
	5	Establishments, Accounts & Budgets
Supply & Transport	6	Supplies
	7	Transport
	8	Clothing & Dress
Farms	9	Farms
Remounts	10	Remounts
Veterinary	11	Veterinary

15 RSOMI is a modern term describing the process by which a force is received into Theatre, is initially administered, issued with additional equipment, conducts specific training, receives operational munitions and then concentrates for battle.

16 There was by early 1914, an informal agreement at British and Indian Government levels that the Indian Army might despatch troops to African and Mediterranean stations to release British forces for Europe.

17 For a description of the work of the General Staff in AHQ, see, Major-General A Hamilton-Gordon CB, 'Share of General Staff in Preparation for War at Army Headquarters in India', *The Army Review*, Vol. VI, No 2 (April 1914). Hamilton-Gordon was well placed as the author, being the Director of Military Operations (DMO).

18 A Punjabi word translatable as *imp*; clearly an oblique reference to imperial.

19 Indian divisions and brigades were, pre-war, all numbered. The War Office directed that those in IEFA should be titled as to prevent confusion with British formations. 3rd (Indian) Infantry Division thus became the Lahore Division and the 7th, the Meerut Division. The brigades of the divisions were also de-numbered and titled, whilst the 9th Cavalry Brigade became the Secunderabad Brigade; TNA WO 95/1088: HQ Indian Corps, GS, WD. To provide clarity, both nomenclatures have been used in the chapter.

continental security. The Viceroy of India reacted furiously when he discovered such a blatant breach of trust had occurred, ordering the scheme abandoned and the plans destroyed.[20] Needless to say, the staffing process disappeared deep into the offices of AHQ, internal office security was significantly tightened and the plans refined, to be dusted off in 1914. In the meantime, practice for a potential deployment moved apace through the annual routines that were vital in generating operational capability within the sub-continent. British Army battalion rotations arrived and departed by sea, whilst many units moved by rail to conduct training. Indian Land Forces had also long been deployed through the 19th and early 20th Centuries outside India, to Aden, East Africa, the Mediterranean, around the Indian Ocean and to Singapore.

In operational terms, the most important recent tasks had been the external deployment of a division of 10,000 troops to China during the Boxer Rebellion in 1900,[21] operations in Somaliland (1901-1904),[22] Tibet (1903-1905), a rare multi-divisional exercise in the Punjab in 1905 and the internal dispatch of 1st Division to Tirah for operations on the North-West Frontier in 1908.[23] In 1911, 1,000 Indian troops from 6th Division sailed to the Makran Coast on the Persian Gulf, whilst in November 1911, the Indian General Staff utilized the mobilization process to support the Delhi Durbar.[24] 50,000 troops, from three infantry divisions, three cavalry brigades and divisional troops plus thousands of army followers were moved in 81 trains to the Delhi railheads.[25] From these operations and exercises, conducted in a variety of climatic and geographic conditions, valuable logistic lessons were identified and experience acquired, much of which proved to be relevant in 1914. In particular, the new Animal Transport (AT) units of the recently established Supply & Transport Corps, formed in 1903 as a result of the Kitchener Reforms, performed efficiently in the Tirah campaign and during the Delhi Durbar but the supply system, whilst credible in internal operations, clearly had inherent structural limitations when matched to the European environment.[26]

As a result of all of these activities, the Indian General Staff, which had only been established in 1910,[27] produced revised expeditionary manuals, whilst rail and sea movement procedures were

20 The scheme was under-written by the Commander-in-Chief India, General Sir O'Moore Creagh and clearly did Douglas Haig no harm because he was awarded the Knight Commander of the Order of the Indian Empire (KCIE) in December 1911.

21 See, General Staff, *Official Account of the Military Operations in China, 1900-1901*, War Office (HMSO: 1903), compiled by Major E W M Norie of the Intelligence Branch. This is the scarcest of the British Official History publications because only 250 copies were printed for official circulation. It has been reprinted in hardcover by the Battery Press (1995) and in soft-back by the Naval & Military Press (2014).

22 General Staff, *Official History of the Operations in Somaliland, 1901-1904*, Vols I & II, War Office (London: HMSO, 1907).

23 See, *Frontier and Overseas Expeditions from India*, Vol. I, *Operations Against the Mohmands 1908*, Intelligence Branch, Army Headquarters India (Calcutta, 1908) and Vol. II, *Operations against the Zakka Khel Afridis 1908*, Intelligence Branch, Army Headquarters India (Calcutta, 1908).

24 The Delhi Durbar was held on Tuesday 12 December 1911 to welcome the King-Emperor, George V, and Queen Mary. The official celebrations supporting the visit taking place 7-16 December.

25 For a concise summary of the unit deployments of the these long forgotten British, Indian and Gurkha regiments and battalions, see, Chris Kempton, *Duty & Fidelity*, Part III (Sect I) *Deployments*.

26 For a summary of AT organization in the Indian Army, see Brunker, *Notes on Organization and Equipment*, pp.111-117.

27 218 officers of the Indian Army had passed the Staff College at Quetta (opened in 1907) by 1914. Contrary to the popular military belief that the Staff Courses contained no logistic content, 23% of the curriculum was devoted to A&Q, or in 21st Century British Army parlance, Combat Service Support (CSS), subjects. There was however, no financial incentive for Indian Army officers and those of the RGA, RE and ASC to attend Camberley or Quetta as many officers lost pay, allowances and regimental seniority. For a detailed explanation of staff training in the pre-Great War British Army, see, the illuminating, Brian Bond, *The Victorian Army and the Staff College 1854-1914* (London: Eyre & Methuen, 1972).

issued as best-practice notes. The 1912 edition of the *Field Service Regulations* (FSR)[28] reinforced this guidance and included a section on army sea movements in co-operation with the Royal Navy. Despite all the training, exercises and operational experience, the Indian Army of 1914 was, in the opinion of its Commander-in-Chief, General Sir O'Moore Creagh, not even properly prepared for an encounter with semi-organized Asiatic enemies,[29] although the Official History[30] was a little less harsh. This scenario was largely the result of political direction and financial parsimony, aspects which the Army had mostly managed carefully for internal tasks but there were three key weaknesses of the Indian Army in relation to operations in a European theatre, which would prove much more testing. First, a very limited combined arms capability; secondly, inadequate administrative arrangements for large-scale overseas deployments and thirdly, dissonance, in comparison with the BEF, in equipment, particularly artillery and the absence of Wheeled Motor Transport (WMT). All of these issues created a series of logistic problems that required solutions in order to enable the IEFA to effectively take to the Field in France.

M-Day

The efficient mobilization of the 3rd (Lahore) and 7th (Meerut) Divisions and the 9th (Secunderabad) Cavalry Brigade, followed by the 1st (Indian) Cavalry Division with their integral artillery and logistic units, for despatch to Egypt, was a major task enabled by the AHQ planning of 1910-1911. The divisional Order of Battle (ORBAT) was based upon the Field Army Allotment Tables After Relief (FAATAR) of 1913-1914, with hot-planning modifications.[31] The distances were immense, with 2,500 miles separating the two units furthest from each other and there were plenty of challenges to keep brigade staff officers and regimental personnel busy.[32] Effective command was therefore, critical and AHQ established CONTROL at Simla to deliver the necessary effect,[33] although divisional staffs quickly discovered that the failure to utilize brigade headquarters as a Command & Control (C2) node, with telegraphic reports from over 20 units being sent directly to divisional headquarters was a serious mistake.[34]

Another taxing issue was the availability of Supply & Transport (S&T) capability and ordnance procured equipment;[35] this was a recurring theme during mobilization,[36] compounded by the reliance, by all but three cavalry regiments, on the *Sillidar* System.[37] Based upon the Yeomanry

28 General Staff, *Field Service Regulations* (FSR) Part I, *Operations*, 1909, War Office (London: HMSO, 1912), Chp III, Movements by Land and Sea.

29 See, O'Moore Creagh, *Indian Studies* (London: Hutchinson, 1919), p.254 and *The Autobiography of General Sir O'Moore Creagh VC*, with an Introduction and Notes by Major-General Sir Charles E Callwell (London: Hutchinson, 1924), p.296.

30 For a pre-war summary of the Army in India, see, Brigadier-General F J Moberly CB CSI DSO psc, BOH, *The Campaign in Mesopotamia*, 1914-1918, Vol. I (London: HMSO, 1923), pp.49-74.

31 TNA WO 95/3932/1: HQ 7th (Meerut) Division, QMG, WD, 8 August 1914.

32 One particular issue for 7th (Meerut) Division HQ staff was ensuring that the movement of the Divisional Photo-Litho and Printing Section remained integral to the HQ to ensure that the HQ was able to issue written orders and instructions. This capability was especially important to the logisticians who relied upon it to print and distribute the detail critical to operations. The important output of the section is lucidly demonstrated by the divisional documents held in the TNA. TNA WO 95/3932/1: HQ 7th (Meerut) Division, QMG, WD, Lessons Identified, August 1914.

33 TNA WO 95/3915/1: HQ 3rd (Lahore) Division, AQMG, WD, 13 August 1914.

34 TNA WO 95/3932/1: HQ 7th (Meerut) Division, QMG, WD, Lessons Identified, August 1914.

35 The Lessons Learned from the deployment and the many operations, which followed it, are encapsulated in the *Indian Army Service Corps (IASC) Manual (War)* (Simla: Government of India Press, 1932).

36 TNA WO 95/3932/1: HQ 7th (Meerut) Division, QMG, WD, entries 9-13 August 1914.

37 For an explanation, see, na, *The Army in India and its Evolution, including an account of the Establishment of the Royal Air Force in India* (Calcutta: Superintendent Government Printing India, 1924), pp.91-96, and Lieutenant-Colonel

model, in which each soldier provided and maintained his own horse, saddlery, equipment and clothing, units were responsible for the provision of nearly all their 1st Line logistic support,[38] except for firearms and ammunition, which was sustainable within the Indian Sub-Continent but introduced clear fragility for operations beyond it. Whilst the transport elements were relatively sound, despite the requirement to mobilize personnel and animals to expand cadre units, the Supply and Ordnance elements certainly had capability limitations. The supply aspects of the expedition were an exacting problem because the Main Effort of the pre-war supply organization[39] was the operation of Supply Depots in the principal cantonments and their smaller supporting sub-depots in the Stations. Much of the work was focused on direct local purchase and contracts because an AHQ Standing Order prohibited the storage of any article, which could be obtained from the civilian market in India; 'Just In Time' and 'Supply Chain Management', are certainly not new concepts. In addition, most Indian personnel were not rationed in peacetime, which meant the complex process of deploying overseas was made more complicated by the requirement to improvise units to supply Indian troops. Mobilization stocks of food and clothing were held at divisional level in a Reserve Depot[40] and further dislocation and inconvenience was created as the issue programme commenced.

As mobilization progressed, some interesting anomalies emerged. The Assistant Quartermaster General (AQMG) staff of 3rd (Lahore) Division suffered some frustration in distributing the classified movement programmes when he discovered the Indian Postal Service would not accept registered mail after 1600 hours[41] on a working day.[42] 33 percent of Indian personnel were on summer leave[43] and because of the monsoon disrupting road communications there were some incredible feats of personal endurance to return to units.[44] There were consequently delays, some Indian units taking two weeks to complete mobilization but 3rd (Lahore) Division was able to depart on ships from Bombay and Karachi during 24-25 August 1914.[45] The 9th Mule Corps was dispersed from its Peace Station at Amballa,[46] which required its Troops to return post-haste, one of which, to meet the time-line, had to march 82 miles in 68 hours in a very trying mid-day heat

E Tennant, *The Royal Deccan Horse in the Great War* (Aldershot: Gale & Polden, 1939), pp.101-105.

38 Lines of Support are used to describe the boundaries of specific elements of logistic functions. Lines of Support was not a term that was in use during the Great War but it appears in various logistic publications and is a simple method of assigning capability to units and formations. 1st Line - organic to a unit; 2nd Line - organic to a brigade or division; 3rd Line - allocated to Corps or Army; 4th Line - provided by the Base. For IEFA, 4th Line was delivered in-Theatre and from the United Kingdom and India.

39 Not including the Leave Reserve, the Supply Branch in 1914 totalled 3,858 staff, which comprised 360 British military personnel, 567 civilians and 2,931 followers. See, *The Army in India and its Evolution*, p.128.

40 One for each division, except for the Burma Division.

41 Whilst the 24 hour clock is used for clarity, this innovation was not officially adopted in the BEF until 1 October 1918.

42 TNA WO 95/3915/1: HQ 3rd (Lahore) Division, AQMG, WD, 11 August 1914.

43 Returns from Garhwali units identified that there might be delays in the return of furlough personnel but units were ready to move by 26 August 1914; TNA WO 95/3932/1: HQ 7th (Meerut) Division, QMG, WD, entries 14 & 26 August 1914.

44 British officers travelling to, on leave in, or returning from, the United Kingdom had various adventures. Some arrived in India to join the IEFA, others joined en-route, whilst many were posted to BEF units or joined the New Armies.

45 Train movements are shown in Movement Appx I in TNA WO 95/3915/1/1: HQ 3rd (Lahore) Division, AQMG, WD, 8 August - 31 December 1914; Appx II, shows the allotment to ships sailing from Karachi.

46 Amballa, also spelt Ambala, is located in the North of India in the State of Haryana and still has a significant military presence. Contemporary British publications often use the name Umballa instead of Amballa. Umballa is the Garrison Town, where in 1898, in an innovative moment of Army veterinary technique, a farrier of the Royal Horse Artillery, allegedly used a fire engine to give an enema to an elephant; Miles Noonan, *Tales from the Mess, A Military Miscellany* (London: Hutchinson, 1983), p.130. By strange co-incidence, 59th Battery RFA sailed to France in the SS *Umbala* (spelling from the source); TNA WO 95/3915/1: HQ 3rd (Lahore) Division, AQMG, WD, 25 August 1914.

of 110°F.[47] The unit was then tasked to mobilize its 200 Army Transport carts, a decision which caused considerable confusion because they were Peace Establishment only equipment. The order was confirmed, thereby creating much work for the muleteers who had never practised the task of stripping the carts for rail and sea movement[48]; fortunately in France, when the carts were moved by rail, they did so, assembled.[49]

British units were generally much quicker to mobilize. 2nd Leicestershire Regiment, a battalion in 7th (Meerut) Division mobilized at Ranikhet on Sunday 9 August, departed on a route march of 52 miles on 11 August to the railhead at Kathgodam, arriving mid-day Saturday 15 August and entraining the same day for Bareilly, the location of the concentration area for the Dehra Dun Brigade.[50] The battalion then spent six weeks at Bareilly and Karachi awaiting equipment and clothing and the arrival of C Company from Delhi, before sailing for France,[51] 7th (Meerut) Division, being phased to deploy in September. Illness and death afflicted British and Indians alike. The 20th Deccan Horse had a brief outbreak of cholera,[52] whilst 1st Connaught Rangers had several soldiers die of heatstroke whilst travelling by rail across the Thar Desert.[53] The 1/39th Garhwal Rifles, serving with 2nd Leicesters in the 20th (Garhwal) Brigade, had to camp for nine days close to a mosquito-infested swamp at the Kotdwara[54] railhead, whilst the 47th Sikhs were placed in quarantine at Pilgrim Camp near Karachi.[55] The movement of the IEFA to the Sea Ports of Embarkation (SPOE) certainly proved how logistically challenging even administrative military activity could be on the Indian Sub-Continent, especially in the oppressive heat and humidity of the summer.

Arrival at the port did not always bring relief; the Other Ranks of the 9th Mule Corps were washed out of their tents by a storm that turned the camp at Cotton Green in Bombay into a quagmire,[56] the Officer Commanding noting that the event was good training for Flanders.[57] The officers did not suffer such discomfort; they were accommodated at the *Taj Mahal Hotel*.[58] The

47 Major H M Alexander DSO, *On Two Fronts, Being the Adventures of an Indian Mule Corps in France and Gallipoli* (London: Dutton, 1917), p.5. 110°F is 43.3°C.

48 Whilst the carts were loaded stripped, which saved space on the ship, this arrangement inevitably led to some assemblies or parts being lost or damaged, which required much work by the artificers to repair, assemble and modify the carts upon arrival in Marseilles; TNA WO 95/3939/8: 7th (Meerut) Division, Indian Mule Transport, WD, 'Notes on Voyage'. The Meerut Indian Mule Transport comprised 11th and 32nd Mule Corps.

49 Alexander, *On Two Fronts*, p.7.

50 TNA WO 95/3945/2: 2nd Battalion Leicestershire Regiment, WD, 1 August 1914 - 31 December 1915.

51 Colonel H C Wylly CB, *History of the 1st & 2nd Battalions The Leicestershire Regiment in the Great War* (Aldershot: Gale & Polden, 1928), pp.106-108.

52 Tennant, *Royal Deccan Horse*, p.9 and TNA WO 95/1187/3: 20th Deccan Horse, WD, 1 August 1914 - 31 December 1916.

53 H Jourdain and E Fraser, *The Connaught Rangers*, Three Volumes (London: Royal United Service Institute, 1924), Vol. I, p.428.

54 This delay was created by the requirement to reorganize rolling stock to move both 3rd Lahore and the 7th Meerut Divisions. Despite the daily issue of five gains of quinine per day per man, a fever broke out, which was probably a mild malaria, with soldiers suffering the effects well into the voyage to France, whilst a few never fully recovered; TNA WO 95/3945/3: 1/39th Garhwal Rifles, WD, August 1914 - November 1915. TNA WO 95/3932/1/1: 7th (Meerut) Division, AQMG, WD, August - October 1914, makes no mention of this delay, or the fever.

55 During the journey to Karachi, a wagon with personnel of the Divisional Supply Column personnel had been attached to the train at Lahore but at Samsatta two of the native followers were diagnosed with cholera; TNA WO 95/3926/1: 8th (Jullundur) Infantry Brigade, WD, 20 August 1914. Fortunately no soldiers in 47th Sikhs were infected; TNA WO 95/3927/4: 47th Sikhs, WD, 1 August 1914 - 31 December 1915.

56 Alexander, *On Two Fronts*, p.9.

57 "Not so my poor men, who were washed out of their tents on the first night by one of the heaviest downpours of rain Bombay had seen for years - four inches during the night of our arrival reducing the camp to an absolute quagmire. Thus early did the men come into contact with the discomforts of active service; it was good training for Flanders;" Ibid p.9.

58 Major Alexander noted, "The management of this hotel had very sportingly offered to put up officers proceeding

20th Deccan Horse, in light bivouacs at the Maiden, having anticipated a period of fine weather with the monsoon passing, faced a similar experience between 8-12 September 1914 before finding accommodation in goods sheds of the Bombay, Baroda and Indian Railway Company (BB&CIR).[59] The contribution of the myriad of companies comprising the Indian Railways remains a key logistic feature of the deployment to the ports and India Command recognized the critical role of the military-civil interface, assigning regimental officers to railway[60] and port liaison[61] posts at the relevant levels, in order to ensure effective coherence and outputs.[62]

P6.1. 7th (Ferozepore) Infantry Brigade Convoy at sea taken from SS *Akbar* owned and operated by the Bombay and Persia Steam Navigation Company. The SS *Akbar* was built by R Napier & Sons of Glasgow in 1889 and was of 4,653 GRT and 2,957 NRT. The ship survived the war but suffered internal engine damage in 1920 because of a failure to adhere to operating procedures. Whilst the deployment was an impressive logistic performance, there were many flaws in execution. (Tom Donovan Collection)

on active service free of charge, so I gladly availed myself of this privilege and spent a week in Bombay in great comfort." Clearly Major Alexander was not a man to unnecessarily share the discomforts of his soldiers but at least he recognized the arrangement; Ibid, p.9.

59 Tennant, *Royal Deccan Horse*, p.9 and TNA WO 95/1187/3: 20th Deccan Horse, WD, 1 August 1914 - 31 December 1916. The BB&CIR is the setting for many of the railway scenes in the film '*Gandhi*' (Columbia Pictures, 1982).

60 The AQMG of 3rd (Lahore) Division appointed three Captains as Railway Transport Officers for Cantt, Rutlam and Samasata within 20 hours of the mobilization order. TNA WO 95/3915/1: HQ 3rd (Lahore) Division, AQMG, WD, 8 August 1914.

61 For example, under the direction of QMG India, QMG 20416/108 WS dated 9 August 1914, nine infantry officers were assigned to port liaison posts, including Assistant Director Rail Transport (ADRT) (Lieutenant-Colonel Home, 1/1st Gurkhas) and Deputy Assistant Director Rail Transport (DADRT) (Major Davidson, 47th Sikhs); TNA WO 95/3915/1: HQ 3rd (Lahore) Division, AQMG, WD, 13 August 1914.

62 Ibid, 8 August 1914.

Across Dark Seas

Whilst the allocated Force Elements were moving to the ports of Karachi and Bombay, AHQ and divisional HQ staffs were busy co-ordinating a multitude of activities to ensure the plans were effectively executed, including the transportation of 36,000 rounds of 13 pdr ammunition and another 2,304 rounds of 4.7 inch from depots to the embarkation ports.[63] A particular challenge from the logistic perspective was the dynamic divisional ORBAT, which changed significantly from the initial Cantonment Division, through the War Division to the Field Formation in France. Approximately 50 percent of the Cantonment infantry battalions from 3rd (Lahore) and 7th (Meerut) Divisions were left in India for Internal Security and Frontier tasks and there were major adjustments to the artillery ORBAT.[64] Logistics required a major re-organization because none of the IEFA divisions had deployable Divisional Trains, Ammunition Parks or Supply Columns, which were essential for operations in France. Nearly all of these units were formed using reservists in the United Kingdom in late August and early September. To complicate the picture further, Territorial Force (TF) battalions[65] and other Indian Army units joined IEFA in France from December 1914 onwards from Egypt, Hong Kong,[66] Malta and the United Kingdom.

The acquisition of shipping was an essential task managed by AHQ Q Staffs, supported by officers from the Royal Navy and Royal Indian Marine, who were practised in dealing with the commercial shipping agents. The 1911 mobilization plans were initiated and the procedures enacted not only to procure cargo and passenger ships but also to allocate the necessary port facilities including wharves, berths, cranes and sheds. At a strategic logistic level, there was great confidence in the maritime capability. In 1914, although 44.4 percent of the World's tonnage of shipping was flagged to the United Kingdom,[67] the key question was whether sufficient vessels of the appropriate type could be acquired to meet the timeframe and of especial concern, was shipping for horses.[68] Arrangements were also made to construct tented camps and convert warehouses to provide suitable staging areas for units transiting the port areas.[69] This was in contrast to the deployment of the BEF to France, which relied on carefully refined scheduling to process units directly from rail to ship, with the minimum of time spent in port facilities. To ensure efficient embarkation, AHQ mobilization plans directed specific regimental officers from deploying units to assume key temporary transportation staff appointments, which complimented the many close professional and personal relationships of commanders and staffs in the pre-war Indian divisions,

63 MEBE, p.421, Table (iii) - Statement of Ammunition sent to France.

64 Of the 22 infantry battalions in 3rd (Lahore) Cantonment Division only 12 were in the IEFA division. For details of the maturing ORBATs, see, Perry, BOH, *Order of Battle of Divisions*, Part 5B.

65 In 3rd (Lahore) Division: 1/4th Londons, 1/4th Suffolks and 4th Kings. In 7th (Meerut) Division, 4th Seaforth Highlanders, 1/3rd Londons and 4th Black Watch. 1/3rd and 1/4th Londons had an interesting itinerary. Participating in Home Defence by guarding key infrastructure on the London & South-Western Railway (LSWR) in August 1914, the battalions sailed to Malta on Friday 4 September 1914 before embarking from the island for Marseilles and arriving there on Wednesday 6 January 1915. Perry, BOH, *Order of Battle of Divisions*, Part 5B.

66 na, *The 40th Pathans in the Great War* (Lahore: The Civil and Military Gazette Press, 1921).

67 The Dominions and Colonies contributed an additional 3.5%, which meant that Britain and the Empire controlled 47.9% of the World's shipping. In 1914, British flagged steam vessels totalled 12,602. Of particular interest, is that 30% of the vessels accounted for 90% of the tonnage, reflecting Britain's economic need to drive costs down in her global trade. Investment was strong too, illustrated by the young age of the fleet; 68% of the ships had been constructed since 1900, 44% since 1905 and 20% since 1910. Sailing ships totalled 2,081. For details, see, *Annual Statement of the Navigation and Shipping of the United Kingdom for the Year 1913*, Command 7616 and Archibald Hurd, BOH, *The Merchant Navy*, Vol. I (London: John Murray, 1921), pp.85-94.

68 For details of maritime horse transportation, see, Major A G Todd, Army Veterinary Corps, 'The Management of Horses on Board Ship', *The Army Review*, Vol. VII, No 4 (October 1914), pp.413-425.

69 7th (Meerut) Division detrained at Karachi 1-4 September 1914 but did not sail until Sunday 20 September; TNA WO 95/3932/1: HQ 7th (Meerut) Division, QMG, WD, September 1914.

which, for the most part generated an atmosphere of co-operation. These arrangements however, were apparently ineffective for 7th (Meerut) Division, whose General Officer Commanding (GOC) wrote to express his dis-satisfaction with a number of areas, not least the lack of tact by the Deputy Assistant Quartermaster General (DAQMG) at Karachi, one Major Winter,[70] whose approach Lieutenant-General Anderson believed had created a great deal of un-necessary friction between the embarkation staff and units.[71]

The requisitioned ships were converted for military use by a small army of fitters provided by the 2nd & 3rd Sappers and Miners supported by artisans mainly contracted from the Great Indian Peninsular Railway.[72] Their tasks included fitting personnel bunks, horse stalls, rifle racks, access ramps and storage containers, although there were a few disputes with ships' captains relating to what might be described as collateral damage.[73] Loading was generally quick for an organized unit, with 45 minutes being recorded for 2/39th Garhwal Rifles boarding the SS *Coconada* on Wednesday 16 September 1914.[74] Most soldiers took time to obtain their sea-legs, which in addition to the temperature and the cramped accommodation,[75] created an unpleasant voyage for many,[76] especially in lively sea conditions.[77] Inevitably, cavalry regiments and mule corps[78] units had the greatest challenges, not only during embarkation but also during the voyage. Many of the ships requisitioned for the transport of horses and mules had limitations for this task,[79] particularly in relation to ventilation, so the soldiers and muleteers had to be innovative in caring for their charges.[80] The 13th Hussars aboard the SS *Dunluce Castle* had an especially trying time with the temperature on the horse decks reaching 133°F: [81]

> You know what the weather has been like, but you can have no conception of what it has been like below in the horse decks: absolute hell. All across the Arabian Sea it was dead calm

70 The DAQMG in Bombay, Major Cummins, had a much better relationship with the embarking units, the OC 9th Mule Corps recording 'Major Cummins, DAQMG, was an ideal Staff Officer, always knowing exactly what we wanted. He was never flurried, always polite, and ready to help……'; Alexander, *On Two Fronts*, p.10.

71 TNA WO 95/3932/1: HQ 7th (Meerut) Division, GOC to Chief of the General Staff Army HQ India, letter dated 2 October 1914.

72 Lieutenant-General Sir William Marshall GCMG KCB KCSI, *Memories of Four Fronts* (London: Benn, 1929), pp. 5-8 and E Sandes, *The Indian Sappers and Miners* (Chatham: Institute of the Royal Engineers, 1948), p.439. Other railways assisted in the provision of artisans and labourers.

73 Modifications to the Ships Taken Up From Trade (STUFT) were a memorable feature of the pre-deployment activity during Operation CORPORATE in 1982. See, Captain Roger Villar, *Merchant Ships at War, The Falklands Experience* (London: Conway, 1984), pp.17-28.

74 Smith & Merewether, *The Indian Corps in France*, p.13.

75 The author of the 8th (Jullunder) Infantry Brigade War Diary recorded: 'The accommodation for officers on the Edavana is very good but as there are two whole battalions on board the men are very crowded'; TNA WO 95/3926/1, entry 29 August 1914. The battalions were 1st Manchesters (8th Brigade) and 1st Connaught Rangers (7th (Ferozepore) Brigade).

76 Despite the heat and the humidity, 8th (Jullundur) Brigade units participated in daily parades of free gymnastics and running drill, recording that 'the troops are all in excellent spirits'; HQ 8th (Jullundur) Infantry Brigade, WD, 7 September 1914.

77 The RMS *Edavana* seemed to be particularly affected by a long swell as the convoy left Karachi and many soldiers of the 1st Connaught Rangers were ill; TNA WO 95/3926/1: HQ 8th (Jullundur) Infantry Brigade, WD, 29 August 1914.

78 The challenges in loading mules to the SS *Castalia* is concisely described in Alexander, *On Two Fronts*, pp.9-10.

79 Officer Commanding (OC) 7th (Meerut) Division, Indian Mule Transport, who was double-hatted as OC 32nd Mule Corps, was of the strong opinion that the ships selected for the move of the Corps were not suitable for the task; TNA WO 95/3939/8: 7th (Meerut) Division, Indian Mule Transport, WD, 'Notes on Voyage'.

80 See, report on SS *Ballarat* dated 28 October 1914 by Major Dennistoun RFA; TNA WO 95/1168/1: 1st (Indian) Cavalry Division, A&Q, WD.

81 Recorded by the Regimental Veterinary Surgeon, whilst horses were being slung into the holds at Bombay; Sir H Mortimer Durand KCMG KCSI KCIE, *The Thirteenth Hussars in the Great War* (Edinburgh & London: William Blackwood and Sons, 1921), p.61. 133°F is 56.1°C.

> and a following wind, and the first day and a half in the Red Sea was even worse. We have worked like slaves with the horses, off and on all day: men stripped, officers in shirt sleeves, and all pouring with sweat; the horses panting for breath, and all we could do by continually moving them, sluicing them with vinegar and water, and all sorts of things to keep them alive. It was heartbreaking. I hope I'll never have to go through such a thing again.[82]

On the SS *City of Sparta*, carrying the mules of the Meerut Indian Mule Transport, there was no outlet on the lower decks for the dung and urine, which had to be carried topside in buckets and large jam tins.[83] The muleteers were not permitted to wash-down the standings or cool the mules with water in order to prevent urine from sluicing into areas of the deck, where rusting of the iron would result; no wonder the OC Mule Transport described the arrangement as 'very bad',[84] although the stench in the heat must have been much worse.[85] The 20th Deccan Horse, embarked on the SS *Egra* and SS *Ellora*, laid coir mats on the ships' decks to enable the horses to have daily exercise[86] but despite their industry, three animals died of pneumonia, whilst commanders, soldiers and muleteers alike were frustrated by the convoy arrangement because it prevented ships turning into wind to freshen the areas below decks.[87] Heat and humidity were not the only dangers. On the SS *Dunluce Castle*, one of the horses of the 13th Hussars having died, was being slung for burial overboard, when it fell from the sling 40 feet into the hold but fortunately only grazing a horse.[88] Horses however, were not the only casualties.[89] On Friday 11 September 1914, the ships conveying 3rd (Lahore) Division placed their engine telegraphs to stop at 1000 LOCAL to bury Captain Mitchell,[90] commanding the SS *Castalia*, who had died during the night,[91] whilst on the RMS *Edavana* during Thursday 24 September, a soldier of 1st Connaught Rangers died of double pneumonia and was buried at sea approximately 420 miles from Marseilles.[92]

As the ships sailed into the Red Sea, commanders and staff had time to take stock.[93] Both

82 An officer of the 13th Hussars to his wife, in a letter quoted in the Regimental History; Durand, *Thirteenth Hussars*, pp.60-61.

83 TNA WO 95/3939/8: 7th (Meerut) Division, Indian Mule Transport, WD, 'Notes on Voyage'.

84 Ibid.

85 Conditions on the SS *Sofala*, were better, with the decks having interconnecting gangways which allowed the mules to roam in batches; Ibid.

86 Tennant, *Royal Deccan Horse*, pp.11-12.

87 The convoys travelled at the speed of the slowest ship, which was often between 7-9 knots. The heat of the Indian Ocean and Red Sea was undoubtedly very trying on the animals in particular. An entry in the HQ 8th (Jullundur) Infantry Brigade War Diary of Monday 7 September 1914 at Aden, noted the oppressive heat on board the RMS *Edavana* at anchor during the night with no wind but during the day the strong sea breeze 'made it nice and cool'. On Wednesday 9 September, 133 miles from Aden in the Red Sea, the convoy was blessed with a 'good head wind'; TNA WO 95/3926/1: HQ 8th (Jullundur) Infantry Brigade, WD, August 1914 - December 1915.

88 Durand, *The Thirteenth Hussars*, p 62.

89 The hardy mules proved more resilient, with only one out of 1,600 from the Mule Transport dying on the voyage. The OC noted that its death was a result of the failure to move all the mules daily and it had remained in the hottest part of the hold for four days; TNA WO 95/3939/8: 7th (Meerut) Division, Indian Mule Transport, WD, 'Notes on Voyage'.

90 Major Alexander, a dining companion, notes Captain Mitchell had served the Anchor Line for over 40 years, although this was the first time he had commanded a troop-ship and it was his last voyage of his service with the company. Major Alexander attributed his death to a heart attack brought on by anxiety; Alexander, *On Two Fronts*, p.21. The War Diary of 7 British Field Ambulance, suggests that heatstroke may have been the cause; TNA WO 95/3920/1.

91 TNA WO 95/3926/1: HQ 8th (Jullundur) Infantry Brigade, WD, 11 September 1914.

92 Ibid, 24 September 1914.

93 Some HQs and units wrote detailed War Diaries whilst at sea; a few made no entries. 21st Century historians are though, well served by the author of the 8th (Jullundur) Brigade War Diary, voyaging on the RMS *Edavana*, who was assiduous in recording ships joining and leaving the convoy, the weather, the sea state and logging the nautical miles sailed each day; TNA WO 95/3926/1: 8th (Jullundur) Infantry Brigade, WD, entries August -

the GOC 1st (Indian) Cavalry Division[94] and GOC 7th (Meerut) Division[95] were industrious in highlighting Lessons Identified. GOC of 1st (Indian) Cavalry Division and his A&Q Staff[96] had a most constructive approach, focusing, perhaps unsurprisingly, on horse care in transit,[97] with specific reference to ventilation.[98] The report raised issues relating to penning, which was preferred to stalls, whilst also examining a series of logistic issues including transit camp improvements, embarkation time reduction and Supply & Transport efficiency measures in the SPOE. The GOC particularly highlighted the insufficiency in strength of the embarkation staff tasked with loading 46 ships and noted the adverse influence of the limitation of rail capacity to the effective delivery of some of the proposals offered by the staff to enhance the process.[99]

GOC 7th (Meerut) Division signed a terse document noting that there appeared to be a failure to adhere to the spirit if not the letter of the key Principles of the *Manual of Combined Naval & Military Operations 1913*, which in his view, was to the Force's disadvantage.[100] He was clearly especially irritated by the Embarkation Staff's failure to grasp the importance of the Desired Order Arrival Staff Table (DOAST),[101] upon which he had not been consulted and the poor recording and stowage of War Stores, especially rations,[102] for the voyage.[103] In addition, the Embarkation Staff allegedly omitted to advise the divisional headquarters of the unit loading plans,[104] of which, he only obtained visibility of by a process of elimination after several days at sea,[105] a problem

September 1914.

94 Major-General M F Rimington. Promoted to Lieutenant-General in December 1914, he commanded the Indian Cavalry Corps until it was disbanded in 1916.

95 Lieutenant-General Sir Charles Anderson. Anderson promoted in September 1915 upon the departure of General Willcocks and commanded the Indian Corps until its departure from France in December 1915. He then commanded XVII and I Corps, before promoting to General in March 1917 on assumption of the post of GOC Southern Army in India.

96 Regrettably, the A&Q staff made no entries in the War Diary whilst the Division was at sea; TNA WO 95/1168/1: 1st (Indian) Cavalry Division, A&Q, WD, 16 October - 10 November 1914.

97 TNA WO 95/1168/1: 1st (Indian) Cavalry Division, A&Q, WD, contains a concise document dated 28 October 1914, written at sea by Major J G Dennistoun RFA, exposing the deficiencies aboard the hired transport SS *Ballarat* in relation to the transportation of horses by sea. The report matches the deficiencies against the requirements of the *Regulations for HM Transport Service, 1908* and *Marine Regulations, India*, Vol. II, 1914. It is clear from the content and detail in the report that Major Dennistoun was a very competent officer in this field.

98 The report noted, 'The congestion was so great and the ventilation so deficient that we were in great danger of losing a large percentage of horses.........Temperatures rose to great heights and it was only by constant and unremitting attention that the percentage of deaths was kept within reasonable limits'; TNA WO 95/1168/1: 1st (Indian) Cavalry Division, A&Q, WD.

99 Ibid, GOC to QMG India Command, letter dated 30 October 1914, written aboard SS *Ballarat* at Port Said.

100 TNA WO 95/3932/1: 7th (Meerut) Division, GOC to Chief of the General Staff Army HQ India, letter dated 2 October 1914.

101 Not identified by the GOC's report but clearly articulated by the OC Meerut Indian Mule Transport, was the issue relating to the allocation of the Mule Corps artificers, who were all placed on one ship, the SS *Sofala*, which was the last Meerut Mule Corps transport to arrive at Marseilles. This meant the carts that had been landed from the other ships could not be assembled because artificers were still at sea, nor was there sufficient manpower to move the cart frames and assemblies from the wharf. TNA WO 95/3939/8: 7th (Meerut) Division, Indian Mule Transport, WD, 'Notes on Voyage'.

102 The Officer Commanding 26th Jacobs Mountain Battery reported that on Sunday 20 September 1914 on the SS *City of Poona*, there was 'great difficulty in finding any rations at all, as there was a very large quantity of ordnance stores which had been dumped on top of the rations'. Copy of a letter from Major J E L Bruce RA to the Adjutant HMHT *City of Poona* dated 30 September 1914 in TNA WO 95/3932/1: 7th (Meerut) Division, QMG, WD, October - December 1914.

103 TNA WO 95/3932/1: 7th (Meerut) Division, QMG, WD, October - December 1914, GOC to Chief of the General Staff Army HQ India, letter dated 2 October 1914.

104 The Meerut Indian Mule Transport had to leave 30 mules at Bombay because there were insufficient stalls on ships allocated to the unit; TNA WO 95/3939/8: 7th (Meerut) Division, Indian Mule Transport, WD, 'Notes on Voyage'.

105 Interestingly, this did not occur in 3rd (Lahore) Division. The 8th (Jullundur) Infantry Brigade War Diary shows a

compounded by absence of signallers or orders for naval and army command interfaces.[106] The failure to produce ships' allotment by unit was almost certainly refuted by the Embarkation Staff because there is, in the A&Q War Diary, a detailed table listing, by vessel,[107] all the units by strength and key equipments.[108] The GOC's temper was obviously not improved after he was informed that inspections on five vessels on Thursday 24 September 1914, three days after departure from Karachi, had declared a significant percentage of the *ghi* rations,[109] unfit for consumption through contamination with coconut oil and kerosene.[110] His report stated:

> I need hardly point out the serious effect which the deprivation of this important portion of their ration, for which there is no substitute may have...........as evidenced by the attached medical report on the health and spirits of the Indian troops.......... I entirely support the opinion of the board that those concerned in the supply of adulterated[111] ghi should be very severely dealt with. Fortunately, it appears the ghi supplied to the troops embarking at Bombay, is good, and I therefore propose to apportion the balance of the ghi of the sea rations as well as of their 30 days' land rations among the whole division.[112]

The GOC also highlighted that no land rations had been shipped for the 4th Brigade Royal Field Artillery (RFA)[113] and that on some ships, insufficient grain and fodder had been loaded,[114] whilst the condition of the livestock on the SS *Torilla* was described as 'disgraceful'.[115] In addition, he forcefully articulated that the sea rations were deficient in protein, quality and quantity and provided evidence that the health of the troops had been adversely affected.[116] Needless to say, the India Command logisticians were given another pasting and QMG India was no doubt relieved when he concluded his examination of the document. Nonetheless, the divisional A&Q Staff raised a series of pertinent Lessons Identified, fully endorsed by the GOC, which lucidly demonstrated the limitations of the Indian Army's supply systems, particularly when exposed to an expeditionary environment, although IEFA was remarkably better served than the other deployed Indian forces.

simple pictogram with all the relevant ships listed by unit, supported by detailed embarkation tables describing the load of each vessel; TNA WO 95/3926/1: HQ 8th (Jullundur) Infantry Brigade, WD, 29 August 1914. Pictorial representation is very rare in war diaries of the period but demonstrates the idea has a long military history.

106 TNA WO 95/3932/1 - 7th (Meerut) Division, QMG, WD, October - December 1914, GOC to Chief of the General Staff Army HQ India, letter dated 2 October 1914.

107 One of the ships was the SS *Braunfels* (5,576 GRT) a German ship seized in port at the outbreak of war. Built by Swan Hunter in 1906, as the SS *Vidovdan* under Yugoslavian registry, she ran aground on Friday 15 December 1939 on Natuna Island NW of Borneo and was declared a total loss.

108 TNA WO 95/3932/1: HQ 7th (Meerut) Division, 'Allotment of Transports by Units of the MEERUT Division', 20 September 1914 signed by the DAA&QMG, Lieutenant-Colonel H Isacke.

109 A type of clarified butter.

110 TNA WO 95/3932/1: HQ 7th (Meerut) Division, QMG, WD, 24 September 1914.

111 This was not solely an Indian problem because the Army was aware that in the United Kingdom in 1909, food inspectors had identified that 10% of butter and 11% of milk samples were adulterated, although not necessarily contaminated; Army Council, *Army Service Corps*, Part II, *Supplies*, War Office (London: HMSO, 1909) (Reprinted 1914 with new Appx XII), p.207. A not uncommon practice of the time was the addition to milk of preservatives, such as salicylic acid, formaline and boracic acid, a procedure, which the Departmental Committee on Food Preservatives had recommended should constitute an offence under the Food and Drugs Act.

112 TNA WO 95/3932/1: HQ 7th (Meerut) Division, GOC to QMG India Command, letter dated 2 October 1914.

113 A regimental grouping comprising 3 x batteries and a Brigade Ammunition Column (BAC).

114 The Meerut Mule Transport had a particular struggle with this problem because the unit was issued with bran and barley. The OC noted: 'Most of my mules are Argentine & heartily dislike either bran or barley'. He noted however, a positive: 'Only the Chinamen scored as they eat anything'; TNA WO 95/3939/8: 7th (Meerut) Division, Indian Mule Transport, WD, 'Notes on Voyage'.

115 TNA WO 95/3932/1: HQ 7th (Meerut) Division, GOC to QMG India Command, letter dated 2 October 1914.

116 Ibid, GOC to QMG India Command, letter dated 2 October 1914.

The GOC also arranged, with an eye to improving the mobility of the division, to dispatch a telegram, via GOC Aden, to the Base Commandant Marseilles, to the effect that the division, upon arrival, needed to be equipped with 'motors, cycles and water supply appliances similar to a British Division'.[117]

Table 6.2
IEFA Deployment Schedule Matrix[118]

Division	Brigade	Depart India	Egypt	Marseilles	Orleans	Divisional Areas
3rd (Lahore) XX	7th (Ferozepore) X 8th (Jullundur) X 9th (Sirhind) X *	24-25 Aug 14	9-19 Sep 14	26 Sep 14	3 Oct 14	21 Oct 14
7th (Meerut) XX	9th (Secunderabad) X+ 19th (Dehra Dun) X 20th (Garhwal) X 21th (Bareilly) X	21 Sep 14	Direct to Marseilles	11 Oct 14	22 Oct 14	29 Oct 14
1st (Indian) Cavalry XX	2nd (Sialkot) X 3rd (Ambala) X 8th (Lucknow) X	16 Oct 14	Direct to Marseilles^1	7 Nov 14	16 Nov 14	26 Nov – 10 Dec 14
2nd (Indian) Cavalry XX	5th (Mhow) X 7th (Meerut) X	19 Nov 14	Direct to Marseilles^2	14-16 Dec 14	20-24 Dec 14	1-4 Jan 15

* Initially remained in Egypt to secure the Suez Canal from Ottoman incursions; arrived Marseilles 1 December 1914.

\+ Independent cavalry brigade.

^1 Convoy called at Suez and Port Said to dis-embark specific units for service in Egypt. Also included 7 ships with approximately 11,727 British regular troops, plus families and civilians bound for the UK.[119]

^2 Convoy called at Suez and Port Said to dis-embark specific units for service in Egypt. Also included 9 ships with approximately 12,219 British regular troops, plus families and civilians bound for the UK.

IEFA could have arrived in France more quickly than the schedule indicates, especially as mobilization and concentration in India were executed remarkably quickly. The delay in the arrival of 3rd (Lahore) Division was caused by the diversion to Egypt,[120] which had been the original destination of IEFA, in preparation for the relief of British garrisons in Egypt, Sudan, Malta and Gibraltar. BEF losses at Le Cateau on Wednesday 26 August 1914 however, created a rapid review of the

117 TNA WO 95/3932/1: HQ 7th (Meerut) Division, QMG WD, 25 September 1914.
118 The information in the table has been collated from Perry, BOH, *Order of Battle of Divisions*, Part 5B and the War Diaries of the Indian Corps divisions.
119 Archibald Hurd, BOH, *The Merchant Navy*, Vol. II (London: John Murray, 1924), pp.93-95.
120 For an outline of the division's movements in Egypt, see, TNA WO 95/3915/1: HQ 3rd (Lahore) Division, AQMG, WD, entries 9-19 September 1914.

options, resulting in the dispatch to France, from the United Kingdom, of 6th Infantry Division in early September, 7th Infantry Division and 3rd Cavalry Division in early October, 8th Infantry Division in early November and the redeployment of the IEFA to France. The reorganization in Egypt and then dispatch of IEFA was, given the time frame, an impressive piece of logistic planning and execution, which deserves more detailed examination. Remarkably, the units at sea discovered the destination of IEFA from a Reuters radio broadcast reporting Kitchener's speech in the House of Lords. Given the secrecy afforded to the despatch of the BEF from the United Kingdom, this was arguably a serious breach of operational security.[121]

Shortage of escorts created by the Royal Navy's global commitments, and in the Indian Ocean, the requirement to escort expeditions to East Africa and the Persian Gulf, whilst also protecting merchant trade against two German cruisers, SMS *Emden* and SMS *Konigsberg*, created a significant delay. Had it not been for this issue, 7th (Meerut) Division would have been hot on the heels of 3rd (Lahore) but the division's ships were held in Karachi for three weeks pending a naval escort. As it transpired, these delays greatly assisted the logisticians in France who were given additional time to plan, prepare and deliver the vital Mediterranean Line of Communication (MEDLOC) without which, IEFA could not have been moved and supported once it entered the European Continent. There was considerable debate within GHQ as to the most effective manner by which, to achieve this task, the alternative being to bring the IEFA ships into Le Havre or Saint Nazaire to utilize the operational BEF LOC. There were many advantages to this concept: clarity, simplicity and efficiency; the latter was of especial concern because establishing a second LOC required the leaning of the main LOC. Interestingly, the decision was influenced by Maritime rather than Land influences; the MEDLOC solution reduced shipping turn-round times and the need for additional naval escorts in the Eastern Atlantic.

Conclusion

So many competing pressures in a dynamic political and military scenario beset the deployment of IEFA that it was always going to be a challenge to deliver an effective result. The logisticians produced a sound plan, which was executed impressively in some areas but failed in others, especially in rationing and forage. The logistic support to the Force was not perfect and a number of issues quickly surfaced as the operation progressed but despite the plethora of problems, which inundated them, logistic staffs at different levels within the Chain of Command, particularly at divisional level, were remarkably adept at creating a fix.

What is especially impressive is how a force, which was not planned, trained, structured or equipped to fight a war in North-West Europe, deployed in short order and, by sound application of Command, Leadership and Management, delivered logistic solutions to a series of complex problems by using basic principles, thoughtful innovations and sound judgement. Key logisticians were certainly keenly aware of the importance of what is now called D QUAD,[122] Destination, Distance, Demand and Duration, even if they found it problematical and sometimes impossible, to meet the requirements. They had more difficulty in bringing coherency to managing materiel reserves, with accountability, mobility and visibility of stocks being particular initial issues but it is clear that both Commanders and Staffs recognized the significance of doing so. GOC 7th (Meerut) Division, Sir Charles Anderson, appears to have been particularly well attuned logistically, an aspect that certainly deserves further study.

121 TNA WO 95/3926/1: HQ 8th (Jullundur) Infantry Brigade, WD, 30 August 1914; message received by the radio operator of the RMS *Edavana*.

122 See, *Army Doctrine Publication* (ADP) Vol. 3, *Logistics*, DGD&D/18/34/63 (UK MOD, 1996), pp.2-3 to 2-5.

In assessing the application of the Principles of Logistics,[123] the logistic planners met, for the most part, despite the hand they had been dealt, an element of each one and scored very highly on flexibility and co-operation, except perhaps for the performance of Major Winter. The deployment to France of IEFA generated many lessons for the logistic support fraternity but one in particular remains pertinent, and was summarized by Colonel Parker in his concluding sentence of his lecture to the RASC Training College in 1920, when he offered these words of advice: '.......it is of the utmost importance that Supply and Transport should be to each other as husband and wife, the one being the complement of the other - Let no man put them asunder'.[124]

123 For more information of the Principles of Logistics, see, Ibid, pp.1-4 to 1-6.

124 Brevet Colonel W M Parker CMG DSO, Supply Services in Mesopotamia, *Royal Army Service Corps Quarterly*, April 1921, p.431.

7

The First I have Heard of Opium

The logistic integration of Indian Expeditionary Force A to the BEF in Autumn 1914

Introduction

The arrival of Indian Expeditionary Force A (IEFA)[1] in France, commencing in late September,[2] with an Order of Battle (ORBAT)[3] consisting of two infantry and two cavalry divisions,[4] whilst introducing fresh operational capability, also brought new logistic responsibilities[5] and in particular, ensuring that the Indian Corps[6] had, where possible, systems and equipment compatible with the

1 Published literature on the IEFA is limited. The IEFA's original commander, General James Willcocks wrote a personal account, *With the Indians in France* (London: Constable, 1920) and apart from the many post-war regimental histories and the unofficial Official History, Smith & Merewether, *The Indian Corps in France*, the story of IEFA was laid to rest until Gordon Corrigan wrote a most enlightening book *Sepoys in the Trenches, The Indian Corps on the Western Front 1914-15* (Staplehurst: Spellmount, 1999). By far the most academically extensive and intellectually expansive analysis, and the most recent, is George Moreton-Jack, *The Indian Army on the Western Front, India's Expeditionary Force to France and Belgium in the First World War* (Cambridge: CUP, 2014), which does full justice to the subject, except for logistics. Shrabani Basu, *For King and Another Country, Indian Soldiers in the Western Front, 1914-1918* (London: Bloomsbury, 2015), beautifully integrates the personal stories of Indian officers and soldiers to the military and social history of the Indian Army in the United Kingdom and France. Chris Kempton, *Duty & Fidelity, The Indian Army 1914-1921*, Three Volumes (Milton Keynes, Military Press, 2009), is impressive in covering the operational history, structure and nomenclature of all divisions, brigades and regiments. Simon Doherty & Tom Donovan, *The Indian Corps on the Western Front: A Handbook and Battlefield Guide* (Brighton: Tom Donovan Editions, 2014), is most illuminating, containing a clear structured resume of the many different IEFA facets and a selection of excellent photographs, whilst Kaushik Roy (Ed.) *The Indian Army in the Two World Wars* (Leiden: Brill, 2011) offers a wider perspective.

2 Robertson was first apprised of the proposal to deploy an Indian Corps to France on Sunday 23 August, as a copy addressee of Telegram 685, from Field-Marshal Kitchener, the Secretary of State for War, to the Commander-in-Chief (C-in-C) BEF, Field-Marshal French; GHQ, QMG, WD, 23 August 1914; TNA WO 95/27/1.

3 For the ORBAT, see, F W Perry, BOH, *Order of Battle of Divisions*, Part 5B, *The Indian Divisions* (Newport: Ray Westlake Military Books, 1993) and Brigadier-General Sir James E Edmonds CB CMG psc (Comp) BOH, *Military Operations, France and Belgium 1914*, Vol. II, *Antwerp, La Bassee, Armentieres, Messines and Ypres, October-November* 1914 (London: Macmillan, 1929), pp.481-486.

4 Indian divisions and brigades were, pre-war, all numbered. The War Office directed that those in IEFA should be titled as to prevent confusion with British formations. 3rd Indian Infantry Division thus became the Lahore Division and the 7th, the Meerut Division. The brigades of the divisions were also de-numbered and titled, whilst the 9th Cavalry Brigade became the Secunderabad Brigade; TNA WO 95/1088: HQ Indian Corps, GS, War Diary. To provide clarity, both nomenclatures have been used in the chapter.

5 This chapter will focus, perforce of space, upon Supply, including Food Services, and Transportation. Remounts, support to the Medical Services, especially medical evacuation and Postal, were all significant logistic activities and deserve further study.

6 This chapter is dedicated to the memory of an Indian Army officer, Lieutenant-Colonel Percy Clare Eliott-Lockhart DSO, Queen Victoria's Own Corps of Guides (Frontier Force) (Lumsden's) Killed on Friday 12 March 1915, aged 47, whilst Commanding 59th Scinde Rifles. At Rest in the Rue-des-Berceaux Cemetery, Richebourg, near Bethune in Grave 11.F.19 and commemorated on the Camberley War Memorial, which is located outside the main entrance of the Royal Military Academy Sandhurst, Percy Eliott-Lockhart was a most distinguished soldier with a wealth of operational experience including two logistic appointments. He authored, *A Frontier Campaign, A Narrative*

British Expeditionary Force (BEF)[7] and were thus commensurate with operations on the Western Front. This process included the creation of a new Line of Communication (LOC) from the Port of Entry (POE) in France, integration of United Kingdom units to the Force ORBAT, specific rations, special equipment, weapon provision, additional clothing requirements and planning around different divisional logistic establishments, as well as the Quartermaster General (QMG) of the BEF, Major-General Wully Robertson, having to personally intervene to arrange the movement of an Indian prince's horse.

Whilst the GHQ BEF General (G) Staff welcomed the news of a major reinforcement, the Administrative (A) & Quartermaster (Q) Staff[8] recognized the issues it would bring; Major-General Robertson certainly had mixed feelings because IEFA was not an homogenous integrated organization deploying to France in a pre-planned operation. The Indian Corps historians summarized the challenge: 'Composed as the Corps was, at various stages of its career, of English, Irish, and Scotch regiments, battalions of Gurkhas, subjects of a foreign state, of units largely formed of Trans-Frontier men, Imperial Service Troops, and even Indian police - a medley of religions and customs, in a foreign country amid strange and depressing surroundings.......'.[9] The arrival of IEFA would certainly create a series of complex logistic challenges at a time when the BEF's logisticians were least able to deliver solutions.

A French Welcome

As the first echelon of IEFA sailed from India, GHQ BEF commenced the planning to create the Mediterranean Line of Communication (MEDLOC) from the Port of Entry (POE)[10] to the BEF's Area of Operations (AOO)[11] although Army Headquarters (AHQ) India retained responsibility for the Sea Line of Communication (SLOC) from India to the POE and dispatching supplies that could only be obtained on the sub-continent, such as *khukuries* and Indian cooking equipment. From the BEF QMG's perspective, the initial French Host Nation Support (HNS) scenario looked none to positive, the QMG writing on Monday 7 September 1914 to his counterpart at the War Office, General John Cowans: "We have no railway of our own but are entirely in the hands of the French authorities. They are more or less off their heads and the railways hereabouts are in a state

of Operations of the Malakand and Buner Field Forces 1897-1898 (London: Methuen, 1898) with Edward Murray Dunmore VC DSO MVO, 8th Earl of Alexander.

7 For an explanation of the BEF's organization, see, Major A F Becke (Comp) BOH, *Order of Battle of Divisions, Part I, The Regular British Divisions* (London: HMSO, 1935). For a description of the strategic construct of which the BEF was a part, see, John Gooch, *The Plans of War, The General Staff and British Military Strategy c1900-1916* (London: Routledge & Kegan Paul, 1974).

8 G in 1914 equates to G2/G3/G5/G6/G7/G9 in 2018, A to G1/G8 and Q, G4.

9 Lieutenant-Colonel J W B Merewether CIE and the Right Honourable Sir Frederick Smith Bart, *The Indian Corps in France* (London: John Murray, 1919), p.401. The authors might have added that this complex mix in France also included soldiers from the British and Indian Army reserves and the United Kingdom's Territorial Force.

10 On Sunday 23 August, Telegram 691, from Field-Marshal Kitchener, the Secretary of State for War, to the Commander-in-Chief (C-in-C) BEF, Field-Marshal French, noted that the Indian Corps would disembark in Marseilles. Given the subsequent work by the staffs of QMG and IGC to resolve the details of the Port of Entry, this may have been an assumption by Kitchener that the French would agree to any request. GHQ QMG WD, entry 23 August 1914; TNA WO 95/27/1.

11 The QMG received confirmation from the War Office on Friday 28 August 1914 through Telegram 728 that the IEFA would comprise 3rd (Lahore) Division, 7th (Meerut) Division and 9 (Secunderabad) Cavalry Brigade; TNA WO 95/27/1: GHQ, QMG, WD, 28 August 1914. A timeline was exposed on Monday 31 August, with the War Office advising that the lead division was expected to arrive at Marseilles on Thursday 17 September, although with the convoy diversion to Egypt, the ships transporting 3rd (Lahore) Division did not arrive until Saturday 26 September.

of chaos, however, we shall no doubt muddle through".[12]

As it transpired, the HNS was a great deal more resilient than expected[13] and the difficulties outlined by the QMG reflected the tactical support to the BEF forward of the Army rear boundary rather than the operational railway capability in the Communication Zones.[14] The initial key task was negotiating with the HN to agree an outline plan. The Sea Port of Debarkation (SPOD) with its associated reception facilities was agreed as Marseilles,[15] although the GHQ QMG staff remained concerned that the French authorities would only permit the deployment of IEFA through the port with sustainment being conducted through either Saint Nazaire or Le Harve, with the concomitant adverse impact upon shipping and naval escorts. The Main Base Area (MBA), in which arriving units were equipped, as far as logistically feasible, to standards appropriate to operations on the Western Front, was located in the environs of Marseilles. An Indian Advanced Base (IAB) was also required, in which formations could be integrated with the additional A&Q capability arriving from the United Kingdom through the SPOD at Saint Nazaire. BEF GHQ identified Fontainebleau as the preferred IAB option but the French were utilizing this area and it was not until 24 September, only two days before IEFA arrived at the SPOD, that the sites at Orleans were agreed.[16]

Efficient reception at Marseilles was an essential component of the planning and the BEF relied upon the HN to grant the estate and infrastructure to create a Base.[17] Allocation of berths and entraining facilities were critical as were areas for the construction of tented transit camps and the provision of buildings for accommodation and storage. The Army Service Corps (ASC) established a significant Base Supply Depot (BSD) eventually comprising a bakery, cold storage installations, sub-depots for forage and Fuel & Lubricants, a goat farm and a mineral water bottling plant.[18] Additionally, the MBA became a haven for all sorts of followers sent by the Government of India to support IEFA. AHQ failed to control the contractors who employed these civilians, as they sought to maximize profits by recruiting more staff.[19] Inevitably, the process and procedures were somewhat basic when the first units arrived but the Base Staff quickly grasped the key issues and created a remarkably solid operation,[20] although one not without its faults. By the time 7th

12 TNA WO 107/13: QMG and IGC Correspondence, Stores and Equipment, letter from Robertson to Cowans dated 7 September 1914.

13 A participant observed, 'The difficulties of the situation are obvious, and they have only been overcome by the exercise of considerable tact by both sides, and the great - and, to many people, unsuspected - talent of the French nation for organization'; Captain R Bonham-Smith, 'Railway Transport Arrangements in France', *Journal of the Royal United Service Institution (JRUSI)*, Vol. LXI (February 1916), p.48.

14 The issues relating to the ability of French rail capacity to support the French Army, an expanding BEF and the national war economy were however, emerging and had been identified by key experts. The acceptance by the British and the French that the BEF needed to assume responsibility for railway operations in its AOR did not mature until mid-1916.

15 TNA WO 95/27/1: GHQ, QMG, WD, entries, September 1914. Clearly, this unease influenced decisions on the deployment of resources to Marseilles to support the operation and the financing of contracts.

16 TNA WO 95/27/1: GHQ, QMG, WD, 24 September 1914.

17 Officers from the Indian Army were assigned to the LOC. Some were drafted from Home Leave in the United Kingdom and others, such as Major Joslin, from the Queen's Own Royal West Kent Regiment seconded, in his case because the 1st Battalion was retained in India for Internal Security duties; C T Atkinson, *The Queen's Own Royal West Kent Regiment, 1914-1919* (London: Simpkin, 1924), p.64. Officers with railway operating and movement experience in India were also posted to assist with the deployment on the Mediterranean Line of Communication (MEDLOC) before being assigned to general railway staff service in the BEF. Heber Alexander relates that the Railway Transport Officer in Marseilles was Colonel Pope, late General Manager of the Oudh & Rohilkand Railway and a former Commanding Officer of the Railway Volunteers at Lucknow; Major H M Alexander DSO, *On Two Fronts, Being the Adventures of an Indian Mule Corps in France and Gallipoli* (London: Dutton, 1917), p.125.

18 Colonel R H Beadon, *The Royal Army Service Corps, A History of Transport and Supply in the British Army*, Vol. II (Cambridge: Cambridge University Press (CUP), 1931), p.88.

19 TNA WO 32/5110: 'Lawrence Report to Kitchener', 10 March 1915.

20 Base Standing Orders by Colonel Fasken, Base Commandant Marseilles, nd; TNA WO 95/3932/2: HQ 7th

(Meerut) Division landed at Marseilles, operations in the MBA were in full swing and a clear routine had been established to process incoming units,[21] although the mix of nationalities and cultures provided an interesting back-drop to the task of delivering effective logistic outputs:[22]

> The scene on the quays was bizarre and incongruous. Working parties of the Indian troops in their sombre but business-like khaki were mixed with assistants in the shape of French seamen, French labourers, stevedores, and our own Army Service Corps men. Nobody understood anyone else's language; parties of Indians could be seen gesticulating and illustrating their wants by vigorous pantomime to sympathetic but puzzled Frenchmen.[23]

The Marseilles MBA[24] controlled British Empire operations within the allotted port and railhead areas, the Base Supply Depot (BSD) in the Traverse de la Pinede and operated nine camps, some of which had a supporting Supply Sub-Depot (SSD) and were located between 0.75 and 10 miles from the docks and railhead.[25] There were occasions when there was insufficient transit accommodation and the services of a local House Agent were utilized to procure suitable buildings,[26] although insufficient attention was paid to the transport arrangements for the distribution of rations, resulting in an requirement for additional HT, which would have been more profitably employed elsewhere in the MBA.[27] The key task of the MBA was to ensure that units were appropriately equipped as far as supply allowed, with 1st Line equipment stores and clothing,[28] commensurate with operations

(Meerut) Division, AQMG, November 1914, Appx 2.

21 TNA WO 95/3932/1: HQ 7th (Meerut) Division, AQMG, Marseilles Disembarkation Orders.

22 This also included soldiers from nearly every part of the French Empire that were stationed in, or transiting through Marseilles, which certainly added to this remarkable mix. See, 'Across the Black Waters', in David Olusoga, *The World's War* (London: Head Zeus, 2014), which places the pertinent cultural aspects of their deployment to France, within the global context of colonial soldiers fighting in a Great Power conflict.

23 Smith & Merewether, *The Indian Corps in France*, p.16.

24 The MBA was commanded by Colonel G F N Tinley who held the post from its formal inception in November 1914 to March 1918, when he was replaced by Brigadier-General R C B Lawrence; Major A F (Retd) Becke (Comp) *History of the Great War, Order of Battle*, Part 4, *The Army Council, GHQs, Armies and Corps, 1914-1918* (London: HMSO, 1945), p.16.

25 Marseilles Base Area - Transit Camps. Table collated from information in TNA WO 95/3932/1: HQ 7th (Meerut) Division, AQMG.

Table 7.1

Marseilles Base Area – Transit Camps

Location	Railhead Distance Miles	Remarks
Campagne Cansolat	3	
Campagne de l'Eveque	4	
La Barasee	8	Supply Depot
La Penne	10	Supply Depot
La Valentine	8	Supply Depot
Marche aux Bestiaux	1	
Parc Borely (Champ de Courses)	3	Supply Depot
Saint-Marcel	7	Supply Depot
Terrain Adjacent a la Scierie Fournier	0.75	

26 Barns, stables and factory complexes were preferred; the hire of private houses was usually avoided; TNA WO 95/1168/1: 1st (Indian) Cavalry Division, A&Q, 'Report on Billets in Marseilles'; nd but probably December 1914. According to the report there was no shortage of suitable buildings. The House Agent is recorded as H Pigeord.

27 Ibid.

28 Lines of Support are used to describe the boundaries of specific elements of logistic functions. Lines of Support

on the Western Front.[29] This seemingly simple process hid a myriad of complex supply issues, which certainly kept officers and staffs of the Army Ordnance Department (AOD) and Army Ordnance Corps (AOC) fully occupied.[30] British units in the Army of India were equipped to higher scales than their Indian counterparts but differently to Home Army Regular units. Bizarrely, the Indian Ordnance Department (IOD)[31] was not responsible for combat clothing, most of which was purchased privately by units to an approved pattern but the Supply & Transport Department furnished Native Troops with full dress uniform.[32] British officers in the Indian Army were not provided, at public expense, with either tentage, field equipment or saddlery, which created a proliferation of different types, most of which, were not suitable for sustained operational service in the North-West European environment. Indian units generally purchased their own cooking, drinking and eating utensils, whilst the ration scales and local market provisioning were designed to tax the most industrious and capable of Regimental Quartermasters. The issue of the incorrect type of food, or catering pot, could easily offend religion or caste, sensitivities lucidly understood by Indian Army officers but rather less so by the hard-pressed supply staffs of the BEF,[33] who were on occasion clearly frustrated by the 'fads of Indians as to what they will and will not eat'.[34] Such differing perspectives were inevitable as logisticians from two separate organizations, cultures and systems, slowly came to comprehend, albeit under considerable stress, how best to integrate and manage a complicated process.

Guns and Treacle

A critical activity was the withdrawal of all Mark II Short Magazine Lee Enfield (SMLE) rifles and supporting ammunition and the issue of the Mark III SMLE and Mark VII operational service rounds.[35] To eliminate errors, Small Arms Ammunition (SAA) and machine-guns were exchanged in bulk immediately after landing[36] and rifles individually, before units left the dock area.[37] Some battalions had their Maxim Machine Guns replaced by the Vickers but not the tripod, the legs of which, had to be cut down to conform to developing tactical practice before new in-service

was not a term that was in use during the Great War but it appears in various logistic publications and is a simple method of assigning capability to units and formations. 1st Line - organic to a unit; 2nd Line - organic to a brigade or division; 3rd Line - allocated to Corps or Army; 4th Line - provided by the Base. For IEFA, 4th Line was delivered in-Theatre and from the United Kingdom and India.

29 Staff officers in headquarters from the IEFA were also involved in the establishment of components of the MBA. The Assistant Director Supplies & Transport (ADST) of 1st (Indian) Cavalry Division, Lieutenant-Colonel Vaughan, noted in the War Diary, 'First engaged in formulating scheme for Advanced Transport Mule Depot at ORLEANS and Base Transport Mule Depot at MARSEILLES'; TNA WO 95/1169/4, HQ 1st (Indian) Cavalry Division, ADST, WD, 26-30 October 1914.

30 For the contribution of the Ordnance Services in supporting the IEFA in France, see, Major-General A Forbes CB CMG, *A History of the Army Ordnance Services*, Vol. Three, *The Great War* (London: Medici, 1929), thereafter, *Army Ordnance Services*.

31 For a resume of the Indian Ordnance Department, see, Major-General A Forbes CB CMG, *A History of the Army Ordnance Services*, Vol. Two, *Modern History* (London: Medici, 1929), pp.201-210.

32 Forbes, *Army Ordnance Services*, p.32.

33 The provision of pots such as the *lotah*, *koratah* and *parat* is an example. See, Forbes, *Army Ordnance Services*, p.34.

34 TNA WO 95/3932/1/1: HQ 7th (Meerut) Division, AQMG, WD, entries 10-14 November 1914.

35 Ibid, entries 13-16 October 1914 and Marseilles Disembarkation Orders, Sect 2 and Appx 1, 'Instructions re Arms, Ammunition and Clothing'; TNA WO 95/3932/2: HQ 7th (Meerut) Division, AQMG, November 1914, Appx 2.

36 Marseilles Disembarkation Orders, Sect 2 and Appx 1, 'Instructions re Arms, Ammunition and Clothing'; TNA WO 95/3932/2: HQ 7th (Meerut) Division, AQMG, November 1914, Appx 2.

37 TNA WO 95/3932/1/1: HQ 7th (Meerut) Division, QMG, WD, entries 13-16 October 1914. Bayonets were not exchanged except for those units equipped with the 'long rifle' and in such cases, new frogs also had to be issued but not slings.

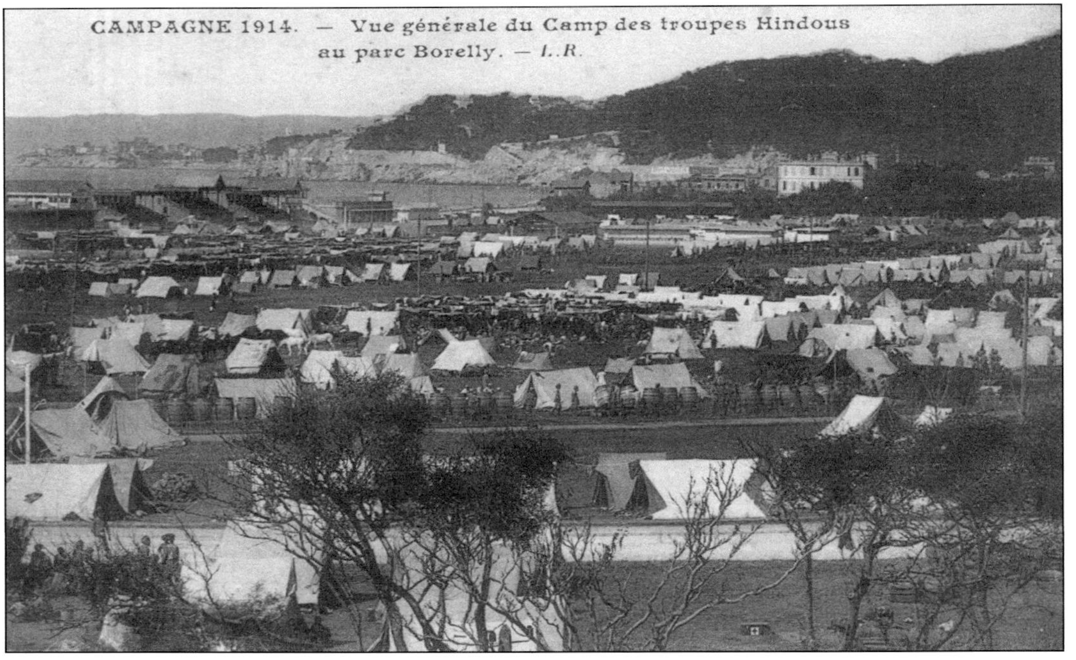

P7.1. Host Nation Support: MBA Marseilles, Parc Borely Transit Camp. The role of the Host Nation in delivering the deployment of IEFA has been effectively forgotten but was crucial to its successful completion and sustainment. (Tom Donovan Collection)

tripods were issued.[38] All pistol ammunition of Indian manufacture was also withdrawn.[39] The issue of winter clothing appears to have been rather haphazard, which may have been the product of availability as units processed through the MBA, so it was helpful that the weather in Marseilles and Orleans was mostly benign in October 1914.[40] In 7th (Ferozepore) Infantry Brigade, 9th Bhopal Infantry were issued with warm underclothing[41] but 57th Wilde's Rifles were not,[42] whilst 58th Vaughan's Rifles[43] in 7th (Meerut) Division were not issued with serge clothing until they arrived in the IAB Orleans. 32nd Mule Corps were certainly well found, the Officer Commanding being effusive in his praise for the quality and the quantity[44] of the items, whilst the 13th Hussars, having insufficient personal load carrying equipment, had to wear the additional clothing and had

38 The War Diary of HQ 8th (Jullundur) Brigade recorded units being issued with the tripod, which had a telescopic front leg and elevating gear, whilst the Brigade was in IAB Orleans; TNA WO 95/3926/1: HQ 8th (Jullundur) Infantry Brigade, WD, entry 18 October 1914.

39 Marseilles Disembarkation Orders, Sect 2 and Appx 1, 'Instructions re Arms, Ammunition and Clothing'; TNA WO 95/3932/2: HQ 7th (Meerut) Division, November 1914, Appx 2. The orders noted, 'Great care must be taken on this point as it is most important'.

40 OC 9th Mule Company recorded that in the last week of September, "The weather was perfect, except for one day when we experienced a Marseilles "mistral". This is a cross between a gale and a dust-storm, and is one of the most unpleasant experiences imaginable;" Alexander, *On Two Fronts*, p.33. HQ 8th (Jullundur) Infantry Brigade, noted that Tuesday 13 October was the first rain experienced since the Brigade had arrived in France on Saturday 26 September 1914; TNA WO 95/3926/1: war diary entry. The weather deteriorated with heavy rain on 14-15 October with camp conditions at Marseilles described as 'very unpleasant', whilst IAB Orleans was 'very wet' 18-20 October; TNA WO 95/3932/1/1: HQ 7th (Meerut) Division, AQMG, WD, entries 14-20 October 1914.

41 TNA WO 95/3923/4: 9th Bhopal Infantry, WD.

42 TNA WO 95/3923/5: 57th Wilde's Rifles, WD.

43 TNA WO 95/ 3948/4: 58th Vaughan's Rifles, WD.

44 Major G Aylmer, 'Indian Mule Transport in this War', *Journal of the United Service Institution of India*, Vol. XLVI, 1917.

difficulty in mounting their horses.[45]

The inability to issue the 1908 pattern Web Infantry Equipment and its associated ancillaries to IEFA units,[46] British and Indian, on arrival at Marseilles was greeted with much disappointment by All Ranks. It also caused not only considerable hardship to the soldiers in the field but also a degradation of operational capability, problems that attracted the personal attention of General Officers Commanding (GOC) Divisions;[47] the absence of a pack and a canteen creating significant difficulties in the carriage of spare clothing and the iron ration. The soldiers though, were not the only part of the IEFA to suffer a shortage of appropriate kit. In October, horse rugs were in short supply leading to an increase in animals with colds, whilst procured commercial saddles and harnesses were often in poor condition. The purchase in India, and then disposal in France, albeit with some monetary compensation, of privately owned kits, caused a good deal of irritation amongst the officers,[48] as well as creating considerable logistic, administrative and financial burdens for the MBA staff, whilst the requirement to store withdrawn regimental and personal equipment generated the need for additional storage facilities within the MBA and the provision of manpower on a scale of one per sub-unit drawn from deploying units.[49]

Religion and caste were important factors in relation to personal supply items, especially rations and cooking equipment, which Ordnance officers with no experience of the Indian Army found a particular challenge.[50] Rationing was a complicated issue in what was a culturally diverse force.[51] From the supply perspective, the Indian ration was an extraordinary one; not only did it include 40 equivalents which could be demanded, but it was, in comparison to the British one, rather complex in relation to the authorized substitutes.[52] The British fresh or frozen daily meat ration was 1 ¼ lb or 1 lb for preserved or salted meat,[53] whilst the Indian ration was only ¾ lb.[54] The vegetable ration for the British soldier was 1 lb in potatoes or its equivalent in greens but the Indian 12 oz in potatoes and ¼ lb in mixed vegetables,[55] with onions being provided as liberally as possible.[56] The ASC staff noted that British soldiers in IEFA were entitled to relaxants at Government expense; a maximum of 2 oz of tobacco per week for those who smoked and ½ gill of issued rum daily,[57] both

45 The Right Honourable Sir H Mortimer Durand KCMG KCSI KCIE, *The Thirteenth Hussars in the Great War* (Edinburgh & London: William Blackwood & Sons, 1921), p.65.

46 For details of this equipment, see War Office, *The Pattern 1908 Web Infantry Equipment* (London: HMSO, 1914).

47 HQ 7th (Meerut) Division, AQMG, Q-92/1 dated 19 December 1914, GOC to DA&QMG Indian Corps in TNA WO 95/3932/2.

48 Durand, *The Thirteenth* Hussars, pp.64-65; the regimental history relates individuals never saw their personal kit again.

49 TNA WO 95/3932/1: HQ 7th (Meerut) Division, Marseilles Disembarkation Orders, Appx B, 'Instructions for Troops Storing Surplus Kits and Baggage'.

50 The comprehensive Army Council, *Army Service Corps*, Training, Part II, *Supplies*, War Office (London: HMSO, 1909) (Reprinted 1914) makes no mention of supplies for the Indian Army.

51 TNA WO 95/74: GHQ, Director of Supplies, WD, 3 November 1914. The Director of Supplies commented: "The feeding of the Indians is becoming very difficult……..As far as I can see in a very short time we shall have at least half a dozen different classes of rations for Indians."

52 Army Council, *Manual of Elementary Military Hygiene*, 1912, War Office, 40/WO/1680, War Office (London: HMSO, 1914), Appx III, Scales of Rations on Active Service.

53 Ibid, Appx III and General Staff, *Field Service Pocket Book 1914* (FSPB 14), War Office (London: HMSO, 1914), p.168.

54 Army Council, *Military Hygiene*, Appx III and FSPB 14, p.171.

55 TNA WO 95/1169/4: HQ 1st (Indian) Cavalry Division, ADST, WD, 26 February 1915.

56 Army Council, *Military Hygiene*, Appx III.

57 Whilst the rum issue was greatly appreciated, especially in wet and cold weather, by those that could consume it, inevitably it was abused. The CO of 7th (Meerut) Divisional Train stopped the rum issue to No 1 Company in early April 1915 because of cases of drunkenness; TNA WO 95/3939/9/1: 7th (Meerut) Divisional Train, WD, 7 April 1915. The War Diary does not explain the cause of the drunkenness, which may have been the result of soldiers

at the discretion of the GOC acting upon the Theatre Medical Officer's recommendation.[58] They also discovered, much to their consternation, that the 6,000 Sikhs serving in the Force were entitled to a daily ration of approximately 1.1 grams[59] of Indian Treacle,[60] which was the Army's 1914 term for opium.[61] The newly appointed Director of Supplies, Major-General Clayton,[62] expressed no disapproval[63] but was certainly surprised by the requirement,[64] especially in view of what, in his opinion, were more pressing needs: "This is the first I have heard of opium. I did not know that it formed part of their ration, nor do I know what stock there is in the country yet."[65] He was clearly relieved though, to learn that there was 1100 pounds of opium in the Base Supply Depot, which at an issue of rate of 15 pounds per day suggested 73 Days of Supply.[66]

The ASC also had a task in resolving problems with the quality and quantity of provisions brought from India. Inspections revealed that tea was unfit for issue, *ghi* was insufficient through having been thrown overboard during the voyage because of contamination and salt was adulterated with sodium sulphate; all of these commodities required replacement. Fortunately, Marseilles being the main POE for France's Eastern trade had a wide variety of Indian products, including *atta*, the flour crucial for flatbreads such as *chapatti*, *roti*, *naan* and *puri*. The acquisition of sufficient goats on the hoof from North Africa and Corsica to support IEFA was an entirely different proposition, which required the assistance of the Foreign Office in London. In the intervening period, tinned mutton was provided, although some Hindu troops rejected this ration because of the labelling, whichŢ, created a hiatus because it included a picture of a cow.[67] Hay had deteriorated at sea and

purchasing alcohol from estaminets, or by the failure to ensure that the rum tot was consumed in the presence of an officer. For an assessment of the issues relating to drink, see the seminal, Craig Gibson, *Behind The Front, British Soldiers and French Civilians, 1914-1918* (Cambridge: CUP, 2014), pp.133-139.

58 Army Council, *Military Hygiene*, Appx III and FSPB 14, p.168. Most of the tobacco used by soldiers in 1914 was smoked in a pipe rather than rolled in cigarettes, these becoming more popular as the war progressed. 21st Century readers will be amazed to learn that Regimental Medical Officers were recommending the issue of smoking tobacco to support health but equally, the tobacco and rum rations were also designed to sustain morale.

59 There is no reference to Indian Treacle in Army Council, *Military Hygiene*, or FSPB 14.

60 See, Ian Malcolm Brown, *British Logistics on the Western Front 1914-1919* (Westport Connecticut & London: Praeger, 1998), p.66. David Omissi (Intro) *Indian Voices of the Great War, Soldiers' Letters, 1914-18* (Basingstoke & New York: Palgrave Macmillan, 1999), however, indicates that whilst opium and cannabis were used, some Indian soldiers requested additional supplies from their families, an activity which the authorities disapproved of.

61 Indian Treacle may not be the only instance of the official use of controlled substances, by the British Army, during the Great War. As part of their Special Operations on the Western Front, it would appear that Military Intelligence used morphia tablets and cocaine as currency for information, and, to suborn German soldiers. See, Michael Occleshaw, *Armour Against Fate, British Military Intelligence in the First World War* (London: Columbus Books 1989), pp.205-209.

62 Frederick Thomas Clayton was a logistician, being late of the ASC and was awarded the KCB and KCMG. Having returned from service in South Africa, he was appointed as Director of Supplies at GHQ BEF in September 1914 before assuming the appointment of IGC in January 1915. He was the first Colonel Commandant of the Royal Army Service Corps (RASC) and Thornhill Barracks in Aldershot, constructed in the period 1926-1928, with additions c1931-39, for occupancy by the RASC, was renamed in his honour in 1929; TNA WO 32/4061: Works and Buildings, Barracks, 'Renaming of Thornhill Barracks as Clayton Barracks, Aldershot'. He died in 1933 and is buried with his wife in the Aldershot Military Cemetery.

63 Having had considerable colonial service, Clayton was used to brushing against many different cultures.

64 Retailers in the United Kingdom were lawfully selling medical kits, which included cocaine or opium for pain relief, to British soldiers and an investigation in 1916 revealed that 40 Canadian soldiers at a camp in Folkestone were addicted to cocaine, leading to the conviction of Horace Dennis Kingsley and Rose Edwards for supplying the drugs. On 11 May 1916, the Army Council used the powers in the Defence of the Realm Act (DORA) of 8 August 1914 to enact Regulation 40B, which prohibited the sale of cocaine, opium, cannabis and other psychoactive drugs to military personnel without an authorised doctor's prescription. The military, social and medical issues relating to these drugs in the Army environment on the Western Front, is an interesting but sensitive subject that requires research.

65 TNA WO 95/74: GHQ, Director of Supplies, WD, 29 October 1914.

66 Ibid, 1 November 1914.

67 GOC 11th Garwhal Brigade reported this particularly sensitive issue created by the issue of tins of mutton to the

P7.2. Fads of IEFA: 9th Gurkhas drawing rations at a farm-house near Saint Floris. IEFA rationing was a constant headache for the BEF's logisticians, creating planning complexities and distribution issues. (Tom Donovan Collection)

replacement stocks had to be procured, whilst barley, an accustomed forage for Indian animals, was no longer preferred by, in particular, the Indian cavalry divisions, once the units identified that oats were available, on demand, through the BEF's supply system. In addition, the French initially requested that customs duty was paid on these imports and although this matter was resolved in the BEF's favour, *octroi*, local taxation on produce brought into towns, was not waived.[68]

Rails to War

Perforce of French railway operating constraints, the rail MEDLOC was a long one. Trains ran West from Marseilles to Toulouse via Cette and Narbonne, thence North via Montaubon, Brive, Limoges, Chateauroux and Vierzon to Orleans Les Aubrais. With a distance of over 600 miles and a journey schedule of 54 hours, the 14 rail paths or marches, allocated to the IEFA daily, had to be programmed to deliver three halts per day. Halt One of 60 minutes for administration, Halt Two for 3 hours to enable a meal to be prepared and served and Halt Three of 60 minutes. As the train departures from Marseilles occurred throughout the 24 hour period, halts were conducted at 15 different stations, each of which had to be provided with facilities for cooking, administration,

troops, which had labels with pictures not only of sheep but also cows; TNA WO 95/3932/1/1: HQ 7th (Meerut) Division, AQMG, WD, entries 10-14 November 1914.

68 Beadon, *Royal Army Service Corps*, p.121.

medical care, potable water for soldiers and animals, and ablutions.[69] Whilst the journey was arduous, there were compensations, which, were clearly appreciated by those that had the fortune to experience them.

> During the journey from MARSEILLES the troops had a magnificent reception from the people. Crowds were gathered at the stations where troop trains stopped & in many places along both sides of the Railway who cheered the troops. Along the whole route fruit of all kinds, coffee, biscuits, flags & flowers were given to the troops by the French people. Nothing could have possibly exceeded the kindness and hospitality with which the French civilians and soldiers received all ranks.[70]

The positive receptions were however, not always quite what they seemed, as the author of the Indian Mule Transport war diary recorded:

> At every stopping place we were received with Guards of Honour, Generals & their Staff & such is the politeness of the French officer, that it was only at the end of the third day - through the officiousness of an interpreter - we discovered we had been signalled all along the line as train des equipage quartier General & been mistaken for a General and his Hd Qtrs.[71]

P7.3. Host Nation Support: French rail movement was vital to the deployment of IEFA and illustrates how important French A&Q co-operation was to the logistic support of the BEF. (Tom Donovan Collection)

69 For an outline deployment schedule, see, Colonel A M Henniker CBE RE, BOH, *Transportation on the Western Front, 1914-1918* (London: HMSO, 1937), p.73.

70 TNA WO 95/3926/1: HQ 8th (Jullundur) Infantry Brigade, WD, 3 October 1914. Such scenes clearly suggest not only the passion with which, the French people perceived the trusted saviours of their Nation but also the remarkable speed of communication in 1914. Surprisingly, the receptions were still going strong in mid-December 1914 as Captain Eve of 13th Hussars noted in his diary; quoted in Durand, *Thirteenth Hussars*, p.63.

71 TNA WO 95/3939/8: 7th (Meerut) Division, Indian Mule Transport, WD, entries 13-20 October 1914.

Rail movement was not however, without its hazards and there were several incidents and accidents as the trains travelled North from Marseilles.[72] The Indian Mule Transport suffered a fatality when a soldier fell from a train during the night and then tried to remount it; the unit was unaware of his fate until the railway company reported the accident. In another incident, a mule jumped from the train as it started but being a hardy creature the mule survived, presumably somewhat chastened, as it was quickly and quietly reloaded to the wagon. OC 9th Mule Corps though, with more than a little cheek, secured a fine seat by riding in the staff-car of the General Office Commanding 3rd (Lahore) Division,[73] which was on a railway wagon on the train, and thus, thoroughly enjoyed the journey to war:

> I travelled in it a good deal of the way, thereby getting a better view of the scenery, which, especially in the valley of the Loire, was gorgeously beautiful. European scenery is always a joy after the hideous monotony of the plains of India, and a better sample than the midlands of France in early October would be hard to find. Altogether the journey from Marseilles to Orleans was a delight.[74]

At IAB Orleans, integration commenced. Ammunition was required for firing practice and the ASC was involved in delivering the whole spectrum of Q from accommodation to rations and fuel to forage. Unit transport deficiencies were also generally resolved, although the shortage of military General Service (GS) Wagons led to the issue of a plethora of civilian commercial varieties from the United Kingdom, including those from the famous R G White Mineral Water company, tradesmens' vans and railway cartage, all with a load capacity of 2000-2500 pounds. Unfortunately, whilst many of these wagons were suitable for operations within the MBA at Marseilles and in IAB Orleans, they were not sufficiently robust to withstand the rigours of operational service.[75] Water carts, being more specialized had to be modified to meet the military requirement; tanks with a capacity of 152–200 gallons and distribution taps were fitted.[76] Assigned British logistic units were also involved in supporting the IAB as the Staff awaited the arrival of the formations.

The training of the Divisional Trains, which were all Horse Transport (HT) and the integration of the recently formed Wheeled Motor Transport (WMT) units, especially the Divisional Supply Columns (DSC)[77] and the Divisional Ammunition Parks (DAP)[78] which were assigned to the Indian divisions, were two key tasks.[79] The Commanding Officer[80] of 7th (Meerut) Divisional

72 Ibid.
73 Lieutenant-General Sir Henry Burton Watkis KCB.
74 Alexander, *On Two Fronts*, p.37.
75 'Vehicles. Non-descript lot, impossible to repair, if break down will have to be abandoned. Wheels sent as spares are useless'; TNA WO 95/3939/9/1: 7th (Meerut) Divisional Train, 'Report to GOC 7th (Meerut) Division GOC by Commandant', copy dated 24 October 1914, through Assistant Director, Supplies & Transport to AQMG.
76 TNA WO 95/3926/1: HQ 8th (Jullundur) Infantry Brigade, WD, 8 October 1914.
77 TNA WO 95/1173: 89 Company ASC, WD. For an interesting personal account of the formation and operations of 89 Company ASC of the 1st (Indian) Cavalry Division Supply Column, see, A M Beatson, *The Motor-Bus in War, Being the Impressions of an ASC Officer during Two and a Half Years at the Front* (London: T Fisher Unwin, 1918). Beatson enlisted as a Private in a Territorial battalion in August 1914, being commissioned into the ASC on Wednesday 28 October 1914.
78 HQ IGC had been tasked by the QMG at the end of August, to examine the issue of replacing the Indian Army HT Reserve Parks with MT; TNA WO 95/27/1: GHQ, QMG, WD, 31 August 1914.
79 TNA WO 95/3932/1: HQ 7th (Meerut) Division, QMG, 'Some Points of Difference Between the Home and Indian Organization and Procedure'; nd but probably late September 1914.
80 The Commanding Officer (CO) was Lieutenant-Colonel H A P Lindsay. The term CO is not used in the War Diary during this period, reference being made to Commandant, Officer Commanding and Commanding. As the Divisional Train was a mounted unit of regimental structure and size with four companies, CO is used for clarity.

Train[81] had an especial challenge because the best of the personnel and equipment had been used to complete the 3rd (Lahore) Train.[82] He was left with recruits who were mostly untrained in animal management, horse transport operations and weapon handling,[83] hired-wagons that were time-expired, water carts that needed urgent modification[84] and harnesses that required replacing.[85] Remarkably, against all the odds, with clear direction from GOC 7th (Meerut) Division[86] and assistance from the logistic staff in his Headquarters, order was brought from chaos.[87]

In addition, the reorganization of the HT assets to create a Brigade Ammunition Column per brigade and the supporting Divisional Ammunition Column was also enacted. For example, 71 Company ASC, the sub-unit allocated as the 9th (Secunderabad) Cavalry Brigade Supply Column (BSC) disembarked with 40 motor lorries[88] at Le Harve on Friday 25 September 1914 arriving at IAB Orleans seven days later on 2 October. In the IAB, the Company Workshop commenced work to repair vehicles and constructed frames so canvas tilts could be fitted to the lorries. 71 Company was also extensively utilized to assist in the establishment and operation of the facilities comprising the IAB.[89] Here they were joined by 72 Company ASC tasked as the Brigade Ammunition Column (BAC)[90] and on Sunday 25 October having loaded with supplies at an Orleans railhead, the BSC and BAC deployed with the brigade to the BEF area of operations, the cool wet weather and the muddy roads making life miserable for the drivers.[91]

The arrival of the 1st (Indian) Cavalry Division in IAB Orleans caused considerable difficulty with the distribution of supplies, especially forage, a problem identified by the Divisional Deputy Director Transport (DDT) who had requested that the Division remain in Marseilles until the Divisional Train[92] had arrived in the IAB from the United Kingdom. The failure by the Chain of Command to support the request created some friction with the logisticians who were attempting

81 To set the scene, the forming Train was so bereft of resources it did not have access to the Army Form C 2118 War Diary or Intelligence Summary pads and the War Diary between 16-31 October was written on pages from a serial numbered notebook; TNA WO 95/3939/9/1: 7th (Meerut) Divisional Train, WD, entries 16-30 October 1914. Four ASC companies were formed on 8 January 1915 to place the 7th (Meerut) Division Indian Supply & Transport Corps Train to formal establishment: 432, 433, 434 and 435.

82 TNA WO 95/3939/9/1: 'Report to GOC 7th (Meerut) Division GOC by Commandant'. Four ASC companies were formed on 8 January 1915 to place the 3rd (Lahore) Division Indian Supply & Transport Corps Train to formal establishment: 428, 429, 430 and 431. The Divisional Train was formed at IAB Orleans, 5-16 November 1914; TNA WO 95/3915/1/1: HQ 3rd (Lahore) Division, AQMG, WD.

83 The Commandant expressed concern that 0.303 Ball rounds had been issued to those who had not passed a Weapon Handling Test and proposed to withdraw ammunition until the identified soldiers had been proved competent in the use of their personal weapon; TNA WO 95/3939/9/1: 'Report to GOC 7th (Meerut) Division by Commandant'.

84 The water tanks had been placed on the fore of the wagon placing undue strain on the cart structure, creating failure and the tanks need to be removed and placed in the centre; TNA WO 95/3939/9/1: 7th (Meerut) Divisional Train, WD, 25 October 1914.

85 TNA WO 95/3939/9/1: 'Report to GOC 7th (Meerut) Division by Commandant'.

86 TNA WO 95/3939/9/1: 7th (Meerut) Divisional Train, WD, entries, 22-25 October 1914.

87 The CO recorded: 'Great difficulty was experienced in evolving order out of confusion'; Ibid, entries 20-23 October 1914. At Bourecq on Wednesday 6 January 1915 at 1000 LOCAL, Lieutenant-General Sir James Willcocks, Indian Corps Commander 'inspected the Train & expressed his satisfaction with all he saw'; Ibid, entry. He might have been less impressed however, by the War Diary scribe incorrectly spelling his name 'Willcox'.

88 By 11 November 1914, 71 Company of 2nd (Indian) Division Supply Column, had 48 lorries of 12 different types; TNA WO 95/1184/2: 71 Company ASC, WD, 11 November 1914.

89 Ibid.

90 TNA WO 95/1184/4: 72 Company ASC, WD.

91 TNA WO 95/1184/2: 71 Company ASC, WD.

92 Lieutenant-Colonel Stone DSO of the Indian Supply & Transport Corps travelled to the UK and returned with 91 x GS Wagons, 24 x Water Carts and 327 x Draught horses, 40 being cast at Southampton Docks from the original 368; TNA WO 95/1168/1: HQ 1st (Indian) Cavalry Division, WD, entries, 26 October - 30 November 1914. The War Diary does not account for the missing horse. The ASC ORBAT for the division comprised 426 (HT) Company as the Train, 82 and 89 (MT) Companies forming the Supply Column and 79 Company providing the Ammunition Park.

to keep a wobbly wheel turning.[93] Further complications were generated when nearly all of the 327 Draught horses brought from the UK developed catarrh fever, with some dying, resulting in additional horses, supplemented by mules, which unfortunately also had fever, being issued from the Remount Depot, thereby delaying the equipping of 2nd (Sialkot)[94] and 8th (Lucknow) Cavalry Brigades and Divisional Troops and thus the operational deployment of the Division.[95]

Once integration at Orleans was complete, IEFA units were moved by rail,[96] from one of four entraining stations,[97] to allocated Indian Corps and divisional BEF railheads, via Juvisy, just South of Paris and, when the BEF base posture was adjusted, via Rouen but in both cases, these arrangements allowed the IEFA LOC to join the BEF LOC from the United Kingdom, thereby creating simplicity and coherency. The operation was however, dynamic because the initial planning assumed the BEF to be located on the Aisne and not, as developing strategic imperatives dictated, on the Northern Flank of the Allied Front in Flanders. Had the 3rd (Lahore) Division arrived in France earlier than 26 September, its move North would almost certainly have been delayed to enable the BEF's three corps and French forces to reposition to the North. As it transpired, the timings were so tight that last minute changes to rail schedules meant that 3rd (Lahore) Division trains running from Orleans overlapped those of I Corps by 12-15 hours and the planned detraining railheads of St Omer, Hazebrouck and Cassel were replaced by Arques,[98] Blendecques and Wizernes,[99] whilst the balance of the IEFA used railheads at Berguette and Lillers.

To Flanders Fields

By early November 1914 both 3rd (Lahore)[100] and 7th (Meerut)[101] Divisions were in the line[102] and the divisional logistic systems were operating, if on occasions, imperfectly but the Indian Corps HQ was at last, in a better position to grip logistic issues.[103] The logistic interfaces were remarkably complex, with units from five divisions integrated to the IEFA ammunition and supply distribution plan in mid-November 1914. Given the rationing arrangements in the IEFA, this caused some

93 TNA WO 95/1168/1: HQ 1st (Indian) Cavalry Division, War Diary, entries, 26 October - 30 November 1914.

94 This is the spelling in the HQ 1st (Indian) Cavalry Division, WD. In Kempton, *Duty & Fidelity*, the spelling is Sealkot. Likewise, in the War Diary, the 3rd Cavalry Brigade is entitled Umballa, in *Duty & Fidelity*, Amballa.

95 TNA WO 95/1168/1: HQ 1st (Indian) Cavalry Division, WD, entries, 26 October - 30 November 1914.

96 7th (Meerut) Division moved from the IAB in 46 trains. The divisional rail departure schedule from the Orleans railheads is shown in an undated manuscript document in TNA WO 95/3932/2: HQ 7th (Meerut) Division, QMG. Advanced Base Standing Orders included a two page instruction, 'Standing Orders on Entrainment at Orleans'; TNA WO 95/3932/2: HQ 7th (Meerut) Division, AQMG, November 1914, Appx 2. Units moved in two types of fixed train consists; '*Train Combattant*' for infantry, artillery and cavalry units and '*Train Parcs*' with additional wagons for MT and HT vehicles to move ammunition columns and divisional trains; WO 95/3915/1: HQ 3rd (Lahore) Division, AQMG, WD, entries, 1-20 October 1914.

97 Les Aubrais, Murlins, Orleans and Port-Sec.

98 TNA WO 95/3926/1: HQ 8th (Jullundur) Infantry Brigade, WD, 20 October 1914. The Brigade War Diary recorded that in each closed wagon, 45-52 men and their personal equipment were loaded, so a few more than the planned 40. Horses were loaded at six Draught horses or eight chargers per wagon. The Brigade move was also delayed by two railway accidents involving other trains moving British and French divisions to the Allied left flank.

99 TNA WO 95/3915/1: HQ 3rd (Lahore) Division, AQMG, WD, entries, 17-21 October 1914.

100 For a concise history of the operations of 3rd (Lahore) Division on the Western Front and then in Mesopotamia, Egypt and Palestine, see, Kempton, *Duty & Fidelity, The Indian Army, August 1914-1921*, Part I, *Divisions*, pp. 23-29 and the constituent brigades, Part II, *Brigades, NW Frontier and Other Theatres*.

101 For a concise history of the operations of 7th (Meerut)) Division on the Western Front and then in Mesopotamia, Egypt and Palestine, see, Kempton, *Duty & Fidelity*, Part I, *Divisions*, pp.53-64 and the constituent brigades, Part II, *Brigades, NW Frontier and Other Theatres*.

102 For a coherent regimental account of the interfaces, see, Colonel L W Shakespear CB CIE, *History of the 2nd King Edward's Own Goorkhas* (Sirmoor Rifle Regiment) Vol. II, 1911-1921 (Aldershot: Gale & Polden, 1924).

103 TNA WO 95/1091: HQ Indian Corps, AQMG, WD, 1 August 1914 - 30 April 1915.

interesting challenges when units were reassigned as part of task organization.[104] One example was the support for the Deccan Horse, a unit in 9th (Secunderabad) Cavalry Brigade of 1st (Indian) Cavalry Division, which had dismounted[105] and been detached to 7th (Ferozepore) Brigade in order to relieve 9th Bhopals in the line. Doctrinally, the support for the Deccan Horse should have been through 7th Brigade but the practical solution was to retain its support through the 9th Brigade Supply Column. The Indian Corps Ammunition Railheads were at Aire and Lillers, which fed the Indian Corps Ammunition Park at Lillers, with the 3rd (Lahore) Division Ammunition Column (AC) Refilling Point (RP) at Estaires[106] and the 7th (Meerut) Division AC RP at Essars.[107] The Corps Supply Railhead was established at Chocques with the respective Divisional Supply Columns supporting each division.[108]

Where possible, divisional railheads were also deployed, reducing the requirement for WMT resources, yet increasing the imperative for staff co-ordination at such an important and complex divisional logistic node because they had a surprising number of moving parts, each controlled by the relevant Subject Matter Expert (SME). Effectively, a divisional railhead[109] was a combination of a Logistic Exchange Point (LXP) where stocks were transferred from rail to road transport, usually Animal Transport (AT)[110] or sometimes WMT and a temporary Field Storage Site (FSS) known as a Dump, from which issues were made. Ammunition, supplies, ordnance stores, casualties, reinforcements, remounts, leave personnel, Prisoners of War (POW) and mail could all pass through a divisional railhead, and with up to 80 motor-lorries allocated to the clearance of an ammunition or supply train, it was busy operation; divisional logistic staff officers paid therefore, specific attention to its effectiveness and efficiency.

A divisional railhead was not however, always a 'Safe Place' in tactical terms. Amongst the many incidents involving enemy artillery bombardments of these sites, the one at the aptly named Dead Cow Farm, serving 7th (Meerut) Division, which was shelled in June 1915 is but one example; fortunately the 1st Seaforth Highlanders' water carts had a lucky escape and no serious damage occurred to the infrastructure.[111] Several staff functions were critical to effective functioning of a divisional railhead, including the coherent interface with the HN, through the *Commissaire Militaire*, responsible for co-ordinating with the BEF Railway Transport Officer (RTO) military rail traffic regulation and support from the local French civil and military authorities.[112] The Railhead Supply Officer (RSO) was responsible for the issue of rations and forage, whilst the Railhead Ordnance Officer (ROO) was, in particular, focused upon Reverse Logistics,[113] with an especial emphasis on salvage and recycling. The Assistant Military Forwarding Officer (AMFO) led on the control of welfare parcels and the return of effects from deceased military personnel, whilst a Field Post Office (FPO) provided the centre for the distribution of divisional mail.

104 TNA WO 95/3915/1: HQ 3rd (Lahore) Division, AQMG, WD, 10 November 1914.

105 The Deccan Horse handed over its horses to the Jodhpur Imperial Service Lancers; Ibid, 10 November 1914.

106 The 3rd (Lahore) Divisional Train, comprising four companies, was billeted in Estaires but hostile shelling resulted in a move; TNA WO 95/3915/1: HQ 3rd (Lahore) Division, AQMG, WD, 7 November 1914.

107 Ammunition Supply Arrangement Diagrams for the Indian Corps, November and December 1914; TNA WO 95/3932/2: HQ 7th (Meerut) Division, QMG, WD. Of interest, is the increasing use of pictorial descriptions to explain logistic operations, which have many similarities with the modern military task synchronization matrix.

108 Supply Arrangement Diagrams for the Indian Corps, November and December 1914; TNA WO 95/3932/2: HQ 7th (Meerut) Division, QMG, WD.

109 For an interesting personal account of railhead operations see, Beatson, *The Motor-Bus in War*.

110 AT consisted of Horse Transport (HT) or Pack Transport (PT), which were mainly mules.

111 TNA WO 95/3932/2: HQ 7th (Meerut) Division, DAA&QMG, WD, 27 June 1915.

112 For a fascinating exposition of the interface with French civilians, see, Gibson, *Behind The Front*.

113 Operations related to the reuse of products and materials, by moving them from their typical final destination of use for the purpose of capturing value or proper disposal.

Inevitably, however, the logistic plans, often carefully crafted, went awry. The rail wagons were often irregularly loaded, thereby degrading efficient unloading, a problem compounded by the wagon labels displaying incorrect content information, whilst the waybills frequently failed to coincide with the materiel.[114] One particular issue, was balancing the requirements for units drawing supplies from the railhead because the deliveries did not always reflect the scales and the deficiencies had to be resolved by issues from a reserve held at the railhead, thereby extending replenishment times.[115] Whilst the front may have been relatively static, logistic operations were remarkably dynamic with key nodes being re-located as the transportation network developed, tactical dispositions were adjusted and divisional tasks amended. For example, in the middle of December 1914, the A&Q Staff of HQ 7th (Meerut) Division were engaged in planning and controlling the interfaces with 5th Infantry Division to enable the 5th Division DAC and DSC to cross 7th (Meerut) Division supply and deployment routes, and to de-conflict the activities of the 5th Divisional Train operating from Hinges. There was also a change to ammunition supply arrangements on Saturday 26 December 1914, when 2nd Infantry Division artillery took over the task of supporting 7th (Meerut) Division.[116]

As the Indian Corps gained practical experience of logistic operations in Flanders, lessons were quickly identified; some could be resolved quickly, others not. Not surprisingly, rough roads tested the civilian carts to the point, in some cases, of destruction and to prevent further serious damage, especially to wheels, axles and suspensions, the cargo-weights had to be reduced, thereby reducing logistic capability. On a more positive note, the Mule Corps Indian carts, the maximum load of which was less at 800 pounds, were much more resilient than the BEF Chain of Command had expected; the sweat and toil in bringing them to France had in the event, been worth the effort. The mules and drivers however, gave mixed impressions to commanders and staffs. Daily hauling around IAB Orleans during the integration phase, supporting divisional activities and training, had clearly honed their skills but morale also played an important role. The Officer Commanding 9th Mule Corps, Major Heber Alexander observed:

> It seems as though the treatment the men received at Marseilles influenced their conduct at the front by giving them an unwonted feeling of pride and confidence. In their own country, despite the hardships they endure and the risks they run, they are classed as 'followers'. Here - however they might be classed - they were treated as fighting men. The result could only tend to increased zeal and efficiency.[117]

The Q staff of 1st (Indian) Cavalry Division[118] were though, much less impressed. The After Action Report on a road move to Bois Des Dames during 11 March 1915 noted:

> The native mule drivers, syces[119] etc are not very satisfactory. For many miles behind the column they wandered along in parties of 2 or 3; they are mostly of miserable physique and in boots 6 sizes too large. Some wearing 5 flannel shirts apiece, 2 coats and a heavy overcoat, lame and exhausted, unable to ask the way, and presented a pitiable appearance.[120]

114 TNA WO 95/1169/4, HQ 1st (Indian) Cavalry Division, ADST, WD, 21 December 1914.
115 Ibid.
116 TNA WO 95/3932/2: HQ 7th (Meerut) Division, DAA&QMG, WD, 27 June 1915.
117 Alexander, *On Two Fronts*, pp.30-31.
118 For a concise history of the operations of 1st (Indian) Cavalry Division on the Western Front, see, Kempton, *Duty & Fidelity*, Part I, *Divisions*, pp.1-3 and the constituent brigades, Part II, *Brigades, NW Frontier and Other Theatres*.
119 A *syce* is a person in India who tends horses.
120 TNA WO 95/1168/1: HQ 1st (Indian) Cavalry Division, A&Q, Appx D (Transport) to an un-referenced After

P7.4. Indian Mule Carts in convoy: the challenge of velocity dissonance. The incompatibility of the Indian Mule Transport with MT and HT during divisional moves and re-supply operations eventually led to its withdrawal from the Western Front. (Tom Donovan Collection)

Their military bearing however, was not entirely the muleteers fault nor was their output because the divisional AT, whilst capable of delivering, with some caveats, the necessary transport support was not appropriately matched on a major formation move, to the speed of HT, resulting in the mules slowing the column of march.[121] This was a structural defect within the division, which was resolved by the removal of the AT, 106 carts and their supporting mules and drivers being returned to Marseilles on 30 March 1915 after being replaced by a British HT unit.[122]

The diverse nature of Indian rations was though, a factor that created several inefficiencies in the logistic system.[123] Whilst clearly procurement and storage in the Base Supply Depots were two aspects, within the divisional areas, it was distribution that caused the most significant delays. Divisional Supply Trains were loaded in bulk for the division and not for brigades or units. Because each Indian unit or sub-unit effectively had a different ration scale,[124] the DSC had to break bulk at the Supply Railhead and again at the Refilling Point,[125] all of which consumed time and thereby, reduced haul capability and flexibility. Divisions were quick to impose

Action Report.

121 Indian AT pace on the march is listed in General Staff, *Field Service Regulations* (FSR) Part I, *Operations*, War Office (London: HMSO, 1909) (Reprinted with Amendments, 1912) Chp III, Movements by Land and Sea, Sect 26, p.50, Pace.

122 TNA WO 95/1168/1: HQ 1st (Indian) Cavalry Division, A&Q, WD, 30 March 1915. The Mule Corps was re-deployed to the Dardanelles; for a personal record, see, Alexander, *On Two Fronts*.

123 The DAA&QMG of 7th (Meerut) Division noted, 'The difficulty of rationing Indian Troops as compared with British Troops is very great......This is increased when the requirements of the different Brigades vary'; TNA WO 95/3932/2: HQ 7th (Meerut) Division, QMG 10/3Q dated 11 November 1914.

124 The administration of the ration was further complicated by the presence of British units within the ORBAT; TNA WO 95/3932/2: HQ 7th (Meerut) Division, QMG, War Diary, entries 10-14 November 1914.

125 Ibid.

solutions,[126] and a key feature of the period, is the work of divisional logistic staff officers, who were much to the fore, not only in their industrious activity but also because of their physical grasp of conditions on the ground. There was plenty to attract their attention. In mid-November there was an increasing shortage of forage deliveries, especially baled hay and oats, arriving at railheads, which necessitated supply by WMT.[127]

As the winter hardened its grip, the IEFA logisticians were tasked to urgently deliver braziers, coke and coal to units, especially those in the trenches, so the soldiers could obtain some warmth and heat tinned rations.[128] By early December, welfare parcels containing clothing, groceries and tobacco were arriving in such numbers that on one day, 3rd (Lahore) Division received 39 packing cases of them, which then had to be distributed.[129] Another service, warmly received by the soldiers, that was arranged by the divisional logistic staff, was hot baths in a private seminary in Bethune at the rate of 400 per day and the laundering and dis-infection of their clothing.[130] By mid-December 1914, 7th (Meerut) Division had established its Divisional Baths in the Brewery at Vieille Chapelle. The Standing Orders[131] for its use are interesting; smoking was prohibited in the establishment and paragraph 3 included a statement very familiar in the 21st Century: 'No money or valuables should be brought to the baths, as the management cannot be responsible for any loss'.[132]

P7.5. At the Front: 58th Vaughan's Rifles in the line at Fauquissar in November 1914. The BEF's logistic focus was to sustain war-fighting capability. (Tom Donovan Collection)

126 TNA WO 95/3932/2: HQ 7th (Meerut) Division, QMG 10/3Q dated 11 November 1914.
127 TNA WO 95/3915/1: HQ 3rd (Lahore) Division, AQMG, WD, 19 November 1914.
128 Ibid, 28 November 1914.
129 Ibid, 3 December 1914. Parcels were distributed to units by supply officers at the Divisional Refilling Point, although the AQMG, Colonel G B Hodson, enjoined the festive spirit by personally presenting some special gifts.
130 Ibid, 19 December 1914.
131 TNA WO 95/3932/2: 'Order for Meerut Divisional Baths', dated 11 December 1914, signed by the DAA&QMG, Lieutenant-Colonel H Isacke.
132 TNA WO 95/3932/2: 'Order for Meerut Divisional Baths', dated 11 December 1914, para 3.

The Deputy Assistant Director Ordnance Services (DADOS) of 3rd (Lahore) Division, Major H W Gardiner RA, aided by Conductor Balchin AOC, had a very personal touch, touring his Area of Responsibility (AOR) in a car. On Friday 4 December 1914, DADOS welcomed 4th Suffolks as they joined 8th (Jullundur) Infantry Brigade, noting that action was required to provide them with new boots.[133] On the same day, he issued 30 x sheep-skin lined coats[134] to 3 Air Squadron Royal Flying Corps (RFC)[135] having met one of their officers at the Divisional Supply Railhead at Chocques[136] and another 158 x coats to the 3rd DSC[137]; he was on the road again on 16 December, issuing 50 x telephones to brigade HQs and divisional units.[138] On Monday 21 December, 129th Baluchis reported 60 x rifles inoperable because of broken extractors;[139] the DADOS discovered 60 x Short Magazine Lee Enfields (SMLE) at a Casualty Clearing Station Collection Point[140] and arranged for their immediate inspection and issue. Clearly, the DADOS was not an officer who would have been content sitting at a computer terminal, although he was equally active in the Divisional HQ. On Wednesday 2 December he issued eight of the 15 hot-water boilers received from the Lord Curzon Fund to battalions. On 4 December he was organizing transport to distribute winter clothing and on Saturday 12 December was discussing, with HQ Indian Corps QMG Branch, the acquisition of an armourer's lorry.[141]

Whilst the logisticians at the Front were using all their energy and skills to keep the Indian Corps supplied, the War Office was hastily improvising logistic units to reinforce it. The decision to form 2nd (Indian) Cavalry Division[142] in France resulted in the requirement to form a DSC and an Ammunition Park, and the requirement to rearrange the units comprising the DSC in 1st Cavalry Division,[143] actions that were initiated by the QMG's staff in the War Office.[144] As the clocks on 31 December 1914[145] ticked towards midnight, with the Indian Corps shrouded by the wet and cold French weather and immersed in the Flanders mud, it is not surprising that the DADOS of 3rd

133 'Received a report that the whole Regiment practically requires new boots owing to the bad quality issued when the Battalion was first mobilized'; TNA WO 95/3917/3: HQ 3rd (Lahore) Division, DADOS, WD, 4 December 1914.

134 Ibid, 4 December 1914.

135 3 Squadron was commanded by Major J M Salmond, later Chief of the Air Staff (CAS) 1930-1933, who was briefly followed as CAS by his brother Geoffrey who died in harness of cancer after 27 days in post, John temporarily succeeding him. For the remarkable story of the Salmond Brothers, see, Anne Baker, *From Biplane to Spitfire* (London: Leo Cooper, 2003).

136 3 Squadron was located at Chocques airfield. The records suggest that in late 1914, divisions hosting RFC squadrons within the divisional Area of Responsibility (AOR) were responsible for supporting them. H A Jones, BOH, *The War in the Air*, Vol. II (Oxford: Clarendon Press, 1928), Appx I.

137 TNA WO 95/3917/3: HQ 3rd (Lahore) Division, DADOS, WD, 4 December 1914.

138 Ibid, 16 December 1914.

139 Ibid, 21 December 1914.

140 Ibid.

141 Whilst the request was supported, there were no surplus lorries available with which, to service the demand; TNA WO 95/3917/3: HQ 3rd (Lahore) Division, DADOS, WD, entries December 1914.

142 For a concise history of the operations of 2nd (Indian) Cavalry Division on the Western Front, see, Kempton, *Duty & Fidelity*, Part I, *Divisions*, pp.5-7 and the constituent brigades, Part II, *Brigades, NW Frontier and Other Theatres*.

143 There is an excellent personal account of the deployment from the United Kingdom to France and the subsequent logistic operations in support of the 1st (Indian) Cavalry Division in Beatson, *The Motor Bus in War*.

144 War Office letter QMG5b 121/934 dated 10 November 1914, in TNA WO 95/1173/1: 89 Company ASC, WD.

145 On the last day of the year not all deaths in IEFA were the result of enemy action. Captain Ernest Kerr Molesworth, aged 36, attached 2nd Queen Victoria's Own Madras Sappers & Miners, was accidentally shot near Norrent being buried on 1 January 1915 at 1430; TNA WO 95/1168: HQ 1st (Indian) Cavalry Division, A&Q, WD, entries 31 December 1914 and 1 January 1915. Aged 36, he was the son of Colonel A O Molesworth of Cruxfield Arms, Berwickshire and husband of Hilda Rosalie, of South Lodge, Hoddesdon, Hertfordshire. The Commonwealth War Graves Commission records his rank as Major and he rests in Saint Hilaire-Cottes Churchyard.

(Lahore) Division chose to avoid emotional hyperbole in the War Diary but wrote of more practical matters: 'Reported that the supply of 2000 pairs of boots size 8 and 1000 size 7 imperative'.[146]

Conclusion

The logistic support to the Force was not perfect and a number of issues quickly surfaced as the operation progressed but despite the plethora of problems, which inundated them, logistic staffs at different levels within the Chain of Command, particularly at division, were remarkably adept at creating a fix. What is especially impressive, is how a force, which was not planned, trained, structured or equipped to fight a war in North-West Europe, deployed in short order and, by sound application of coherent Command Leadership and Management, delivered logistic solutions to a series of complex problems by using basic principles, thoughtful innovations and sound judgement.

In assessing the application of the Principles of Logistics,[147] the A&Q officers met, for the most part, despite the hand they had been dealt, an element of each one and scored very highly on flexibility and co-operation. What is especially interesting from the perspective of the 21st Century, is the focus of the divisional Q staff in not only co-ordinating the output of logistic assets to create maximum effect but also their ability and willingness to deploy on the ground in order to do so. That the smaller divisional AORs of 1914-15 enabled this approach is clear but the entries in the War Diaries consistently reinforce the operational significance and logistic effect created by staff officers who knew their business and utilized it to generate timely solutions based upon their expertise and knowledge.

146 TNA WO 95/3917/3: HQ 3rd (Lahore) Division, DADOS, WD, 31 December 1914.

147 For more information about the Principles of Logistics, see, *Army Doctrine Publication* (ADP) Vol. 3, *Logistics*, pp.1-4 to 1-6.

8

Sustaining The Storm

An analysis of the challenges to logistic planning in preparation for the Battle of the Somme in 1916

Introduction

Saturday 1 July 1916 was a catastrophic day for the British Army, with the Fourth Army and elements of the Third, suffering the loss of 57,470, men, killed, wounded, missing and taken prisoner, a figure which, equates to approximately 70% of the establishment of the British Army in 2016. 18,247 of these casualties were fatal,[1] a rate of 31.7 percent. In many respects, these enormous losses became more deeply seared into the collective National Memory[2] than the military one[3] but the lessons of this battle became the foundation for future operations on the Western Front.[4] Many books[5] have been written about the Battle of the Somme but unsurprisingly logistics does not feature as a prominent component of any of them.[6] One thing is certain however, logistics

1 Casualty figures extracted from Brigadier-General Sir James E Edmonds CB CMG & Major A F Becke, BOH, *Military Operations, France and Belgium, 1916*, Vol. I, *Sir Douglas Haig's Command to the 1st July: Battle of the Somme* (London: Macmillan, 1932), p.483.

2 See, William Philpott, *Bloody Victory, The Sacrifice on the Somme and the Making of the Twentieth Century* (London: Little, Brown, 2009), pp.592-629. It is instructive to remember that at 0730 on Thursday 1 July 1976, barely a soul stood at Lochnagar Crater near La Boiselle for the 60th anniversary of the start of the battle; indeed there may have been no one. 10 years later, at 0730 on the bright sunny morning of Tuesday 1 July 1986 and to the tunes of a lone Scottish piper, there were, on the white chalk rim of Lochnagar Crater, over 200 people who bowed their heads as the Cross of Remembrance was dedicated to commemorate the courage of thousands of young men who gave their lives 70 years before to the minute. Amongst the mourners were a handful of veterans who had fought on the Somme and at least one, Billy, aged 90, from the 36th (Ulster) Division, who had gone over the top as the whistles blew on 1 July. Later, immaculately dressed in a dark suit on a hot day, he pointed out the area of the trench from which he climbed to advance and the tears rolled down his cheeks; 70 years were indeed, to quote Sir Paul McCartney, 'In the Blink of an Eye'. The Lochangar Crater was purchased by Richard Dunning MBE in July 1978 and is now a memorial, which receives around 200,000 visitors annually.

3 One remarkable aspect discovered during the research for this work, was that the often detailed, comprehensive and erudite War Diary of the Deputy Director Supplies & Transport (DDST) at HQ Fourth Army, contains not one overt reference to the preparations for the Battle of the Somme, concentrating exclusively upon the efficient and effective delivery of the technical operations within his domain. Even on 1 July, the entry relates solely to a reconnaissance for the site of a proposed Forward Supply Depot at Ferme du Rosel. Given the scale and scope of the plans for the offensive and the very significant role of DDST in supporting them, the absence from the record is a mystery but the entries provide a fascinating wealth of information relating to the issues affecting the logistic outputs. TNA WO 95/4541: HQ Fourth Army, DDST, WD, May - June 1916.

4 From the British perspective, the Western Front was the Area of Responsibility (AOR) of the British Expeditionary Force in France and Flanders but more generally, the whole of the Allied front from Switzerland to the Channel Coast.

5 For a focused summary, see, Gary Sheffield, *The Somme* (London: Cassell, 2003). For a Soldier's perspective, Martin Middlebrook, *The First Day on the Somme* (London: Allen Lane, 1971). For a detailed analysis, see, Robin Prior and Trevor Wilson, *The Somme* (New Haven & London: Yale University Press, 2005). For a description of the operations, see, Edmonds, BOH, *France and Belgium, 1916*, Vol. I and Appendices, and Captain Wilfred Miles (Comp), BOH, *France and Belgium, 1916*, Vol. II, and Appendices and Maps, *2nd July 1916 to the End of the Battles of the Somme* (London: Macmillan, 1938).

6 Ian Malcolm Brown, *British Logistics on the Western Front, 1914-1919* (Westport Connecticut & London: Praeger,

played a very significant role in the preparations for the Battle and it is the aim of this chapter to expose its contribution by analysing the preparations of the Fourth Army.[7]

Logistic planning for the offensive was a major challenge at every level because apart from its specific requirements, the sustainment of the British Expeditionary Force (BEF) had by 1916, reached prodigious proportions. To place this into perspective, in October 1916, the daily tonnage delivered to railheads was estimated to be 40,424,[8] equating to an average 1,684 tons per hour, of which 27 percent was ammunition, 37 percent construction materials and 3.7 percent railway equipment, a level of activity that required 26,430 Standard Gauge Railway (SGR)[9] railway wagons to be in circulation to support it. Another key aspect that has been forgotten, which was essential to the Fourth Army's logistic planning, was co-ordination with the Host Nation, which lucidly demonstrates that whilst the Somme is mostly viewed as an entirely British battle, the French played a pivotal role in enabling the effective delivery of Fourth Army logistics.[10]

To examine every aspect of the logistic contribution to preparations for the Battle of the Somme would, in a study of this length, be impossible and for this reason, it focuses upon transportation and supply, although discussion of functional activities of the logistic corps of the day,[11] and their organizational structures, have been omitted. Logistic planning of the Medical[12] and Veterinary Services, except for the medical evacuation[13] of casualties, has not been included either; the scope, scale and significance are such that it demands its own examination. Finally, the reader may be surprised that there is, in this essay, only this reference to the tank. One advantage accruing to those planning the logistic support to the initial Battle of the Somme had, was that they did not have to support them. The logistic preparations though, were very significant and required an enormous amount of manual labour, much of which had to be undertaken, in the main, by infantry

1998) is a notable exception, concentrating on the strategic aspects.

7 'Support to Man and Machine' was one of five themes explored during the British Army's Operation REFLECT Battle of the Somme Exploitation Conference, held at the Tidworth Garrison Theatre on Tuesday 27 September 1916. I am indebted to Major General Tyrone Urch CBE, General Office Commanding Force Troops Command, for the opportunity to attend this important seminar and to Dr Chris Pugsley, the academic lead on the theme for his contribution post discussion.

8 Colonel A M Henniker CBE RE (Comp) BOH, *Transportation on the Western Front, 1914-1918* (London: HMSO, 1937). Figures extracted from wagon numbers to support British Army Traffic in October 1916, pp.188-189. *Transportation on the Western Front* is also held in the TNA in ZLIB 29/455 (Text) and 456 (Maps).

9 The Track Gauge on a railway is the distance between the inside edges of the heads of the two rails, measured just below the running surface, the corners of which are rounded. In 1918, Standard Gauge was 4 feet 8 ½ inches (1435mm) and Narrow Gauge, anything less. In 2018, Standard Gauge is rated between 1432mm and 1435mm to account for those SGRs, which have reduced their gauge by 3 mm, to improve the ride of high-speed trains.

10 HQ Fourth Army, A&Q, War Diary is replete with entries relating to co-ordination with the French Army on a variety of matters, including rail construction, road maintenance, Fourth Army access to and use of roads and railways, authorization for railheads and ammunition dumps and the delivery of ammunition to French units using BEF resources. TNA WO 95/441/2.

11 For the Royal Engineers, see, Major-General H L Pritchard (Ed.) *The History of the Corps of Royal Engineers*, Vol. V, *The Home Front, France, Flanders and Italy in the First World War* (Chatham: Institution of the Royal Engineers, 1952), pp.153-668. For Army Service Corps (ASC) operations, see, Colonel R H Beadon CBE psc, *The Royal Army Service Corps, A History of Transport and Supply in the British Army*, Vol. II (Cambridge: Cambridge University Press (CUP), 1931), pp.83-155. For the Army Ordnance Corps (AOC) see, Major-General A Forbes, CB CMG, *A History of the Army Ordnance Services*, Vol. Three, *The Great War* (London: The Medici Society, 1929), pp.3-147. For labour, see, K W Mitchinson, *Pioneer Battalions in the Great War, Organized and Intelligent Labour* (London: Leo Cooper, 1997) and covering a much wider spectrum, the comprehensive John Starling & Ivor Lee, *No Labour, No Battle, Military Labour During the First World War* (Stroud: Spellmount, 2009).

12 For details of the medical issues, see, Major-General Sir W G Macpherson KCMG CB LLD, BOH, *Medical Services*, Vol. III, *Medical Services during operations on the Western Front in 1916, 1917 and 1918; in Italy; and in Egypt and Palestine* (London: HMSO, 1924), pp.11-53.

13 Medical evacuation is the medically controlled process of moving any person who is wounded, injured or sick to, from, or between Medical Treatment Facilities (MTF).

soldiers.[14] Haig summarized the logistic tasks in his Despatches, which highlights, in particular, the importance of logistic engineering.

> Vast stocks of ammunition and stores of all kinds had to be accumulated beforehand within a convenient distance of our front. To deal with these many miles of new railways-both standard and narrow gauge-and trench tramways were laid. All available roads were improved, many others were made, and long causeways were built over marshy valleys. Many additional dug-outs had to be provided as shelter for the troops, for use as dressing stations for the wounded, and as magazines for storing ammunition, food, water and engineering material……….Except in the river valleys, the existing supplies of water were hopelessly insufficient to meet the requirements of the numbers of men and horses to be concentrated in this area as the preparations for our offensive proceeded. To meet this difficulty many wells and borings were sunk, and over one hundred pumping plants were installed. More than one hundred and twenty miles of water mains were laid, and everything was got ready to ensure that an adequate water supply as our troops advanced.[15]

P8.1. Logistic Engineers: The role of the logistic engineers in delivering the BEF's war-fighting capability, and in particular, the preparations for the Battle of the Somme, was fully appreciated in 1916, if not in 2016. Sapper Arthur Stanley Hill, a post-war architect and Second World War railway engineer, is Front Row, 2nd from left of picture, ones of thousands who made victory possible. (Courtesy of Edwina Maginniss)

14 Divisional and regimental histories record little of the logistic preparations, which given the involvement of the soldiers in delivering a significant part of the manual labour in the trenches to deliver components of it, is perhaps surprising. The regimental history of the Somerset Light Infantry Regiment, for example, records nothing of the work of its soldiers, relying on paraphrasing Haig's Despatches to explain the activities; see, Everard Wyrall, *The History of the Somerset Light Infantry (Prince Albert's) 1914-1919* (London: Methuen, 1927), pp.114-115.

15 Lieutenant-Colonel J H Boraston OBE (Ed.), *Sir Douglas Haig's Despatches, December 1915 - April 1919* (London:

Diagram 1
British Expeditionary Force
Supply Chain Outline

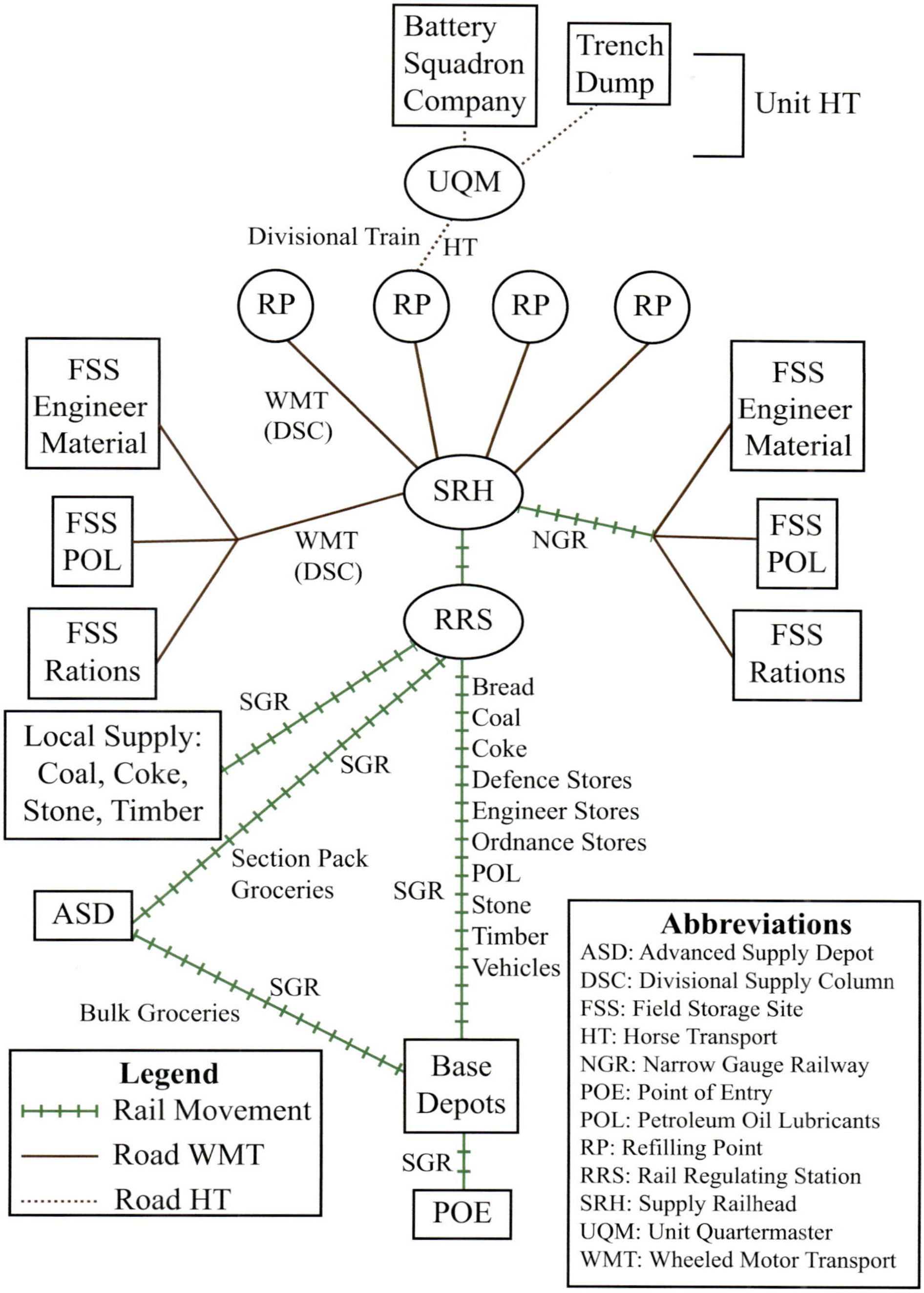

Source: Beadon, Royal Army Service Corps

Graphics: Hollie Barrett

Diagram 2
British Expeditionary Force Ammunition Supply

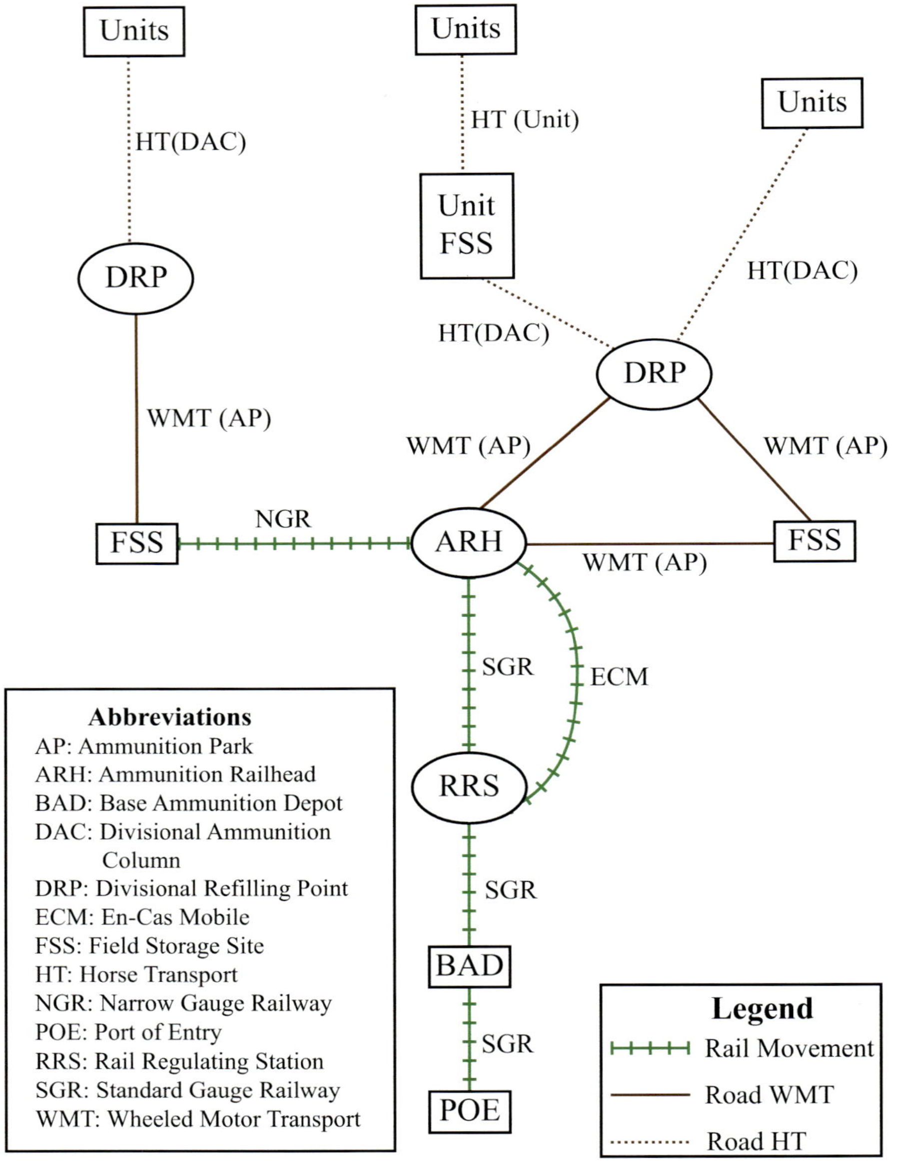

Note: Field Storage Sites controlled by Army, Corps, or Division had minimal or no technical staff to supervise the care of ammunition. The contemporary terminology was 'Dump'.

Source: Beadon, Royal Army Service Corps

Graphics: Hollie Barrett

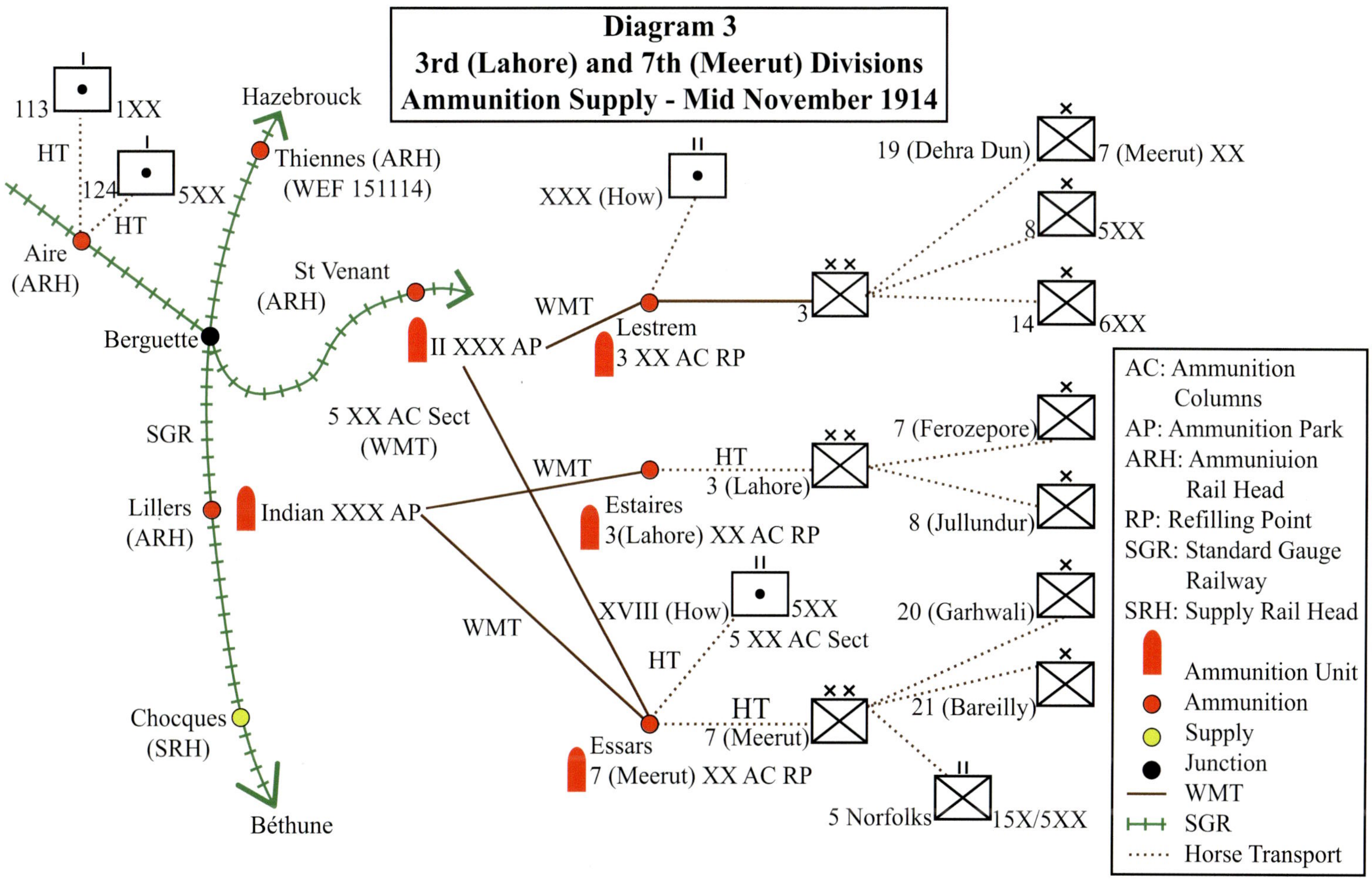

Source: TNA WO 95/3922/2, Becke, Divisions Part 1, & Perry, Divisions, Part 5B

Graphics: Hollie Barrett

Unit and Formation Map Symbols

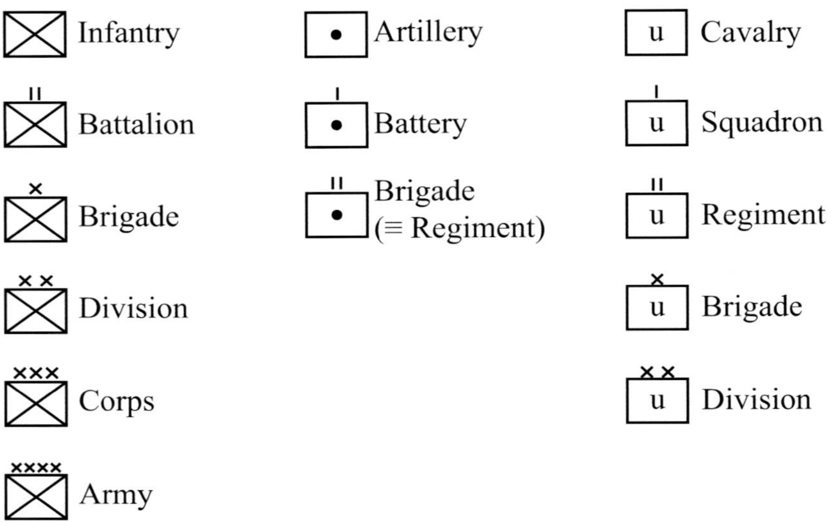

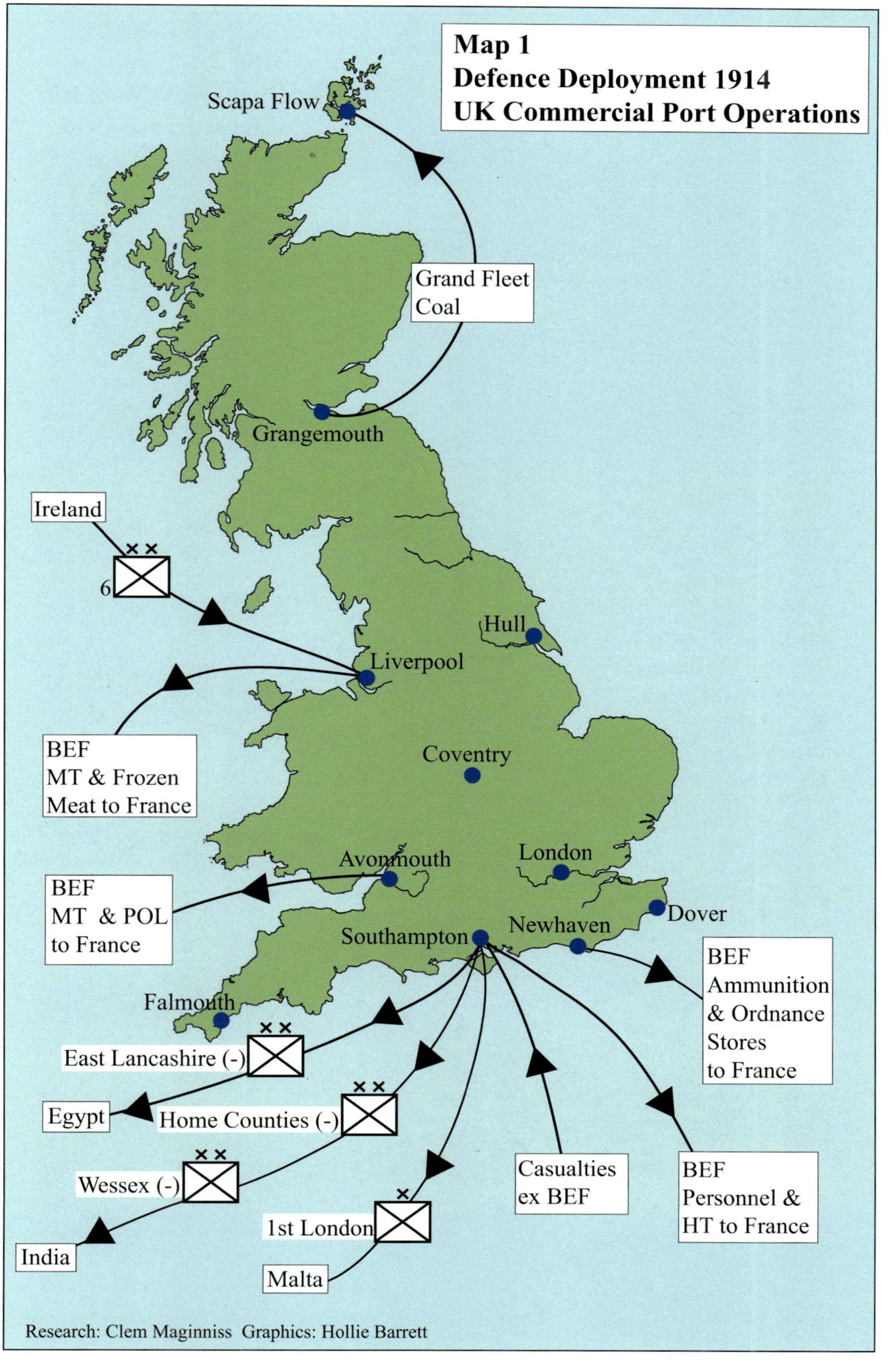
Map 1
Defence Deployment 1914
UK Commercial Port Operations
Scapa Flow
Grand Fleet
Coal
Grangemouth
Ireland
6
Hull
Liverpool
BEF
MT & Frozen
Meat to France
Coventry
Avonmouth
London
BEF
MT & POL
to France
Dover
Southampton
Newhaven
BEF
Ammunition
& Ordnance
Stores
to France
Falmouth
East Lancashire (-)
Egypt
Home Counties (-)
Wessex (-)
India
1st London
Malta
Casualties
ex BEF
BEF
Personnel &
HT to France
Research: Clem Maginniss Graphics: Hollie Barrett

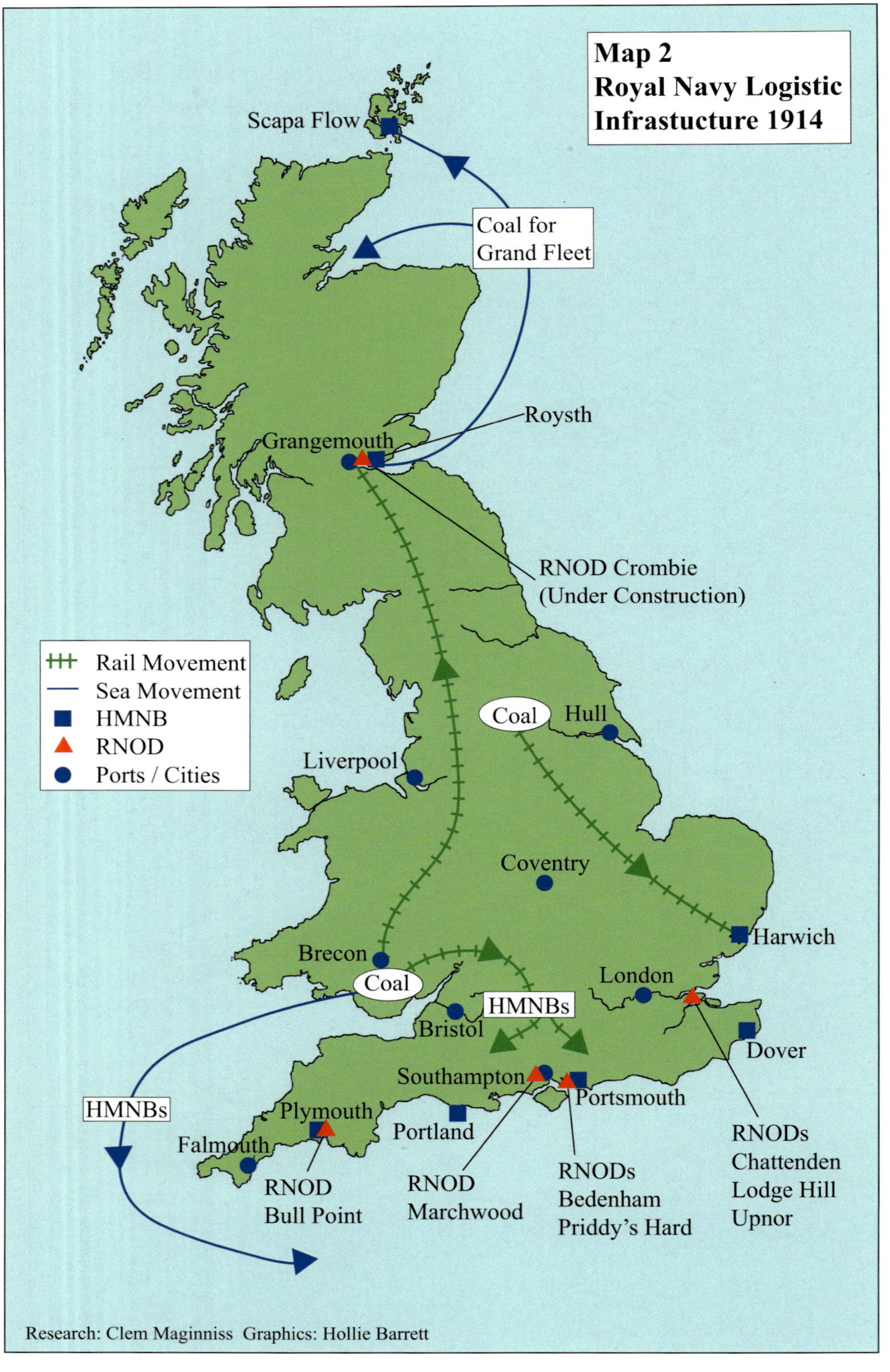
Map 2
Royal Navy Logistic
Infrastucture 1914
Scapa Flow
Coal for
Grand Fleet
Roysth
Grangemouth
RNOD Crombie
(Under Construction)
Rail Movement
Sea Movement
HMNB
RNOD
Ports / Cities
Coal
Hull
Liverpool
Coventry
Harwich
Brecon
Coal
London
HMNBs
Bristol
Dover
Southampton
Portsmouth
HMNBs
Plymouth
Portland
Falmouth
RNOD
Bull Point
RNOD
Marchwood
RNODs
Bedenham
Priddy's Hard
RNODs
Chattenden
Lodge Hill
Upnor
Research: Clem Maginniss Graphics: Hollie Barrett

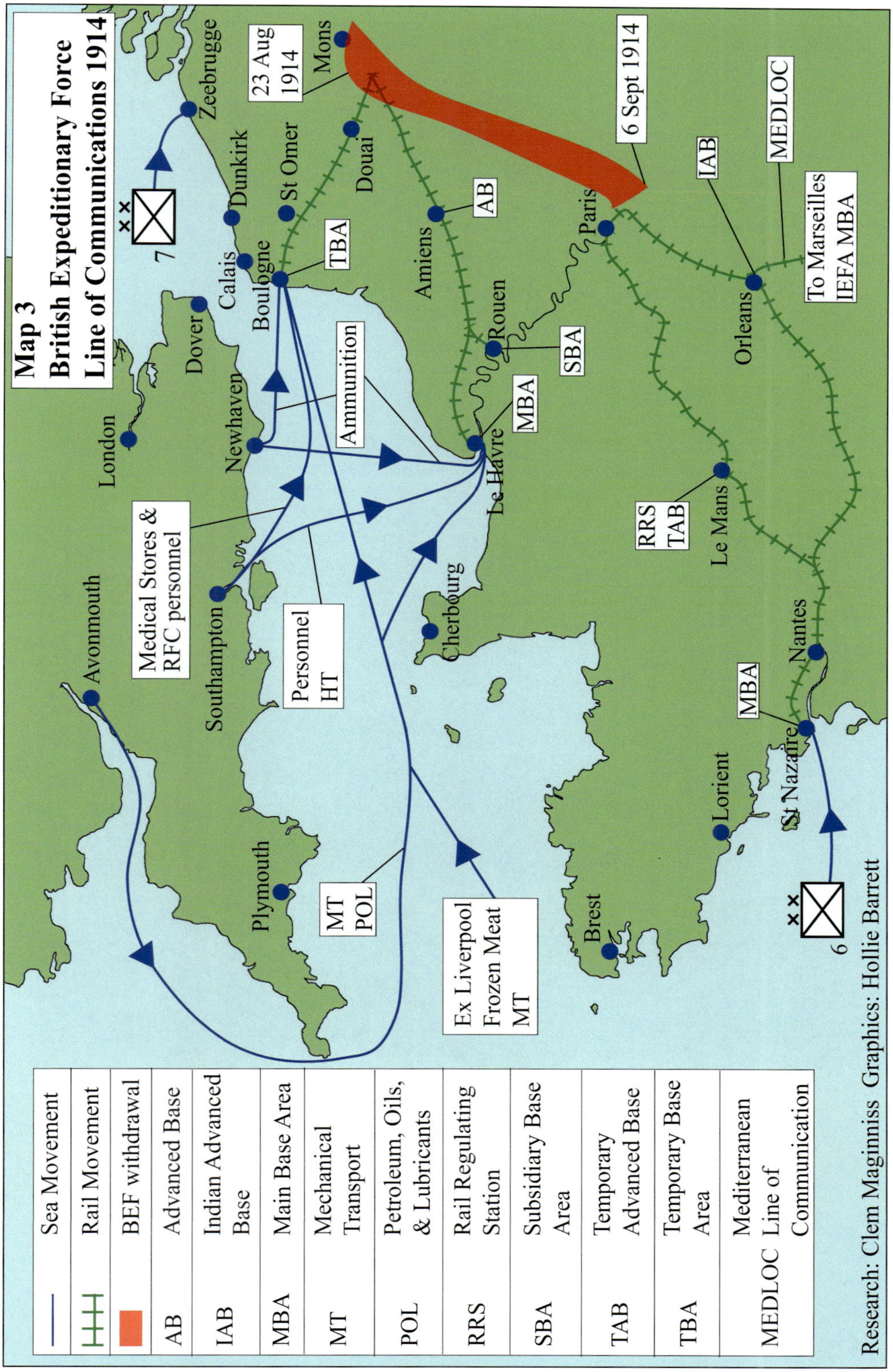
Map 3
British Expeditionary Force
Line of Communications 1914
Zeebrugge
Dunkirk
Calais
Boulogne
Dover
London
Newhaven
Southampton
Avonmouth
Plymouth
St Omer
Douai
Mons
23 Aug 1914
6 Sept 1914
Amiens
AB
TBA
Rouen
SBA
Paris
Le Havre
MBA
Ammunition
Medical Stores & RFC personnel
Personnel HT
Cherbourg
MT POL
Ex Liverpool Frozen Meat MT
Le Mans
RRS TAB
Orleans
IAB
MEDLOC
To Marseilles IEFA MBA
Nantes
MBA
St Nazaire
Lorient
Brest
7
6
Sea Movement
Rail Movement
BEF withdrawal
AB Advanced Base
IAB Indian Advanced Base
MBA Main Base Area
MT Mechanical Transport
POL Petroleum, Oils, & Lubricants
RRS Rail Regulating Station
SBA Subsidiary Base Area
TAB Temporary Advanced Base
TBA Temporary Base Area
MEDLOC Mediterranean Line of Communication
Research: Clem Maginniss Graphics: Hollie Barrett

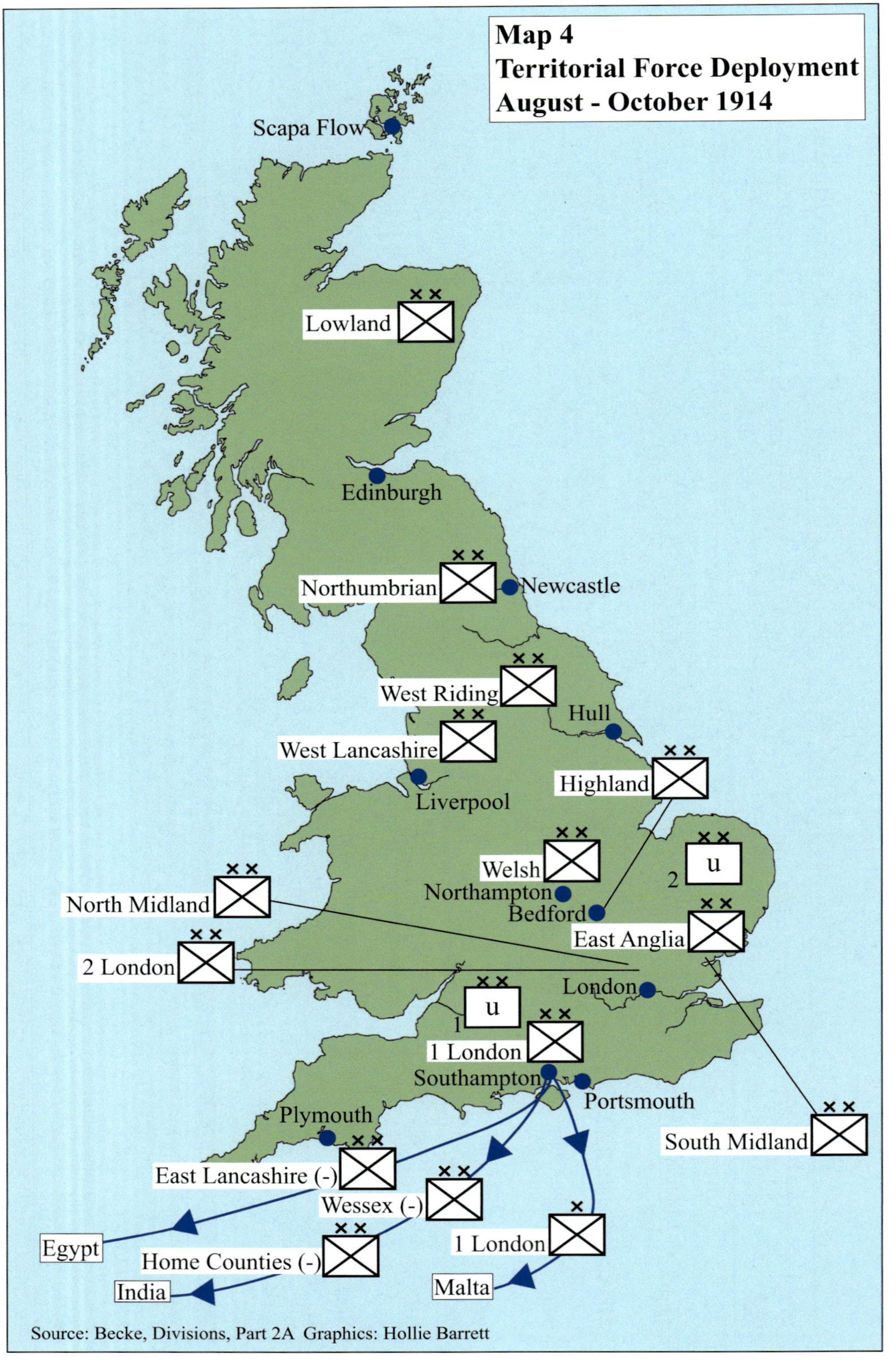
Map 4
Territorial Force Deployment
August - October 1914
Scapa Flow
Lowland
Edinburgh
Northumbrian
Newcastle
West Riding
Hull
West Lancashire
Liverpool
Highland
Welsh
u
2
Northampton
Bedford
East Anglia
North Midland
2 London
London
u
1
1 London
Southampton
Portsmouth
Plymouth
South Midland
East Lancashire (-)
Wessex (-)
1 London
Egypt
Home Counties (-)
India
Malta
Source: Becke, Divisions, Part 2A Graphics: Hollie Barrett

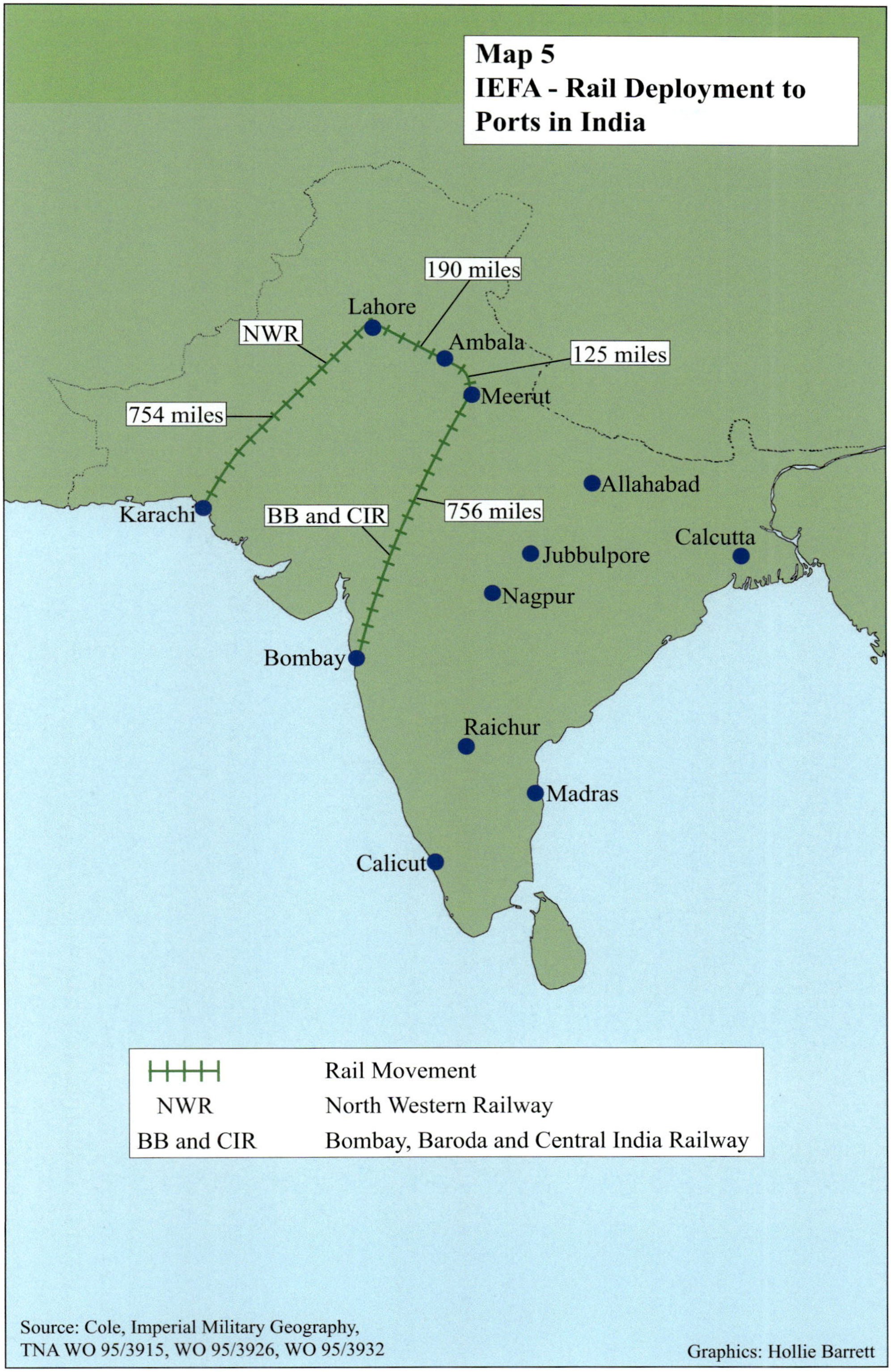
Map 5
IEFA - Rail Deployment to Ports in India
190 miles
Lahore
NWR
Ambala
125 miles
754 miles
Meerut
Allahabad
Karachi
BB and CIR
756 miles
Calcutta
Jubbulpore
Nagpur
Bombay
Raichur
Madras
Calicut
Rail Movement
NWR North Western Railway
BB and CIR Bombay, Baroda and Central India Railway
Source: Cole, Imperial Military Geography,
TNA WO 95/3915, WO 95/3926, WO 95/3932
Graphics: Hollie Barrett

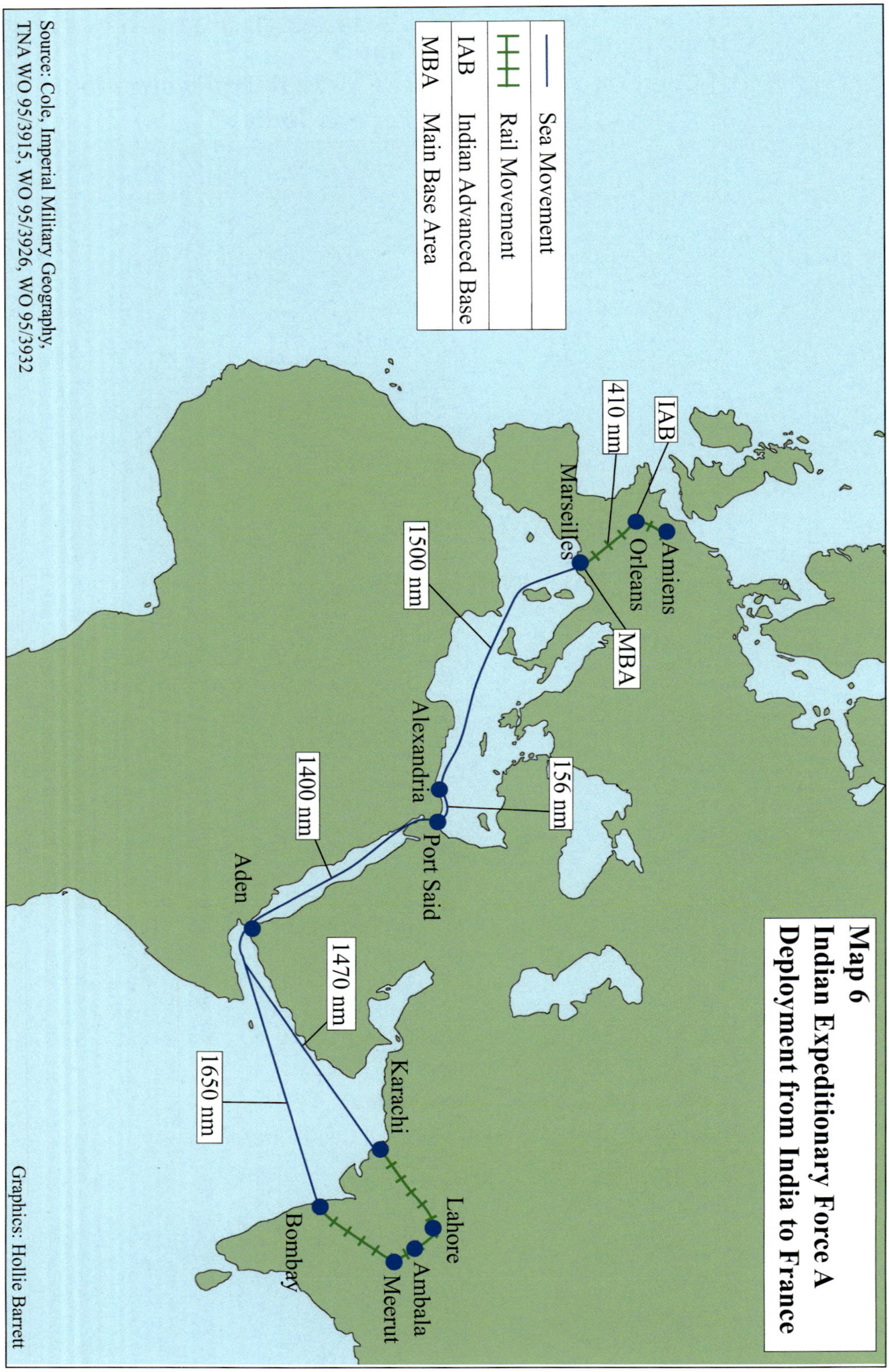

Map 6
Indian Expeditionary Force A Deployment from India to France

Source: Cole, Imperial Military Geography, TNA WO 95/3915, WO 95/3926, WO 95/3932

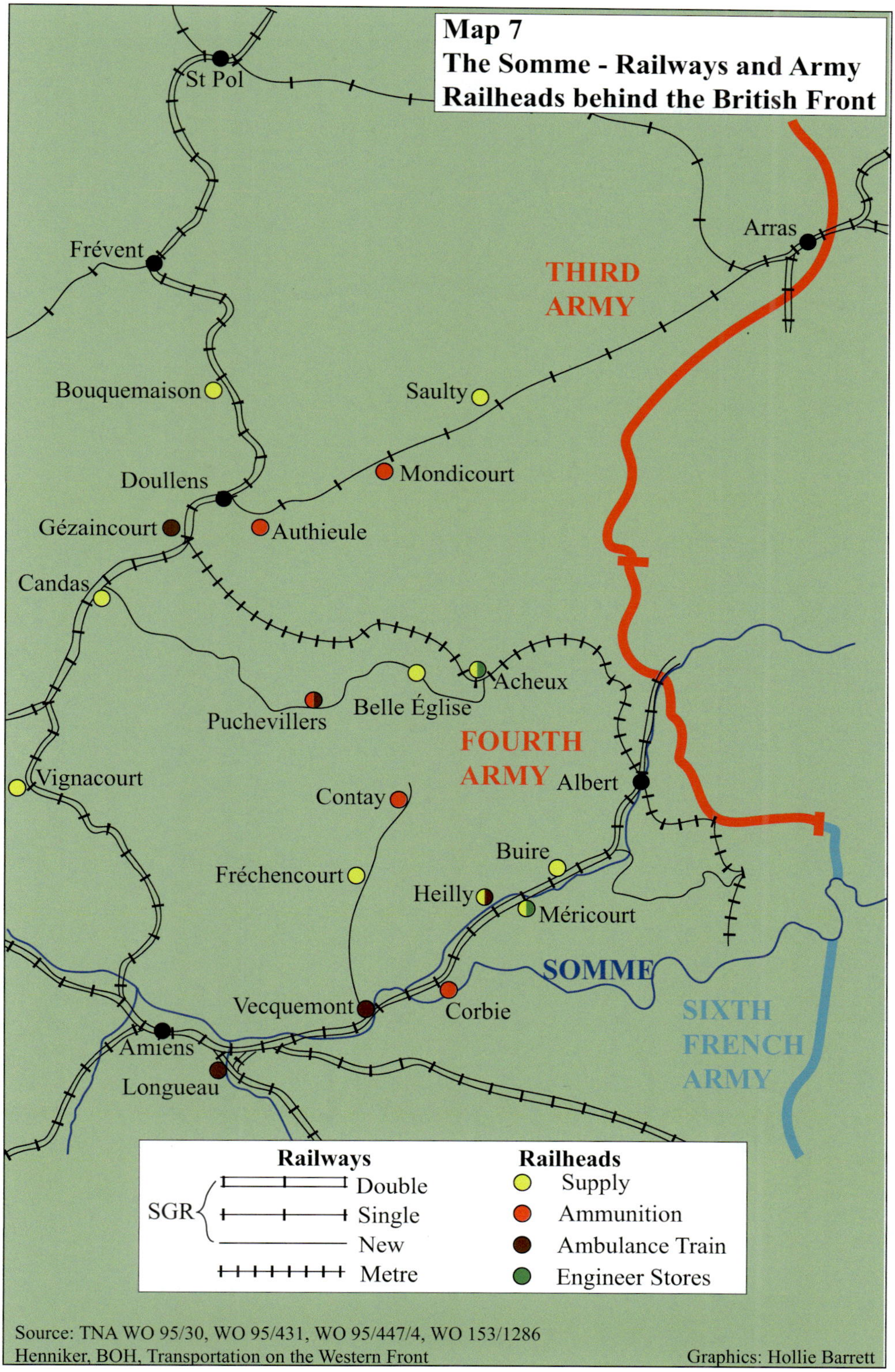
Map 7
The Somme - Railways and Army Railheads behind the British Front
St Pol
Frévent
Arras
THIRD ARMY
Bouquemaison
Saulty
Doullens
Mondicourt
Gézaincourt
Authieule
Candas
Acheux
Belle Église
Puchevillers
FOURTH ARMY
Albert
Vignacourt
Contay
Fréchencourt
Buire
Heilly
Méricourt
SOMME
Vecquemont
Corbie
SIXTH FRENCH ARMY
Amiens
Longueau
Railways
SGR
Double
Single
New
Metre
Railheads
Supply
Ammunition
Ambulance Train
Engineer Stores
Source: TNA WO 95/30, WO 95/431, WO 95/447/4, WO 153/1286
Henniker, BOH, Transportation on the Western Front
Graphics: Hollie Barrett

Map 8 Third Army Traffic Map: April 1918 - France (Lens) 1: 100,000

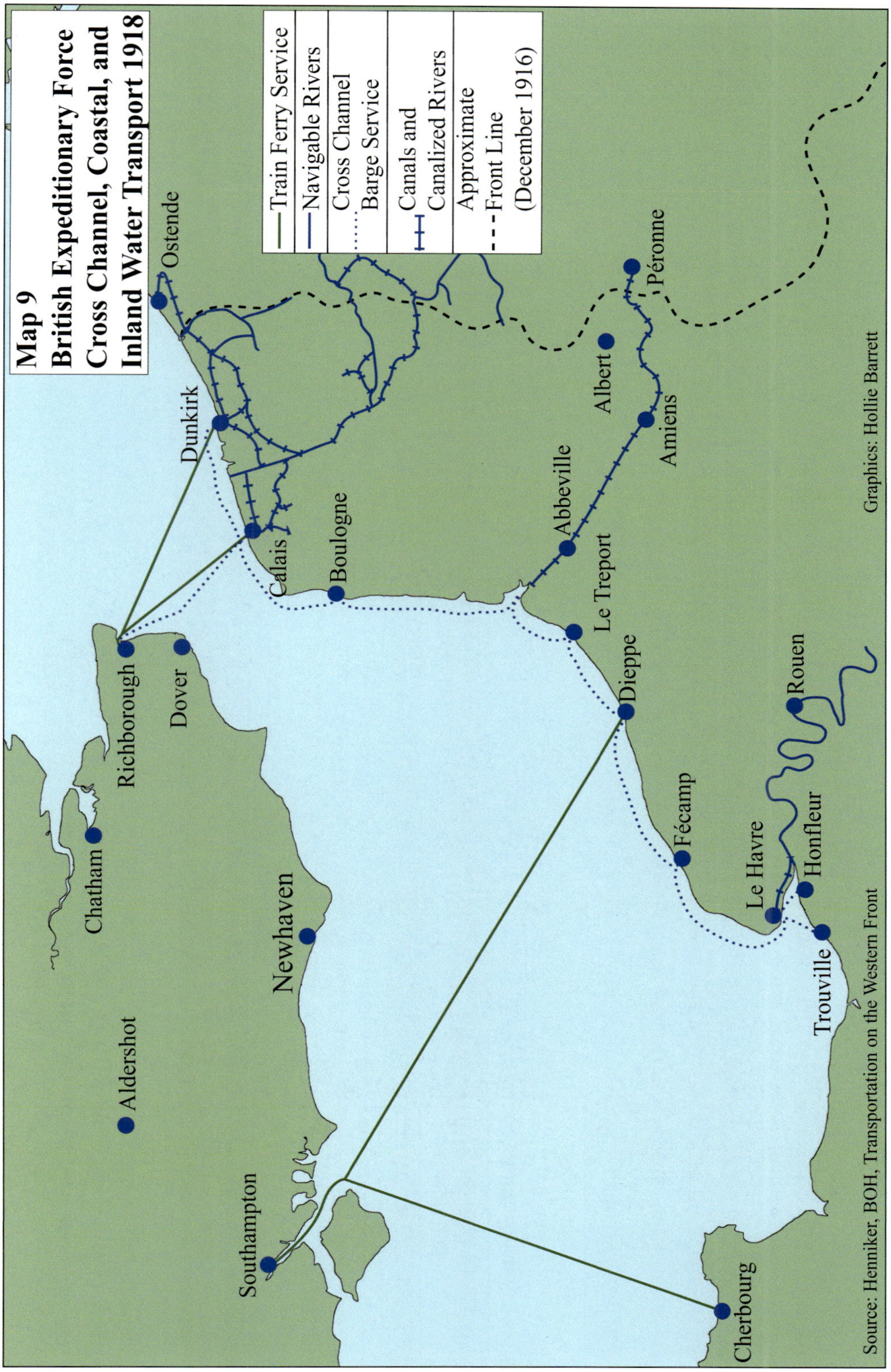
Map 9
British Expeditionary Force
Cross Channel, Coastal, and
Inland Water Transport 1918
Train Ferry Service
Navigable Rivers
Cross Channel
Barge Service
Canals and
Canalized Rivers
Approximate
Front Line
(December 1916)
Ostende
Dunkirk
Calais
Boulogne
Abbeville
Le Treport
Dieppe
Fécamp
Le Havre
Honfleur
Trouville
Rouen
Amiens
Albert
Péronne
Richborough
Dover
Chatham
Newhaven
Aldershot
Southampton
Cherbourg
Graphics: Hollie Barrett
Source: Henniker, BOH, Transportation on the Western Front

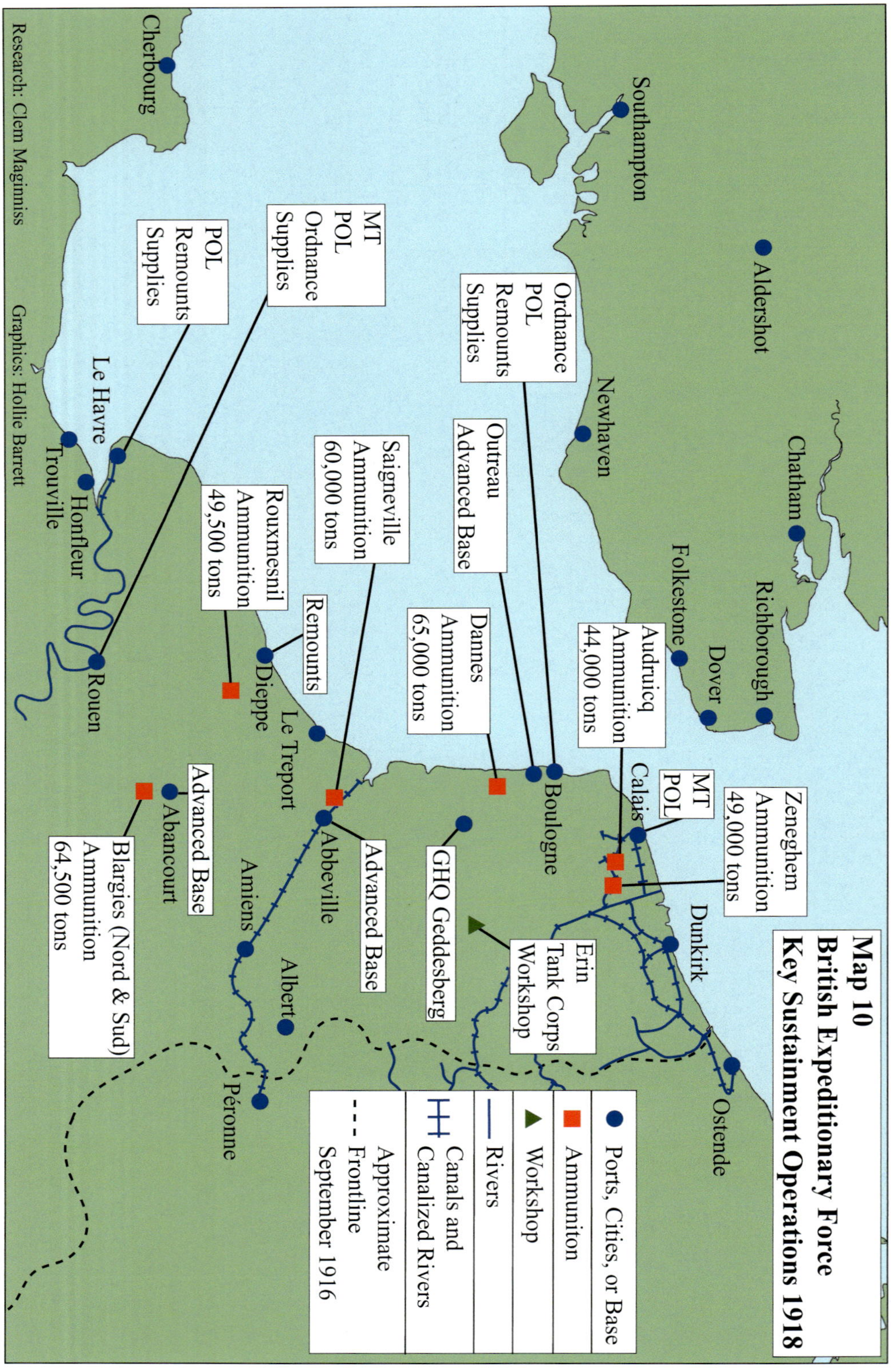
Map 10
British Expeditionary Force
Key Sustainment Operations 1918
Ports, Cities, or Base
Ammuniton
Workshop
Rivers
Canals and Canalized Rivers
Approximate Frontline September 1916
Southampton
Aldershot
Chatham
Richborough
Dover
Folkestone
Newhaven
Cherbourg
Ordnance POL Remounts Supplies
MT POL Ordnance Supplies
POL Remounts Supplies
Le Havre
Trouville
Honfleur
Rouen
Outreau Advanced Base
Saigneville Ammunition 60,000 tons
Rouxmesnil Ammunition 49,500 tons
Remounts
Dieppe
Le Treport
Dannes Ammunition 65,000 tons
Audruicq Ammunition 44,000 tons
Boulogne
Calais
MT POL
Zeneghem Ammunition 49,000 tons
Dunkirk
Ostende
GHQ Geddesberg
Erin Tank Corps Workshop
Abbeville
Advanced Base
Advanced Base
Abancourt
Blargies (Nord & Sud) Ammunition 64,500 tons
Amiens
Albert
Péronne
Research: Clem Maginniss
Graphics: Hollie Barrett

P4.2. Railway Motive Power was critical to BEF deployment and sustainment. The WF Plan required through running to meet the schedules so it was critical that allocated locomotives could run upon different railway company metals. A Class 27 locomotive, of the Lancashire & Yorkshire Railway, a type introduced in 1889, still steaming on the North Norfolk Railway in 2011. (Author)

P8.1. Logistic Engineers: The role of the logistic engineers in delivering the BEF's war-fighting capability, and in particular, the preparations for the Battle of the Somme, was fully appreciated in 1916, if not in 2016. Sapper Arthur Stanley Hill, a post-war architect and Second World War railway engineer, is Front Row, 2nd from left of picture, ones of thousands who made victory possible. (Courtesy of Edwina Maginniss)

The construction of the dug-outs and shelter facilities on the Somme was a superb piece of long-forgotten logistic engineering, which was a critical to Force Protection, enhancing logistic capability whilst crucially improving soldiers' morale. The planning of this work is testament to the diligence of engineers and logisticians, whilst its execution, sometimes conducted under artillery fire, a demonstration of their determination. Then, as now, much of the activity was hidden from view but the task clearly demonstrated the vital role of manual labour on the exposed surface and in the confined subterranean tunnels, in excavating the thousands of tons of spoil and handling the heavy timbers, corrugated iron sheets, steel shutters, bags of cement and boxes of nails, without which, the facilities would never have been completed. Many of these underground shelters remain, suggesting that there is more Great War archaeology below ground on the Western Front than there is above.[16]

Estimate and Planning

Whilst terms such as 'Mission Analysis'[17] and 'Logistic Estimate'[18] were not used in 1916, similar processes were used to assess key tasks. Fundamentally, the task of the Staff and the logisticians was the Logistic Preparation of the Battlefield (LPB)[19] a function clearly understood today but just as significant in 1916. Although historians have not articulated its importance, the work that was enacted to prepare logistic capability in the Fourth Army area confirms that not only was the requirement for LPB was lucidly recognised by the Staff but also very significant resources were dedicated to its successful delivery at the tactical level. The Q planners at BEF General Headquarters (GHQ)[20] were however, only just being beginning to comprehend the wider logistic operational and strategic implications of supporting five Armies in the Field[21] and the logistic tasks involved in mounting offensive operations involving nearly 20 divisions. At the Army level and below, in common with many battles on the Western Front, the logisticians had two clear objectives:

J M Dent & Sons, 1919), p.21.

16 Whilst the work of the tunnelling companies in placing mines under German defences and conducting counter-mining against the Germans is relatively well known, see, Alexander Barrie, *War Underground, The Tunnellers of the Great War* (London: Frederick Muller, 1961), the exploits of the RE in building significant logistic and defence facilities, especially in the Ypres area where the clay and the high water table posed exceptional challenges, has almost been airbrushed from history. Pritchard, *Corps of Royal Engineers*, Vol. V, p.479 offers half a page on the subject, whilst the Royal Engineers Institute, *Work of the RE in the European War of 1914-19, Work under the Director of Works (France)* (Chatham: W & J Mackay, 1924) grants no insight into this fascinating work. For a modern assessment, based upon practical discovery below ground, see, Peter Barton, Peter Doyle & Johan Vandewalle, *The Tunnellers' War 1914-18* (Staplehurst: Spellmount, 2004).

17 A process by which, a commander and his Staff makes an initial analysis of what outputs are required by analysing the mission, which has been given, with particular reference to the superior commander's intent; *Army Doctrine Publication* (ADP) Vol. 2, *Command*, HQDT/18/34/51, Army Code No 71564 (UK MOD, 1995), pp.3-10.

18 A Logistic Estimate is an analysis tool through which, all the relevant factors relating to the logistic requirement can be evaluated, leading to an assessment of tasks, consideration of a number of Courses of Action and then concluding with the commander's decision, from which, the Staff then create a plan. Ibid, pp.3-12 to 3-13.

19 LPB was originally a United States Army concept and the term summarizes the process of the Logistic Estimate: 'The process of gathering data against pertinent battlefield components, analysing their impact on sustainment and integrating them into tactical planning so that support actions are synchronised with manoeuvre. It is a conscious effort to identify and assess those factors, which facilitate, inhibit, or deny support to combat forces'. *Army Doctrine Publication* (ADP) Vol. 3, *Logistics*, DGD&D/18/34/63, Army Code No 71566 (UK MOD, 1996), para 0323. LPB has now been expanded to assess supporting issues, the US Army using the term 'Sustainment Preparation of the Operational Environment'.

20 For a personal view of the work of GHQ, and in particular its Q staff, see, GSO [Frank Fox] *GHQ (Montreuil-Sur-Mer)* (London: Phillip Allan, 1920).

21 For details of the formation, commanders, key senior staff officers and significant operations of each Army, see, Major A F Becke (Rtd) (Comp) BOH, *Order of Battle*, Part 4, *The Army Council, GHQs, Armies and Corps, 1914-1918* (London: HMSO, 1945), pp.71-120.

first, to provide support to the break-in and break-through battle and secondly, should it occur, to sustain the breakout. In effect, this provided a two-phase sequential operation, the concept of which appears alluringly simple but in the conditions appertaining on the Western Front in 1916, the first was a major challenge, whilst the second was usually unachievable but the logisticians were clear about the difficulties of the logistic engineering required to build the connecting roads and new railways across the German defensive areas once they were captured.[22]

Odd though it may now seem, the influence of the enemy upon logistic operations in 1916 was a relatively minor factor in the logisticians' calculations, and the relatively static nature of the Western Front led to stocks being held well forward. This arrangement reduced the potential for shortages during offensive operations, a deduction reinforced by the fact that there were no Special, parachute or helicopter forces to create flank or rear threats, and no chance of surprise deep penetration operations by manoeuvre forces.[23] Artillery was however, an increasing problem, especially if directed from aircraft or kite balloons, so although small effectively camouflaged dumps might be relatively safe, transport moving during the day was usually vulnerable to indirect enemy fire as were any logistic operations that could be viewed by the enemy. Of but two examples, the engineer stores railhead at Acheux was shelled three or four times in the first week of June, prompting the Army Chief Engineer to request a new siding to be constructed at Lealvillers,[24] whilst XV Corps ceased using the Dermancourt-Bray railway extension because of shelling,[25] thereby disrupting the artillery ammunition dumping programme. Aircraft were identified as posing a potential threat to freedom of movement, although there was lively debate about their capability to effectively disrupt generic logistic activity. In 1916 the *Fliegertruppen des deutschen Kaiserreiches* (FDK)[26] had no success in interdicting the logistic concentration for the Somme, the Royal Naval Air Service (RNAS) apparently making the only offensive strike in the Fourth Army area.[27]

The enemy though, affected logistics in rather more benign ways than one might expect. Improvements to German aerial observation capability generated an increasing requirement to store and issue camouflage material, and reinforced the need for logistic units to make use of it.[28] In addition, the focus on improving Anti-Aircraft Artillery (AAA)[29] initiated the need to procure,

22 TNA WO 95/441/2: HQ Fourth Army, A&Q, WD, 24 June 1916, in relation to the repair of the Albert-Arras railway line. See, also, Initial report from Geddes to Lloyd George in a Private and Confidential letter dated 15 September 1916; Sir William Guy Granet Papers, held in the Modern Records Centre University of Warwick Library (MRCUWL) GB 152, MSS.191/3/3/ 10. Geddes proposed that specially equipped and trained Light Railway units were the Way Ahead to enable the 3-6 miles of 'devastated zone' to be logistically 'bridged'.

23 The British experience in 1940 was however, to be very different. See, Lieutenant Colonel C H Maginniss, 'The Most Unkindest Cut: The Impact of Manoeuvre Warfare upon Logistics in 1940', *British Army Review* No 117, UK MOD (December 1997), pp.16-29.

24 TNA WO 95/441/2: Fourth Army, A&Q, WD, 4 June 1916.

25 Ibid, entry 10 June 1916.

26 The German Air Force was not an independent organization but the air arm of the German army, in the same way as the RFC in the British Army until the formation of the Royal Air Force. The *Deutsche Luftstreitkrafte* (DLK) was formed in October 1916 from the *Fliegertruppen des deutschen Kaiserreiches* (FDK) the Imperial German Flying Corps. The German Imperial Air Service (GIAS) is often used in British sources as the term for the *Luftstreitkrafte* and its predecessor but neither German title translates thus. See, Peter Grey and Owen Thetford, *German Aircraft of the First World War*, 2nd Edn (London: Putnam, 1979), p.xxix.

27 The FDK was conspicuous by its absence over the Fourth Army logistic areas during the preparations for the Somme offensive; Edmonds, BOH, *France and Belgium, 1916*, Vol. I, p.286-297. It is interesting that H A Jones, BOH, *War in the Air, Being the Story of The part played in the Great War by the Royal Air Force*, Vol. II (Oxford: Clarendon Press, 1928), makes no mention of this good fortune, presumably because of the German inaction rather the RFC's air defence operations, of which, there is no record either BOH.

28 TNA WO 95/441/2: HQ Fourth Army, A&Q, WD, 31 May 1916.

29 HQ Fourth Army A&Q War Diary for May and June 1916, records the trickle arrival of AA units; TNA WO 95/441/2. In particular, 15 AA Section, Q Battery; TNA WO 95/483/8: WD.

transport, store, inspect and repair an expanding array of AA weapons,[30] and the supporting munitions. Overall though, the enemy threat to logistics was low if the activity was outside German artillery range, and dispositions and procedures reflected the risk. Operational security (OPSEC)[31] was harder to achieve because some civilians were living in the corps and divisional rear areas where much of the logistic activity was clear for everyone to see.[32] Whilst there were some restrictions on movement, and the passage of information was slow, there remained the possibility that the preparations being conducted by Fourth Army might be reported to the enemy. Of more immediate logistic effect was pilfering by civilians of coal, forage and rations from dumps.[33] Security at these sites was generally weak because there was insufficient manpower to guard them all and there was a growing need to secure those items deemed Valuable and Attractive, or 'V&A' in Army parlance, in buildings, whilst fencing was sometime erected for bulk items, or stocks greatly reduced, to enable security measures to be more effective.[34] Pilfering was certainly a consistent irritation, which, in addition to reducing the availability of military supplies, whilst increasing the cost to the British taxpayer, did little improve relations between the British Army and the local populace.[35]

The enemy attack upon logistic infrastructure was compounded by the BEF's dis-aggregated control of the transportation system, especially the railways, which created plenty of opportunity for innovative but incoherent solutions to the challenges of a rapidly expanding logistic system.[36] This process, known in 1916 as 'ad-hocism'[37] created an underlying fragility in the BEF's logistic system, which was not fully exposed until the Battle of the Somme was underway and the structural flaws only became an issue after the BEF began to expand. That the system continued to operate was the product of two factors: the logisticians' remarkable ability to improvise, which masked the inherent failure to plan for sustained expansion and the munitions shortage of 1915. It appears highly probable that had artillery ammunition been available in the quantities desired by the General Staff, the transportation system would have reached criticality in mid-1915 and not mid-1916.[38]

30 For details of AAA on the Western Front, see, Brigadier N W Routledge, OBE TD, *History of the Royal Regiment of Artillery, Anti-Aircraft Artillery, 1914-55* (Woolwich: The Royal Artillery Institution, 1994), pp.3-26.

31 The importance of OPSEC is explained in *Army Doctrine Publication (ADP)* Vol. 1, *Operations*, HQDT/18/34/46, Army Code No 71565 (UK MOD, 1994), p.4-23; fn 6, 'The aim of OPSEC is to provide a military operation or exercise an additional form degree of security, using active or passive means, to ensure that knowledge of friendly dispositions, capabilities, intentions and vulnerabilities are denied to the enemy'. OPSEC measures concentrate on identifying those aspects of a plan which are considered vital to the success of an operation.

32 For a fascinating assessment of the interface between French civil society and the soldiers of the BEF, see the seminal, Craig Gibson, *Behind the Front, British Soldiers and French Civilians, 1914-1918* (Cambridge: CUP, 2014).

33 DDST Fourth Army recorded a particular issue at the Forward Supply Depot (FSD) Canaples, which only had one sentry patrolling and villagers were taking the opportunity to remove increasing amounts of coal, oats and rum; TNA WO 95/454/1: HQ Fourth Army, DDST, WD, 14 April 1916.

34 Ibid.

35 This issue is carefully explored in Gibson, *Behind The Front*. It has been a timeless feature of deployed British military operations and GHQ was alive to consequences of soldiers responding with draconian local retaliatory measures. Prevention was deemed to be better than cure but the imposition of effective security required resources, the deployment of which was usually influenced by the amount of what commercial suppliers and retailers call 'shrinkage', although the decision was not always driven by the financial imperative. The frustrations caused by pilfering and theft and the response to it by particular units during Operation TELIC were brought to public prominence by the media, although uncontrolled human depredation is an enduring military problem of which, the adverse effects upon capability were well known to Great War logisticians.

36 Inland Water Transport (IWT) was used widely in supporting preparations for the Somme. Operations included the non-urgent delivery of water, fresh meat, oats, defence stores, ammunition, timber, stone for road and railways and also medical evacuation. IWT is another aspect of BEF logistic capability that has had little light shed upon it. For a recent academic review, see, Christopher Phillips, 'Logistics and the BEF: The Development of Waterborne Transport on the Western Front, 1914-1916', *British Journal of Military History*, Vol. 2, No 2 (2016), pp.42-58.

37 'Ad-hocism' is a termed used by Ian Malcolm Brown in *British Logistics on the Western Front*, to describe what he assesses to be continual short-term solutions to the BEF's structural logistic problems.

38 Given the outcome of the later failure, it is fascinating to speculate on how operations might have developed had

In 1916, the General Staff planned the opening battles on the Somme without regard for the wider transportation implications as part of the Logistic Preparation of the Theatre and the adverse results were a direct, although not complete correlation of this failure. In the post-war years, the consequences of separating tactical thought and supply arrangements became a prime lesson in staff training in the Q arena but it was hard-won from the experiences of 1916-1918. The *1933 Manual of Movement (War)* summarized them:

> The degree of mobility possessed by a force in the field is governed by the facilities for adequate maintenance of personnel and material, which cannot be effected without ample facilities for movement..........A study of the resources available for movement in a theatre of war is therefore a primary consideration when a plan of campaign is being formulated, and remains the first importance in every phase of subsequent operations.[39]

The Fourth Army[40] was not formed until February 1916.[41] As it transpired, this left less than four months for the Headquarters to plan and execute the preparations on and across ground, which

the transportation crisis been identified and resolved in 1915 instead of 1916.

39 Army Council, *Manual of Movement (War)* 26/Manuals/1297, War Office (London: HMSO, 1933), p.1.

40 The ORBAT of the Fourth Army commanded by General Sir Henry Rawlinson on 1 July 1916 is shown in the table. 46th (North Midland) Division (TF) and 56th (London) Division (TF) comprised VII Corps (Lieutenant-General Sir T D'O Snow) in Third Army (General Sir E Allenby). 111th and 112th Brigades of 37th Division were attached to 34th Division. GOC ranked as a Major-General and Corps Commanders, Lieutenant-General. For details of the ORBATs including HQ Staffs and Combat Service Support units see, Major A F Becke (Comp), BOH, *Order of Battle*, Parts 1-4 (London: HMSO, 1935-1945). Middlebrook, *The First Day on the Somme*, Appx 1, Order of Battle of British Infantry Units, 1 July 1916, provides an excellent summary to battalion level.

Table 8.1

Fourth Army – 1 July 1916
Corps ORBAT and Commanders

Corps	Divisions	Status	GOC	Corps Commanders
III	8th	Regular	H Hudson	Sir W P Pulteney
	19th (Western)	NA	G T M Bridges	
	34th	NA	E C Ingouville-Williams	
VIII	4th	Regular	Honourable W Lambton	Sir A G Hunter-Weston
	29th	Regular	H de B de Lisle	
	31st	NA	R Wanless O'Gowan	
	48th (South Midland)	TF	R Fanshawe	
X	32nd	NA	W H Rycroft	Sir T L N Morland
	36th (Ulster)	NA	O S W Nugent	
	49th (West Riding)	TF	E M Perceval	
XIII	18th (Eastern)	NA	F I Maxse	Sir W N Congreve VC
	30th	NA	J S M Shea	
XV	7th	Regular	H E Watts	Sir H S Horne
	17th (Northern)	NA	T D Pilcher	
	21st	NA	D G M Campbell	

41 HQ Fourth Army was formed at Tilques before relocating to the *Querrieu Chateau* on the Amiens to Albert Road; it is open to the public. Army Service Corps officers and clerks were reporting to the latter by Wednesday 23 February 1916; TNA WO 95/441/2: HQ Fourth Army, A&Q, WD, entries late February and early March 1916.

was mostly unfamiliar territory, for what was, at that point, the largest land offensive that any British field force had undertaken in history, which was certainly taking a considerable risk.[42] In mitigation, the preparatory timeframe became compressed and from the perspective of early 1916, the perception was that challenges as great had been surmounted.[43] Whilst therefore, the decision to direct a new headquarters, which had little time to integrate and mature, to plan and execute such a major operation might be adjudged fundamentally flawed, the achievement of the staff officers, and particularly those engaged in logistic planning,[44] in delivering a significant offensive, especially given all the limitations with which they were faced, is testimony to the determination, if not the cohesive experience of the participants.[45] To compound the problem, 56 percent of the divisions in

42 The British divisions participating in the Battle of the Somme on the first day are shown in the table. Details compiled from information in Becke, BOH, *Order of Battle*, Parts 1-4.

Table 8.2
British Divisions – 1st Day on the Somme

Division	Type	Deployment to France	Previous Location	Remarks
4th	Regular	August 1914	UK	Initial BEF deployment
7th	Regular	October 1914	UK	Units from Empire Garrison Duties
8th	Regular	November 1914	UK	Units from Empire Garrison Duties
17th (Northern)	New Army (K2)	July 1915	UK	
18th (Eastern)	New Army (K2)	May 1915	UK	
19th (Western)	New Army (K2)	July 1915	UK	
21st	New Army (K3)	September 1915	UK	
29th	Regular	April 1916	Gallipoli*	*March 1915-March 1916
30th	New Army (K4)	November 1915	UK	
31st	New Army (K4)	March 1916	Egypt*	*December 1915-March 1916
32nd	New Army (K4)	November 1915	UK	
34th	New Army (K4)	January 1916	UK	
36th (Ulster)	New Army (K5)	October 1915	UK	
46th (North Midland)	Territorial Force	March 1916	Egypt*	*December 1915-January 1916
48th (South Midland)	Territorial Force	March 1915	UK	
49th (West Riding)	Territorial Force	April 1916	UK	
56th (London)	Territorial Force	January 1916	UK	

43 One example was the rapid expansion of its personnel. Manpower in the BEF rose from 270,000 in December 1914 to 858,000 in August 1915, a factor of 3.17 in 8 months. In the 24 days between 1-24 August, 96,000 personnel joined the BEF and the expansion continued, with its strength rising to 1.029 million in February 1916. Figures from War Office, *Statistics of the Military Effort of the British Empire during the Great War, 1914-1920* (MEBE) (HMSO, 1922), p.64 (iii), Table (ii) -Estimated Strength of the Expeditionary Forces - France and Italy. This is a remarkable rate of growth, which, has rarely been achieved by any organization and, although perhaps not finely executed in every area, created a confidence that 'big' problems could be surmounted.

44 DA&QMG: Major-General H C Sutton; Chief Engineer: Major-General R U H Buckland; Deputy Director Supplies & Transport: Colonel F M Wilson; Deputy Director Ordnance Services: Colonel J A Stewart, who was replaced by Colonel H S Bush on 21 May 1916; Director Medical Services: Major-General O'Keeffe; Deputy Director Veterinary Services: Lieutenant-Colonel F W Hunt and Deputy Director Lieutenant-Colonel W E Matcham. All these officers were appointed to post within a three-week period, 5-27 February 1916 and clearly had a significant challenge in developing their incoming staffs, generating Standard Operating Procedures and integrating their Branches under the direction of the Major-General General Staff (MGGS), Major-General A A Montgomery (from 1926 Montgomery-Massingberd), within the headquarters, to achieve the necessary effect. Major A F (Retd) Becke (Comp) *History of the Great War, Order of Battle*, Part 4, *The Army Council, GHQs, Armies and Corps, 1914-1918* (London: HMSO, 1945), pp.99-100.

45 Colonel F M Wilson, HQ Fourth Army DDST, recorded that the Senior Staff Officer (SSO) of a New Army

the Fourth Army were from the New Army (NA)[46] most of which, required more training,[47] whilst 70 percent had yet to be tested in battle.[48] This matter was exacerbated by the lack of experienced staff officers,[49] which pervaded all parts of the BEF because even seasoned campaigners,[50] from the pre-war Army, had never been involved in planning or controlling logistics[51] on such a scale.[52] This did not however, prevent some NA logistic units reaching high standards of competence in technical skills and equipment care, with the Trains of 19th (Western) and 36th (Ulster) Divisions receiving outstanding commendations from the Deputy Director Supplies & Transport (DDST)

formation, 31st Division, had informed him that in relation to the deployment of the division into the Fourth Army Area, he was 'entirely strange to this kind of work and had very little idea as to how he should proceed'; TNA WO 95/454/1: HQ Fourth Army, DDST, WD, 8 March 1916. The SSO was, presumably, the GSO1, Lieutenant-Colonel H R Cumming.

46 This equally applied to the logistic capability of a division at every level. The Assistant Adjutant and Quartermaster General (AA&QMG) of 17th (Northern) Division of XV Corps in June 1916, Lieutenant-Colonel Colonel Walter Norris Nicholson CMG DSO, was especially cognizant of this issue and particularly of the logistic lynchpin in a unit, the Regimental Quartermaster (RQM). 'New Army quartermasters proved a weak link in our organization. A good Regular quartermaster is a first rate fellow; his one thought is the comfort of his men, and he lets nothing stand in his way to getting it'; Colonel W N Nicholson CMG DSO, *Behind the Lines, An Account of Administrative Staff-work in the British Army 1914-1918* (London: Jonathan Cape, 1939), p.203.

47 49th Divisional Supply Column, a Territorial Force unit, which had been in the BEF for only a month was assessed by DDST in May: 'This is the best unit I have seen so far. Everything, including lorries, workshop accounts, and comfort for the men being in very good order'. 56th DSC, another TF unit, received a rather different report: This is without exception the dirtiest Supply Column I have yet seen'. TNA WO 95/454/1: HQ Fourth Army, DDST, WD, entries 22 May and 3 November 1916.

48 The NA divisions are 56% of the total, Regular 22% and Territorial Force (TF) 22%. Whilst therefore, the NA divisions were the largest component, it was only just over half the force. Additionally, 33% (6) of the divisions participating in the battle had arrived within 6 months of the attack and 22% (4) had deployed to France 3 months before. Of these late arrivals, the 29th Division (Regular) had been fighting at Gallipoli for nearly 12 months, whilst the 31st (NA) and 46th (TF) had been in Egypt, a location in which, they spent little time before being redeployed to the Western Front. Clearly, these moves were a major disruption to formation integrity, organization, training and efficiency, reducing the capability of all the units, not least those from the logistic corps.

49 The problem was compounded by the severe shortage of Camberley 'Passed Staffed College' (psc) graduates. In July 1914, there were only 447 psc officers serving in the Army, many of whom became casualties in the battles of September and August of that year, a scenario exacerbated by the Regimental focus of the pre-1914 Army. Staff appointments were not sought by the majority of officers, who were content to leave the task to those with the coveted psc qualification, a culture that had a most detrimental effect on the conduct of operations and the delivery of logistic support in the early part of the war. For an analysis of these issues, in the period 1900-1914, including the formation of the General Staff and development of the Staff College, see, Brian Bond, *The Victorian Army and the Staff College, 1854-1914* (London: Eyre Methuen, 1972), pp.212-295.

50 Colonel Walter Norris Nicholson CMG DSO was one of these seasoned campaigners. He commissioned into the Suffolk Regiment in 1900, commanding the 1st Battalion in the period 1924-1929, and was Colonel of the Regiment between 1939 and 1947. He spent however, much of his career in A&Q appointments, including Deputy Assistant Adjutant and Quartermaster General (DAA&QMG) at the Cape of Good Hope in 1912, and then DAA&QMG of the Highland Division of the Territorial Force in 1914. He took over as Assistant Adjutant and Quartermaster-General (AA&QMG) of 17th (Northern) Division in June 1916, and was promoted to Assistant Quartermaster-General (AQMG) of XIII Corps in April 1918.

51 The AA&QMG of 17th (Northern) Division in June 1916, Lieutenant-Colonel Nicholson, made a most pertinent observation on this issue: 'The trained staff may have had no knowledge of practical administration when the war started; but they learnt far quicker than anyone else, and having learnt they taught'; Nicholson, *Behind the Lines*, p.177. Nicholson was a Camberley graduate and may therefore, have been biased but his administrative experience suggests that his gravitas reinforced his opinions in illustrating the significance and capability of quality psc officers, especially with regard to the influence of their mentorship.

52 After the GHQ Army Commanders meeting held at HQ First Army on Saturday 6 May, Rawlinson discussed with Maxwell, the requirement to strengthen the Q Staff at HQ Fourth Army; TNA WO 95/441/2: Fourth Army, A&Q WD, 6 May 1916. Lieutenant-Colonel Colonel Nicholson described how quality staff officers could improve on the 'very good'. "We were a very good administrative division before 'Quack' Philips arrived; but he might well be likened to the highly salaried expert who is brought into a firm to substantially increase the profits. He emphatically succeeded;" Nicholson, *Behind the Lines*, p.181. Frank Philips was a character as well, wearing bright yellow gloves as he cut around the headquarters of 17th (Northern) Division.

Fourth Army, Colonel F M Wilson, an officer with an eye for detail,[53] a particular dislike of shirkers and slackers,[54] and a very strong belief in the importance of capable, active, technically competent commanders, whose personal charisma, energy and example motivated their soldiers to not only achieve high standards but also to generate excellent morale.[55]

Hidden from view in most histories, are the constant changes to the Fourth Army Order of Battle (ORBAT) as formations and units arrived and departed, or were relocated at Corps level. As an example, as Fourth Army prepared to mount the largest offensive by the BEF to date, GHQ issued an order[56] to its HQ to prepare 7th (Meerut) Cavalry Brigade[57] of 2nd (Indian) Cavalry Division,[58] of the Indian Expeditionary Force A (IEFA)[59] for a rail move to Marseilles, for deployment to Mesopotamia, whilst replacing it with the Canadian Cavalry Brigade, thus creating another round of logistic planning tasks for the A&Q Branch. Also concurrent with offensive operational planning were significant structural reorganizations, one of which was the disbandment of Brigade Ammunition Columns by absorbing them into the Divisional Ammunition Columns[60] to make more efficient use of resources.[61]

The challenges of G, A and Q Staff,[62] particularly at Army level, interfacing internally in the relevant headquarters was complex enough but to do so externally with corps and divisional HQs

53 It is clear from his excursions and inspections, Colonel F W Wilson was a man of vitality and curiosity, who left no stone unturned in the execution of a wide range of logistic tasks. His commitment and diligence has left the 21st Century historian and logistician with a wealth not only of detail but a splendid review of his remarkable and wide-ranging bailiwick. TNA WO 95/454/1: HQ Fourth Army, DDST, WD.

54 Inspecting the 36th Divisional Train on 2 May 1916, he wrote "I saw 10 pairs and wagons on parade which were without exception the best turns out I have seen in my Service," and a month later on 2 June, "I inspected the 19th Divisional Train which is perhaps the best I have seen." TNA WO 95/454/1: HQ Fourth Army, DDST, WD, entries 2 May and 2 June 1916.

55 There are several entries in the War Diary, in which Colonel Wilson highlights the success of units to these qualities in commanders and equally, several where the absence of them, had created failure; TNA WO 95/454/1: HQ Fourth Army, DDST, WD, February - June 1916.

56 GHQ Q /5231 dated 17 June 1916, 'Move of Meerut Brigade 19/20 June 1916 to Marseilles', in TNA WO 95/30/3: GHQ, QMG, WD. The instruction directed that the Brigade was to embark with 396 rpg for 13 pdrs, 300 rpg SAA for rifles, 4,600 per Hotchkiss MG and 17,000 per Vickers MG. All horses on HT were to be replaced with mules. One rather quaint but clear instruction related to MT: 'No government motor cars will be taken, but any private cars belonging to Indian Princes may be embarked'.

57 7th (Meerut) Cavalry Brigade arrived in France in December 1914 and formed with 3rd (Ambala) 5th (Mhow) and 9th (Secunderabad) Cavalry Brigades, 2nd (Indian) Cavalry Division. For a short history of these brigades, see, Chris Kempton, *Duty & Fidelity, The Indian Army, August 1914-1921*, Part II (Milton Keynes: The Military Press, 2009), pp.2-8.

58 2nd (Indian) Cavalry Division arrived in France in December 1914 and formed with 1st (Indian) Cavalry Division, the Indian Cavalry Corps, which was dispersed in March 1916 and the 2nd Division was allocated to Fourth Army for trench holding operations. For a short history, see, Kempton, *Duty & Fidelity*, Part I, pp.5-7.

59 Indian divisions and brigades were, pre-war, all numbered. The War Office directed that those in IEFA should be so titled as to prevent confusion with British formations. 3rd Indian Infantry Division became the Lahore Division and the 7th, the Meerut Division. The brigades of the divisions were also de-numbered and titled, whilst the 9th Cavalry Brigade became the Secunderabad Brigade; TNA WO 95/1088: HQ Indian Corps, GS, WD. To provide clarity, both nomenclatures have used in the chapter.

60 HQ Fourth Army, Q Branch Summary No 70 dated 8 May 1916, para 132; TNA WO 95/441/2. The reorganization created two echelons with the DAC, one of which was under command of the division and the other controlled by the Corps unless released as a divisional asset, thereby generating logistic capability controlled by Corps HQ. Ammunition holdings in front of the divisional railhead therefore decreased by 99 rpg for the 18 pdr but increased by 22 rpg for the 4.5 inch Howitzer, reflecting the growing significance of the heavier munitions.

61 HQ 35th Division noted that it was intended to save 265 personnel, 310 horses, and 44 x GS wagons, although it reduced the amount of ammunition on wheels for the 18 pounder. Whilst this outcome was sustainable during the relatively static operations of 1916, the mobile warfare of 1918 created a very different challenge. Lieutenant-Colonel H M Davson CMG DSO RA, *The History of the 35th Division in the Great War* (London: Sifton Praed & Co, 1926), p.19.

62 In 2018 parlance, the G Staff equates to G2/3/5/6/7/9, the A Staff to G1/G8 and Q to G4/8.

as well, was a remarkable, although by no means perfectly achieved activity.[63] Inevitably, therefore, there were failures in the command and staff chain, as each sought to conduct its tasks to the best of their capabilities. In this respect, it is clear that the HQ Fourth Army sought advice from other formations in the BEF and DDST recorded members of his staff attending a briefing by Lieutenant-Colonel Honourable M A Wingfield, AA&QMG 7th Division, on the experiences at the Battle of Loos,[64] which focused particularly upon traffic control, the delivery of supplies in the advance and medical evacuation. The DDST noted: 'The lecture was extremely interesting as showing the enormous detail which necessitated before a battle takes place under the present conditions of trench warfare by a Division staff, and also brings out very vividly very many loopholes left for mistakes, which if made will very seriously affect the success, or otherwise, of the operation'.[65] Linked to this issue was the increasing challenges created by the continuing expansion of the BEF and the consequent dilution of experience, which inevitably initially reduced effectiveness and efficiency.[66]

Foremost, was the failure of the G Staff, especially at GHQ, to comprehend the how the capabilities and limitations of the transportation system would affect the freedom to conduct operations. Major-General Harding Newman,[67] commenting post-war upon the plan to position the divisions for the offensive, which required approximately 3,240 train paths to be planned to support the movement of 85-90 trains per division, wrote: 'No staff adequately educated in railway operations could have envisaged concentrating a quarter of a million men for the purpose of battle in front of such a bottleneck'.[68] The difficulties generated by this problem, are well illustrated by a document issued by GHQ in February 1916 entitled, *Preparatory measures to be taken by Armies and Corps before undertaking offensive operations on a large scale*.[69] It appears, at first glance, to contain much sound advice but to a professional officer of 1914, most of the content would have been a blinding glimpse of the obvious. That GHQ issued such a document in this format is confirmation that, in perception at least, even the Staff at Army and Corps level, had to be led by the hand. Perhaps the most telling evidence relating to the misunderstanding of the importance of logistics amongst many members of the G Staff is the content of the summary of XIII Corps Plan of Operations[70] consisting of 30 pages, only 28 lines outlined the logistic arrangements, which certainly failed to meet the direction of the GHQ directive issued in February.

63 Major-General R U H Buckland, Commander Royal Engineers (CRE) in writing to the Engineer-in-Chief at BEF GHQ makes an interesting observation in relation to the staff work and clerical resources within the Engineer Branch at Army HQ, noting that: 'I send you a narrative written from memory but its accuracy in points of detail is not be relied upon..........It is impossible to keep detailed records at A.H.Q but in many cases these could be turned up in the diaries of Corps, Divisions and units'; TNA WO 95/451/1: HQ Fourth Army, Engineer General Report, 'Letter Buckland to Engineer-in-Chief dated 24 February 1919'.

64 The War Diary of DDST Fourth Army is comprehensive, neatly typed and a fascinating read. TNA WO 95/454/1: HQ Fourth Army, DDST, WD, February - December 1916.

65 HQ Fourth Army, DDST, WD, 21 April 1916.

66 Fourth Army DDST made an interesting observation, with more than a hint of irritation: ' OC 36th Div Train came to see me and discussed various matters of minor importance'; TNA WO 95/454/1: HQ Fourth Army, DDST, WD, 26 February 1916.

67 In 1918, Brigadier-General Harding Newman late Essex Regiment was the Deputy Adjutant & Quartermaster-General (DA&QMG) of IX Corps, Fourth Army; Becke, BOH, *Order of Battle*, Part 4, p.185. He had a swift promotion, being a Brevet Major in March 1915, when he was appointed a Temporary Lieutenant-Colonel back-dated to 16 October 1914; *London Gazette*, 22 March 1915, p.2833.

68 Major-General J C Harding Newman CB CMG, *Modern Military Administration, Organization and Transportation* (Aldershot: Gale and Polden, 1933), p.6.

69 GHQ General Staff OB 1207 dated 2 February 1916, 'Preparatory Measures to be taken by Armies and Corps before undertaking Offensive Operations on a large scale, with appendices - Principal Points to be Attended to in making Preliminary Arrangements'. The main document devoted eight of 17 pages to A&Q. Edmonds, BOH, *France and Belgium 1916*, Vol. I, Appx 16.

70 Edmonds, BOH, *France and Belgium, 1916*, Vol. I, Appx 21, pp.152-181.

The Somme was not an area with which, the BEF was familiar, so logistic reconnaissance and intelligence were particularly significant factors. The greatest constraint for the logisticians was the timeframe, which allowed insufficient scope to ensure the most effective and efficient use of resources but detailed assessments were produced that highlighted the vital issues that resulted in an ever expanding number of logistic tasks. The time to complete them, however, was reduced by at least two months when the pressures of war intervened to draw the 'ready for offensive operations' date forward from the original assessment of Thursday 31 August 1916 to late mid-June. To achieve the mission therefore, corners were cut, tasks eliminated and expedients utilized to the full, and, inevitably, there were failures.

Third and Fourth Armies took over the line from the French, and in doing so, imported 18 divisions,[71] all of which had to be supported. The task was undoubtedly a most significant logistic undertaking and provided the units and headquarters with much needed experience in a raft of activities but was a very significant learning burden whilst attempting prepare for such a major action.[72] In addition, deployment of British divisions on the Somme unbalanced the manner in which the BEF had structured its LOC, which had to be adjusted to account for the new arrangements. This not only involved much staff work at GHQ and co-ordination with the French, to ensure that the appropriate railway infrastructure and capability were made available but also generated a requirement for more resources to operate the extension to the LOC.

To add yet more challenges, the Somme was, in early 1916, a 'Quiet Sector' and the logistic infrastructure was incapable of supporting a major offensive by Fourth Army; this constraint entailed therefore, a very significant effort from the logistic services to resolve. In anticipation of the battle, the Fourth Army had to construct new roads and improve others, build railways, create and enhance accommodation, lay water pipes, establish ammunition storage sites, excavate under-ground shelters for various types of occupancy, dig trenches and bury communication cables.[73] To execute these tasks, GHQ could only provide five labour battalions, totalling 5,000 men. The gargantuan requirement for dedicated labour to support these projects, which were a critical aspect of sustaining the force, was in the Spring of 1916, not fully understood and resulted in soldiers from infantry units that were training for battle, being deployed to assist in logistic and construction tasks.[74]

In addition to these tasks, there was a multitude of lesser yet important logistic work required to keep the Fourth Army's wheels turning and in this respect, the officers and soldiers serving in the Deputy Director Ordnance Services (DDOS) Branch had much to keep them occupied. The activities are too many to describe in the detail but a seasoning offers a taste of the tasks, which include the allotment of 6,000 additional gumboots,[75] the provision of Gas Warfare (GW) defence equipment,[76] the issue of additional blankets for the arriving 31st

71 For the outline ORBAT see, Edmonds, BOH, *France and Belgium,* 1916, Vol. I, pp.498-502.

72 The constant changes to the Fourth Army Order of Battle (ORBAT) during May and June 1916 are lucidly illustrated by the daily Q Branch Summaries in TNA WO 95/441/2. To ensure appropriate routine logistic support in such a dynamic environment was undoubtedly a challenge.

73 Keeping this range and intensity of activity secret was clearly an important task and the management of the OPSEC aspects of this very significant series of logistic and engineering projects, deserve study.

74 This was not confined to infantry units. 500 troopers from cavalry regiments formed working parties to dig 3,088 yards of trench for a water-pipeline at Montauban; RE Institute, *Work of the RE in the European War of 1914-19, Water Supply - France* (Chatham: W & J Mackay, 1924), p.66. DDMS Fourth Army offered, as labour, the whole staffs of the CCSs, although presumably the female Nursing Staff were excused the duty, and some personnel from Field Ambulances, to assist the Royal Engineers in constructing CCS hardstands, accommodation and water distribution systems, noting that apart from some carpenters, medical units had few personnel with constructional experience or qualifications. HQ Fourth Army, DDMS FA 19/34 dated 24 April 1916 in TNA WO 95/447/3: DMS, Fourth Army, April 1916.

75 TNA WO 95/452/1: HQ Fourth Army, DDOS, WD, 8 March 1916.

76 Ibid, 9 March 1916.

Division,[77] the procurement of mono-wheels carts for the carriage of trench mortars,[78] retention of mackintosh capes for military policemen,[79] and the acquisition of replacement firing mechanisms for 2 inch mortars.[80] The improvements to the issued covers for steel helmets, a matter about which, the Army Commander was 'very anxious' and hoped for a solution 'which will look better than the ones supplied from Base', inevitably involved the DDOS, who directed that the work be conducted by the Ordnance Workshops. Rawlinson was greatly concerned that the issue covers and the paint on the helmets were much too conspicuous and examples of the modifications were dispatched to the QMG at GHQ.[81] Another issue, now long forgotten, was, given the proposed depth of the advance, the planning and preparations to support and feed the civilian population in liberated areas, [82] which resulted in an instruction from GHQ to all Armies a week before the assault began.[83]

Feeding the Guns

Last but not least was the debate and uncertainty relating to the concept of operations.[84] General Rawlinson,[85] Commander Fourth Army, initially opted for an operation with a limited objective,[86] supported by an artillery bombardment,[87] with a duration of 50-60 hours.[88] This type of attack would ensure that the artillery could support the assault through each phase, although clearly security and surprise would be reduced, if not forfeited.[89] The importance of artillery to the Fourth Army attack was clearly articulated by Rawlinson[90] but he was sanguine about the shortage of

77 Ibid, 11 March 1916.

78 TNA WO 95/452/1: HQ Fourth Army, DDOS, WD, 29 May 1916.

79 This was refused by GHQ; TNA WO 95/452/1: HQ Fourth Army, DDOS, WD, 10 June 1916.

80 TNA WO 95/452/1: HQ Fourth Army, DDOS, WD, 27 June 1916.

81 Ibid, entries 3-7 April 1916.

82 Strategically GHQ assessed it would be necessary to plan for a penetration of up to 60 miles, although clearly this did not necessarily reflect the operational intentions at Army level. Indeed, the logistic resources available to Fourth Army precluded such an outcome. GHQ Q 4072/A (SECRET) 'Note on Meeting of Committee on Feeding Liberated Populations', held on 11 May 1916 in TNA WO 95/30/3: GHQ, QMG, WD, Appendices, May 1916.

83 GHQ Q 4072/B dated 24 June 1916 in TNA WO 95/30/3: GHQ, QMG, WD. The plan involved the Belgian and French authorities delivering relief supplies to nominated rail stations for delivery to forward railheads. Commanders were authorised to use military personnel and rations to support liberated civilian populations until the establishment of civil agencies in the areas.

84 Key correspondence with GHQ on plans and objectives are in Edmonds, *France and Belgium, 1916*, Appendices. TNA WO 153/546: Fourth Army, Battle of the Somme Objectives, contains details of the proposed objectives as at 5 April, 26 May and 5 June 1916.

85 For a summary of his military life up to 1918, see, Ian F W Beckett, 'Henry Rawlinson', in Ian F W Beckett & Steven J Corvi (Eds.) *Haig's Generals* (Barnsley: Pen & Sword Military, 2006), pp.164-182. The standard biography is Fredrick Maurice, *The Life of General Lord Rawlinson of Trent*, (London: Cassell, 1928). Robin Prior & Trevor Wilson, *Command on the Western Front* (Oxford UK & Cambridge USA: Blackwell, 1992), whilst not a biography in the conventional sense, was upon publication, a major re-evaluation of Rawlinson as a battlefield commander and also a significant contribution to the understanding of the military 'learning process' on the Western Front. His last appointment was Commander-in-Chief India and he died in harness in Delhi on 28 March 1925 aged 61, having been taken ill after playing polo and cricket. He was the Commandant of the Army Staff College Camberley 1903-1906 and was remembered by the naming of the central lecture theatre, constructed in 1913, Rawlinson Hall.

86 'Bite and Hold' is a common nomenclature applied to this style of operation.

87 For a recent assessment of the role and development of the BEF's artillery capability in the Battle of the Somme, see the seminal Sanders Marble, *British Artillery on the Western Front, The Infantry cannot do with a gun less*, Ashgate Studies in First World War History (Farnham: Ashgate, 2013), pp.129-153.

88 General Sir Martin Farndale KCB, *History of the Royal Regiment of Artillery, Western Front, 1914-18* (Woolwich: The Royal Artillery Institution, 1986), pp.141-157.

89 The Commander-in-Chief (C-in-C) Field-Marshal Haig believed however, that not only was surprise essential but that the 'Bite and Hold' operation proposed by Rawlinson was not ambitious enough, and suggested that a hurricane bombardment would be the better option, followed by deep penetration.

90 'It is capital country in which to undertake an offensive when we get a sufficiency of artillery, for the observation is excellent and with plenty of guns and ammunition, we ought to be able to avoid the losses which the infantry

heavy artillery, the movement of the ammunition and the means to deliver it accurately.[91] The tactical and operational issues, which are central to this debate, and which are carefully analysed in *Command on the Western Front*,[92] had a key impact upon logistic planning. Clearly, a preparatory bombardment of three or four days[93] would require much greater logistic activity for a longer period than a 'hurricane' one of three-four hours.[94] As it transpired, the bombardment lasted not three to four days but seven, and highlighted the problem of supplying artillery ammunition for an additional two days above the planned five.[95] From this may be deduced an important fact because whilst the detail of staff planning was nowhere near as refined as it became in 1917 and 1918, calculations relating to ammunition expenditure were standard practice in 1916. Estimated from the weight of shell required to destroy each yard of trench, the calculation was a fundamental component of planning and the significance of accuracy is lucidly demonstrated when gauged to firing rates of nearly 9,000 rounds per hour. Consumption at this rate created very significant problems for the logisticians and it was essential that structure and coherency was generated if the supply chain was to meet the demand.

Table 8.3

Fourth Army – Battle of the Somme Artillery Ammunition Allocations[96]

Nature	Projected 1 May 1916	Projected 1 June 1916	Actual 25 June 1916*	*Stock on LOC
18 pdr	2,000,000	3,000,000	2,600,000	2,870,962
4.5 inch How	350,000	500,000	260,000	281,196
4.7 inch & 60 pdr	120,000	200,000	156,000	54,451
6 inch How	100,000	150,000	100,000	84,467
8 inch and 9.2 inch	60,000	100,000	60,000	11,262
9 inch and 12 inch	0	0	750	3,026

* Artillery ammunition stock on LOC listed in the right hand column is extracted from MEBE, p.433, Table (xi) - Ammunition on the Lines of Communication. Figures based on holdings on Thursday 22 June 1916, by which time the in-load of the corps and divisional dumps was almost complete.

have always suffered on previous occasions'; Rawlinson to Wigram 27/2/16, Rawlinson Papers, 5201/33/18 NAM quoted in Prior & Wilson, *Command on the Western Front*, p.139.

91 'I very much doubt if any kind of artillery fire however accurate and well sustained will have the desired effect unless it is sufficient to bury the garrisons in the deep dug-outs they have now constructed and this is a matter of chance'. Rawlinson in a letter to First Army dated 21 June 1916; TNA WO 95/710: IV Corps, WD, June - August 1916.

92 Prior & Wilson, *Command on the Western Front*, pp.138-153.

93 In relation to the artillery preparation for an infantry assault, General Staff, *Notes for Infantry Officers on Trench Warfare*, War Office, March 1916, Sect 45, Preliminary Bombardment noted, 'The bombardment will probably take a long time......'

94 In 1916, the BEFs artillery was incapable of delivering hurricane bombardments but they were perfected by late 1917, creating many logistic and operational advantages.

95 HQ Fourth Army planners examined two options. An intense bombardment of 5-6 hours and a methodical one of 48-72 hours; Rawlinson selected the latter. The Fourth Army 'Artillery Programme of Preliminary Bombardment' dated 5 June 1916, is at Appx 19 of Edmonds, BOH, *France and Belgium, 1916*, Vol. I, Appendices.

96 GHQ proposed an initial ammunition allocation to Fourth Army based upon projected availability shown in the table in GHQ OAD 644 dated 26 March 1916 and signed by the CGS, Lieutenant-General Kiggell; TNA WO 158/321: Battle of the Somme, Preparations.

The need for greater destructive capability drove the requirement for more heavy guns. From the logistic perspective, this increase created two problems: moving the artillery and handling the munitions. The latter was a particularly difficult problem to solve because not only was industry producing an increasing number of heavy shells but also nearly all of them were subject to manual handling throughout the supply chain,[97] compounded by the need to transfer some ammunition from SGR to NGR and WMT to reach the assigned ammunition dumps.[98] The significant increase in artillery ammunition arriving in France as a result of the industrial production,[99] whilst very

97 Projectile weights extracted from War Office, *Treatise on Ammunition*, 10th Edition (HMSO, 1915), Table 15, p.15. The table clearly illustrates the increasing problem; as a contemporary comparison, a 155 mm L15 HE shell weighs 96 pounds.

Table 8.4
British Artillery – Projectile Weights

Artillery Piece	Projectile Weight (lb)
18 pdr	18.50
4.7 inch	46.50
60 pdr	60.00
6 inch	100.00
8 inch	200.00
9.2 inch Howitzer	290.00
9.2 inch Gun (Railway)	380.00
12 inch	714.00

98 TNA WO 95/441/2: HQ Fourth Army, WD, 4 May 1916, concerning a conference between key logistic and engineer staff officers from XIII and XV Corps to discuss potential sites for the storage of ammunition on the Metre Gauge line Derancourt - Bray and Derancourt - Meaulte.

99 The headline overall increase was nearly 307% over four months, which lucidly illustrates the very significant rise in industrial production. Of especial significance, is the increase in heavy shell for the 6, 8 and 9.2 inch howitzers; figures compiled from MEBE, p.434, Ammunition sent to France.

Table 8.5
Artillery Ammunition sent to France
May to August 1916

Nature	May (a)	June (b)	July (c)	August (d)	% increase (e)	Total
13 pdr QF	70,480	142,556	173,584	162,348	230.30	548,968
18 pdr QF	1,298,634	2,926,360	2,413,800	3,871,121	298.09	10,509,915
4.5 inch QF	341,148	487,850	599,236	878,392	257.48	2,306,626
60 pdr BL	80,552	167,982	165,674	301,714	374.55	414,208
4.7 inch QF	18,100	34,902	54,716	45,339	250.50	153,057
6 inch BL Gun	5,500	4,250	8,750	15,600	283.63	34,100
9.2 inch Gun	200	550	482	569	284.50	1801
6 inch How	46,198	212,429	154,233	302,185	654.10	715,045
15 inch How	0	375	802	575	153.33	1,752
12 inch How	0	3,300	6,758	9,255	280.45*	21,065
9.2 inch How	15,852	34,728	93,259	110,557	697.43	254,396
8 inch How	7,740	54,913	91,952	85,551	1105.30	240,156
15 pdr BLC	0	5,000	0	0	00.00	5,000
3 inch QF 20 cwt	0	0	0	1,064	00.00	1,064
Total	1,884,404	4,075,195	3,763,246	5,784,270	306.95%	15,207,153

Notes:

(a) Four weeks ending 27 May 1916.
(b) Five weeks ending 30 June 1916.
(c) Four weeks ending 29 July 1916.
(d) Five weeks ending 31 August 1916.
(e) May to August 1916
* From June

positive from the operational perspective, generated the need for more munitions storage,[100] with a concomitant requirement for estate,[101] construction, rail capacity, labour and trained technical staff but with the constraint of ensuring improved resilience and safety.[102] The most vulnerable aspect of the ammunition supply chain in the Theatre had always been munitions storage and it came as no surprise to some of the more experienced ammunition technical staff, when a German aerial bomb caused a fire that destroyed 9,000 tons of ammunition[103] at Audruieq[104] on Friday 21 July 1916.[105] Surprisingly, the attack had little effect on operations because in the month preceding the explosion,[106] although expenditure was running at nearly 5,000 tons per day, artillery ammunition was flowing through the supply chain[107] supported by copious forward reserves.[108] Given the

100 This was though, a dynamic process. 101,771 tons of ammunition arrived in France between 24 June and 23 July 1916 but in the same period 148,00 tons were expended, creating storage for 46,000 tons. Forbes, *Army Ordnance Services*, p.125.

101 The acquisition of estate for ammunition depots became a serious issue because of the competing demands of location, terrain, railway access, construction resources, materials, safety and the need to negotiate with the Host Nation. TNA WO 95/30/4: GHQ, QMG, WD, July 1916, 'Summary of Requirements for Ammunition Storage Facilities', Appx A1.

102 The BEF took enormous risks in the storage of munitions. Initially, in August 1914, quantities of Small Arms Ammunition (SAA) and small numbers of artillery rounds and charges were stored in the port areas, sometimes in sheds with other ordnance stores. This practice continued as more ammunition arrived, with stocks being retained at ports in case of the need for evacuation, a lesson reinforced during August and September 1914 during the withdrawal of the BEF and the consequent readjustment of the Line of Communication. At Rouen by early 1916, 20,000 tons of munitions were stored in the port area and had a serious explosion occurred, the port and the town would have suffered very significant damage, with the concomitant loss of logistic capability. Forbes, *Army Ordnance Services*, pp.123-124.

103 The loss included 500,000 rounds of 18 pdr and 10,000 rounds of 8 and 9.2 inch howitzer; Miles, BOH, *France and Belgium,* 1916, Vol. II, p.112. Whilst the BOH suggests there was no impact upon operations, the loss of 500,000 rounds of 18 pounder certainly depressed the LOC stock holdings, which had reached 653,395 on 8 July before falling to around 450,000 until late 1916. The 8 inch and 9.2 inch howitzer stocks were quickly replaced, rising from 28,552 and 24,748 respectively on 22 July to 44,925 and 47,339 on 1 August 1916. MEBE, p.433, Ammunition on the Lines of Communication in France.

104 Located 11 miles North-West of Saint Omer. The explosions were so powerful that live shells were found two miles from the depot, most of the trench mortar ammunition detonated and one oblong shaped crater was 60 feet deep; Forbes, *Army Ordnance Services*, pp.126-127.

105 The Court of Enquiry held on 23-24 July 1916 identified that the initiation involved no more than five small aerially delivered weapons and probably only one. The immediate Lessons Identified covered the design of future depots, fire-fighting equipment, ammunition packaging, splinter protection, decoy sites and the positioning and operation of railheads within ammunition depots. The financial loss was assessed at £3.5M in 1916 prices; which in 2016, based on the *Measuring Worth UK* Project Economy Cost as a share of the Gross Domestic Product (GDP) is £2.08 billion. The clearance of damaged munitions, many of them unstable, took months. Correspondence in TNA MUN 4/3077: Reports on Fire in France at Audruicq, including the 'Report of the Court of Enquiry' and 'Instructions in regards to Storage of Ammunition', GHQ QMG Loose Minute dated 8 August 1916. See, also, Forbes, *Army Ordnance Services*, pp.125-127.

106 It did however, have a significant effect upon the design of ammunition depots. New sites were constructed away from other installations and were designed to have greater internal dispersion. This resulted in a depot planned to store 30,000 tons requiring at least 1,000 acres of estate and 50 miles of internal railway to serve it; Henniker, BOH, *Transportation on the Western Front*, pp.322-323. 1,000 acres equates to an area one third of size of London Heathrow airport, which provides a clear illustration of the estate required for these depots and the staff work with the French and civilian authorities which, was required to acquire the land and the authority to store such large quantities of munitions.

107 In the week 18-24 June 1916, the BEF imported 21,980 tons of ammunition and 631 tons of explosives; TNA WO 95/30/4: GHQ, QMG, WD dated 1 July 1916. In August 1916, 54,560 tons were exported to the BEF just from Southampton; TNA MT 23/671: Shipment of Ammunition from Southampton to N. France, T96838/1916, 'Ammunition Ships - Southampton to France'. In the five weeks from 28 May to 30 June 1916, 4,075,195 rounds of artillery ammunition were exported to the BEF, of which, 2,926,360 were 18 pdr gun rounds; MEBE, p.434, Table (xii) - Ammunition sent to France.

108 The catastrophic incident on Sunday 2 April 1916 at the Uplees Marshes Gunpowder Mill in Kent operated by the Explosives Loading Company and the Cotton Powder Company resulting in the deaths of 109 people and extensive damage to infrastructure, is a lucid example of the risks that were being run, knowingly or otherwise, to generate

quantities involved, the requirement for labour, just to store and distribute artillery ammunition along the LOC was enormous, and any activity that reduced the requirement to handle it made clear savings in manpower.

The preliminary artillery bombardment was a critical component of the plan and in the seven days before the assault, 1,492,158 rounds, exclusive of trench mortars, were fired, an average of 213,165 rounds per day, equating to 8,881 per hour. Whilst the daily rate was exceeded in later battles,[109] it was the largest and longest bombardment in British Army history to that date, and the logistic operation matched its scale. The dumping programme began on Wednesday 7 June 1916,[110] with the commencement of the rail in-load,[111] and a key component of this process was to ensure that an even flow was generated to prevent the distribution system sloughing.[112] Seven trains, each carrying between 370-400 tons of munitions, arrived daily at Fourth Army Ammunition Railheads (ARH) until Thursday 15 June, when, with the possibility that the bombardment might commence on 20 June, the in-load rate was increased to 10 trains per day.[113] Such was the importance of the rail in-load and especially the swift removal of ammunition from the ARH that Ordnance Staff from HQ Fourth Army were visiting the ARHs almost daily.[114]

By 20 June, the corps and divisional dumps, the ammunition columns, the unit echelons and the gun position locations were in-loaded and arriving ammunition was stored at the railheads until the bombardment and thus the replenishment, started, by which time, nearly 50,000 tonnes of ammunition[115] had been delivered.[116] Also transported to the construction sites, and then carried

the rapid increase in munitions production that the BEF required. TNA MUN 4/1731: Report of enquiry on Explosion at Faversham factory.

109 The highest expenditure of artillery ammunition on the Western Front in a period of 24 hours was achieved between 1200 on 28 September to the same time on 29 September 1918 and amounted 943,947 rounds, a rate of 39,326 rounds per hour. MEBE, p.481, Table 5 - Approximate Cost of Gun Ammunition and Number of Rounds Expended by the British Armies in France from Noon, 28th September, to Noon, 29th September 1918.

110 War Diary entry Wednesday 7 June 2016, Fourth Army, Deputy Director Ordnance Services (DDOS) in TNA WO 95/452/1; Colonel J A Stewart AOD held the DDOS appointment. HQ Fourth Army, War Diary states 8 June; TNA WO 95/441/2. The post of DDOS is sometimes shown as Assistant Director Ordnance Services (ADOS).

111 The Assistant Director Ordnance Services (ADOS) War Diary recorded on Thursday 8 June 1916: 'All arrangements made proved satisfactory and ammunition unloaded on to lorries and got away in good time.........OK train arrived 4 hours late'. In-loading at ARH OK was clearly a problem because the train was late the next day; TNA WO 95/452/1, 9 June 1916.

112 TNA WO 95/452/1: HQ Fourth Army, DDOS, WD, 13 June 1916: 'Alteration of table of dumping to take place from 15th instant - Ten trains a day now allotted' and on Wednesday 14, 'Further alteration of table of dumping Trains'.

113 TNA WO 95/441/2: HQ Fourth Army, A&Q, WD, 14 June 1916, entry, 'Dumping of ammunition accelerated'.

114 TNA WO 95/452/1: HQ Fourth Army, DDOS, WD, entries, June 1916.

115 The table summarizes the planned artillery ammunition holdings at each level; it is instructive to note that stocks were well forward to reduce the effects of a failure in the transportation system during what was perceived to be a critical period. For example, 62% of the 18 pdr ammunition was held in the gun dumps.

Table 8.6
Fourth Artillery Ammunition – Rounds Per Gun Dumping Plan

Nature	Corps	Division	Ammunition Column*	Gun Dumps
18 pdr	Nil	250	354	1,000
6 inch	200	Nil	200	650
8 inch	Nil	Nil	90	500

*Including Battery stocks.

116 TNA WO 95/452/1: Fourth Army, DDOS, WD, Tuesday 20 June 2016.

by men deep under the German lines, were nearly 100 tons of explosive, packed in bags, which were used in the mines that were timed to explode immediately before the assault.[117] Ammunition storage at corps and divisional dumps however, posed a series of issues to safety and maintenance, resulting in explosions which caused loss of military and civilian life,[118] destroyed property and degraded operational capability. Conditions were more austere than in the Base depots and there were usually no Army Ordnance Department and Corps ammunition technical staff on site, although these two aspects were offset to a limited extent because of reduced storage periods before issue. Reliability of munitions' components became an increasing issue because wooden storage boxes were not weatherproof and the damp particularly affected fuzes, which were critical to the correct functioning of the artillery shells and several issues with them were identified in the four weeks before the offensive commenced.[119] Corroded safety pins in grenades created another hazard.[120] Separation and dispersion, even by the field standards of the day, were rarely enforced and inspections revealed open fires and smoking in these sites were common practice, whilst empty wooden boxes were stored amongst live munitions.[121]

Senior Commanders were certainly keenly aware of the importance of artillery but not always its limitations, nor the supply issues relating to its use. XV Corps for example, exceeded its daily artillery ammunition allotment on 27 and 28 June,[122] which inevitably caused concern amongst those who understood the fragility of the distribution system.[123] One particularly serious issue was the shortage of High Explosive (HE) 18 pdr rounds,[124] which was a significant operational constraint, although the most frustrating aspect of the bombardment was that approximately 30 percent of the shells failed to detonate.[125] In logistic terms this was a massive loss of capability; to have manufactured, stored, issued, transported and fired a large number of shells, 30 percent of which did not explode,[126] much less inflict damage on the enemy, was a very significant contribution

117 The programme totalled 19 mines; eight large and 11 small. The large mines were at Beaumont Hamel, Mametz, La Boiselle, Lochnagar and the Tambour. Edmonds, BOH, *France and Belgium,* 1916, Vol. I, p.286. Lochnagar, near La Boiselle, is the largest mine crater on the Western Front and was created by the detonation of nearly 27 tons of explosive placed in two chambers and is 70 feet deep and 300 feet in diameter.

118 For a description of the concomitant financial claims, managed by the BEF's Claims Commission, see, Gibson, *Behind the Front,* pp.222-242.

119 On Wednesday 31 May 1916, DDOS reported that No 87 fuzes, with the exception of those manufactured by RC, were found to be deficient of washers; TNA WO 95/452/1: HQ Fourth Army, DDOS, WD entry. On Monday 12 June 1916, DDOS issued an instruction that the No 102 fuze was not to be used; Ibid, entry. A GHQ instruction then ordered the replacement of all No 102 fuzes with the No 100 fuze; Ibid, entry, 15 June 1916. On 22 June DDOS reported to GHQ that the No 100 fuzes for 6 inch and 8 inch shells were in an 'unsatisfactory' state.

120 A tragic incident before zero hour on 1 July 1916 involved pins being dislodged when a box of grenades fell to the floor of a trench occupied by C Company 14th Battalion Royal Irish Rifles. 20 year old 14/18278 Rifleman William MacFadzean was awarded a posthumous Victoria Cross for saving the lives of his comrades by throwing himself across the grenades; he is commemorated on the Thiepval Memorial.

121 Forbes relates finding a soldier collecting howitzer charge remnants whilst puffing away on a pipe below a NO SMOKING sign, whose action upon being brought to book, was to empty the hot tobacco amongst the loose cordite on the floor; Forbes, *Army Ordnance Services*, pp.140-143.

122 TNA WO 95/441/2: HQ Fourth Army, A&Q, WD, 29 June 1916. This over-expenditure was of sufficient significance for Haig to note it in his diary on 30 June; Gary Sheffield & John Bourne (Eds.) *Douglas Haig War Diary and Letters, 1914-1918* (London: Weidenfeld & Nicolson 2005), p.195.

123 TNA WO 95/441/2: HQ Fourth Army, A&Q, WD, 16 June 1916, noting that the dumping of heavier calibre shells (6 inch, 8 inch and 9.2 inch) was not progressing satisfactorily.

124 On 1 July 1916, the LOC holdings of 18 pdr shells totalled 3,218,00, which appears healthy but only 568,563 were HE, the balance being shrapnel. HE stocks rose 8.7% to 653,395 within a week through imports from production; MEBE, p.433, Table (xi) - Ammunition on the Lines of Communication in France.

125 On average, approximately 70 tonnes of unexploded munitions, including chemical rounds, are recovered annually from what was the Western Front.

126 Damp fuzes were a particular problem, often caused by the wooden storage boxes being stacked directly to wet ground; Forbes, *Army Ordnance Services*, p.141.

Left: P8.2. British Factory to German Fire-Trench: Lochnagar Crater, 1 July 1986. 27 tons of explosive detonated 52 feet below the surface at 0728 on Saturday 1 July 1916 to create the largest crater on the Western Front. The crater, designed to have tactical effect, was the product of a significant series of logistic activities. (Author)

Below: P8.3. Still live: a failure of Quality Assurance in 1916 but potentially lethal in 2016. The clearance of the Somme battlefields continues a Century on. (Author)

to the degradation of British military effect.[127] At the other end of the spectrum, some of the ammunition exploded all too easily,[128] sometimes in the artillery tube,[129] or more benignly created excessive barrel wear[130] through poorly controlled tolerance during manufacture or equally from improper storage in the field.[131] From the logistic perspective, all these issues created a requirement to handle far more material than should have been needed for the task.[132] Indeed, the post-war Ordnance Corps history summarized the issue, which is equally applicable and important in the 21st Century: 'In fact ammunition of immense value to the amount of many thousands of tons, that consumed our man-power in the making and whose sole object was to destroy enemy man-power, was exposed to avoidable risk and rendered substantially less effective because there was no trained staff to look after it'.[133]

Gas, Fire, Air and Water

By the time the Battle of the Somme commenced, the BEF's Gas Warfare (GW) logistic components in France had started to assumed industrial proportions, with a phosgene factory near Calais operated by the Ministry of Munitions and a cylinder depot at Les Attaques.[134] Whilst the capability was growing, Rawlinson was cautious about its use in the offensive, particularly in view of his perception of the effectiveness of German defensive measures, unpredictable wind and the requirement for British troops to wear respirators in the assault.[135] Gas was however, used during the preparatory period, mainly on the defensive fronts, which sometimes had a degrading effect upon German logistic activities up to six miles behind the front trenches. The amount delivered,[136]

127 This issue has resonance with the degradation of the effect of the RAF's strategic air offensive during the Second World War, caused by poor bombing accuracy.

128 At Quevilly on Friday 10 March 1916, a box of 4.5 inch shell exploded whilst being unloaded from the second train to arrive at the new depot. The resulting fire spread, causing the deaths of three people and loss of all 600 tons of ammunition held in the site, although there was fortunately relatively little damage to the depot, as most of it was confined to the area of the railhead. It was certainly fortunate that Quevilly was not filled to its designed capacity of 44,000 tons. The inquiry established that ten rounds of 4.5 inch of ammunition from one batch had been dropped whilst loading a ship at Newhaven, which had probably damaged a No 100 fuze. Lieutenant Reed AOC was awarded the Military Cross for fighting the fires. Forbes, *Army Ordnance Services*, p.123.

129 32nd Division reported that during the bombardment, four 4.5 inch howitzers had suffered premature shell explosions; '32nd Division Report on Preparations and Actions during Operations of July 1916' in TNA WO 95/2368: 32nd Division, WD, July 1916.

130 Equipment maintenance was critical to capability. In mid-June 1916, HQ 7th Division requested that its artillery be exchanged for new guns because of continual shorting in range. A DDOS technical inspection revealed that whilst repairs were necessary, all the pieces were serviceable, which almost certainly indicates that the inexperience of unit personnel was creating a degradation of operational capability. TNA WO 95/452/1: HQ Fourth Army, DDOS, WD, 23 June 1916.

131 Dirty and rusty shells, some with missing rope grummets and others chipped driving bands, all contributed to barrel wear and reduced accuracy; Forbes, *Army Ordnance Services*, p.141.

132 The soldier of 2018 needs to be reassured that he or she will not be making pointless journeys under fire to deliver munitions or equipment that do not function correctly when fired or used. Quality Assurance, with checks in manufacture, storage and inspection are as important now as they were then and we forget the significance of correctly conducting these tasks at another's peril.

133 Forbes, *Army Ordnance Services*, p.141. Given the cost of munitions, the impact upon military operations if they fail to function correctly and the potential damage if they do unexpectedly, the logic of ensuring appropriate personnel training and suitable storage is compelling.

134 For a description of the industrial aspects of the British Army's Gas Warfare (GW) operations, see, Ministry of Munitions, *The Official History of The Ministry of Munitions* (MOM) Vol. XI, *The Supply of Munitions*, Part II, *Chemical Warfare Supplies* (HMSO, 1922) and TNA MUN 5/337/160/11/2.

135 Notes of Special Gas Brigade, GX 3/2 dated 27 May 1916 in TNA WO 158/321: Preparations for the Battle of the Somme.

136 The total for June 1916 was 398 tons from 13,260 cylinders, calculated from a bar diagram in TNA SUP/10/292, 'Report on Activity of the Special Brigade' dated 19 December 1918.

whilst dwarfed by later operations, was not inconsiderable[137] and by Friday 30 June, 20,000 cylinders[138] had been positioned for operations.[139] Between 23-30 June 1916, 3,772 rounds of 4.5 inch SK were fired and 9,165 cylinders of mainly White Star were discharged.[140] Chemical shells amounted to only 0.25 percent of the daily firing rate for the artillery, which places the logistic requirement into perspective and most of the gas was discharged from heavy steel cylinders, approximately 5 feet 6 inches high, each of which had to be manually handled in the confines of complex trench systems during darkness;[141] for those providing the labour, it was tough and dangerous work.[142]

Another logistic task, almost completely forgotten, was the work undertaken in the XIII Corps sector, to emplace and supply, four Livens Large Gallery Flame Projectors (LGFP)[143] to support the right of 53rd Brigade and the left of 55th Brigade both of 18th (Eastern) Division, during the assault in the area of Casino Point to Breslau Trench to the East of Mametz.[144] Weighing 2.5 tons and 56 feet long, the projectors were entrenched by 183 Tunnelling Company RE, with the equipment and fuel for each system being carried to site in 200-300 man loads, which is yet another example of the immense importance of manual labour to BEF operations on the Western Front. The logistic support requirement involved the provision and delivery of high-pressure gas cylinders[145] and the fuel mix.[146] This was an amazing achievement given that the LGFP systems and

137 The classic period account is Major-General C H Foulkes CB CMG DSO, *"Gas", The Story of the Special Brigade* (Edinburgh & London: William Blackwood, 1934), although its 'Boy's Own Paper' style lacks modesty and is a mixture of technical precision and historical confusion. The seminal text is L F Haber, *The Poisonous Cloud, Chemical Warfare in the First World War* (Oxford: Clarendon Press, 1986). For a recent analysis of British chemical operations on the Western Front, see, Albert Palazzo, *Seeking Victory on the Western Front, The British Army and Chemical Warfare in World War I* (Lincoln & London: University of Nebraska Press, 2000).

138 Foulkes, *"Gas"*, p.122.

139 Fourth Army were allocated seven of the 20 companies in the Special Brigade, with Z Company assigned upon its arrival from the United Kingdom; Ibid, p.122.

140 Figures extracted from TNA WO 142/266: 'List of Special Brigade Operations'. SK was a lachrymatory consisting of 75% Ethyl Iodoacetate and 25% Ethyl Alcohol. White Star was a mix of Chlorine (50%) and Phosgene (50%). The BEF also had stocks of Red Star (Chlorine) and Blue Star (80% Chlorine and 20 % Sulphur Chloride).

141 On Monday 26 June 1916, in the Boiselle-Fricourt sector (21st and 34th British Divisions), 1,043 cylinders were discharged and 970 at Beaurains, on the 18th Division front, on Tuesday 27 June 1916; *"Gas", The Story of the Special Brigade*, pp.131-132.

142 On Friday 16 June 1916, at Laventie, a German shell struck a cylinder and in addition to the trauma injuries, 80 men were gassed, of whom 11 died; TNA WO 142/87: Chemical Warfare Department, Physical Data Book I, AGD 36 A-E.

143 Of the four LGFP detrained, only three were deployed. These projectors were damaged by German artillery fire but the two that fired, in conjunction with a mine and an enfilading fire from a machine gun, appear to have been very effective in reducing British casualties in the supported units. Edmonds, BOH, *France and Belgium, 1916*, Vol. I, p.331, describes the action, stating that the use of the LGFP enabled 8th Norfolks of 53rd Brigade to advance with relative ease, although there is no mention of the ½ Battalion of 7th Buffs in 55th Brigade attacking on the right shoulder of 8th Norfolks. Neither the 18th Division history (Captain G H F Nichols, *The 18th Division in the Great War* (Edinburgh and London: William Blackwood & Sons, 1922)), the regimental histories or the unit war diaries make mention of the LGFP, although F Lorraine Petre OBE, *The History of the Norfolk Regiment*, Vol. II, *4th August 1914 - 31st December 1918* (Norwich: Jarrold, nd but c1925) p.217, notes light casualties and ascribes this good fortune to the British barrage. It certainly seems strange that weapon designed to deliver shock and awe, has left so little impact upon unit records.

144 The LGFP at Casino Point was struck twice by German artillery fire; parts were recovered for use elsewhere and the site abandoned. An archaeological dig at the site in May 2010, by the Centre for Battlefield Archaeology at the University of Glasgow, directed by Peter Barton and Jeremy Banning, revealed the remains of a Livens LGFP. See, Time Team, '*The Somme's Secret Weapon*', Channel Four TV, aired 2100 Thursday 14 April 2011.

145 Foulkes, *"Gas"*, p.112, states the propellant gas was 'de-oxygenated compressed air' (nitrogen) and not air, in order to decrease flammability of the mix during handling. Each LGFP required 12 cylinders; assuming the equivalent of the British Oxygen 'G' size, each of them when filled, weighed 86 pounds.

146 The fuel mix was one part light oil, to two parts heavy; "*Gas*", p.112. The mix was probably kerosene (49.9 lbs per cubic foot) and fuel oil (58 lbs per cubic foot) or, as used in the Time Team re-enactment, diesel (varying density).

the majority of the Z Company manpower from the Special Gas Brigade had only been detrained at Corbie on Monday 26 June 1916, transported 15 miles by 3 ton lorries, then by soldiers to the firing positions in Russian saps at Casino Point and astride the Carnoy-Monauban Road,[147] assembled, fuelled and pressurized, and all under artillery fire.[148] What is even more incredible, is that all the LGFPs were damaged during assembly when the saps were blown in by German shells on 28 June and the firing team at Casino Point had to be dug out by 183 Tunnelling Company.[149]

Whilst aerial operations were in their infancy in 1916, there is no doubt of their increasing importance,[150] and concomitantly the increasing significance of the logistic support systems that enabled them to be conducted.[151] IV RFC Brigade, consisting of 68 aircraft in six squadrons plus one Kite Balloon Squadron supported the Fourth Army, and in so doing created a series of new support tasks. The key logistic unit supporting IV RFC Brigade was Fourth Army Air Park (AAP),[152] which held complete aircraft ready for issue and co-ordinated the raft of spares and maintenance required to ensure that the aviation units could execute their operations, including the provision of compressed hydrogen for the balloons. Much more mobile than its predecessor, the AAP still required up to 10 railway wagons to moves its technical stores;[153] the war was making increasingly challenging demands upon logistics. The aircraft of 1916 were not complex by the standards of the 21st Century but an effective supply chain was still essential to capability, and it is remarkable how quickly the logisticians of the day developed systems and processes to support this new force. Where possible, airfields were built close to a railhead, although in theory the Wheeled Motor Transport (WMT) vehicles in an aviation squadron were capable of sustaining it up to 25 miles from one. The biggest problem was usually aviation spirit; on a busy day, one squadron might consume 500-600 gallons. During an intensive day's operations IV RFC Brigade might use nearly

Three 10 second shots, required approximately 280 gallons of fuel, and thus 140 two gallon cans to be carried into the sap.

147 In contrast to the introduction of a weapon of industrial scale, approximately 800 yards to the East of the double LGFP site, an entirely different act of war took place at Zero Hours on 1 July 1916, when Captain W P Nevill, Officer Commanding B Company 8th East Surreys and Private A A Fursey kicked two footballs in the direction of the German trenches, although Nevill suffered a fatal gunshot wound having moved only 20 yards; Nichols, *The 18th Division in the Great War*, p.40. The Commonwealth War Graves Commission records Wilfred Percy Nevill as buried in Carnoy Military Cemetery in Grave E.28, his headstone bearing the badge of his Regiment, the East Yorkshires. Of the two footballs, Nevill's was lost on 29 April 2015, in the fire at the National Trust's Clandon Park House near Guildford, which housed the Surrey Infantry Museum, whilst Fursey's is held in the Museum of The Princess of Wales' Regiment and Queen's Regiment at Dover Castle.

148 With the assistance of the Royal Engineers at the Royal School of Military Engineering (RSME) Chatham, Time Team constructed a working replica. The range of the projectors is recorded in publications being between 330 and 210 feet. MOM, Vol. XI, *The Supply of Munitions*, Part 1, *Trench Warfare Supplies*, p.97 states 330 feet, *Corps of Royal Engineers*, Vol. V, p.88, 300 feet and Foulkes, *"Gas"*, p.111, 210 feet but under operational conditions the two successful LGFP shoots astride the Carnoy-Montauban Road near Mametz, achieved 282 and 261 feet respectively; Ibid, pp.163-164.

149 Foulkes, *"Gas"*, p.163.

150 For a recent assessment, see, E R, Hooton, *War Over The Trenches, Air Power and the Western Front Campaigns*, 1916-1918 (Hersham: Midland Ian Allan, 2010).

151 For an excellent short analysis, see, Peter Dye, 'The Genesis of Modern Warfare: The Contribution of Aviation Logistics', in Gary Sheffield & Peter Grey (Eds.) *Changing War, The British Army, The Hundred Days Campaign and the Birth of the Royal Air Force, 1918,* Birmingham War Studies (London: Bloomsbury, 2013), pp.171-190 and his comprehensive and illuminating, *The Bridge to Air Power: Logistics Support for Royal Flying Corps Operations on the Western Front, 1914-18* (Annapolis: Naval Institute Press, 2015).

152 The Officer Commanding Third Army Air Park was Major Kirby, who was awarded the Victoria Cross in 1900 during the Boer War, whilst serving as a Corporal in a mounted troop of the Royal Engineers. He was appointed a Regimental Sergeant Major in 1906 and commissioned to be a Quartermaster in 1911, attending the first course at the Central Flying School in 1912. He retired in 1926 as a Group Captain having also been awarded a CBE and a DCM.

153 The AAP was restricted to holding no more than 14-28 days of spares, depending upon the item, to ensure that its mobility remained within the constraints of the transportation plan. Jones, BOH, *The War in the Air*, p.189.

5,000 gallons, which may not appear to be a large quantity, except that it required the manual handling of around 2,500 x 2 gallon cans.

Then, as now, the provision of water was a critical logistic task and one led by the Royal Engineers.[154] Water was required for drinking, Bath & Laundry, hospitals, personal hygiene, steam locomotives, fire-fighting, cooling Vickers machine guns, vehicle and wagon wash-down, MT,[155] liquid-cooled aero-engines, animals, mainly horses, and catering. At Army level, a Water Supply Officer (WSO) controlled a small planning team,[156] which in Fourth Army, had an especially challenging task because apart from the Rivers Somme and Ancre, and a small stream between Vadencourt and Contay, there was no surface water near or on the battlefield, and none within the area planned for the initial advance.[157] With horses consuming 5-10 gallons per day,[158] this was a serious concern and Rawlinson issued a directive that 'not a single animal more than necessary should be kept forward in the salient',[159] which of course, constrained the positioning of the 1st Cavalry Division, with its 7,700 plus horses consuming up to 77,000 gallons, weighing 343.75 tons, of water per diem.[160]

Water was obtained from a variety of sources including open wells, artesian wells[161] and rivers, using a selection of equipment for pumping and purification, including water-supply barges[162] and fire engines.[163] Distribution was achieved through 4 inch and 6 inch pipelines,[164] WMT and HT. Of particular importance, was the creation of an Army Water Column (AWC),[165] a WMT 3rd Line mobile water purification and distribution capability,[166] with a lift of 131,585 gallons to work the

154 For details of water supply operations, see, RE Institute, *Water Supply - France*.

155 WMT required water to fill the engine coolant systems and Steam Transport (ST), the boilers.

156 Major H S Rogers RE, assisted by Lieutenant B M Owen, headed this cell, supported by Colonel W A Liddell from the GHQ Engineer-in-Chief staff; TNA WO 95/451/1: Fourth Army CRE Report, February 1916 - November 1918.

157 The issue was not the same across all parts of the Fourth Army area. In April 1916, the provision of water was deemed to be satisfactory in XV Corps but not XIII Corps; TNA WO 158/321: Preparations for the Battle of the Somme, 'Notes from an Fourth Army A&Q Conference held at Fourth Army Headquarters on Friday 28 April 1916' attended by Commander Fourth Army, GOCs XIII and XV Corps their supporting A&Q staffs and Corps Chief Engineers. The attendance of senior commanders at an A&Q meeting is proof that they understood the importance of logistics to the operation.

158 Horses consume significant quantities of water, drinking, depending on the weather, diet and work; General Staff, *Field Service Pocket Book 1914* (FSPB 14), (London: HMSO, 1914), p.52. There were 5,592 horses on the establishment of a 1914 infantry division, requiring an upper figure of 55,920 gallons of water per day, or in weight, 249.64 tons. In the context of 15 divisions in the Fourth Army AOR, this equates to a minimum of 838,800 gallons or 3,745 tons of water per day.

159 Ibid, 'Notes from an Fourth Army A&Q Conference held at Fourth Army Headquarters on Friday 28 April 1916.'

160 Based on 7,718 to establishment of a three brigade 1914 cavalry division; FSPB 14, p.2. The Pocket Book shows a four brigade ORBAT, so an adjustment has been calculated.

161 An artesian well is one, which does not require a pump to bring the water to the surface, the pressure in the aquifer, the permeable or porous rock holding the water, being sufficient for it to naturally occur.

162 Water-supply barge units were moored on the River Somme and were fitted with equipment capable to producing 4,000 gallons of potable water per hour, which was then pumped into the pipeline system; RE Institute, *Water Supply - France*, p.59. No 3 and 4 Barge Units, each consisting of a filtration barge, a chemical barge and four water barges arrived at Sailly Lorrette on Friday 26 May 1916; TNA WO 95/441/2: HQ Fourth Army, Q Branch Summary No 86 dated 26 May 1916, paragraph 158 (iv).

163 To assist in planning the utilization of these steam and petrol driven equipments, Lieutenant Hamilton-Gordon, late of the London Fire Brigade, was attached to the Water Supply Team; TNA WO 95/451/1: HQ Fourth Army, CRE Report, February 1916 - November 1918.

164 For technical details of the operations, see, RE Institute, *Water Supply - France*, pp.57-67.

165 Despite the importance of this capability, the unit was still training and experimenting with its new equipment in early May 1916. Of particular note, was the requirement to modify the carriage section of the water lorries to accommodate supporting fittings such as pipes and pumps. TNA WO 95/454/1: HQ Fourth Army, DDST, WD, 6 May 1916. DDST inspected the unit in November 1916 and reported: 'This unit is in a high state of efficiency both as regards vehicles, workshops and interior economy. The state of the unit reflects great credit on the Officer Commanding'; TNA WO 95/454/1: HQ Fourth Army, DDST, WD, 3 November 1916.

166 The Fourth Army AWC initially supported five corps and comprised an MT Water Tank Company with a lift of

loop between Initial and Forward Water Points and the divisional water carts.[167] It was expected that the AWC would not become an effective operational asset until roads had been constructed through the German defensive system, which transpired to be an accurate assessment.[168] To assist the carriage of water at company and platoon level, the DDOS authorised a trial, to test the carriage of empty petrol tins on water carts,[169] and was involved in progressing a contract with a French company at Amiens for the provision of 15,000 canvas water bags.[170]

Medical Evacuation

A controversial issue on 1 July 1916 has always been the failure to provision sufficient medical evacuation,[171] with Fourth Army HQ and sometimes its commander, receiving the blame. Medical evacuation planning was influenced by a number of factors, not least the competition for rail and road-space,[172] and real estate, for the delivery of other logistic functions and the movement and positioning of combat units. One issue was the prohibition placed by HQ Fourth Army upon the movement of ambulance trains from Vecquemont to Contay on the newly constructed SGR because of the requirement to use Contay as an ARH and to the South, Frenchencourt for supplies.[173] This restriction was a particular frustration as Contay provided a convenient and desirable central location to site at least one if not two, Casualty Clearing Stations (CCS).[174] Another constraint was in Amiens, where although the CCS was only 200 yards from the railway station, patients had to be moved by motor-ambulance, three miles to the Ambulance Train Railhead (ATR) at Longueau.[175]

The wounded were to be evacuated from the CCSs mainly by ambulance trains, supported by canal barges and by road, using Motor Ambulance Convoy (MAC) assets. According to the BOH,[176] the medical staff under the Director Medical Services (DMS) Fourth Army,[177] estimated that the greatest number of wounded that could be treated in one day was 24,000. This calculation was predicated upon 9,500 being in the CCSs, 10,000 in Field Ambulances and 4,900 being evacuated

25,985 gallons, consisting of 111 x 1 ton lorries with 135 gallon tanks, 20 x 3 ton lorries with 550 gallon tanks, with 19 clarifying and 11 de-poisoning lorries, reinforced by 192 x 3 ton lorries with 550 gallon tanks, of 105,600 gallons capacity. In addition to the Army asset, there were 165 x HT GS wagons, each carrying 200 gallons and providing a lift of 33,000 gallons allocated to reinforce divisional capability and 160 x Regimental Water Carts to supplement unit capacity; RE Institute, *Water Supply - France*, p.67.

167 The AWC was inspected at Saint Ouen on Tuesday 9 May by the DA&QMG, Major-General H C Sutton and the AQMG (Lieutenant-Colonel R S May) of HQ Fourth Army and visited on Wednesday 31 May by the AQMG to view operations at Hennencourt; TNA WO 95/441/2: HQ Fourth Army, A&Q, WD, entries 9 and 31 May 1916.

168 The maximum operating distance from a Forward Water Point to a Regimental Water Point was assessed to be 10 miles with another three miles for a short period, using the additional Regimental Water Carts allocated to the Army; RE Institute, *Water Supply - France*, p.67 and Part II, Plate III, Fourth Army Water Column.

169 TNA WO 95/441/2: HQ Fourth Army, DDOS, WD, 28 May 1916.

170 Ibid, entries, 6-7 June 1916.

171 For a description of the medical arrangements for the Battle of the Somme, see, Macpherson, BOH, *Medical Services*, Vol. III, pp.11-53. For a recent academic assessment, see, Mark Harrison, *The Medical War, British Military Medicine in the First World War* (Oxford: Oxford University Press (OUP), 2010), pp.65-78.

172 Competition for road-space was a significant issue. An infantry battalion required 800 yards and an infantry division 14.66 miles; FSPB 14, pp.41-42. Planning and executing the moves of divisions on the march became routine but failure to include factors such as the weather, road conditions, soldier and animal fitness, equipment state and the influence of logistic activities on the route, could easily unravel the most detailed plan.

173 Macpherson, BOH, *Medical Services*, Vol. III, p.29. This restriction was lifted in August 1916; for details of the subsequent re-deployment of medical units, see, pp.32-33.

174 Ibid, p.29.

175 Ibid.

176 Ibid, p.43.

177 Surgeon-General M W O'Keeffe. Lieutenant-Colonel H B Fawcus was the Deputy Assistant Director Medical Services (DADMS).

in ambulance trains, generating a requirement for seven Permanent Ambulance Trains (PAT) and three Temporary Ambulance Trains (TAT).[178] The published record is therefore, at variance with the HQ Fourth Army files,[179] which reveal that the HQ Fourth Army medical staff had calculated that there would be an initial requirement to evacuate, daily, 10,000 casualties by train, which is double the figure in the BOH, generating a need for 12 Permanent Ambulance Trains (PAT) and six Temporary Ambulance Trains (TAT) per diem.[180] The HQ Fourth Army assessment of its medical evacuation requirement though, was much higher than other Armies in the BEF, which was not perhaps, positively received in GHQ.[181] Whether prompted by his Director Medical Services (DMS) or intuition,[182] Rawlinson wrote to Lieutenant-General Maxwell, the BEF's Quartermaster-General:

> I should like to be assured that this number of trains will be available, as I am informed that the total number of ambulance trains is only 30, of which 6 are employed solely at the Bases, and that the total number of improvised trains is only 6. It appears to be necessary that the number of trains available for Fourth Army should be increased, if the delay which I understand occurred during the Loos fighting in September last is to be avoided.[183]

Maxwell replied[184] four days later stating that 'It is not anticipated there will be any difficulty in meeting the needs of Fourth Army during active operations' yet Rawlinson and his Staff cannot have been assured by other parts of the reply articulating that ambulance trains would be regulated by GHQ,[185] 'according to the needs of the moment and it is not considered advisable to allot them to Armies beforehand' and although there was no limit to the numbers of improvised ambulance that could be used, they would be brought into use 'as and when necessary'. Such comments certainly did little to convince Fourth Army planners that these key assets would be allocated in a timely manner and as Fourth Army was the Main Effort for the offensive, General Rawlinson could have been forgiven for not being assured, a position reinforced by Maxwell's final sentence, 'No reports of any delays in the evacuation of the wounded during the fighting around LOOS can be traced to this office'.[186]

178 Macpherson, BOH, *Medical Services*, Vol. III, p.43.

179 A note in TNA WO 95/447/3: Director Medical Services (DMS) Fourth Army, June 1916, clearly states the Fourth Army requirement as 12 PAT and six TAT.

180 This assessment was supported by *Field Service Regulations* (FSR), which stated that there should be one ambulance train mobilized for each division; General Staff, *Field Service Regulations*, Part II, *Organization and Administration*, War Office (London: HMSO, 1909) (reprinted with amendments to October 1914), Chp XI - The Medical Service, Sect 94, Ambulance Railway Trains, p.125.

181 The G, A and Q staff at GHQ should have been well versed in this issue as the importance of evacuating the Casualty Clearing Stations (CCS) had been lucidly highlighted in early 1915 by the War Office Advisory Committee on Ambulance Trains, which observed that 'carrying capacity to be increased to the utmost. It is better to carry many patients with some discomfort than to delay evacuating the Casualty Clearing Station'. TNA WO 158/10: Ambulance Trains, 'Advisory Committee on Ambulance Trains, Minutes of Meeting, 20 March 1915'.

182 Mark Harrison believes that Haig had witnessed over-crowding at CCSs and mentioned this to Rawlinson after he was appointed as Commander Fourth Army on 24 January 1916, which is certainly plausible. The primary sources suggest that the DMS was pushing against an open door in discussions with Rawlinson. The note that Haig commanded Fourth Army is presumably a typographical error because he commanded First Army and the Fourth was not formed until after Haig had been appointed as Commander-in-Chief BEF; Harrison, *The Medical War*, p.69.

183 HQ Fourth Army 19/47 dated 14 June 1916 in TNA WO 95/447/3: DMS Fourth Army, June 1916.

184 GHQ QMG Rys/1167B dated 18 June 1916 in TNA 95/447/3: DMS Fourth Army, June 1916.

185 This was reinforced by two detailed memoranda issued on 20 June 1916 relating to the 'Regulating of Ambulance Trains in Times of Pressure'.

186 It is probable that Rawlinson was referring to the first day of the action, in which 13,910 casualties were admitted to the divisional Field Ambulances and 7,464 into the Casualty Clearing Stations (CCS) but ambulance trains only evacuated 1,894 and effectively the same problem would occur on 1 July 1916. To resolve this issue, First Army DMS arranged with the Assistant Director Railway Transport (ADRT) to run trains to Noeux-les-Mines and

As it transpired, Rawlinson and his DMS had every right to be concerned. By 2359[187] on Saturday 1 July, only five of the 12 ambulance trains requested had arrived in the Fourth Army area, three of which had been positioned before the assault began. Of the 2,165 casualties evacuated to ATRs, only 1,670[188] were cleared, leaving 495 to await trains on Sunday 2 July, with an increasing number of casualties not being cleared from Casualty Clearing Stations (CCS),[189] which was exactly what Rawlinson and his DMS feared would occur.

Table 8.7

Casualties Evacuated by Ambulance Trains – 1 July 1916[190]

PAT No	ATR	Destination	Officers	OR	Total
3	Gezaincourt	Rouen	18	329	347
8	Heilly		21	428	449
15	Heilly		0	463	463
18	Puchevillers		0	188	188
20	Vecquemont		21	202	223
Total	All ATR		60	1,610	1,670

That ambulance trains were critical to mass evacuation capability is lucidly illustrated by their performance; from a poor start on 1 July, they lifted 93 percent[191] of all the casualties and sick[192] from the CCSs,[193] during July.

Bethune to clear the Field Ambulances; Macpherson, BOH, *Medical Services*, Vol. III, p.467.

187 Whilst the 24 hour clock is used for clarity, this innovation was not officially adopted in the BEF until 1 October 1918.

188 Figures extracted from the 'Casualty Return from IVth Army and Table of Evacuations', in TNA WO 95/447/4: DMS Fourth Army, July 1916.

189 By Monday 3 July, ambulance trains were arriving promptly at ATRs and evacuations from CCSs began to exceed admissions; HQ Fourth Army, DMS WD, 3 July 1916 in TNA WO 95/447/4. Ambulance train evacuations were 13,556 in 17 x PATs and six TAT, which was the highest figure for any 24 hour period during BEF operations on the Western Front; Macpherson, BOH, *Medical Services*, Vol. III, p.46.

190 Figures extracted from the 'Casualty Return from IVth Army and Table of Evacuations' in TNA WO 95/447/4: DMS Fourth Army, July 1916. The medical BOH quotes 2,317, which is closer to the 'evacuated to' but not 'from' the ATR figure; Macpherson, BOH, *Medical Services*, Vol. III, p.46.

191 The total figure was 104,121 of which, ambulance trains transported 96,878.

192 One often forgotten aspect is the evacuation of those with psychiatric illness, caused, or exacerbated, by their military service. By 1917, orders were issued relating to the provision of capability on ambulance trains: 'three compartments are to be set aside for mental cases, and.......bars are to be fitted over all [windows].....the doors should be capable of being locked'; TNA WO 158/11: Ambulance Trains: Sub-Committee, 'Ambulance Train, Continent Sub-Committee, Minutes of Meeting, 7 May 1917'.

193 Each CCS was established for only three 3 ton lorries, which undertook a multitude of tasks including the delivery of potable water and aggregate for building and maintaining the hard-tracks and pads at the CSS, whilst also providing a reinforcement evacuation lift for casualties. With availability only averaging 66%, the GHQ Director General Medical Services (DGMS) staff proposal to reduce the establishment from three to two met with stiff resistance. HQ Fourth Army DMS 16/18 dated Monday 12 June 1916 in TNA WO 95/447/3: DMS Fourth Army, June 1916.

Table 8.8

Medical Evacuations from Fourth Army – July 1916[194]

Transport	Officers	OR	Total	Remarks
PAT	2,394	71,892	74,286	
TAT	160	22,432	22,592	
Barge	655	2,838	3,493	
MAC	47	2,821	2,868	1-3 July only
Buses	8	874	882	1-3 July only
Totals	3,264	100,857	104,121	

The medical BOH places the blame for this firmly on the failure of Fourth Army DMS to give sufficient notice to Fourth Army Assistant Director Railway Transport (ADRT) of the first day's ambulance train requirement,[195] although during 1 July, the HQ Fourth Army Medical Branch War Diary explicitly notes increasing concerns relating to their non-arrival at the nominated ATRs.[196] It seems most unlikely that after the estimate conducted by the Medical Branch and Rawlinson's intervention to increase the numbers of trains allocated to Fourth Army for the offensive, that DMS would not have been pressing for early arrival.[197] Placing aside direct blame, there is a nuance, absolutely relevant today, relating to logistic support to the Main Effort. Rawlinson recognized that Fourth Army was the BEF's Main Effort during the offensive and required the concomitant medical evacuation resources, whilst GHQ was not prepared to commit them unless the need matured.[198] In this respect, there appears to have been dissonance between the QMG and DGMS Directorates because the GHQ Deputy Director General Medical Services (DDGMS) was sufficiently concerned about the resilience of the QMG ambulance train solution to generate a contingency plan using barge[199] and road[200] transport, whilst also instructing First and Second Armies to move their much

194 Figures compiled from 'Casualty Return from IVth Army and Table of Evacuations' in TNA WO 95/447: DMS, Fourth Army, July 1916.

195 Macpherson, BOH, *Medical Services*, Vol. III, p.45.

196 HQ Fourth Army, DMS, WD dated 1 July 1916 in TNA WO 95/447/3. DMS directed Motor Ambulance Convoys (MAC) and the *char-a-banc* (open-top single deck buses) reserve to cover some of the shortfall, which transferred 2,868 and 882 patients respectively in the first three days before reverting to their tasks of evacuating the Field Ambulances and transferring patients from the CSS to the ATR.

197 TNA WO 95/441/2: HQ Fourth Army, A&Q, WD, 29 June 1916 states that 'the siding of hospital trains appears to be quite satisfactory'. 'Siding' refers to positioning and 'hospital' refers to ambulance.

198 As a result of the outcome, the BEF's Director General Medical Services (DGMS) Lieutenant-General Sir Arthur Sloggett, issued a memorandum on Monday 10 July 1916 to the DMS of each Army, listing the Lessons Identified. In particular, he noted the importance of refining casualty estimates with the G Staff and matching it to the ambulance train requirement. Whilst all the points were absolutely valid, O'Keeffe can only have read it with mounting frustration because he had executed his plan thus. Macpherson, BOH, *Medical Services*, Vol. III, pp.47-48.

199 No 3 Ambulance Flotilla was transferred from the Aire-La Basee Canal to the Somme Canal to reinforce No 4 Flotilla; TNA WO 95/441/2: HQ Fourth Army, Q Branch Summary No 78 dated 16 May 1916, para 146 (iii). Each flotilla had six barges capable of transporting 30-32 stretcher cases and were used where comfort was more important than speed; Macpherson, BOH, *Medical Services*, Vol. III, p.44. FSR noted: 'Water transport is well adapted for the removal of serious cases. Every use will be made of this form of transport throughout the evacuating zone when suitable waterways exist and the necessary boats or barges can be obtained'; FSR, Part II, Chp XI -The Medical Service, Sect 94 (5).

200 No 1 Motor Ambulance Convoy (MAC) was assigned to clear the CSSs in the Doullens area at a rate of 1,000 patients per day and No 26 MAC at Saint Omer tasked to be prepared to move to the Fourth Army Area; Macpherson, BOH, *Medical Services*, Vol. III, pp.44-45. 15 *char-a-bancs* to transfer sitting casualties were allocated from LOC resources to be held at readiness in Abbeville and CCSs were tasked to ensure unit lorries, of which there were only three established for each CCS, were to be fitted with seats to offer some reinforcement capability. 'Notes

smaller numbers of casualties by road[201] to hospitals at Saint Omer, whilst Third Army was directed to use allocated MACs to evacuate casualties to Etaples.[202] It seems that the concept of the Main Effort was conceptually embedded but the full and timely application of it failed.

Iron Ways

Commanders and Staffs were well aware that the Standard Gauge Railway (SGR) was the fundamental component of logistic support for the Somme offensive,[203] clearly understanding that only the railway could deliver the immense tonnages of materiel and numbers of soldiers in the timeframe but not being cognizant of its fragility and limitations. A key feature was the almost complete reliance upon the French to operate and maintain the mainline railway system, which supported the BEF, whilst failing to comprehend that its ability to sustain the ongoing expansion was almost exhausted. The potential requirement therefore, to take over this huge operation to enable the French to support operations elsewhere on the Western Front came a major shock to the planning staff.

Estimates indicated that Fourth Army would, when in action, need 70 trains per day, and Third Army, only part of which, was to be involved, another 58. Only two railway lines approached the front, both running into Albert. The lateral, North-South, communication, in particular, was poor, its capacity for military traffic being greatly reduced because of coal[204] trains running from Artois to other parts of France; military planners constantly forget that economies still operate during conflict. 17 miles of SGR line were therefore, constructed between Candas and Acheux, providing an additional four or five Supply Railheads (SRH),[205] whilst 10 miles of SGR was built from Daours to Contay to create three more. In total, to support the Somme offensive, 54.88 miles of new railway were constructed in the three months from April - June 1916,[206] which considerably diminished British stocks of railway construction material, there being, on 1 July 1916, only sufficient, to construct another 10 miles of track. Had there been a significant breakthrough by Fourth Army in early July 1916, the challenges of delivering the necessary logistics to an advancing force of 15 divisions are all too clear, a factor often forgotten by tactical analysts and historians.

from a meeting held at HQ Fourth Army on Monday 19 June 1916 between GHQ Deputy Director General Medical Services (DDGMS) DMS Fourth Army and Deputy Adjutant and Quartermaster General (DA&QMG) Fourth Army' in TNA WO 95/447/3: DMS, Fourth Army, June 1916.

201 A key fragility in this plan was that motor ambulances were each manned with one driver plus a 25% reserve. Both DMS and DDST Fourth Army were of the view that this level was insufficient to support a major offensive; TNA WO 95/454/1: HQ Fourth Army, DDST, WD, 23 April 1916.

202 Macpherson, BOH, *Medical Services*, Vol. III, p.43.

203 For details, see, Henniker, BOH, *Transportation on the Western Front*, pp.119-146.

204 The BEF was also a consumer of coal, using by 1918, nearly 2,000 tons per day. Coal was used mainly for transportation (railway locomotives and steam lorries) and heating. Other essential needs included hot water for cooking, washing, laundry and dis-infection. An interesting issue relating to the application of logistic detail occurred in 49th Division in March 1916 when the GOC pressed the DDST for an increase in the coal allowance to assist in reducing an outbreak of scabies by enhancing laundry and washing capability. An investigation revealed that the Division was using house coal for the steam boilers, thereby generating decreased output and increased consumption. TNA WO 95/454/1: HQ Fourth Army, DDST, WD, 11 March 1916.

205 A world away from Army operational logistic plans, the Railhead Supply Detachment (RSD) at SRH Heilly caused the DDST (Colonel F M Wilson) to intervene on their behalf after the Fourth Army Administrative Commandant Railheads complained that the soldiers did not undertake route marches or physical drill. After an investigation and a personal visit, the DDST declined to take action, noting that with the exception of three NCOs, the average age of the men in the RSD was 50 years and in the light of a nine hour day, a significant part of which, included heavy manual labour, he concluded that the daily work was sufficient to keep his soldiers reasonably fit. TNA WO 95/454/1: HQ Fourth Army, DDST, WD, 8 May 1916.

206 This comprised 35.58 miles of main line track and 19.30 miles of sidings; Henniker, BOH, *Transportation on the Western Front*, p.126.

Narrow Gauge Railways (NGR)[207] were not widely used by the BEF in France forward of SGR railheads until early in 1917, although their use in field storage sites and depots was becoming increasingly common.[208] Indeed, the BEF's first meaningful exposure to the concept in the forward areas came from the experience acquired when the Fourth Army took over the systems operated by the French Army. Interestingly though, a GHQ instruction *Preparatory measures to be taken by Armies and Corps before undertaking offensive operations on a large scale* of 2 February 1916 included the following note: 'The provision of light railways to supply ammunition to heavy guns and howitzers and of trench tramways[209] for stores to the front line will save roads and may be necessary'.[210]

P8.4. Still serving: Decauville NGR rail panels in use as a fence on the Somme in 1986. It is remarkable how the logistic materiel of a Century ago still has application. (Author)

207 Many documents refer to Narrow Gauge Railways (NGRs) as Light Railways, which, whilst not inaccurate, is not technically correct. There is no official international definition of a light railway but it may be described as one which is constructed to a lesser standard than that required for main or branch line operations; it may be broad, standard, or narrow gauge. NGRs, by the nature of their construction, are usually defined as light, but this may not necessarily be the case, whilst some of the Standard Gauge Railways (SGR) constructed in France to support military operations during the First World War, could certainly be described as light. Railways are therefore, in this context, best described by gauge rather than engineering construction standards. For the technical definitions, and a short history of Light Railways, see, Jack Simmons and Gordon Biddle (Eds.) *Oxford Companion to British Railway History* (Oxford & New York: OUP, 1997), pp.263-265.

208 The Official History is held in TNA WO 158/852: Director-General Transport: History of Light Railways. For the classic history of British NGR during the Great War, see, W J K Davies BA AKC, *Light Railways of the First World War, A History of Tactical Rail Communications on the British Fronts 1914-1918*, (Newton Abbot: David & Charles 1967). For two excellent illustrated histories, see, Keith Taylorson, *Narrow Gauge at War* (Brighton: Plateway Press, 1987) and *Narrow Gauge at War*, Vol. 2 (Brighton: Plateway Press, 1996).

209 In the pre-war period, French farmers used wooden tramways to to support agricultural activities. The history of the 8th Division records that the divisional, AA&QMG, Lieutenant-Colonel H M de F Montgomery DSO had noted in late 1914 that they might have military application and that the practice was spreading to other parts of the Front; Boraston, J H, Lieutenant-Colonel, CB OBE and Bax, E O, Cyril, Captain, *The Eighth Division in War, 1914-1918* (London: The Medici Society, 1926), p.8. The role of the 8th Division in developing the system is corroborated by an entry in the AA&QMG War Diary of 23 February 1915; TNA WO 95/1680.

210 Edmonds, BOH, *France and Belgium 1916*, Vol. I, Appx 16, p.104.

The reluctance to build NGR forward of the SGR railheads was predicated on logistic efficiency and effectiveness, a point lucidly demonstrated by pre-Somme preparatory construction, which totalled only 0.69 miles of Metre gauge sidings.[211] In defence, it was assessed that NGR operations would be more vulnerable to artillery fire than MT and HT, whilst creating additional rigidity in the system. In the offensive, the effort involved in extending them to support the advance was deemed to be a waste of resources because NGR could never carry the supplies that were required and as the SGR was brought forward, NGR would become redundant and would require redeployment. The Staff therefore, considered that resources were much better employed in constructing SGR. What was not clear in 1916 though, was how difficult it would be to extend SGR across the battle area, and how in 'Bite and Hold' operations, which became in the norm in 1917, that the need was best met through initially extending NGR.

The tonnage per mile of front to be transported from railheads was, in this period, 1,934 tons per day, which equated to a total of 22,000 tons per diem for Fourth Army to support offensive operations at intense rates of fire.[212] Consequently, railheads were usually well forward to reduce the requirement for WMT and HT in the loop between the railheads, field storage sites and units. As the war progressed and artillery ranges increased, the siting of railheads became a compromise between logistic efficiency and security. The Somme however, posed a constraint to the distribution of materiel from the railheads, which relied, increasingly on WMT. Mainly agricultural in nature, the roads of the Somme were however, not suited for sustained use by WMT and plans were initiated to upgrade the road system.[213] Suitable stone was not available locally, which meant importing it from quarries elsewhere in France and the United Kingdom, creating another burden on the logistic system, whilst the Staff had to accept that procuring the full labour requirement to support this major project would interrupt work on other essential tasks.[214]

211 Henniker, BOH, *Transportation on the Western Front*, p.126.

212 Figures extracted from Henniker, BOH, *Transportation on the Western Front*, p.157. The table illustrates the balance of munitions natures, supplies and materiel, with ammunition being 62% of the task by weight.

Table 8.9

Mile of Front v Materiel Tonnages per day

Ammunition & Materiel	Tonnage (tons)	Remarks
Heavy Artillery Ammunition	500	6 inch and above
Medium Artillery Ammunition	88	4.7 inch and 60 pdr
Light Artillery Ammunition	450	18 pdr
SAA & Trench Mortar Ammunition	176	
Engineer Stores	50	
Stone	400	
Ordnance Stores & Rations	270	
Total	1,934	

213 Geddes highlighted the importance and the issues relating to road maintenance, with particular reference to Fourth Army; Initial report from Geddes to Lloyd George; Granet Papers, MRCUWL, GB 152, MSS.191/3/3/ 8. The Fourth Army logistic planners were though, ahead of the game and by the end of August 1916 the Army had been issued with 18 miles of NGR track, five locomotives and 60 wagons to reduce the road traffic; Davies, *Light Railways*, p.44. The Fourth Army CRE was scathing in his Armistice Engineer Report: 'The true cause of the failure to keep the roads fit for use was the that the highest authorities before the war had not realised that the upkeep of the roads in winter under modern conditions of traffic entailed, and, in consequence, the necessary labour - especially skilled road men, had not been provided'; TNA WO 95/451/1: HQ Fourth Army, CRE Report, February 1916 - November 1918.

214 Geddes highlighted the labour issue, 'The handling of roadstone is undoubtedly wasteful of labour. The plant at the disposal of the engineers is not the most suitable'; Initial report from Geddes to Lloyd George; Granet Papers, MRCUWL, GB 152, MSS.191/3/3/ 8. The shortage of road repair capability was such that 29th and 31st

The critical necessity for stone[215] was such that it was raised in a personal meeting between Rawlinson and Maxwell,[216] whilst its delivery to the construction sites was a constant concern for the logisticians and engineers within HQ Fourth Army.[217] Road construction and repair was further complicated by the arrangements for its execution.[218] Forward of Corps HQ, it was a BEF responsibility, whilst in the Corps Rear Area and beyond it was undertaken by a Joint Anglo-French organization entitled *Sous Commission d'Armee du reseau routier*. The result of this scenario was a decision to utilize more HT, which created less damage to the roads, especially in wet conditions,[219] and to restrict the use of WMT to levels that matched the import of stone and labour.[220] It also reduced the need to distribute motor spirit and lubricants. These issues were all exacerbated by the very limited mobility of WMT, which meant building hard-tack pads for units to operate from, which often resulted in long drives to complete tasks.[221]

Congestion on the roads is not a new phenomenon and was a critical constraint in sustaining operations on the Somme. Indeed, the Fourth Army War Diary has constant references to high traffic densities on the roads, which was so significant during the preparatory period in late June that the Army Commander specifically directed his Corps Commanders to note the 'necessity of keeping roads clear of mechanical transport during operations'.[222] The reason for this is not clear. It may have been related to reducing damage or Rawlinson's perception of the velocity dissonance between WMT and HT. Both were issues. Rawlinson certainly appears to have had a *bete-noire* about WMT operating forward from railheads because that was the key message given to DDST[223] by the DA&QMG, when the former arrived at HQ Fourth Army in February 1916.[224] Whatever

Divisional Supply Columns were, for a period in April reassigned from out-loading railheads to support RE work; TNA WO 95/454/1: HQ Fourth Army, DDST, WD, 20 April 1916.

215 Stone became such a precious commodity that a CCS upon moving in preparation for the battle, dug out all the paths and pads and transferred the 20 lorry-loads of material to the new site; Middlebrook, *The First Day on the Somme*, p.83. The movement of stone by unit CCS lorries with the Red Cross caused considerable forthright discussion in HQ XIII Corps between the A&Q staffs and the RAMC, which seems to have reached the level of a spat. The Q staff argued that because the stone was used solely to enable the evacuation and treatment of the wounded, then the activity was in accordance with the Geneva Convention; the Corps Surgeon-General took a different view and the Red Crosses were removed and ASC drivers replaced RAMC personnel; see, Nicholson, *Behind the Lines*, p.53.

216 TNA WO 95/441/2: HQ Fourth Army, A&Q, WD, 6 May 1916.

217 Stone was also delivered using Inland Water Transport (IWT) because of French requirements to prioritise the use of the railway from Ailly-sur-Somme and Guillaucourt; TNA WO 95/441/2: HQ Fourth Army, A&Q, WD, 1 May 1916.

218 Geddes identified this as a key issue, noting that because the Corps moved within the BEF, interest in maintaining the roads was focused on the short-term; Initial report from Geddes to Lloyd George; Granet Papers, MRCUWL, GB 152, MSS.191/3/3/ 7.

219 A week before the offensive commenced, DDST Fourth Army recorded his experience of a journey to inspect logistic operations, which offers a very clear picture of the challenges to operating WMT in support of the preparations for the offensive: 'the roads were in a most appalling state, one part of the road in fact being, in a dangerous condition owning to the greasy mud'; TNA WO 95/454/1: HQ Fourth Army, DDST, WD, 24 June 1916.

220 Such decisions have in the past, sometimes been misconstrued as either a failure to understand the capabilities of WMT or a conservative approach to new technology. The reality is that it was a considered judgement based on experience and practicality.

221 In one of many examples, during July 1916, the III Corps Ammunition Park was located at Franvillers. One of its tasks was to out-load munitions from the Edgehill Ammunition Railhead (ARH) to a dump two miles away. To achieve the task, the WMT travelled light for seven miles, collected the ammunition, moved loaded for two miles and then returned to Franvillers on a nine mile route, thereby completing 18 miles but only two miles under load; Henniker, BOH, *Transportation on the Western* Front, pp.157-158.

222 TNA WO 95/441/2: HQ Fourth Army, A&Q WD, 22 June 1916.

223 Colonel F M Wilson late ASC, who, post-war, was Director of Supplies & Transport in India in the rank of Major-General.

224 Major-General H C Sutton to Colonel F M Wilson, verbal discussion, recorded in TNA WO 95/454/1: HQ Fourth Army, DDST WD, 26 February 1916.

Rawlinson's thinking, it clashed with contemporary doctrine, which was predicated upon Supply Columns, equipped with WMT, clearing the railheads, unless the railheads were sufficiently far forward to enable HT to complete the daily loops to the divisional Refilling Points or dumps.[225]

Whilst Rawlinson was reluctant to utilize the capability, the importance of WMT in supporting offensive operations is lucidly illustrated by increase in size of the Fourth Army fleet. This almost doubled between April and September 1916, rising from 3,784 to 6,755 vehicles, with the most significant rise, 235%, in lorries from 2,025 to 4,671.[226] In addition, based solely on the assets of the 15 divisions within the Fourth Army AOR, and without Corps and Army units, there were approximately 84,000 horses,[227] 13,000 HT wagons,[228] over 270,000 soldiers and an increasing number of heavy artillery tractors, nearly all of which, used the roads at some point, so the importance of traffic control and road repair to prepare for and to sustain operations, is lucidly apparent.[229] A traffic census at Fricourt Cemetery during a 24-hour period on 21-22 July 1916, illustrates the demands made upon the roads, which was a major reason why the BEF required 11,520 tonnes of stone per day. Passing the Census Point were 26,500 men on foot, 3,756 horse drawn wagons, 5,400 riding horses, 813 trucks, 95 buses, 330 motor ambulances and 63 guns.[230] The rapid expansion of WMT capability also created another logistic problem in supplying the vehicles with Petrol Oil and Lubricants (POL) and spares to ensure that operations could be conducted. In the summer of 1916, the consumption of motor spirit in Fourth Army was approximately 12,000 gallons per day,[231] requiring the distribution and recycling of approximately 6,000 x 2 gallon cans, each of which required manual-handling on several occasions as it passed through the supply chain.

What is difficult for the logisticians of today to appreciate is the incredible task involved in supplying the soldiers at 1st Line in the trenches.[232] No matter how efficient the transportation systems on the LOC, corps and division, there came a time, when the logistic system relied entirely on the Man. There were some trench tramways and aerial ropeways constructed to ease the burden but for the most part, the soldier had to bear the load.[233] At some point, nearly all the paraphernalia of war had to be carried, often at night, under artillery and small arms fire, in pouring rain, through a maze of mud-bound trenches by a man in khaki who was cold, tired, wet, thirsty, probably hungry and possibly wearing a respirator. Then, in order to support the assaulting troops, there was

225 Wilson suggested to the DA&QMG that the solution in this instance would be to await the allotment of the Corps to the Army and assess the options; TNA WO 95/454/1: HQ Fourth Army, DDST, WD, 26 February 1916.

226 In early April 1916, these figures were: 2,025 lorries, 434 cars, 386 ambulances (combined total: 820) and 1,636 motorcycles, increasing in September, to 4,671 lorries, 1,145 cars and ambulances and 1,636 motorcycles; TNA WO 95/454/1: HQ Fourth Army, DDST, WD, 2 April 1916. There is an error in the table in the WD, which reads a total of 810 cars and ambulances, when the sum figure is 820; a most unusual error by the DDST Staff!

227 Calculated solely upon the assets of divisions in the Fourth Army and based on a 1914 infantry division, which had an establishment of 5,592 horses, thereby totalling 83,880 in the Fourth Army AOR; FSPB 14, p.6.

228 Excluding gun carriages and limbers, each division had an establishment of 876 HT vehicles, equating to 13,140 HT wagons for Fourth Army; Ibid, p.6.

229 These are recurrent themes in the HQ Fourth Army WD entries during May and June 1916; TNA WO 95/441/2. These include comments from the Army Commander reinforcing the need for traffic control, eliminating unnecessary vehicle movement, transferring loads to rail and the importance of maintaining the roads.

230 Edmonds, BOH, *France and Belgium 1916*, Vol. I, p.283.

231 Henniker, BOH, *Transportation on the Western Front*, p.158.

232 Lines of Support are used to describe the boundaries of specific elements of logistic functions. Lines of Support was not a term that was in use during the Great War but it appears in various logistic publications and is a simple method of assigning capability to units and formations. 1st Line - organic to a unit; 2nd Line - organic to a brigade or division; 3rd Line - allocated to Corps or Army; 4th Line - provided by the Base. For the BEF, 4th Line was delivered in-Theatre and from the United Kingdom.

233 One interesting innovation was niche investment in the traditional Tumpline, a porterage system promoted by 1st Canadian Division, which created the 11th Canadian Infantry Brigade Tumpline Company; Major F R Phelan, *The Tumpline as a Means of saving Manpower*, Field Publication, early 1917, courtesy Tom Donovan.

another part of the logistic sequence to be enacted. Once the advance had begun, supplies had to be carried by the soldiers of the battalion, across what had been No Man's Land, to the remnants of platoons and companies attempting to hold positions that had been seized in the assault. The range of supplies and stores was extensive: SAA, trench mortar bombs, duckboards, iron pickets, barbed wire, sandbags, rations, medical items, mail, tools, timber and water to name a few. Most of these items were heavy or bulky or both; one Imperial Gallon of fresh water weighs 10 pounds,[234] plus the can. If soldiers only consumed two pints of water per day for drinking, a battalion of a 1000 soldiers in the line required 1.12 tons every 24 hours. In a 21st Century military environment awash with 20 foot containers, Quadcons, Load Handling Systems, and pallets, it is probably almost impossible to grasp how tough and dangerous this work was, and the 1st Line logisticians have never been given the recognition they deserve.

P8.5. 70th Anniversary of the Somme: but who remembered the logisticians? (Author)

Conclusion

The Battle of the Somme was, for the British Army, a watershed in military operations, planning, scale, casualties, artillery and logistics. From the operational perspective, the lessons and experiences of the Somme created the basis for a much more capable army and one, which eventually matured to make a most significant contribution to victory in 1918. If therefore, the Somme was the making of this army, then it was also the casting of a very different approach to logistics,[235] without

234 10.02 pounds at 39.2° F (4°C), the temperature at which, fresh water is most dense.
235 For an examination of how this developed, see, 'The Transportation Mission to GHQ, 1916', Keith Grieves, *Look to Your Front, Studies in the First World War* by the British Commission for Military History (Staplehurst: Spellmount, 1999) pp.3-78.

which, the successes of 1918 could never have been achieved.

The preparation for the Battle of the Somme clearly exposed for the first time, the fundamental importance of appropriately resourced transportation capability in supporting operations on the Western Front. Initially an activity taken for granted, it was only after the realization in late July 1916 when the system was reaching its limit of expansion, GHQ recognized that transportation needed to be planned, executed and sustained at a strategic rather than a tactical level. This acceptance, supported by the C-in-C, was fundamental in ensuring that action was taken to resolve the inherent failures within the system.

Logistic operations on the Somme also clearly reinforced the need for the effective integration of logistic activity. Whilst functions remained the responsibility of particular directorates and staffs, the immense significance of co-ordination at every level became lucidly apparent. Indeed, one of the most striking features of the period, is the recognition that executing the function was far more important that reinforcing the lines of demarcation through the Regimental System. There was little point in the railway delivering 400 tons of ammunition to a railhead if there was no WMT to transport it to Refilling Points, or the Royal Engineers pumping thousands of gallons of water from a well if it could not be distributed to Water Points. The control of the many facets of logistics became a key task of the various Staffs at Army, Corps and Division to ensure that logistics were delivered as effectively and efficiently as possible. In this respect, it is pertinent to remember that even in major conflicts, the British Army has rarely had an embarrassing surplus of resources, and that the rigorous use of them is as important now as it was in the Great War.

Equally important was the need for quality assurance in production and an effective storage and maintenance regime, especially for munitions and in particular, fuzes. The criticality of the Equipment Support task enabled by trained and experienced personnel, in units and workshops and supported by a resilient spares supply chain was also reinforced.[236] In addition, by 1917, the logisticians were searching for ways to create reserves to ensure more flexibility without increasing the requirement for more material. The Somme was though, the first time in British military history, that a major logistic operation was planned and executed in a manner that would become familiar not only to the soldiers of the Great War but also to those in the Second and their successors in the Cold War and beyond.[237]

236 According to HQ Fourth Army DDOS, four days before the Somme offensive, there was only one spare Plunger G available, located in England, for the 15 inch howitzers in the BEF; TNA WO 95/452/1: HQ Fourth Army, DDOS, WD, 26 June 1916.

237 To those conversant with the British Army of the Rhine (BAOR) Rail Movement Instruction (MI) 45 in BAOR the transportation planning for the Somme would be instantly recognizable.

Part III

Innovation and Improvisation

9

Getting over Military Prejudices

The dynamics and frictions of employing civilian logistic consultants in the BEF

Introduction

Whatever the operational and tactical successes or failures of the BEF throughout the war, its logistics and administration were generally sound at the beginning of the conflict and at the end, with what might be described as a developing crisis in the middle. The most difficult period was from Spring 1915, when the BEF's expansion began to accelerate, and Autumn 1916, when the resources and procedures to support a force of one million plus personnel,[1] in an overseas theatre of operations became clearly understood and the challenges began to be surmounted. Of these, transportation was the most significant and potentially the most fragile issue.

The historical logistic focus has generally been upon the military component but there is a clear commercial thread throughout the war that was critical to military success, a process which commenced with the pre-war planning to deploy the British Expeditionary Force (BEF) and was in full flow in various guises at the Armistice. This aspect has particular resonance in 2018 as the British Army seeks to reduce its costs and improve its capability by introducing commercial practice in the logistic environment, utilizing contractors to deliver specific outputs, and importing civilian consultants to improve efficiency.[2] Whilst there may be positive outcomes, these activities often create risk, especially in manoeuvre operations,[3] so the level and depth of their implementation, remains controversial. This chapter seeks to explore the BEFs experience in relation to the contribution of commercial practice and commercial consultants to enhancing military capability and the internal frictions it created within the Army hierarchy.[4]

By mid-1916, the 'Elephant in the Room' was the crisis in transportation within the BEF's Area of Operations (AOO) whilst, concomitantly, the most significant contribution of Contractor Support to Operations (CSO) in the BEF was the revision of Theatre logistic and transportation planning by a relatively small number of contracted civilian experts embedded within the BEF's General Headquarters (GHQ).[5] The Three Ms, 'Men-Munitions-

1 The strength of the BEF rose from 993,368 on 1 January 1916, to 1,343,457 on 1 June and 1,546,474 on 1 October. War Office, *Statistics of the Military Effort of the British Empire during the Great War*, 1914-1920 (MEBE) (HMSO, 1922), p.64 (iii), Table (ii) - Estimated Strengths of the Expeditionary Forces.

2 Contractors were used extensively during Operation HERRICK, the British Army's deployment to Afghanistan.

3 The British Army describes *Manoeuvre* as the employment of forces on the battlefield (using movement) in combination with fire or fire potential to achieve a position of advantage in respect to the opposition in order to accomplish the mission. See, *Army Doctrine Publication* (ADP) Volume 1, *Operations*, HQDT/18/34/46, Army Code No 7156 (UK MOD, 1994), pp.3-17 to 3-19.

4 For a wider assessment of the utilization and impact of civilian expertize in the British Army during the Great War, see, Aimee Fox, *Learning to Fight, Military Innovation and Change in the British Army, 1914-1918* (Cambridge: Cambridge University Press (CUP) 2018), pp.164-203.

5 For a personal account, which focuses mainly on A&Q, of the work of GHQ, see, GSO [Frank Fox] *GHQ,*

Movements',[6] were crucial to the BEF's future operational capability but the success in expanding the first two areas, had created a crisis for the third, which was highlighted by the logistic problems in sustaining the Somme offensive.

The GHQ Transportation Staff understood there was problem but arguably did not have the volumetric capacity to grasp the complex interlocking factors that were generating it, or create effective solutions, whilst also labouring to keep the wheel turning, although post-war assessments were sometimes more self-critical: "And one cannot evade the truth that we could have foreseen it and taken measures to meet it *before*[7] the battle, had we only studied earlier the science of transportation and is practicable application to war."[8] The introduction of CSO capability however, created an additional resource, backed by innovative approaches and under-pinned by experts who had wide-ranging of experience of tackling major logistic issues in the commercial arena and, equally importantly, the influence to obtain the assets which were a critical component of the solution.

Changing Step

The problem in early 1916 was that whilst operations and production had most certainly reached those of the mass era, the methods to bridge the gap from 'Factory to Fire-Trench' were in effect, more of a cottage industry. In May 1915, the failure and losses involved in the Battle of Aubers Ridge exposed,[9] what was in effect, a government and commercial miscomprehension of the developing scale for the expanding munitions requirement,[10] and in its wake, the Ministry of Munitions was established.[11] As a result of this reorganization, ammunition production increased rapidly. In 1914, filled artillery shell production was 526,300; in 1915 it rose to 7,332,886, and then in 1916, to 52,943,913 rounds.[12]

Whilst the problems of production were being resolved,[13] two important aspects in the process of 'Factory to Fire-Trench', had not: Cross-Channel movement and transit from corps and divisional railheads to the dumps and gun-lines. Transportation of munitions by rail within the United Kingdom to the South Coast ports, although growing, had not reached the railways' capacity to handle it. Military operations in France and Belgium had reduced economic activity from these ports to the Continent and the railways were, initially, able to sustain the major increase in

Montreuil-Sur-Mer (London: Philip Allan & Co, 1920). Fox was an Australian pre-war artillery reservist, author and journalist who worked for *The Morning Post* as News Editor and then War Correspondent. He was twice wounded during actions on the Somme before serving as a Staff Captain at GHQ in the QMG's Branch and then the General Staff at the War Office, being awarded the OBE for his services. Post-war he supported a number of causes including the Empire Rheumatism Council and the British Empire Cancer Campaign, being knighted in 1926. Obituary, *The Times*, 9 March 1960, Official Website, accessed 11 July 2017.

6 This *buzz-phrase* is attributed to Douglas Haig but was almost certainly in staff officer circulation within GHQ.

7 *Italics* in the original.

8 Colonel M G Taylor CMG DSO, 'Land Transportation in the Late War', *Journal of the Royal United Service Institution* (*JRUSI*), Vol. LXVI (November 1921), p.705.

9 See, Adrian Bristow, *A Serious Disappointment, The Battle of Aubers Ridge 1915 and the Munitions Scandal* (London: Leo Cooper, 1995).

10 In the Land context, munitions were those items of materiel destined for military use including ammunition, explosives, small arms, artillery, aircraft, tanks, Gas Weapons, vehicles and railway equipment.

11 For the detailed history of the Ministry, see *The History of the Ministry of Munitions* (MOM) Vols I - XII, HMSO, 1921-1922, reprinted by the Naval & Military Press and Imperial War Museum, nd but 2008. See, also, the immediate post-war narrative, George A B Dewar, *The Great Munition Feat, 1914-1918* (London: Constable, 1921).

12 MEBE, p.477, Gun Ammunition - Output of Empty and Filled Shell.

13 The detailed complexities in resolving the issues with munitions production are lucidly exposed in *The History of the Ministry of Munitions.*

military movement.[14] Whilst the carefully crafted Cross-Channel deployment of the BEF had been orchestrated with precision, the massive increase in the shipping requirement and the associated movement processes to support a rapidly growing Continentally based army continued to frustrate the Trade Department of the Admiralty. The focus on what might be described as 'Front Line First', created a tendency for supplies to be moved to the UK Channel Ports for immediate dispatch to the Continent, regardless of whether suitable shipping was available to move it, or whether transport was available in France to transfer it within the BEF's AOO. This resulted in congestion in the sheds and quays, with a concomitant delay in loading and a reduction in asset tracking accuracy but an increase in loss through damage or pilfering.[15]

The pace and scope of BEF port operations, even in Spring 1916, is well illustrated by the entries for 13 hours in the war diary for Thursday 16 March 1916 of the Rail Transport Officer (RTO) at *Quai Ouest* at Calais.[16] In the period, the RTO controlled the shunts and dispatch of wagons and trains for coke, charcoal, slag, engineer stores, sand, meat, groceries, postal mails, railway stores, petroleum, supplies, flour, bread and the receipt of No 14 Ambulance Train with 84 casualties. He was liasing with the RTOs at *Quai Est*, Ambulance Trains and Medical Triage, the Military Landing Officer *Quai Ouest*, the Postal Quartermaster Sergeant, the Master Baker[17], the French railway *Sous-Chef* and Navy and the *Gare Maritime* staff. In addition, at 0945 he hosted the Deputy Assistant Director (DAD) Railways from GHQ and at 1835 attended the *commission militaire* conference at Calais Ville, with one pressing issue in particular, the acquisition of SSY wagons to clear the SS *Harmattan* of railway stores. Clearly, this was not an appointment for the faint-hearted, the idle or the incompetent.

The establishment, in November 1915, of the Port and Transit Executive Committee,[18] consisting of representatives from the Admiralty, War Office and Board of Trade was supplemented by a number of senior commercial managers from the transportation industry.[19] This committee, which by subsuming the Admiralty Committee on the Diversion of Shipping and the Board of Trade Committee on Congestion in Docks but then including the War Office, was a significant advance in logistic co-ordination, creating not only a Joint approach between the Royal Navy and the Army but also a much stronger military-civil interface. Whilst its focus was on port operations on the West Coast of the United Kingdom, its output did much to alleviate some of the delays in the Channel Ports. The Committee met weekly but a Standing Sub-Committee gathered each day to consider the implications of the daily reports received from the 43 principal UK ports. The

14 Not all the problems affecting the railways were man-made. On Sunday 19 December 1915, ground movement East of the Martello Tunnel on the main line of the South Eastern and Chatham Railways (SECR) between Folkestone and Dover, distorted the Permanent Way for nearly two miles. This important route was closed for the duration of the war and had it been achieved by enemy action, would have been a major military coup. One result of the closure was that the twin bores of the Shakespeare's Cliff Tunnel were used for the storage of ammunition trains waiting to load to ships at the South East Ports (SEP). See, O S Nock, *The South Eastern & Chatham Railway* (London: Ian Allan, 1961), pp.154-155.

15 Despite the introduction of electronic tracking systems, asset visibility remains a challenge. Operations in Iraq, 1990-91, on Operation GRANBY, clearly exposed the issues, not all of which had not been fully resolved by the time of the second deployment to Iraq, Operation TELIC, in 2003, with container control being an especial problem.

16 Colonel A M Henniker CBE (Comp) BOH, *Transportation on the Western Front, 1914-1918* (London: HMSO, 1937), pp.517-520. This publication is also held in the TNA in ZLIB 29/455 (Text) and 456 (Maps).

17 The BEF had installed a bakery in a cellulose factory within the dock complex. Flour was received from ships to the bakery and bread exported by rail; Henniker, BOH, *Transportation on the Western Front*, p.517.

18 For details of its composition and work, see, C Ernest Fayle, BOH, *Seaborne Trade*, Vol. II, *Submarine Campaign*, (London: John Murray, 1920), pp.197-204.

19 The Committee included Sir Frederic Bolton of Lloyds; J G Broodbank of the Port of London Authority; Sir Sam Fay, General Manager of the Great Central Railway and a member of the Railway Executive Committee and Sir A Norman Hill, Liverpool Steam Ship Owners' Association.

Situation Reports (SITREP) detailed the state of berths, rates of discharge, warehouse facilities, cold storage capability, transit shed capacity, availability of labour, railway movements, barges, harbour craft, trucks, sheets and cartage, thereby enabling the most effective use of the assets to be generated by combining planning with tasks and resources.

One of the recommendations of the Committee was the formation of a Transport Workers' Battalion to provide a mobile reserve of military labour in order to support the civilian dockers in ports where military transit operations were being constrained because of a shortage of manpower.[20] The War Office was though, in November 1915, reluctant to allocate military personnel to what was perceived to be a commercial activity and it was not until March 1916 that the Army Council authorized the formation of such a unit with a personnel establishment of 647 All Ranks. Surprisingly, given that the Royal Engineers (RE) were responsible for dock operating, the War Office entitled the new unit 16th York & Lancaster Regiment,[21] with the manpower enlisted from men allocated to Home Defence units, preferably volunteers with port operations experience.

Many challenges had to be surmounted before the unit was effective. The Transport Workers' Federation was suspicious lest this mobile force became a source of cheap labour[22] and it was agreed that when employed in the docks, the Non Commissioned Officers and soldiers would be paid the equivalent civilian rates appertaining to the relevant responsibilities.[23] Recruiting was slow, with many physically unfit men being posted to the battalion by Commanding Officers keen to dispense with their services but by July 1916, the unit had seven companies, deploying in excess of 600 personnel on a regular basis. Haig recognized the importance of dock labour,[24] military and civilian, wherever it was located, in delivering logistic capability, recording in his diary:

> Mr Ben Tillett[25] came to see me. He calls himself a 'Socialist Revolutionary' but has rendered very valuable service in keeping the dockers and other operatives at work, and has inspired them with determination to beat the Germans. It seems extraordinary how he can impress his audiences, although he knows very little about his subject. To please 'Ben', I was photographed alongside of him![26]

20 Lord Derby raised the first Dockers' Battalion for service in the Liverpool Docks.

21 Regimental Headquarters (RHQ) was in the village of Colsterdale, approximately 9.3 miles North West of Ripon in North Yorkshire; the nearest railhead was at Masham, on the North Eastern Railway, about 3.7 miles to the East. Colsterdale appears to be an odd location for a Dock Operating Unit but there was method in selection. First, it was central to many of the key ports on the West and East Coast in Northern England. Secondly, its location, a significant distance from any port, allayed the fears of union representatives that a military unit might become a permanent feature within its confines.

22 The London Dock strike of 1889 and the national dock and transportation strikes of 1911 and 1912 had focused the minds of politicians, government officials and military planners on the effects of the withdrawal of labour. See, TNA WO 3232/5289 and 5290: Defence of the Realm Acts, for powers possessed by the Government under the Regulation of the Forces Act, 1871 and National Defence Act, 1888, to secure the distribution of essential supplies, including food, by rail. See also, the 'Report of the Standing Sub-Committee of the Committee of Imperial Defence on the Internal Distribution of Supplies in Time of War' (SECRET 152B) dated 12 June 1912 in TNA WO 32/5290.

23 In addition, the employer assumed responsibility for death and disablement allowances as provided in the Workmen's Compensation Act; see, Fayle, BOH, *Seaborne Trade*, Vol. II, p.288.

24 See, E J Hobsbawn, *Labouring Men, Studies in the History of Labour* (London: Weidenfeld & Nicolson, 1964), Chp 11, National Unions on the Waterside.

25 Ben Tillett was the leader of the Dock, Wharf, Riverside and General Labour Union, which was the largest union forming the Transport & General Workers' Union in 1922. Tillett played a prominent role in the London dock strike of 1889 and the national dock strikes of 1911 and 1912 and was Labour Member of Parliament for Salford North 1917-1924 and 1929-1931. He also had an interesting personal life, having nine children with his wife Jane Tompkins and four with his mistress, the Australian opera singer, Eva Newton. See, Juliet Nicolson, *The Perfect Summer, England 1911, Just Before The Storm* (London: John Murray, 2006).

26 Diary entry, Wednesday 25 October 1916 in Gary Sheffield & John Bourne (Eds.) *Douglas Haig, War Diaries and*

A Growing Challenge

Far more serious however, was the growing delay in the North French Channel Ports. Not only were there insufficient railway wagons available to move the stocks unloaded from the ships but also the operational efficiency of these sites was adversely affected by the command and manpower arrangements. Many of the military officers, although capable logisticians were inexperienced in handling such a massive inflow of material, whilst a significant proportion of the operating personnel and labourers were not suitably trained. Initially, these matters were not deemed to be critical but as the BEF expanded, the flaws in the structure began to appear, although equally measures were in hand to resolve them.

Logistically, the result of the failures to grip the Theatre transportation issues began to have strategic outfalls; the key downstream affect being a reduction in available shipping as ships lay alongside waiting for discharge, although this was often caused not by any failure by the BEF's logisticians but by the ships' stowage, the significance of which, the War Office did not comprehend, despite clear direction from Inspector General Communications (IGC) BEF.[27] Interestingly, it was not the War Office that initiated external action but a body of senior commercial executives, forming the Shipping Control Committee,[28] which considered that immediate investigative action was required into the question of why more shipping was being utilized on the Cross-Channel routes than the volume of material appeared to warrant.

On 10 June 1916, Thomas Royden, Deputy Chairman of the Cunard Steamship Company, accompanied by two advisors, T H Underwood[29] of the Great Central Railway[30] and L A P Warner, Assistant Manager of the Mersey Docks and Harbour Board, proceeded to France to conduct the investigation.[31] The Royden Commission visited the key Northern Ports: Boulogne, Calais, Dieppe, Dunkirk, Le Harve, Rouen and St Valery-sur-Somme. In addition, by arrangement with the Inspector-General of Communications (IGC),[32] although he was not content with their presence in these facilities, the Mission also inspected advanced bases and railway regulating sidings.

From the strategic perspective, the report made depressing reading. Ship offloads were half the potential rate, there were insufficient railway wagons, the French Railways were slow in returning stock and the tally process was inefficient. In addition, the Movement Staffs were unable to plan the flow of supplies from the port areas because manifests arrived with the ships instead of being telegraphed in advance. The Commission also identified that there was insufficient railway export capacity within the ports in proportion to the number of berths, which meant that it was the

Letters 1914-1918 (London: Weidenfeld & Nicolson, 2005), p.247.

27 Remarks on the 'Report of the Commission sent out by the Shipping Control Committee' (the Royden Report) by IGC, Lieutenant-General Clayton, dated 30 July 1916, in Sir William Guy Granet Papers held by the Modern Records Centre University of Warwick Library (MRCUWL) GB 152 MSS.191/3/3/22-23. Clayton highlighted the poor stowage of ships from Canada that had upon arrival in February 1916, taken, 'weeks to unload'.

28 The establishment of the Shipping Control Committee was approved by the Prime Minister, Herbert Asquith on 27 January 1916. A small body, its members were Lord Curzon (Chairman); Lord Faringdon (Chairman of the Great Central Railway); Thomas Royden (Deputy Chairman, Cunard Steam Ship Company); F W Lewis (Deputy Chairman of Furness, Withy and Company) with Captain Clement Jones, Director of the Booth Line, as Secretary. For its terms of reference and operation, see, Fayle, BOH, *Seaborne Trade*, Vol. II, pp.229-230.

29 Underwood also held a commission, as a Lieutenant-Commander, in the Royal Naval Volunteer Reserve (RNVR).

30 As the Western District Traffic Manager of the Great Central Railway (GCR) in 1905, Underwood's salary was £600; £220,700 at 2016 values, using Labour Earnings (*Measuring Worth UK*). See, George Dow, *Great Central*, Vol. Three, *Fay Sets The Pace*, 1900-1922 (London: Ian Allan, 1965), p.38.

31 Fayle, BOH, *Seaborne Trade*, Vol. II, pp.293-294.

32 IGC responsibilities and tasks are shown in General Staff, *Field Service Regulations* (FSR), Part II, *Organization and Administration*, War Office (London: HMSO, 1909) (reprinted, with amendments to October, 1914) pp.32-34.

P9.1. Port Clearance: crucial to efficient logistics. Civilian consultants identified the need to resolve inefficiencies in port operating, the resolution of which, reinvigorated outputs. (RLC Museum: AB/000783D)

railways and not the number of ship berths, which represented port capacity.[33] A key element of this process was the importance of clearance from the port and not solely the unloading of ships. Experience suggested that a ship could discharge onto the quay between two to five times the rate the material could be cleared from the quay, whilst the quay could be cleared between three and five times the rate from the transit sheds.[34] Instead therefore, of being facilities for the collation of consignments, the ports became reserve rear depots, accumulating significant stocks of various items that were needed elsewhere and reducing the capacity of the quays to handle offloading.[35] All these matters appeared obvious to the Royden Commission but the approach and tone of the report cut no ice with the IGC, Lieutenant-General[36] Clayton,[37] whose comments upon it, so concisely describes the equally cool relationship between military commanders and commercial managers:

33 Taylor, 'Land Transportation in the Late War', p.719.

34 Lieutenant-Commander H B Tuffill, commenting upon Taylor, 'Land Transportation in the Late War', p.717.

35 The problem was exacerbated by the failure to comprehend the unit establishments, which rightly did not provide large numbers of staff to execute depot functions such as receipt, inspection and storage.

36 Clayton was a substantive Major-General and held the temporary rank of Lieutenant-General; *The Edinburgh Gazette*, 16 February 1917, announcing his award, by His Majesty the King of the Belgians, of the *Commandeur de l'Ordre de Leopold*.

37 Frederick Thomas Clayton was a logistician, being late of the Army Service Corps (ASC) and was awarded the KCB and KCMG. Having returned from service in South Africa, he was appointed as Director of Supplies at GHQ BEF in September 1914 before assuming the appointment of IGC in January 1915. He was the first Colonel Commandant of the Royal Army Service Corps (RASC) and Thornhill Barracks in Aldershot, constructed in the period 1926-1928, with additions c1931-39, for the RASC, was renamed in his honour in 1929; TNA WO 32/4061: Works and Buildings, Barracks, 'Renaming of Thornhill Barracks as Clayton Barracks, Aldershot'. He died in 1933 and is buried with his wife in the Aldershot Military Cemetery.

> Right through the Report not one word is said about maintaining the Army and keeping it provided with supplies, stores, ammunition, horses and men. The only conclusion one can come to after reading it is, that it is impossible for the ordinary business civilian to understand what are the conditions under which we have to work and that it is a mistake to allow them to interfere with an Army business that most of us have studied all our lives.[38]

This was not the first time the importation of external advisors had caused friction within the GHQ environment and there appears to have been a general distrust of them.[39] Certainly, the outfall from the Royden Report lucidly illustrates the creative tension between not only the differing cultures but also the procedures and imperatives. General Clayton's comments are mostly defensive seeking to expose the immense positive industry being undertaken by the BEF's logisticians, whilst also reflecting his concerns that the whole working logistic system supporting the BEF in France, so carefully created, was about to be replaced by an untried one, constructed by a group of civilian amateurs who were likely to erode, if not eliminate the BEF's combat capability. He expressed his frustration and existence in one clear note: "but the one object I am here for is to see that the Army is supplied promptly and regularly with all it requires whether it is a 15" shell or a bootlace, and this work has been carried out so far without a single hitch or complaint…."[40]

Clayton was also annoyed about the report's comments relating to military labour in the docks, noting in his remarks that perforce of circumstances, the BEF's soldiers, whilst not as effective as professional waterside labourers, were working 65-70 hours week, with 'no strikes or complaints, which is more than can be said of labour, however good, working in the Docks in England'.[41] In the circumstances, it is perhaps as well that Haig hosted Ben Tillett and not Clayton;[42] indeed, the arrangement may have been deliberate. Clayton's comments about soldiers working 'overtime',[43] clearly indicates a comprehension of the sensitivities in this arena, which illustrates that Senior Officers by default, were not blind to the increasingly 'unionised' flavour of many military logistic activities, and Clayton was in agreement with the observations of the Transportation Mission,[44] about the necessity to improve its output and technical management.[45] There are though, also specific elements in the report, the critical movement of ammunition being one, which had been

38 IGC remarks dated 30 July 1916 on the Royden Report in the Granet Papers, MRCUWL, GB 152, MSS.191/3/3/14. It probable that Clayton had identified from a professional perspective, that civilian consultants posed a potential threat to the credibility of military logisticians and possibly to the post of IGC or equally, personally, to him as the incumbent. In the former, he was partially correct because the post was abolished.

39 Clayton may also have been influenced by the outfall from the Girouard Report of October 1914, on railway arrangements in France by a military railway officer, in which his predecessor Maxwell had been embroiled.

40 IGC remarks dated 30 July 1916 on the Royden Report, Granet Papers, MRCUWL, GB 152, MSS.191/3/3/23.

41 Ibid, MSS.191/3/3/18.

42 Haig hosted a remarkable number of inspectors and visitors from the United Kingdom and many other nations, representing a wide spectrum of society, professions and activity. Of particular note in relation to this chapter, was the visit of the financial editor of the influential US *Saturday Evening Post*, Issac Frederick Marcosson, who was granted access to the relevant GHQ directorates and given a guided tour to view the BEF's logistic operations. As a result of his visit, he wrote a most illuminating book entitled, *The Business of War* (London: John Lane, The Bodley Head, 1918). For his description of his meeting with Haig, see, pp.229-257.

43 IGC remarks dated 30 July 1916 on the Royden Report, Granet Papers, MRCUWL, GB 152, MSS.191/3/3/18.

44 For a detailed analysis, see, 'The Transportation Mission to GHQ, 1916', by Keith Grieves in *Look to Your Front, Studies in the First World War* by the British Commission for Military History (Staplehurst: Spellmount, 1999), pp.63-78.

45 IGC remarks dated 30 July 1916 on the Royden Report, Granet Papers, MRCUWL, GB 152, MSS.191/3/3/18 and Initial report, Geddes to Lloyd George in a Private and Confidential letter dated 15 September 1916; Granet Papers, MRCUWL, GB 152, MSS.191/3/3/4. Geddes reported: "From my preliminary investigation and observations, there is no doubt a constructive policy on the use of labour, and a proper consideration - given by experts - to conditions under which labour handles materials and commodities conveyed by road, rail, etc is called for. A very considerable saving in the use of labour required could be effected."

overtaken by developments and were no longer accurate, which rightly irritated the IGC and he left no doubt of his position on its output:[46]

> We cannot have civilians, who know nothing of the Military situation, interfering because we are not unloading our ships on commercial lines; they do not know what is required. The Royden Commission, I think, with the best intentions in the word, only looked upon our work at the Ports from a purely civilian standpoint. The military aspect, as I have said before, did not appeal to them because they had not the knowledge to understand it, and for that reason we should not allow in future any civilian Commission to come out here and criticise our work;[47] when we fail in any way to keep the Army supplied it will be time for criticism.

As it transpired, he was in for a significant and unwanted surprise but Clayton, as he later accepted, was not entirely correct in his perception but equally he was right to be concerned based upon the manner in which, the Commission appears to have presented its approach. 'Just in Time' logistics is very much a 21st Century concept yet the Royden Commission was espousing the same in 1916, in order to generate faster ship turnarounds and thus, more capacity.[48] Where the lacuna lay, was in the Commission's apparent failure to comprehend the critical importance of stock reserves to the military operation in France, the risk the Commander-in-Chief was willing to take with the levels of those reserves, and thus the BEF's logistic lay-down, a point, which Clayton felt compelled to articulate:

> To supply an Army in the Field it is necessary that certain reserves of supplies, stores, ammunition, horses and men should be kept close at hand and in order that no interruption should be made in the daily regular flow to the Armies (by closing of Ports etc) the number of days is fixed by the Commander-in-Chief...........This point was not touched on by the Commission, as probably they were not aware that reserves were necessary, and from a civilian point of view it is quite natural that it should not have been realised.[49]

The Royden Mission is long forgotten but its work lucidly articulated the growing movement problems within the BEF created by tactical rather than strategic logistic planning. Resolving the issues within the docks did not however, remove all the inefficiencies and an investigation on behalf of the Minister of Munitions, Lloyd George, indicated other reasons for the problem, concerns, which became more focused when he assumed, upon the death of Lord Kitchener, the appointment of Secretary of State for War.[50] The result was the formation and despatch of the Transportation Mission to GHQ, led by Eric Geddes,[51] Deputy Director General of Munitions Supply and

46 IGC remarks dated 30 July 1916 on the Royden Report, Granet Papers, MRCUWL, GB 152, MSS.191/3/3/20-23.
47 Ibid, MSS.191/3/3/23.
48 Clayton was unimpressed, noting that of the stated 12-15 ships awaiting berths at Cherbourg, there were none; IGC remarks dated 30 July 1916 the Royden Report, Granet Papers, MRCUWL GB 152, MSS.191/3/3/16-17.
49 Ibid, MSS.191/3/3/16.
50 Lord Kitchener was drowned on Monday 5 June 1916, when the ship, the armoured cruiser HMS *Hampshire*, in which he was travelling to Russia, was mined West of the Orkney Islands.
51 Later Sir Eric Geddes GCB GBE PC (1875-1937). After leaving school, Geddes went to the USA, working as a lumberjack and steel-worker before joining the Baltimore and Ohio Railroad. In 1895, he moved to India and served with the Rohilkund & Kumaon Railway becoming Superintendent in 1901. Joining the North Eastern Railway (NER) in the UK in the newly created post of Claims Agent, he became the Deputy Chief Goods Manager in 1906, Chief Goods Manager in 1907, before being appointed Deputy General Manager in 1912. Usually remembered for his involvement in reducing post-war government expenditure by wielding the 'Geddes Axe', he

P9.2. Just Too Much Logistics? The Royden Mission created tension between senior military logisticians and the civilian consultants about the level of reserves that should be held. (RLC Museum: AB/000783B)

late Deputy General Manager of the North Eastern Railway (NER).[52] One of the largest UK enterprises in 1913, the NER employed 50,000 people but more significantly for the BEF, its staff, under its General Manager between 1891-1906, Sir George Stegmann Gibb,[53] pioneered the use of new management systems,[54] inter-modal transportation, traffic forecasts, statistical analysis,[55] the effective provision of bulk mineral freight operations[56] and the introduction of high capacity wagons.[57] All these processes were to be key elements in enhancing the BEF's logistic capability.

also held the appointments of First Lord of the Admiralty and Minister for Transport before retiring from political life and government service, to become a director of Dunlop Rubber and then, in 1924, the Chairman of Imperial Airways, dying in harness, aged 61, in 1937.

52 His impact upon the operations of the NER was not highlighted in the company history to 1914, his only entry being in the list of Goods Managers; W W Tomlinson, *The North Eastern Railway, Its Rise and Development* (Newcastle-upon-Tyne: Andrew Reid & Co, 1914), p.772.

53 I am indebted to Andrew Gibb for his time in sharing his family knowledge of his Great-Grandfather.

54 The Traffic Apprenticeship scheme at the NER created the opportunity for a broad management perspective and early responsibility for selected candidates, in preparation for entry into general management. Whilst generally excluding technical staff and focusing upon exceptional personality criteria, it was still an unusual approach before 1914. See, *The Ability to Manage: A Study of British Management 1890-1990*, S P Keeble, (Manchester: Manchester University Press, 1992), pp. 140-141.

55 Tomlinson, *North Eastern Railway*, pp.731-733. Some of the Indian railways had been utilizing statistics to improve traffic efficiency since the mid-1870s but remarkably, the NER was the first railway company in the UK to compile them for this purpose.

56 In 1914, the NER had 59,815 wagons dedicated to bulk mineral operations; its closest commercial competitor, the Midland Railway, although possessing 1,000 more wagons in total, had only 18,309 vehicles of this type; C J Allen, *The North Eastern Railway* (London: Ian Allan, 1964), p.210.

57 See, R J Irving, *The North Eastern Railway Company, 1870-1914* (Leicester: Leicester University Press), pp.213-266

On Tuesday 8 August 1916, Lloyd George wrote to the Commander-in-Chief BEF:

> There are three points in particular, which I should like Sir Eric Geddes to talk over with you. One is the question of transport facilities for the very considerably increased quantity of ammunition and other stores, which we are expecting to send to you.[58] Another is the difficulty that has arisen over the great shortage of petrol. I am really afraid that, unless we are able to effect some economy in petrol,[59] we shall be faced with a shortage or curtailment of the motor bus services, which the working classes are so largely dependent upon, and which would to a great extent interfere with getting work-people to and from the large munitions factories. The third is the question of repair and working of ports, railways, canals and roads in the case of an advance, having regard to the difficulties as to men and materials in this country.[60]

P9.3. A pioneer for BEF logistics: the innovative systems of the North Eastern Railway were to be key elements in enhancing the BEF's logistic capability. (Author)

and Tomlinson, *North Eastern Railway*, pp.726-731.

58 For example, in the four weeks ending 27 May 1916, 1,884,404 rounds of artillery ammunition were shipped to France. This increased to 4,075,195 in June, 6,376,406 in December and peaked at 9,051,253 in June 1918; MEBE, p.435, Table (xii) - Ammunition sent to France.

59 Deputy Director Supplies & Transport (DDST) at Fourth Army at a meeting with his fellow DDSTs at GHQ, identified a quick win to assist in providing a solution to this problem by persuading MT drivers to switch off their engines when they were waiting for tasking; TNA WO 95/454/1: HQ Fourth Army, DDST, WD, 3 May 1916. As an issue, it seems to have been gripped, at least in Fourth Army. In September 1918, the Deputy Provost Marshal reported only one offender in the month; TNA WO 95/445/5: HQ Fourth Army, A&Q, 'D.P.M's. Report for Week Ending 28-9-18'. It is a problem that lives on in the 21st Century British Army, although contemporary drivers have little excuse because the self-start ignition has replaced the starting-handle.

60 Henniker, BOH, *Transportation on the Western Front*, pp.183-184.

Management or Command?

Inevitably, the Geddes' Mission was a dilemma for Haig, particularly in his relationship with Clayton. Haig recorded of Geddes, upon his arrival in France, "A most pleasant and capable man. He is afraid that the Inspector General of Communications (General Clayton) resents his visit![61] I said that I am glad to have practical hints from anyone capable of advising!"[62] The results of the Geddes' Mission,[63] however, were a turning point for the BEF and Haig's decision, perhaps a little reluctantly initially, to accept the recommendations, was a courageous step and clearly demonstrates that whatever historians may write about him as the C-in-C, the Nation and the Army were immensely well served by his decision.[64] Without doubt however, it is clear that Haig believed that action needed to be taken to resolve the growing transportation issues and, if Geddes is to be believed, other senior officers within GHQ took the same view.[65] Indeed, without it, the BEF would not have been able to sustain any major offensive operations in 1917, nor been able to react so adeptly to the German offensives in 1918. First and foremost, the Mission reflected the quest for professional technical experts with the necessary skills and experience to control and manage the BEF's logistic support infrastructure within the Line of Communication. In doing so, it lucidly demonstrated the perceived cultural differences between the military and commercial logisticians, with Geddes offering much sympathy to the Army's predicament:

> Generally speaking, the soldier, as opposed to the civilian, asks for less than he really ought to have-and in my private opinion-this is due to the way in which he has been made to cheespare, and the fear he has of the Treasury, on account of the lean years before the war; throughout the soldier has almost consistently put forward demands far below the real needs of the situation.[66]

In 1916, the term 'consultant', so familiar today in the management environment was not widely in use but the Royden and Geddes Missions' were composed of them, which demonstrates, even from the perspective of 2018, how perceptive Haig was in pursuing what was perceived by some, as a revolutionary approach to the growing logistic crisis, even if some of the reports, written by a civilian and offering somewhat adverse observations on military output, made uneasy reading: Geddes writing, "I am aware that the officers who are responsible for the work out there will say -

61 Perhaps unsurprisingly, Geddes had detected, probably through Royden, that the IGC was not especially enthusiastic about his visit. Diary entry, Wednesday 25 October 1916, Sheffield & Bourne, *Haig, War Diaries and Letters*, p.223.

62 Even from the perspective of 2018, it would be engaging to learn of his reaction to the Geddes Mission, especially when he discovered that Haig was apparently so receptive to it. No doubt, the Commander-in-Chief found it necessary to put an arm around a proverbial shoulder.

63 The reception Clayton gave to Geddes is not revealed in Geddes' initial report to the Secretary of State for War but Geddes was most effusive about his visit: "I have received great kindness from Sir Douglas Haig and the Quartermaster-General, and as much information as I have asked for has been placed at my disposal by the Directorates concerned." Initial report, Geddes to Lloyd George, Granet Papers, MRCUWL, GB 152, MSS.191/3/3/4.

64 Haig was politically aware and his decision may have been influenced by his perception of future relationships within this arena. If this was the case however, he fought a long battle with the War Office over the command arrangements for the new directorate, which won him few friends on the Army Council.

65 "I understand that the Commander-in-Chief is anxious about the transportation of his Army…….I must say that I share his anxiety and several officers in positions of responsibility and knowledge at G.H.Q. think alike;" Initial report, Geddes to Lloyd George; Granet Papers, MRCUWL, GB 152, MSS.191/3/3/10.

66 Letter, Geddes to Granet, 19 October 1916, in Ibid, MSS.191/3/3/49-59. His comments here are in stark contrast to his actions when tasked with reducing post-war public expenditure.

"Has the Army ever wanted for anything in these last two years of fighting?" My answer to that is that if the Army has not wanted for anything, it is because it has been a stationary Army."[67]

In this respect, Geddes had alighted upon the third component of Haig's 'Three Ms', Movements,[68] but whilst his examination of dock and railway operations was perceived to be within his remit, his expansion into the Combat Zone created precisely the unease that GHQ and IGC logisticians were sensitive to. In particular, Geddes proposed that specially equipped and trained Light (Narrow Gauge) Railway units were the Way Ahead,[69] to enable the 3-6 miles of 'devastated zone' to be logistically 'bridged',[70] which although it had its merits, was not a tank that many senior logistic military officers wanted parked on their lawn.

Secondly, there was a focus upon assessing capabilities through the collection of data and obtaining a clear view of requirements to support future operational plans. The use of statistics was a critical component of improving the efficiency and effectiveness of the transportation systems sustaining the BEF[71] but also a significant advance in military logistic planning and essential to the control and use of resources, factors absolutely relevant to military operations in the 21st Century.[72] A vast array of information was collected including, in the railway arena, the unloading times of each type of train at railheads, demurrage under fire,[73] traffic densities per mile under fire and not under fire, and the numbers of empty wagons passing through Advanced Supply Depots.[74] The centralization of port control through a Docks Directorate ensured that ports became part of the movement process where stocks transferred swiftly from ship to rail instead of accumulating in transit sheds or worse, on the dockside.[75]

An example of improving performance created by the use of analysis of statistics and working practices, related to port discharge, which rose from 10 tons per ship per hour in port in February

67 Initial report, Geddes to Lloyd George; Ibid, MSS.191/3/3/ 9.

68 "This is a war of Armies backed by machinery and "movement" and I do not think "movement" has received sufficient attention in anticipation of the advance;" Ibid, MSS.191/3/3/10-11.

69 Ibid, MSS.191/3/3/8-9.

70 Constructing and operating the Narrow Gauge Railway (NGR) system was no sinecure and in the period 1917-1918, the units suffered 45 fatal casualties. In one of many incidents, 127th Railway Battalion, 2nd Battalion Canadian Railway Troops, Canadian Expeditionary Force, suffered casualties from German artillery fire amongst its infantry labour force on Thursday 15 February 1917 near Acheux, whilst on the same day, work ceased on the Ancre Valley Line because 63rd (Royal Naval) Division did not supply the requisite labour. On Friday 13 April, a mine exploded under NGR track near Achiet-le-Grand making a crater 35 feet deep and 80 feet across. On Saturday 14 April, a German artillery shell struck a Narrow Gauge locomotive near Avesnes-lez-Bapaume, destroying the track, holing the boiler and badly scalding Sapper Nicholson. Lieutenant Colonel H M Jackson MBE ED, *The 127th Battalion CEF, 2nd Battalion, Canadian Railway Troops* (West Montreal: Industrial Shops for the Deaf, nd but 1957), p.9 & p.19. For the Roll of Honour, see, pp.169-170.

71 For a summary of the importance of statistics to transportation in France, see, Sir George Beharrell DSO, 'The Value of Full and Accurate Statistics, as Shown under Emergency Conditions in the Transportation Service in France, A Paper', *The Railway Gazette*, Special War Transportation Number, 21 (September 1921), pp.37-39.

72 Brigadier (Retired) Peter Foxton, late Chief Executive of the Defence Storage and Distribution Agency: "If you cannot measure, you cannot manage it;" advice to the author in October 2004. See also, his book, P D Foxton, *Powering War: Modern Land Force Logistics* (London: Brassey's, 1994).

73 Demurrage is, in the railway context, the payment of financial compensation for undue detention of a wagon, and was introduced as an inter-company transaction by the Railway Clearing House in 1842. For the most part, whilst the concept was sound, this was one area of commercial practice that failed to create the desired efficiency on the railways because the allowances were too generous to prevent companies using the wagons from other companies as temporary storage facilities. Philip Bagwell, *The Railway Clearing House in the British Economy 1842-1922* (London: George Allen & Unwin, 1968). In the BEF context, by compiling statistics on demurrage under fire, Geddes's staff were assessing the adverse impact of enemy operations upon the circulation of wagons.

74 Marcosson, *Business of War*, p.277. Marcosson makes several references to the importance of statistics in managing logistics.

75 Taylor, 'Land Transportation in the Late War', pp.711-712 & p.715.

P9.4. Mass of Material: The challenge of visibility and accounting. To ensure effective and efficient use of material, the BEF had to import more rigorous methods of checking, control and analysis. (RLC Museum: AB/000768A)

1917, to 37.5 tons by March 1918.[76] In addition, the rate of handling per man per hour was monitored, each port being compared with its previous performance on similar cargoes, in order to identify potential areas for improvements to personnel supervision and handling equipment.[77] This work reinvigorated the Docks Tonnage Programme, which allocated the ten ports in use by the BEF, amounts of material by type and specified whether it was to be moved from the quay by rail or road, or loaded directly to Inland Water Transport (IWT).[78] In February 1917, the weekly allocation to these ports was 168,599 tons. The table below shows the allocation for each port and clearly illustrates the scale of the logistic support to the BEF.

76 *The Railway Gazette*, p.37.

77 Ibid, pp.37-38.

78 IWT made a significant contribution to the BEF's transportation capability. Having been initiated in September 1915, by May 1916, it had moved over 400,000 tons and evacuated over 16,000 sick and wounded; TNA WO 95/56: Director of Inland Water Transport, 'Memo No 2, Inland Water Transport, 5 May 1916'. By the end of 1916, IWT was moving 100,000 tons per month using 564 vessels, mainly barges. TNA WO 95/56: Director of Inland Water Transport, 'Memo No 3, Inland Water Transport, December 1916' and 'Memo No 4, 29 April 1917'. IWT is another component of BEF logistics that requires greater exposure. For a recent academic assessment, see, Christopher Phillips, 'Logistics and the BEF: The Development of Waterborne Transport on the Western Front, 1914-1916', *British Journal of Military History*, Vol. 2, No 2 (2016), pp.42-58.

Table 9.1

BEF Ports – Weekly Tonnage Allocation: February 1917[79]

Port	Tonnage	Remarks
Boulogne	36,036	
Calais	23,614	
Cross-Channel Barge	2,661	No port discharge - movement by canal
Dieppe	13,877	
Dunkerque	21,750	
Etaples	Nil	
Fecamp	1,000	
Le Harve	24,998	All tank movement was via Le Harve
Rouen	42,588	
St Valery	1,940	General Supplies only
Treport	135	Fuel Supplies only
Total	**168,599 tons**	

Thirdly, the Mission resisted attempts to retain the compartmentalization of the three key In-Theatre surface transportation elements, rail, road and IWT, seeking to promote an integrated system by initiating the co-ordination of planning, resources and utilization.[80] There were however, limits to the capabilities of the consultants. They had an impressive knowledge of railway, dock and IWT operations and some in Horse Transport (HT) but the mass use of Mechanical Transport (MT) and especially Wheeled Motor Transport (WMT) was a process that few had any experience of. This was an area therefore, that the military had to learn through practical utilization on the ground although at GHQ, a consultant civil engineer was appointed to head the Roads Directorate.[81] Last but certainly not least, was the momentous decision for GHQ to accept responsibility for operating the rail LOC. This was the backbone of the BEF's transportation capability, which hitherto had been completely or partially delivered by Host Nation Support (HNS). The change was a step that on the one hand was gratefully agreed by the French but on the other, had very significant resource implications both in manpower,[82] training and equipment[83]

79 Compiled from figures in the Dock Tonnage Programme table in Henniker, BOH, *Transportation on the Western Front*, between pp.232-233.

80 The major railway companies of the period were complex commercial enterprises, the focus of which was the carriage of freight and passengers by rail. To support these activities, they operated road transport, hotels, ports and ships. For a contemporary introduction to their business, see *The Railway Year Book for 1913, The Whitaker of the Railway Service* (London: The Railway Publishing Company, 1913).

81 Brigadier-General (later Sir) Henry Percy Maybury GBE KCMG CB (1864-1943) was a civil engineer who was appointed the BEF's Director of Roads on 20 October 1916, retaining the post for the remainder of the war. His employment started with a five-year post in the Chief Engineer's Office of the Shrewsbury & Hereford Railway and his professional ability advanced him to become, in 1921, the first president of the Institute of Transport and, in 1933, the President of the Institute of Civil Engineers.

82 TNA WO 107/69: 'Report Upon the Work of the Quartermaster-General's Branch of the Staff and Directorates Controlled, British Armies in France and Flanders', Major G E Pitt (DAQMG GHQ) (Comp), pp.16-17. MEBE, p.600 (i), Table (iii), Military Railways, Personnel - All Theatres, Establishment and Strength of Railway Personnel Employed in the Various Theatres, quotes an Operating Personnel establishment of 15,744 and a strength of 14,224, for 1 June 1918, with a deficiency of 1,511.

83 At the beginning of 1915, the BEF's Railway Operating Division (ROD) had commenced operations with seven Standard Gauge Railway (SGR) locomotives loaned by the South Eastern & Chatham Railways (SECR) increasing to 59 locomotives and 675 personnel in December. By the Armistice in November 1918, the figures totalled

for the British.[84]

Time and Motion

These improvements focused upon ensuring the most effective use of existing equipment and resources through structural and cultural adjustments, whilst obtaining the necessary hardware from industry to generate the capability that was required. In this respect, Geddes fully comprehended the importance of 'Big Logistics' (Big L),[85] which generated the capability to deliver Theatre military logistics, 'Small L', at scale. As some of the initial additional equipment had to come from the railway companies rather than production, to oil the wheels, Geddes brought to France, senior railway managers so they could view the scale of the operations and of course, be exposed to the 'Geddes effect'.[86]

The missing aspect, was the technological logistic innovation which, would have revitalized the supply chain, especially for the secure distribution of smaller high value items, namely the transferable container, a capability that had appeared on the railways of Britain in 1849.[87] This commercial activity[88] was however, not translated into the military field, so an opportunity was lost to not only enhance logistic capability but also to reduce the need for labour.[89] The implementation of the Mission's recommendations marked a fundamental change in the manner in which, logistic operations were planned and conducted, an output received positively by the C-in-C.[90] The abolition of the IGC post, removed one of the potential primary challenges to streamlining Q operations within the BEF, whilst the new arrangements completed the rationalization of the

1,486 SGR locomotives and 18,500 personnel; TNA WO 107/69: 'Report Upon the Work of the Quartermaster-General's Branch of the Staff and Directorates Controlled, British Armies in France and Flanders', pp.16-17. MEBE, p.607, Table (i) Military Railways, Material and Traffic - France, Progress of Transportation in France since January 1917, records an average of 1,398 SGR locomotives in traffic for November 1918 and 1,421 for December. The difference from TNA WO 107/69 may be the total strength against those available for operations.

84 'Progress Report - Personnel Provided by the War Office, Week Ending 7th October 1916', Granet Papers, MRCUWL, GB 152, MSS.191/3/3/99.

85 'Big Logistics', 'Big L': the mobilization of industrial resources and production to support the defence requirement, with the interface with 'Small L' at Theatre level. 'Big L' is an American term, which neatly describes the activity. For an analysis of United States 'Big L' during the Second World War, see, Alan Gropman (Ed.) *The Big L, American Logistics in World War II* (Washington DC: National Defense University Press, 1997).

86 Marcosson, *Business of War*, p 276. Geddes also focused upon the deployment of railway specialist railway battalions from Canada.

87 For more details, see, Jack Simmons & Gordon Biddle (Eds.) *The Oxford Companion to British Railway History* (Oxford & New York: Oxford University Press (OUP), 1997), p.108.

88 The same occurred in the inter-war period. By 1939, new concepts of materiel handling were being introduced by the civil sector, albeit with some caution. The Big Four Railway Companies in the United Kingdom, prompted by increasing road haulage competition, used one ton containers on an increasing scale for rail-road inter-modal operations, whilst the Fork Lift Truck (FLT) began to appear on industrial premises. The introduction of the container for inter-modal transport in the United Kingdom began in the 1920s but once again, the military did not seize the opportunities it offered.

89 The introduction of the modern international inter-modal transportation container was a result of the innovation and initiative of the American road transport entrepreneur Malcom Purcell McLean. Commencing a coastal US service in 1956 using two converted tankers, his company Sea-Land was relatively slow to expand but attracted the attention of the US Government, which contracted it to operate a military container service to support operations in Vietnam. The concept expanded and has revolutionized international trade, particularly in reducing transportation costs, although there are under-developed countries where the infrastructure cannot support inter-modal operations and the distribution arrangements reflect this constraint, with manual labour being essential to output. See, Marc Levinson, *The Box: How the Shipping Container Made the World Smaller and the World Economy Bigger* (Princeton New Jersey: Princeton University Press, 2006).

90 Marcosson observed of one example of the step-change, 'Again you have the parallel with trade, because the whole enterprise is operated just as if it were the annex of a private business that must be conducted at maximum productivity and with the minimum overhead cost'; *Business of War*, p.126.

transportation structure at GHQ, thereby creating the opportunity to generate synergy between forecasting and delivery.

Eric Geddes[91] was also appointed as Director General of Military Railways (DGMR) at the War Office and he accepted the post on Thursday 21 September 1916. He worked as a Deputy to the Quartermaster General (QMG) drawing expressions of opposition from two members of the Army Council, a situation not defused by Geddes receiving the temporary, although honorary, rank of Major General.[92] On 22 September, Haig requested that Geddes be sent to France as Director-General Transportation (DGT)[93] at GHQ, which effectively created a fourth Principal Staff Officer,[94] ranking with the Chief of the General Staff (CGS) the Adjutant General (AG) and the QMG. DGT[95] was responsible for all the BEF's transportation services: Standard Gauge Rail (SGR) Narrow Gauge Rail (NGR)[96] IWT, road transport, and later, port operating. To complete the jigsaw, Geddes retained his post as DGMR at the War Office, which whilst appearing to have disadvantages, enabled him to co-ordinate resources at a national strategic level rather than a Theatre one; in today's terminology, Geddes was a 'Transportation Czar'. Geddes summarised the issue:

> In my opinion it is desirable that the transportation question as a whole should be placed under one selected man, he should be in touch with the man power and supply questions at home and with the transportation in France……There is no-one who can tell you throughout where his weak places are, or co-ordinate the policy and resources, present and future, of the various means of transit. It is not possible for the Commander-in-Chief or the Q.M.G. in France to do it; it is alone a big job for the best man you can find. [97]

Colonel A M Henniker of the Royal Engineers, during the Great War, Deputy Assistant Director (DAD) Railways in the BEF, summarized, post-war, the conditions of the appointment: 'He was specialist called in on an emergency to undertake a special task and given an exceptional position to enable him to perform it. While the emergency lasted the normal army organization had to be

91 Despite Geddes's important role in the development of his military railways in the BEF, most of correspondence and papers relating to this work have not survived. The Modern Records Centre (MRC) at the University of Warwick holds the Papers of Sir William Guy Granet for the period, which also contain a number of fascinating documents relating to Geddes and his work for the BEF, under the reference GB 152, MSS.191, which Granet's grand-daughter, Mrs David Yorke, deposited with the MRC in 1978. ADM 116 in the TNA contains seven volumes of Geddes's correspondence and thanks to the industry of Ian Malcolm Brown two or three letters have been found to relate to the BEF's transportation operations. See, Ian Malcolm Brown, *British Logistics on the Western Front, 1914-1919* (Westport Connecticut & London: Praeger, 1998), p.151, fn 1.

92 Geddes had a taste for military rank. In his political appointment as First Lord of the Admiralty, he carried the rank of Honorary Vice-Admiral.

93 Geddes had experience of working with the military. He was involved in planning troop movements on the Indian railways during the reinforcement of the North West Frontier in 1904 to repel a potential Russian invasion and was a member of the Railway Executive Committee (REC) in 1913-1914, responsible for advising the War Office on mobilization timetables. He was also a member of the Engineer and Railway Volunteer Staff Corps holding the substantive rank of Lieutenant-Colonel.

94 Sheffield & Bourne observe that Haig was initially dubious about Geddes' appointment but quickly came to appreciate his qualities; *Haig, War Diaries and Letters*, p.223, fn 1.

95 Ronald and Christensen have suggested that a military officer, Sir Edouard Percy Cranwill Girouard (1867-1932) KCMG DSO, who had significant colonial and industrial railway expertise, was proposed for the post. See, Colonel David Ronald (Retd) & Mike Christensen OBE, *The Longmoor Military Railway, A New History*, Vol. One: *1903-1939* (Lydney: Lightmoor Press, 2012), p.33.

96 For an examination of the NGR on the Western Front, see, TNA WO 158/852: History of the Light Railways. Examples of NGR wagons, motive power equipment and Permanent Way (PW) can be seen at the Imperial War Museum at Duxford in Cambridgeshire.

97 Initial report, Geddes to Lloyd George; Granet Papers, MRCUWL, GB 152, MSS.191/3/3/11-12.

altered to suit the circumstances. The arrangement he should have direct access to the C-in-C was made at the suggestion of the C-in-C himself'.[98] Post-war, the Assistant Director of Movements at the War Office[99] summarized Geddes' contribution:

> Sir Eric Geddes came over and saw what was wrong and devised the full organization for the transportation which was required. He linked up ports to railways, railways to roads, inland waterways to both. He secured the regulation of sea transport with direct reference to port capacities and to the possibilities of clearance from ports inland. He developed ports, railways, and roads by construction until they could reasonably be expected to carry out the work required by them, and he brought the whole under one unified control responsible for co-ordination of effort. He showed what transportation meant, and how each variation in one process of movement must inevitably have its effects on the others, and he secured from home men and plant, in sufficient quantities and of the right type to relieve the situation entirely both for us and our Allies.[100] Finally, he, as Director-General of Transportation, took command, got it into running order, and controlled its operations until it found its own feet.[101]

Lost though, in these analyses, is the constructive commercial hand of Sir George Stegmann Gibb,[102] whose view on controlling transportation conglomerates must have had a powerful influence upon Geddes. The NER history recorded: 'Sir George Gibb declared with all the force of experience and authority that there was no belief connected with railway policy and administration which he held with firmer confidence than that each great district, should, in the public interest, be served by one undertaking under one management, thereby securing the highest combination of efficiency with economy of effort'.[103]

With authority however, came responsibility, and Geddes was tasked with staffing the new directorate.[104] Not surprisingly, he recruited key civilian experts into the new organization, most of whom, were invested with temporary military rank.[105] Phillip Nash, late of the Great Northern

98 Henniker, BOH, *Transportation on the Western Front*, p.194.

99 Colonel M G Taylor CMG DSO.

100 Geddes' positive contribution to military logistics is lucidly illustrated by the expanding BEF railway capability. SGR locomotives increased from 401 in March 1917 to over 1400 by December 1918. In the same period, operating miles rose from 148 miles to 833; wagons in traffic from 10,546 to 52,494 and monthly loaded trains from 1,253 peaking at 1,931 in August 1918. MEBE, pp.606-607, Table (i) Progress of Transportation in France since January 1917.

101 Statement by Colonel M G Taylor CMG DSO, Assistant Director of Movements at the War Office, during his lecture on 'Land Transportation in the Late War' on Wednesday 5 October 1921 at the Royal United Service Institute, with the Quartermaster-General to the Forces, General Sir T E Clarke KCB KCMG in the Chair. The QMG makes no adverse comment on the statement during the post-presentation discussion, only reinforcing his experience as the BEF's QMG on the importance of co-ordinating transportation in order to create efficiencies, maximize resources and ensure economy, although by the time Clarke assumed his BEF appointment, Geddes had left and the transportation empire had been returned to the QMG bailiwick. As Clarke was Taylor's senior superior at the War Office, one must assume that he was in agreement with Taylor's position. 'Land Transportation in the Late War', pp.705-706 and pp.720-721.

102 For an examination of the positive role of Gibb in the NER, see, Cecil J Allen, *The North Eastern Railway* (London: Ian Allan, 1964), pp.231-234. Allen makes particular note of the 'team spirit' created by Gibb.

103 Tomlinson, *North Eastern Railway*, p.760.

104 Marcosson described Geddes as 'England's War Efficiency Engineer'; *Business of War*, p.258. Given his contribution to improving the effectiveness and efficiency of transportation operations on the Western Front, it is a strange co-incidence that the BOH, *Transportation on the West Front*, should be published in the same year as Geddes' death, 1937.

105 For an examination of the increase of experts in government during the Great War, see, J Turner, 'Experts and interests. David Lloyd George and the dilemmas of the expanding state, 1906-1919' in R MacLeod, *Government and Expertise: Specialists, Administrators and Professionals, 1860-1919* (Cambridge: Cambridge University Press

Railway (GNR) and East Indian Railways became Deputy Director–General of Transportation at GHQ, with the temporary rank of Brigadier-General. Sir Guy Granet, General Manager of the Midland Railway (MR)[106] was appointed Deputy Director General of Military Railways at the War Office, whilst Director Docks was R L Wedgewood, Chief Goods and Passenger Manager at the NER.

Functioning Friction or Creative Tension?

At face value, one might have expected considerable hostility between the military and commercial ethic but moderating influences had a positive effect. Friction with the General and QMG Staff in GHQ was, to an extent, reduced by the Directorate's location at Monthouis, which was known initially as 'Geddesburg' and then, when Phillip Nash took over, 'Nashville'.[107] The Unity of Purpose in delivering logistic capability was clearly significant, as indeed was the arrangement by which, commercial managers had been loaned to the State from their companies and were therefore, sufficiently divorced from their commercial allegiances for them to be part of the military logistic team. In addition, the approximately 100 Royal Engineer and civilian transportation officers who worked in this geographically distanced Directorate never seriously challenged the position of the traditional mainstream non-technical officer corps based at GHQ Main Montreuil and were therefore, able to execute their tasks with relatively little interference from them.[108]

The involvement of commercial business managers in controlling high-level military logistic operations, whilst necessary, was received with little enthusiasm in some parts of the military bureaucracy. The Director of Movements at the War Office, Brigadier-General A R Montagu-Stuart-Wortley,[109] an officer who should, professionally, have been focused on a creating a close working relationship with Geddes, had, according to Lord Derby, an intense dislike of him.[110] In a broader sense, the interface between military officers and commercial managers was neatly summarized by the Military Attache in Paris, Colonel Le Roy-Lewis who wrote on 8 November 1916, to Lloyd George, informing him that: 'You can never get over military prejudices. The

CUP, 1988), p.206.

106 Sir William Guy Granet GBE (1867-1943) was unusual as a senior railway manager, having graduated from Balliol College Oxford in Modern History in 1889 before being called to the bar in 1893 and entered railway management having held the post of Secretary to the Railway Companies Association from 1900-1905. Appointed as Assistant General Manager of the Midland Railway (MR) in 1905, he was appointed General Manager in 1906 upon the resignation of the incumbent, John Mathieson. Whilst revolutionizing heavy freight operations and concomitantly its profit, his traffic control solutions impeded MR locomotive development, much to its, and the railway's, future detriment. He became Deputy Chairman of the London Midland & Scottish Railway upon grouping in 1923 and its Chairman, 1924-1927.

107 Major-General Phillip Nash CB (later Sir) did not hold the dual appointment of DGMR and DGT BEF, being assigned only to the second post.

108 There was always the potential for friction. In GSO, *GHQ*, p.228, Fox observed that the QMG, Lieutenant-General Sir Travers Clarke, who assumed the post in December 1917, 'did not like about him, men however clever, who had not seen fighting'.

109 Brigadier-General A R Montagu-Stuart-Wortley late KRRC had, pre-war, been the Assistant Director of Movements in QMG 2 and was a key staff officer crafting the With-France plan. He was appointed to command 68th Brigade in 23rd Division in February 1917 and was temporary GOC 19th Division April - May 1917 and then 32nd Division in June. Whether though, an infantry officer was best suited the post of Director of Movements within the arena of enhanced transportation professionalism and commercialisation is a fair question. Knighted in 1918 for his services in Mesopotamia as DQMG, he retired from the Army, as a Lieutenant-General, in 1927. His papers for 1916 are held at Warwick University Modern Records Centre in GB 152, MSS.191/3/4/20-29. His older brother, Major-General The Honourable Edward James Montagu-Stuart-Wortley CB CMG DSO MVO, was dismissed from command of the 46th (North Midland) Division as a result of its failure on 1 July 1916, although the decision remains controversial; see, Alan MacDonald, A *Lack of Offensive Spirit?* (Iona Books, 2008).

110 House of Lords Record Office, Lloyd George MSS E1/1/6 Lord Derby to Lloyd George, 15 September 1916; quoted in Grieves, 'The Transportation Mission to GHQ', *Look to Your Front*, p.71.

appointment of anyone who does not belong to the military Trade Union is as welcome to soldiers, as the appointment of a bishop drawn from the ranks of stockbrokers would be to the clergy.'[111]

In this respect, the Officers' Trade Union[112] in GHQ had, at first, rather been given to cold-shouldering the dilutees from the Territorial Force and New Army who were posted there, on the basis that they had not undertaken their apprenticeship, nor indeed paid their union fees.[113] No doubt similar feelings arose, when commercial staff appeared, especially when they received military rank.[114] The creation of a Fourth Directorate, outside the scope and control of the QMG, brought a raft of adverse comment from the War Office and staff officers within GHQ. The BEF's QMG, Lieutenant-General Sir Ronald Maxwell[115] argued that neither he, nor his Staff, could be held responsible for the maintenance of the Army unless he controlled the transportation system and he noted that *Field Service Regulations* supported his position.[116] Haig, determined that improvement could only be effected by Geddes having the authority to deliver all the relevant changes throughout the relevant components, was clear that DGT would not be subordinated to QMG, and Sir Ronald tendered his resignation,[117] although Haig chose not to accept it and opted to clarify their respective responsibilities,[118] recording, with one suspects, more than a little annoyance but certainly crystal practicality:

> There is a good deal of criticism apparently being made at the appointment of a civilian like Geddes to an important post in the Army. These critics seem to fail to realise the size of this Army, and the amount of work which the Army requires of a civilian nature. The workings of the railways, the upkeep of the roads, even the baking of bread and 1000 other industries go on in peace as well as in war![119] So, with the whole nation at war, our object should be to employ men on the same work in war as they are accustomed to in peace. Acting on this principle, I have got Geddes at the head of all the railways and transportation with the best practical engineers under him. At the head of the road directorate is Mr Maybury, head of the road board in England. The docks, canals etc are being managed in the same way i.e. by men of practical experience. To put soldiers into such positions, merely because they are generals and colonels, would be to ensure failure![120]

Haig's support for the introduction of civilian advisors was revolutionary enough but to grant them executive positions within the command structure, and with military ranks, was an incredible

111 Quoted in, Ibid, p.68.

112 It is instructive to see Colonels referring to organized labour in their correspondence and memoirs, and associating terminology from it with their own profession. Whether this is a subtle recognition of its importation into the military, especially in the logistics arena, or whether it illustrates that Colonels were cognizant of the fact that they too, as part of the Regular Officer Corps, had interests and status to protect and needed to act as a Corporate Body, could be an interesting area of research.

113 GSO, *GHQ*, p.182.

114 Fox, in GHQ, recorded: 'Brigadier-General-----------, the eminent expert in------------, who became a General very suddenly, was reported to around partly in dreadful, partly in proud anticipation of a guard turning out for him when he wandered from GHQ area'; Ibid, p.182.

115 For an review of Maxwell's time as QMG, see, na, 'Lt-General Sir R Maxwell, QMG, BEF, France, Jan 1915 - Dec 1917', *Royal Army Service Corps Quarterly*, Vol. 13 (December 1924), pp.536-542.

116 FSR, Part II, Chp III, Functions of the Forces in the Field, pp.44-48.

117 Maxwell remained as QMG until he was replaced by Lieutenant-General Sir Travers Edwards Clarke GBE KCB KCMG (1871-1962) who served as QMG to the BEF until 1921. Commissioned into the Royal Inniskilling Fusiliers in 1890, Clarke's last appointment was on the Army Council as QMG to the Forces. He retired from the Army in 1926.

118 Diary, Monday 30 October 1916, Sheffield & Bourne, *Haig, War Diaries and Letters*, p.249.

119 Haig, like many of his contemporaries, was promiscuous with the use of the exclamation mark!

120 Diary, Friday 27 October 1916, Sheffield & Bourne, *Haig, War Diaries and Letters*, pp.248-249.

action, which not only ruffled a few feathers but also, for many senior officers, placed the fox firmly in the chicken coop. The QMG to the Forces, General John Cowans,[121] was certainly of this view; his biographers, summarized his position:

> It is quite another matter with supplying armies in the field. That can only successfully be done by a Staff Officer who knows intimately every branch of the service, the special and peculiar needs of every section of the Army, and the exact conditions under which they carry out their work. No civilian can possibly know all this........Moreover, the good Staff Officer must have himself been a serving soldier and, as such, seen all these problems from the point of view of the serving soldier and the Commanding Officer in the field.[122]

In terms of logistics in operational formations at Army level or below, Cowans was absolutely correct in his assessment but at the Theatre level, Haig was equally so. Cowans however, was certainly not adverse to civilian advisors as the efficiency of the army postal service, the veterinary corps and the clothing department all bore testimony to his use of them in a consultancy role, although he rebuffed the suggestion that Geddes investigate railway operations in France during January 1915;[123] had he taken a more positive tack, efficiencies and thereby effectiveness could probably have been generated much earlier.[124] The issue was however, subject to the influence of internal military politics. The proposal to despatch Geddes, a civilian, in 1915 had been preceded by a review by a military railway officer,[125] Brigadier-General[126] Sir E P C Girouard,[127] under the direction of Lord Kitchener. Girouard's report elicited a very cool response from Maxwell, the IGC and Robertson, the BEF's QMG:[128] "In my opinion it would have been well if Sir P Girouard had

121 General Sir John Stephen 'Jack' Cowans GCB GCMG (1862-1921) was commissioned into the Rifle Brigade in 1881 and died in 1921 as a result of complications arising from a kidney operation. He was the only member of the Army Council to remain in post throughout the Great War, serving as QMG between 1912 and 1919. His biographers summarized his contribution to the British Army during the Great War thus: 'No Quartermaster in history is even faintly comparable to him in achievement', Major Desmond Chapman-Huston & Major Owen Rutter, *General Sir John Cowans, GCB GCMB, The Quartermaster General of the Great War*, Vols I & II (London: Hutchinson, 1924), Vol. II, p.324. Sir Arthur Yapp, Director of the YMCA, described him as a 'genial autocrat'; Ibid, p.250. Jack Cowans was a most interesting character and a very able administrator, whose industrious contribution to the British Army's capability during the Great War has, effectively, been forgotten; his time as QMG certainly deserves a modern study. See also, RHB, 'Sir John Cowans, The Greatest Quartermaster General', *Royal Army Service Corps Quarterly*, Vol. 13 (April 1925), pp.189-197 and for a short recent reappraisal of his life, particularly as QMG, see, Keith Grieves' examination in the *Oxford Dictionary of National Biography* (Oxford: OUP, 2004).

122 Chapman-Huston & Rutter, *Quartermaster General of the Great War*, Vol. II, p.206.

123 Ibid, p.102.

124 Marcosson clearly ascribes the proposal for Geddes to visit France in January 1915 to Kitchener and equally its failure to mature, to the 'Red Tape Octopus' squeezing out his scheme; Marcosson, *Business of War*, p.267.

125 CONFIDENTIAL, 'Report upon Rail Transport arrangements of the British Army on the Continent' by Brigadier-General Sir E P C Girouard in TNA WO 32/5144.

126 In Cowans biography and Major-General (Ed.) H L Pritchard, *History of the Corps of Royal Engineers*, Vol. V, Girouard is ranked as a Colonel, whilst in TNA WO 32/5144 and Henniker, BOH, *Transportation on the Western Front*, he is graded as a Brigadier-General. He reached the rank of Major-General, when he was appointed as Director War Office Munitions in 1916. See, Ronald & Christensen, *The Longmoor Military Railway*, Vol. I, p.33.

127 Sir Edouard Percy Cranwill Girouard (1867-1932) KCMG DSO was a Canadian railway engineer commissioned into the Royal Canadian Engineers and then, in 1888, to the Royal Engineers. Posted to 10 Company RE at Woolwich, he was appointed the Traffic Manager of the Woolwich Arsenal Railway (1890-1895) before impressing Kitchener during the Sudan campaigns, the demanding railway construction projects for which he was responsible, delivering military success. President of Egyptian State Railways and Alexandria Harbour in 1898, he was Director of Imperial Military Railways in South Africa during the Boer War, followed by Colonial Office appointments until 1912 when he took a commercial appointment as the Director of the Elswick Works of Armstrong Whitworth, remaining until after the Great War except for brief military or government attachments, mainly initiated by Kitchener. For a resume of his military career, see, Ronald & Christensen, *Longmoor Military Railway*, Vol. One, pp.25-33.

128 Girouard may have irritated Maxwell and Robertson but he was an experienced railway engineer and operator,

restricted himself to what he was told to do. He has far exceeded his instructions. He was not told to produce a scheme for uprooting organisations deliberately laid down after deep deliberation."[129]

As a result of this, it is understandable that Cowans chose to stay his hand in pushing a Geddes-style review at this point. There was also another factor because in the background there was a potentially more sinister issue because Cowans became increasingly concerned that it was the intention of Ministers to replace the military QMG with a civilian head or place the Department within a Commission,[130] which might explain his strong opposition to the concept of imported civilian managers from commerce or government departments who were not directly subordinate to military command.[131] Haig though, did have a strong hand, not only because of his appointment as C-in-C and the challenges the BEF's were grappling with but also because in 1916, the civilian managers he was proposing for the posts were not fast track whizz-kids but men who had acquired practical experience in the rough and tumble of their business, although in a sense, this scenario created an even greater concern for Cowans.[132] If the railways functioned more effectively under imported civilian management than military leadership, the imperative to civilianize the control of QMG responsibilities in the War Office would almost certainly increase.[133]

The War Office though, was determined that DGT would be subordinated to the QMG and a struggle ensued between it and the C-in-C. Timing is said to be everything and the War Office senior staff believed that the appointment of a regular Royal Engineer officer, Major-General Crookshank,[134] to the post of DGT BEF,[135] was an opportune moment to resolve the issue. In June 1918, the Army Council issued a letter to Haig informing him of the new command arrangements based on the premise that the control of all the relevant resources must be vested in the officer responsible for the maintenance of the army in the field, namely QMG BEF. Haig replied, commenting that whilst he agreed in principle with the proposal, it was not timely to enact it. Pressured by the Army Council, GHQ promulgated a note informing Army Staffs of the forthcoming change but noting a delay, whilst organizational changes were confirmed.[136] There, the matter rested; a Civil Service solution, delivered by a military man to sustain a commercial creation.

whose principles generated success in many transportation arenas. His report exposed a whole series of issues that matured later as the BEF expanded but as Chapman-Huston and Rutter observe in Cowan's biography, the issue was rather less the report's content and rather more that neither the IGC nor the QMG were ready for change, combined with their distrust of interference from the War Office. See, Chapman-Huston & Rutter, *Quartermaster General of the Great War*, Vol. II, p.102.

129 Letter from Maxwell to Robertson, dated 17 October 1914 in TNA WO 32/5144: 'Report upon Rail Transport arrangements of the British Army on the Continent'. Robertson attached a covering letter to Cowans dated 23 October 1914. There may also have been some antipathy because Girouard was a 'Kitchener Man'.

130 Chapman-Huston & Rutter, *Quartermaster General of the Great War*, Vol. II, p.163, p.206 & p.324.

131 That a Business Manager was installed in the War Office working in parallel with him cannot have made Cowans feel any more comfortable, although he appears to have outwardly accepted the appointment in order to ensure the Army was appropriately supported; Ibid, pp.199-200.

132 Cowans's biography, especially Vol. II, covering his time as QMG, although dated, is for logisticians, compelling reading because it gives a very powerful feel for not only the depth and breadth of his appointment and its immense global responsibilities but also exposes a remarkable level of logistic detail and his gracious personal touch.

133 Chapman-Huston and Rutter, noted: 'A very slender knowledge of recent history would have served to remind the supporters of the civilian idea that in the old days, before the establishment of the Army Service Corps, the Supply department had not only never been a success but had developed into a scandal'; *Quartermaster General of the Great War*, Vol. II, p.206.

134 Sir Sydney D'Aguilar Crookshank KCMG CB CIE DSO MVO (1870-1941) was a RE officer with colonial and Indian Army experience, including service with the Indian Public Works Department. He had meteoric promotion during the war, being a Major in May 1915, commanding the 2nd Indian Field Squadron, and, when he was appointed Chief Engineer of XV Corps in January 1917, Brigadier-General. In his diary, Haig spells the name as Cruickshank.

135 19 March 1918; Major A F (Retd) Becke (Comp) BOH, *Order of Battle*, Part 4, *The Army Council, GHQs, Armies and Corps, 1914-1918* (London: HMSO, 1945), p.12.

136 Henniker, BOH, *Transportation on the Western Front*, pp.195-197.

The military and civilian staff of DGT made a very major contribution to the capability of the BEF; indeed, without their forethought, innovation and planning, the war would almost certainly have continued much longer, with all the concomitant adverse military, economic and social consequences that would have followed. Haig was clearly enthused by the success of the organization, writing in his diary in August 1917,

> Everything has gone extremely well. The number of trains to rail-head has increased to an excessive number: 30 more per diem than we had calculated for, and told the French we would want!'. The number is now 220 per diem, in addition to L of C trains. To avoid the risk of breakdown, he is reducing the number of trains to what can be reasonably be run. I agreed of course.....[137]

As an illustration of the immense tasks the Directorate underwrote, the table below lists the tonnages of all the key weekly imports to the BEF from the UK and abroad in February 1917, all of which had to be moved from the ports to depots and divisions. Ammunition accounted for 27 percent of the weight; as a comparison, the tonnage of ammunition shipped to the Gulf during Operation GRANBY in 1990-91 was 76,000,[138] the equivalent of 11.6 days total material shipments to the BEF in February 1917.

Table 9.2

BEF Average Weekly Key Materiel Import Tonnage – February 1917[139]

Materiel	Tonnage	Remarks
General Supplies	56,742	
Fuel	11,468	Solid & Liquid
Coal	4,500	For railways and IWT operations
Ordnance Stores	8,500	
Tanks	270	10 tanks
MT Equipment	693	
Expeditionary Forces Canteens	2,000	
Ammunition	45,800	
RE Stores (General)	9,000	
Timber (RE)	9,000	
Timber (Railway Construction)	8,000	
Medical & Veterinary Stores	165	
Railway Track	11,500	
Aviation Material	800	For Royal Flying Corps
Inland Water Transport Stores	91	
Explosives	70	By Cross Channel Barge Service
Total	**168,599 tons**	

137 Diary entry, relating to a discussion with DGT, Major-General Philip Nash, Tuesday 7 August 1917, in Sheffield & Bourne, *Douglas Haig, War Diaries*, p.311. Haig thought highly of Nash's professional capabilities.

138 Nigel Pearce, *The Shield and the Sabre, The Desert Rats in the Gulf 1990-91* (London: HMSO, 1992), p.26, states a figure of 80,000 tons. The MOD, QMG Ops & Plans calculation provided for the publication was 76,000; author's memory.

139 Docks Tonnage Programme table in Henniker, BOH, *Transportation on the Western Front*, between pp.232-233.

Full Circle

The involvement of commercial business managers in controlling military logistic operations was a revolutionary concept in 1916. What is remarkable though, is the acceptance of the C-in-C in not only implementing new ideas and command arrangements but also sustaining them for so long against opposition from senior advisors in his HQ and the War Office. The introduction of the DGT provided though, the bridge between the industrial base in the United Kingdom and the operational forces in France and Belgium, thereby creating the final conduit for the process of 'Factory to Fire-Trench'.[140] Whilst not involved in procurement, DGT's Staff were essential to creating the conditions to move the results of production and DGT acquired the necessary expertize, communications and authority to ensure an effective result.

DGT's Staff were the first to grapple with strategic logistic planning, reaching out to ensure the resources were there to meet the task, even if the activity was 12 months ahead. This process was a fundamental change to what had been an unwritten military policy, which functioned on the minimum and the ad-hoc. Geddes was clear that war on a national industrial scale could not be effectively conducted with a minimalist approach and clearly Haig took the same view. He and his Staff used statistics and data to assess performance, and to re-allocate equipment and manpower, whilst other key processes, which have become fundamental military principles, were also driven forward by the DGT Staff. 'Can Consignee Accept' was a critical question if unloading in France was to be efficient, whilst the issue of ships' cargo manifests in advance was an essential factor in enabling meaningful material movement planning to be enacted. In turn, this returned the port areas to their transit function, speeded transportation to the depots and reduced the numbers of railway wagons being utilized for storage. All these activities are as important today, as they were in 1918.

For political, military and financial reasons, logisticians rarely have the opportunity to practise their skills and develop their experience to meet the contingencies of a major deployment, and many have to learn on the job;[141] as true in 2018 as it was in 1914. Commerce though, played a key role in creating training opportunities in this environment. Ports, road haulage, railway companies and major supply distributors all offered exposure to scale, which the Army could rarely match on a regular basis, then as now. Whilst business practice may or not be pertinent to deployed operations, the Army relies on industrial output and commercial support to deliver its capability, and logisticians should always be ready to assess whether new systems might be applied to enhance effectiveness.

The logisticians of 1914 did a spectacular job in deploying and supporting the regular BEF but were overwhelmed by its subsequent rapid expansion. In this respect, whilst the organization may have required restructuring and reorientation, many of the senior logistic officers were capable professional officers who knew their business, albeit that they had to gain the experience of scale at a time of rapid expansion, which inevitably created demanding challenges and in some cases over-faced the incumbents. In 1917, an independent observer remarked of the BEF's Director of Transport: 'General Boyce[142] is a fine type of the clear-cut efficiency that you invariably discover in the high executive British Army places'[143] and of the Director of Supply, 'Like his stalwart colleague,

140 Geddes had clearly articulated this issue in his initial report: 'It is beyond argument there is today no one who controls the continuous transit from this country to the front'. Initial report, Geddes to Lloyd George in Granet Papers, MRCUWL, GB 152, MSS.191/3/3/12.

141 The Gulf Wars of 1990-91 and 2003 are recent examples but in logistic terms are insignificant in comparison to the BEF. See, Major General M S White (Ed.) *Gulf Logistics, Blackadder's War* (London: Brassey's, 1995).

142 Brigadier-General W G B Boyce late ASC, assumed the appointment of Director of Transport on 30 November 1914 and remained in post for the rest of the war; Becke, *Order of Battle*, Part 4, p.13.

143 Marcosson clearly knew his man because the post-war Royal Army Service Corps regimental history recorded of him, 'a strong and able organiser, who possessed that merit somewhat rare in the British Army of knowing when

General E E Carter,[144] who rules the Domain of Supply,[145] he is a graduate and member in good standing of the Army Service Corps - a conspicuous figure in the Army Behind the Army'.[146] Clearly, such individuals must have favourably impressed a man who, whilst perhaps tasked with placing a constructive spin on British achievements, was lucidly conversant with the concept of 'Big L' and thus unlikely to have over promoted their abilities.

Conclusion

The effective use of resources will always be a challenge because in many situations the process of retaining critical mass will be fragile and the capability to deliver expansion disappears. The devil may be in the detail but at a national level, logistics is about economies of scale. In two years, the BEF's logisticians, under the guiding hand of Geddes and his successors, moved from the tactical solutions to which they were wedded because they lacked the correct resources and were afraid to ask for them, to delivering logistic support on a massive scale at a strategic level. Indeed, the reverse became true, with significant requests for men and equipment and Geddes sometimes adding a round figure.[147]

Historians may assess that it was the ability of Geddes, Haig and the GHQ logistic Staff to start 'Thinking Big' that created the solution to the BEF's logistic problems but it was not so much the thought that solved the problem, than the delivery and there must be a clear case that the influence of George Stegmann Gibb and the operations of North Eastern Railway did more for the British Army in France than they have ever been given credit for.[148] Haig stands tall in the arena; not only did he take the risk of accepting civilian advisors, against a background of potential intrigue but was prepared to place suitably qualified non-military people into senior Director appointments in order to bring coherency and focus to a critical area. His vision in accepting that the specific logistic components of the BEF had as much to do with commercial industrial output as it had with tactical soldiering placed him at odds with those who viewed the issues from a solely military perspective.

to dismiss subordinates, who, however agreeable in other respects, did not satisfy him professionally'; Colonel R H Beadon, CBE psc, *The Royal Army Service Corps, A History of Transport and Supply in the British Army*, Vol. II (Cambridge: CUP, 1931), p.86.

144 Brigadier-General E E Carter was another long-serving appointee, commencing his service in the post on 27 January 1915. He was a pre-war contributor to the logistic debate including an article on the new transport system: Lieutenant-Colonel, E E Carter CMG MVO psc ASC, 'The New Transport System: its Principles and their Application', *Journal of the Army Service Corps* (May 1912), pp.671-707 and 'The Services of Maintenance in the Field: Some Object Lessons from the Army Exercise 1913', *The Army Review*, Volume VI, No 2 (April 1914), War Office, pp.471-489.

145 Becke, *Order of Battle*, Part 4, p.13, notes that the appointments of Director Transport and Director Supply were ranked as Brigadier, although other sources clearly state both officers held the rank of Major-General. Becke, BOH, *Order of Battle, Part 4*, p.13 states Brigadier-General, whilst Marcosson, *Business of War*, notes Major-General. More definitively, in 1918, Brigadier-General F M Wilson (promoted in post from Colonel on 16 October 1917) the Deputy Director Supplies & Transport (DDST) Fourth Army records Boyce as a Major-General; TNA WO 95/454/4: HQ Fourth Army, A&Q, war diary, entry 12 October 1918. Boyce was knighted for his services. Temporary and Acting rank was common throughout the BEF in the Great War and promotion, sometimes to substantive rank, likewise; these arrangements usually account for such differences in the sources.

146 Marcosson, *Business of War*, p.127.

147 See, T Jones, *Lloyd George* (Oxford: OUP, 1951), p.74 and also, TNA WO 32/5145: 'Preliminary Statement of personnel necessary to carry out light railway recommendations of the Commander-in-Chief', E Geddes, 26 September 1916.

148 Given Stegmann's significant contribution to the development of NER operations, the company history was rather measured in its summary of his work; 'By his readiness to carry out new ideas and modern methods, he made his personality felt, not only on the North Eastern but throughout a much wider area, and.....under his vigorous management, many improvements in working were successfully introduced'; Tomlinson, *North Eastern Railway*, p.726. As the history was published in 1914, the author could not know how prophetic his words were to be.

10

Four Wheels on my Wagon

The influence of Wheeled Motor Transport upon British Army operations on the Western Front 1914-1918

Introduction

Wheeled Motor Transport (WMT) was not a war-winner on its own[1] but it supported components of the All-Arms battle, particularly infantry and artillery that were.[2] The contribution it made to the Allied victory was certainly a most significant one, and one that could not have been achieved without the relevant synergy between headquarters, units, logisticians and most importantly, industry. Many aspects of the British Expeditionary Force's (BEF) developing operational art on the Western Front have been examined but the influence of WMT has not been the subject of a widely published assessment.[3]

Much was achieved in the period 1900-1914,[4] with expansion and progression in the military and civil sectors at a pace that equalled that of aviation.[5] The introduction of WMT to replace the horse was initially slow but there were logical reasons for this approach. Significant funding for the development of WMT awaited assessments of its potential, and, until 1910, the emphasis on motive power for large road goods vehicles in the civil sector vehicles was steam, although the War Office Mechanical Transport Committee (MTC)[6] was not convinced that this was the most

1 Referring to WMT, as well as a number of supporting military mechanically driven systems, Haig noted: 'Immense as the influence of mechanical devices might be, they cannot by themselves decide a campaign'; Lieutenant-Colonel J H Boraston OBE (Ed.), *Sir Douglas Haig's Despatches, December 1915 - April 1919* (London: J M Dent & Sons, 1919), p.330.

2 For a detailed examination of how these systems were integrated and controlled, see, Tim Travers, *How The War Was Won, Command and Technology on the Western Front 1917-1918* (London: Routledge, 1992).

3 For technical details of vehicle types, see, David Fletcher, *British Military Transport 1829-1956* (London: The Stationery Office, 1998), pp.27-41.

4 TNA WO 161/7: History of Military Mechanised Transport.

5 Whilst there were many high profile events demonstrating the capability of WMT, there was an unseen but nonetheless significant expansion in the commercial arena, in which the Army took a growing interest. Cars were first used by the Army in 1901 and proved sufficiently successful, for the War Office to authorize, in 1903, the establishment of the first Army Service Corps (ASC) Mechanical Transport (MT) Company (Number 77) and the formation of the Motor Volunteer Corps (MVC). In 1904, 78 MT Company ASC formed in Aldershot, and the MVC became established for 40 motor-cycles, although with the progression of MT in the Regular Army, the MVC was disbanded in 1906. The War Office procured the first Motor Ambulance in 1906 and the concept of the MVC was revived upon the formation of the Territorial Force (TF) in 1908, when some of its members joined the Army Motor Reserve (AMR), which was established in the Special Reserve (SR). For more details, see, Colonel R H Beadon, CBE psc, *The Royal Army Service Corps, A History of Transport and Supply in the British Army*, Vol. II (Cambridge: Cambridge University Press (CUP), 1931) and Michael Young, *Army Service Corps 1902-1918* (Barnsley: Leo Cooper, 2008).

6 The War Office Mechanical Transport Committee (MTC) was formed during the Boer War and consisted of representatives from the Royal Artillery, Royal Engineers and the Army Service Corps, with four sub-committees reporting to it. MTC annual reports are held by the Royal Logistic Corps Museum.

effective future military system.[7] Whilst the engineers, inventors and enthusiasts plied their ideas and equipment, the MTC authorized various experiments and trials to test the concept of utilizing WMT for military operations, including the deployment of motor ambulances to Garrisons[8] and 30 cwt lorries for the Royal Flying Corps (RFC),[9] a developing Arm, which was determined, culturally and technologically, not to be bound by the past but to be driven by the vision of the future.

Early Days

Before the Great War, the British Army conducted several high profile exercises and smaller trials in the United Kingdom involving Mechanical Transport (MT). Over the weekend of Saturday 19 - Sunday 20 December 1908, 500 Territorial Force (TF)[10] soldiers were moved by 24 buses of the London General Omnibus Company, from Warley in Essex, to Shoeburyness,[11] to oppose an to an imaginary hostile landing on the Thames Estuary.[12] Whilst the newly formed TF and the WMT performed well, officials in the War Office were concerned to discover that all the buses were of European manufacture; for Senior Army Officers of a nation that was the centre of the British Empire, this must have come as an uncomfortable surprise. In March 1909, the Automobile Association (AA)[13] staged an interesting operation, in which 500 hundred of their members, driving 316 private cars,[14] moved a composite battalion from the Brigade of Guards, from London to Hastings, with unit baggage being transported in 21 lorries from Napier & Sons. Whilst march discipline left much to be desired, the spectacle of 337 motor vehicles,[15] in several convoys, must have been inspiring to planners, participants and onlookers, whilst also generating much positive publicity for the AA.

The 1910 Annual Army Manoeuvres (AAM) were a milestone in the development of Army MT[16] because the exercises confirmed that steam power imposed tactical fragile constraints upon

7 The Internal Combustion Engine (ICE) was a potentially interesting solution but in the period 1900-1908, the War Office technical advisers assessed petrol and paraffin ICE capability to be effectively unreliable for military employment and the diesel engine had yet to be accepted by the motor industry in the United Kingdom. It was not until around 1909-1910 that an effective petrol ICE power-plant, capable of hauling heavy loads, proved itself, but petrol and paraffin were not readily available, nor was expertize to operate the equipment. Water and coal though, were plentiful, as was the skilled labour to operate and maintain the steam equipment; those tasked with making recommendations and taking decisions had therefore, a series of often conflicting issues to consider, much of which related to technology and systems of which, they had little, if no, experience.

8 Before the Great War, the provision of motor ambulances was surprisingly high on the War Office list of priorities, and by 1911, the following garrisons had them: Aldershot, Bulford, Curragh, Devonport, Edinburgh, Malta, and Portsmouth.

9 For an examination of pre-war British military aviation, see, Walter Raleigh, *BOH, The War in the Air, Being the Story of The part played in the Great War by the Royal Air Force*, Vol. I (Oxford: Clarendon Press, 1922) and Hugh Driver, *The Birth of British Military Aviation: Britain 1903-1914*, The Royal Historical Society (Woodbridge: The Boydell Press, 1997).

10 Consisting of 14 divisions, the Territorial Force (TF) was, after considerable opposition, formed on 1 April 1908, from the Volunteer and Yeomanry components of the Auxiliary Forces, with the Militia being disbanded, although on occasions the complete strength of a Militia unit transferred to the Special Reserve. See, the first annual return of the TF, *The Annual Return of the Territorial Force for the Year 1908,* Command 4496 (London: HMSO, 1909).

11 Shoebury Garrison was an important military facility in the town. Much of the infrastructure has been sympathetically redeveloped for residential use, although Defence retains a contracted munitions test and evaluation facility, including proofing ranges, within the Ministry of Defence (MOD) Shoeburyness site.

12 Beadon, *Royal Army Service Corps*, p.33. Each bus carried 26 men and their equipment and officers noted the potential for buses to evacuate casualties.

13 Beadon, *Royal Army Service Corps*, p.33.

14 Ibid, p.33, states 316. Fletcher in *British Military Transport*, p.17 based upon photographic evidence, suggests 500 cars moving 1,000 soldiers. Based on three soldiers per car instead of two, 316 could have provided the lift.

15 Or 521, if Fletcher, rather than Beadon is correct.

16 For details of ASC vehicles by type in service in 1910, see, Young, *Army Service Corps 1902-1918*, Annex F, pp.220-225.

military road transport operations.[17] Not only did the glare from fireboxes and sparks from smoke-stacks attract the attention of the opposing forces but it could take an hour to steam up once boiler fires were drawn. Clearly, such limitations might impose significant operational constraints but expediency outlived this perspective during the Great War because steam vehicles were deployed to the Western Front until the end of the conflict.[18] Whilst Steam Transport (ST) vehicles did a splendid job in supporting road repair and heavy haulage in the rear areas, there were problems in provisioning water, and during the German offensive of March 1918 the tactical limitations were lucidly exposed. Another key factor was that Spark Ignition (SI) ICE had become the power-plant of choice in the civil sector.[19] SI ICEs were improving in reliability and power, whilst petrol had become increasingly available, resulting it being the principal fuel used by the commercial haulage industry, public transport and private cars. In the light of these developments, the MTC recommended that not only should the British Army make a radical change in the type of Mechanical Transport (MT)[20] to be employed in the service but also that a commitment be made, to a programme, which would almost completely mechanize the Army,[21] despite the small industrial base in the UK producing such vehicles, exacerbated by the almost complete absence of component manufacturers.[22] The idea was therefore, a most significant proposal, especially as the horse was the major player in the Nation's road transport system;[23] indeed, Horse Transport (HT) moved, at some point in its transit, at least 85 percent of the United Kingdom's freight.[24] Indeed, the conceptual risk that the Army Council took is lucidly illustrated by the use of MT by the commercial railway companies; even in 1918 the combined MT fleet totalled only 191 units,

17 The 1910 exercises also exposed defects in the Subsidy Scheme, on which the bulk of mobilized military MT was to be obtained. Many of the vehicles were poorly maintained, and there was little standardization, and almost no spares. If the Subsidy Scheme was to be militarily effective, standards and incentives needed to be addressed.

18 In November 1918 the BEF (excluding the RAF) had on strength, 725 x steam lorries and 65 x steam tractors; War Office, *Statistics of the Military Effort of the British Empire during the Great War, 1914-1920* (MEBE), (HMSO, 1922), p.595, Table (i) (a) - Monthly Census of Mechanical Transport Vehicles in All Theatres.

19 For a resume of UK civil motor transport development in the pre-Great War period, see, Philip S Bagwell, *The Transport Revolution from 1770* (London: B T Batsford, 1974), pp.199-208.

20 Wheeled, tracked, or semi-tracked land vehicle utilised in a logistic context to move men and materiel to, on or from the battlefield and powered by the Internal Combustion Engine (ICE) either Spark Ignition (SI) or Compression Ignition (CI) fuelled by petroleum spirit or diesel oil respectively, or by steam (Steam Transport (ST)). Often abbreviated to MT, it does not include combat vehicles, such as tanks, Armoured Personnel Carriers (APC) or Self-Propelled Guns (SPG). Motor Transport (MT) included Wheeled or tracked or semi-tracked land logistic vehicle powered by the ICE but to provide specific clarification for wheeled vehicles, the term Wheeled Motor Transport (WMT) is used.

21 The British Army did not declare its expeditionary components motorized until 1937, although in 1939 the 1st Cavalry Division deployed mounted via France to Palestine; TNA WO 106/2042, 'Plan MCD, Move of the 1st Cavalry Division to Palestine from the UK'. See also, Denis C Bateman, 'Goodbye to Boots and Saddles, The Twilight of the British Cavalry', *British Army Review*, No 114, UK MOD, (December 1996), pp.75-89. The Royal Indian Army Service Corps (RIASC) deployed to the BEF in France in 1940, as part of Force K6, four Animal Transport (AT) Mule Transport Companies totalling 1,536 mules and 528 two-wheeled carts, whilst from the Middle East, came two Pack Transport Companies with Cypriot muleteers. These AT units were specifically imported for operations in the Saar because it was assessed that WMT might not able to operate in some areas and the BEF had no tracked logistic carriers. In 2017, the British Army still has more horses (485 for ceremonial duties) than tanks (227 x Challenger 2) or helicopters (102).

22 F W Lanchester recorded of 1905 that 'owing to the fact that no ancillary trades had been developed we had to do *everything* [sic] ourselves, chassis, magnetos, wheels, bodywork etc, everything except the tyres'; P W Kingsford, *F W Lanchester, A Life of an Engineer* (London: Edward Arnold: 1960), p.47. Amongst his many innovations in aeronautic and automotive engineering was the development, pre-Great War, of hybrid petrol-electric vehicles.

23 Commercially there was a clear dissonance in application. By 1913, in London, whilst 94% of passenger vehicles plying for hire were MT, it only provided 12% of trade and freight vehicles; H Wyatt, *The Motor Industry, Its Growth, Its Methods, Its Prospects, Its Products* (London: Sir Issac Pitman & Sons, 1917), pp.5-6.

24 Some freight was never moved by road in the UK; exported coal being a good example.

compared to 32,657 HT vehicles.[25]

Despite the MTC's enthusiasm for full mechanization,[26] the War Office assessed, correctly, that until MT and WMT in particular, could operate off-road, it would be essential to retain HT[27] in units and in the 2nd Line Divisional Train. Whilst Commanders and Staff were understandably culturally reluctant to replace a proven system with an untried technology, many were also cognizant of the limitations of early MT and its ability to reduce rather than enhance logistic capability if it was deployed injudiciously. Some historians have suggested that senior officers failed to fully grasp the potential of the new systems but their decision to retain both was wise and fully supported by events on the Western Front.[28] Their perception was certainly reinforced by the 1912 AAM[29], held in the United Kingdom, which confirmed the potential of Motor over other forms of MT in the military operational environment[30] but also exposed its mobility limitations in comparison to HT.

The introduction of WMT was therefore, a process of evolution, although some elements of the logistic operation were about to dramatically alter, with one of the major changes being the employment of WMT to refill the divisional dumps from the railhead, thereby replacing two echelons of HT. The Assistant Director of Transport at the War Office, noted that: 'Road transport will be considered as the organisation by means of which supplies of all descriptions in war are conveyed from the railways, or other sources, to field units, and which also undertake the evacuation of sick and wounded, and the conveyance to the rear of impedimenta no longer required at the front'.[31] Major De Pree of the Royal Field Artillery was effusive in his assessment of its possible impact: 'War Establishments published with Army Orders in February 1912 have sanctioned the conversion of the old divisional ammunition column into a divisional ammunition park, the transport of which is to be motor lorries. The first step has thus been taken in what will probably revolutionize the supply of ammunition in European war'.[32]

25 na, *The Motor Industry of Great Britain*, Society of Motor Manufacturers and Traders, 1926 edn, p.30.

26 The term 'mechanized' in the British Army is often used to describe the introduction of Mechanical Transport, most of which was Wheeled Motor Transport. In the pre-Second World War, 'mechanize' was often used to describe the re-equipment of horsed cavalry regiments with tanks, infantry battalions with the equipment emphasis on tracked carriers, whilst those equipped with WMT for the carriage of combat troops were termed motor-battalions, a capability created through the motorization programme.

27 HT, whilst having limitations, still had a significant lift, much flexibility and good cross-country mobility and could often traffic roads impassable by WMT. The General Service (GS) Wagon Mark X introduced in 1905, could carry a wide variety of stores in various configurations, examples included: 108 x 18 pdr rounds, 66 x 4.5 inch, 200 x camp kettles, 600 x ground-sheets (cased), 640 x GS shovels, 350 x RE spades and 4 x hospital marquees. The detail of the types and quantities of other loads may be found in the General Staff, *Field Service Pocket Book 1914* (FSPB 14), (London: HMSO, 1914), p.134.

28 In early November 1918, the Fourth Army Major-General General Staff (MGGS), Major-General A A Montgomery concluded: 'In the forward area, where the roads had been destroyed by mine craters, the infantry had outstripped the forward limit of the lorries, and it became necessary to use additional horse transport from the ammunition columns; it was quite obvious, therefore, that if the army continued to advance a complete breakdown in the supply organisation must result before long'. Major-General Sir Archibald Montgomery KCMG CB, *The Story of the Fourth Army in the Battles of the Hundred Days, August 8th to November 11th 1918* (London: Hodder and Stoughton, 1919), p.vii.

29 For an analysis of the 1912 AAM, see, Simon Batten, *Futile Exercise?, The British Army's Preparations for War 1902-1914* (Warwick: Helion, 2018), pp.99-131.

30 For a summary of the development of MT in the period 1900-1914, see, Beadon, *Royal Army Service Corps*, pp.24-45.

31 A reference to what is called in the 21st Century, Reverse Logistics. Colonel G R C Paul, 'Notes on Recent Developments in Road Transport', *Army Service Corps Quarterly*, Vol. 4 (October 1911), pp.535-551.

32 Major H De Pree RFA, 'The Supply of Ammunition and Motor Transport', *Journal of the Royal United Service Institute* (*JRUSI*) Vol. LVI (414), August 1912, pp.1149-1164. Of particular note, is his calculation relating to the importance of the motor lorry in delivering artillery ammunition at a rate of 432 rounds per gun per day (rpgpd) for 13 and 18 pdr, 256 rpgpd for field howitzers and 280 for the 60 pdr. Given the stocks held in July 1914, this equated to the following Days of Supply (DOS) at Intense Rates: 4.4 for the 13 pdr and 3.5 for the 18 pdr. See,

These developments not only gave greater flexibility to the supply of ammunition but they also offered the opportunity to route, through the military supply chain, fresh bread and meat that in the past could only be provided to units from local sources. At the same time, the requirement for forage[33] was reduced, the supply and distribution of which, was expected to be a very significant task in the emerging Expeditionary Force (EF).[34] The storage and transportation of petroleum products to support these new vehicles created fresh issues but unlike forage, the stocks did not suffer depredation from the activities of various rodents, although pilfering became an increasing problem. Another concern was the impact of civil regulations upon the military planning for the use of WMT. The carriage of ammunition upon the Public Highway in lorries powered by SI ICE was a good example because until 1912, a Home Office directive prohibited it.[35] The result of these influencing factors meant that HT remained a key component of the logistic system throughout the Great War, with MT, which was almost entirely WMT, complimenting but not replacing it.[36]

Wagons Roll

MT and especially WMT, was an emerging technology in 1914 which, was by no means proven in the military environment, whilst there was no guarantees for the industrial production of equipment nor the availability of Petroleum, Oils and Lubricants (POL).[37] In addition, there were challenges concerning provision of new vehicles, storage, maintenance, repair, spares and the training of operators and Equipment Support[38] personnel.[39] It is therefore, perhaps surprising

BOH, *History of the Ministry of Munitions* (MOM) Vol. I, Part I, *Munitions Supply*, HMSO, 1922, pp 87-88. See also, John Hussey, 'Without an Army, and Without any Preparation to Equip One, The Financial and Industrial Background to 1914', *British Army Review* No 109, UK MOD, (April 1995), pp.76-84.

33 Forage consisted of oats and hay. In barracks, heavy draught horses were allocated 15 lbs of oats per day, others between 10 and 12. Draught horses were rationed for 16 lbs of hay per day, the rest, 12 lbs. See, FSPB 14, p.169.

34 This reduction was relative. On 1 August 1918, there were 395,941 horses and mules in the BEF, each consuming an average of 22.2 pounds of forage per day, the daily account being a staggering 3,924 tons. This figure is a calculation based upon the number of horses and mules multiplied by 22.2 lbs but is at variance with 60,000 tons per month and thus 2,000 tons per day. MEBE, p.485, Table 11 - Stores Shipped to France for the British Expeditionary Force, 9 August 1914 -10 November 1918, records 2,978,301 tons of oats and 2,460,301 tons of hay, totalling 5,438,602 tons, generating a daily average of 3,500 tons over 1554 days. Given there were reductions in the forage ration, fluctuations of animal numbers and inevitably forage losses, the figure of around 4,000 tons per day at peak seems a reasonable equivalent planning figure.

35 The fear of a fuel fire, followed by an ammunition explosion in a residential area, was not something the civil servants of the day were prepared to accept. Given that vehicles of the period usually had wood cabs, leaking fuel lines and exposed hot engine components, the caution is entirely understandable. The new regulations, introduced in 1912, permitted the carriage of ammunition but only if there was a sheet-metal firewall between the load and the engine.

36 In 1914, there were 876 HT vehicles established in a division; FSPB 14, p.6, declining by only 6% to 822 by 1918. The numbers of horses, of various types, and mules in the BEF, lucidly illustrates their importance, despite the rapid expansion of WMT. On 31 August 1917 there were in the BEF, 368,149 horses and 81,731 mules, a total of 449,880 animals. The numbers of horses equated to 62.25% of those in service with the British Army, whilst the BEF's mules represented 38.31% of the total. See, MEBE, p.400, Animals in All Theatres.

37 The current British Army term is Fuel and Lubricants (F&L). For the wider issues relating to the delivery of petroleum products required by the United Kingdom, see, Mark Gibson, *Britain's Quest for Oil, The First World and the Peace Conferences* (Solihull: Helion, 2017), pp.48-70.

38 Equipment Support (ES) includes the preparation and repair of equipment for battle and the repair and recovery of equipment battle casualties and failures. The ES staff have a vital role in monitoring the serviceability of critical equipments in a formation to ensure that combat power is maintained; *Army Field Manual* (AFM) Vol. 1, *Combined Arms Operations*, Part 6, *Combat Service Support*, DGD&D 18/34/44, Army Code No 71344 (UK MOD, 1998), p.viii.

39 The importance of vehicle maintenance in delivering operational capability was clearly understood in 1914. FSPB 14 noted: 'Whenever mechanical transport is employed, arrangements must be made to have efficient artificers with the necessary tools to execute all repairs and adjustments at the end of each day's work'; p.133.

that in 1914, when the British Expeditionary moved to France, the Army had a large contingent of motor transport, totalling 1,852 vehicles,[40] although all but 80 were impressed from the civil sector.[41] 500 vehicles were allocated to the Army Service Corps (ASC)[42] Supply Columns, 650 to the Divisional Ammunition Parks (DAP) and 50 to base operations. Between September and December 1914, to support WMT operations, an average of 140,000 gallons of petrol per month[43] was issued from the Base Supply Depots (BSD) at Le Harve and Rouen,[44] which demonstrates the significant use of WMT.[45] Such a major contribution, so early in the conflict, from a new system, was a risk, and confirms that far from being wedded to the horse as a mode of transport, the British Army was looking very much to the future.[46]

A contemporary observer noted the results of a rapidly expanding capability: 'Thousands of Army Service Corps motor-lorries, painted service grey-green, line the roads behind the trenches in France and Flanders. Petrol is surely the key to modern warfare. Operations on such a gigantic scale could not be carried on without it'.[47] By November 1918, there were 55,473 WMT vehicles in the BEF,[48] of which, 26,809 were load-carrying 3 ton and 30 cwt lorries[49] that were consuming, with combat vehicles such as tanks and armoured cars and petrol powered equipments,[50] approximately 10.5 million gallons[51] of petrol per month, requiring the movement and handling of 33,398 tons of fuel,[52] mostly in cans.[53] In addition, there was a variety of workshops to repair this vast array of ICE equipments, salvage teams to recycle parts, depots to store new and reconditioned vehicles

40 'MT with the EF' document dated 2 October 1914 in TNA WO 107/18: New Armies: Mechanical Transport Statement and Returns, indicates the total comprised 1,468 lorries, 326 cars and 58 ambulances. Beadon, *Royal Army Service Corps*, p.90, cites a total of 1,200; 950 lorries and cars, and 250 motor-cycles. Perhaps inevitably some of the figures quoted do not agree; time frames and vehicle groupings probably account for most of the differentials.

41 The Subsidy Scheme was initiated in 1911. For details of its enactment and operation, see, Major R Campagnac RASC and Major P E C Hayman 15/19 KRH, *The Second World War, 1939-1945, Army, Fighting, Support and Transport Vehicles and the War Office Organization for their Provision*, Part II - *Unarmoured Vehicles* (War Office, 1951), pp.9-39. It was not a successful concept before the Great War, with only 80 vehicles being subscribed to the scheme. Most of the civilian vehicles used by the BEF in August 1914 were requisitioned or donated.

42 For a regimental perspective, see, Beadon, *Royal Army Service Corps* and Young, *Army Service Corps*.

43 Calculated from figures in Beadon, *Royal Army Service Corps*, p.87. At the 2017 average price of £5.46 pounds Sterling per gallon, this equates to £764,400. The movement of this fuel required 70,000 x 2 gallon cans.

44 Ibid.

45 For a brief summary of the logistic issues relating to the early part of this period, see, Roger G Miller, 'The Logistics of the British Expeditionary Force, 4 August to 5 September 1914', *Journal of Military Affairs*, XLIII (3), (October 1979), pp.133-138.

46 At divisional 2nd Line however, HT remained a key component for the rest of the war, illustrated by the 1914 motor vehicle establishment for only 9 motor-cars and 9 motor-cycles.

47 A M Beatson, *The Motor-Bus in War, Being the Impressions of an ASC Officer during Two and Half Years at the Front* (London: T Unwin Fisher, 1918), pp.14-15. Beatson enlisted as a Private in a Territorial battalion in August 1914, being commissioned into the ASC on 28 October 1914 and later serving as a Temporary Lieutenant in 89 Company in the Mechanical Transport Supply Column of the 1st (Indian) Cavalry Division.

48 Extracted from MEBE, p.595, Table (ii) (a) - Monthly Census of Mechanical Transport Vehicles in All Theatres.

49 In the last week of September 1918, the Fourth Army 3 ton and 30 cwt lorry availability rate based upon Establishment was 77.5%, with an average of 3,314 vehicles on task each day; TNA WO 95/445/5: HQ Fourth Army, A&Q, Note 842, 'MT Situation in Fourth Army on 28-09-18'.

50 These equipments included petrol powered NGR locomotives and electrical generators.

51 Figure calculated from information in Beadon, *Royal Army Service Corps*, p.87, listing the maximum monthly petroleum issues in gallons from the Supply Depots at Calais (7,919,384) Le Harve (225,610) and Rouen (4,673,024) totalling 12,591,633 gallons, of which 1.5 million gallons were aviation spirit.

52 Based on a Specific Gravity (SG) of 0.7125 for Motor Spirit. Professor Henry Spooner records the SG of Petrol, Motor Spirit, Petroleum Spirit, Gasoline or Benzine as distillates of Crude American Petroleum to be between 0.680 and 0.745. Henry Spooner, *Motors and Motoring* (London, T C & E C Jack, 1909), 1916 Edn, Sect 25, Table II - Commercial Distillates of Crude American Petroleum.

53 There was no military specification two gallon can in the Great War with cans being procured directly from commerce. Initially, the cans were in company colours but as the war progressed, MT cans were painted an enamel grey and aviation spirit cans red, with A stencilled in black letters, 3 inches high, on each large face.

and spares and a spectrum of drivers, mechanics, fitters and storekeepers to keep the vast machine working, including an increasing number of women undertaking a variety of technical and non-technical trades.[54] An American commercial observer summarized the arrangements that were necessary to deliver this effect:

> On a chart about three feet square, which hangs on the wall in General Boyce's office at General Headquarters is a layout of the whole system from factory to field.[55] At the bottom is Production, which may be factories in the United States or England, where mobilisation of transport, drivers and mechanics is effected. Beyond this lies France, where you go from the Base Mechanical Transport Depots to the Advanced Mechanical Transport Depots, past the Heavy Repair Shops and Tire Presses, up to the Mobile Work Shops in the field where the cars damaged by shell fire or wrecked on the roads in the zone of the armies come for repair.[56]

Vehicles seriously damaged in accidents or by enemy kinetic action such as artillery, mines or aerially delivered ordnance were collected at Vehicle Casualty Parks (VCP) where an assessment was conducted to shape a decision as to repair or salvage. Psychology played a key part in determining site layout, with damaged vehicles being screened from passing WMT traffic. Whilst the sight of damaged vehicles might have played a part in improving road safety and thus capability, the remains of lorries and ambulances shredded by exploding artillery shells were deemed to have a depressing effect upon soldiers' morale. An American journalist who had the privilege of an official visit to BEF logistic operations, observed, 'It is precisely like the effect produced upon a man who goes into hospital for an operation and is required to pass through the morgue on the way to his room'.[57]

The rapid expansion of WMT was as remarkable as it was timely because the logistic requirements of the Western Front grew significantly.[58] WMT produced key capability forward from the railhead by transporting fresh and composite rations,[59] water, canned fuel, trench and village stores[60] and infantry ammunition natures,[61] to Refilling Points (RP) from where, HT transported the stocks.

54 In the MT environment, this included driver-mechanics, fitters, welders, machinists and electricians; War Office, *Regulations for the Queen Mary's Auxiliary Corps* (War Office,1918), pp.32-39.

55 Brigadier-General W G B Boyce late ASC assumed the appointment of Director of Transport on 30 November 1914 and remained in post for the rest of the war; Major A F (Retd) Becke (Comp) BOH, *Order of Battle*, Part 4, *The Army Council, GHQs, Armies and Corps, 1914-1918* (London: HMSO, 1945), p.13.

56 Issac Frederick Marcosson, *The Business of War* (London: John Lane, The Bodley Head, 1918), p.153.

57 Ibid, p.129.

58 A census at Fricourt Cemetery on Saturday 22 July 1916, a not especially busy day, revealed that over 7,300 HT and MT vehicles passed the Traffic Post in 24 hours. This survey recorded an average of 5.07 vehicles per minute, increasing to 7.95 between 0900 and 1500. These vehicles had to share the road with 26,536 troops and 5,404 riding horses. Henniker, BOH, *Transportation on the Western Front*, p.157 and Brigadier-General Sir James E Edmonds CB CMG (Comp) BOH, *Military Operations, France and Belgium 1916*, Vol. I, *Sir Douglas Haig's Command to the 1st July: Battle of the Somme*, (London: Macmillan, 1932), p.283.

59 Fresh rations included uncooked meat, bread and vegetables, whilst composite rations were comprised of tinned and dried foods, including the emergency ration and Maconochie's 'Patent Army Ration'. For details, see, Army Council, *Army Service Corps*, Part II, *Supplies*, War Office (London: HMSO, 1909) (Reprinted 1914 with new Appx XII).

60 Trench Stores included combat items such as sniper-scopes, rocket signals, mortars, ammunition, grenades and entrenching tools, although the Assistant Adjutant & Quartermaster-General (AA&QMG) of 17th (Northern) Division related that in one sector, a cow was included in the weekly returns. Village Stores generally included home-comforts, such as stoves, hurricane lamps, building tools and occasionally china and glass. Colonel W N Nicholson CMG DSO, *Behind the Lines, An Account of Administrative Staff-work in the British Army, 1914-1918* (London: Jonathan Cape, 1939), p.202.

61 Infantry ammunition natures included Small Arms Ammunition (SAA) of 0.455 inch rounds for pistols, 0.303 inch rounds for rifles and machine guns, hand and rifle grenades, mortar bombs and flares. For details of packing,

WMT also transported artillery ammunition, ordnance stores and engineer stores from railheads to dumps, whilst also moving stone and building materials to construction sites. Railheads were therefore, critical logistic nodes, the operation of which, required careful planning, good drills and clear control, if the WMT circulating within it was to be effectively and efficiently managed. Operating a railhead during the day, out of the range of German guns, was a routine, if nonetheless important task but at night, with enemy artillery active, it could be a very different proposition, with crafted plans rapidly unravelling. An Army Service Corps officer recorded such an event in September 1916:

> Our time for loading was usually about midnight, and at about this hour on the night of the 17th the weather changed, and the heavens began to pour forth rain and continued to do so throughout the night. We were not the only Division to be loading at the time and the chaos of the traffic in the pitch-blackness and pouring rain can only be described as appalling.[62]

WMT also made a significant contribution to tank operations, delivering canned POL products, ammunition, spares, rations and water to dumps near, or at, tankodromes,[63] although ironically, because of the poor off-road capability of WMT, HT was sometimes required complete the delivery. WMT was also essential to road construction and maintenance projects across the BEF's Area of Responsibility (AOR).[64] Most WMT had no meaningful off-road capability, thereby reducing efficiency because WMT required hard-standings to operate from, so not infrequently units were located some distance from the task. In July 1916, the III Corps Ammunition Park was located at Franvillers. One of its tasks was to out-load munitions from the Edgehill Ammunition Railhead (ARH) to a dump two miles away. To achieve the task, the WMT travelled light for seven miles, collected the ammunition, moved loaded for two miles and then returned to Franvillers on a nine-mile route, thereby completing 18 miles but only two miles under load.[65] An even more extraordinary operation involved a Third Army Divisional Supply Column (DSC) driving 40 miles a day, of which only five or six miles were with supplies from the railhead to the Brigade RP, which was located two miles distant.[66] The Q Staff of II (ANZAC) Corps generated much improved WMT efficiency by co-ordinating the assets on a Corps circuit, which included the railheads, thereby reducing non-loaded mileage.[67]

The failure to create at least some off-road capability, generated inefficient WMT utilization, decreased outputs, initiated additional Equipment Support requirements, increased road congestion, enhanced fuel usage and produced the need for more road maintenance, which in turn generated

content differentials and box markings, see, War Office, *Treatise on Ammunition*, 10th Edition (HMSO, 1915).

62 Beatson, *The Motor-Bus in War*, p.195.

63 A tankodrome, a title closely associated with the RFC's aerodrome, was an area allocated to tank training but was also used to describe a site used in the field for final logistic preparations prior to operations, particularly field maintenance, refuelling and 'bombing-up' with ammunition, although the descriptor 'Tank Park' was also used. Some tankodromes and aerodromes were rail-served. Whilst tankodrome has passed from the British Army's lexicon it survives in the Indian Army and in the Czech Republic, there is privately operated military style training area advertised as *Tankodrom Milovice*.

64 The task was so important that WMT units, such as ammunition sub-parks allocated to the delivery of artillery ammunition were directed to support road repair. The 180 Company history records that in March 1917, 75% of its effort was devoted to hauling road materials and 25% to artillery ammunition. G Lispcombe, *Historical Record of 180 Coy, Royal Army Service Corps (Mechanical Transport)* RASC (Aldershot: Gale & Polden, 1919), p.63.

65 Henniker, BOH, *Transportation on the Western* Front, pp.157-158.

66 Ibid, p.158.

67 Lipscombe, *Historical Record of 180 Coy*, p.48.

the requirement for more WMT. The non off-road capability also created operational security (OPSEC)[68] issues because the preparation of hard-standings was always of interest to German aerial reconnaissance, which duly noted the activity for future reference. When 180 Mechanical Transport Company ASC[69] occupied a prepared site near Lunaville Farm North-West of Ypres in mid-October 1917, as part of a divisional plan to reduce mileage and congestion on the roads by positioning the Company near to its ammunition in-load tasks, the location was shelled by German artillery and suffered air attack[70] with fragmentation bombs;[71] these two assaults were of such intensity that withdrawal was the only sensible option.[72] Daily transport movement could be equally hazardous, as an Army Service Corps officer observed in recording the control measures to partially counter the threat to WMT moving by day on a road from Bray-sur-Somme to Suzanne:

> The German gunners had registered its range accurately, and no transport was allowed along it in daylight without a special pass or permit from Divisional Headquarters. We frequently took convoys along it by day, however, without any mishap of any kind, always taking the precaution, of course, to keep the lorries a good two or three hundred yards apart from one another. Taking these precautions, the possibility of a shell putting the whole convoy or any part of it out of action is reduced to a minimum.[73]

Once the deployment of the BEF became relatively static, WMT developed to support it. There was rapid expansion in 1915, in line with the BEF, with many vehicles being impressed from the civil sector. Much local initiative was evident and whilst this had many advantages in solving immediate problems, it created a wealth of long-term ones. There were many different vehicle types, a grave shortage of spares, a flagging supply system and an establishment process that was fast disintegrating. Unit Establishments were resolved first, with the various special units being assessed and equipped to meet their specific tasks. Type aggregation was the next task; vehicles of the same type were grouped in units, to generate greater coherency in training[74] and to improve maintenance, and

68 The importance of OPSEC is explained in *Army Doctrine Publication (*ADP) Vol. 1, *Operations*, HQDT/18/34/46, Army Code No 71565 (UK MOD, 1994), p.4-23; fn 6, 'The aim of OPSEC is to provide a military operation or exercise an additional form degree of security, using active or passive means, to ensure that knowledge of friendly dispositions, capabilities, intentions and vulnerabilities are denied to the enemy'. OPSEC measures concentrate on identifying those aspects of a plan which are considered vital to the success of an operation.

69 180 Company was a New Army unit, the history of which has been fortunately recorded, in a neatly illustrated document, *Historical Record of 180* Coy, which apart from being most informative and engaging and having several useful tables containing logistic statistics, is unusual in being written by a NCO, Mechanist Sergt-Major G Lipscombe. The title however, is incorrect, as during the period it covers, the Company was Army Service Corps, the Royal prefix not being awarded until 27 November 1918. The author, who joined shortly after its formation on 21 January 1915, served until the Company's amalgamation with 179 Company ASC on 13 March 1918.

70 Lipscombe, *Historical Record of 180 Coy*, p.79 notes 'The night raids were the worst evil the unit had to contend with, and it cannot be truthfully stated that any person maintained his usual sang-froid whilst the enemy planes were overhead'. This unease was usually created because the soldiers were unable to take effective shelter during raids.

71 180 Company was fortunate. The neighbouring 47 Ammunition Sub-Park was less so, suffering four killed and eight injured in a night fragmentation bombing air attack; Ibid, pp.76-77. 180 Company as 18 Ammunition Sub-Park was also fortunate on the night of 31 October 1917, when 12 of its lorries were leaguered with 35 Ammunition Sub-Park, which came under air attack. 35 Ammunition Sub-Park lost one killed and three wounded with 13 lorries burnt out but Corporal H W Wilmot of 18 Ammunition Sub-Park moved his company vehicles from the conflagration; Ibid, pp.79-80.

72 Ibid, pp.77-79.

73 Beatson, *The Motor-Bus in War*, p.153.

74 Of particular note, is that even as late as July 1918, MT training was developing, with, in this month, the opening of the Fourth Army Lorry Driving School; TNA WO 95/454/4: HQ Fourth Army, DDST, WD, entries 23-27 July 1918.

P10.1. 3 tonners: The Logistic Workhorse. The expansion of WMT had a very significant impact not only upon operational capability of the BEF but also the manner in which, it had to adjust its training and logistics to support the emerging reliance upon the WMT system. (RLC Museum: MT Collection)

thereby, operational effectiveness. By 1916, the 3 ton lorry had become the preferred carrier and the majority of vehicles sent to the BEF from British and American manufacturers were of this type.[75]

As the fleet grew, the imposition of traffic control regulations became imperative,[76] and the Staff tackled these issues with vigour. Maps were produced showing which roads had two-way traffic, whilst one-way systems were created to enhance movement flows, which sometimes increased route distances.[77] In addition, directives instructed WMT to keep to metalled roads, speed limits were introduced to reduce the accident rate,[78] anti-skid chains issued and much effort devoted to traffic and convoy control measures. Despite these precautions, adverse weather, especially rain,[79] snow

75 In November 1918, 48.3% of all WMT in the BEF was inventoried in the 3 ton - 30 cwt category. Figure calculated from MEBE, p.595, Table (ii) (a) - Monthly Census of Mechanical Transport in All Theatres, November 1918; excludes MT vehicles allocated to the RAF.

76 As an example, on 1 September 1916, Fourth Army had on strength, 4,671 lorries, 1,145 cars and ambulances and 1,636 motor-cycles; Henniker, BOH, *Transportation on the Western* Front, p.157.

77 A Third Army Traffic Map of April 1918, at a scale of 1 inch to 1.58 miles (1: 100,000) published by 3 Field Survey Company RE, clearly shows the permitted and restricted routes in the Third Army AOR. Most of the lateral routes were uni-directional, although there were dispensations for officers on duty travelling in staff cars, Despatch Riders and, if in possession of a Provost or Assistant Provost Marshal's pass, Box Cars, which were vans of 30 cwt or less. Horses and mules were not to be exercised on restricted or uni-directional roads. Of interest, is the reference to the Royal Air Force (RAF), so recently formed and in particular, RAF tenders, which although usually lorries of 3 tons and above, were authorized to travel as Cars, which suggests their importance in movement priorities.

78 The speed limits in the Third Army AOR were: Lorries and buses (spelt 'busses' in the notes) 10 mph in the country and 6 mph in village or on poor roads; for cars and ambulances, the limits were 20 and 10 mph respectively. This simple measure also increased vehicle availability, whilst reducing workshop tasking, the requirement for spares, vehicle wear and road surface damage.

79 In late June 1916, a week before the Somme offensive commenced, Colonel F M Wilson, Deputy Director Supplies & Transport (DDST)) Fourth Army recorded his experience of a journey to inspect logistic operations, which offers a very clear picture of the challenges to operating WMT: 'the roads were in a most appalling state, one part of the road in fact being, in a dangerous condition owning to the greasy mud'; TNA WO 95/454/1: HQ Fourth Army, DDST, WD, 24 June 1916.

and fog, all created additional hazards.[80]

The last change came late in the war, during the winter of 1917-1918 and was a radical reorganization of MT in the BEF. With a few exceptions for specialist work, all the WMT in the BEF was to be scaled for 'pool operations'. In place of ammunition sub-parks, army, corps and divisional supply columns, and auxiliary patrol companies, and similar units, WMT companies were organized on a universal establishment of a Headquarters (HQ) plus a number of sections,[81] each of which, had 16 lorries. Divisional MT companies consisted of five sections, and those of corps troops, two sections, and these units were allocated in the proportion of one to each division and one to each corps. One company was allotted to each Army Headquarters for army troops, and one to GHQ. These measures produced a major economy in personnel and vehicles, which was used to create a pool of 12 General Reserve Companies, each comprising a HQ and six sections. Each company had an establishment of 96 lorries, and the General Reserve totalled 1,152.[82] The reorganization was indeed timely; without the General Reserve Companies, the logisticians would have struggled to sustain the BEF during the German Spring offensive of 1918, which caused significant disruption to the strategic rail network.[83] There was though, inherent risk in reorganizing in this way because the effective utilization was predicated upon the C2 becoming more agile to improve efficiency.[84]

Technical Challenges

WMT was comprised of Low Mobility Load Carriers (LMLC), which although having some interesting innovations, also had limitations. Many vehicles had a respectable load capacity of 3 tons, and there were four-wheel drive systems in service,[85] but most of the lorries had solid rubber tyres, which though relatively robust, gave poor off-road performance. Pneumatic tyres became increasingly common on light vehicles but punctures were common, and the solid tyre remained a feature of load carriers until the 1920s. Wheeled vehicle cross-country capability was therefore, non-existent, a technological failure, which created one of the greatest paradoxes of the war once operational mobility was restored in 1918.[86] Until then, cross-country capability had been largely irrelevant because WMT had operated on roads in the Base, Army, Corps and Divisional areas, and

80 Lipscombe, *Historical Record of 180 Coy*, pp. 61-62, records a peculiar incident after which, a lorry was unofficially named 'U-30, (*Untersee* Boat). Frost had frozen a large pond next to a regularly travelled route upon which, snow had fallen. The road had a sharp bend to avoid the pond, which now appeared to be part of the road and the vehicle drove onto it, sinking as it stopped in the snow. Fortunately, the crew escaped with a chilly ducking, which cannot have been very pleasant and the lorry was recovered, remarkably leaving the scene under its own power.

81 In the ASC during the Great War, a sub-section equated to 4-6 vehicles and a section, a troop of 16-24.

82 Young, *Army Service Corps*, p.105.

83 For details of the logistic impact of the withdrawal, see, Henniker, BOH, *Transportation on the Western Front*, pp.402-419 and from the German perspective, David T Zabecki, *The German 1918 Offensives* (London: Routledge, 2006).

84 Lipscombe. *Historical Record of 180 Coy*, p.49, records that in the winter of 1916-1917, and well before this organization took place, 180 Company, although an ammunition sub-park, was hauling railway stores, pit-props, trench stores and moving personnel, and so, had in effect, become a General Transport (GT) unit. Many of the pit-props were to support tunnelling operations during the excavations for the British mines on the Messines Ridge and to preserve the secrecy of this vital operation, 180 Company drivers were told it was for trench improvements, whilst delivery to the construction sites was undertaken solely at night.

85 Nearly all the Four Wheel Drive vehicles came from the USA: FWD, Nash, Jeffery-Quad and Knox were the leaders. 55,000 were produced in the USA before the war finished. For a comprehensive contemporary review of US industrial support to the Western Front, see, Benedict Crowell & Robert Forrest Wilson, *How America Went to War, The Armies of Industry, Our Nation's Manufacture of Munitions for a World in Arms*, Vols I & II, (New Haven: Yale University Press, 1921).

86 This was however, an excellent example of an operational and industrial compromise; solid tyres were resilient and simple to maintain, requiring little Equipment Support input in comparison to pneumatic tyres.

no wheeled vehicle was expected to cross the terrain surrounding the trenches.

As the advance of the Hundred Days[87] progressed, the BEF discovered that the German counter-mobility plan had made many roads impassable to WMT.[88] Construction teams refurbished roads between the railheads and the road-heads, which were usually 10-15 miles behind unit administrative echelons,[89] thereby enabling WMT to run the loops between the railheads and the road-heads. It was however, not feasible to upgrade, within the operational timeframe, the roads forward from the road-heads to support motor traffic to the forward infantry echelons.[90] Having therefore, placed so much emphasis on the role of the motor lorry, with its serious cross-country limitations, the BEF had to rely on HT from the divisional trains to provide the last link in the logistic chain, in order to Maintain Momentum in the advance.

A particular shortfall in logistic vehicle capability was the availability of Heavy Equipment Transporters (HET)[91] capable of moving tanks and other armoured vehicles. Whilst the tank was not the war-winner that some commanders hoped it would be, it was a significant component in the growing capability of the BEF. It is therefore, ironic that whilst mechanization created a potentially powerful new capability, it failed to deliver the operational movement flexibility that was needed to generate the greatest effect. Whatever the technical capability of the emerging armoured force, deployment remained dependent upon the railway, whilst recovery of tanks in the advance had to await the arrival of a SGR railhead.[92] In the set-piece 'Bite & Hold' operations of 1917, the reliance upon the railway to deliver tanks to corps and divisional areas had relatively little risk but during mobile operations the delivery of armoured units to the battle-space in a timely manner was much more difficult.

87 It was 96 days. The use of 100, apart from having a fine resonance, was probably linked to the famous Hundred Days campaign of Napoleon in 1815, during which a British Army, in a coalition, achieved victory.

88 The Germans destroyed bridges, cratered roads and laid delayed-action mines in culverts, requiring Royal Engineer teams to defuse the Improvised Explosive Devices (IED) before repairs could commence. General Staff, *Field Service Regulations* (FSR) Part 1, *Operations*, War Office (London: HMSO, 1909) (Reprinted 1912), p.213 had highlighted this particular problem before the Great War. In particular, it noted: 'The destruction of even small bridges may delay mechanical transport greatly'.

89 Whilst the British Army is constantly reorganizing and re-equipping, the concept of the unit echelon system has stood the test of time remarkably well, although the composition and nomenclature have varied over the years. The F Echelon contains the fighting forces, inclusive of personnel, weapons, vehicles and the allocated Combat Service Support (CSS), then termed A&Q, such as Equipment Support (ES) and Medical. A1, the first Administrative Echelon is designed to provide immediate CSS to fighting capability and usually includes reserves of combat supplies and some ES. A2, the second Administrative Echelon, contains technical stores and some ES and the Regimental Aid Post (RAP) may be in the battle-space. The B Echelon holds the non-urgent capabilities, such as clothing, stores, administrative staff; unit B Echelons were often grouped at brigade level. In the Great War on the Western Front, A1 and A2 is often identified as the 1st Line Regimental Transport and Trench Dumps, whilst the B Echelon is the Quartermaster's Store.

90 The burden of road repair and construction in 1918 is clearly illustrated by the rise in the weekly average outputs controlled by Director-General Transportation in the LOC and Army AORs. DGT's responsibility did not include all roads in the AORs nor any roads forward of Brigade rear boundaries; see, Henniker, *Transportation on the Western Front*, pp.345-346. New and re-made road in square yards peaked at 81,803 in March and then averaged 60,000 square yards per week until October. Road re-surfacing rose from 41,554 in April peaking at 161,847 square yards in August and 96,647 in October. MEBE, p.608, Table (i) - Progress of Transportation in France.

91 Until the mid-1990s, British Army vehicles capable of transporting tanks were termed Tank Transporters. Since then, the US Army nomenclature of Heavy Equipment Transporter (HET) has become standard.

92 Mounting an armoured assault on the scale of Cambrai or Amiens was a massive logistic undertaking; four weeks of intensive preparations were required for the former involving the movement of 436 tanks, which was planned and executed with meticulous care.

From the perspective of 2018, it seems incredible that the BEF of 1918 fielded so many tanks with no HETs,[93] which makes the logistic feat of moving them all the more impressive.[94] Despite this lacuna, WMT played a crucial role in sustaining tank operations, HQ V Tank Brigade recording in an After Action Report from the Battle of Amiens, 'The only safe method of supplying tanks for any length of time during a moving Battle, is to have a mobile dump of at least 50 fills of petrol, oil and grease, loaded on lorries and standing by in some central place ready to move at a moments notice in any required direction'.[95] This plan of course, was predicated on the assumption that the WMT would be able to traffic the route, HQ V Tank Brigade noting in an instruction, 'The difficulties of using M.T. owing to the bad state of the roads must be borne in mind, when selecting sites for supplies to be sent to'.[96]

Gunbuster

If the operational deployment of armour was to tax the logistic system, sustaining the artillery battle was to provide an even greater challenge, and one in which WMT played a major part.[97] Whilst armour, Close Air Support (CAS)[98] and Air Interdiction (AI)[99] were emerging aspects of the All Arms Battle, the artillery, supported by air reconnaissance, was, for the most part, a finely honed and vital part of British tactical operations,[100] which made massive demands on the logistic chain, especially the transportation of artillery ammunition. Between Thursday 8 August and Friday 6 September 1918, 9,807,000 rounds, weighing 242,350 tons were fired by the BEF,[101] whilst the

93 What is remarkable though, from an historical perspective, is that the British Army has fielded only five distinct types of military HET capable of transporting tanks since 1927. These are: Scammell Pioneer (UK), the Diamond T (USA), Thornycroft Antar (Mks 1 & 3 - UK), Scammell Commander (UK) and the Oshkosh 1070F (USA). The Antar tractor (FV 12000) was originally designed to support oilfield construction operations, the prototype being trialled in Iraq in 1952.

94 This was also true of the BEF in 1939-1940. Despite the experiments during the 1920s, it was not until 1927 that two Scammell 6 x 4 Pioneer Transporters, came into service, both of which had been purchased to move the Vickers Mk II Medium Tank. This acquisition did little to prompt an expansion of this essential capability and clearly indicated that the importance of a having a capable HET had still not been grasped in the mid-1930s. As a result, the BEF in 1939-1940 deployed 704 tanks to France, yet fielded only two military HETs, plus 23 impressed civilian variants. In 1940, many failed or damaged tanks could not be recovered because there were insufficient HETs with winches to move them. The lessons were however, eventually learnt and the deployment and recovery of armour, often under fire, was a skill finely honed in the Western Desert. See, G N Georgano, *World War Two Military Vehicles (Transport and Half-Tracks)* (London: Osprey Automotive, 1994).

95 TNA WO 95/112/2: '5th Tank Brigade, Report on Operations with Australian Corps from 8th August to 15th August 1918', para 3, Supplies.

96 TNA WO 95/112/2: '5th Tank Brigade, Order No 1dated 19 September 1918, Administrative Instructions', para 2, Supplies.

97 For a pre-war perspective on ammunition supply to divisional artillery, see, Brevet Major C N Buchanan-Dunlop RA, 'Ammunition Supply', *JRUSI*, Vol. LVII (January 1913), pp.87-92. Of particular note, is that the Brigade Ammunition Columns did not exist in peace except in India, so it was not possible to conduct field training for expeditionary operations as the units were only authorised on the War Establishment. Major Buchanan-Dunlop argued that the Brigade Ammunition Column should absorb the relevant 1st Line Regimental Wagons to create a more flexible capability.

98 Close Air Support (CAS) is air action against hostile targets, which are in close proximity to friendly forces and which, require detailed integration of each air mission with the fire and movement of those forces; *Air Publication* (AP) *3000, British Air Power Doctrine*, 3rd Edition, Directorate of Air Staff (UK MOD, 1999), p.3.13.2.

99 Air Interdiction (AI) is an air operation conducted to destroy, neutralize or delay the enemy's military potential, before it can be brought to bear effectively against friendly forces at such a distance from friendly forces, that detailed integration of each air mission with the fire and movement of friendly forces is not required; *Air Publication* (AP) *3000*, p.3.13.1.

100 For a seminal examination of its role in supporting the BEF, see, Sanders Marble, *British Artillery on the Western Front, The Infantry cannot do with a gun less*, Ashgate Studies in First World War History (Farnham: Ashgate, 2013).

101 Including, 5,372,000 rounds of 18 pdr, 1,443,000 of 4.5 inch, and 1,566,800 of 6 inch howitzer and 145,700 of

highest recorded expenditure of artillery ammunition in 24 hours in the BEF was between 1200 on Saturday 28 September to the same time on Sunday 29 September 1918, was an enormous 943,947 rounds.[102] Whilst NGR was used to move gun ammunition from SGR railheads to dumps, from the middle of 1916, WMT played an increasingly important role in this task, and from March 1918, when mobility was restored to the Western Front, it became an essential component during various phases of operations. In the advance, the logistic staffs had two major problems to contend with. First, moving the guns to a position where they were able to support the battle, and secondly, supplying the ammunition; WMT played an increasing role in both. Some 18 pdr guns, usually horse drawn, were, in the latter stages of the war, towed by WMT, or carried portee, solutions driven by the transfer of horses to the American Expeditionary Force (AEF)[103] whilst WMT became increasingly important to bridge the gap between railheads and forward artillery ammunition dumps.

MT also played a crucial role in the deployment of Anti-Aircraft Artillery (AAA). From the beginning of its development, AAA was mounted on, and fired from, WMT because it was perceived this was the best solution, predating the concept of the artillery Self Propelled Gun (SPG). The driver was the dynamic of the threat; aeroplanes were mobile and so the defence needed to be as well. Whilst the lorry mounted equipment of the day could not usually operate in the forward areas because the terrain and the tactical situation,[104] WMT mounted AAA was deployed to protect Vital Points within the Base, along the Line of Communication (LOC) and Army Areas to the Divisional Rear Boundaries.[105] Near the end of the war, an attempt was made to produce an equipment capable of operating in the more challenging terrain of the forward battle area and a 3.6 inch weapon was trialled, mounted on a tracked trailer, to permit deployment off-road,[106] which started an affair with trailer-mounted AAA, which was to last over 100 years. Once mobility was restored to the battlefield in Spring 1918, WMT AAA was able to contribute more effectively to ground operations but for various reasons, the integration of AAA into the All-Arms battle was slow to mature and the Armistice stopped its development. Nonetheless, WMT had made its mark in a new area of military endeavour.[107]

WMT made a critical contribution to the capability of military aviation by enabling the delivery of an effective and efficient logistic system. From its foundation in 1912, the Royal Flying Corps (RFC) as befitting the emergence of a state of the art technology, sought to ensure its mobility and support in the field not by HT but the provision of a wide range of WMT vehicles; indeed, the

9.2 inch howitzer; MEBE, p.481, Munition Notes, Table 4 - Ammunition Expenditure in France from 8th August to 6th September 1918.

102 Ibid, p.481, Munition Notes, Table 6 - Approximate Cost of Gun Ammunition and Number of Rounds Expended in France from Noon, 28th September to Noon, 29th September 1918. The cost of this ammunition in 1918 prices was £3,871,000, which in 2016, based on the *Measuring Worth UK* Project Economy Cost as a share of the Gross Domestic Product (GDP) is £1.511 Billion. Given that the average daily cost of the war to the United Kingdom in this period was £7,443,000 in 1918 prices (£2.906 Billion in 2016 values), this was massive investment; MEBE, p.561, Table (b) - Average Daily Expenditure of the War.

103 For an examination of this issue, see, the seminal, Graham Winton, *Theirs Not to Reason Why, Horsing the British Army*, 1875-1925, Wolverhampton Military Studies (Solihull: Helion, 2013), pp.333-339.

104 On the occasions that it did, German artillery was usually quick to respond. Needless to say, infantry units within German artillery range, were not enthused by having lorry mounted AAA in location.

105 Lipscombe, *Historical Record of 180 Coy*, p.76, records that AA shell fragments were a hazard unless soldiers were accommodated in dug-outs.

106 For details, see, Ian V Hogg, *Allied Artillery of World War One* (Marlborough: The Crowood Press, 1998), pp.150-164.

107 In November 1918, there were, in the BEF, 234 x 13 pdrs and 103 x 3 inch (9 & 20 cwt). For details, see, Brigadier N W Routledge OBE TD, *History of the Royal Regiment of Artillery, Anti-Aircraft Artillery 1914-1955* (London & New York Brasseys, 1994), pp.3-27.

RFC was the first fully motorized corps in the Army. By October 1917, there were approximately 2,700 WMT vehicles on the Western Front operating in direct support of air operations.[108] The key vehicle grouping was of 3 ton and 30 cwt lorries, comprising 94 percent of the total and which, included specialist repair workshop systems. The 2,533 lorries were therefore, around 10 percent of the BEF's total lorry inventory, a remarkable figure given that the RFC represented only 1.1 percent of the BEF's manpower[109] and a clear illustration of its importance to the Corps. WMT enabled the formation of flexible Air Ammunition Columns responsible for the delivery of munitions, sometimes direct from railheads to airfields and in September 1917, the creation of Reserve Lorry Parks (RLP) for each RFC brigade to generate an operational reserve.[110] Its significance was lucidly demonstrated during the German Spring offensive in 1918,[111] when operational RAF squadrons suffered relatively modest losses of Ground Support Equipment (GSE) despite the rapidity of the German advance because units were able to evacuate equipment and stores,[112] a lesson that had to be re-learnt during operations in France in the Spring of 1940.[113]

Moving The Troops

The movement of troops by bus in the United Kingdom before the war provided valuable experience for the BEF. In 1914 and 1915, movement, although well planned, focused on routine lifts, often only at the battalion level. As the war progressed, troop lift by road became more important and complex, so GHQ BEF allocated every Army, an Auxiliary Omnibus Company (AOC)[114] each comprising 50 vehicles, to support moves within the Army area[115]. There was however, no unit capable of lifting a brigade or a division from one Army to another, and all operational moves were conducted by rail, or occasionally, on foot. The Battle of the Somme in 1916 clearly reinforced the increasing complexities of operating within an operational rather than a tactical level, and prompted a review of how the BEF conducted its divisional and corps deployments.

Part of the study examined the French system, which at the time, was well ahead of the British one and the BEF solution was based on their experience. The result was that the five omnibus companies in France were placed under one command, the Auxiliary Omnibus Park (AOP), which

108 TNA AIR 1/1155/204/5/2428: Quarterly returns of engines and vehicles held by the RAF in the field.

109 TNA WO 394/20: Summary of Statistics, 1914-1920.

110 This re-organization reflected similar readjustments in other parts of the BEF's logistic system, the RLPs being created by a reduction in the lorry establishments of operational squadrons and Army Air Parks; TNA AIR 1/520/16/12/1: Pt III - Air Policy: Expansion and Organization of the RFC and RAF.

111 Major-General John Salmond, recently appointed GOC RFC in France, observing the effects of the German Spring offensive on his command noted: "The transport has stuck it all right so far, but I visualize a large number of moves in the future and I shall be obliged for the extra vehicles of the extra Lorry Park;" TNA AIR 1/475/15/312/201: 'Copies of letters from General Salmond to Trenchard on operations during German offensive'. Salmond had taken over as GOC from Trenchard, who became Chief of the Air Staff.

112 In the four days, 21-25 March 1918, the RFC abandoned or destroyed 4,300 hydrogen cylinders, 1,500 bombs, 40 light aircraft tents, one car, two lorries and two light tenders; TNA AIR 1/475/15/312/201.

113 On 15 May 1940, HQ British Air Forces France (BAFF) supporting the BEF's Air Component and the Advanced Air Striking Force (AASF) assessed that the air forces in France were only semi-mobile even based on units being to establishment for WMT. That on this date, however, deficiencies totalled 600 vehicles and to create a more effective mobility the AASF had to borrow WMT from the Host Nation and reduce the number of its bomber squadrons from ten to six, clearly illustrates how the lessons of the Great War had failed to appropriately influence planners and financiers. *The Second World War, 1939-1945, Royal Air Force, Maintenance,* CD 1131 (Air Ministry, 1954), CONFIDENTIAL, downgraded to UNCLASSIFIED, March 1966, pp.63-67.

114 The early buses were owned by London omnibus companies and arrived in France complete in their liveries and displaying adverts extolling the virtues of particular safety razors, soaps and matches. Some also had adverts for a popular London comedy play of the time about two American Jewish businessmen in New York called 'Potash & Perlmutter', whom French soldiers and civilians assumed were two BEF generals. Marcosson, *Business of War,* p.125.

115 Beadon, *Royal Army Service Corps,* p.140.

was controlled by GHQ. The AOP was concentrated at St Valery-sur-Somme during October and November 1916, being supplemented by additional equipment and two newly formed units: one company of Troop Carrying Lorries (TCL) and one company of single deck *charabancs*.[116] Each double-deck omnibus could lift 25 men, and each of the 271 x TCLs, 20. The AOP, at full strength consisted of 650 task vehicles, operated by 1800 All Ranks, and was capable of moving, in a one-time lift, all the dismounted troops of a division, including the machine gun and the pioneer battalion. The HQ Company normally lifted the divisional troops, with the task companies moving half a brigade each.

The AOP was normally on 60 minutes Notice To Move (NTM) with orders being given to the AOP HQ by telephone and confirmed by hard-copy delivered by a Despatch Rider (DR). GHQ produced a combined traffic embussing and debussing map for the whole of the BEF's frontage, showing Army areas and the direction of traffic on all roads. All embussing and debussing points were numbered, and marked on the ground.[117] Embussing was honed to a fine art and by mid-1918 a division could be collected within 30 minutes of arrival at the Pick Up Point (PUP). The record for an infantry brigade was 4 minutes and 30 seconds.[118] The work of the AOP was critical during the German offensive of March 1918 during which, it moved elements from 16 BEF divisions and two French, lifting 211,213 men and travelling 855,638 miles.[119] The emplacement, during defensive operations, of 12th (Eastern) Division, less its organic artillery, from the First Army, into the gap at Albert during an overnight move from Busnes was especially noteworthy.[120]

Official recognition highlighted the importance of these successful logistic operations. The Commanding Officer of the AOP[121] received warm letters of thanks from not only the QMG but also the Commander-in-Chief, Field Marshal Sir Douglas Haig[122] and the soldiers were recognized with a wealth of awards.[123] In the offence, the AOP positioned most of the Australian and Canadian Corps from Arras to Amiens for the Allied assault, although poor staff planning by Fourth Army Roads Officers supporting the Canadians,[124] resulted in lengthy delays, compounded by accidents caused by tired drivers operating in the dark.[125] Nonetheless, its fine work was recognized by name in the C-in-C's despatches,[126] the AOP being the only ASC unit in the BEF to receive this distinction during the war, thereby demonstrating the capability of an agile mobile logistic

116 Ibid, p.141. The *charabanc* was an open top, single deck bus.
117 Ibid, p.141.
118 Ibid, p.142.
119 Young, *Army Service Corps*, p.124.
120 See, Major-General Sir Arthur B Scott KCB DSO & P Middleton Brumwell MC CF, *History of the 12th (Eastern) Division in the Great War* (London: Nisbet & Co, 1923), pp.167-168.
121 Lieutenant-Colonel G L H Howell ASC was the AOP's first Commanding Officer, having been posted to the appointment from the 13th Corps Ammunition Park.
122 For transcripts of the letters, see, Young, *Army Service Corps*, pp.124-125.
123 The Commanding Officer was awarded the CMG and the Adjutant, the DSO; 21 NCOs and soldiers were awarded the MM. For details, see, Ibid, p.125. Haig commented to the CO that his soldiers had, 'greatly assisted the operations of our troops and have contributed in no small degree to the frustration of the enemy's plans'.
124 Most of these operations were conducted at night, with bus drivers behind the wheel for 60 hours without rest, which clearly which impaired efficiency and safety, yet was vital to meet the operational imperative. Beadon, *Royal Army Service Corps*, p.142.
125 For details of the interaction between the AOP and the Canadian Corps, see, Rob Thompson, 'Delivering the Goods, Operational Landovery Castle: A Logistical and Administrative Analysis of Canadian Corps Preparations for the Battle of Amiens 8-11 August 1918', in Gary Sheffield and Peter Gray (Eds.), *Changing War, The British Army, The Hundred Days Campaign and the Birth of the Royal Air Force, 1918*, Birmingham War Studies (London: Bloomsbury, 2013), p.46.
126 Lieutenant-Colonel J H Boraston OBE (Ed.), *Sir Douglas Haig's Despatches, December 1915 - April 1919* (London: J M Dent & Sons, 1919), p.239 & p.306. The despatch noted that in the advance, the AOP had lifted nearly 800,000 troops and travelled over 2,500,000 miles.

P10.2. Motor Ambulances: a very significant improvement in patient care. Improvements to battlefield ambulance design continue in the 21st Century. (RLC Museum: Masters Collection)

transport reserve in delivering critical operational output.[127] Whilst the AOP was a critical GHQ asset, divisional WMT companies, including ammunition sub-parks, were frequently involved in transporting infantry and pioneer units.[128]

An often forgotten contribution of WMT was its role in improving medical evacuation.[129] From a global army total of 15 ambulances in August 1914, the BEF had 3,527 in November 1918.[130] From late August to late September 1914, the small but growing number of motor ambulances in the BEF were mainly deployed in the base areas but it became obvious from operational experience that WMT had a much more significant role to play and by the Armistice WMT ambulances were widely deployed through the BEF's Area of Responsibility (AOR). In August and September 1914, as directed by *Field Service Regulations* (FSR) many casualties were evacuated by returning supply lorries,[131] a process, which, whilst lucidly demonstrating that WMT

127 Lieutenant-Colonel G L H Howell ASC was also mentioned by name as the AOP Commanding Officer, in the C-in-C's Final Despatch published in the *London Gazette* on Thursday 10 April 1919, p.4711, which noted that the AOP was 'controlled with great ability by its commander'. This entry is unique because although two other Lieutenant-Colonels are mentioned both were staff officers in GHQ.

128 Lipscombe, *Historical Record of 180 Coy*, p.49, records that the II (ANZAC) Corps were especially keen 'to eliminate "marching" as much as possible' and in the BEF there was always a requirement for WMT to reposition divisions. Lipscombe recorded the movement of troops not in numbers but rather unusually, in tons.

129 For details of the medical issues, see Major-General Sir W G Macpherson KCMG CB LLD & Major T J Mitchell DSO RAMC, BOH, *Medical Services, General History*, Vol. IV, *Medical Services during Operations on the Gallipoli Peninsula; in Macedonia; in Mesopotamia and North-West Persian East Africa; in the Aden Protectorate and in North Russia. Ambulance Transport during the War* (London: HMSO, 1924).

130 MEBE, p.595, Table (ii) (a) - Monthly Census of Mechanical Transport Vehicles in All Theatres.

131 'The empty wagons of supply columns and ammunition parks returning to replenish at the railhead may be utilized

had utility in this arena, disrupted the distribution of ammunition and material.[132] In addition, whilst WMT generally provided faster evacuation than horse ambulance, the level of patient care was well below emerging standards. GHQ issued instructions that Motor Ambulance Convoys (MAC) each of 50 ambulances, were to be established to provide a more coherent response to the increasing requirement for improved medical evacuation.

It soon became apparent that the motor ambulance had many advantages over HT, particularly with regard to patient comfort and timeliness, both of which are essential to casualty survival rates, as indeed was the courage of the drivers, with one, Private Masters ASC,[133] being awarded the VC.[134] Clearly, there were many challenges to be tackled in order to produce a suitable and capable motor ambulance that would be Fit For Role; indeed the quest continues today as the threat changes and aspirations for patient care rise.[135] An emerging issue was the initial growth of the numbers of motor ambulances,[136] which resulted in a fleet comprising vehicles from 20 different manufacturers, which from the Equipment Support perspective was unsustainable.[137] Pneumatic tyres, which had inner inflatable tubes and outer covers and were preferred for ambulance duties because they provided a more comfortable ride, were vulnerable to punctures, whilst their supply, distribution and fitting, created another logistic chain.

Clinically, the early ambulances had many limitations but as the war progressed, design specifications generated a wide range of improvements, including springing, interior lighting, ventilated casualty compartments with heating, driver-attendant communication, rear steps, attendant's folding seat, locking stretcher racks, padded seating, floor drains, tool box and petrol can stowage. Two trials are of note. One attempted to offer some protection against shrapnel to the patient compartment,[138] whilst the other focused upon the provision of transportation for specialist surgical cases and serious

for this purpose, sufficient personnel from the clearing hospitals being sent forward with the supply columns, &c, to take over the sick and wounded'; and General Staff, *Field Service Regulations, Part II, Organization and Administration*, War Office (London: HMSO, 1909) (reprinted, with amendments to October, 1914), p.123.

132 This option remained in use throughout the war, most usually for walking wounded. An interesting aside to this activity was the voluntary deployment of members of 180 Company to 34 Casualty Clearing Station (CCS) to assist with the registration of patients, the provision of refreshments and the loading of ambulance trains. For a brief summary of the involvement of 180 Mechanical Transport Company (18 Ammunition Sub-Park) in these tasks, during the Battle of the Somme, see, Lipscombe, *Historical Record of 180 Coy*, p.43 & p.45.

133 Pre-war, Masters was, between 1898-1900, with W Birtwistle, the cycling World record holder for the tandem at ¼ and ½ miles. George Masters had three children with his wife Alice, who died in 1943, being reunited with her on 4 April 1963 when he passed away at Southport aged 86. They are buried together in the churchyard at Saint Cuthbert's, Southport. Information collated from documents in the RLC Museum.

134 Private Richard George Masters ASC, attached to 141 Field Ambulance Royal Army Medical Corps as an motor ambulance driver, was awarded the VC for his courage and determination in evacuating nearly 200 casualties to a dressing station, whilst driving an Austin Ambulance (No 21) whilst under artillery and machine gun fire and air attack. The action took place near the village of Gorre, approximately two miles East of Bethune in Northern France on Tuesday 9 April 1918. He was also awarded the Croix de Guerre and received a Mention in Despatches (MID) for other actions. His hand-written memoir of his service in the Great War is held by the Royal Logistic Corps Museum and he describes his delight and surprise in receiving the VC from King George V at First Army Headquarters, and afterwards being walked around the chateau garden with another VC recipient by General Horne, Commander First Army, who had his arms round their shoulders. Memoirs of M2/048544 Private George Masters VC, RLC Museum.

135 See, Lieutenant Colonel C H Maginniss BA RLC, 'One Four Bravo, An analysis of the imperatives for the design of military ambulances supporting ground force operations in the 21st Century', *British Army Review*, No 150, UK MOD (Winter 2010-2011), pp.73-81.

136 Some of these ambulances were gifted by private individuals, societies, philanthropic organizations and commercial companies.

137 Macpherson & Mitchell, BOH, *Medical Services*, Vol. IV, p.618.

138 Marcosson wrote of the effects of artillery upon ambulances, 'A riddled ambulance shows how an errand of succour was halted by shrapnel that knows no mercy or charity'; Marcosson, *Business of War*, p.152.

P10.3. Logistic VC: Private George Masters. Masters was the only badged logistician to be awarded a VC in the Great War, whilst conducting an in-role task. (RLC Museum: Masters Collection)

fractures; unfortunately neither of these projects were entirely successful, capability being limited by the contemporary technology but the projects certainly demonstrated the Chain of Command commitment to enhancing in-transit patient care.[139] Motor ambulance operations were one of the components of WMT operations in which, women played a key role, with many vehicles in the base and LOC areas, and sometimes forward of the Army Rear Boundaries, being operated by amongst other organizations, the First Aid Nursing Yeomanry (FANY).[140]

MT Musings

It is remarkable how quickly the Army embraced WMT as a capability and a technology, which demolishes the myth that senior commanders and staff officers were fundamentally conservative

139 Two successful components of the specialist care ambulance were the Coleman-Newall Sling Stretcher and the Clark-Doherty Suspension Apparatus; Macpherson & Mitchell, BOH, *Medical Services*, Vol. IV, p.626.

140 See, Irene Ward DBE MP, *FANY INVICTA* (London: Hutchinson, 1955), Janet Lee, *War Girls, The First Aid Nursing Yeomanry in the First World War* (Manchester: Manchester University Press, 2005) and Diane Atkinson, *Elsie and Mairi Go to War, Two Extraordinary Women on the Western Front* (London: Preface Publishing, 2009).

in their thinking and reactionary in their approach. Whilst there were some that were in this category, for the most part, their perspective was from one of three schools: enthusiastic, pragmatic or cautious. The enthusiasts were generally over optimistic, assigning early WMT a capability that it could not deliver, although it improved as the war and technology progressed. The pragmatic school saw a system that needed to be developed whilst the cautious highlighted the challenges, of which there were many.

Some figures give a flavour of the problem. In August 1914, the British Army had a global total of 443 WMT vehicles,[141] including 124 lorries (3 ton and 30 cwt). By February 1916, there were 352 types of WMT vehicle supported by 281,000 lines of spares. In November 1918, the BEF in France and Belgium had on charge 26,809 lorries. The BEF's WMT inventory certainly impressed an American observer in 1918 who noted that it was 'more than one-sixth of all the commercial motor vehicles in use in the United States'.[142] The table below clearly illustrates the exponential increase of WMT equipment, which provided a raft of opportunities and problems for commanders and staffs.

Table 10.1
Expansion of WMT Vehicles in the BEF 1914–1918[143]

Vehicle Type	Army - August 1914	BEF - November 1918
Ambulances	15	3,527
Cars	45	5,137
Lorries - Disinfector	0	90
Lorries - General Transport (3 ton & 30 cwt)	124	26,809
Lorries - Stores	0	904
Lorries - Workshop	18	708
Motorcycles - Solo & Sidecar	24	14,328
Vans	0	2,526
Various	217	1,444
Total WMT Vehicles	**443**	**55,473**

The effective management and utilization of this fleet could not have been achieved without senior officers embracing the developing culture and the emerging technology, which given that their military experience was almost entirely railway transportation or Animal Transport (AT) demonstrates how impressive the achievement was. That this group was able to transfer its professional skills obtained mainly through its experience of HT to WMT, makes the transition even more remarkable, especially as throughout the conflict it was essential to master and maintain both capabilities.[144] That key officers were of outstanding quality did not escape the notice of

141 415 vehicles were in UK with 28 overseas; Egypt: 1 x ambulance; South Africa: 2 x cars and Malta: 1 x car, 1 x ambulance, 1 x motorcycle, 18 x wheeled trucks and 4 x various. See, Young, *Army Service Corps*, Annex I, p.230. In addition, the Army possessed 57 steam tractors, 7 of which were in Malta, for a total mechanical transport fleet of 507.

142 Marcosson, *Business of War*, p.18.

143 Figures for August 1914 compiled from Young, *Army Service Corps*, Annex I, p.230 and for November 1918, from MEBE, p.595, Table (ii) (a) - Monthly Census of Mechanical Transport in All Theatres, November 1918; excludes MT vehicles allocated to the RAF.

144 As an example, Colonel F M Wilson, Deputy Director Supplies & Transport (DSST) at HQ Fourth Army appears

independent observers, one of whom remarked of the BEF's Director of Transport, 'General Boyce[145] is a fine type of the clear-cut efficiency that you invariably discover in the high executive British Army places.'[146]

In generating the introduction of a very significant WMT capability, there was a requirement to apply what is now called 'Defence Lines of Development' (DLOD).[147] Whilst the process was not as complex as it is in 2018,[148] the War Office was responsible for assessing a wide range of issues relating to the fielding of equipment but in the first half of the war it was overwhelmed by the need to deploy assets to operational theatres; indeed the procurement of thousands of WMT vehicles during the war was probably the most challenging Urgent Operational Requirement (UOR) project in the British Army's history.[149] As the war progressed however, these areas were refined to generate a more coherent delivery of the requirement.[150] One issue that was never resolved was a direct consequence of the need for quantity, which inevitably resulted in a plethora of different types from many manufacturers,[151] thereby generating a host of logistic issues, especially in relation to the delivery of ES.[152] Training the soldiers was another major problem and it took some time before the challenges relating to the many components of the process started to be improved. With remarkable foresight however, the ASC had, pre-war, devoted a complete handbook to WMT operations,[153] which, combined with some agile military planning, enabled the ASC to form 12

not only at ease in dealing with HT and MT issues but also has a lucid grasp of their strengths and limitations. Of especial interest, is his application of basic principles of transport management in creating output in both arenas, covering key aspects such as training, equipment care, utilization and support. TNA WO 95/454: HQ Fourth Army, DDST, WD, entries, February 1916 - December 1918.

145 Brigadier-General W G B Boyce late ASC, BEF Director of Transport. The records relating to his rank are at variance because he promoted to Major-General in post. Becke, BOH, *Order of Battle, Part 4,* p.13 states Brigadier-General, whilst Marcosson, *Business of War,* notes Major-General. More definitively, in 1918, Brigadier-General F M Wilson (promoted in post from Colonel on 16 October 1917) the DDST Fourth Army records him as a Major-General; TNA WO 95/454/4: HQ Fourth Army, A&Q, WD, 12 October 1918. Boyce was knighted for his services.

146 Marcosson, *Business of War,* p.127. Marcosson clearly knew his man because the post-war Royal Army Service Corps regimental history recorded of him, 'a strong and able organiser, who possessed that merit somewhat rare in the British Army of knowing when to dismiss subordinates, who, however agreeable in other respects, did not satisfy him professionally'; Beadon, *Royal Army Service Corps,* p.86.

147 Usually summarized as TEPID OIL: Training, Equipment, Personnel, Information, Doctrine, Organization, Infrastructure, Logistics.

148 If it had been, there seems little doubt that the urgent effect could not have been achieved but equally in the longer-term the need to compress the process inevitably created downstream issues.

149 Whilst in-service WMT in the Second World War far exceeded that of the Great War, the British Army had to overcome far greater challenges in terms of industry building a manufacturing base and the War Office creating the critical operating, supply, equipment support and training capability. For a description of British WMT procurement and production in the Great War, see TNA MUN 5/340/160/12/4: MOM, Vol. XII, Part IV, *Mechanical Transport Vehicles.* For a summary of British defence WMT production figures in the Second World War, see, Central Statistical Office, *History of the Second War, Statistical Digest of the War* (London: HMSO, 1951), Table 127, p.149.

150 One example was the refinement of production programmes through the Ministry of Munitions, which was based upon weekly outputs for each type of vehicle. The issue of 'spot' demands, mainly comprising small numbers of specialist equipments, such as generator trailers, water carriers and signalling vehicles at short notice, in addition to the programme, was a constant demand in 1918, and in July, for example 100 extra cars were requested. TNA MUN 5/340/160/12/4: MOM, Vol. XII, Part IV, *Mechanical Transport Vehicles,* pp.20-22.

151 Ibid, p.3, cites 23 British WMT manufacturers whose vehicles were in service in significant numbers, plus others producing specialist equipments. Marcosson recorded that in late 1917, there were vehicles from over 50 manufacturers in service with the BEF, with one lorry capacity type having 67 marques from several manufacturers, requiring an inventory of 4,000 spares items; *Business of War,* p.137.

152 One outcome of this problem was that vehicles and spares from American manufacturers were held in the Northern Base Mechanical Transport Depot (BMTD) at Calais, whilst the British assets were held at the Southern BMTD at Rouen; Marcosson, p.146.

153 Army Council, *Army Service Corps, Part IV, Mechanical Transport,* War Office (London: HMSO, 1909) (Reprinted

P10.4. MT Training: Vital for logistic capability. The expansion from 443 MT vehicles in the Army in 1914 to 55,473 in the BEF in November 1918, created an equal requirement for training to support the capability. (RLC Museum: MT Collection)

WMT companies[154] between 28 August and 19 September 1914.[155]

The problems and lessons relating to this contribution to fighting power were many, varied and sometimes complex. Doctrinally, the ASC had embedded direction on the utilization of WMT remarkably early in its technological existence, although the Army, through the medium of FSR[156] offered little guidance as to its employment. That WMT had potential though, was clearly illustrated by the FSR of 1909 outlining the opportunities of utilizing motor-cars for reconnaissance and the use of motor-cycles,[157] for DRs;[158] these aspects were developed on the Western Front. Motor-cycles[159] became an essential tool for traffic control and the delivery of documents and

with amendments, 1914).

154 The ASC termed these companies MT for Mechanical Transport, even if the vehicles were wheeled.

155 44 and 66-76 Companies. Lispcombe, offers an informative and engaging but sadly all too brief explanation of the formation and training of 180 Company ASC, which was based at Hungerford in Berkshire in the period late January to late July1915, until its deployment to France; Lipscombe, *Historical Record of 180 Coy*, pp.1-13.

156 FSR, Part I, *Operations* Office and Part II, *Organization and Administration*.

157 FSR, Part 1, *Operations*, Appx I, pp.221-223.

158 For a personal account of the life of a DR, see, David Venner, *Despatch Rider on the Western Front 1915-1918, The Diary of Sergeant Albert Simpkin MM* (Barnsley: Pen & Sword, 2015).

159 Then, as now, motor-cycles were not the safest form of road transport and accidents were legion. 180 MT Company was remarkably fortunate in 1918 in having no casualties from enemy action and almost no recorded sickness, so the untimely death of M2/175106 Private John Wilson, aged 22, a Despatch Rider, en-route from Frevent to Doullens on Friday 22 February 1918 as a result of a head-on collision with a car, was an especial blow; TNA WO 95/803: 180 Mechanical Transport Company ASC, War Diary. The unit history recorded, 'His death created a very painful impression, as it seemed but a few minutes before that he was, as usual, indulging in cheery and good-humoured sallies, for which he was particularly noted and well liked. He was interred in the Military Cemetery, Doullens on the Monday 25 February, 1918, many of the company and also civilian friends being present, who placed floral tributes on the grave of another well-esteemed comrade of 180 Coy A.S.C M.T'. Apart from being an emotional tribute to a soldier in a unit his, the comment of Private Wilson having civilian friends is certainly of social interest; Lipscombe, *Historical Record of 180 Coy*, pp.93-94.

orders,[160] whilst Staff Cars[161] enabled senior commanders and staff officers to inspect units, training activities and logistic operations with more flexibility and to meet personally or in conference, thereby improving their knowledge and enhancing efficiency through improved liaison and co-ordination. There were occasions however, when their enthusiasm, quest for information or poor Situational Awareness placed them in tactically embarrassing positions. As an example, on Thursday 8 August 1918 on the first day of the Battle of Amiens, a staff car from HQ Fourth Army was engaged by German forces at La Flaque, a location so far beyond forward elements of BEF infantry that it was seen by vehicles of the 17th Armoured Car Battalion.[162] Logistic commanders in the Base were able to take especial advantage of the capability because the road network that connected these facilities was usually more suitable for car traffic than that in the divisional areas.[163] That MT and particularly, WMT, was able to flourish despite the lacuna in the doctrine, says much for its contribution, the inherent flexibility of FSR and the determination of the practitioners.

Inevitably, this flexible mobility came at a cost in casualties, some of whom were senior officers. In one particular incident, the President of the BEF Claims Commission, Brigadier-General Colquhoun Grant Morrison CMG, late Royal Dragoons, was fatally injured in motor traffic incident near Querrieu on Tuesday 23 May 1916 whilst travelling to HQ Fourth Army for a meeting to discuss the hire of land for training.[164] The incident was initiated by the failure of a front suspension spring, causing the driver, who was travelling at 'excessive speed' to lose control of the vehicle and collide with a tree.[165] DDST came to an interesting conclusion: 'I do not consider the driver can be blamed for the excessive speed as after all the passengers if senior to the driver, are responsible for the pace'.[166]

Marcosson, in *The Business of War*, attributes much of the BEF's WMT operational success to what he describes as 'Vehicle Intelligence'[167] and in particular, its excellent inventory control, repair and registration recording systems and noted that its database, the 'Motor Census of the Army Mechanical Transport' was a 'notable industrial document', which 'would be worth its weight in gold to any motor manufacturer'.[168] Another major issue resulting from the expansion of WMT in the BEF was the rapidly increasing requirement to procure, receipt, inspect, store and issue spares,[169] the under-pinning basis of appropriate provision being the Motor Census. By 1918, this activity was being conducted on an industrial scale,[170] with the two Base Mechanical Transport

160 The BEF had 14,328 motor-cycles (solo & sidecar) on its inventory in November 1918; MEBE, p.595, Table (ii) (a) - Monthly Census of Mechanical Transport Vehicles in All Theatres.

161 The BEF had 5,137 motor-cars on its inventory in November 1918; Ibid, p.595.

162 TNA WO 95/112/2: 5th Tank Brigade WD, 'Report on Operations with Australian Corps from 8th August to 15th August 1918'.

163 Roads, particularly in the divisional areas, were subject to intense use by marching troops, WMT, MT, HT, tracked vehicles, including tanks and caterpillar tractors, and riding horses, as well as the attentions of German artillery.

164 TNA WO 95/441/2: HQ Fourth Army, A&Q, WD, 23 May 1916. He is buried in Saint Pierre Cemetery, Amiens in Grave VB7. Senior French officers attended his funeral on Thursday 25 May and the records suggest he had a professional and friendly relationship with them. Morrison was the AA&QMG in Gibraltar before his appointment to the BEF Claims Commission but had been involved in claims adjustment during the Boer War; TNA WO 95/27/5, GHQ, QMG, WD, 14 November 1914, Appx 8. His death is not recorded in Frank Davies and Graham Maddocks, *Bloody Red Tabs, General Officer Casualties in the Great War, 1914-1918* (London: Leo Cooper, 1995). His successor was Major-General Right Honourable L B Friend, who assumed the post on 23 June.

165 TNA WO 95/454/: HQ Fourth Army, DDST, WD, 23 May 1916.

166 Ibid.

167 Marcosson, *Business of War*, p.165.

168 Ibid, p.166.

169 The British Army in 2018 uses the acronym PRISMA to describe these tasks: Provision, Receipt, Issue, Store, Manage and Account.

170 This is in terms of range of items and quantity. Marcosson noted that the spares range for one type of American lorry consisted of 1,140 different parts ranging from a nut to an axle and that in one shed he visited at the Northern

Depots[171] at Rouen (No 1) and Calais (No 2)[172] being the two key storage and distribution hubs. On the evening of Sunday 11 August 1918, the *Deutsche Luftstreitkrafte*,[173] bombed No 2 Base Mechanical Transport Depot[174] at Calais, and the resulting fire[175] destroyed the spares[176] for nearly 20,000 vehicles, equivalent to 40 percent of the British fleet in France.[177] Operationally, this attack had some profound effects on the logistic system, generating a staff assessment for replacements,[178] reallocation of UK and BEF spares priorities,[179] adjustment of industrial priorities to produce more MT parts, a reduction in training in UK and a re-evaluation of storage dispersal,[180] whilst issues to Theatres other than the BEF were reduced.[181]

BMTD, he viewed 44,00 pneumatic tyre covers, 40,000 inner tubes and 17,000 solid tyres; *Business of War*, p.136 and p.144. He also noted that the Northern BMTD stocked 32,000 non-interchangeable spares totalling 1.7 million items, pp.137-138.

171 The main tasks of the BMTDs were the receipt, inspection, storage, maintenance and issue of WMT and the related spares.

172 Marcosson recorded his impressions of the inventory control infrastructure at the Northern Base Mechanical Transport Depot: 'Go into its huge counting room - it looks precisely like the office of a great factory with its clicking typewriters, card indexes, ledger accounts, adding machines and other aids to business'; *Business of War*, p.134.

173 The German Air Force was not an independent organization but the air arm of the German army, in the same way as the RFC in the British Army until the formation of the Royal Air Force. The *Deutsche Luftstreitkrafte* was formed in October 1916 from the *Fliegertruppen des deutschen Kaiserreiches*, the Imperial German Flying Corps. The German Imperial Air Service (GIAS) is often used in British sources as the term for the *Luftstreitkrafte* and its predecessor but neither German title translates thus. See, Peter Grey and Owen Thetford, *German Aircraft of the First World War*, 2nd Edn (London: Putnam, 1979), p.xxix.

174 The aerial attack on the Northern BMTD was part of an operation against the Allied logistic complexes in the Calais area. A water pumping station was wrecked, a Belgian MT depot gutted and a French timber yard set ablaze, in addition to the fire at the British BMTD. Railways were attacked as well, creating new challenges for those tasked with the security of the Lines of Communication. For an outline description of the British response to DLK attacks on the railway and port facilities, see, Henniker, BOH, *Transportation on the Western Front*, pp.313-326.

175 Marcosson records positive observations about the fire precautions taken in the Depots and Parks he visited. On this occasion, the deployment of Calais fire-fighting forces to tackle other conflagrations in the Base Area resulted in the Depot staff being unable to contain the blaze.

176 Destroyed were the spares for 6,497 motor-cars and ambulances and 12,270 lorries, including 26,000 inner tubes and 16,000 tyres. This loss represented an inventory loss of spares for 55% of the motor-cars and ambulances in the BEF and 40% of the lorries. Most of the losses related to spares for American vehicles. Jones, BOH, *The War in the Air*, Vol. VI, p.430. The financial loss in 1918 prices was £1,250,000, equating in 2016 values, based on the *Measuring Worth UK* Project Economy Cost as a share of the Gross Domestic Product (GDP) to £0.488 Billion.

177 Jones, BOH, *The War in the Air*, Vol. VI, pp.429-432.

178 This resulted in a trawl of spares from across the Armies. HQ Fourth Army was remarkably swift in responding, the comprising Corps of the Army (III, Australian and Canadian) dispatching their quotas by Thursday 15 August 1918; TNA WO 95/454/4: HQ Fourth Army, DDST, WD, 15 August 1918.

179 Training in the United Kingdom was curtailed as spares were directed to the BEF, whilst on the Continent, the Unit Repair Scale (URS) was reduced in order to enhance stocks at 2nd, 3rd and 4th Line.

180 The vulnerability of depots now became an issue, with dispersion and protection key activities, although given the limited amount of estate available the former was a considerable challenge. The risk had been carried since March 1918 when, as a result of the German offensives, the materiel in the Advanced Mechanical Transport Depot at Abbeville had been evacuated to Calais, from which, it had been intended to re-deploy the capability once the operational scenario stabilized.

181 Jones, BOH, *The War in the Air*, Vol. VI, p.431, states that in Macedonia, this had a clear and adverse operational impact because the British contribution to the final offensive in September 1918 was conditioned by the shortage of MT spares, particularly tyres and inner tubes. Neither Beadon, *Royal Army Service Corps*, nor Captain Cyril Falls (Comp), BOH, *Military Operations, Macedonia*, Vol. II, *From the Spring of 1917 to the End of the War* (London: HMSO, 1935) mention this issue, with Falls noting that most of the transportation difficulties were created by limitations in rail capacity and road repair facilitation, whilst the key supply concern related to specific types of artillery ammunition (pp.113-117 and pp.122-123). It is possible that the appearance of the spares issue in *War in the Air* was a subtle expose of the perceived impact of operational Air Interdiction in one Theatre having a strategic logistic influence in another, thereby reinforcing the utility of the RAF on operations.

Trucking Thoughts

One of the inevitable consequences of the expansion of the BEF and its concomitant support requirements was an insatiable demand for transport. Had WMT not existed, the solution would have been to acquire more HT, and place greater reliance on SGR and NGR. In the former case, there would have been an growth in the requirement for animals, forage and remount services, all of which would have been increasingly difficult to procure,[182] whilst the latter solution would have reduced logistic flexibility. WMT was therefore, a timely system that solved what would have been a very considerable challenge for the logisticians.

Given the low mobility of most of the WMT, one might have deduced that a significant proportion of the load carriers would be employed in the Base or on the LOC; a study though, of the deployment reveals a very different scenario. From November 1916 to November 1918, only approximately 3.5 percent of the 3 ton fleet was operating in the Base Areas and a similar proportion in the LOC, as the table below illustrates, whilst in November 1916, Fourth Army had 30.5 percent of the 3 ton lorries in France.[183] The Centre of Gravity (COG) for WMT operations in the BEF was forward of Army Rear Boundaries, with around 85 percent of 3 ton lorries being deployed there and most of them were allocated to Army and Corps tasks. The increase of 3 tonners in the LOC proved to be most fortuitous once mobile operations began, particularly when rail operations were disrupted by the German offensives in March 1918.

Table 10.2
BEF – Allocation of 3 ton Vehicles by Percentage November 1916-January1918[184]

Period	Lorries	Base	Depot Reserve	LOC	Army Areas
November 1916	15,291	3.83	5.06	0.46	90.65
April 1917	18,674	3.28	5.03	2.70	88.89
October 1917	22,248	3.57	5.60	4.20	86.63
January 1918	21,709	3.92	6.20	7.15	82.73

One particularly interesting aspect of the development of WMT on the Western Front was the correlation with the attempts by the Army to replace manpower with technology. This process is a recurrent theme in many recent analyses, which highlight that the Army slowly matured its original focus upon numbers of people to overcome the enemy, by replacing human and equine resources with technology: machine guns, chemical weapons, artillery, tanks and aircraft, all controlled by more effective Command, Control, Communications (C3) systems, although the communications aspect of the latter, proved to be the most challenging to deliver. What is missing from the piece is

182 The equine issue was a serious one, which generated much correspondence between the War Office and GHQ. Not only was it believed by many, that the cavalry divisions and brigades had too many horses but they also consumed a too greater logistic slice in relation to their operational effectiveness. To illustrate the point, a cavalry division in late 1914 had 9,815 horses and an infantry division 5,592. Given the enormous requirement for forage and water and a double echelon of WMT to transport them, which, added to the additional equine resources to support artillery and ASC units in terrain where WMT could not operate, especially in the forward areas, the concerns of operational logisticians are obvious.

183 Figure calculated from information in Henniker, BOH, *Transportation on the Western* Front, p.157 and MEBE, pp.593-594, Table (i) - Mechanical Transport in France.

184 Calculations based on figures extracted from MEBE, pp.593-594, Table (i) - Mechanical Transport in France.

WMT, which was, by default, executing this process by reducing the numbers of people and horseflesh required to deliver the capability. Indeed, this process had started in the mid-19th Century when the military had first used the growing capabilities of the railways. Strangely though, having made these two major advances, other parts of the logistic system, especially inter-modal transfer and storage, relied on the man until well into the mid 1960s and beyond.[185] During the Great War, the introduction of WMT to supplement HT demonstrated the efficiencies of mechanization and it is surprising that it found little wider application across the logistic arena. Very significant numbers of people were employed in Labour Companies[186] to handle the gargantuan volume of supplies throughout the distribution system[187] and if more technology had been employed to reduce the labour requirement, this could have had a significant constructive effect.

There were many lessons from the employment of WMT in the BEF. First and foremost, was its cross-country performance, which initiated a search for more capable vehicles during the Twenties and Thirties, especially for colonial service, particularly on the North-West Frontier,[188] although with the exception of some specialist trucks, the Army of 1939 deployed to France with an emphasis on 4 x 2 capability and many impressed civilian vehicles. The experience of the BEF on the Western Front was therefore, a Lesson Identified rather than a Lesson Learned, although the impressments system was a measure forced on the War Office to meet the short-notice political requirement for a Continental Expeditionary Force in 1939. Secondly, the importance of the engineering effort to construct and maintain roads was critical to the execution of WMT operations forward of Army Rear Boundaries; in this respect, whilst rail played a key role in the delivery of material, it was the use of WMT that enabled the work to be executed. Thirdly, the establishment of a Bureau of MT Technical Intelligence to collate all relevant information was an excellent idea, which of course, did not survive contact with demobilization. Fourthly, the outline organization of WMT stood the test of the war and few major restructuring actions were necessary. The assignment of specific vehicle types to generic WMT companies was one important change, which reduced the training bill, whilst creating efficiencies in repair and the adoption of general task grouping created much greater operational flexibility and capacity. In the winter of 1917-1918, this process was taken further by the abolition of Corps and Divisional Supply Columns, Ammunition Sub-Parks and Auxiliary Patrol Companies.[189] This re-organization pooled the assets, forming Divisional Mechanical Transport Companies, generating not only a saving in personnel and vehicles but also improvements in logistic lift, with a particular focus on producing a reserve to replace or reinforce railway movement in specific sectors if required.[190] Last but not least, was the importance of reserve stocks of vehicles

185 The loading of supplies, to ships, by lines of hand-balling soldiers, in preparation for Operation CORPORATE in 1982 is an excellent illustration; see, David Brown, *The Royal Navy and the Falklands War* (London: Leo Cooper, 1987), p.66. The photograph also demonstrates timeless logistic dockyard humour relating to salvage. Despite the introduction of a suite of Materials Handling Equipment (MHE) from Container Handling Equipment to Hand Pallet Trolleys, the soldier of the 21st Century is still involved in breaking-bulk, especially within the Fighting Echelons of units where it is necessary to load ammunition, rations and water from pallets and Unit Load Containers (ULC) to platforms such as SPG, tanks and Infantry Fighting Vehicles.

186 Labour Corps personnel peaked at 142,323 in January 1918, declining to 107,481 in November; MEBE, p.64 (iii), Table (ii) - Estimated Strengths of the Expeditionary Forces.

187 For a clear analysis of the role of labour in supporting operations on the Western Front, see the excellent and comprehensive, John Starling & Ivor Lee, *No Labour, No Battle, Military Labour During the First World War* (Stroud: Spellmount, 2009), pp.79-162.

188 During operations in the period 1936-1937, the Indian Army employed two mechanical transport companies, nine independent mechanical transport sections and a motor ambulance company in addition to the equivalent of 18 animal transport companies; *Official History of Operations on the NW Frontier of India, 1936-37* (Delhi: Government of India, 1943), pp.viii-ix.

189 For a unit perspective of this amalgamation, see, Lispcombe, *Historical Record of 180 Coy*, pp.96-100.

190 Beadon, *Royal Army Service Corps*, pp.138-139.

and spares to buffer In-Theatre operational and accidental loss, a reduction in industrial output, allocation of assets to other theatres and interruption of supplies from the UK Base and the USA.

Conclusion

WMT made a major contribution to the operations of the BEF in every area from the ports to the Fighting Echelon. Its niche work in supporting Base activities enabled HT to be reduced and its delivery of road construction material from railheads was vital to the BEF's ability to exist, develop and operate. Whilst much of the artillery ammunition was moved by SGR and NGR, WMT was a critical component in the provision of logistic support to mobile operations. HT, even in 1918, remained a significant component of logistic capability[191] but there was a clear recognition, that WMT, in its various guises, was the Way Ahead[192], although as it transpired, the maturing balance of HT, WMT and a small number of tracked armoured logistic vehicles, served the BEF extremely well in the Hundred Days.[193]

The expansion and exploitation of WMT during the Great War was incredible. Indeed, it is impossible to think of another technology, which was so widely applied to so many aspects of military activity in such a short period of time. For most of the war, WMT made a subtle impact upon military operations complimenting and reinforcing HT and occasionally replacing it, depending upon the logistic task, geographical environment and tactical scenario. As it did so, the vehicles became more reliable, the operators more experienced and the capability concomitantly grew that much greater. What was hidden though, by the nature of operations, was its inherent flexibility, which was demonstrated on the Aisne in September 1914 but was not fully exposed until mobility was restored in 1918; Commanders and Staffs had though recognized that WMT was not purely a base logistic operation but a potential deliverer of survival and then possibly, victory. In this respect, the key output was to integrate a new technology into the Order of Battle (ORBAT) and utilize its capacity whilst maturing its capability.

The AOP played a significant role during the German offensive and the Allies would have been pressed to react to the German advance with the flexibility they showed, without access to the growing and developing WMT capability, whilst, without it, the British advance during the Hundred Days could not have been achieved in the manner it was. The BEF of late 1918 was by all contemporary comparisons, the most capable and effective land force that the British Army has ever fielded and WMT was an essential component of its success. Although SGR was the key factor in generating the lift capacity to support the advance, it was the coherent and effective use of WMT, which provided the flexibility to deliver the stocks forward and deploy the forces. To this extent, WMT was not just a logistic activity; it provided the moving arm joining the powerful shoulder and the mailed fist, and thus enabled the development of the winning Operational Art of War in the British Army.

191 The complex issues relating to the supply and movement of horses are clearly exposed in na, 'National Horse Supply and our military requirements, *JRUSI*, Vol. LII (362), April 1908, pp.510-531 and Major A G Todd Army Veterinary Corps, 'The Management of Horses on Board Ship', *The Army Review*, Vol. VII, (4), War Office (October 1914), pp.413-425. For a comprehensive examination of the role of horses in delivering military capability in the period and their interface with WMT, see, Winton, *Theirs Not To Reason Why*.

192 The debate about horses or trucks continued after the Great War. Interestingly, the drive to motorize was driven not so much by the Army Council but by commerce because by 1922 many of the Light Draught horses, which were essential to military mobilization were being replaced by the motor lorry, many of which were ex British Army and RAF vehicles, an imperative lucidly recognized by the Inspector of Remounts. See, Brigadier-General T R F Bate CMG, 'Horse Mobilization', *JRUSI*, Vol. LXVII (465), (February 1922), pp.16-25.

193 Brevet Major O W White DSO, Dorsetshire Regiment, 'The Abolition of Horse Transport in the Administrative Services', *JRUSI*, LXVI (461), (February 1921), pp.58-80, is clear on the advantages of moving to a WMT based road transport operation for conventional expeditionary operations.

11

Without Trucks to Move Them

The role of logistics in delivering armoured capability in the BEF

Logistics and the Rhomboid

The employment of tanks on the Western Front has received much attention over the years but it was, for the most part, logistics,[1] which controlled the operational deployment of armour during the Great War and in three areas in particular.[2] Whilst the tank had a tactical mobility in excess of all other military systems, with perhaps the exception of the horse in certain circumstances, its strategic and operational mobility was effectively zero, and in the Great War, only the railway was capable of enabling it in these two arenas. More critically, for the first time in ground operations, a heavy self-propelled equipment was deployed, in significant numbers, not on the Line of Communication or in Divisional Rear Areas but to engage the enemy with direct fire weapons in the Combat Zone, which clearly brought new challenges for the enactment of movement, re-supply, repair and recovery. Mounting an armoured assault on the scale of Cambrai or Amiens was a massive logistic undertaking; four weeks of intensive preparations were required for the former,[3] and, even with this experience, it took three weeks to prepare for the latter.

A key challenge was the operational deployment of the tanks because their sustainable track mileage on *pave* roads was usually no more than 20 miles, and, as there were no road Heavy Equipment[4] Transporters (HET),[5] tanks had to travel by Standard Gauge Railway (SGR) because the Narrow Gauge Railway (NGR) systems, which were often essential to transporting supplies and equipment within some of the trench zones, were incapable of moving them, although in Bite and Hold operations in 1917, NGR played a significant role in in-loading the Tank Brigade dumps with supplies.[6] To reach an operational area for an attack, tanks had therefore, to be moved by SGR to

1 For a description of the industrial aspects, see, *The Official History of The Ministry of Munitions* (MOM) Vol. XII, *The Supply of Munitions* (HMSO, 1922), Part III, Tanks.

2 For assessments of the role of armour in the Hundred Days, see, J P Harris, *Men, ideas and tanks, British military thought and armoured forces, 1903-1939* (Manchester University Press, 1995), pp.159-194 and David J Childs, *A Peripheral Weapon? The Production and Employment of British Tanks in the First World War* (Westport Connecticut & London: Greenwood, 1999), pp.171-189.

3 432 tanks were moved to the front by nine trains of 12 tanks each, per day for four consecutive days (15-18 November 1918) a total of 36 trains. The last four tanks followed later, making a total of 436.

4 Until the mid-1990s, British Army vehicles capable of transporting tanks were termed Tank Transporters. Since then, the US Army nomenclature of Heavy Equipment Transporter (HET) has become standard.

5 Despite the experiments with tanks during the 1920s, it was not until 1927 that two Scammell 6 x 4 wheel drive, Pioneer Transporters came into service, both of which had been purchased to move the Vickers Mk II Medium Tank. See, G N Georgano, *World War Two Military Vehicles (Transport and Half-Tracks)* (London: Osprey Automotive, 1994), p.49. Had road transporters been available, the Main Supply Routes (MSRs) would have required very significant improvement, as even small load carriers had poor off-road performance. The same applies in 2018; few tank transporters in any army have true cross-country capability.

6 In preparation for the Battle of Cambrai, NGR in the Third Army area carried, amongst many items, 165,000

a detraining Tank Railhead (TRH) close to, or within, an assembly area, which was preferably out of German artillery range, in order to prepare for the offensive operation. Once an advance had been made, the follow-up deployment of heavy tracked armour, which was partly dependent for large scale operations, upon the recovery and repair of tanks from the last offensive, had to await the movement forward of an SGR TRH, in order to deploy tanks from the reserve and recover damaged or failed ones from the battlefield.

P11.1. Barnham Station 2017: it is difficult to believe this was once one of the most secret places in the UK in 1916. (Author)

The first tanks to be shipped to the British Expeditionary Force (BEF) in France were moved to the Elvedon Explosives Area (EAA)[7] in Suffolk during June 1916 to conduct trials and

gallons of petrol in 82,500 tins, 55,000 lbs of grease, 54,000 rounds of 6 pdr shell and 5,000,000 rounds of 0.303 inch SAA; Colonel J F C Fuller DSO, *Tanks in the Great War, 1914-1918* (London, John Murray, 1920), p.143.

7 The Elvedon Explosives Area (EEA), a title hopefully encouraging the curious to stay away, was based mainly upon the estate of Lord Iveagh, although part of the complex was outside it. Lord Iveagh, an Anglo-Irish brewing magnate, had purchased it at a bargain price in 1892 from the India Office, after its previous owner, Maharajah Duleep Singh, the last King of the Punjab, had renounced his government pension in order to offer his services to the Czar of Russia to assist in the invasion of India. The land was acquired through the Defence of the Realm (Lands Acquisition) Act 1916 and the removal of the population and the sealing of the area, including the closure of the road between Thetford and Mildenhall, provided a precursor to the development of the Stanford Battle Area between Thetford and Watton in Norfolk during the Second World War, although unlike the EEA, the Stanford Training Area (STANTA) remains in military use. The War Office created on the EEA, an area designed to replicate a part of the BEF's Western Front, with the trenches based upon the Loos Pattern. See, Christy Campbell, *Band of*

training.[8] The vehicles arrived by rail at Barnham Station,[9] on the Great Eastern Railway (GER) line between Thetford and Bury Saint Edmunds, after dark on Sunday 18 June[10] to be offloaded by 711 (Mechanical Transport) Company ASC,[11] and were then tracked to Bernersfield Farm, the HQ of C Company, 5.47 miles[12] to the South West.[13] The night move,[14] an operation which, became frequent on the Western Front, was to preserve secrecy,[15] but unloading in these conditions was certainly a challenge to the inexperienced ASC drivers. The movement by rail of the Mark I-III tanks was complicated by the loading gauge envelope, which meant the sponsons housing the armament had to be removed from the tank and travel on separate wagons. As each sponson weighed 3.5 tons, the task not only required lifting tackle but also much labour, sweat and muscle. On Tuesday 15 August, the tanks[16] departed from the EAA for Avonmouth,[17] for shipping to Le Harve,[18] the port closest to the BEF's rail centre of Amiens and one with a 60 ton

Brigands, The First Men in Tanks (London: Harper Press, 2007), pp.118-122.

8 For a summary of the trials and training, see, Campbell, *Band of Brigands*, pp.118-132 and Stephen Pope, *The First Tank Crews, The Lives of the Tankmen Who Fought at the Battle of Flers-Courcelette*, 15 September 1916 (Solihull: Helion, 2016), pp.17-20.

9 Barnham Station closed in 1953. The site (UK Ordnance Survey (OS): TL 862791) is occupied by a small industrial estate but the line of the track-bed to the North-North East can be clearly seen. The Second World War also brought military traffic to Barnham; in 1939, RAF Barnham was opened as a railed served chemical munitions site. In the period, 1956-1963, nuclear weapons were stored in a road-served special compound, constructed immediately adjacent to the South West of the chemical site. The nuclear storage site has several buildings with listed status, although the complex is used as a light industrial estate. See, Landranger Map Sheet 144, *Thetford & Diss*.

10 The first tank to arrive, on 4 June 1916, was His Majesty's Land Ship (HMLS) Centipede, later known as *Mother*; Pope, *The First Tank Crews*, p.18.

11 For a summary of the activities of 711 Company ASC, see, Michael Young, *Army Service Corps, 1902-1918*, Institute of the Royal Army Service Corps and Royal Corps of Transport (London: Leo Cooper, 2000), pp.100-104 and for its wider involvement in tank operations, Pope, *The First Tank Crews*.

12 Bernersfield Farm is extant. UKOS: TL 786749; Landranger Map Sheet 144, *Thetford & Diss*. Childs, in *A Peripheral Weapon?*, states that the farm was located near Barnham Station; see, p.108.

13 The tracking distance was much further. Whilst the route is not known, it was probably around 10-12 miles.

14 Sunset was approximately 2020 Greenwich Mean Time (GMT) or ZULU in current military parlance, on 18 June and Sunrise around 0340 on 19 June, so in practical terms, there would not be full darkness. As a result of the Summer Time Act 1916, Daylight Saving Time (DST) came into to effect on 21 May, so the times were 2120 and 0440 respectively. In comparison to 2018, in 1916, even in June, the darkness of the countryside around Elvedon, would have been deepened because there was no ambient light from towns and villages. The darkness at night in the centre of STANTA gives a fair feel for the conditions of 1916 but almost certainly Elvedon and its woodlands were darker. See, *The Nautical Almanac 1997* (London: HMSO, 1996), p.123 and also, Pope, *The First Tank Crews*, pp.17-20.

15 Within the Area of Responsibility (AOR) of the 69th (East Anglian) Division with its HQ at Thetford, the EEA was, in June 1916, one of the most secret places in the United Kingdom, with security being provided by regular cavalry and infantry and 450 officers and soldiers of the Royal Defence Corps, an organization created in March 1916 from infantry regiment Home Service Battalions and manning them with soldiers medically unfit for active service overseas. It was clearly a sensitive military area as the crew of a RFC aircraft discovered when it penetrated the airspace above it and was met with anti-aircraft fire from ground based machine-guns. See, Major Clough Williams-Ellis MC & A Williams-Ellis, *The Tank Corps* (London: Country Life, 1919), p.18. Major Clough Williams-Ellis was an architect by profession and his work included the famous Italianate village at Portmeirion in North Wales.

16 The soldiers departed from Thetford Bridge Station for Liverpool Street before marching to Waterloo and then thence by the London & South Western Railway to Southampton for Le Harve; Pope, *The First Tank Crews*, p.20. It seems strange that the troops did not depart from the loading station at Barnham, although in July 1916, a two-track Government Siding with a central loading platform had been constructed near Culford Lodge Farm (UKOS: TL 8575), which was used for tank entrainment but possibly not passengers. Barnham Station is though, approximately two miles nearer to Culford Sidings than Thetford Bridge, so the extra march may have been created by the wish to improve security by reducing the military foot-print at Barnham.

17 Portsmouth was used for latter shipments, reducing the shipping requirement and reducing the exposure to U-Boat attack. The crane at Portsmouth was capable of lifting a tank from a rail flat into a ship's hold.

18 Boulogne was the alternative.

crane.[19] At Le Harve, up to 26 tanks arrived in each ship but at Boulogne, a limit of 20 per ship was imposed and, depending upon type, a maximum of 40-45 in the port.[20] The tanks were then dispatched to the Tank Depot at Erin, where they were lifted from the flats by an overhead gantry crane, although unloading using an end-ramp or side-loading platform, was introduced. In 1918, the final refinement in armour movement came with the introduction of the Cross-Channel rail ferry services Richborough-Calais[21] and Southampton-Dieppe,[22] enabling tanks to be railed from factories and depots in the United Kingdom to the Tank Depot in France.

Railways to the Rescue

The introduction of the tank to the battlefield,[23] posed a significant challenge to logisticians. Movement, supply and maintenance were critical to combat capability but were untested operational tasks, whilst height, weight and width were three constraints during rail transportation. When the first tanks arrived in France, various expedients were adopted, none of which, were particularly effective or efficient. The Mark I Male tank weighed 28 tons combat ready[24] and had a width of 13 feet 9 inches,[25] thereby exceeding the loading gauge of the United Kingdom and Continental railways. The sponsons were however, detachable, which enabled the width to be reduced to 8 feet 7 inches, although with a time penalty for preparation and re-assembly. The Mark IV tank however, had sponsons, which swung inboard, thereby reducing loading time, administrative inconvenience and planning detail and was an excellent example of strategic movement constraints affecting the design of military equipment.

The *Nord* Railway possessed a suitable flat but with a load capacity of only 20 tons, which was clearly exceeded by most tanks and, unsurprisingly, there was concomitant damage to the suspension systems of many wagons, when they were overloaded. In addition, whilst tanks on the flat met the loading gauge on the *Nord* system, that of the *Etat* system, which served Le Harve, was less permissive.[26] The *Etat* system had 50 wagons designed to move a load of 25 tons, and tanks

19 TNA: MUN 4/2794: Mechanized Warfare: 'Dock and transport facilities for tanks, 27 November - 1 December 1916'.

20 Colonel A M Henniker CBE, BOH, *Transportation on the Western Front, 1914-1918* (London: HMSO, 1937), p.306. *Transportation on the Western Front* is also held in the TNA in ZLIB 29/455 (Text) and 456 (Maps).

21 Richborough Military Port was a very significant wartime development in Kent, served by the South Eastern & Chatham Railways (SECR) that by the time of the Armistice, covered 2,200 acres between Pegwell Bay and Sandwich, with 60 miles of PW and 35 locomotives. In June 1918, the port was handling, through the ferry service, 28,000 tons a month of military exports and 12,000 tons of imports, whilst the overall port capacity was 120,000 tons per month. To service the train ferries, an adjustable steel-girder link-span bridge was constructed, the gantry of which, after the Great War was purchased by the Great Eastern Railway (GER) and moved to Harwich where it resides in 2018. The complex included the Royal Engineer (RE) Inland Water Transport (IWT) Base, Depot and training centre, a RAF Salvage Depot and dump employing 700 women and 200 discharged soldiers plus supporting welfare facilities, with a total of around 28,000 personnel on site. See, Edwin A Pratt, *British Railways and the Great War, Organization, Efforts, Difficulties and Achievements*, Vol. II (London: Selwyn & Blount, 1921), pp.1106-1114 and Robert Butler, *Richborough Port* (Ramsgate: Ramsgate Maritime Press & East Kent Maritime Trust, 1999). Post war, it was sold to the Port of Queenborough Development Company but the financial and commercial viability was unsustainable and it was returned to Government ownership in 1923 before sale to a consortium of Pearson, Dorman & Long. See, TNA MUN 4/5081: Land and Property: 'Richborough (Sandwich Haven) Agreement for sale of port to Port of Queenborough Development Company'.

22 The Richborough - Calais service commenced on Sunday 10 February 1918 and Southampton - Dieppe, Friday 22 February 1918.

23 See, Childs, *A Peripheral Weapon?*

24 The Mark VIII had a combat weight of 37 tons; David Fletcher, *Landships, British Tanks in the First World War*, (London: HMSO, 1984), p.48.

25 Ibid, p.48.

26 Henniker, BOH, *Transportation on the Western Front*, p.306.

P11.2. Logistic Innovation: Sheeted tanks on the Cross-Channel Train Ferry. The introduction of Train Ferry capability reinforced the concept of Factory to Fire-Trench. (Tank Museum: 0883/5)

weighing up to 28 tons were carried, supporting the concentration for Cambrai in November 1917 but the consequential damage to 28 of the 43 wagons utilized, resulted in them being removed from service for a deep repair suspension overhaul. Rail carrying wagons were also used for the carriage of tanks. The British imported wagons of this type from the UK, capable of carrying 45 tons, for Permanent Way (PW)[27] work but had to modify them for tank movement,[28] in particular, to prevent the ends being damaged during loading. Attempting to withdraw the planned 60 wagons from PW tasks in order to support the Cambrai offensive proved to be a more difficult task and only 24 were ready to support the operation.[29]

Given that deliveries of tanks were expected to rise to 280 per month by September 1917,[30] the BEF's Director General of Transport (DGT),[31] first requested that 50 wagons of 25 tons

27 Permanent Way (PW) is a 19th Century term, sometimes abbreviated to PWay, which encapsulates all the guidance and support systems for the railway. This includes the rails, sleepers, ballast, blanketing and drainage. In the Victorian period PW referred to the completed works, whilst the Temporary Way was the track laid to assist in the construction of the PW.

28 After the Second World War, some of the Warwells built to move high vehicles and armour, ordered by the War Department, were converted, by the London Midland & Scottish Railway (LMS) to carry rail; R J Essery, D P Rowland and W O Steel, *British Goods Wagons, From 1887 to the Present Day* (Newton Abbot: David & Charles, 1970), p.104.

29 Henniker, BOH, *Transportation on the Western Front*, p.306.

30 2,818 operational tanks of various types, including gun, infantry and supply carriers, were produced in the United Kingdom during the Great War; *Statistics of the Military Effort of the British Empire during the Great War* (MEBE), *1914-1920*, War Office (HMSO, 1922), p.479, Table (e) - Output of Tanks.

31 Major-General Philip A M Nash, late of the Great Northern Railway (GNR) and East Indian Railways and

load capacity be acquired from the Great Western Railway (GWR) and a contract was let for an additional 26 to be manufactured. It was however, rapidly realized, that these wagons would not be suitable to handle the dynamic developments in tank modifications. Orders were therefore, placed for a special flat, which became the basis of all the War-Flats which have been produced since; those in service in the 21st Century conceptually being direct descendants of those used in France in 1918.[32] 905[33] Rectanks,[34] varying slightly in size and capacity, were built[35] and nearly 400 of them were in service on the Western Front by November 1918.[36] The GWR built 78 x 38 ton wagons in three lots in early 1918,[37] the Midland Railway constructed 40 x 35 ton wagons in April 1918[38] and the Leeds Forge Company, 787 wagons in the period late 1917 to mid-1918.[39] These wagons were fitted with screw-jacks on both sides of the wagon at each end, which, when in position, took the weight of the tank as it passed over the bogies, in order to protect the suspension.

As the new wagons did not begin to arrive in Theatre until early 1917, there was a shortage of suitable flats for major moves, so the importance of honing the timetables and generating rapid turnarounds through swift loading and unloading drills, were essential to the maintenance of the deployment schedules. Tank train routing was dependent upon wagon type, with for instance, the *Etat* Railway serving Le Harve, requiring a low-flat for the tanks to meet the loading gauge. Initially, tank movement depended upon the requirement to transport them matched to the capacity available, so trains were not standardized. In order to properly support major operations, standard train formations based upon the type of tanks with which, brigades were equipped, became a feature of military planning. During May 1917, in preparation for the Battle of Messines, the movement of II Tank Brigade armour comprising 72 combat tanks and 12 supply tanks, from the Tank Depot at Erin to the Second Army TRH, was conducted using eight trains, each of a standard consist.[40]

Table 11.1
II Tank Brigade – Train Consists

Trains 1-6	Trains 7-8
12 x Flats (Tanks)	6 x Flats (Tanks)
3 x 20 Ton Wagons (Stores)	3 x 20 Ton Wagons (Sponsons)
1 x Coach (30 x Officers)	1 x Coach (10 x Officers)
6 x Covered Wagons (200 x Other Ranks)	2 x Covered Wagons (80 x Other Ranks)
2 x Brake Vans	2 x Brake Vans

previously Deputy Director General of Transportation at GHQ. Nash assumed the appointment effective from 7 June 1917. Major A F (Retd) Becke (Comp) BOH, *Order of Battle*, Part 4, *The Army Council, GHQs, Armies and Corps, 1914-1918* (London: HMSO, 1945), p.12.

32 TNA MUN 4/3138: Railway Material: 'Wagons for the conveyance of tanks in France'.

33 Childs in *A Peripheral Weapon?* suggests that 240 wagons were constructed for the American Expeditionary Force (AEF); see, p.121.

34 The nomenclature, *Rectank*, came from the Railway Executive Committee (REC), which was the organization responsible for running the British railway system during the First (and the Second) World War. The Rectank was supplemented by the Stableford 40 ton Well-Wagon, which was built in small numbers in early 1918, and was capable of moving the German A7V tank.

35 Remarkably, British Railways constructed another 78 wagons in 1960, which were almost identical to the Rectank design, some of which were later converted to carry nuclear waste containers; Essery, Rowland & Steel, *British Goods Wagons*, p.112.

36 Henniker, BOH, *Transportation on the Western Front*, p.307.

37 Don Rowland, *British Railway Wagons* (Newton Abbot: David & Charles, 1985), p.125.

38 R J Essery, *Illustrated History of Midland Wagons*, Vol. II (Sparkford: Oxford Publishing, 1980), p.168.

39 *Special War Transportation Number, The Railway Gazette*, 21 September 1920, p.20.

40 Henniker, BOH, *Transportation on the Western Front*, pp.308-309.

This arrangement however, introduced logistic and tactical fragility to the plan because all the sponsons travelled on two trains and the tanks were not operational without them. The introduction of the Mark IV, with sponsons designed to swing inboard for rail movement, solved this problem. Experience gained in 1917 preparing for Arras, Messines, Ypres and Cambrai, refined the arrangements, and all trains carried 12 tanks with the supporting stores and personnel. Trains were given a Rail Movement Number (RMN) and the 'consist',[41] allocated specific loads for each trip, the set of wagons[42] then being run to a plan to execute the delivery.

In preparing for the Battle of Cambrai, the requirement was to move to the allocated Third Army TRHs, 436 tanks. From Thursday 15 to Sunday 18 November 1917, there were nine trains per day, each of 12 tanks, totalling 432 vehicles with four trains following later. The TRHs were forward and reached by PW constructed to the minimum safe standards, which inevitably meant operating risk involving minor hitches and accidents, that resulted in delays later in the movement plan. Additional fragility was created by having to use some *Etat* wagons, which travelled loaded in excess of the maximum permitted gross weight. Whilst there were no critical failures, having to remove these wagons from the train sets, would inevitably have reduced the availability of tanks for the operation,[43] so with the import of new higher capacity flats from the United Kingdom, the *Etat* wagons were gradually withdrawn from tank movement tasks. Such was the pressure though, to ensure that rail movement continued with the minimum of delay, the Standard Operating Procedure (SOP) in the case of a derailed loaded wagon was for the tank to swing 90 degrees and dismount the wagon, regardless of any damage to the wagon or tank. Once the wagon had been disconnected from the rake,[44] the tank was to pull the wagon clear of the track, any damage to the PW would then be repaired and the train would recommence its journey.[45] The recovery of the tank would of course pose another interesting logistic challenge but the other eight would be ready for offensive operations.

Unexpected Challenges

In addition to the challenges of loading and unloading, the movement of tanks by rail to recently completed forward TRHs, created some interesting problems. The introduction of fascines,[46] to the armoured inventory, generated a number of logistic issues, not least of which was manufacturing, moving and recovering them. For the Cambrai offensive, 220 rail wagons containing 21,500 bundles of wood, weighing 400 tons,[47] were delivered to the Central Tank Workshops,[48] which

41 The composition of a train, by wagon or coach, with the designation starting at the locomotive and ending at the brake van.
42 Usually a complete train, including locomotive and wagons or coaching stock, or a mix of both, assembled to undertake a rail movement task. A 'Set' was usually associated with a recurring task.
43 Tanks were deemed a crucial component of the Battle of Cambrai. Objective 1 stated: 'to break the enemy's defensive position by a *coup de main* with the help of tanks'. Captain Wilfred Miles (Comp), BOH, *Military Operations, France and Belgium, 1917*, Vol. III (London: HMSO, 1948), p.17.
44 A group of coupled wagons, not necessarily of the same type, deemed either to be ready for movement or for future tasking.
45 Henniker, BOH, *Transportation on the Western Front*, p.310.
46 In military operations during 1917-1918, a fascine was a bundle of brushwood or similar material bound together and used to fill ditches and trenches or be placed onto marshy ground, thereby creating restoring mobility, especially for tracked vehicles. The British Army still uses fascines, usually deployed by Royal Engineer vehicles, although they are now normally constructed from heavy-duty plastic pipes.
47 Miles, BOH, *France and Belgium, 1917*, Vol. III, p.15.
48 In December 1916, it was decided to expand the Heavy Repair Workshop and Stores. The French proposed that the Central Workshops be sited at Saint Pol near Ramecourt, although Erin was the selected location. Construction of the seven acres of railway sidings and six acres of buildings commenced in early January 1917 but was delayed by

were then chopped to a specific length. Between 60-100 bundles were then bound, using a special fixture to tighten the binding with chains,[49] by two tanks pulling on it, in opposite directions.[50] Rolling the completed fascine, on the level, which weighed between 1.50 and 1.75 tons,[51] required 15-20 labourers, who were mostly Chinese. Entraining and moving tanks with fascine loads was not without its difficulties. The height of the top of a fascine carried by a tank was planned, from the top of the rail level, to be 15 feet 6 inches, comfortably inside the loading gauge, to avoid telephone wires across the railway, which were set at 18 feet above rail height.[52] After the first major rail moves with fascines from Plateau, it was discovered that the shape and diameter of the fascines and their positioning on the tank, varied to the point, where some of the loads were in excess of 18 feet and many telephone wires were removed by the fascines,[53] causing not only potentially critical disruption to communications but also generating more repair tasks for the Signal Sections.

The movement of tanks from the TRH to the tankodromes,[54] which was the first phase of the 'Approach March' from the TRH to the 'start' or 'jumping-off' point, was a critical task with a number of logistic implications, especially as this activity was normally conducted at night to enhance operational security. Traffic control, route suitability, repair and recovery were all important planning tasks, as indeed, was ensuring each tank had sufficient fuel to complete the journey. The challenges and hazards of executing these night moves must not be underestimated; even in the 21st Century with night vision equipment, conducting, in the dark, the off-loads, marshalling and movement, against the constant roar of engines and tracks, requires careful planning, sound training, practised drills and clear control, which makes the work of the Great War planners and soldiers, all the more remarkable.[55] The Tank Reconnaissance Officers (TRO) were responsible for much of this work,[56] which was complex from the planning perspective because company and battalion movement incorporated corps and divisional routes.[57] The acquisition of road space, was a particular issue, causing potential delays to other operations, especially re-supply. Damage was

adverse weather and a shortage of materials and labour. The initial manning establishment was 13 officers and 630 men. Central Stores were initially co-located until the Workshops were transferred to Teneur in 1918, a site of 20 acres, 1 ½ miles from Erin. For a brief resume, see, Fuller, *Tanks in the Great War*, pp.125-129.

49 Another challenge was the procurement of the 12,000 feet of chain from the UK; Miles, BOH, *France and Belgium, 1917*, Vol. III, p.15.

50 The tension exerted by the binding chain was such that an infantryman, in search of firewood, having filed through the chain, was allegedly killed, having suffered traumatic injuries from the fascine springing open; Williams-Ellis & Williams-Ellis, *The Tank Corps*, p.103.

51 Various publications either state 1.50 tons or 1.75. There will of course, have been variations in weight between fascines. Tactically, the fascine capability created one particular limitation, in that it obscured the view of the forward periscope.

52 The erection of wires across the railway was a noted issue. In preparation for the Battle of Arras, the 37th Division Instructions, No 6, stated: 'Signal sections are particularly warned about putting up lines which cross the permanent ways without ample clearance'; 'Administrative Arrangements (Q) 2 April, 1917 Section IX (1)' in Captain Cyril Falls (Comp), BOH, *Military Operations, France and Belgium, 1917*, Vol. I (London: Macmillan, 1940), *Appendices*, p.116.

53 Childs, *A Peripheral Weapon?*, p.114.

54 A tankodrome, a title closely associated with the RFC's aerodrome, was an area allocated to tank training but was also used to describe a site used in the field for final logistic preparations prior to operations, particularly field maintenance, refuelling and 'bombing-up' with ammunition, although the descriptor 'Tank Park' was also used. Some tankodromes and aerodromes were rail-served. Whilst tankodrome has passed from the British Army's lexicon it survives in the Indian Army and in the Czech Republic, there is privately operated military style training area advertised as *Tankodrom Milovice*.

55 The BEF tank crewman of 1918 would certainly be highly impressed by Challenger 2 and its Thermal Imaging (TI) capability but probably wonder in amazement at the fluorescent green jackets worn by the soldiers and the yellow flashing lights atop of the turrets.

56 For details, see, Colin Hardy, *The Reconographers, Intelligence and Reconnaissance in British Tank Operations on the Western Front 1916-18*, Wolverhampton Military Studies (Solihull: Helion, 2016), p.120.

57 TNA WO 95/101: 2nd Tank Brigade, WD, Appx A, February - December 1917.

always a concern, not only to road surfaces but also to communication cables,[58] so liaison with the Royal Engineers was critical to prevent disruption to other road movements and signals capability.

Another issue was ensuring that tanks, when crossing railway lines, did so at prepared sites with temporary level crossings, created by laying railway sleepers or comparable timber, parallel and next to the rails of each side of the track, in the Four-Foot,[59] and where necessary, packing around the sleepers with additional ballast, to improve resilience of the PW. Without the relevant preparation, the rotating tank tracks would distort the rails, damage elevation and compromise the gauge, leading to, at worse, derailments, or at best, disruption to traffic, until repairs were completed. Despite constant reminders in formation and unit orders and instructions, the problem remained an issue until the Armistice, much to the frustration of commanders, staff officers, railway operators, civil engineers and PW gangs. Whilst SGR and NGR were vulnerable to damage, NGR because of its lighter construction was especially susceptible.[60] Additionally, in forward areas, tanks sometimes used the NGR PW as a road, straddling the lines but in doing so,[61] damaging the ballast formation. Many road bridges were equally vulnerable to damage or collapse through the passage of tank traffic, either because the bridge was not designed to take the weight, or the structure had been weakened by enemy action, flooding or constant military use.[62] SGR bridges were much more resilient, being designed to support 100 ton plus locomotives, with single axle loads of 25 tons but without very significant engineer preparation, tanks damaged the PW by distorting the gauge, and also in some cases, the bridge decking.

Ramping it Up

At a TRH, it was essential to have a side or an end-ramp to facilitate offloading but railheads did not always have this infrastructure,[63] and it was necessary to build end-ramps using wooden railway sleepers.[64] This was a slow process, which took, in daylight, 20 men 10 hours to construct the 1 in 7 gradient ramp, plus the sleeper carpet extension to ensure that the tanks, as they descended the ramp did not nose into the ground, damaging the PW and creating ruts into which, the following tanks might stall. Building the ramp at night usually prevented detection from aerial reconnaissance but took longer and in the summer, there were only six to eight hours of darkness. These ramps and platforms used scarce labour and resources, constrained detraining TRHs to fixed points and could compromise security.[65] In addition, the Direction of Travel (DOT) of the train became a

58 TNA WO 95/112/2: 5th Tank Brigade, WD, '5th Tank Brigade, Preliminary Instructions No 2 dated 7 August 1918, Administrative Instructions Confirming Verbal Orders', para 1, Tanks Destroying Communications.

59 On a Standard Gauge Railway, the distance between the inner sides of the two rails is usually 4 feet 8 ½ inches (1435mm and reduced to 1432mm for high speed running). This gap is known colloquially, if inaccurately, as the 'Four-Foot' and the term is also often used on NGR when the gauge might only be 3 feet or less.

60 This is as true in 2018 as it was in 1918.

61 Tank units were not the only offenders in illegally using the railway as a route. Of but many examples, a battalion history records that a SGR trackbed was utilized for a company move to a worksite, although it was probably more of a straggle because marching on the ballast and the sleepers is remarkably difficult; Captain G K Rose MC, *The Story of The 2/4th Oxfordshire and Buckinghamshire Light Infantry* (Oxford: Blackwell, 1920), p.35.

62 Tanks were, in comparison to other mechanical vehicles of the period, heavy equipments, whilst most of the bridges had been designed and built for HT. The British Mark I-III Male tanks had a combat weight of 28 tons and the Mark VIII, 37 tons. See, Fletcher, *Landships*, p.48.

63 End or side platforms were rare on the pre-war Continental railways; Henniker, BOH, *Transportation on the Western Front*, p.312.

64 *Royal Corps of Transport Training*, Vol. IV, *Transport Operations - Rail Transport*, A/26/GS Trg Publications/2921, Army Code No 70443 (UK MOD, 1975), Annex K, Appx 2, pp.267-269, explains the concept and the construction.

65 Such facilities would certainly attract German interest and comprise the offensive, although equally the British might integrate the facility to a deception plan.

critical planning issue because it was essential to ensure that when it arrived at the TRH, the tanks could drive off the flats. Careful routing was therefore, required to ensure that the train arrived at the detraining TRH with the tanks facing in the correct direction for the end-ramp, which might mean reversing the train to change direction en-route, or ensuring there were bi-directional ramps. The sleeper ramps, whilst effective, were relatively easy to damage with a moving 600 ton plus train and it was essential to shunt the flats with care to ensure a gentle buffer to the ramp; not an easy task at night in heavy rain. Neither did the ramps survive continuous use; after unloading 50 tanks, repair was usually necessary.

All these issues generated a requirement for a much more flexible and effective solution, which transpired in the form of a Tank Ramp Wagon (TRW), which could travel with the train, carrying the materials and railway sleepers that were required to prepare the off-loading site and then be used to off-load the tanks by removing the one axle and lowering one end of the wagon to rail level. As an experiment, six were constructed in France from old wagons and were so successful another 21 were built in the UK. The advent, in Spring 1918, of the Ramp Wagon System (RWS),[66] enabled armour to off-load at any suitable site, with the minimum of construction work, and a reduced risk of detection; the latter was not only important for the protection of the equipment, but also to ensure the security of the operation.[67]

The DOT issue remained because only one axle and therefore, end, of the TRW could be lowered, although if necessary, a TRW could be attached to each end of the train. Upon arrival at the de-training site, the TRW would be lowered by removing the axle, the sleeper carpet to protect the rails laid and the screw-jacks at the ends of the tank flats positioned and then unloading would begin. The manpower for these operations consisted of two supervisors from the Chief Mechanical Engineer's Department of the Railway Operating Division (ROD) who travelled with each train, whilst 25 men of the Tank Corps[68] vehicle party completed the labouring tasks. Off-loading could be remarkably quick. In September 1918, from the arrival of a train of 12 tanks, preparing the site for off-load and positioning the RWS to the clearance of the last tank over it, took an average of one hour and 20 minutes.[69]

Gas and Guns

The introduction of the tank created many more challenges for the logisticians than rail movement. The official fuel consumption for the Mark IV tank was two gallons[70] per mile[71] but this was on flat hard ground. Cross-country, with a full combat load, the 12 gallons per mile suggested by a tank

66 The Ramp Wagon System (RWS) was a sound concept and an effective design, which remained in service, with new equipments, until the end of the 20th Century and still has application in 2018. For details of the design and operation of the Ramp Wagon System (RWS) see, *Royal Corps of Transport Training*, Vol. IV, Annex K, Appx 1, pp.264-265.

67 The importance of OPSEC is explained in *Army Doctrine Publication* (ADP) Vol. 1, *Operations*, HQDT/18/34/46, Army Code No 71565 (UK MOD, 1994), p.4-23; fn 6, 'The aim of OPSEC is to provide a military operation or exercise an additional form degree of security, using active or passive means, to ensure that knowledge of friendly dispositions, capabilities, intentions and vulnerabilities are denied to the enemy'.

68 The Tank Corps was not formed until Friday 27 July 1917. Before this date, it was called the Heavy Section Machine Gun Corps (MGC) and then Heavy Branch MGC. During August 1916, the Heavy Section was organized into four companies, A, B, C and D each of which had four sections. Companies were allocated 25 tanks: 6 tanks per section, with one spare per company. For a history, see, Captain B H Liddell Hart, *The Tanks, The History of the Royal Tank Regiment and its predecessors*, Vol. I, 1914-1939 (London: Cassell, 1959).

69 Henniker, BOH, *Transportation on the Western Front*, p.313.

70 Miles, BOH, *France and Belgium 1917*, Vol. III, p.385 and Fletcher, *Landships*, p.48.

71 At 2017 pump prices, £5.46 pence per gallon, this would cost £10.92 per mile in fuel; petrol for a Tank Brigade therefore, amounted to £786 per mile. The Amiens operation cost, in 2017 prices, £4,761 per mile for tank fuel.

P11.3. A Ramp Wagon System (RWS) operated by 79 Railway Squadron RCT in Holt II Sidings in Monchengladbach, Germany in 1982 with a FV 438 Swingfire anti-tank vehicle loading. That the RWS was in use 90 years after it was introduced demonstrates how outstanding the concept and the design was. (Author & UK MOD)

officer,[72] seems entirely plausible. With only 70 gallons in the tank, its mileage at best on one fill was a maximum of 35 miles and at the higher consumption rate, moving across country, around 5.8 miles.[73] These figures lucidly indicate that whilst the heavy tanks of the Great War introduced tactical mobility, their contribution to creating mobile warfare was relative to the previously static conditions imposed by the enemy defences.[74] From a logistic perspective, the task of constantly refuelling tanks with such short range to enable them to maintain momentum in the advance was effectively impractical with the resources to hand. As an example, to refill 72 tanks in a brigade after an advance,[75] would require 5,040 gallons of petrol in 2,520 two gallon cans,[76] every one of which, needed manual labour to load to vehicles, whether MT or HT, unload at a dump, issue to companies and then to individual tanks. The fragility imposed by these technical and logistic

72 Captain D M F Sheryer, *The War Experiences*, Tank Museum Bovington, RH 86/T.C./42688.

73 These are mathematical calculations, which require practical application. As with modern vehicles, there is usually a point when gravity or the pump ceases to produce fuel from the tank, depending upon the attitude of the platform.

74 An After Action Report (AAR) from the Battle of Amiens, compiled by V Tank Brigade assessed that the Mark IV tanks were capable of fighting a continuous action to a depth of 8,000-10,000 yards (4.54 -5.68 miles). For a narrative of the actions of the 17th Armoured Car Battalion, see, TNA WO 95/112/2: 5th Tank Brigade, WD, '5th Tank Brigade, Report on Operations with Australian Corps from 8th August to 15th August 1918', para 11, deductions, which accord with Captain Sheryer's assessment.

75 This is illustrative. On no occasion did 72 tanks leaving a Brigade Start Line all complete the mission but it demonstrates the logistic demand.

76 The tanks were allocated a low grade fuel of 45 octane, traded commercially as 'US gasoline'; David Fletcher, *Great War Tank, Mark IV Owners Workshop Manual, An insight into the history, development, production and role of the British Army's main tank of the First World War* (Sparkford: Haynes, 2013).

constraints, which could all too easily result in fuel exhaustion, with concomitant tactical defeat, was a critical consideration in planning the support of armoured operations.

The wheeled Truck Tanker Fuel (TTF) or bowser, with a carrying capacity of 600 gallons, appeared to be obvious solution but its low mobility and slow fuel pumping rate,[77] meant it was unsuitable for refuelling tanks on mobile operations and reliance was placed on the more flexible two gallon can. In order to prepare for the Battle of Cambrai, for each of the three tank brigades,[78] a special POL dump[79] was established, comprising 30,000 gallons of petrol, 7,500 gallons of oils and 2.23 tons of grease, which required two trains to deliver,[80] totalling six for the three brigades. Each tank brigade thus had 15,000 cans of petrol in its dump, plus all the oils and greases, the delivery and stacking of which, was a significant logistic task and one entirely reliant on manual handling. As each tank brigade at this time consisted of 72 tanks,[81] this was a considerable achievement, equating to six petrol fills per tank[82] but was a much larger task for V Tank Brigade at Amiens in August, preparing the 142 tanks in its four battalions.[83]

To be combat ready, each Mark IV Rhomboid[84] required a 'fill' consisting of 60 gallons of petrol,[85] 10 gallons of oil and 20 gallons of water. In addition, the ammunition requirement for each tank consisted of 30,080 x 0.303 inch for the Females, or for the Males, 332 rounds of 6 pdr, plus 6,272 rounds of 0.303 inch,[86] all of which, had to be manually loaded and stowed in the vehicle. In addition, many tanks were issued with fascines, each weighing between 1.50 and 1.75 tons. Ensuring the Combat Supplies and engineer materiel arrived at the right time and in the right place, required detailed staff-work and much effort from Movement Control staffs and unit personnel. Another factor, often forgotten now, was the logistic burden inherent in the post operation recovery; after Cambrai, the return movement from Ruyaulcourt to Plateau in the period 1-14 December 1917, required 28 trains moving 336 tanks,[87] whilst at the end of the first day of action at Amiens, V Tank Brigade had only 47 (33 percent) operational tanks from the 142 that had crossed the start line.[88]

Whilst the tonnages of materiel involved in supplying armoured operations were much smaller than that for artillery, there were a variety of other tasks, not least of which, was providing Combat

77 In this respect, its capability was the reverse of the Unit Bulk Refuelling Equipment (UBRE) of the 1970s and 1980s. To quote Major Stephen Barr RCT, SO2 Transport & Movements (Logistic Mobilization Plans) HQ British Army of the Rhine, 1985-1987, it was, "all pump and no juice."

78 I, II and III. For a contemporary summary of the tank operations at Cambrai, see, Fuller, *Tanks in the Great War*, pp.140-153 and Williams-Ellis & Williams-Ellis, *The Tank Corps*, pp.100-120.

79 A dump is a temporary storage area, usually in the open, for munitions, equipment, or supplies; see, *Army Doctrine Publication* (ADP) Vol. 3, *Logistics*, DGD&D/18/34/63, Army Code No 71566 (UK MOD, 1996), p.xiii.

80 Miles, BOH, *France and Belgium 1917*, Vol. III, p.41.

81 As a TTF carried 600 gallons, it could fill 8.57 tanks. A tank brigade therefore, required, in mathematical terms, 8.4 x TTF lifts to deliver a brigade fill. Assuming though, each Mark IV tank had 10 gallons remaining, this reduced to 7.2 x TTF lifts. A UBRE could only refill 4.96 Chieftain tanks.

82 The British Army uses the term Fuel Consumption Unit (FCU) when planning fuel requirements. A FCU can apply to vehicles, formations, units, generators, and heating and cooking equipment, the calculation for each being defined by task, time and intensity. For example, a FCU for a logistic wheeled vehicle is defined as quantity of fuel required for a vehicle with a standard load, to travel a defined distance on a specified surface at specified speed.

83 TNA WO 95/112/2: 5th Tank Brigade, WD, '5th Tank Brigade, Report on Operations with Australian Corps from 8th August to 15th August 1918'.

84 Rhomboid described the shape of the early British tanks. The Whippet had a fixed turret.

85 Assuming the fuel tank was empty, it required 70. Many documents refer to 60 gallons as the planning figure.

86 Fletcher, *Landships*, p.48.

87 Henniker, BOH, *Transportation on the Western Front*, p.310.

88 TNA WO 95/112/2: 5th Tank Brigade, WD, '5th Tank Brigade, Report on Operations with Australian Corps from 8th August to 15th August 1918', Summary of Action. The figure was 44 at the end of operations on 11 August; Ibid, Report for 11th August 1918 dated 23 August 1918.

Supplies[89] once contact with the enemy had been made, [90] the logisticians utilizing a combination of the Old and the New to keep the tracks turning. Forward dumps were in-loaded,[91] supply tanks positioned in reserve, petroleum products and ammunition held on wheels,[92] and additional WMT allocated to tank battalions for rations and water.[93] In an After Action Report (AAR) from the Battle of Amiens, HQ V Tank Brigade recorded, 'The only safe method of supplying tanks for any length of time during a moving Battle, is to have a mobile dump of at least 50 fills of petrol, oil and grease, loaded on lorries and standing by in some central place ready to move at a moments notice in any required direction'.[94] HT also played its part in planned operations, with assets being tasked from Corps to provide resilience in delivering Combat Supplies and to salvage ammunition[95] from immobilized tanks for re-distribution.[96] Whilst the actions, near Amiens on 8 August 1918, of the 12 Austin armoured cars of the 17th Armoured Car Battalion,[97] and the 96 Medium A (Whippet)[98] tanks and in particular, 'Musical Box' of 6th Tank Battalion, in support of the Cavalry Corps, demonstrated the capability of mobile armour in the exploitation role, it also illustrated the lacuna in the logistic plan.[99] If armoured operations were to be conducted

89 Combat Supplies are ammunition, POL, rations and water. Although the modern term Combat Supplies was not current in the British Army during the Great War, it neatly summarizes the items that were the most important in delivering direct military effect in the front-line. Ammunition included, in the Great War context, small arms ammunition, artillery ammunition, specialized infantry natures, chemical weapons and explosives. POL covered all liquids fuels, lubricants (oils and greases) and antifreeze. Rations included food for personnel and forage for animals.

90 On 8 August 1918, three of the four tank battalions in V Tank Brigade used 1,670 rounds of 6 pdr and 66,000 rounds of SAA; TNA WO 95/112/2: 5th Tank Brigade, WD, '5th Tank Brigade, Report on Operations with Australian Corps from 8th August to 15th August 1918', Appx C, Ammunition expended.

91 In preparation for the Battle of Amiens, V Tank Brigade POL Field Storage Site (FSS) held 350 fills, which was two fills for each tank in the Brigade, plus five dumps allocated to specific units totalling 168 fills. The Brigade ammunition FSA held 3,000 rounds of HE and 1,000 rounds Caso shot (canister) for the 6 pdr, 500,000 rounds SAA, and 5,000 rounds PW. TNA WO 95/112/2: 5th Tank Brigade, WD, '5th Tank Brigade, Preliminary Instructions No 1 dated 6 August 1918, Administrative Instructions', para 3, Supplies and para 4, Ammunition.

92 V Tank Brigade held on WMT, reserves of POL reserve totalling 100 fills and 1,000 rounds of 6 pdr, 5,000 rounds PW plus additional SAA, which are described as 'mobile dumps' in the instructions; Ibid, para 3, Supplies and para 4, Ammunition.

93 TNA WO 95/112/2: 5th Tank Brigade, WD, '5th Tank Brigade, Order No 1dated 19 September 1918, Administrative Instructions', para 2, Supplies.

94 TNA WO 95/112/2: 5th Tank Brigade, WD, '5th Tank Brigade, Report on Operations with Australian Corps from 8th August to 15th August 1918', para 3, Supplies. This plan of course was dependent upon the ability of the WMT to traffic the route.

95 TNA WO 95/112/2: 5th Tank Brigade, WD, '5th Tank Brigade, Preliminary Instructions No 1 dated 6 August 1918, Administrative Instructions', para 2 (b) Horse Transport. These arrangements were not specific to Amiens and details of the requirement appear in successive Administrative Instructions issued by HQ V Tank Brigade.

96 By late September 1918, the salvage of rations, ammunition, supplies and equipment had become more organized with detailed instructions being issued as to execution, and co-ordinating the use of supply tanks, WMT and HT to effect the task; TNA WO 95/112/2: 5th Tank Brigade, WD, '5th Tank Brigade, Policy of Supply & Salvage of Equipment', A.Q 308 dated 27 September 1918.

97 For a narrative of the actions of the 17th Armoured Car Battalion, see, TNA WO 95/112/2: 5th Tank Brigade, WD, '5th Tank Brigade, Report on Operations with Australian Corps from 8th August to 15th August 1918', para 10, Action of 17th Armoured Car Battalion.

98 The Medium A (or Whippet) weighed 14 tons, with a maximum speed of 8.3 mph, and a fuel capacity of 70 gallons and on a level track, had a maximum range of 80 miles, at 1.14 gpm, which at first glance, appears impressive. Assuming however, a maximum of three times the road fuel consumption for cross-country travel at 3.42 gpm, the 80 gallons would power it for about 20 miles, so it was not a deep penetration system unless it had appropriate logistic support. Fletcher, *Landships*, p.49.

99 HQ V Tank Brigade AAR recorded that an armoured car from 17th Battalion penetrated the German defences to the point where it 'followed an enemy's lorry for a considerable distance without the lorry driver noticing it', creating 'an opportunity for the use of Armoured Cars.....which if timed at the right moment, can do enormous amount of damage to the enemy's rear organisation and reserves'; TNA WO 95/112/2: 5th Tank Brigade, WD, '5th Tank Brigade, Report on Operations with Australian Corps from 8th August to 15th August 1918', para 10, Action

in depth, how were the vehicles to be re-supplied, or if they failed mechanically, repaired or recovered?[100]

Repairing the Damage

Armoured operational capability relied greatly upon the ability to deliver, what in the 21st Century, the British Army calls Equipment Support (ES).[101] Whilst the systems and nomenclature may have changed, the ES tasks for tanks are remarkably similar and are summarized as 'prepare, repair, recover and recondition', to restore their combat capability as quickly as possible and therefore, maximize equipment availability.[102] Before the introduction of heavy mechanized equipment to the British Army, the ES function, whilst equally important and conducted in various ways, was usually delivered within the unit by specialized trades or by the Ordnance services in a central facility.

Most equipment could be repaired in situ, or easily recovered and even with the arrival of the motor lorry, this process remained extant. The tank however, added a new dimension to the ES task in three discrete areas. First, whilst most of the components of the tank were in military service, although in some aspects as relatively unproven technologies, the key development was the integration of them to a complete system, with the characteristic ES complexities involved in maintaining power-plants, transmissions, armament, optical equipment and the armour. The effective support to this new system was immediately degraded because there was no coherent system in place for the programming, procurement of distribution of spares,[103] which inevitably introduced extempore measures, with all the inherent fragility of these solutions. This arrangement is placed firmly in context against one 1917 calculation that a Mark IV tank travelling an average of three miles per day for 14 days required 20 tons of spares,[104] which lucidly demonstrates, not only the issues with reliability[105] but also the importance of ensuring a robust ES system to maintain

of 17th Armoured Car Battalion. The dislocation of the enemy's logistic system in a divisional area during such an action, was almost at hand.

100 Ibid, para 10, notes that the key issue was an Equipment Support (ES) one; a fundamental failure in mechanical reliability caused by an unsuitable chassis, resulting in seven out of 16 cars being, at various times, out of action, which constrained the tactical outcomes.

101 ES includes the preparation and repair of equipment for battle and the repair and recovery of equipment battle casualties and failures. The ES staff have a vital role in monitoring the serviceability of critical equipments in a formation to ensure that combat power is maintained; *Army Field Manual* (AFM) Vol. 1, *Combined Arms Operations*, Part 6, *Combat Service Support*, DGD&D 18/34/44, Army Code No 71344 (UK MOD, 1998), p.viii. A key component of ES is Equipment Support Management (ESM) which is the process of controlling the allocation, repair policy, refurbishment, redesign and replacement of, and re-supply of material for, an equipment throughout its service life; ADP, Vol. 3, p.xiii.

102 The Tank Corps categorized maintenance as the replacement of damaged parts and repair as the mending of broken parts, with the doctrine espousing two key ES principles: maintenance was to be conducted in the field by crews and repair was to be centralized at the Tank Workshops. Fuller, *Tanks in the Great War*, pp.125-126.

103 This issue was clearly articulated by the Tank Technical Advisor in France, Lieutenant-Colonel Frank Searle in a letter to General Hugh Elles at the War Office. In his communication, he also lucidly highlights a fundamental logistic principle of ES in 2018 that the critical issue is to have enough of the right spares of the right quality at the right time in the right place. His last paragraphs stand the test of a 100 years: "Under these circumstances, and considering the urgency of the needs of the Country in other engineering directions, I feel it would be a crime to manufacture and send to this country, machines which there is no possibility of maintaining. With modifications in design, the quantity of spares necessary could be halved; of this I am positive, and the other Engineering Officers of this Unit are of the same opinion, but I understand that the Ministry do not agree." TNA WO 158/838: Tanks: 'Technical Advisor's Report dated 24 March 1917'.

104 *A Peripheral Weapon?* p.94; Childs does not reference this figure.

105 Manufacturing flaws in sprockets and wheel-hubs were but two of many issues that created poor reliability. For an analysis, see, Childs, *A Peripheral Weapon?* pp.102-104. Sheryer in *The War Experiences*, recounts that the life of a Mark IV Daimler 105 bhp engine was about 60 miles.

operational capability.[106]

Secondly, as there was no single organization in the Army or the BEF responsible for the repair of equipment,[107] it is of little surprise that a niche organization, internal to the Tank Corps, emerged to deliver ES, with many parallels to that of military aviation,[108] particularly in relation to field support, Reverse Logistics and centralized reconditioning.[109] The key difference however, was maturity because although military aviation was a relatively new capability, most of its ES systems had structure, were embedded within the BEF's operational matrix and generally had the relevant manning and equipment to execute the work, which the emerging tank capability did not; machine tools being a prime example. Indeed, during the winter of 1916-1917, without the support of the Royal Flying Corps's workshops, armour plate could not have been cut, nor mountings for the Lewis Light Machine Gun (LMG) been fabricated.[110] Thirdly, the tank was the first heavy self-propelled ground equipment to be designed to engage in direct fire with the enemy in a hazardous and demanding combat zone, which generated a host of challenges in maintenance, repair and recovery, all of which, were essential to sustaining combat effectiveness of armoured units. In particular, there were initially no Repair and Recovery tanks,[111] which limited forward ES operations in mobility, protection and output, creating reliance on manpower based solutions when a mechanized one was needed.

Ensuring that tanks were issued to units fit for battle became a key task of the centralized tank depot, through the work of the Central Workshops and the Central Stores,[112] although units might add particular refinements upon receipt. The forward maintenance of tanks, particularly beyond the TRH and in the Combat Zone became increasingly important tasks to sustain fighting power. Tanks were not always damaged or immobilized through enemy action[113] but suffered mechanical

106 This issue is crucial to present military and commercial operations. In the military environment, reliability reduces the supply, transportation and maintenance burden, whilst generating high levels of operational capability and enabling the ES system to focus on repairing battle damage. In addition, transportation assets can be released for the movement of operational equipment and Combat Supplies. In the commercial sector, reliability drives down costs, delivers reputation and generates customer confidence.

107 ES capability was delivered mainly in-house, especially in the technical corps and to a lesser extent by the artificers of the Royal Artillery and developing Tank Corps; the Army Ordnance Corps Engineering Branch was responsible for other Arms and Services. Progression of this issue had to wait until the Second World War, when the experience of the campaign in France and the Western Desert, generated a series of reviews in relation to the delivery of ES capability, culminating in the formation of the Royal Electrical and Mechanical Engineers (REME) in 1942. For a detailed explanation of the issues, see, Major-General Sir E Bertram Rowcroft KBE CB (Comp), *The Second World War, 1939-1945, Army, Royal Electrical and Mechanical Engineers*, Vol. I, *Organization and Operations* (War Office, 1951), pp.1-12 and Brigadier B B Kennedy CBE & Colonel J A Tatman, *Craftsmen of the Army, The Story of the Royal Electrical and Mechanical Engineers* (London: Leo Cooper, 1970), pp.148-166.

108 For a description of the industrial aspects, see, BOH, MOM, Vol. XII, Part 1, Aircraft.

109 Whilst there was clearly a strong engineering element to this process, recovery, reconditioning and refurbishment relied entirely on transportation to deliver the output.

110 Major S G Brockbank, *War History of the Central Workshops*, Tank Corps, Chp 2, p.27; held in the Tank Museum Bovington, RH 86/T.C./CW/557-60.

111 A number of tanks were later fitted with cranes to assist in salvage and recovery, whilst two tracked Gun Carriers were also modified for these tasks, which were the predecessors of the 21st Century Armoured Repair and Recovery Vehicles (ARRV). See, Fletcher, *Landships*, p.27 and Philip Ventham and David Fletcher *Moving the Guns, The Mechanization of the Royal Artillery 1854-1939* (London: HMSO, 1990), pp.18-20.

112 The term Central Stores offers the impression of a large warehouse containing shelves of small items but was the nomenclature of what was the BEF's Base Tank Depot, responsible for receiving, inspecting, maintaining, storing and issuing tanks.

113 Of the 142 tanks in V Tank Brigade, which crossed the start line on the first day of the Battle of Amiens on 8 August 1918, 40 (28%) received strikes from direct or indirect fire and 3 (2%) were immobilized by mines; TNA WO 95/112/2: 5th Tank Brigade, WD, '5th Tank Brigade, Report on Operations with Australian Corps from 8th August to 15th August 1918', Summary of Action.

failures[114] and terrain embarrassment[115] and crews returning from action to the Brigade Rallying Point were directed to make every effort to recover these vehicles.[116] The restoration of platform mobility was critical, either through engineering intervention by the repair of motive and drive systems, or recovery from ditching or bogging.[117] In the Combat Zone, unit personnel conducted these tasks. Tanks deemed irrecoverable were left in situ but with subsequent salvage of all accessible operational components.

Repair and salvage work, often conducted during darkness in the Combat Zone to reduce the risks to the personnel, was certainly hard work and sometimes dangerous, with parties coming under direct and indirect fire. Many damaged tanks were only accessible by foot or Animal Transport (AT) and tools for the task, and the recovered spares or equipment, had to be carried or hauled by soldiers, horses or mules, often using improvised sleds made from duckboards or metal sheets, to a site where WMT could collect it, a distance occasionally measured in miles.[118] Tools were a critical issue, and even in September 1918, were a constraint to the delivery of effective and efficient ES.[119] Salvage teams went to remarkable lengths to recover tanks, including the use of hand-grenades to apply explosive effect to re-shape metal components; their persistence and determination to complete their tasks is amazing:

> This tank (it was number 711) was in the front line.....it was useless to attempt to bend the plate with a sledge-hammer or a jack, but a few hand-grenades judiciously applied at the correct distance did the trick. It was a long business as the track and other parts had to be removed while the bombing was being done, also all work had to be carried out in the dark and even so the party often attracted a heavy bombardment. After a week's work No 711 was able to move to a more sheltered spot, and eventually onto a rail head under her own power.[120]

Between Friday 22 December 1916 and Thursday 25 January 1917, a party of two officers and 18 men, equipped with two lorries and a van, salvaged 32 x 6 pdr guns, each nine feet long and weighing 1,008 pounds, from tanks located on the Somme battlefield.[121] If a tank could not be mobilized under its own power, it would then have to be towed to the nearest suitable TRH to await a train. Loading these un-powered tanks was no easy task because they required to be hauled by an operational one onto a tank flat, whilst the challenges presented to wagon loading by failed tanks with locked tracks are obvious, with an equal problem during unloading at the de-training TRH, unless the tank was dispatched to a location with an overhead gantry, such as the Tank Depot at Erin. The towing vehicle might then have to be extracted by shunting the wagons, so it

114 Of the 142 tanks in V Tank Brigade, which crossed the start line on the first day of the Battle of Amiens on 8 August 1918, 23 (16%) came out of action because of mechanical failure, the AAR assessing that 'taken as a whole the mechanical troubles experienced in action were of a very minor nature'; TNA WO 95/112/2: 5th Tank Brigade, WD, '5th Tank Brigade, Report on Operations with Australian Corps from 8th August to 15th August 1918', Appx C, Report on Mechanical Efficiency of Mark V Tanks in Action.

115 In April 1918, 10th Tank Battalion, after an action involving eight tanks, had only three operational but none of the five casualties was from enemy action. Three were ditched, one had a failed gearbox and fifth broken drive sprockets. Major E R Parson, *Experiences in the Tank Corps*, 1916-1918; held in the Tank Museum, RH 86/T.C/2549.

116 TNA WO 95/112/2: 5th Tank Brigade, WD, '5th Tank Brigade, Preliminary Instructions No 2 dated 7 August 1918, Administrative Instructions' Confirming Verbal Orders, para 1, Clearing of Battlefield.

117 The introduction of the wooden un-ditching beam for the Mark IV tank generated an element of self-recovery capability, although positioning it under fire was, for those undertaking it, a hazardous one.

118 Captain R P Butler, 'Reminiscences of Salvage Work', *The Royal Tank Corps Journal*, 1932, p.40.

119 Parson, *Experiences in the Tank Corps*, p.12.

120 Butler, 'Reminiscences of Salvage Work', pp.42-43.

121 Ibid, p.41.

could unload and be returned to duty at the TRH. Mark V tanks struck by artillery shells were particularly susceptible to fire, resulting in serious damage. Recovering these vehicles to the Central Workshops and reconditioning them, was an especial challenge.[122]

Whilst field maintenance and reconditioning would be completed at a 'tankodrome', base overhaul and refurbishment was conducted at the Central Workshops, which had a critical role in delivering re-furbished tanks to combat. Between Thursday 8 August and Sunday 20 October 1918 General Elles stated that there were 830 tank casualties from all causes, of which 300 had been recovered, repaired and reissued.[123] Indeed, one tank having suffered combat damage from artillery was repaired and issued three times in five weeks during September and October 1918.[124] Central Workshops were also involved in the production and fitting of special modifications or accessories to meet urgent operational requirements.[125] Examples of these, were the manufacture of fascines, the fitting of Lewis LMG mounts, locking levers for doors and revolver ports, conversion of ammunition racks from the belt-fed Vickers and Hotchkiss[126] machine-guns to the drum magazine Lewis LMG,[127] with some of this work being contracted to an agricultural machine repair company at Blangy-sur-Ternoise.[128] Whilst these appear to be relatively small engineering tasks, it is pertinent to note that the 1,500 sets of locking devices for the revolver ports, each consisted of 25 parts, which had to be forged, drilled and fitted, whilst the reversion to the Hotchkiss machine-gun, within a month of the War Office decision to fit the Lewis LMG, created yet more work for the Central Workshops to reinstall the ammunition racks, which no doubt caused much irritation to officers and soldiers alike. Operational experience also generated requests for modifications, such as the provision of fuel gauges, lights for oil pressure gauges and clock cases.[129]

Workshop capacity was always being challenged, with tradesmen, materials and machines constantly at a premium. On occasions, personnel were dispatched to Paris to purchase oxygen cylinders to sustain oxy-acetylene cutting operations, whilst special tools were fabricated in the workshop.[130] Labour was key to every aspect of Logistic and Equipment Support in the BEF and

122 Brockbank, *Central Workshops*, Chp 2, p.2; repairs to fire damaged tanks were assessed to require 50% more man-hours than those without.

123 'Summary of Tank Operations, 8th-20th October 1918'; General H Elles, extract from a letter to GCS from Tank Corps HQ dated 29 October 1918, held in the Tank Museum Bovington.

124 Brockbank, *Central Workshops*, Chp 4, p.2.

125 In 2018, the British Army describes the acquisition of such capability as an Urgent Operational Requirement (UOR). One important tactical ES modification raised by V Tank Brigade was to reduce the heat signature of the tank engine silencer, which glowed red at night and, if pierced by bullet or shell fragments, issued flames, by fitting a larger gas expansion chamber protected by asbestos rope. TNA WO 95/112/2: 5th Tank Brigade, WD, '5th Tank Brigade, Report on Operations with Australian Corps from 8th August to 15th August 1918', Appx C, Report on Mechanical Efficiency of Mark V Tanks in Action.

126 The Hotchkiss machine-gun was of French design and manufactured in Coventry at the Arno Motor Works in Gosford Street, under licence from *Societe Hotchkiss*. After the Great War, the factory built Morris car engines, produced armaments in the Second World War, survived three major aerial attacks 14-15 November 1940, 8-9 and 10-11 April 1941 and rather less well, two fires in 1964 and 1966. Having been also occupied at various times by the Ministry of Pensions and National Insurance and the Blood Transfusion Service, it was acquired by Coventry University in 2000, and, after extension and refurbishment, houses, as the William Morris Building, the Faculty of Engineering and Computing.

127 The decision by the War Office, to adopt, albeit briefly, the Lewis LMG to replace the Hotchkiss and Vickers is examined in Childs, *A Peripheral Weapon?* pp.78-79. The Lewis did not fit easily into the loopholes and the drum magazine reduced its arcs of fire. Operational experience also identified that the barrel jacket of the Lewis LMG was more susceptible to damage from small arms fire and shell splinters than the Hotchkiss.

128 Brockbank, *Central Workshops*, Chp 2, pp.4-6.

129 TNA WO 95/112/2: '5th Tank Brigade, REPORT on Operations of 18th September 1918 by 2nd Tank Battalion with IIIrd, Australian and IXth Corps', para 12 (iii), Lessons and Suggestions, which also suggests irritation with the failure to resolve the problem: 'This had been put forward on several occasions'. Document under cover of HQ 5th Tank Brigade, G50/45 dated 16 October 1918.

130 Brockbank, *Central Workshops*, Chp 2, p.7.

the Central Workshops was no exception. Re-organization sought to increase productivity and utilize scarce tradesmen more effectively, whilst tank crews were taught more complex maintenance tasks to reduce the specialist ES burden.[131]

Another solution was the use of men from the Chinese Labour Corps (CLC), the first 200 arriving on Wednesday 8 August 1917,[132] to undertake trade appointments, although a significant number were found to be unsuitable. Indeed the Central Workshops was the key unit in the BEF, which employed members of the CLC in skilled trades and their work included the repair of all sprocket wheels and radiators. Labourers were also needed and 270 arrived on Saturday 25 August and they were crucial to the production of fascines in November to support the Cambrai operation. By March 1918 there were 248 CLC members employed as tradesmen or semi-skilled men at the Central Workshops,[133] including blacksmiths, tinsmiths, riveters, track-breakers, carpenters and electricians.

Conclusion

Major armoured operations, were, because of logistic support constraints, extraordinarily difficult to mount,[134] and although in the context of late 1918 it was possible for armour to be integrated to the tactical Combined Arms Battle, at the operational level, it was a major logistic challenge. The outfall was that once the Battle of Amiens was over, GHQ discovered that pausing to prepare another large armoured operation[135] would have interrupted, rather than supported the Maintenance of Momentum. *En-masse*, tracked armour could not keep up with the operational pace of the advance,[136] and despite various grandiose schemes, which suggested that the BEF might begin conducting the beginnings of ground manoeuvre warfare,[137] in late 1918 the equipment, doctrine and logistics were insufficiently honed to bring it to fruition.[138] The introduction of more tactically agile tanks compounded the logistic support challenge, an issue, which emerged again for the British Army, during operations in the Western Desert during the Second World War.[139]

131 HQ V Tank Brigade had noted in its Amiens AAR that 'It is obvious from actions in which we have been engaged, that Tanks have failed due to minor faults which crews have either been unable to diagnose or trace'; TNA WO 95/112/2: 5th Tank Brigade, WD, '5th Tank Brigade, Report on Operations with Australian Corps from 8th August to 15th August 1918', Appx C, Report on Mechanical Efficiency of Mark V Tanks in Action.

132 Plus four officers and twelve NCOs. 51 Company of the Labour Corps was assigned to Erin and 69 Company to Teneur.

133 Childs, *A Peripheral Weapon?*, p.66.

134 Williams-Ellis & Williams-Ellis, *The Tank Corps*, pp.192-193.

135 Tanks continued though, to be used to large numbers, in support of assaults. Between 11 August and 20 October 1918, more than 100 were used on three occasions, and over 50 on six. The largest post-Amiens armoured operation, involving 183 tanks, was in support of the Third Army's attack on Bucquoy.

136 An AAR in late September 1918 from HQ V Tank Brigade noted the tactical and logistic fragility of employing small number of tanks, 'A Battalion of 20 Tanks spread over a frontage of 14 Miles is extremely difficult to put into action'; TNA WO 95/112/2: 5th Tank Brigade, WD, '5th Tank Brigade, REPORT on Operations of 18 th September 1918 by 2nd Tank Battalion with IIIrd, Australian and IXth Corps', para 12 (i) (d), Lessons and Suggestions. Document under cover of HQ 5th Tank Brigade, G50/45 dated 16 October 1918.

137 The British Army describes 'Manoeuvre' as 'the employment of forces on the battlefield (using movement) in combination with fire or fire potential, to achieve a position of advantage in respect to the opposition in order to accomplish the mission'; *Army Doctrine Publication*, Vol. 1, *Operations*, pp.3-17 to 3-19.

138 The vision of the British Army theorists of 1918 has matured in the logistic capability of the US Army's armoured and mechanized manoeuvre forces, which conducted deep penetration operations during Operation IRAQI FREEDOM in 2003.

139 One interesting area of potential study is the development of logistics to support experimental British Army mechanised and mobile forces during the inter-war period. For an assessment of the armoured doctrine, see, Harold R Winton, *To Change an Army, General Sir John Burnett-Stuart and British Armored Doctrine, 1927-1938* (Lawrence: University Press of Kansas, 1998).

Equally, by February 1918, armour moves had progressed to the point where tanks could be moved factories and depots from the United Kingdom to TRHs in France, via a rail ferry service, without a change of wagon. This was an impressive capability, which reinforced the industrialized concept of 'Factory to Fire-Trench'. Militarily however, the strategic and operational movements of tanks relied entirely on SGR and in particular the location of the TRHs, which constrained the offensive capability of the tank, an issue exacerbated by its limited range, although the advent of the RWS created greater deployment flexibility. From the perspective of 2018, it seems incredible that the BEF of 1918 fielded so many tanks with no HETs, which makes the logistic feat of moving them all the more impressive even if they had to be supplied by HT.[140] What is clear however, from the records, is that Commanders and Staff Officers in the Tank Corps were acutely aware of the criticality of robust logistics in armoured operations and its vital role in delivering combat effectiveness.

140 TNA WO 95/112/2: 5th Tank Brigade, WD, '5th Tank Brigade, Preliminary Instructions No 1 dated 6 August 1918, Administrative Instructions' para 2 (b) Horse Transport.

12

Heads of Steel

Logistic challenges and innovation during the BEF's mobile All Arms Battle: July - November 1918

Introduction

In late 1918, on the Western Front, the British Army was conducting All-Arms mobile warfare, without the aid of computers, in a chemical environment, with Close Air Support (CAS),[1] which, from the military perspective, was nothing short of a revolution.[2] Whilst John Laffin may have described British generals as 'Butchers and Bunglers,'[3] the creation of an organization, capable, after four years of fighting, to defeat the German Army in the field was an impressive feat of arms,[4] a view clearly articulated by a senior contemporary participant in 1919:[5] 'There is no period in the history of the Great War which is of such transcendent interest to the soldier as that covered by this book [*The Story of the Fourth Army in the Battles of the Hundred Days*]. It is not too much to say that the events that took place in France during August, September and October, 1918, constitute the greatest military triumph the world has ever seen'.[6]

Whilst GHQ British Expeditionary Force (BEF) was unable to fully seize the opportunity to integrate state of the art technology[7] into new doctrine before the

1 Close Air Support (CAS) is air action against hostile targets which are in close proximity to friendly forces and which require detailed integration of each air mission with the fire and movement of those forces; Air Publication (AP) 3000, *British Air Power Doctrine*, 3rd Edn, Directorate of Air Staff (UK MOD, 1999), p.3.13.2.

2 This issue was the subject of a presentation by Dr Paul Harris of the Royal Military Academy Sandhurst (RMAS) War Studies Department: 'FM Haig and the technological revolution in the BEF during the 100 Days, 1918' at a study day hosted by RMAS, entitled 'Field Marshal Sir Douglas Haig and the Western Front', on Saturday 21 May 2011.

3 John Laffin, *British Butchers and Bunglers of World War I* (Stroud: Alan Sutton, 1988).

4 Robin Neillands, takes a very different view to John Laffin, and has challenged the popular myth of the incompetence and callousness of the Great War generals; see, *The Great War Generals on the Western Front, 1914-18* (London: Robinson, 1999).

5 General Lord Rawlinson GCB GCVO GCSI KCMG. Whilst Rawlinson, as Commander Fourth Army, may have a personal interest in promoting the success of his Command, given the operational outcome, his statement is a concise and appropriate comment.

6 Major-General Sir Archibald Montgomery KCMG CB, *The Story of the Fourth Army in the Battles of the Hundred Days, August 8th to November 11th 1918* (London: Hodder and Stoughton, 1919), p.vii. This publication, whilst not an Official History, was compiled by the staffs of HQ Fourth Army and the supporting HQs of the Corps and Divisions within it, a point recognized, in his introduction by Major-General Montgomery, who was Major-General General Staff (MGGS) of Fourth Army; see, pp.xi-xii. Given though, its detail, exhaustive content, structure and access to official documents, it is effectively an Official rather than regimental history.

7 Haig, when describing the interaction of these new capabilities, including tanks, offered a balanced view of their strengths and limitations, which resonates today, recording: 'It should never be forgotten however that weapons of this character are incapable of effective independent action. They do not in themselves possess the power to obtain a decision, their real function being to assist the infantry to get to grips with their opponents. To place them in a reliance out of proportion to their real utility, to imagine for example, that tanks and aeroplanes can take the place of infantry and artillery, would be to do, a disservice to those who have the future of these weapons most at heart by robbing them of the power to use them to their best effect'. Lieutenant-Colonel J H Boraston OBE (Ed.), *Sir Douglas Haig's Despatches, December 1915 - April 1919* (London & Toronto: J M Dent & Sons, 1919), p.329.

Armistice,[8] should not overshadow the achievement but the outcome serves to remind us that there will always be a balance of risk between tried methods and new ideas.[9] Much has been written about the Last[10] Hundred[11] Days,[12] and though there have been a number of analyses,[13] which have projected new light on a raft of operational topics,[14] few have touched upon the subject of logistic innovation.[15] Clearly though, mobile warfare, even in 1918, could not have been conducted without a comprehensive and resilient logistic capability, its importance being summarized post-war by a contemporary wartime Australian participant who was not a professional soldier:[16]

> Although the "Q" work was less spectacular, on its excellence depended the effective realization of the aims of the General Staff. Without regular and sufficient supplies of food, water, ammunition and battle stores, no troops can be maintained in any position, however admirable it may be from a tactical point of view........The greater the depth of an advance the greater is the strain thrown upon the supply and transport organisation.[17]

That logisticians were integral to the process should perhaps, be obvious. Often hidden though, from the historical and popular view for over 100 years, has been their ability to sustain trench warfare for nearly four years, before engaging in the most significant withdrawal[18] the BEF had experienced

8 See, *The Division in the Attack - 1918*, SS 135 T/1635 40/WO/7036 (Shrivenham: Strategic and Combat Studies Institute, 2008).

9 An interesting innovation was the use of the 24 hour clock for timings, which was officially adopted in the BEF on 1 October 1918.

10 As described in Brigadier-General Sir James E Edmonds CB CMG and Lieutenant-Colonel R Maxwell-Hyslop, BOH, *Military Operations France and Belgium 1918*, Volume V, *26th September - 11th November, The Advance to Victory*, (London: HMSO, 1947), p.xxxiii.

11 It is 96 days. The use of 100, apart from having a fine resonance, linked it to the famous Hundred Days campaign of Napoleon in 1815, during which a British led Army in a coalition, achieved victory.

12 In the BOH, *Military Operations, France and Belgium*, out of a total of 14 volumes devoted to the Western Front, five volumes were dedicated to 1918, two of which, cover the Last Hundred Days. See, Brigadier-General Sir James E Edmonds CB CMG, BOH, *Military Operations, France and Belgium*, Vols IV & V (London: HMSO, 1947).

13 In particular, see, Jonathon Boff, *Winning and Losing on the Western Front, The British Third Army and the Defeat of Germany* (Cambridge: Cambridge University Press (CUP), 2012) *and* Gary Sheffield and Peter Grey (Eds.) *Changing War, The British Army, The Hundred Days Campaign and the Birth of the Royal Air Force, 1918*, Birmingham War Studies, (London: Bloomsbury, 2013).

14 For a contemporary account, see, Montgomery, *The Story of the Fourth Army.* For a modern assessment, J P Harris with Niall Barr, *Amiens to the Armistice, The BEF in the Hundred Days' Campaign*, 8 August - 11 November 1918 (London & Washington: Brasseys, 1998). The authors make no apology for including little on logistics, doing so for sound reasons and explaining why, whilst briefly highlighting the importance of administration and logistics in supporting the operations.

15 A notable exception is the seminal *British Logistics on the Western Front, 1914-1919*, Ian Malcolm Brown (Westport Connecticut & London: Praeger, 1998) and the most valuable work of Geoff Clarke, *Supplying The Battlefront: British Frontline Transport in Mobile Warfare 1918*, Unpublished MA dissertation (Birmingham: University of Birmingham, 2006) and Christopher Phillips, *A Modern Industrial Organization: A Case Study of Fourth Army during the battles of the Hundred Days*, Unpublished MA dissertation (Birmingham: University of Birmingham, 2009).

16 Captain A D Ellis MC, a pre-war schoolmaster and later an officer in 29th Battalion Australian Imperial Force.

17 Captain A D Ellis MC, *The Story of the Fifth Australian Division, Being an Authoritative Account of the Division's Doings in Egypt, France and Belgium* (London: Hodder and Stoughton, nd but c1920), p.326.

18 For the operational perspective, see, Brigadier-General Sir James E Edmonds CB CMG, BOH, *Military Operations France and Belgium, 1918*, Vol. I, *The German Offensive and its preliminaries* (London: Macmillan, 1935) and Vol. II, *March - April: Continuation of the German Offensives* (London: Macmillan, 1937). For a recent critical analysis based on German records, see, David T Zabecki, *The German 1918 Offensives* (Abingdon: Routledge, 2006). For the British soldiers' view of the battles, see, Martin Middlebrook, *The Kaiser's Battle: 21 March 1918, The First Day of the German Spring Offensive* (London: Allen Lane, 1978) and Lyn Macdonald, *To The Last Man: Spring 1918* (London: Viking, 1998).

during the war,[19] and then grasping the challenge of supporting All-Arms mobile warfare. That they were successful in enabling the victory in November 1918 is clearly demonstrated by the outcome, and had the logisticians been unable to sustain the force as it advanced, there would have been no offensive campaign upon which, to bring the conflict to an end.[20] In this respect, the efforts of the logisticians have been taken for granted but the intellectual, structural and practical changes, which enabled these activities to be successfully conducted, were immense, and those who enacted them have never been given the credit they deserve. The BEF's QMG,[21] an officer assessed by one contemporary observer,[22] as a 'ruthless reformer',[23] was however, clear about the criticality of logistics to the advance, noting of the challenge and the opportunity of 8 August 1918: 'The problem of effective pursuit will largely be one of supplies and transport ....to convert a German withdrawal into a decisive German defeat, the necessity is to follow the enemy up not only with men, but with a vast tonnage per day per mile of front'.[24]

In addition, there is the impression offered in some material, that the Hundred Days were less operationally demanding than the rest of the war; the opposite is true.[25] Between August and November 1918, there was some ferocious fighting,[26] and this is reflected in the enormous number of casualties[27] and a prodigious expenditure of artillery

19 For details of the logistic impact of the withdrawal, see, Colonel A M Henniker CBE (Comp), BOH, *Transportation on the Western Front, 1914-1918* (London: HMSO, 1937), pp.402-419. This BOH is also held in the TNA in ZLIB 29/455 (Text) and 456 (Maps).

20 Harris and Barr make this clear in *Amiens to the Armistice*, p.55.

21 Lieutenant-General Sir Travers Clarke GBE KCB KCMG took over as QMG in late 1917 having served for 18 months as the QMG in Salonika and four months as the Deputy Adjutant General in GHQ. At 46, he was young for the post and according to Frank Fox, an officer on his Staff, was only a substantive Major; [Frank Fox] GSO, *GHQ, Montreuil-Sur-Mer* (London: Philip Allan & Co, 1920), p.226. Fox recorded, "T.C. had the ideal personality for a military leader. You were always dreadfully afraid of him and sincerely fond of him"; pp.227-228. Clarke's first wife, Mary Jordan died in 1918, although he remarried in 1921 to Irene Roe (nee Cross), the widow of an officer in his regiment, the Royal Inniskilling Fusiliers. From 1919-1923, he was QMG to the Forces.

22 Major Frank Fox was an Australian pre-war artillery reservist, journalist and author, who worked, pre-war, for *The Morning* Post, as News Editor and then War Correspondent. He was twice wounded during actions on the Somme before serving as a Staff Captain at GHQ in the QMG's Branch and then the General Staff at the War Office, being awarded the OBE for his services. Post-war, he supported a number of causes including the Empire Rheumatism Council and the British Empire Cancer Campaign, being knighted in 1926. Obituary, *The Times*, 9 March 1960, Official Website, accessed 11 July 2017.

23 GSO, *GHQ*, p.226.

24 TNA WO 95/39: GHQ QMG, WD, June - August 1918, 'Explanatory Review, July 1918', pp.1-2.

25 Arguably, it was the logistic units that faced the greatest challenges, and the increased hazards associated with them, involved in mobile, rather than static operations. Of the 33 Army Service Corps (ASC) officers killed during the Great War who were Gentlemen Cadets at Sandhurst, 16 (48%) were killed in 1918. They are commemorated in the Royal Military Chapel on the Royal Army Service Corps plaque. On 27 November 1918, His Majesty King George V conferred upon the ASC, the prefix Royal, for its outstanding work in the war. It was decided therefore, that ASC officers would be remembered by a Corps, they had given their lives to create, rather than the one in which, they had served.

26 On 4 November 1918, during hedgerow fighting on the edge of the Forest of Mormal, casualties (Killed In Action, Died from Wounds, Wounded and Prisoners of War) from 9th Battalion Duke of Wellington's Regiment totalled 13 officers and 226 Other Ranks from strengths of 15 and 584; A Hilliard Atteridge, *History of the 17th (Northern) Division* (Glasgow: University Press, 1929), p.457. This casualty list is sadly one that would appear more in keeping with the First Day on the Somme (1 July 1916) than the last week of the war. In the last 23 hours of the conflict, the BEF fired the following rounds of artillery ammunition: 1,189 x 13 pdr, 52 x 3 inch AA, 1,831 x 18 pdr, 374 x 4.5 inch howitzer, 510 x 60 pdr and 1,756 x 6 inch howitzer; *Statistics of the Military Effort of the British Empire, during the Great War, 1914-1920* (MEBE) War Office (HMSO, 1922), p.416, Table (ii) - Expenditure of Gun Ammunition in France (by Weeks) since 2 January 1916.

27 October 1918 was the last full month of the Great War, and during it, British Empire forces in the BEF suffered the staggering total of 121,046 soldiers Killed In Action (KIA), Died, Wounded, Injured, Missing & POW. This equates to 3,905 soldiers per day and lucidly illustrates the intensity of the fighting. MEBE, p.270, Table (iii) - Approximate Casualties by Month in the Expeditionary Force, France. For an analysis, see, Major T J Mitchell DSO MD RAMC and Miss G M Smith MBE, BOH, *Medical Services, Casualties and Medical Statistics of the Great*

ammunition.[28] The transition from trench to mobile warfare created mixed results for the logisticians. Demands for trench stores continued,[29] despite the operational requirement effectively evaporating and units recognizing that the new order needed a different approach,[30] which sometimes generated urgent requests for different equipment.[31] The use of artillery attracted the attention of Colonel Walter Nicholson,[32] the Assistant Quarter-Master General (AQMG) of XIII Corps,[33] who observed:[34]

> Every gun was given a maximum amount of ammunition to fire,[35] just as if we were still at our old trench warfare of the previous year. Commanders failed to shake themselves clear of trench warfare traditions...............We gave ourselves an objective of some few thousand yards, arranged a colossal barrage to cover our advance; then stopped when the guns slackened.[36]

Whilst Colonel Nicholson's view is valid from a logistic perspective, and was probably borne of frustration to effect change, there were two key issues which, led to continued heavy artillery ammunition expenditure. First, commanders and staffs were cognizant of the importance of reducing casualties to a minimum, and heavy concentrations of artillery remained part of this process. Secondly, in order to attack the German reserves, great emphasis was placed on the deeper battle, which relied on larger tubes, and therefore, heavier shells; the logistic demands therefore,

War (London: HMSO, 1931), Chp X, pp.166-175.

28 Prodigious did not always mean effective, and there were several instances during the Hundred Days, when the number of shells fired did not mirror the effect of artillery support. The relaying of target acquisition information to the guns was a particular problem, especially during mobile operations, whilst the efficiency of aerial observation could be quickly reduced by poor visibility.

29 Lieutenant-Colonel J W S Sewell, 'The Supply of Bulk Stores in War', The RE Journal, 35 (1922), p.46, attributes this to staff officers accustomed to the practice of continually indenting for them. Equally, engineers and soldiers may have been preparing for the expected winter 'dig-in'. Either way, these stores not only failed to add any value to offensive capability but also degraded it, by using precious transport. DDOS Fourth Army, whilst expecting entrenchment, took a logisticians' 'Just in Time' perspective noting 'Jerkins and Gum Boots will only be useful when Trench Warfare starts again'; TNA WO 95/452/1: HQ Fourth Army, DDOS, WD, 19 August 1918.

30 'The war of movement upset the accustomed trench economy established during years of siege warfare. Picks and shovels were not now trench stores, companies had to take theirs in and out on relief. Billhooks and axes had been issued to cut brushwood for flooring posts and trenches. Thermos food containers came into use again, and bivouac sheets appeared as a store on company charge'. Captain J C Dunn DSO MC & Bar DCM RAMC, *The War The Infantry Knew, 1914-1919, A Chronicle of Service in France and Belgium* (London: Janes, 1987), p.558.

31 In late October, HQ Fourth Army actioned a request for 2,000 billhooks for forest fighting and on 30 October, a requirement for 4,500 lifebelts for water crossings; TNA WO 95/452/1: HQ Fourth Army, DDOS, WD, 26 October 1918.

32 Colonel Walter Norris Nicholson CMG DSO was commissioned into the Suffolk Regiment in 1900, commanding the 1st Battalion in the period 1924-1929, and was Colonel of the Regiment between 1939 and 1947. He spent however, much of his career in A&Q appointments, including Deputy Assistant Adjutant and Quartermaster General (DAA&QMG) at the Cape of Good Hope in 1912, and then DAA&QMG of the Highland Division of the Territorial Force in 1914. He took over as Assistant Adjutant and Quartermaster General (AA&QMG) of 17 Division in June 1916, and was promoted to Assistant Quartermaster-General (AQMG) of XIII Corps in April 1918.

33 XIII Corps was transferred from Fifth Army and assigned to Fourth Army for October and November 1918.

34 For more detail, see, Colonel J B A Bailey MBE, 'British Artillery in the Great War' in Paddy Griffiths (Ed.) *British Fighting Methods in the Great War* (London & Portland Oregon: Frank Cass, 1996).

35 Pritchard (Ed.) *The History of the Corps of Royal Engineers*, Vol. V (Chatham: The Institution of the Royal Engineers, 1952), p.639, describes these artillery units as 'munitions gourmets'.

36 Colonel W N Nicholson CMG DSO, *Behind the Lines, An Account of Administrative Staff-work in the British Army 1914-1918* (London: Jonathan Cape, 1939), p.214. *Behind the Lines* is a fascinating read; amusing, erudite, informative and forthright. *The Army Quarterly*, Volume 38, stated that: Every officer, certainly every aspiring staff officer, should read this book. *Behind the Lines* was reprinted in 1989, with new historical notes, by the Strong Oak Press and Tim Donovan Publishing (ISBN 1-871048-16-8).

remained high. Commanders and Staffs faced very significant challenges and it is no surprise that not every aspect of operations was brought to a peak of finesse, so even in Fourth Army, an organization rated for its logistic outputs,[37] a host of issues were constantly attracting the attention of its HQ.[38]

Heads of Steel[39]

To effect operations, the BEF required enormous quantities of material,[40] all of which had to be procured, stored, transported, inspected, receipted and issued. This material, was, for the most part, delivered to Standard Gauge Railway (SGR)[41] railheads,[42] by rail, whence it was transferred to units by Mechanical Transport (MT),[43] mainly Wheeled Motor Transport (WMT), Horse Transport (HT) and the NGR network,[44] with Inland Water Transport (IWT) making a significant

37 The attention to detail and constant investigative activity by A&Q staff officers is remarkable. As an example, in the week ending 28 September 1918, the Instructor in Catering of Fourth Army visited 14 units, noting that catering was not subject to supervision by an officer, many units were not in possession of SS 615, 'Cooking in the Field', nor following the instructions contained therein and 10 units had failed to report details of surplus dripping; TNA WO 95/445/5: HQ Fourth Army, A&Q, Note 763, 'Catering, Week Ending 28-9-18'. The return of dripping was not a small logistic issue. In September, Fourth Army collected 97,906 lbs (43.70 tons) at its railheads; TNA WO 95/445/5: HQ Fourth Army, A&Q, Note 785a, 'Statement of Dripping returned to Railheads by Army and Corps Troops & Divisions during the month of September 1918'. It is of interest that the Fourth Army was conducting Q inspections of RAF combat and logistic units; TNA WO 95/445/5: HQ Fourth Army, A&Q, Note 788, 'Catering, Week ending 5 October 1918' and that the Instructor of Catering noted that the BEF had much to learn from the Americans in the arena of food services; TNA WO 95/454/4: HQ Fourth Army, DDST, 'Q Conference Notes, 18 October 1918'.

38 The Fourth Army DDST War Diary contains a fair share of issues relating to unsatisfactory field storage areas, poor equipment care, improper maintenance and weak stores accounting; TNA WO 95/454/4: HQ Fourth Army, DDST, WD, entries July - November 1918. An example was a review of the Corps Reserve supply dumps in August 1918, which were described by the DDST as 'unsatisfactory', with the Canadian Corps dump being especially bad, an inspection revealing that the stocks had been dumped by the roadside with no attempt at stacking nor were there any tarpaulins to cover the supplies from observation or the elements. TNA WO 95/454/4: HQ Fourth Army, DDST, WD, 17 August 1918.

39 The 'Head of Steel' was defined as the furthest point on the Permanent Way to which, railway services could be conducted, although this point was not necessarily a railhead. Beyond the 'Head of Steel' there might be another 10-12 miles of track under construction that could support the operation of slow moving engineer trains loaded with railway materiel, ballast and water.

40 In 1918, weekly imports to the BEF ranged from a low of 160,216 tons in January to a peak of 189,446 in October, declining post-Armistice to 157,443 tons in November and then 112,224 tons in December. Exports had a low of 4,068 tons in February, peaking at 12,517 tons in August. MEBE, p.607, Table (i) - Progress of Transportation in France.

41 In 1918, Standard Gauge was 4' 8 ½ inches (1435mm) and Narrow Gauge, anything less. In 2018, Standard Gauge is rated between 1432mm and 1435mm to account for those SGRs, which have been reduced in gauge by 3 mm, to improve the ride of high-speed trains.

42 The *Field Service Pocket Book* of 1914 defines a railhead as: 'a locality on the railway where ammunition and supplies are transferred to ammunition parks and supply columns.' General Staff, *Field Service Pocket Book 1914* (FSPB 14) (London: HMSO, 1914), p.xi.

43 Wheeled, tracked, or semi-tracked land vehicle utilised in a logistic context to move men and materiel to, on or from the battlefield and powered by the Internal Combustion Engine (ICE) either Spark Ignition (SI) or Compression Ignition (CI) fuelled by petroleum spirit or diesel oil respectively, or by steam (Steam Transport (ST)). Often abbreviated to MT, it does not include combat vehicles, such as tanks, Armoured Personnel Carriers (APC) or Self-Propelled Guns (SPG). Motor Transport (MT) included Wheeled or tracked or semi-tracked land logistic vehicle powered by the ICE but to provide specific clarification for wheeled vehicles, the term Wheeled Motor Transport (WMT) is used.

44 Many documents refer to Narrow Gauge Railways (NGRs) as Light Railways, which, whilst not inaccurate, is not technically correct. There is no official international definition of a Light Railway but it may be described as a one which is constructed to a lesser standard than that required for main or branch line operations; it may be broad, standard, or narrow gauge. NGRs, by the nature of their construction, are usually defined as light, but this may not necessarily be the case, whilst some of the Standard Gauge Railways (SGR) constructed in France to support

contribution in specific traffic flows from the Base.[45] These activities were not sustained by mass alone. The war diary of the Fourth Army Deputy Director Supplies & Transport (DDST) is replete with entries recording inspections and audits of logistic units and a wide range of materiel, regimes designed to enhance operational capability, whilst driving down waste and cost.[46] In this respect, routine logistic tasks were as equally important to the BEF's capability as planning and delivering combat logistics for major operations, facts revealed in its headquarters and unit war diaries.[47]

The importance of the railway to the BEF's advance in the Hundred Days went beyond its role in logistics because on occasions, the security of Allied rail routes became the operational imperative, [48] whilst equally, the Allies sought to disrupt German logistic capability by attacking battlefield railway nodes with light armour.[49] The attack on Amiens was an example because one of the key aspects of the attack was to secure, from German interference, three *lignes de rocade*[50] deemed vital to future Allied operations.[51] General Foch's orders began: '1. The object of the operations is to disengage Amiens and the Paris-Amiens railway, also to defeat and drive back the enemy established between the Somme and Avre'.[52] One of the key reasons why the logisticians were capable of generating cross-Army support, so vital to the advance from August onwards, was the large railway construction and rehabilitation programme undertaken by the Allies in response the German attacks in the Spring of 1918, which created critical logistic flexibility.[53] From the planning perspective, a significant logistic debate before the advance was whether, in the event of major territorial gains, the establishment of new SGR railheads were to take precedence over the rehabilitation or construction of NGR. An ingenious idea, which made the best of limited resources, was to utilize captured German NGRs, a concept, which had many initial advantages. It was though, only effective in those areas where the Germans had a system to support their trench zones, and even then, the German NGR might only run between 7-10 miles to the rear. The use of the German NGR was therefore, a useful method of providing support but only for a relatively short distance. The process by which this was achieved was simple; having prepared the ground, which might be a significant task, engineers would lay a 60 centimetre[54] track[55] between the BEF's

military operations during the Great War, could certainly be described as Light. Railways are therefore, in this chapter, described by gauge rather than engineering construction standards. For the technical definitions, and a short history of Light Railways, see, Jack Simmons and Gordon Biddle (Eds.) *The Oxford Companion to British Railway History* (Oxford & New York: Oxford University Press, 1997), pp.263-265.

45 Between March and November 1918, IWT was moving an average of 56,000 tons per week, peaking at 66,368 tons in October; MEBE, p.613, Inland Water Transport, Table (iii) - France and Cross-Channel Services.

46 TNA WO 95/454/4: HQ Fourth Army, DDST, WD.

47 Examples in the A&Q arena include the price of beer in army canteens, shortages of salt, the type of tobacco ratio, petrol allowances for Church Army cars, the supply of wine and wafers for the sacrament, quality of lubricating oils, coal for bath units, use of army biscuits in cooking, provision of medical comforts, procurement of soap, and additional rations for WMT operators working excessive hours; TNA WO 95/454/4: HQ Fourth Army, DDST, WD, entries July - December 1918.

48 Henniker, BOH, *Transportation on the Western Front*, pp.371-376.

49 TNA WO 95/112/2: '5th Tank Brigade, Order No 2, G26/34 dated 26 September 1918', para 5, Role of 17th Armoured Car Battalion.

50 *Ligne de rocade*, a term derived from 'castling' in chess, were routes allocated for lateral movements; Henniker, BOH, *Transportation on the Western Front*, p.xxxii.

51 The rail links were the lines Paris-Chalons, Paris-Avricourt and Paris-Amiens. These three railways were essential to the rapid movement of Allied reserves up and down the front, either to repel enemy attacks, or more to the current purpose, to position reserves for the advance.

52 Edmonds, BOH, *France and Belgium 1918*, Vol. IV, p.2.

53 Henniker, BOH, *Transportation on the Western Front*, pp.411-419.

54 60cm was known as *Decauville*. In Northern France, 60cm track from the Great War can still be seen because sections of it are used for fencing.

55 60cm was not the only NGR gauge to be used by the Allies. One metre was a common commercial gauge in North-

NGR and the German system.[56] After careful consideration of experience gained in 1917, it was decided that should the advance exceed 12-15 miles[57] then the Main Effort (ME) would be the projection of SGR railheads,[58] rather than the extension of NGR systems.[59]

The pressure to open lines and railheads to meet this requirement is clearly illustrated in the Fourth Army[60] Administrative Arrangements[61] issued for the commencement of the Battle of Amiens. Whilst the SGR Main Effort did not stop the transportation staffs from adopting a number of differing applications on the ground if they believed it to be appropriate,[62] there is no doubt that based upon train capacity and materiel clearance, the decision was the correct one for the BEF. Standard trainloads on SGR were usually around 300 tons, whilst on the NGRs, net trainloads rarely exceeded 60 tons, and in the battle area only 30; this meant that to clear an SGR train onto NGR took 5-10 trains. Whilst there were occasions when it was effective to transfer SGR loads for extended movement by NGR, for the most part, the mathematics suggested a different solution. The NGRs had made an immense contribution to the logistic support of operations during 1917, and, in the base and rear areas, continued to do so until the BEF completed its draw-down after the Armistice. Tactically, the use of NGR, rather than roads in the battle area, was certainly sound because during dry weather there was almost no dust generated by the transportation operations, whilst the requirement to repair the roads was also reduced. The use of NGR to support the advance was however, restricted to supporting the move through the German main defensive areas; once into open country it became more cost effective to extend the SGRs. It was anticipated though, that the SGR would probably not keep up with the pace of the advance, and, in order to ensure the 'Maintenance of Momentum', Armies were allotted a reserve of WMT to run forward stocks from the Army railhead to a road-head. From here, a supply column transported it to a Refilling Point, which reinforced the importance of effective and timely

East France before the war, whilst Belgium had a network of One metre gauge of over 2,500 miles, a little less than the Standard Gauge Railway (SGR) system. One metre gauge was however, considered unsuitable for a tactical rail communication system. Having examined the possibility of using, the gauge of 2 feet 6 inches (76cm) of which the Royal Engineers had a small stock, it was decided to opt for the 60cm gauge used by the French and Germans.

56 An early example of this technique was the work by No 2 Army Tramway Company, which, in November 1917, linked the BEF's NGR at Gouzeau with the German one at La Vacquerie; Edmonds, BOH, *France and Belgium 1917*, Vol. III, p. 41. HQ 8th Division was full of praise for the engineer work undertaken to support its operations by connecting British and German systems in July 1918; see TNA WO 95/1679: War Diary and Narrative of Operations, July 1918 - June 1919.

57 The Fifth Army was an exception. In mid-October 1918, it was operating NGR 20 miles behind its front.

58 TNA WO 95/39: GHQ, QMG, WD, June - August 1918, 27 August 1918. For a description of railway operations in the period August - November 1918, see, Henniker, BOH, *Transportation on the Western Front*, pp.420-461. By the first week of October 1918, Fourth Army planned or active SGR construction was 143.69 miles, whilst NGR totalled only 1.42; TNA WO 95/445/5: HQ Fourth Army, A&Q, Note 770, 'Broad Gauge Railway Construction, Week Ending 2-10-18' and Note 769, 'Light Railway Construction, Week Ending 4-10-18'.

59 TNA WO 95/445/5: HQ Fourth Army, A&Q, Note 769, 'Light Railway Construction, Week Ending 4-10-18'.

60 The logistic operations of Fourth Army are a strong thread in this chapter. The dynamic ORBAT, which included the British III, IX, XIII and Cavalry Corps, and the Australian and Canadian Corps, make it of particular interest, as a British 'Empire' Army, whilst the inclusion of II American Corps creates the Coalition dimension. The logistic implications of the inclusion of the latter, deserves study. For the changing ORBAT, see, Major A F Becke (Rtd) (Comp) BOH, *Order of Battle*, Part 4, *The Army Council, GHQs, Armies and Corps, 1914-1918* (London: HMSO, 1945), pp.106-107 and the excellent 'Tartan Diagram' in Montgomery, *The Story of the Fourth Army*, facing p.262, which shows the employment of assigned Corps and Divisions in Fourth Army during the Hundred Days.

61 Fourth Army Administrative Arrangements, dated 6 August 1918, Edmonds, BOH, *France and Belgium 1918*, Vol. IV, Appx VII, Sect A - Railways, pp.559-560.

62 The Canadian Corps instructions for the offensive in support of the BEF's attack on the *Hindenburg Line* were very specific about the requirement, and the reason, to extend NGR in their sector. Para 25 (iv) stated: 'The light railways will be pushed forward over the canal with all possible speed in order that artillery ammunition may be delivered east of the canal by light railway and thus reduce the amount of wheeled traffic over the bridges'; Edmonds, BOH, *France and Belgium 1918*, Vol. V, p.633.

road maintenance. There were however, even early in the advance in mid-August, occasions when the shortage of WMT became so acute[63] that the salvage,[64] reconditioning and use of captured German WMT became an option.[65]

Storm of Steel

If the operational deployment of armour was to tax the logistic system, the sustainment of the artillery battle was to provide an even greater challenge.[66] Whilst armour and CAS were emerging aspects of the All Arms Battle, the artillery, supported by air reconnaissance, was, for the most part, a finely honed and vital part of British tactical operations,[67] which made massive demands on the logistic support chain.[68] There was though, the recognition that if firepower, and artillery in particular, was to make up for the increasing shortfall in manpower within the BEF, the logistic system had to deliver the materiel to the right place, at the right time, in the right amount and in the right order. In this respect, critical reforms, including the introduction of commercial practices, the reorganization of the BEF's transportation system in late 1916 and early 1917, reviews of logistic establishments, adjustments to the allocation of resources and a ruthless approach to salvage and economy were fundamental to the BEF's capability in 1918.[69] In the intervening period, the increasing effectiveness and efficiency of transportation also had a very positive impact upon tactical operations, operational doctrine and strategic decisions.[70] Artillery was a vital component in tactical and more significantly, operational success, and its capability was limited by the logistic support allocated to it. That the artillery was able to achieve the success it did, was the direct result of the logisticians' ability to deliver the shells from British Factory to German Fire-Trench:

> Abundant ammunition supplies allowed commanders to experiment with firepower approaches to the tactical and operational problems facing them..........and proved to be the

63 TNA WO 95/454/4: HQ Fourth Army, DDST, 'Notes on Conference at "Q" 6.45 pm, 28 August 1918': 'Situation with regard to lorries very serious in view Boche retreat behind Somme........It is not possible at present to move up any Supply Dumps as lorries not available'. This problem was still extant in October; 'Large quantities of boxed ammunition are lying about the area in various dumps. 'Q' knows of this but state that the necessity of economy in lorries makes it compulsory for ammunition to be drawn from Railheads first'; TNA WO 95/452/1: HQ Fourth Army, DDOS, WD, 19 October 1918.

64 One aspect that would benefit from more research is the subject of the control of the acquisition of trophies from the enemy, a matter, which appeared as a key issue during Operation GRANBY (Gulf War) in 1991. DOS GHQ for example, directed that II (American) Corps follow British Army directives; TNA WO 95/452/1: HQ Fourth Army, DDOS, WD, 19 August 1918.

65 TNA WO 95/454/4: HQ Fourth Army, DDST, 'Notes on Conference at "Q" 6.45 pm, 30 August 1918'. Captured German artillery was also reconditioned and utilized. In September, the Australian Corps was issued 12 x 77mm, 2 x 105 mm, 2 x 150mm and 1 x 210mm howitzer; TNA WO 95/452/1: HQ Fourth Army, DDOS, WD, 15 September 1918.

66 For a seminal examination of its role in supporting the BEF, see, Sanders Marble, *British Artillery on the Western Front, The Infantry cannot do with a gun less*, Ashgate Studies in First World War History (Farnham: Ashgate, 2013).

67 For a detailed description of British artillery on the Western Front in the period, see, General, Sir Martin Farndale KCB *History of the Royal Regiment of Artillery, Western Front, 1914-18* (Woolwich: The Royal Artillery Institution, 1986), pp. 287-331 and for key lessons, pp.335-336. For an assessment of its role in the Hundred Days, see, Marble, *British Artillery on the Western Front*, pp.228-248.

68 In just the last week of September 1918, the BEF expended 3,462,763 rounds of artillery ammunition; MEBE, p.421, Table (ii) - Expenditure of Gun Ammunition in France (by Weeks) since 2 January 1916.

69 Frank Fox was of the view that without these reforms, the BEF would have been incapable of defeating the German Army in the Field; GSO, *GHQ*, p.231.

70 For evaluations of the British Army's tactical and operational doctrine, see, Paddy Griffith, *Battle Tactics on the Western Front, The British Army's Art of Attack 1916-18* (New Haven & London: Yale University Press, 1994) and Griffith, *British Fighting Methods in the Great War*.

> appropriate one to 'solve' the dilemma of the trenches; firepower in large but controlled quantities provided the operational 'umbrella' under which the infantry could begin to reassert its role on the battlefield. By so freeing the infantry, Geddes's transportation system by early 1917 allowed the BEF to advance its battlefield doctrine in whatever fashion it chose.[71]

In the advance, the logistic staffs had two major problems to contend with. First, moving the guns to a position where they were able to support the battle, and secondly, supplying the ammunition. The first problem was overcome in a number of ways. 18 pdrs were usually horse drawn, although an increasing number were, in the latter stages of the war, towed by MT, or carried portee, solutions which also sought to assist the American Expeditionary Force (AEF) in horsing its units, whilst maintaining the operational mobility of the BEF.[72] Artillery pieces up to the calibre of the 60 pdr could be moved by NGR, whilst larger systems were towed by Army Service Corps (ASC) Siege Park Company tractors, or positioned, in part at least, by SGR. An ingenious solution to the movement of artillery was the introduction, in July 1917,[73] of the Gun Carrier Mark I, designed to move the 6 inch and 60 pdr guns on tracks,[74] although its significant logistic capability of transporting 200 shells weighing 10 tons across country, prompted its use as an ammunition and supply carrier. The BEF also developed a sled, which could be towed behind a tank, capable of mounting a wheeled artillery piece; trials were completed, but the system was not deployed operationally.[75]

Expenditure rates, which rose on some occasions, to exceed those of the Somme in 1916, or Ypres in 1917, compounded the difficulties inherent in the second task. Between 8 August and 6 September 1918, the following rounds were expended: 5,372,000 of 18 pdr, 1,443,000 of 4.5 inch, and 1,566,800 of 6 inch.[76] The highest expenditure of artillery ammunition[77] on the Western Front in a period of 24 hours was achieved between 1200 on 28 September to the same time on 29 September 1918 and amounted to 943,947 rounds.[78] The financial cost was just as prodigious; the 1918 value of the shells was £3.871 million, which equates to £1.47 Billion at 2016 prices.[79] The damage to environment was equally high, creating a psychological and practical impact upon the

71 Brown, *British Logistics on the Western Front*, p.174.

72 For an examination of this issue, see, the seminal, Graham Winton, *Theirs Not to Reason Why, Horsing the British Army*, 1875-1925, Wolverhampton Military Studies (Solihull: Helion, 2013), pp.333-339.

73 Their first major action was the Third Battle of Ypres; Fuller, *Tanks in the Great War*, p.167.

74 Based upon the components of a Mark I tank, the Gun Carrier Mark I, was tracked and armoured, and mounted a 6 inch 26 cwt BL howitzer, or a 60 pdr BL Mark I gun. With its mobility and protection, it was able, in theory, to provide the seamless artillery support to infantry and armour, which, in the advance, other artillery systems were unable to do. In practice, the concept was never developed to its logical conclusion, and only 48 were produced. The 6 inch version was the World's first Self Propelled Gun (SPG) and although it was used, at night, to snipe at enemy gun positions, from locations inaccessible to other artillery, this impressive technical equipment was never integrated into a doctrinal framework. The vehicle was operated by soldiers from the Gun Carrier Companies of the Tank Corps, whilst the guns were served by detachments of the Royal Garrison Artillery; see, Philip Ventham and David Fletcher, *Moving the Guns, The Mechanization of the Royal Artillery 1854-1939* (London: HMSO, 1990), pp.18-20.

75 For an explanation of the system and its operation, see, Ibid, p.22.

76 MEBE, p.481, Table 4 - Ammunition Expenditure in France from 8th August to 6th September 1918.

77 For a comprehensive survey of the BEF's artillery ammunition and fuzes, see the CONFIDENTIAL *Handbook of Ammunition*, May 1918, Royal Laboratories, reprinted by the Naval and Military Press, nd but 2017.

78 MEBE, p.481, Table 5 - Approximate Cost of Gun Ammunition and Number of Rounds Expended by the British Armies in France from Noon, 28th September, to Noon, 29th September 1918. Fourth Army received a 'pat on the back' for having the lowest ammunition demands in the BEF on account of salvage operations within the AOR, although this did require the allocation of 100 lorries for transportation; TNA WO 95/452/1: HQ Fourth Army, DDOS, WD, 15 September 1918. In October, the shortage of WMT led to a reversion to focus upon drawing ammunition from railheads; TNA WO 95/452/1: HQ Fourth Army, DDOS, WD, 19 October 1918.

79 Based on the *Measuring Worth UK* Economic Cost measuring the relative share of the project as a percentage of the output of the economy.

BEF's logisticians,[80] as the territory the BEF advanced into was 'completely destroyed by shellfire and there were no huts or houses, even trees......the battlefields; they are absolutely beyond description: nothing but ruin, desolation and death for miles and miles'.[81] Maintaining the momentum of the advance in these conditions required not only effective combat power but also very significant logistic and engineering capability.

Challenges continued to emerge. The high expenditure rates reflected the expanding involvement in the advance, of almost all of the BEF's divisions during the Hundred Days and to replace Fourth Army ammunition stocks required over 100 trains, so perhaps it was no surprise that there were problems in moving the munitions forward from the railhead at Templeux-le-Guerard.[82] The demands made on the logisticians were exacerbated by the variety of artillery pieces and ammunition natures,[83] which, were in service and the planning considerably complicated, by the requirement to store, transport and issue chemical munitions.[84] The complexity of the transport requirement could be destabilizing to the point of failure, a point highlighted by the AQMG of XIII Corps: 'Another transport lesson that must never be forgotten. Never juggle; simplicity in plan and execution is the keynote of success. During these last operations I worked on the simplest lines; as soon as anything became complicated I started to unravel it, cutting my losses and bringing it back to simplicity'.[85]

Onwards and Upwards

Motivated to 'Maintain Momentum', logisticians became more adventurous in their approach to logistic support. The plan to sustain the 4th (Australian) Division[86] attacking Hamel on the Somme on 4 July 1918 is instructive.[87] Two hours after Zero (0310) at 0510, with Allied Forces consolidating their positions, RE 8 planes from 9 Squadron,[88] began an air-drop of Small Arms

80 The history of 42nd (East Lancashire) Division recorded depressing sights during the move: 'they [the soldiers] were met by straggling groups of refugees, women, children, and old men, hastening with the more portable of their poor possessions out of the reach of Hun savagery and rapacity. Some of these homeless wanderers appeared haggard and despairing; some numbed and hopeless; others imply bewildered. It was pitiful and pathetic sight'; Frederick P Gibbon, *The 42nd (East Lancashire) Division* (London: Country Life, 1920), p.129.

81 J Sambrook, *With the Rank and Pay of a Sapper: the 216 (Nuneaton) Army Troops Company Royal Engineers in the Great War* (Nuneaton: Paddy Griffiths Associates, 1998), p.205.

82 In the period 26-29 September 1918, 45 ammunition trains arrived at the railhead. Ammunition expenditure included 32,000 rounds of mustard agent shells.

83 For a comprehensive review, see, Ian V Hogg, *Allied Artillery of World One* (Marlborough: The Crowood Press, 1998).

84 There were 14 different types of chemical shell and six types of gas cylinder; for details, see, *Gas Attack, Chemical Warfare 1915 - The Present Day*, William Moore (London: Leo Cooper, 1987), Appx B and the Royal Laboratories Handbook of Ammunition, 1918.

85 Nicholson, *Behind the Lines*, p.215.

86 There were also troops from the 3rd (Australian) Division, and four companies from the 33rd (American) Division.

87 One feature of the Fourth Army DDST War Diary in this period is the record of the dynamic interfaces with key logistic staff officers from the comprising Corps: Cavalry, Tanks, Australian and Canadian. Clearly, without this co-ordination, logistic coherency would have disintegrated. TNA 95/454/4: HQ Fourth Army. DDST, WD, August - November 1918.

88 For details of the RE 8, see, Francis K Mason, *The British Bomber since 1914* (London: Putnam, 1994), pp.60-62 and J M Bruce, *The Aeroplanes of the Royal Flying Corps Military Wing*, 2nd Edn (London: Putnam, 1992), pp.458-464. The RE 8 was nick-named in the RFC in rhyming slang as 'Harry Tate' after a contemporary music hall comedian.

Ammunition (SAA).[89] By the end of the day, they had delivered 112,000 rounds in 93 boxes,[90] for the loss of two aircraft,[91] an operation, which clearly demonstrated the flexibility of air power,[92] although generating a future 'creative-tension' in relation to the hazards of air logistic support to ground operations. Four supply tanks,[93] each with a unloading party of four infantry and a Junior NCO,[94] then arrived on the position, delivering 496 coils of barbed wire, 1,720 picquets, 180 corrugated iron sheets, 600 Stokes mortar bombs, 40,000 rounds of SAA and 400 gallons of water.[95] The manpower to lift these stores would have amounted to 1,250 soldiers.[96] The tanks were crewed by 24 personnel, an efficiency improvement factor of 50; the war appeared to have moved on except for the requirement to create a specially organized train of pack mules to carry Combat Supplies[97] across terrain that HT and WMT could not traverse.[98] Another forgotten logistic task was to deliver sufficient canvas, wood and wheel assemblies to the 1st and 4th (Australian) Divisions to construct dummy tanks, which were used to support Fourth Army operations in the area of Cologne Farm on 18 September.[99] The successful enactment of logistic operations, required though, careful and detailed planning by experienced staff officers and the Hamel operation was but a tiny part of a massive and complex activity.

In preparation for the Battle of Amiens, Fourth Army planners, mindful of the importance of ensuring that logistic operations did not compromise operational security, directed that all rail and road movement in support of the offensive was conducted at night, with only routine administrative activity continuing by day.[100] In addition, the RAF flew daylight patrols over the Fourth Army area

89 C E W Bean, *Australian Official History of the War* (AOH) *1914-1918,* Vol. VI, *The Australian Imperial Force in France during the Allied Offensive, 1918* (Sydney: Angus and Robertson, 1942), p.270. Fn 71 states that Rawlinson had been exposed to the concept from an intercepted German communication and requested Brigadier-General L E O Charlton, commander V Brigade RAF to investigate, who tasked 3 Squadron Australian Flying Corps (AFC) to conduct trials.

90 The boxes were dropped at specific agreed locations and on any large V laid on the ground in white cloth within Australian Corps boundaries; Ibid, p.270.

91 H A Jones, BOH, *The War in the Air, Being the Story of The part played in the Great War by the Royal Air Force,* Vol. VI (Oxford: Clarendon Press, 1937) pp.416-417.

92 To support the Amiens offensive, 9 Squadron RAF was assigned the mission of dropping machine gun ammunition to units of III and Australian Corps on their 2nd and 3rd objectives; Montgomery, *The Story of the Fourth Army,* p.24. Each box contained 1,000 rounds of 0.303 inch ammunition and descended on a small parachute, the procurement and distribution of which, was another logistic activity.

93 Edmonds, BOH, *France and Belgium 1918,* Vol. III, p.203, describes these vehicles as 'supply tanks' but Bean, *Australian Imperial Force in France,* p.270, fn 72 is clear that they were Gun Carriers, specifically noting they were designed to transport a 60 pdr artillery piece.

94 Bean, AOH, Vol. VI, *Australian Imperial Force in France,* p.270.

95 Major-General J F C Fuller CB CBE DSO, *Memoirs of an Unconventional Soldier* (London: Nicholson & Watson, 1935), p.289.

96 Edmonds, BOH, *France and Belgium 1918,* Vol. III, p.203.

97 Combat Supplies are ammunition, POL, rations and water. Although the modern term Combat Supplies was not current in the British Army during the Great War, it neatly summarizes the items that were the most important in delivering direct military effect in the front-line. Ammunition included, in the Great War context, small arms ammunition, artillery ammunition, specialized infantry natures, chemical weapons and explosives. POL covered all liquids fuels, lubricants (oils and greases) and antifreeze. Rations included food for personnel and forage for animals.

98 Bean, AOH, Vol. VI, *Australian Imperial Force in France,* p.271.

99 These decoys were used because of the shortage of tanks for the operation and were deployed to draw German anti-tank and artillery fire away from live equipment, a task in which, they were generally successful; Montgomery, *The Story of the Fourth Army,* p.125. Decoys were used by IX Corps to support an attack by 71st and 137th Brigades during the early morning of 11 October; Edmonds, BOH, *France and Belgium,* Vol. V, p.248 but this appears to be the only mention in the BOH of their use, although photographs in the Tank Museum archive suggest they were used regularly to support set-piece attacks. Moving the decoys became a problem in the mud as they were thin-wheeled and normally towed by horses whilst negotiating winding village streets required care.

100 Montgomery, *The Story of the Fourth Army,* p.28.

to confirm that unauthorized movements and activities were not occurring, a critical task which became embedded in future preparations,[101] whilst at night, aircraft flew sorties to screen the noise of tank movement forward of the railheads.[102] Logistic planners, recognizing the importance of support to armour, had arranged the in-load of stocks to IV Brigade at Saleux and V Brigade at Poulainville, with 4th Line stocks arriving from the Base at Rouen on Thursday 8 August 1918 as the Fourth Army reserve located at Prouzel but with 12 wagons allocated to IV Brigade for delivery to the railhead at Longueau. This is particularly interesting because it was allocated as one of the Ambulance Train Railheads for the Australian, Canadian and Cavalry Corps.[103]

Table 12.1
Battle of Amiens
Fourth Army Tank Brigades POL Inload[104]

Product	IV Brigade	V Brigade	Reserve Stocks	Total
Petrol A (Gallons)	80,000	80,000	40,000	200,000
Price's Engine Oil (Gallons)	4,000	4,000	2,000	10,000
Steam Cylinder Oil, Thick (Gallons)	10,000	10,000	5,000	25,000
Vacuum A, Oil (Gallons)	8,000	8,000	4,000	20,000
Grease (Tons)	8.93	8.93	4.46	22.32

In addition to POL, the Tank Corps Ammunition Railhead (ARH) at Flesselles held a reserve of 50,000 rounds of 6 pdr High Explosive (HE), 5,000,000 rounds of 0.303 inch of various types and 100,000 rounds of pistol ammunition. The supply requirements extended to a wide range of items across Fourth Army, including issues of five tons of Chloride of Lime,[105] 111,000 Iron Rations, 2,400 gallons of rum,[106] 3,000 rations for Prisoners of War (POW), 50,000 packs of Pea Soup & Oxo and 23,200 petrol tins for the carriage of water.[107] All of this materiel required manual labour and clerical staff to move, account for, and issue it.

There were occasions however, when critical items failed to be delivered in a timely manner. On 4 August 1918, less than four days before the Amiens offensive, 1st (Canadian) Division had not

101 TNA WO 95/112/2: '5th Tank Brigade, Order No 3, G23/34 dated 26 September 1918' in preparation for the attack on the *Hindenburg Line*, para 9, Secrecy.

102 Montgomery, *The Story of the Fourth Army* p.19 and TNA WO 95/112/2: '5th Tank Brigade, Preliminary Instructions No 2 dated 7 August 1918, Administrative Instructions Confirming Verbal Orders', para 6 (3).

103 Fourth Army Administrative Arrangements dated 6 August 1918; Edmonds, BOH, *France and Belgium 1918*, Vol. IV, Appx VII, Sect B - Table 1 Railheads on Zero Day, p.561. This may have been a sequential operation, the stocks being cleared before the arrival of the ambulance trains.

104 Table compiled from information in Fourth Army Administrative Arrangements dated 6 August 1918, Edmonds, BOH, *France and Belgium 1918*, Vol. IV, Appx VII, Sect F - Supplies, p.564.

105 Chloride of Lime was used for a variety of essential tasks including the neutralization of liquid chemical warfare agents, dis-infection procedures, water purification and laundering.

106 The scale was 300 gallons of rum per week per division in the line; TNA WO 95/454/4: HQ Fourth Army, DDST, 'Notes on Conference at "Q", 8th July 1918'. Rum was stored and transported in one gallon stone jars with a stopper that was wax sealed, in wood crates. This meant, on this occasion, handling at the point of final delivery, 2,400 jars. Jars had the abbreviation SRD marked upon them, denoting Supply Reserve Depot. The soldiers suggested in a manner, which is timeless, other meanings, such as 'Soon Runs Dry' or 'Seldom Reaches Destination'. Each jar held the per diem rum ration of ½ gill for 64 soldiers, thus 2,400 jars provided 153,600 rations. Rum was not an entitlement nor was it issued daily to each soldier, with the ration usually being authorized by the GOC of a Division upon the advice of the Senior Medical Officer, although some divisional commanders chose not to exercise their discretion.

107 Edmonds, BOH, *France and Belgium 1918*, Vol. IV, Appx VII, Sect F - Supplies, p.564.

received the authorised in-load of infantry ammunition natures, including rifle and hand grenades, mortar bombs, SAA and flares, a problem repeated across the Corps in varying degrees.[108] This issue was not generated by a shortage of ammunition but the means to clear materiel from the ARHs, a situation created by a number of interlocking factors embedded in the allocation and use of WMT within Fourth Army. This understandably focused upon the delivery of artillery ammunition but left insufficient lift for infantry natures, a problem that could have been reduced by using HT assets. The concentration of tanks, aircraft and additional WMT for the attack compounded the complexity, by rapidly increasing the requirement for petrol within the Area of Responsibility (AOR). This induced a shortage, with a concomitant need for more WMT to collect additional POL stocks from the railheads, whilst the extra vehicle movements and weak traffic control exacerbated road congestion. This one example lucidly demonstrates how complex the logistic issues in the BEF were and how readily failure could emerge.[109] In this instance, the fragility came close to delaying the Canadian Corps participation in the offensive,[110] a scenario only saved by the professional and swift intervention of logisticians at every level of command.

With the BEF maintaining 4,106 miles of road in August 1918,[111] there were insufficient resources to immediately upgrade the roads between the road-heads and the units. So, having placed so much emphasis on the role of the motor lorry, the BEF had to rely on HT from the divisional trains to provide the last link in the chain.[112] In places, the logistic system was unable to provide ammunition and rations by road in sufficient quantities to advanced elements and the logisticians turned to the RAF to deliver these items by air. In one operation, on 2-3 October 1918, WMT dumped 15,000 rations weighing 13 tons at the dispatch airfields, and in a joint operation with the Belgians, stocks were air-dropped to Belgian and French troops in the areas of Oostnieuwkerke and Stadenburg, by 80 RAF and Belgian aircraft.[113] In another operation, on 13 October 1918, Armstrong-Whitworth FK 8 aircraft of 35 Squadron RAF, dropped two tons of bully beef and biscuits to troops and civilians around Le Cateau.[114]

Race to the Swift

As the advance progressed, the BEF's logisticians grappled with the immense challenges in supporting the greater part of five Armies moving to bring the enemy to battle. Key to this success was the critical role of the Railway Operating Division (ROD),[115] a significant organization, employing,

108 For an examination of the A&Q issues, see, Rob Thompson, 'Delivering the Goods, Operation Landovery Castle: A Logistical and Administrative Analysis of Canadian Corps Preparations for the Battle of Amiens 8-11 August 1918', in Gary Sheffield and Peter Gray (Eds.), *Changing War, The British Army, The Hundred Days Campaign and the Birth of the Royal Air Force, 1918*, Birmingham War Studies, (London: Bloomsbury, 2013), pp.37-54.

109 The railhead was a critical logistic node, the capability of which, was greatly dependent upon the speed of transhipment between rail and road transport assets, itself a product of sound planning, good drills, command grip and the timely arrival and departure of WMT and HT.

110 For a comprehensive and most engaging examination of the Administrative aspects of the Canadian Corps A&Q picture, see the seminal Kenneth Radley, *Get Tough, Stay Tough, Shaping the Canadian Corps 1914-1918*, Wolverhampton Military Studies (Solihull: Helion, 2014).

111 TNA WO 95/39: GHQ, QMG, WD, June - August 1918, 'Explanatory Review, August 1918', p.3.

112 The numbers of horses on strength, lucidly illustrate the importance of HT to BEF capability. On 17 October 1918, Fourth Army for example, had 50,570; TNA WO 95/445/5: HQ Fourth Army, A&Q, 'Wastage in Horses during the Week Ending 17-10-18'.

113 For details, see, *A Short History of the Royal Air Force*, Air Publication 125 (Air Ministry, September 1929), pp.316-317 and BOH, *The War in the Air*, Vol. VI, p.534. The RAF allocated two squadrons to the task: 82 flying the Armstrong-Whitworth RK 8 and 218 equipped with the De Havilland DH 9.

114 See, *Airlift, Military Air Transport The Illustrated History*, Richard Townshend-Bickers (London: Osprey, 1998), p.17. This operation is not mentioned in either, *A Short History of the Royal Air Force* or *The War in the Air*, Vol. VI.

115 For details of ROD operations, see, Henniker, BOH, *Transportation on the Western Front*, Pritchard, *Royal Engineers*,

in June 1918, 18,235 operating and workshop personnel, with another 14,080 involved in SGR construction and maintenance,[116] supporting the operation of 1,247 SGR locomotives, increasing to 1,421 by December.[117] It has a sound claim to be the largest Lieutenant Colonel's command that there has been in the British Army, as the appointment of Commanding Officer ROD, was held by Temporary Lieutenant-Colonel Sir Guy Paget, Bart CMG DSO, late Superintendent of the Midland Railway. The ROD was not the whole story because it did not include approximately 16,000 troops operating NGR,[118] or the 21,905 personnel involved in headquarters, survey, movements, quarrying or labouring units, which were directly supporting railway operations.[119] By late 1918, there were therefore, probably a strength of about 71,000 personnel,[120] from an establishment of 74,950, involved in delivering or supporting BEF railway activity,[121] which equates to approximately 3.77 percent of the BEF's manpower,[122] a figure, that belies the crucial part the ROD played in the combat capability of the BEF. Significant SGR works continued throughout the period of the BEF's advance. Work included enhancements to the main lines, advancing the railheads and improvements to loops and sidings. Planned or on-going projects in the Fourth Army Area in the first week of October 1918, totalled 143.69 miles of construction or refurbishment including new sidings at Tincourt for armour,[123] ambulance and ammunition trains, of 0.3 miles and 2.30 miles respectively, 3.14 miles of additional sidings in the Chemin-Vert Yard and 8.25 miles between Maricourt and Peronne.[124]

As the ROD pushed the railheads forward, road repair teams refurbished roads between the railheads and the road-heads,[125] which were usually 10-15 miles behind the unit B echelons.[126] The Germans, as part of their Counter-Mobility plan had cratered and mined many of the roads, creating

Vol. V and the illustrated work, William A T Aves, *ROD, The Railway Operating Division on the Western Front, The Royal Engineers in France and Belgium, 1915-1919* (Donington: Shaun Tyas, 2009).

116 MEBE, p.600 (i), Table (iii) -Establishment and Strength of the Railway Personnel Employed in the various Theatres of War.

117 The two key sources are at variance. TNA WO 107/69: 'Report Upon the Work of the Quartermaster-General's Branch of the Staff and Directorates Controlled, British Armies in France and Flanders', pp 16-17, states the total in November 1918 was 1,486 SGR locomotives and 18,500 personnel. MEBE, pp.606-607, Table (i) - Progress of Transportation in France since January 1917, quotes an average of 1,398 SGR locomotives in traffic for November 1918 and 1,421 for December. The difference from TNA WO 107/69 may be the total strength against those available for operations, as some locomotives were hired from the Belgian Railways.

118 16,407 in June 1918; MEBE p.600 (i), Table (iii) - Establishment and Strength of the Railway Personnel Employed in the various Theatres of War.

119 Ibid.

120 Ibid.

121 A deficiency of 4,323 against establishment; Ibid.

122 Figure calculated from tables in MEBE, p.600 (i), Table (iii) - Establishment and Strength of the Railway Personnel Employed in the various Theatres of War.

123 Tincourt was an active railhead, particularly so during the adjustment of Fourth Army in preparation for the attack on the Hindenburg Line. One important move in the period 20-22 September 1918 was the arrival of 98 tanks from Achiet Boisleux and Erin, from 8th, 13th and 15th Tank Battalions and No 5 Supply Tank Company. TNA WO 95/112/2: '5th Tank Brigade, Order No 1, dated 19 September 1918'.

124 TNA WO 95/445/5: HQ Fourth Army, A&Q, Note 770, 'Broad Gauge Railway Construction, Week Ending 2-10-18'.

125 The burden of road repair and construction in 1918 is clearly illustrated by the rise in the weekly average outputs controlled by Director-General Transportation in the LOC and Army AORs. DGT's responsibility did not include all roads in the AORs nor any roads forward of Brigade rear boundaries; see, Henniker, *Transportation on the Western Front,* pp.345-346. New and re-made road in square yards peaked at 81,803 in March and then averaged 60,000 square yards per week until October. Road re-surfacing rose from 41,554 in April peaking at 161,847 square yards in August and 96,647 in October. MEBE, p,608, Table (i) - Progress of Transportation in France.

126 The B Echelon holds the non-urgent capabilities, such as clothing, stores, administrative staff; unit B Echelons were often grouped at brigade level. In the Great War on the Western Front, A1 and A2 is often identified as the 1st Line Regimental Transport and Trench Dumps, whilst the B Echelon is the Quartermasters' Store.

P12.1. Logistic Challenge: WMT limited mobility. The failure to produce off-road WMT vehicles generated many in-efficiencies in employment, outputs and fuel usage, and resulted in the requirement to retain HT. (RLC Museum: MT Collection)

an urgent requirement for the BEF to clear,[127] repair and maintain these routes, whilst conducting Mobility tasks in constructing, rebuilding or by-passing blown bridges,[128] which reinforced the critical importance of this logistic engineering capability.[129] The material required to execute this work was very significant, totalling, just for road repair, 7,838 tons in the Fourth Army Area during last week of September 1918,[130] whilst in the period August - October, the BEF's engineers had erected 326 steel bridges and constructed over 200 from timber and salvaged materials, sometimes with the assistance of French contractors or Locally Recruited Workers.[131] These tasks had an especial imperative because the WMT fleet was composed of Low Mobility Load Carriers (LMLCs),[132] which, although

127 Albert was for example, cleared by RE Tunnelling Companies of 100 small road mines and 30 large ones, all without incident; TNA WO 95/451/4: HQ Fourth Army, CRE, 'III Corps Engineering Work during Operations August/ September 1918', nd.

128 To ensure the maintenance of momentum in the advance, the requirement for the co-ordination of Engineer Explosive Ordnance Disposal, combat engineer assets and labour became paramount.

129 The assessment of the bridging requirement was the subject of a two year study by the staff of the GHQ Engineer-in-Chief, which commenced in May 1915. The acquisition of the material and specialist equipment, such as the Hopkins and Inglis bridges commenced in early 1917, with the advances of 1917 creating what was in effect, a rehearsal of bridging operations in the Hundred Days. Transportation of course, was essential to deliver the assets to the sites. On the subject, Institution of the Royal Engineers Institute, *Work of the RE in the European War of 1914-19,* Bridging (Chatham: W & J Mackay, 1921) is comprehensive. See also, J H Joiner, *One More River to Cross, The Story of British Military Bridging* (Barnsley: Leo Cooper, 2001).

130 TNA WO 95/445/5: HQ Fourth Army, A&Q, 'Road Metal Issues Week Ending 28-9-18'. Of this total, 7,408 tons was macadam, 90 tons soling, 30 tons chipping and 310 tons gravel.

131 Joiner, *One More River to Cross,* p.87.

132 In this respect, the experience of the Great War was quickly forgotten. This fact being demonstrated by the mixture of vehicles in the British Army of 1939-40, which was influenced by the Crosland Committee, formed in 1934 to consider to what extent the 3 ton 6 x 4 lorry could be replaced by a civilian 4 x 2 model. It exceeded though, its initial Terms of Reference (TOR) by taking into consideration the Western Plan for deployment to the Continent, which was to undergo many revisions before it was enacted as Deployment Plan W4 in the autumn of 1939. In doing so, the Committee recommended that over 50% of military 6 x 4 vehicles should be replaced by 4 x 2 civilian types, on the basis that, as the Army would deploy to an operational theatre with good roads and railways, the

having some interesting innovations also had many limitations,[133] the key one being poor off-road performance.[134] Units other than those from the Royal Engineers also contributed to repairs in order to maintain the momentum of the advance.[135] It was in this arena that HT came into its own because it was able to operate off-road, negotiate watercourses and pass obstructions, although in early November 1918, a new threat appeared when there were a series of incidents involving horses hooves striking unexploded shells and initiating them.[136] In addition, to these problems, there were plenty of dangers for the unwary:

> Movement in the Forest (of Mormal) was a hazardous business, since booby traps for the unwary abounded. Special explosives experts from the Engineers were attached to infantry units to look out for, and render harmless, all such snares laid for the careless and the inquisitive.[137] Passage for transport was likewise a problem because the main tracks were mined or blown up. Much RE reconstruction work was necessary before heavy vehicles and guns could use the rides and tracks.[138]

The transport of 1st Line Combat Supplies through the enemy's defensive zone was the subject of much discussion and innovation. The reasons were simple; not only was WMT and to a lesser extent Horse Transport (HT) often incapable of traversing the ground but they were vulnerable to the destructive effects of artillery. Not surprisingly, the planners opted to use modified tanks and gun carriers as supply vehicles because not only were they armoured, but also they were tracked;[139] the two key challenges were therefore conceptually, if not practically, immediately solved, and the first use of supply tanks took place at Messines in June 1917.[140] The modified vehicles had though, many disadvantages and before the war ended, a few specialist supply platforms were

importance of capable military specials had declined. See, Major R Campagnac RASC & Major P E C Hayman 15/19 KRH, *The Second World War, 1939-1945, Army, Fighting, Support and Transport Vehicles and the War Office Organization for their Provision*, Part II-*Unarmoured Vehicles* (War Office, 1951), pp.7-14.

133 One assumption the Crosland Committee made, which perpetuated the focus on LMLC, was that the Army would not require them to operate in terrain such as Passchendaele. No doubt this assumption also provided a strong argument against those proposing a requirement for tracked logistic vehicles. Lieutenant Colonel C H Maginniss BA RLC, 'Everybody's Trucking, The Expansion of the British Army's Logistic Vehicle Task Fleet 1938-1940', *RLC Review*, Regimental Association of the Royal Logistic Corps (1998), pp.64-71.

134 Many types had a respectable load capacity of 3 tons and there were four-wheel drive systems in service, but most of the vehicles had solid rubber tyres, which though robust, gave poor off-road performance. Pneumatic tyres became increasingly common on light vehicles but punctures were frequent, so the solid tyre remained a feature of load carriers until the 1920s. Nearly all the Four Wheel Drive vehicles came from the USA: FWD, Nash, Jeffery-Quad and Knox were the leaders.

135 18th Corps Cyclists serving with the Cavalry Corps, did sterling work in making the Premont - Maretz road passable after a brick bridge over a stream was blown, and supported 25th Divisional Engineers by filling a crater on the Searin - Premont crossroads; TNA WO 95/451/4: HQ Fourth Army, CRE, Cavalry Corps G.X.471/122, nd, 'Notes on R.E. work with the Cavalry Corps during operations towards LE CATEAU October 8th - 12th, 1918'.

136 Home, Archibald, Brigadier-General, Sir, KCVO CB CMG DSO, *The Diary of a World War I Cavalry Officer* (Tunbridge Wells: D J Costello, 1985), p.189.

137 Hazards that the British Army is all too well more recently acquainted with, from operations in Northern Ireland, Iraq and Afghanistan.

138 Dunn, *The War the Infantry Knew*, p.566.

139 Originally Mark I and Mark II tanks were converted to the supply role, the work being undertaken at the Tank Corps Central Workshops.

140 Tank battalions had six vehicles at 1st Line (two per company) whilst supply companies supporting armoured units at 2nd Line on the Western Front in 1918, were established for 30 armoured tracked logistic carriers; Edmonds, BOH, *France and Belgium 1918*, Vol. IV, p.24. Colonel J F C Fuller DSO, *Tanks in the Great War, 1914-1918* (London, John Murray, 1920), p.169 noted that the attachment at battalion level 'did not work well' owing to the Company HQ being 'left in the air'.

designed and built.[141] To enhance the lift capacity of each tank, trials with wooden sledges towed behind the tanks,[142] led to their operational use in September 1917 and 110 were deployed at Cambrai in November 1917,[143] although V Tank Brigade abandoned the concept after series of failures at Amiens, resulting in them being described as 'absolutely useless',[144] whilst 3 Tank Supply Company dragging sledges loaded with bridging materiel for the Canadian Corps Engineers had a similar experience.[145]

P12.2. Logistic Innovation: armoured high mobility. A Tracked Supply Carrier, converted from the Gun Carrier, Mark I. Remarkably, despite various proposals since 1918, to introduce a tracked armoured logistic vehicle into the British Army, the BEF remains unique in having the capability. (Tank Museum: 883/B1)

141 The Mark IX was designed in 1916 as an Armoured Personnel Carrier (APC) but because of production difficulties, models did not reach France until October 1918. Only 36 vehicles were built, 25 of them in late 1918.

142 The trials proved that each tank could tow three sledges with a total cargo capacity of 14 tons. American forces in the Pacific, as part of their operations to support island assaults, used wooden sledges loaded with Combat Supplies to create unit loads. On the Base Islands, they were usually moved with Fork Lift Trucks (FLTs) but during the assault phase of an operation, they were dragged off the landing craft with tractors or bulldozers. For more details, see, Alvin P Stauffer, *US Army in World War II, The Technical Services, The Quarter-Master Corps: Operations in the War Against Japan* (Washington DC: Office of the Chief of Military History, Department of the Army, 1956), pp. 263-265.

143 The manufacture of these sledges by the Central Tank Workshops consumed 70 tons of wood; Fuller, *Tanks in the Great War*, p.129.

144 TNA WO 95/112/2: '5th Tank Brigade, Report on Operations with Australian Corps from 8th August to 15th August 1918', para 3 (a) Tank Supplies, recorded that the towing cables failed, sometimes with empty sledges, the sledges disintegrated under tow, the Mark IV tank engine was not sufficiently powerful to tow the sledges across rough ground and it was almost impossible to tow the sledges through the winding village streets. The concept however was revived in the Second World War. In 1944-45, the Royal Engineer Armoured Vehicles Royal Engineers (AVRE) towed armoured sleds, rated at 4 tons capacity, carrying stores, fascines, explosives or an infantry section; see, *79th Armoured Division, Final Report* (21 Army Group Printing Service, July 1945), p.53 & p.225.

145 Fuller, *Tanks in the Great War*, p.169.

As the BEF had so few armoured supply vehicles, replenishment operations in the advance usually took place at night unless they were out of enemy artillery range.[146] The effect of artillery fire on a logistic tank hide could be devastating and much effort was expended in ensuring good camouflage and concealment practices were enacted, especially during the preparations for a set piece attack. No matter how much care was taken though, mis-fortune could still intervene and V Tank Brigade suffered a particularly unfortunate loss[147] on the late afternoon of Wednesday 7 August 1918. No 1 Gun Carrier Company,[148] comprising 19 tanks[149] loaded with Combat Supplies[150] and defence stores[151] for the infantry,[152] was in a camouflaged tactical hide in an orchard near Villers Bretonneux, when a German shell struck a supply tank.[153] The resulting fire set the camouflage nets alight and the heat detonated some of the trench mortar ammunition, with the smoke and explosions adding to the expanding conflagration,[154] which destroyed, 14 tanks complete with their loads.[155] The vulnerability of logistic capability was not however, confined to the field of battle. On the evening of Sunday 11 August 1918, the *Deutsche Luftstreitkrafte* (DLK),[156]

146 Montgomery, *The Story of the Fourth Army*, p.19.

147 This particular incident is an excellent illustration of the frustrations of defining some of the logistic detail because the primary and secondary sources are at variance on numbers present, the divisional allocations, losses and the loads carried.

148 No 1 Gun Carrier Company was assigned to carry infantry supplies, as follows: two tanks each to 2nd and 3rd Australian Divisions and nine tanks each to 4th and 5th Australian Divisions, totalling 22. TNA WO 95/112/2: '5th Tank Brigade, Report on Operations with Australian Corps from 8th August to 15th August 1918', para 1(e), Allotment of Tanks.

149 The sources are at variance as to the numbers of tanks in the orchard. TNA WO 95/112/2: '5th Tank Brigade, 'Report on Operations with Australian Corps from 8th August to 15th August 1918', para 2 (d) Lying Up Places, states that 14 were lost and five saved, thus totalling 19.

150 TNA WO 95/112/2: '5th Tank Brigade, Report on Operations with Australian Corps from 8th August to 15th August 1918', Appx E, lists SAA in boxes and ready to use Lewis gun panniers, Stokes 3 inch mortar rounds, grenades, explosives, flares, iron rations, biscuits, preserved meat and water in tins.

151 Ibid, Appx E lists shovels, picks, pickets, barbed wire and sandbags.

152 Ibid, Appx E lists in detail the loads carried by the 11 Carriers of 1 Company and the 12 from 5th Supply Company. Ellis, *The Story of the Fifth Australian Division*, p.326 records that one tank was loaded with 100 rounds of trench mortars, 40,000 rounds SAA, 50 water cans, 4 larges boxes of food, 200 shovels, 100 picks, 5,000 sandbags, 300 screw pickets and 50 coils of barbed wire. This may be an example load as none of the tanks in Appx E match the load list.

153 Ellis, *The Story of the Fifth Australian Division*, p.328.

154 The sources are at variance as to the cause of the destruction. Montgomery, *The Story of the Fourth Army*, p.28, fn 1, Edmonds, BOH, *France and Belgium 1918*, Vol. IV, p.25, and Bean, AOH, *1914-1918*, Vol. VI, p.523, all state that smoke, flame and explosions caused by the stray shell caused the Germans to an initiate a directed bombardment on the orchard, whilst noting that the sole fatality was an Australian Gunner, J S Bannon, who was mortally wounded whilst fighting a fire in a tank. Ellis, *The Story of the Fifth Australian Division*, p.328 is clear that the resulting destruction was the result of one shell, whilst the TNA WO 95/112/2: '5th Tank Brigade, Report on Operations with Australian Corps from 8th August to 15th August 1918', para 2 (d) Lying Up Places states the loss was initiated by 'a chance shell'.

155 The sources are at variance as to losses. Montgomery, *The Story of the Fourth Army*, p.28, fn 1 and Edmonds, BOH, *France and Belgium 1918*, Vol. IV, p.25, both state 25 tanks were destroyed, suggesting nine supply and 16 combat but Bean, AOH, *1914-1918*, Vol. VI, p.523, notes that there were 16 supply tanks, of which 13 were destroyed. Ellis, *The Story of the Fifth Australian Division*, p.328, is specific that there were only 18 in the orchard, thus indicating its allocated nine supply tanks and nine combat. *Tanks in the Great War*, p.169, states that of 22, only six were saved. The War Diary of V Tank Brigade states that 14 supply tanks were destroyed but only listed 11 loaded tanks in 1 Gun Carrier Company when it had 22; TNA WO 95/112/2: '5th Tank Brigade, Report on Operations with Australian Corps from 8th August to 15th August 1918', para 2 (d) Lying Up Places. Williams-Ellis & Williams-Ellis, *The Tank Corps*, p.195, records that Second-Lieutenant Henderson Smith was awarded the MC for his actions in attempting to save the tanks from the explosions and fire.

156 The German Air Force was not an independent organization but the air arm of the German army, in the same way as the RFC in the British Army until the formation of the Royal Air Force. The *Deutsche Luftstreitkrafte* was formed in October 1916 from the *Fliegertruppen des deutschen Kaiserreiches*, the Imperial German Flying Corps. The German Imperial Air Service (GIAS) is often used in British sources as the term for the *Luftstreitkrafte* and its predecessor but neither German title translates thus. See, Peter Grey and Owen Thetford, *German Aircraft of the First World War*, 2nd Edn (London: Putnam, 1979), p.xxix.

bombed No 2 Base Mechanical Transport Depot[157] at Calais, and the resulting fire destroyed the spares for nearly 20,000 vehicles,[158] equivalent to almost half the British mechanized force in France.[159] The monetary loss at 2016 values amounted to nearly £474 million,[160] which, although a very significant sum, almost pales into insignificance when it is set against the daily cost of the war in the period April - October 1918: £2.820 Billion at 2016 valuations.[161] Logistic degradation was not however, caused solely by the enemy because looting was a persistent problem,[162] even extending to NGR operations in Fourth Army in October 1918.[163]

Operationally though, the attack had some profound effects on the logistic system, and it is instructive to examine how the staff approached the problem. The BEF's QMG Staff had to assess the requirement for restocking, and, once their bids were forwarded, the War Office had much work to do to progress them. Industrial priorities were changed to generate greater production of MT parts, whilst issues to Theatres other than the BEF were reduced. Training in the United Kingdom was curtailed as spares were directed to the BEF, whilst on the Continent, the Unit Repair Scale was reduced in order to enhance stocks at 2nd, 3rd and 4th Line. The vulnerability of depots now became an issue, with dispersion and protection being reviewed, although given the limited amount of estate available the former was a considerable challenge. The *War in the Air* offered an interesting comment upon the balance of risk, which the logisticians faced.

> It must be admitted that we showed a general reluctance to make allowance for the bombing menace. Surveying the whole field of war, it can be argued that the likelihood of a hit on this or that particular objective was small, and the British character inclines to the taking of a sporting chance in preference to making fussy and apparently endless preparations for something which may never happen. Such an attitude of mind has its advantages, but it can also be merely stupid, or worse.[164]

Gas Warfare (GW) operations,[165] offensive and defensive, were integral to logistic activities until the end of the war, although by late August 1918 the manner in which the British conducted offensive

157 The railways were attacked as well, creating new challenges for those tasked with the security of the Lines of Communication. For an outline description of the British response to DLK attacks on the railway and port facilities, see, Henniker, BOH, *Transportation on the Western Front*, pp.313-326.

158 Losses included, spares for 6,497 motor-cars and ambulances, 12,270 lorries and 799 tractors, representing 55%, 40% and 93% of the assets respectively. Also destroyed, were 26,000 inner tubes and 16,000 tyres. Jones, BOH, *The War in the Air*, Vol. VI, p.429-432.

159 This resulted in a trawl of spares from across the Armies. Fourth Army were remarkably swift in responding, the comprising Corps of the Army (III, Australian and Canadian) dispatching their quotas by Thursday 15 August 1918; TNA WO 95/454/4: HQ Fourth Army, DDST, WD, 15 August 1918.

160 DDOS Fourth Army was therefore, delighted to report to GHQ that site of No 5 Ordnance Mobile Workshop (Heavy) at La Flaque captured by the Germans in the Spring offensives, had been retaken with the store of vehicle parts almost untouched; TNA WO 95/452/1: HQ Fourth Army, DDOS, WD, 28 August 1918. Fourth Army used the site for an Advanced Gun Park.

161 Both these sums are based on the share of GDP evaluations. The annual cost would be approximately £1,061 Billion in 2016 values based on the daily cost of the war in the period April - October 1918 of £2.906 Billion, which was £7,443,000 in 1918 values. See also, MEBE, p.561.

162 The effect of military and civilian looting and pilfering upon the BEF's logistic system and upon the Nation's finances deserves study.

163 Authorizing reinforcements and soldiers returning from leave, to travel on NGR supply trains, generated this issue. The problem ceased when travel was forbidden. TNA WO 95/454/4: HQ Fourth Army, DDST, WD, 15 October 1918.

164 Jones, BOH, *The War in the Air*, Vol. VI, pp.431-432.

165 Gas Warfare (GW) was the contemporary term for Chemical Warfare (CW). For an academic assessment of the BEF's GW capability, see, Albert Palazzo, *Seeking Victory on the Western Front, The British Army and Chemical Warfare in World War 1* (Lincoln & London: University of Nebraska Press, 2000). Donald Richter, *Chemical Soldiers, British*

operations had changed. Until the August offensives, use was made of the NGR to support major beam gas attacks on the Germans, culminating in single operations using in excess of 2,500 cylinders.[166] These operations could be highly effective but for the Special Brigade soldiers and the railwaymen, it was often a mind concentrating experience. From arrival at the pooping site to withdrawal from location, could often be as much as an hour, with the poop taking 15 minutes.[167] During this period there was every possibility of enemy shelling, which could be devastating, and on occasions, machine-gun fire. The transit period could be just as exciting; leaking cylinders created a constant hazard, whilst the possibility of a derailment within range of German artillery, added to the dangers.[168] Fourth Army logisticians were also involved in planning the reconditioning of some German 77mm artillery pieces and the issue of captured Blue Cross chemical shells filled with diphenylchloroarsine for use by the Royal Artillery.[169]

The use of mustard[170] created a particular problem for forward NGR and road transport operations because unlike many other chemicals used in combat during the Great War, it was a persistent agent. During offensive operations, it was often necessary to negotiate contaminated ground, with all the inherent hazards such activity entailed and for the logisticians, it added to the many hidden dangers, which they faced. Then, as now, driving at night, wearing a respirator and under artillery fire was not for the faint-hearted; the *History of the 36th (Ulster) Division* summarized the challenge:

> The lorry-driver, who stuck for fifteen hours at his wheel amid the ruts and turmoil of the Menin Road, as many of them did, with bombs crashing down at night; the section of the Divisional Train bringing up its wagons through valleys wreathed and stinking of gas, these men in truth deserved well of the infantryman facing the bullets further forward, and were in truth their companions-in-arms.[171]

Broad Front - Fixed Railheads

By late October 1918, the logisticians were focused on ensuring the BEF was properly supported as it advanced on a broad front but the problems inherent in pushing forward the railheads became more obvious as operations continued.[172] On 9 September 1918, GHQ issued a directive that all reconstruction work was to be focused upon two main rail routes in direct support of the advance.

Gas Warfare in World War One (Lawrence: University Press of Kansas, 1992) offers a wider regimental perspective. The classic text is L F Haber, *The Poisonous Cloud, Chemical Warfare in the First World War* (Oxford: Clarendon Press, 1986). Major-General C H Foulkes CB CMG DSO, *"Gas!" The Story of the Special Brigade* (Edinburgh & London: William Blackwood & Sons, 1934) is the key historical account.

166 Beam Attacks were also known as Retired Cylinder Attacks.

167 Poop was the term used to describe the release of the gas. Each cylinder had a detonator on the valve, which was exploded electrically, thereby obtaining, in theory at least, a simultaneous release of gas. A good poop was a release, which not only soaked the enemy in gas, but also involved no German reaction, and was free from accidents with the cylinders or derailments.

168 By late August, the ability to enact beam attacks had reduced as the availability of suitable NGRs across the enemy's front had declined. In addition, as the BEF advanced, and the Germans retreated, it became increasingly difficult to co-ordinate the attacks with other arms. The BEF also began to encounter French civilians, and it was this factor that finally spelled the demise of beam attacks.

169 TNA WO 95/452/1: HQ Fourth Army, DDOS, WD, 13 September 1918.

170 As a casualty producer, mustard (dichlorethylsulphide) was 36 times as effective (weight for weight) as high explosives; it remains an efficient chemical warfare agent in 2018. The introduction of mustard was a quantum leap in chemical warfare, as, for the first time, the whole body required protection.

171 Cyril Falls, *The History of the 36th (Ulster) Division* (Belfast: M'Caw Stevenson & Orr, 1922), p.279.

172 TNA WO 153/581: Fourth Army, Administrative Maps, Roads, Railheads, Dumps etc, 1 October - 30 November 1918.

Boulogne-Arras-Douai-Valenciennes-Mons to support First Army and Saint Quentin-Busigny-Le Cateau-Maubeuge-Charleroi line serving Third and Fourth Armies.[173] The re-construction plan,[174] delivered by a prioritised engineering operation,[175] enabled the Heads of Steel (HOS) to keep pace with the advance but enemy action often prevented the use of railheads.[176] A HOS reached Marcoing on 4 October and 250 yards of siding were built there the same day. Enemy shelling prevented further work until 10 October when 950 yards of sidings were laid and 1,000 yards were completed at Rumilly the same day. These impressive outputs enabled one train per day to be unloaded from 11 October.[177] Unfortunately, the Germans made widespread use of Delayed Action Mines (DAM),[178] which caused disruption to the delivery of materiel,[179] although DLK air attacks on railway facilities, including junctions, sidings, stock and railheads, which had been of increasing concern to GHQ planners in June and July,[180] started to decline as the dynamics of the DLK offensive changed as the BEF's advance gained momentum, with much greater emphasis on Close Air Support over Air Interdiction.[181] Inevitably a few attacks caused degradation to traffic but equally, the demands of operating in darkness over recently built track, constructed to minimal operational standards, often led to minor but nonetheless disruptive derailments.

As the BEF advanced, the road loop beyond the railheads and the divisional Refilling Points began to extend to the point where a perfect storm began to brew because of all the mounting problems: mine clearance, insufficient resources for road repair, decreasing traffic-ability, vehicle accidents and overwhelmed workshop recovery, repair and salvage capacity, all of which, was of course, why it was so important to open forward railheads. Colonel Nicholson, eruditely and forcefully, expressed the many frustrations[182] and intricate challenges of supporting the Corps in the advance, and especially the importance of roads to the advance.

173 Henniker, BOH, *Transportation on the Western Front*, p.437. To facilitate these tasks, rails were removed from less important routes and sidings.

174 Henniker, BOH, *Transportation on the Western Front*, pp.432-439.

175 The construction of SGR and to a much lesser extent, NGR, continued apace up to the Armistice. Fourth Army railway construction outputs for autumn 1918 are shown in TNA WO 95/445: HQ Fourth Army, A&Q, WD.

176 Henniker, BOH, *Transportation on the Western Front*, p.xix. HQ Fourth Army recorded on 4 November that mine craters on the PW beyond Saint Quentin had caused the closure of all railheads after Fresnoy, placing more burden on overworked WMT; TNA WO 95/454/4: HQ Fourth Army, DDST, WD. There was better news on 6 November when all the supply trains arrived; Ibid.

177 Henniker, BOH, *Transportation on the Western Front*, pp.458-459.

178 In 21st Century terminology, the DAM in this context would be described as Improvised Explosive Devices (IED). The Army had plenty of experience with this threat, most notably in South Africa during the Second Boer War but also on the North-West Frontier of India. See, Institution of the Royal Engineers, *Detailed History of The Railways in the South African War, 1899-1902*, Vol. I, (Chatham: W & J Mackay, 1904), p.95.

179 24 mines were discovered in the Third and Fourth Army areas up to Sunday 27 October 1918 and were removed by RE Tunnelling Companies. On the Saint Quentin to Busigny railway line, 13 mines exploded between Fresnoy and Busigny between, 2-4 November. The damage could be serious. One incident created a crater 27 feet in depth and 90 feet in diameter and on Thursday 31 October 1918, a mine that exploded on the line between Cambrai and Awoingt, blew a crater 20 feet deep and 40 feet across, seriously damaging a PW train, although the line re-opened with a deviation inserted, 10 hours after the explosion; another impressive piece of logistic engineering. Henniker, BOH, *Transportation on the Western Front*, pp.440-441.

180 In May 1918, the DLK mounted a series of attacks on the Allied railways in the Etaples area, including the Canche Viaduct, which carried around 100 trains per day, resulting in significant damage on the night of 30-31 May 1918; Henniker, BOH, *Transportation on the Western Front*, pp.324-325.

181 Ibid, pp.325-326.

182 Given his immense responsibilities, the AQMG was probably un-impressed to discover that the four reckless driving offences reported in Fourth Army for the week ending 26 October 1918, were from XIII Corps; TNA WO 95/445/5: HQ Fourth Army, A&Q, 'D.P.M's. Report for the Week Ending 26-1018'.

> In October 1918, responsible for the supply of the four divisions[183] and corps troops[184] of XIII Corps, I sat at a table with a map in front of me. The map became more and more attenuated as we advanced; for our railheads remained fixed while our front reached farther and farther away from them. All my interest was centred on the long thin line which joined my railheads with my front, and hardly any of my interest concerned actual fighting. I spent many hours calculating the number of lorries I could raise, working out the amount of ammunition that could be carried forward, planning roads and traffic circuits, watching the light railway[185] gradually move forward and the repairs to the broad gauge[186]..........The number of complications in such a problem is inconceivable. A time mine on the railway, the wrong side of Epehy, which delayed an ammunition train some twenty hours, lost me one hundred and fifty lorries and robbed me of an ammunition reserve just before a battle....... but worst of all was the ignorance of the General Staff on the Q work that kept the advance moving......roads - the General Staff did not seem to realize their vital relation to an advance.[187]

At the end of October 1918, of the approximately 20,000 lorries deployed in the Army areas, 3,600, 18 percent, were Vehicle Off the Road (VOR) chiefly because of broken springs.[188] Whilst the road surface conditions must have contributed to this decline in availability,[189] the suspicion was that WMT drivers were operating their vehicles in a manner, which was not conducive to future availability nor sustaining the road surface, resulted in closer supervision and the introduction of speed patrols.[190] Indeed the WMT capability was so stretched that by the Armistice, HT from Divisional Ammunition Columns was tasked to assist.[191] The Fourth Army Major-General General Staff (MGGS) concluded:

> In the forward area, where the roads had been destroyed by mine craters, the infantry had outstripped the forward limit of the lorries, and it became necessary to use additional horse transport from the ammunition columns; it was quite obvious, therefore, that if the army continued to advance a complete breakdown in the supply organisation must result before long.[192]

183 XIII Corps was in the Fourth Army during October and November 1918, consisting of the 18th, 25th, 50th and 66th Divisions. Each division had the following 2nd Line Logistic Support assets: Ammunition Company, Divisional Train (4 x companies ASC) a Pioneer Battalion and an Employment Company.

184 A Corps had the following 3rd Line Logistic Support assets: Corps MT Column (4 x MT Companies) Heavy Artillery Company ASC and an Area Employment Company.

185 NGR - 60cm.

186 Standard Gauge 1435mm or 4 feet 8 ½ inches.

187 Nicholson, *Behind the Lines*, pp.214-215.

188 TNA WO 95/40: GHQ, QMG, WD, 1 September - 30 November 1918, 'Explanatory Review, October 1918', p.3. One ES response to generate greater output efficiency was to centralize all vehicle spring repair in one Army workshop, which could focus upon the task with a trained workforce.

189 Fourth Army had mixed fortunes in this respect. IX Corps WMT appeared to be in a particularly poor state, whilst XIII Corps was able to make improvements, reaching 79% availability by 1 November 1918, which was in line with the BEF average. TNA WO 95/454/4: HQ Fourth Army, DDST, WD, 1 November 1918. The trend however was clearly one of decline, with DDST noting on 10 November, a summary of his letters CR 1200/15479 31 October and CR 1200/1547/3, 7 November 1918, to the Army DA&QMG explaining that 'the M.T situation was serious, that it was due to the lorries being overworked.....and that in future the D. of T. would only be able to replace complete casualties due to enemy act, collisions etc'. TNA WO 95/454/4: HQ Fourth Army, DDST, WD.

190 The Fourth Army's DPM weekly reports for October show charges for excessive speed in the Fourth Army area totalled less than 10 per week but clearly relatively lower speeds on rough roads could damage vehicle suspensions. TNA WO 95/445/5: HQ Fourth Army, A&Q Notes, October 1918.

191 Henniker, BOH, *Transportation on the Western Front*, p.461.

192 Montgomery, *Story of the Fourth Army*, p.260.

With HT having to replace WMT to keep pace with the infantry, mounting an attack with a concentration of armour was clearly impractical, an issue which been maturing since the Battle of Amiens in August.[193] This situation lucidly demonstrated that whatever the tactical combat capability of the tank was, its application at the operational level was entirely dependent upon the strategic extension of SGR. That the Fourth Army A&Q war diary for October 1918[194] barely mentions logistic support for tanks[195] but notes tank trains were being used to recover damaged WMT[196] and is replete with entries concerning the numbers of Prisoners of War (POW),[197] evacuation of casualties,[198] the availability of WMT[199] and wastage rates for horses[200] and mules,[201] is a clear illustration of its declining mass contribution during latter part of the Hundred Days.

Whilst the BEF advanced, Reverse Logistics was also gaining momentum. In October 1918, salvage returns in one week from one Army, the Fourth, were costed at approximately £2,000,000, which in 2016 prices would equate to an economic output cost to the Nation of nearly £0.781 Billion. Included in the return were 5,345,000 rounds of SAA, 49,492 artillery shells,[202] 152,686 brass shell cases, 148 Machine Guns, 13,161 rifles, 12,660 steel helmets, 9,928 respirators and 10,459 petrol tins.[203] One particular issue was accounting for and processing, captured materiel,[204] with ammunition being an especial problem,[205] whilst transporting food and coal for the civilian

193 In preparation for the Battle of Epehy, Fourth Army was allocated 2nd Tank Battalion. The Corps allotments however, were small. III Corps were assigned eight tanks, IX Corps six and the Australian Corps, nine. Montgomery, *The Story of the Fourth Army*, p.125.

194 TNA WO 95/445/5: HQ Fourth Army, A&Q, WD, October 1918.

195 One note from the weekly Fourth Army Q Conference states, 'Are petrol and oils coming up all right for tanks'; TNA WO 95/454/4: HQ Fourth Army, DDST, 'Notes on Conference at "Q" 23-9-18'.

196 TNA WO 95/454/4: HQ Fourth Army, DDST, WD, 27 October 1918.

197 The flow of POWs was higher in the first half of October with 3,026 being captured or surrendering on 4 October; TNA WO 95/445/5: HQ Fourth Army, A&Q, WD. Logistic innovation was applied to this problem, with salvaged coils of barbed wire being used to construct POW cages; HQ Fourth Army, A& Q Note No 828, October 1918.

198 Medical evacuation of Fourth Army wounded, injured and sick averaged approximately 1,000 personnel per day in October, with 2,527 on 24 October; TNA WO 95/445/5: HQ Fourth Army, A&Q, WD.

199 In the last week of September 1918, the Fourth Army 3 ton and 30 cwt lorry availability rate based upon Establishment was 77.5%, with an average of 3,314 vehicles on task each day; TNA WO 95/445/5: HQ Fourth Army, A&Q, Note 842, 'MT Situation in Fourth Army on 28-09-18'.

200 In the third week of October 1918, the horse wastage rate in Fourth Army was 2.56% per week, compared to 1.74% in the same week in September, illustrating the demanding nature of the advance. Of the 1,295 losses, shell fire accounted for 382 killed or destroyed (291 in the same week in September), whilst 21 died from wounds or disease and 892 were evacuated; TNA WO 95/445/5: HQ Fourth Army, A&Q, 'Wastage in Horses during the Week Ending 17-10-18'. In the previous week, the wastage rate was 2.44%, with the Cavalry Corps at 4.42% and Fifth Army, 0.64%.

201 In the third week of October 1918, the mule wastage rate in Fourth Army was 0.98% per week, compared to 1.05% in mid September. Of the 176 losses, shell fire accounted for 39 killed or destroyed, with one killed by an aerial bomb, whilst four died from wounds or disease and 112 were evacuated; TNA WO 95/445/5: HQ Fourth Army, A&Q, 'Wastage in Mules during the Week Ending 17-10-18'. In the previous week, the wastage rate was 1.21%, with the Cavalry Corps at 0.22% and Fifth Army, 0.31%.

202 Salvage at scale was certainly not a new activity. In August 1917, the four batteries of XV Artillery Brigade tasked with artillery materiel salvage, recovered from a relatively small area at Ypres, 14 x 18 pdr pieces, 6 x 4.5 inch howitzers, 9,327 rounds of 18 pdr, 3,507 rounds of 4.5 inch, 177 rounds of 60 pdr, 227 rounds of 6 inch, 38,366 x brass 18 pdr cases and 214 x boxes of SAA. 1/1 Warwickshire Battery RHA (TF), Royal Artillery Historical Society Autumn Meeting, 22 October 2008 at Larkhill.

203 TNA WO 95/445/5: HQ Fourth Army A&Q, Note 787, October 1918.

204 The utilization of captured supplies developed into a Coalition issue because the Germans had requisitioned much of the food and the fodder from French civilians and HQ Fourth Army was instructed by GHQ to suspend all issues of these items to units; TNA WO 95/454/4: HQ Fourth Army, DDST, WD, 30 October 1918.

205 The BEF captured thousands of tons of German ammunition, with the handling of chemical munitions being an especial problem: 'as to the disposal of large quantities of German Gas Shell in the area.......At present only possible to put up danger boards as quantities are to large to handle with existing personnel'; TNA WO 95/452/1: HQ Fourth Army, DDOS, WD, 28 August 1918. The enormous task of disposal during this period and post conflict

population,[206] as well as feeding, moving and accommodating thousands of POWs became significant tasks.[207]

Critical to sustaining the advance, Reverse Logistics and the emerging support to civilians and POWs was the SGR. In August and September, the numbers of trains arriving daily at railheads averaged 153, but by the middle of October this had dropped to 133, the equivalent loss of 6,000 tons of materiel every 24 hours.[208] In addition, some WMT columns clearing railheads to road-heads were taking 72 hours instead of 24 to complete the loop.[209] Despite the best efforts of its logisticians and engineers, the BEF was becoming less capable but not incapable, of maintaining its forward momentum on a broad front,[210] without pauses to consolidate its logistic posture.[211] The BOH summarized the position:

> The deciding factor of the pace at which the pursuit of the enemy could now be carried on by the Fourth, Third and First Armies was supply. Although the railways had by now been constructed from Busigny to Wassigny, from Cambrai nearly to Solesmes, and had reached Valenciennes, explosions of time mines made it necessary to use railheads farther back, and from these supplies and ammunition had to be brought forward by motor transport. The ever-lengthening distances involved and the gradual deterioration of the roads as the weather grew worse, the demolitions more frequent and the traffic heavier, imposed a severe strain on the transport vehicles and their drivers. The mobile workshops found it almost impossible to deal with the abnormal amount of repairs due to bad roads and to excessive use. The infantry had now got beyond the forward limit of lorries, reckoned at about thirty miles, and beyond that limit the divisional horse transport bringing up supplies, although reinforced from the ammunition columns, was beginning to feel the extra strain involved in the hilly country which the Armies were now entering.[212]

Transportation on the Western Front was more succinct: 'Until the railways could deliver further forward and the roads made fit for MT it was no longer possible for the [Fourth] Army to advance at full strength; little more than a thin screen to keep touch with the retreating enemy could have been kept supplied'.[213]

Analysis of the BOH reveals that the statements focus not upon on the inability of the BEF to advance, but on the velocity and mass of its forward momentum. There were pauses prior to the attack on the Hindenberg Line in late September, another on the Selle between 11-17 October and one before the assault on the Sambre and Oise Canal, 25 October - 4 November. On 5 November 1918, with the gap between the front line and the railheads now 30 miles in Third Army and 50 miles in the Fourth, the difficulties were not decreasing and the result was a reduction in the

is another area ripe for study.

206 TNA WO 95/454/4: HQ Fourth Army, DDST, WD, 18 October 1918.

207 Between 18 July 1918 and 11 November 1918, the BEF captured 188,700 Prisoners of War, an average of 1,613 per day. Figures quoted from Edmonds, BOH, *France and Belgium 1918*, Vol. V, p.557.

208 Henniker, BOH, *Transportation on the Western Front*, p.456.

209 Ibid, p.461.

210 Edmonds, BOH, *France and Belgium 1918*, Vol. V, p.559.

211 As the advance continued, one key issue that developed was the growing difficulty of out-loading the ammunition FSSs. The lorry establishment of ammunition carrying WMT, was, as the DDST recorded, based upon the requirement to move munitions from railheads and not from FSSs. With little reserve WMT to hand and loop times increasing to the divisional rear areas, the opportunities to resolve it without a logistic pause decreased. TNA WO 95/454/4: HQ Fourth Army, DDST, WD, 31 October 1918.

212 Edmonds, BOH, *France and Belgium 1918*, Vol. V, pp.518-519.

213 Henniker, BOH, *Transportation on the Western Front*, p.461.

tonnage of stores being delivered to divisions. In the period 5-10 November 1918, the operational scenario was changing rapidly as German resistance declined, which resulted in a reduction in the amount of artillery ammunition required,[214] whilst the immense logistic and engineering capability of the BEF, with support from the *Nord* Railway, pushed forward the railheads and repaired the roads but the supply chain was struggling to cope and on 9 November, Fourth Army received no supply trains.[215] The pause created by the Armistice arrived at a timely moment thus enabling the resilience of the logistic loop to be improved and on Wednesday 13 November 1918, the BEF's QMG stated that the logisticians were capable of sustaining 40 divisions engaged in offensive operations on the German frontier.[216] This was a remarkable achievement but one entirely in keeping with the operational logistic scenarios of the previous three months, during which the BEF had paused on a number of occasions to consolidate its supply chain.[217]

Winding Down?

The BEF of late 1918, although it had some failures, was probably the most capable field force the British Army has deployed. It contained battle experienced soldiers[218] equipped with state of the art weapons and a command structure able to seize at least some of the opportunities offered by the internal combustion engine for conducting mobile warfare and delivering logistic capability. Whilst the logistic efficiency and effectiveness of divisions varied, in the round, the BEF's logistics were robust and innovative and capable of supporting an advance equating to an average of 28 miles per month during the Hundred Days. The Fourth Army did much better, with an average of 34 miles per month, whilst between 8-10 November, Second Army advanced an amazing 22 miles. Whilst these distances were exceeded by the 50 miles per month of the fully mechanized Allied Armies in France in the period June 1944 to February 1945, they were higher than the average monthly advance in Italy between September 1943 and May 1945.[219] These were impressive achievements

214 As late as 31 October - 2 November 1918, the Canadian Corps artillery fired 2,419 tons, an amount greater than British and Boer forces expended in the Boer War 1899-1902. The last 23 hours of the war were not quiet either; from 101200 to 111100 November 1918, the BEF fired 8,863 artillery rounds; MEBE, p.420.

Table 12.2
Artillery Expenditure: 101200-111100 November 1918

Type	Rounds
13 pdr	1,800
3 inch	89
18 pdr	3,704
4.5 inch How	374
60 pdr	1,140
6 inch How	1,756
Total	8,863

215 TNA WO 95/454/4: HQ Fourth Army, DDST, WD, 9 November 1918.

216 Edmonds, BOH, *France and Belgium 1918*, Vol. V, p.559.

217 The logistic planners however, had not been pausing. In early September, DDOS Fourth Army had, in preparation for another winter campaign, indented for additional blankets for Indian labourers and had requested GHQ to authorize the stocking of winter unclothing to meet the strength of Fourth Army; TNA WO 95/452/1: HQ Fourth Army, DDOS, WD, 8 September 1918.

218 An example of their experience and confidence is the increasing amount of significant fighting conducted by the BEF at night, where motivation and drills, then, as now, were most important if operations were to be successful.

219 25 miles per month.

for a semi-mechanized Army.

By mid-1918, the logisticians had spent three and a half years supporting siege warfare operations, managed a significant withdrawal and then provided the assets to support major offensives in the advance. They had been an integral part of the massive expansion in WMT operations, sustained a 48 fold increase in petrol consumption, and a 150 fold one for aviation spirit. They had ensured a continuous flow of artillery ammunition in defence, withdrawal and attack, and had adapted their systems to support the new era of armoured operations. They seized the initiative, developed and enacted new concepts, some of which were way ahead of their time, and in doing so, took a variety of risks. They executed all of these activities, whilst retaining a focus on the Main Effort, which was the projection of SGR railheads in the advance. They were however, cognizant of the importance of the role of WMT, the coherent utilization of which enabled some impressive advances during the closing stages of the war. In short, they balanced the tried and tested, with the new and the unknown; some of the planners certainly had great vision but were limited by the technology of the day.

The logisticians were clear on how to best achieve the task, and there was an enormous engineer effort to reconstruct the railways and roads,[220] with bridging being an especial challenge, which whilst enabling the distribution of stocks to the advancing Armies, clearly demonstrated the criticality of logistic engineering to operational combat capability and the shortage of resources to enact the tasks. Also of import, was the dissonance between the controlled commercial transportation and supply regimes in the Bases and the dynamic logistic operations in the Field, a feature, which is as relevant in 2018 as it was in 1918. When the fighting ceased on 11 November 1918, the logisticians could rightly be congratulated on a job well done,[221] although the fragility of some components of the machine had been exposed. It was however, one of the ironies of war, that no sooner had the logistic process successfully overcome the greatest challenges the British Army had faced, then new demands,[222] created by the Armistice, appeared, requiring major adjustments to the structure, system and organization.[223] The demobilization and restructuring of the BEF,[224] occupation of the Rhineland and assistance to civil governments were all significant activities which had to be enacted with declining resources, of which the hand back of the railway system to civilian control[225] was a most significant one.[226] The logisticians though, as true professionals, were ready for the new challenge.

220 An additional key task was the construction and maintenance of roads in FSSs. Fourth Army had for example, at considerable time and effort, constructed a rail-served Gun Park built but the ash tracks failed to cope with WMT traffic and the RE had to lay more substantial roads; TNA WO 95/452/1: HQ Fourth Army, DDOS, WD, 19 August 1918.

221 Whilst the logisticians could indulge in a few self-congratulations, the war diary of the Fourth Army DDST suggests that for most of them, it was very much business as usual; TNA WO 95/454/4: HQ Fourth Army, DDST, WD, November - December 1918.

222 One of those demands was ill-discipline, which included looting of military supplies on a considerable scale. On Saturday 23 November 1918, there was a serious incident at Vaux Andigny SRH involving Australian soldiers and repatriated English and Italian POWs. TNA WO 95/454/4: HQ Fourth Army, DDST, WD, 23 November 1918.

223 One telling action was the reversion to office hours in HQ Fourth Army A&Q, which from Saturday 21 December 1918 were to be 0930-1300 and 1700-1930, except for Saturday afternoons and the whole of Sunday when the A&Q offices were closed; TNA WO 95/454/4: HQ Fourth Army, DDST, WD, 20 December 1918.

224 It is perhaps ironic that on 31 December 1918, the Fourth Army "Q" Conference should focus upon the proposed disposal and sale of materiel. Of particular note, is that DDST observed: 'It was decided these Sales required a great deal of expert management and that G.H.Q. should be asked either to carry them out or to supervise them, also that we should tell them to ask for a representative of the Financial Adviser's Dept. to be on the spot'. TNA WO 95/454/4: HQ Fourth Army, DDST, WD, 31 December 1918.

225 Henniker, BOH, *Transportation on the Western Front*, pp.487-488.

226 For the logistic aspects, see, Brigadier-General Sir James E Edmonds, CB CMG (Comp) BOH, *Military Operations, France and Belgium, The Occupation of the Rhineland, 1918-1929*, CONFIDENTIAL edn (London: HMSO, 1944; Public edition, London: HMSO, 1987), pp.14-22.

Conclusion

Logistics remains for the most part, a hidden history of the British Army's operations on the Western Front. Whilst the chapters of *An Unappreciated Field of Endeavour* have exposed some of the facets and their importance, there are many elements that require research if the full contribution of logistics is to be written.[1] 'Big Logistics', Big L, effectively unknown as a concept or an application in 1914, was fundamental to the capability of British Army in the Great War and underpinned the BEF's deployment, expansion and operational success. The BEF's crowning achievement, the defeat of the German Army in the field on the Western Front, was, in the view of a contemporary industrial observer, George Dewar, enabled by the 'masterly skill' of the BEF and 'Big Logistics' production.[2] The process started at the point the War Office planners embedded the commercial sector as a critical element to its plans for deploying the BEF to France and grew to include very significant government intervention and control of the complete range of defence production, including the formation of the Ministry of Munitions to ensure that capability was sustained by the effective and efficient use of national resources. The introduction of commercial statistical analysis to effectively control BEF logistic resources was a critical component of its operational success and the ability of the United Kingdom to fight a global war.

BEF logistic operations on the Western Front grew to an industrial scale and in so doing imported processes, cultures and people that were, to the pre-war soldier, rather unmilitary. The inclusion of consultants, commercial managers, contractor support and female labour, all of which were key features of the commercial and industrial sectors, to the military stage, were but four elements of a dynamic logistic transformation on the Western Front that were critical components of creating a new 'Small L' within the military environment. The introduction of these actors was certainly a change but arguably it was the scale rather than the concept, which was more dramatic because in each of the areas there had been pre-war progression at various levels that included these groups in the logistic matrix. The deployment of Indian Expeditionary Force A to France in 1914 also demonstrated that even under the most arduous of operational scenarios, the BEF's logisticians, were, in co-operation with a Host Nation, sufficiently agile in innovation and resilient in determination, to improvise a solution to generate force capability.

The technical logistic aspects are equally important. The railway remained the key strategic transportation mode on the Western Front, without which, the BEF could not have been sustained and it was therefore, appropriate that given the vital role that the railways had played in enabling the Allied victory, the Armistice was signed in a railway carriage.[3] Wheeled Motor Transport

1 The 'Big L - Small L' interface, Anglo-French Joint A&Q operations, Reverse Logistics, the Supply Investigation Department, logistic planning and delivery at Army, Corps and divisional level and the post-war battlefield clearance, recovery and salvage operations are but six areas that would significantly add to our knowledge of BEF Great War logistics on the Western Front.

2 George A B Dewar, *The Great Munition Feat, 1914-1918* (London: Constable, 1921), p.viii.

3 The railway still has a key role in supporting military capability, although the lesson in the British Army requires to be refreshed. This point was raised by Major General (Retired) Mungo Melvin at the British Army's Operation

(WMT) played an increasingly important role at the operational level, its tactical contribution being limited by the failure to create an effective cross-country capability, leaving the few expensive tracked logistic vehicles to cover the ground, which, for the most part, only Horse Transport could traverse. The crucial challenge was therefore, to restore mobility across enemy defensive systems and thereby, allow logistic capability to support the advance. This required the direction of logistic engineering resources to restore road and rail connections, with offensive forces in the intervening period being maintained with a mixture of improvised tracked vehicles, pack and horse transport, the occasional air-drop and the soldier.

The enormous requirement for ammunition reinforced the importance of maintaining quality control in mass production and the provision of trained personnel to store and maintain it;[4] the resulting outcomes being munitions failing to function upon delivery to the enemy or doing so all too readily in storage or transit. Reverse Logistics, initiated by the Royal Flying Corps (RFC) for expensive reusable aircraft sub-systems such as aero-engines, encompassed, by 1918, nearly every item on issue from tank-tracks to boots-laces, whilst recovery, salvage and reclamation remained a significant post-war task. The introduction of aircraft and tanks to the combat inventory generated a concomitant and significant increase in the logistic requirement for the procurement, storage and distribution of improved fuels, technical spares and an expanding inventory of munitions and a growing need for specialist infrastructure and transportation. In a much broader context, for the first time in an operational British Army theatre of war, women in uniform were involved in the delivery of logistic capability, a situation generated not by politically driven social engineering but a clear military imperative, which arguably created a far more progressive foundation for supporting the enhancement of Women's freedoms than the Suffragette Movement achieved.

Given the logistic challenges of the 21st Century, there is much to be learned from an era in which, such activities were enacted through cable, clerk and pencil, and relied upon clear structures and robust procedures to be effective. Never in the history of the British Army, had the process of 'Factory to Fire-Trench' been so important to its operational success and its significance is as vital today as it was in 1918. A future QMG to the British Expeditionary Force of 1939 wrote in 1926: 'Movement must be viewed as a single continuous process from its commencement, say in England, to the delivery of the goods to the soldier in the front line,[5] and including also the return of the means of conveyance - ship, railway wagon, lorry or limber - to its starting point ready for a fresh load'.[6] Yet without the integrated support from the French as Host Nation, British 'Big L' and 'Small L' would have been very much the poorer. Whilst the Anglo-French coalition struggled to bring order to Joint Logistics in the combat arena, the creation of an effective professional relationship in the A&Q area was critical to the delivery of BEF capability and is a subject worthy of further study. Through a combination of committees, working groups, liaison teams, military missions and personal friendships, the two armies created a system that was able to agree a solution on issues such the allocation of estate for ammunition sites, the control of port facilities, the prioritisation of troop movements during the German Spring offensive and payment for services rendered and compensation for damages done.

REFLECT Battle of the Somme Exploitation Conference, held at the Tidworth Garrison Theatre on Tuesday 27 September 1916.

4 This was a problem throughout the war. In August 1918, DDOS Fourth Army had to intervene when he discovered that both the Australian and Canadian Corps were salving 18 pdr rounds by crimping the NCT cartridge mouths onto the shell but without understanding that the failure of the seal may have caused the charge to become damp; TNA WO 95/452/4: HQ Fourth Army, DDOS, WD, entry 2 August 1918.

5 Even in 2018, the process is not quite seamless but with the introduction of the inter-modal container and the Unit Load Container (ULC), Lindsell would be professionally impressed.

6 Major (Temporary Lieutenant-Colonel) W G Lindsell DSO OBE MC, 'Administrative Lessons of the Great War', psc RA, *Journal of the Royal United Service Institution*, Vol. LXXI (February 1926), p.713.

It is of course, the lot of logisticians, regardless of rank and appointment, to be forgotten.[7] In this respect, it definitively applies to the finest British Army logistician of the period, General Sir John Stephen 'Jack' Cowans.[8] Great War history is replete with well-known Generals whose names spring quickly to mind but Cowans is not one of them and yet his biographers were full-some in their praise: 'No Quartermaster-General in history is even faintly comparable to him in achievement'.[9] Jack Cowans was most certainly an interesting character and a very able administrator, whose industrious contribution to the British Army's capability during the Great War has evaporated from the military time-space continuum; his service as QMG deserves, without doubt, a modern study.[10] Indeed, Cowans was not the only British Army logistician to be forgotten since the Great War, as the phenomenon was current at the time. A contemporary American observer remarked, 'There are dozens of British Generals better known to the average man in England than General Cowans, but none, not even Field Marshal Sir Douglas Haig himself, has a more important task'.[11]

In many respects though, the greatest logistic feat of the war was not industrial production, transport across the thousands of miles of ocean, storage in the United Kingdom or distribution on the LOC to armies, corps and divisions but the work of 'Tommy Loggie'. He was often not a member of a logistic corps but he was the last and most enduring link in the supply chain. Had he failed to deliver over the last two miles of tortuous ground under the most appalling conditions, the industrial might and military power of the Allies would have been emasculated. Historians often forget the challenges of the Quartermaster and his men in the Trenches but if it failed there, all the effort elsewhere was wasted. The logisticians of the Great War were not supermen and the majority were not professional soldiers by vocation but they proved equal to the task and they deserve to be remembered for it. That the oldest known British soldier to be killed by enemy action during the Great War was not only a logistician but also a man who had never served in the Armed Services before the Great War,[12] is a fitting tribute to their courage and their commitment to their Country.[13]

7 As a Regimental Quartermaster wryly observed, 'no one gives a s**t about logistics until the toilet paper runs out'.

8 General Sir John Stephen 'Jack' Cowans GCB GCMG (1862-1921) was commissioned into the Rifle Brigade in 1881 and died in 1921 as a result of complications arising from a kidney operation. He was the only member of the Army Council to remain in post throughout the Great War, serving as QMG between 1912 and 1919 and promoted the employment of uniformed women, particularly in the logistic services.

9 Major Desmond Chapman-Huston & Major Owen Rutter, *General Sir John Cowans, GCB GCMB, The Quartermaster General of the Great War*, Vols I & II (London: Hutchinson, 1924), Vol. II, p.324.

10 This was not the case post-war; see, RHB, 'Sir John Cowans, The Greatest Quartermaster General', *Royal Army Service Corps Quarterly*, Vol. 13, April 1925, pp.189-197. For a recent but short reappraisal of his life, particularly as QMG, see, Keith Grieves' examination in the *Oxford Dictionary of National Biography* (Oxford: Oxford University Press (OUP), 2004).

11 Issac F Marcosson, The *Business of War* (London: John Lane, The Bodley Head, 1918), p.18.

12 Lieutenant Henry Webber was not an administrator in the Base but the Transport Officer of the 7th Battalion South Lancashire Regiment, 56th Brigade, 19th (Western) Division, a combat unit in the front line. He had three sons serving in the Army, one a Colonel and two Majors and had worked in the London Stock Exchange for 42 years before he was commissioned. He was 67 when he was fatally wounded in the head by a fragment of a German 210mm shell, which exploded during a Battalion Orders Group in Mametz Wood on Friday 21 July 1916. He is buried in Dartmoor Cemetery Becordel-Becourt in grave IE 54.

13 The Commonwealth War Graves Commission records list 239 Great War Armed Services deaths of personnel aged 65 or over. Marcosson, writes of meeting a 71 year old Second-Lieutenant from the Army Service Corps working at a Base Supply Depot, the Commanding Officer of which, was his son; *Business of War*, p.80.

Bibliography

Primary Sources:

United Kingdom – The National Archives (UK TNA)

ADM 116/1043B	Expeditionary Force, RN War Plans.
ADM 116/1324	Expeditionary Force, inter-dept Conference.
ADM 116/1331	Expeditionary Force Arrangements.
ADM 116/1370	HMS Bulwark Explosion and Loss.
ADM 116/1804-1810	First Lord of the Admiralty (Geddes) Correspondence, 1917-1919.
ADM 116/3107	Organization of East Coast Defences.
ADM 265/28	History of development of oil burning fuel in HM Service.
ADM 265/29	Admiralty, Architectural and Engineering Works Department.
AIR 1/475/15/312/201	Copies of letters from General Salmond to Trenchard on operations during German offensive.
AIR 1/520/16/12/1	Pt III, Air Policy: Expansion and Organization of the RFC and RAF.
AIR 1/1155/204/5/2428	Quarterly returns of engines and vehicles held by the RAF in the field.
CAB 3/1/20	Committee of Imperial Defence, Home Defence Memoranda.
CAB 3/2/56	Fixed Defence of Ports on the West Coast.
CAB 3/2/66	Committee of Imperial Defence, Home Defence Memoranda.
CAB /3/2/74	Committee of Imperial Defence, Home Defence Memoranda.
CAB 17/25	Committee of Imperial Defence - Correspondence and Memoranda, Home Defence, Channel Tunnel.
CAB 17/30	Internal Distribution of Supplies in time of War.
CAB 37/132/17	Ardeer Explosion 1913.
CAB 37/115/24	Admiralty Notes: Problems of Overseas Attack.
CAB 38/19/49	Committee of Imperial Defence - Minutes of the 114th Meeting: 23 August 1911.
CAB 38/28/34	Channel Tunnel: Memorandum by Field-Marshal Sir J D P French.
MT 23/671	Shipment of Ammunition from Southampton to N. France, T96838/1916, 'Ammunition Ships - Southampton to France'.
MUN 4/203	Transport: 'Census & Control of rail tank wagons'.
MUN 4/1731	Report of enquiry on Explosion at Faversham factory.
MUN 4/3077	Reports on Fire in France at Audruicq.
MUN 5/337/160/11/2	*The Official History of The Ministry of Munitions* (MOM) Volume XI, *The Supply of Munitions*, Part II, *Chemical Warfare Supplies*.
MUN 4/2794	Mechanized Warfare: Dock and transport facilities for tanks.
MUN 4/3138	Railway Material: Wagons for the conveyance of tanks in France.
MUN 4/5081	Land and Property: Richborough.

SUP/10/292	Report on Activity of the Special Brigade.
WO 32/3116	Training - Lessons of the 1914-1918 War.
WO 32/5110	Lawrence Report to Kitchener.
WO 32/5144	Report upon Rail Transport arrangements of the British Army on the Continent by Brigadier-General Sir E P C Girouard.
WO 32/5289	Defence of the Realm Acts, Powers possessed by the Government.
WO 32/5290	Defence of the Realm Acts, Railways and Supplies.
WO 32/5300	Channel Tunnel.
WO 32/7087	Coastal Defence - Flooding as a Means of Defence.
WO 32/9133	Revised railway arrangements for transport of horses to Aldershot on mobilization.
WO 32/13745	Legal Authority for Military and Police guarding railways to challenge and fire upon people.
WO 33/462	Appreciation of the Situation in the in the Event of Hostilities with a European Maritime Power.
WO 33/606	Expeditionary Force Tables, November 1912.
WO 33/654	Western Command, Home Defence Railway Plan.
WO 33/657	Southern Command, Mobilization Railway Time Tables.
WO 33/661	Mobilisation - Scottish Command Scheme, Railway and Steamship Programmes, January 1914.
WO 33/670	Irish Command, Home Defence Railway Plan.
WO 33/676	Eastern Command, Mobilization Railway Time Tables, Horses.
WO 33/679	Eastern Command, Mobilization Railway Time Tables, Reservists.
WO 33/684	Eastern Command, Mobilization Railway Programme, Parts I and II.
WO 33/692	Distribution of Home Defence Forces, 1914.
WO 33/694	Central Force Scheme for Home Defence, 1914.
WO 33/713	Telegrams, European War, France.
WO 79/63	Private Papers of Sir A J Murray.
WO 92/25	GHQ, AG Branch, War Diary, 1914.
WO 95/27	GHQ, QMG Branch, War Diary, 1914.
WO 95/30	GHQ, QMG, War Diary, May - July 1916.
WO 95/34	GHQ, QMG, War Diary, 1917.
WO 95/74	GHQ, Director of Supplies, War Diary.
WO 95/101	2nd Brigade Tank Corps, War Diary.
WO 95/112	5th Brigade Tank Corps, War Diary.
WO 95/441/2	Fourth Army, A&Q, War Diary, May - June 1916.
WO 95/445/5	Fourth Army, A&Q, War Diary, October 1918.
WO 95/447	Fourth Army, Director Medical Services, War Diary, May - July 1916.
WO 95/451/4	Fourth Army, CRE Report, February 1916 - November 1918.
WO 95/452/4	Fourth Army, DDOS, War Diary, July - November 1918.
WO 95/454/1	Fourth Army, DDOS, War Diary, March - December 1916.
WO 95/454/4	Fourth Army, DDST, War Diary, February 1916 - May 1919.
WO 95/483/8	15 Anti-Aircraft Section, Q Battery, War Diary.
WO 95/710	IV Corps, War Diary, June - August 1915.
WO 95/803	180 Mechanical Transport Company, ASC War Diary.
WO 95/1088	HQ Indian Corps, GS, War Diary.
WO 95/1091	HQ Indian Corps, AQMG, War Diary, 1 August 1914 - 30 April 1915.

WO 95/1168	HQ 1st (Indian) Cavalry Division, A&Q, War Diary.
WO 95/1169	HQ 1st (Indian) Cavalry Division, ADST, War Diary.
WO 95/1173	89 Company ASC, War Diary.
WO 95/1184/2	71 Company ASC, War Diary.
WO 95/1184/4	72 Company ASC, War Diary.
WO 95/1187/3	20th Deccan Horse, War Diary, 1 August 1914 - 31 December 1916.
WO 95/2040/1	8th Norfolk Regiment, War Diary, July 1915 - February 1918.
WO 95/2368	32nd Division, War Diary, July 1916.
WO 95/2653/2	428, 429, 430 & 431 (Horse Transport) Companies ASC, War Diaries.
WO 95/3915	HQ 3rd (Lahore) Division, AQMG, War Diary.
WO 95/3917	HQ 3rd (Lahore) Division, DADOS, War Diary.
WO 95/3920/1	7 British Field Ambulance, War Diary, 1 August 1914 - 31 December 1915.
WO 95/3923/4	9th Bhopal Infantry, War Diary.
WO 95/3923/5	57th Wilde's Rifles, War Diary.
WO 95/3926	HQ 8th (Jullundur) Infantry Brigade, War Diary.
WO 95/3927/4	47th Sikhs, War Diary, 1 August 1914 - 31 December 1915.
WO 95/3932	HQ 7th (Meerut) Division, QMG, War Diary.
WO 95/3938/8	7th (Meerut) Division, Indian Mule Transport, War Diary, September - December 1914.
WO 95/3939/9/1	7th (Meerut) Divisional Train, War Diary, October 1914 - December 1915.
WO 95/3945/2	2nd Battalion Leicestershire Regiment, War Diary, 1 August 1914 - 31 December 1915.
WO 95/3945/3	1/39th Garhwal Rifles, War Diary August 1914 - November 1915.
WO 95/ 3948/4	58th Vaughan's Rifles, War Diary.
WO 95/3949	IGC, War Diary, August - October 1914.
WO 95/3950	IGC, War Diary, November 1914.
WO 95/4052/8	8 Railway Company, War Diary.
WO 95/4052/11	10 Railway Company, War Diary.
WO 95/4594	1/7th Battalion Lancashire Fusiliers, War Diary, 1 August 1914 - 30 April 1915.
WO 95/4595	1/5th Battalion East Lancashire Regiment, War Diary 1 August 1914 - 31 May 1915.
WO 95/5460	432, 433, 434 & 435 (Horse Transport) Companies ASC, War Diaries.
WO 106/46	British Military Action in case of War with Germany.
WO 106/49A/1	History of the Growth of the Wilson-Foch Scheme.
WO 106/49A/2	Expeditionary Force to France, Revision of Programme, Remarks of Directorates.
WO 106/49A/2	Expeditionary Force to France, i, Factors affecting plan of movement and Staff work.
WO 106/49A/2	Expeditionary Force to France, ii, Outline of Scheme and Staff arrangements.
WO 106/49A/2	Expeditionary Force to France, iii, Mobilization.
WO 106/49A/2	Expeditionary Force to France, iv, Home Railway Movements.
WO 106/49A/2	Expeditionary Force to France, v, Sea Transport.
WO 106/49A/2	Expeditionary Force to France, vi, Disembarkation.

WO 106/49A/2	Expeditionary Force to France, vii, Movement by rail to area of concentration, Detrainment and Billeting.
WO 106/49A/2	Expeditionary Force to France, viii, Organization of Lines of Communication.
WO 106/49A/2	Expeditionary Force to France, ix, Mechanical Transport.
WO 106/49A/2	Expeditionary Force to France, x, Supplies.
WO 106/49A/2	Expeditionary Force to France, xi, Medical Service.
WO 106/49A/2	Expeditionary Force to France, xii, Ordnance Stores.
WO 106/49A/2	Expeditionary Force to France, xiii, Mark vii Small Arms Ammunition.
WO 106/49A/2	Expeditionary Force to France, xiv, Director of Works.
WO 106/49A/2	Expeditionary Force to France, xv, Telegraphs.
WO 106/49A/2	Expeditionary Force to France, xvi, Postal.
WO 106/49A/3	Organization and Working of Military Operations Directorate in times of strained relations and War.
WO 106/49/A5	Expeditionary Force to France.
WO 106/49A/6	Entrainment and Movement to Areas of Concentration.
WO 106/49A/7	Instructions for 1st and 2nd Army Commanders and Officers of Advanced Parties and Railway Transport Establishment.
WO 106/49A/8	Expeditionary Force Tables and details of the War Establishment of Units.
WO 106/49A/9	Mobilization Appointments, A1590 dated April 1914 - Part I Expeditionary Force.
WO 106/49B/1	Expeditionary Force to France, Instruction for Entrainment and Embarkation (Short Voyage) for Units of the Expeditionary Forces.
WO 106/49B/2	Interdepartmental Conference, Slade Committee.
WO 106/49B/3	Expeditionary Force Railway Timetables.
WO 106/49B/4	Expeditionary Force to France, Serial Tables, Southampton.
WO 106/49B/5	Expeditionary Force to France, Detrainment and Billeting Table D.
WO 106/49B/6	Expeditionary Force to France, Detrainment and Billeting Table D.
WO 106/49B/7	Expeditionary Force to France, Disembarkation Tables.
WO 106/49B/8	Mobilization Remount Statement.
WO 106/50	Areas required for depots at Bases.
WO 106/50	Embarkation and Ports of Embarkation.
WO 106/50	Military Mobilization Railway Programmes.
WO 106/50	Naval Requirements - Railway Services.
WO 106/50	Ports of Disembarkation.
WO 106/2042	Plan MCD, Move of the 1st Cavalry Division to Palestine from the UK.
WO 107/13	QMG and IGC Correspondence, Stores and Equipment, 1 September - 31 December 1914.
WO 107/13	QMG and Correspondence, IGC Stores and Equipment, 1 January 1915 - 30 June 1915.
WO 107/18	New Armies: Mechanical Transport Statement and Returns.
WO 107/69	Report Upon the Work of the Quartermaster-General's Branch of the Staff and Directorates Controlled, British Armies in France and Flanders.
WO 142/87	Ministry of Munitions, Trench Weapons and Chemical Warfare Reports.
WO 142/266	Anti-gas production and work: reports.
WO 142/266	List of Special Brigade Operations.

WO 153/115	Distribution of Home Forces, 31 August 1914.
WO 153/117	Projected and Actual Concentration of BEF, August 1914.
WO 153/546	Fourth Army: Battle of the Somme Objectives.
WO 153/581	Fourth Army, Administrative Maps, Roads, Railheads, Dumps etc, 1 October - 30 November 1918.
WO 158/10	Ambulance Trains: Advisory Committee; Minutes.
WO 158/11	Ambulance Trains: Sub-Committee; Minutes.
WO 158/321	Battle of the Somme, Preparations.
WO 158/838	Tanks: Technical Advisor's Reports.
WO 158/852	Director-General of Transport: History of Light Railways.
WO 159/6	Private Office Papers of Lord Kitchener.
WO 163/13	Army Council Minutes, 1908.
WO 394/20	Summary of Statistics, 1914-1920.
ZLIB 29/455	Transportation on the Western Front (Text).
ZLIB 29/456	Transportation on the Western Front (Maps).

University of Warwick Library - Modern Records Centre

GB 152 MSS.191	Papers of Sir William Guy Granet.

Tank Museum

Experiences in the Tank Corps, 1916-1918, Major E R Parson - RH 86/T.C/2549.
History of 17th (Armoured Car) Battalion.
Summary of Tank Operations, 8th - 20th October 1918.
The War Experiences, Sheryer, D M F, Captain, - RH 86/T.C./4288.
War History of the Central Workshops Tank Corps, Brockbank, Major S G - RH 86/T.C/CW/557-60.
War Diary - 6th Tank Battalion.
War Diary - 10th Tank Battalion.

Royal Logistic Corps Museum – Royal Corps of Transport Archive

Allotment of ASC Units; with amendments to 25 November 1916 - B1/8210.
Fletcher, David, *War Cars: British Armoured Cars of the First World War*, London: HMSO, 1987 - B1/8392.
Hobbs, P E F, Colonel, CMG, 'The New System of Transport as carried out by the Blue Forces during Army Manoeuvres 1912', *The Army Review*, Volume IV, No 2, War Office, April 1913, pp.412-30 - C3/1643.
Memoirs of M2/048544 Private George Masters VC.
Mobilisation of Motor Transport; French Organisation of Services - A1/0752-4.
Motor Transport Corps reports, 1090-1913 - A6/8921-24.
Royal Corps of Transport Training, Volume IV, *Transport Operations - Rail Transport*, A/26/GS Trg Publications/2921, Army Code No 70443, UK Ministry of Defence, 1975.
Royal Logistic Corps, Rail Transport, Railway Operating, Army Code 71680A, UK Ministry of Defence, 2004.

Stewart, Herbert, A, DSO, *From Mons to Loos: The Diary of a Supply Officer*, London: Blackwood and Sons, 1916 - B2/7705.

The Royal Logistic Corps, Volume 1, Pamphlet 1, *Logistic Support Doctrine*, UK Ministry of Defence, 1997.

Official Military Publications:

A & Q, or Military Administration in War, Colonel W G Lindsell DSO OBE MC psc RA, Aldershot: Gale & Polden, Third Edition, 1933.

Administration in the Field, A26/GSTP/3351, Army Code No 71024, UK Ministry of Defence, 1975.

Admiralty, *The Navy List for October 1918*, corrected to 18th September 1918, London: HMSO, 1918.

Admiralty, *Navy Losses and Merchant Shipping (Losses)* London: HMSO, 1919.

Air Publication (AP) *3000, British Air Power Doctrine*, 3rd Edition, Directorate of Air Staff, UK Ministry of Defence, 1999.

Army Council, *Army Service Corps,* Part I, *Training*, War Office, London: HMSO, 1909 (Reprinted with amendments, 1915).

Army Council, *Army Service Corps,* Part II, *Supplies*, War Office, London: HMSO, 1909 (Reprinted 1914 with new Appendix XII).

Army Council, *Army Service Corps Training,* Part III, *Transport*, War Office, London: HMSO, 1909 (Reprinted with amendments, 1915).

Army Council, *Army Service Corps,* Part IV, *Mechanical Transport*, War Office, London: HMSO, 1909 (Reprinted with amendments, 1914).

Army Council, *Manual of Elementary Military Hygiene 1912*, 40/WO/1680, War Office, London: HMSO, 1914.

Army Council, *Manual of Movement (War)* 26/Manuals/1297, War Office, HMSO, 1933.

Army Council, *Medical Service, Army, Regulations*, London: HMSO, 1906 (Reprinted, with amendments, 1914).

Army Doctrine Publication (ADP) Volume 1, *Operations*, HQDT/18/34/46, Army Code No 71565, UK Ministry of Defence, 1994.

Army Doctrine Publication (ADP) Volume 2, *Command*, HQDT/18/34/51, Army Code No 71564, UK Ministry of Defence, 1995.

Army Doctrine Publication (ADP) Volume 3, *Logistics*, DGD&D/18/34/63, Army Code No 71566, UK Ministry of Defence, 1996.

Army Field Manual (AFM) Volume 1, *Combined Arms Operations*, Part 6, *Combat Service Support*, DGD&D 18/34/44, Army Code No 71344, UK Ministry of Defence, 1998.

A Short History of the Royal Air Force, Air Publication 125, Air Ministry, September 1929.

CB 1515 (24) *The Technical History and Index*, Volume 2, Part 24, Storage and Handling of Explosives in Warships, Admiralty, October 1919.

Critical Study of the Campaign in Mesopotamia up to April 1917, Part 1 - Report, compiled by Officers of the Staff College Quetta, October - November 1923, Calcutta: Government of India Press, 1925.

General Staff, *Field Service Pocket Book*, War Office, London: HMSO, 1908 & 1914.

General Staff, *Field Service Regulations,* Part I, *Operations*, War Office, London: HMSO, 1909 (reprinted, with amendments, 1912).
General Staff, *Field Service Regulations,* Part II, *Organization and Administration*, War Office, London: HMSO, 1909 (reprinted, with amendments to October, 1914).
General Staff, *Handbook of the French Army*, 1914, War Office, HMSO, 1914.
General Staff, *Manual of Field Engineering 1911*, War Office, London: HMSO, 1911.
General Staff, *Notes for Infantry Officers on Trench Warfare*, War Office, March 1916.
General Staff, *Order of Battle of the British Armies in France*, GHQ, 11 November 1918.
General Staff, *Railway Manual (War)*, War Office, HMSO, 1911 (reprinted with amendments 1914).
General Staff, *Report on Foreign Manoeuvres* in1912, CONFIDENTIAL, War Office, 1913.
General Staff, *Small Wars, Their Principles and Practice*, Colonel C E Callwell, Third Edition, War Office, London: HMSO, 1906.

Handbook of Ammunition, May 1918, Royal Laboratories, reprinted by the Naval and Military Press, nd but 2017.

Indian Army Service Corps (IASC) Manual (War) Simla: Government of India Press, 1932.

King's Regulations and Orders for the Army 1912, War Office, London: HMSO, 1914.

Manual of Combined Naval and Military Operations (A1674) War Office, 2 September 1913.
Military Organization and Administration, Major-General Sir W G Lindsell DSO OBE MC idc psc RA, Aldershot: Gale & Polden, 23rd Edition, 1941.
Modern Military Administration, Organization and Transportation, Major-General J C Harding-Newman CB CMG, Aldershot: Gale and Polden, 1933.

Notes for Commanding Officers, Aldershot: Gale & Polden, 1918.

Ordnance Duties, Course of Three Lectures given to the Army Class, London School of Economics, Lent Term, 1925, Lieutenant-Colonel B A Hill DSO RAOC, London: HMSO, 1926.

Report of His Majesty's Commissioners Appointed to Inquire into the Military Preparations and Other Matters connected with the War in South Africa, Command 1789, London: HMSO, 1903.

Standing Orders of the Warwickshire Yeomanry, The Regiment, Warwick: Hugh Rees, Ltd, 1912.

The Annual Return of the Territorial Force for the Year 1908, Command 4496, London: HMSO, 1909.
The Army in India and its Evolution, including an account of the Establishment of the Royal Air Force in India, Calcutta: Superintendent Government Printing India, 1924.
The Division in the Attack - 1918, SS 135 T/1635 40/WO/7036, Shrivenham: Strategic and Combat Studies Institute, 2008.
The Second World War, 1939-1945, Army, Manpower Problems Major-General A J K Pigott CB CBE (Compiler), War Office, 1949.
The Second World War, 1939-1945, Army, Royal Electrical and Mechanical Engineers, Volume I, *Organization and Operations*, Major-General Sir E Bertram Rowcroft KBE CB (Compiler), War Office, 1951.

Second World War, 1939-1945, *Army, Fighting, Support and Transport Vehicles and the War Office Organization for their Provision*, Part II - *Unarmoured Vehicles*, Major R Campagnac RASC and Major P E C Hayman, 15/19 KRH, War Office, 1951.

The Second World War, 1939-1945, Army, Personnel Selection, Colonel B Ungerson CBE BSc (Compiler), War Office, 1953.

The Second World War, 1939-1945, Royal Air Force, Maintenance, CD 1131, Air Ministry, 1954, CONFIDENTIAL, downgraded UNCLASSIFIED, March 1966.

War Office, *Regulations for the Queen Mary's Auxiliary Corps*, 1918.

War Office, *The War Office List and Administrative Directory for the British Army 1910*, C Newman Knight, London: HMSO, 1910.

War Office, *Treatise on Ammunition*, 10th Edition, HMSO, 1915.

War Office, *Technical Notes, R.F.C.* WO 43/FS/436, London: HMSO, 1916.

War Office, *Statistics of the Military Effort of the British Empire during the Great War, 1914-1920*, HMSO, 1922.

UK Defence in Numbers, UK Ministry of Defence, September 2016.

Official Histories and Despatches:

Admiralty, *Narrative of the Battle of Jutland*, London: HMSO, 1924.

Army Headquarters India, Intelligence Branch, *Frontier and Overseas Expeditions from India*, Volumes I & II, *Operations Against the Mohmands 1908*, Calcutta: Government Printer, 1908 and 1910.

Bean, C E W, *Australian Official History of the War 1914-1918*, Volume VI, *The Australian Imperial Force in France during the Allied Offensive, 1918*, Sydney: Angus and Robertson, 1942.

Becke, A F, Major (Retired) (Compiler) *History of the Great War, Order of Battle of Divisions*, Part 1, *The Regular British Divisions*, London: HMSO, 1935.

Becke, A F, Major (Retired) (Compiler) *History of the Great War, Order of Battle of Divisions*, Part 2A, *The Territorial Force Mounted Divisions and the 1st Line Territorial Force Divisions (42th-56th)* London: HMSO, 1936.

Becke, A F, Major (Retired) (Compiler) *History of the Great War, Order of Battle of Divisions*, Part 2B, *The 2nd Line Territorial force Divisions (57th-69th) with the Home Service Divisions (71th-73rd) and 74th and 75th Divisions*, London: HMSO, 1937.

Becke, A F, Major (Retired) (Compiler) *History of the Great War, Order of Battle of Divisions*, Part 3A, *New Army Divisions (9th-26th)* London: HMSO, 1938.

Becke, A F, Major (Retired) (Compiler) *History of the Great War, Order of Battle of Divisions*, Part 3B, *New Army Divisions (30th-41st) & 63rd (RN) Division*, London: HMSO, 1945.

Becke, A F, Major (Retired) (Compiler) *History of the Great War, Order of Battle*, Part 4, *The Army Council, GHQs, Armies and Corps, 1914-1918*, London: HMSO, 1945.

British Documents on the Origins of the War, 1898-1914, Volume III, *The Testing of the Entente, 1904-1906*, London: HMSO, 1938.

Butler, A G, Colonel, DSO VD BA MB ChB (Camb) *The Official History of the Australian Army Medical Services in the War of 1914-1918*, Volume II, The Western Front, Canberra: Australian War Memorial, 1940.

Carbery, A D, Lieutenant Colonel, CBE, *New Zealand Medical Services in the Great War*, Auckland & Christchurch: Whitcombe & Tombs, 1924.

Central Statistical Office, *History of the Second World War, Statistical Digest of the War*, London: HMSO, 1951.

Corbett, Sir Julian, S, *History of the Great War, Naval Operations*, Volume I, *To the Battle of the Falklands December 1914*, London: Longmans, Green & Co, 1920.

Edmonds, James, E, Brigadier-General Sir, CB CMG (Compiler) *History of the Great War, Military Operations, France and Belgium, 1914*, Volume I, *Mons, The Retreat to the Seine, the Marne and the Aisne, August-October 1914*, London: Macmillan, 1923.

Edmonds, James, E, Brigadier-General Sir, CB CMG (Compiler) *History of the Great War, Military Operations, France and Belgium, 1914*, Volume II, *Antwerp, La Bassee, Armentieres, Messines and Ypres, October-November 1914*, London: Macmillan, 1929.

Edmonds, James, E, Brigadier-General Sir, CB CMG (Compiler) *History of the Great War, Military Operations, France and Belgium, 1916*, Volume I, *Sir Douglas Haig's Command to the 1st July: Battle of the Somme*, London: Macmillan, 1932.

Edmonds, James, E, Brigadier-General Sir, CB CMG (Ed.) *History of the Great War, Military Operations, France and Belgium, 1918*, Volume I, *The German Offensive and its preliminaries*, London: Macmillan, 1935.

Edmonds, James, E, Brigadier-General Sir, CB CMG (Ed.) *History of the Great War, Military Operations, France and Belgium, 1918*, Volume II, *March - April: Continuation of the German Offensives*, London: Macmillan, 1937.

Edmonds, James, E, Brigadier-General Sir, CB CMG (Ed.) *History of the Great War, Military Operations, France and Belgium, 1918*, Volume III, *May - July: The German Diversion Offensives and the First Allied Counter-Offensive*, London: Macmillan, 1939.

Edmonds, James, E, Brigadier-General Sir, CB CMG (Ed.) *History of the Great War, Military Operations, France and Belgium, 1918*, Volume IV, *8th August - 26th September, The Franco - British Offensive*, London: HMSO, 1947.

Edmonds, James, E, Brigadier-General Sir, CB CMG (Compiler) *History of the Great War, Military Operations, France and Belgium, 1918*, Volume V, *26th September - 11th November, The Advance to Victory*, London: HMSO, 1947.

Edmonds, James E, Brigadier-General Sir, CB CMG and Davies, H R, Major-General (Compilers) *Military Operations, Italy, 1915-1919, History of the Great War, Military Operations, Italy, 1915-*1919, London: HMSO, 1949.

Edmonds, James, E, Brigadier-General Sir, CB CMG (Compiler) *History of the Great War, Military Operations, France and Belgium, The Occupation of the Rhineland, 1918-1929*, CONFIDENTIAL edition, London: HMSO, 1944; Public edition, London: HMSO, 1987.

Ellis, A D, Captain MC, *The Story of the Fifth Australian Division, Being an Authoritative Account of the Division's Doings in Egypt, France and Belgium*, London: Hodder and Stoughton, nd but c1920.

Falls, Cyril, Captain (Compiler) *History of the Great War, Military Operations, Macedonia*, Volume II, *From the Spring of 1917 to the End of the War*, London: HMSO, 1935.

Falls, Cyril (Compiler) *History of the Great War, Military Operations, France and Belgium, 1917*, Volume I, *The German Retreat to the Hindenberg Line and the Battles of Arras* & Appendices, London: Macmillan, 1940.

Fayle, Ernest, C, *History of the Great War, Seaborne Trade*, Volume III, *The Period of Unrestricted Submarine Warfare*, London: John Murray, 1924.

General Staff, *Official Account of the Military Operations in China, 1900-1901*, War Office, HMSO, 1903.

General Staff, *Official History of the Operations in Somaliland, 1901-1904*, Volumes I & II, War Office, London: HMSO, 1907.

Government of India, *Official History of Operations on the NW Frontier of India, 1936-37*, Delhi: Manager of Publications, 1943.

Henniker, A M, Colonel, CBE RE (Retired) (Compiler) *History of the Great War, Transportation on the Western Front, 1914-1918*, London: HMSO, 1937.

Historical Committee of the Committee of Imperial Defence, *Official History of the Russo-Japanese War*, Part II, *From the Battle of the Ya-Lu to Liao-Yang Exclusive*, General Staff, London: HMSO, 1908.

Hurd, Archibald, *History of the Great War, The Merchant Navy*, Volumes I-III, London: John Murray, 1921, 1924 and 1929.

Jones, H A, *History of the Great War, Being the Story of The part played in the Great War by the Royal Air Force*, Volumes II-VI, Oxford: Clarendon Press, 1928-1937.

Macphail, Andrew, Sir, Kt MRCS LRCP FRSC OBE, *Official History of the Canadian Forces in the Great War, 1914-1919, The Medical Services*, Ottawa: F A Acland for Canadian General Staff, 1925.

Macpherson, W G, Major-General, Sir, KCMG CB LLD, *History of the Great War, Medical Services, General History*, Volume II, *The Medical Services on the Western Front, and during operations in France and Belgium in 1914 and 1915*, London: HMSO, 1923.

Macpherson, W G, Major-General Sir, KCMG CB LLD, *History of the Great War, Medical Services, General History*, Volume III, *Medical Services during operations on the Western Front in 1916, 1917 and 1918; in Italy; and in Egypt and Palestine*, London: HMSO, 1924.

Macpherson, W G, Major-General Sir, KCMG CB LLD and Mitchell, T J, Major, DSO RAMC, HMSO *History of the Great War, Medical Services, General History*, Volume IV, *Medical Services during Operations on the Gallipoli Peninsula; in Macedonia; in Mesopotamia and North-West Persian East Africa; in the Aden Protectorate and in North Russia; Ambulance Transport during the War*, London: HMSO, 1924.

Miles, Wilfred, Captain, (Compiler) *History of the Great War, Military Operations, France and Belgium, 1916*, Volume II, *2nd July 1916 to the End of the Battles of the Somme*, London: HMSO, 1938.

Miles, Wilfred (Compiler) *History of the Great War, Military Operations, France and Belgium, 1917*, Volume III, *The Battle of Cambrai*, London: HMSO, 1948.

Ministry of Munitions, *The Official History of The Ministry of Munitions*, Volumes I-XII, HMSO, 1922. Reprinted by the Naval & Military Press in 2008.

Mitchell, T J, Major, DSO MD RAMC and Smith, G M, Miss, MBE MA, *History of the Great War, Medical Services, Casualties and Medical Statistics of the Great War*, London: HMSO, 1931.

Moberly, F J, Brigadier-General, CB CSI DSO psc, *History of the Great War, The Campaign in Mesopotamia*, 1914-1918, Volume I, London: HMSO, 1923.

Newbolt, Henry, *Naval Operations*, Volume IV, London: Longmans, Green & Co, 1928.

Parker, H M D, *History of the Second World War, Manpower, A Study of War-time Policy and Administration*, London: HMSO, 1957.

Pearce, Nigel, *The Shield and the Sabre, The Desert Rats in the Gulf, 1990-91,* London: HMSO, 1992.

Perry, F W (Compiler) *History of the Great War, Order of Battle of Divisions*, Part 5A, *The Divisions of Australia, Canada, and New Zealand and those in East Africa*, Newport: Ray Westlake Military Books, 1992.

Perry, F W (Compiler) *History of the Great War, Order of Battle of Divisions*, Part 5B, *Indian Army Divisions*, Newport: Ray Westlake Military Books, 1992.

Pratt, Edwin, A, *British Railways and the Great War, Organization, Efforts, Difficulties and Achievements*, Volumes I & II, London: Selwyn & Blount, 1921.

Raleigh, Walter, *History of the Great War, The War in the Air, Being the Story of The part played in the Great War by the Royal Air Force*, Volume I, Oxford: Clarendon Press, 1922.

Stauffer, Alvin, P, *US Army in World War II, The Technical Services, The Quarter-Master Corps: Operations in the War Against Japan*, Office of the Chief of Military History, Washington DC: Department of the Army, 1956.

Divisional, Regimental and Unit Histories:

Adderley, H A, The Honourable (Compiler) *The Warwickshire Yeomanry in the Great War*, Warwick: W H Smith & Son, 1922.

Addison, Colonel G H (Compiler) CMG DSO MA, *The Work of the Royal Engineers in the European War 1914-1918, Miscellaneous*, Chatham: Royal Engineers Institute, W & J Mackay 1927.

Atkinson, C T, *The Queen's Own Royal West Kent Regiment, 1914-1919*, London: Simpkin, 1924.

Atkinson, C T, *The Devonshire Regiment, 1914-1918*, Exeter: Eland Brothers, 1926.

Atkinson, C T, The Seventh Division 1914-1918, London: John Murray, 1927.

Atteridge, A Hilliard, *History of the 17th (Northern) Division*, Glasgow: University Press, 1929.

Beadon, R H, Colonel, CBE psc, *The Royal Army Service Corps, A History of Transport and Supply in the British Army*, Volume II, Cambridge: Cambridge University Press, 1931.

Boraston, J H, Lieutenant-Colonel, CB OBE and Bax, E O, Cyril, Captain, *The Eighth Division in War, 1914-1918*, London: The Medici Society, 1926.

Davson, H M, Lieutenant-Colonel, CMG DSO RA (Retired), *The History of the 35th Division in the Great War*, London: Sifton Praed & Co, 1926.

Dudley Ward, C H, Major, DSO MC (Compiler), Regimental Records of the Royal Welch Fusiliers, Volume III, 1914-1918, France, London: Forster Groom, 1928.

Durand, Mortimer, Sir H, KCMG KCSI KCIE, *The Thirteenth Hussars in the Great War*, Edinburgh & London: William Blackwood and Sons, 1921.

Falls, Cyril, Captain, *The History of the 36th (Ulster) Division*, Belfast: M'Caw Stevenson & Orr, 1922.

Farndale, Martin, General, Sir, KCB, *History of the Royal Regiment of Artillery, Western Front 1914-18*, Woolwich: The Royal Artillery Institution, 1986.

Farndale, Martin, General, Sir, KCB, *History of the Royal Regiment of Artillery, The Forgotten Fronts and the Home Base, 1914-18*, Woolwich: The Royal Artillery Institution, 1988.

Foulkes, C H, Major-General, CB CMG DSO, *"Gas", The Story of the Special Brigade*, Edinburgh & London: William Blackwood, 1934.

Forbes, A, Major-General, CB CMG, *A History of the Army Ordnance Services*, Volume Three, *The Great War*, London: The Medici Society, 1929.

Fuller, J F C, Colonel, DSO, *Tanks in the Great War, 1914-1918*, London, John Murray, 1920.

Gibbon, Frederick P, *The 42nd (East Lancashire) Division*, London: Country Life, 1920.

Jackson, H M, Lieutenant Colonel, MBE ED, *The 127th Battalion CEF, 2nd Battalion, Canadian Railway Troops*, West Montreal: Industrial Shops for the Deaf, nd but 1957.

Jourdain, H and Fraser, E, *The Connaught Rangers*, Three Volumes, London: Royal United Service Institution, 1924.

Keith-Falconer, Adrian, *The Oxfordshire Hussars in the Great War*, London: John Murray, 1927.

Kennedy, B B, Brigadier CBE & Tatman, J A, Colonel (Compilers) *Craftsmen of the Army, The Story of the Royal Electrical and Mechanical Engineers*, London: Leo Cooper, 1970.

Latter, J C, Major-General, CBE MC, *The History of the Lancashire Fusiliers, 1914-1918*, Major General J C Latter CBE MC, Volume I, Aldershot: Gale & Polden, 1949.

Liddell Hart, B H, Captain, *The Tanks, The History of the Royal Tank Regiment and its predecessors*, Volume One, 1914-1939, London: Cassell, 1959.

Lipscombe, Mechanist Sergt-Major, G, RASC *Historical Record of 180 Coy, Royal Army Service Corps (Mechanical Transport)* Aldershot: Gale & Polden, 1919.

Montgomery, Archibald, Major-General, Sir, KCMG CB, *The Story of the Fourth Army in the Battles of the Hundred Days*, London: Hodder and Stoughton, 1919.

na, *The 40th Pathans in the Great War*, Lahore: The Civil and Military Gazette Press, 1921.

Nichols, G H F, Captain, *The 18th Division in the Great War*, Edinburgh and London: William Blackwood & Sons, 1922.

Petre, Lorraine F, OBE, *The History of the Norfolk Regiment*, Volume II, *4th August 1914 - 31st December 1918*, Norwich: Jarrold, nd but c1925.

Pritchard, H L, Major-General (Ed.) *The History of the Corps of Royal Engineers*, Volume V, *The Home Front, France, Flanders and Italy in the First World War*, Chatham: The Institution of the Royal Engineers, 1952.

Richards, Walter, *His Majesty's Territorial Army*, Walter Richards, London: Virtue & Co, 1909 (Four volumes).

Rose, G K, Captain, MC, *The Story of The 2/4th Oxfordshire and Buckinghamshire Light Infantry*, Oxford: Blackwell, 1920.

Routledge, N W, Brigadier, OBE TD, *History of the Royal Regiment of Artillery, Anti-Aircraft Artillery 1914-1955*, London & New York: Brasseys (UK) 1994.

Royal Engineers Institute, *Detailed History of The Railways in the South African War, 1899-1902*, Volumes I & II, Chatham, W & J Mackay, 1904.

Royal Engineers Institute, *Work of the RE in the European War of 1914-19, Bridging*, Chatham: W & J Mackay, 1921.

Royal Engineers Institute, *Work of the RE in the European War of 1914-19, Water Supply - France*, Chatham: W & J Mackay, 1924.

Royal Engineers Institute, *Work of the RE in the European War of 1914-19, Work under the Director of Works (France)*, Chatham: W & J Mackay, 1924.

Sambrook, J, *With the Rank and Pay of a Sapper: the 216 (Nuneaton) Army Troops Company Royal Engineers in the Great War*, Nuneaton: Paddy Griffiths Associates, 1998.

Sandes, E, *The Indian Sappers and Miners*, Chatham: Institute of the Royal Engineers, 1948.

Sandilands, H R, Brigadier, CMG DSO, *The Fifth in the Great War: A History of the 1st & 2nd Northumberland Fusiliers, 1914-1918*, Edinburgh & London: G W Grigg & Son, 1938.

Scott, Arthur, B, Major-General Sir, KCB DSO, and Brumwell, P Middleton, MC CF, *History of the 12th (Eastern) Division in the Great War*, London: Nisbet & Co, 1923.

Shakespear, L W, Colonel, CB CIE, *History of the 2nd King Edward's Own Goorkhas* (Sirmoor Rifle Regiment) Volume II, 1911-1921, Aldershot: Gale & Polden, 1924.

Simpson, Major-General, C R, CB, *The History of the Lincolnshire Regiment, 1914-1918*, London: The Medici Society, 1931.

Sneddon, John Mason, *The Devil's Carnival, The First Hundred Days of Armageddon, 1st Battalion Northumberland Fusiliers, August - December 1914*, Brighton: Reveille Press, 2012.

Tennant, E, Lieutenant Colonel, *The Royal Deccan Horse in the Great War*, Aldershot: Gale & Polden, 1939.

Thomas, Alun, *Unfailing Gallantry, 8th (Regular) Division in the Great War 1914-1919*, University of Wolverhampton Military Studies, Solihull: Helion, 2017.

Townsend, C E C, Major (Retired) TD, *All Rank and No File, A History of the Engineer and Railway Staff Corps RE*, 1865-1965, London: The Engineer and Railway Staff Corps RE (TAVR) 1965.

Willcox, Walter Temple, Lieutenant Colonel, CMG, *The 3rd (King's Own) Hussars in the Great War, 1914-1919,* London: John Murray, 1925.

Williams-Ellis, Clough, Major, MC and Williams-Ellis, A, *The Tank Corps*, London: Country Life, 1919.

Wylly, H C C B, Colonel, *History of the 1st & 2nd Battalions The Leicestershire Regiment in the Great War*, Aldershot: Gale & Polden, 1928.

Wyrall, Everard, *The History of the Somerset Light Infantry (Prince Albert's) 1914-1919*, London: Methuen, 1927.

Wyrall, Everard, *The History of the King's Regiment (Liverpool) 1914-1919*, Volume I, 1914-1915, London: Edward Arnold, 1928.

Wyrall, Everard, *The Gloucestershire Regiment in the War, 1914-1918*, London: Methuen, 1931.

Wyrall, Everard, *The History of the Duke of Cornwall's Light Infantry, 1914-1919*, London: Methuen, 1932.

Books: Naval & Military Pre and Great War

Appleby, Catrina, Cocroft, Wayne and Schofield, John (Eds.) *The Home Front in Britain, 1914-18, An Archaeological Handbook*, York: Council for British Archaeology, 2015.

Ash, Eric, *Sir Frederick Sykes and the Air Revolution 1912-1918*, London & Portland Oregon: Frank Cass, 1999.

Atkinson, Diane, *Elsie and Mairi Go to War, Two Extraordinary Women on the Western Front,* London: Preface Publishing, 2009.

Barrie, Alexander, *War Underground, The Tunnellers of the Great War*, London: Frederick Muller, 1961.

Barton, Peter, Doyle, Peter and & Vandewalle, Johan, *The Tunnellers' War 1914-18*, Staplehurst: Spellmount, 2004.

Basu, Shrabani, *For King and Another Country, Indian Soldiers in the Western Front, 1914-1918*, New Delhi: Bloomsbury, 2015.

Batten, Simon, *Futile Exercise? The British Army's Preparations for War 1902-1914*, Warwick: Helion, 2018.

Beckett, Ian, F W and Simpson, Keith (Eds.) *A Nation in Arms, A social study of the British army in the First World War*, Manchester: Manchester University Press, 1985.

Beckett, Ian, F W, *The Army and the Curragh Incident, 1914*, Army Records Society, London: The Bodley Head, 1986.

Beckett, Ian, Bowman, Timothy & Connelly, Mark (Eds.), *The British Army and the First World War*, Armies of the Great War, Cambridge: Cambridge University Press, 2017.

Bird, Antony, *Gentlemen, We Will Stand and Fight, Le Cateau, 1914*, Marlborough: Crowood Press, 2008.

Black, Nicholas, *The British Naval Staff in the First World War*, Woodbridge: The Boydell Press, 2009.

Boff, Jonathon, *Winning and Losing on the Western Front, The British Third Army and the Defeat of Germany*, Cambridge: Cambridge University Press, 2012.

Boghardt, Thomas, *Spies of the Kaiser, German Covert Operations in Great Britain during the First World War Era*, Basingstoke & New York: Palgrave Macmillan, 2004.

Bond, Brian, *The Victorian Army and the Staff College, 1854-1914*, London: Eyre Methuen, 1972.

Boraston, J, H, Lieutenant-Colonel OBE (Ed.) *Sir Douglas Haig's Despatches, December 1915 - April 1919*, London & Toronto: J M Dent & Sons, 1919.

Bowman, Timothy and Connelly, Mark, *The Edwardian Army, Recruiting, Training and Deploying the British Army*, Oxford: Oxford University Press, 2012.

Bristow, Adrian, *A Serious Disappointment, The Battle of Aubers Ridge 1915 and the Munitions Scandal*, London: Leo Cooper, 1995.

Bruce, J M, *The Aeroplanes of the Royal Flying Corps Military Wing*, 2nd Edition, London: Putnam, 1992.

Brunker, H M E, Lieutenant-Colonel, *Notes on Organization and Equipment*, 6th Edition, London: William Clowes and Sons, 1909.

Campbell, Christy, *Band of Brigands, The First Men in Tanks*, London: Harper Press, 2007.

Cassar, George, *The Forgotten Front, The British Campaign in Italy, 1917-1918*, London & Rio Grande: The Hambledon Press, 1998.

Cassar, George, H, *Kitchener's War, British Strategy from 1914-1916*, Washington DC: Brassey's, 2004.

Childs, David J, *A Peripheral Weapon? The Production and Employment of British Tanks in the First World War*, Westport Connecticut & London: Greenwood Press, 1999.

Corrigan, Gordon, *Sepoys in the Trenches, The Indian Corps on the Western Front 1914-1915*, Staplehurst: Spellmount, 1999.
Corum, James, S, *The Luftwaffe, Creating the Operational Air War, 1918-1940*, Lawrence: University Press of Kansas, 1997.

Dennis, Peter, *The Territorial Army, 1907-1940*, The Royal Historical Society, Woodbridge: The Boydell Press, 1987.
Dillon, John, *Allies are a Tiresome Lot, The British Army in Italy in the First World War*, University of Wolverhampton Military Studies, Solihull: Helion, 2015.
Dittmar, F J and Colledge, J J, *British Warships, 1914-1919*, London: Ian Allan, 1972.
Doherty, Simon and Donovan, Tom, *The Indian Corps on the Western Front: A Handbook and Battlefield Guide*, Brighton: Tom Donovan Editions, 2014.
d'Ombrain, Nicholas, *War Machinery and High Policy, Defence administration in peacetime Britain, 1902-1914*, Oxford Historical Monographs, Oxford: Oxford University Press, 1973.
Driver, Hugh, *The Birth of British Military Aviation: Britain 1903-1914*, The Royal Historical Society, Woodbridge: The Boydell Press, 1997.
Dunlop, J K, Colonel, OBE MC TD, *The Development of the British Army, 1899-1914, From the Eve of the South African War to the Eve of the Great War, with Special Reference to the Territorial Force*, London: Methuen, 1938.
Dunn, J C, Captain, DSO MC & Bar DCM RAMC, *The War The Infantry Knew, 1914-1919, A Chronicle of Service in France and Belgium*, London: PS King Ltd, 1938. 2nd Impression, London: Janes, 1987.

Escoli, David, *The Mons Star, The British Expeditionary Force 1914*, London: Harrap, 1981.
Ehlert, Hans, Epkenhans, Michael & Cross, Gerhard P (Eds.) *The Schlieffen Plan, International Perspectives on the German Strategy for World War I*, Kentucky: University Press of Kentucky, 2014

Fletcher, David, *Landships, British Tanks in the First World War*, London: HMSO, 1984.
Fox, Aimee, *Learning to Fight, Military Innovation and Change in the British Army, 1914-1918*, Cambridge: Cambridge University Press, 2018.

Gardner, Nikolas, *Trial By Fire, Command and the British Expeditionary Force in 1914*, Westport Connecticut & London: Praeger, 2013.
Garsia, Clive, Lieutenant-Colonel, DSO MC *A Key to Victory, A Study in War Planning*, London: Eyre and Spottiswoode, 1940.
Gibson, Craig, *Behind the Front, British Soldiers and French Civilians, 1914-1918*, Cambridge: Cambridge University Press, 2014.
Gibson, Mark, *Britain's Quest for Oil, The First World and the Peace* Conferences, Solihull: Helion, 2017.
Gilbert, Adrian, *The Challenge of Battle, The Real Story of the British Army in 1914*, Oxford: Osprey, 2013.
Gooch, John, *The Plans of War, The General Staff and British Military Strategy c1906-1916*, London: Routledge & Kegan Paul, 1974.
Green, Andrew, *Writing the Great War, Sir James Edmonds and the Official Histories, 1915-1919*, London & Portland Oregon: Frank Cass, 2003.

Greenhalgh, Elizabeth, *Victory through Coalition, Britain and France during the First World War*, Cambridge: Cambridge University Press, 2005.

Grey Peter and Thetford, Owen, *German Aircraft of the First World War*, 2nd Edition, London: Putnam, 1979.

Griffiths, Paddy, *Battle Tactics on the Western Front, The British Army's Art of Attack 1916-18*, New Haven & London: Yale University, 1994.

Griffiths, Paddy (Ed.) *British Fighting Methods in the Great War*, London & Portland Oregon: Frank Cass 1996.

Grimes, Shaun T, *Strategy and War Planning in the British Navy, 1887-1918*, Woodbridge: The Boydell Press, 2012.

Grotelueschen, Mark Ethan *The AEF Way of War, The American Army and Combat in World War 1*, Cambridge: Cambridge University Press, 2012.

GSO [Frank Fox] *GHQ, Montreuil-Sur-Mer*, London: Philip Allan & Co, 1920.

Haber, L F, *The Poisonous Cloud, Chemical Warfare in the First World War*, Oxford: Clarendon Press, 1986.

Hamilton, Richard, F and Herwig, Holger, H (Eds.) *War Planning 1914*, Cambridge: Cambridge University Press, 2010.

Hampshire, A Cecil, *They Called it Accident*, London: William Kimber & Co, 1960.

Hardy, Colin, *The Reconographers, Intelligence and Reconnaissance in British Tank Operations on the Western Front 1916-18*, Wolverhampton Military Studies, Solihull: Helion, 2016.

Harris, J P, *Men, ideas and tanks, British military thought and armoured forces, 1903-1939,* Manchester: Manchester University Press, 1995.

Harris, J P, with Barr, Niall, *Amiens to the Armistice, The BEF in the Hundred Days Campaign, 8 August - 11 November 1918*, London & Washington: Brassey's, 1998,

Hart, Peter, *Fire and Movement, The British Expeditionary Force and the Campaign of 1914*, Oxford: Oxford University Press, 2015.

Hartcup, Guy, *The War of Invention, Scientific Developments, 1914-1918*, London: Brassey's, 1988.

Hervig, Holger, H, *The Luxury Fleet*, London: Allen & Unwin, 1980.

Herwig, Holger, H, *The Marne, 1914, The Opening of World War 1 and the Battle that changed the World*, New York: Random House, 2009.

Hogg, Ian, V, *Allied Artillery of World War One*, Marlborough: Crowood Press, 1998.

Holmes, Richard, *Riding the Retreat, Mons to the Marne Revisited 1914*, London: Jonathan Cape, 1995.

Holmes, Richard, *Tommy, The British Soldier on the Western Front 1914-1918*, London: Harper Collins, 2004.

Home, Archibald, Brigadier-General, Sir, KCVO CB CMG DSO, *The Diary of a World War I Cavalry Officer*, Tunbridge Wells: D J Costello, 1985.

Hooton, E R, *War Over The Trenches, Air Power and the Western Front Campaigns*, 1916-1918, Hersham: Midland Ian Allan, 2010.

James, E A, OBE TD, *British Regiments, 1914-1918*, London: Samson Books, 1978.

Jones, Spencer, *From Boer War to World War, Tactical Reform of the British Army, 1902-1914*, Norman: University of Oklahoma Press, 2012.

Jones, Spencer (Ed.) *Stemming The Tide, Officers and Leadership in the British Expeditionary Force 1914*, University of Wolverhampton Military Studies, Solihull: Helion, 2013.

Kempton, Chris, *Locations of Regiments and Battalions of the British Army, 1 August 1914 and 1 September 1939*, Milton Keynes: Military Press, 2000.

Kempton, Chris, *Duty & Fidelity, The Indian Army, August 1914-1921*, Parts I-III, Milton Keynes: The Military Press, 2009.

Kennedy, Paul (Ed.) *The War Plans of the Great Powers, 1880-1914*, London: George Allen & Unwin, 1979.

Lambert, Nicholas, A, *Sir John Fisher's Naval Revolution*, Columbia: University of South Carolina Press, 1999.

Lambert, Nicholas, A, *Planning Armageddon, British Economic Warfare and the First World War*, Cambridge Massachusetts & London: Harvard University Press, 2012.

Lengel, Edward, G, *Thunder and Flames, Americans in the Crucible of Combat, 1917-1918*, Lawrence: The University Press of Kansas, 2015.

Lucy, J F, *There's a Devil in the Drum*, London: Faber & Faber, 1938.

Macdonald, Lyn, *To The Last Man: Spring 1918*, London: Viking, 1998.

Mallinson, Allan, *Fight the Good Fight, Britain, The Army & the Coming of the First World War*, London: Bantam Press, 2013.

Marble, Sanders, *British Artillery on the Western Front, The Infantry cannot do with a gun less*, Ashgate Studies in First World War History, Farnham: Ashgate, 2013.

Marder, Arthur, J, *From The Dreadnought To Scapa Flow*, Volume I, *The Road to War, 1904-1914*, London: Oxford University Press, 1961.

Marshall, William, Lieutenant-General, Sir, GCMG KCB KCSI, *Memories of Four Fronts*, London: Benn, 1929.

Marwick, Arthur, *Women at War, 1914-1918*, London: Fontana Paperbacks, 1977.

McCartney, Innes, *Jutland 1916, The Archaeology of a Naval Battlefield*, London: Bloomsbury, 2016.

Merewether, J W B, Lieutenant-Colonel CIE and Smith, Frederick, Right Honourable Sir, Bart, *The Indian Corps in France*, London: John Murray, 1919.

Messenger, Charles, *Call To Arms, The British Army 1914-1918*, London: Weidenfeld & Nicolson, 2005.

Middlebrook, Martin, *The First Day on the Somme, 1 July 1916*, London: Allen Lane, 1971.

Miller, Geoffrey, *Straits, British policy towards the Ottoman Empire and the origins of the Dardanelles Campaign*, Kingston-upon-Hull: University of Hull Press, 1997.

Miller, Geoffrey, *The Millstone, British Naval Policy in the Mediterranean, 1900-1914, the Commitment to France and British Intervention in the War*, Kingston-upon-Hull: University of Hull Press, 1999.

Mitchinson, K W, *Defending Albion, Britain's Home Army, 1908-1919*, Basingstoke & New York: Palgrave Macmillan, 2005.

Mitchinson, K W, *England's Last Hope, The Territorial Force, 1908-1914*, Basingstoke & New York: Palgrave Macmillan, 2008.

Morton-Jack, George, *The Indian Army on the Western Front, India's Expeditionary Force to France and Belgium in the First World War*, Cambridge: Cambridge University Press, 2014.

Murland, Jerry, *Retreat and Rearguard 1914, The BEF's Actions from Mons to the Marne*, Barnsley: Pen & Sword, 2011.

Murland, Jerry, *The Battle on the Aisne, The BEF and the Birth of the Western Front*, Barnsley: Pen & Sword, 2012.

Neillands, Robin, *The Great War Generals on the Western Front, 1914-18*, London: Robinson, 1999.
Neillands, Robin, *The Old Contemptibles, The British Expeditionary Force 1914*, London: John Murray, 2004.

Occleshaw, Michael, *Armour Against Fate, British Military Intelligence in the First World War*, London: Columbus Books 1989.
Olusoga, David, Across the Black Waters, *The World's War*, London: Head Zeus, 2014.
Omissi, David, (Introduction) *Indian Voices of the Great War, Soldiers' Letters, 1914-18*, Basingstoke & New York: Palgrave Macmillan, 1999.
Owen, David, *The Hidden Perspective, The Military Conversations*, 1906-1914, London: Haus Publishing, 2014.

Padfield, Peter, *The Great Naval Race: Anglo-German Naval Rivalry 1900-1914*, London: Hart Davis, 1974.
Palazzo, Albert, *Seeking Victory on the Western Front, The British Army and Chemical Warfare in World War I*, Lincoln & London: University of Nebraska Press, 2000.
Philpott, William, *Bloody Victory, The Sacrifice on the Somme and the Making of the Twentieth Century*, London: Little, Brown, 2009.
Pope, Stephen, *The First Tank Crews, The Lives of the Tankmen Who Fought at the Battle of Flers-Courcelette*, 15 September 1916, Solihull: Helion, 2016.
Prior, Robin and Wilson, Trevor, *Command on the Western Front*, Oxford UK & Cambridge USA: Blackwell, 1992.
Prior, Robin and Wilson, Trevor, *The Somme*, New Haven & London: Yale University Press, 2005.

Radley, Kenneth, *Get Tough, Stay Tough, Shaping the Canadian Corps 1914-1918*, Wolverhampton Military Studies, Solihull: Helion, 2014.
Railway Companies Association, *St Paul's Cathedral Service in Memory of Railwaymen, In Memory of the Railwaymen of Great Britain and Ireland who have Died in the Service of their Country during the War, 1914-1919*, 1919.
Rawson, Andrew, *British Army Handbook 1914-1918*, Stroud: Sutton Publishing, 2006.
Richter, Donald, *Chemical Soldiers, British Gas Warfare in World War One*, Lawrence: University Press of Kansas, 1992.
Robbins, Simon, *British Generalship on the Western Front, Defeat into Victory*, London & Portland Oregon: Frank Cass, 2005.
Richards, Frank, DCM MM, *Old Soldiers Never Die*, London: Faber & Faber, 1933.
Roy, Kaushik (Ed.) *The Indian Army in the Two World Wars*, Leiden: Brill, 2011.
Ruger, Jan, *Great Naval Game, Britain and Germany in the Age of Empire*, Cambridge: Cambridge University Press, 2007.

Saunders, Anthony, *Dominating the Enemy, War in the Trenches, 1914-1918*, Stroud: Sutton Publishing, 2000.
Saunders, Anthony, *Reinventing Warfare, 1914-18, Novel Munitions and Tactics of Trench Warfare*, Continuum Studies in Military History, London & New York, Continuum, 2012.
Seligmann, Matthew, S, *Spies in Uniform, British and Naval Intelligence on the Eve of the First World War*, Oxford: Oxford University Press, 2006.
Seligmann, Matthew, S (Ed.) *Naval Intelligence from Germany, The Reports of the British Naval Attaches in Berlin, 1906-1914*, Aldershot: Ashgate (for the Naval Records Society) 2007.

Seligmann, S, *The Royal Navy and the German Threat, 1901-1914, Admiralty Plans to Protect British Trade in a War Against Germany*, Oxford: Oxford University Press, 2012.

Sheffield, Gary, *The Somme*, London: Cassell, 2003.

Sheffield, Gary and Todman, Dan (Eds.) *Command and Control on the Western Front, The British Army's Experience, 1914-1918*, Staplehurst: Spellmount, 2004.

Sheffield, Gary and Gray, Peter (Eds.) *Changing War, The British Army, The Hundred Days Campaign and the Birth of the Royal Air Force, 1918*, Birmingham War Studies, London: Bloomsbury, 2013.

Sheffield, Gary, *Command and Morale, The British Army on the Western Front, 1914-1918*, Barnsley: Pen & Sword, 2014.

Simkins, Peter, *From the Somme to Victory, The British Army's experience on the Western Front, 1916-1918*, Barnsley: Pen & Sword, 2014.

Simpson, Andy, *Directing Operations, British Corps Command on the Western Front, 1914-1918*, Stroud: Spellmount, 2006.

Snow, Dan and Pottle, Mark, *The Confusion of Command, The Memoirs of Lieutenant-General Sir Thomas D'Oyly 'Snowball' Snow, 1914 –1918*, London: Frontline Books, 2011.

Snyder, Jack, *The Ideology of the Offensive, Military Decision Making and the Disasters of 1914*, Ithaca & London: Cornell University Press, 1984.

Sondhaus, Lawrence, *The Great War at Sea, A Naval History of the First World War*, Cambridge: Cambridge University Press, 2014.

Spears, E L, Brigadier-General, CB CBE MC, *Liaison 1914, A Narrative of the Great Retreat*, London: William Heinemann, 1930.

Travers, Tim, *The Killing Ground, The British Army, The Western Front and the Emergence of Modern Warfare, 1900-1918*, London: Allen & Unwin, 1987.

Travers, Tim, *How The War Was Won, Command and Technology on the Western Front 1917-1918*, London & New York: Routledge, 1992.

West, Nigel (Ed.) *MI5 in the Great War*, London: Biteback Publishing, 2014.

Wilson, Trevor, *The Myriad Faces of War, Britain and the Great War, 1914-1918*, Cambridge: Polity Press, 1986.

Williamson, Samuel, R, *The Politics of Grand Strategy, Britain and France Prepare for War, 1904-1914*, Cambridge Massachusetts: Harvard University Press, 1969.

Woodward, David R, *Field-Marshal Sir William Robertson: Chief of the Imperial General Staff in the Great War*, Westport Connecticut & London: Praeger, 1998.

Zabecki, David T, *The German 1918 Offensives*, Abingdon: Routledge, 2006.

Zuber, Terence, *Inventing the Schlieffen Plan, German War Planning, 1871-1914*, Oxford: Oxford University Press, 2002.

Zuber, Terence, *The Mons Myth, A Reassessment of the Battle*, Stroud: The History Press, 2010.

Zuber, Terence, *The Real German War Plan, 1904-14*, Stroud: The History Press, 2011.

Books: Great War Logistics

Alexander, Heber Maitland, Major, DSO, *On Two Fronts, Being the Adventures of an Indian Mule Corps in France and Gallipoli*, London: William Heinemann, 1917.

Aves, William A T, *ROD, The Railway Operating Division on the Western Front on the Western Front, The Royal Engineers in France and Belgium, 1915-1919*, Donington: Shaun Tyas, 2009,

Beatson, A M, *The Motor-Bus in War, Being the Impressions of an ASC Officer during Two and a Half years on the Front*, London: T Fisher Unwin, 1918.

Brown, Ian Malcolm, *British Logistics on the Western Front, 1914-1919*, Westport Connecticut & London: Praeger, 1998.

Butler, Robert, *Richborough Port*, Ramsgate: Ramsgate Maritime Museum & East Kent Maritime Trust, 1999.

Clifton-Shelton, Alfred, *On the Road from Mons, With an Army Service Corps Train, By its Commander*, London: Hurst and Blackett, 1916.

Crowell, Benedict and Wilson, Robert Forrest, *How America Went to War, The Armies of Industry*, Volumes I & II, *Our Nation's Manufacture of Munitions for a World in Arms*, New Haven: Yale University Press, 1921.

Darroch, G R S, *Deeds of a Great Railway, A Record of the Enterprise and Achievements of the London and North Western Railway Company during the Great War*, London: John Murray, 1920.

Davies, W J K, *Light Railways of the First World War, A History of Tactical Rail Communications on the British Fronts, 1914-1918*, Newton Abbot: David & Charles 1967.

Dewar, George, A B, *The Great Munition Feat, 1914-1918*, London: Constable, 1921.

Dye, Peter, *The Bridge to Air Power: Logistics Support for Royal Flying Corps Operations on the Western Front, 1914-18*, Annapolis: Naval Institute Press, 2015.

Ellis, John, *Eye Deep in Hell, The Western Front, 1914-1918*, London: Purnell Book Services, 1976.

Fletcher, David, *British Military Transport, 1829-1956*, London: The Stationery Office, 1998.

Hamilton, J A B, *Britain's Railways in World War 1*, London: George Allen & Unwin Ltd, 1967.

Harrison, Mark, *The Medical War, British Military Medicine in the First World War*, Oxford: Oxford University Press, 2010.

Higgins, Jeremy, *Great War Railwaymen, Britain's Railway Company Workers at War 1914-1918*, London: Uniform Press, 2014.

Hooper, Colette, *Railways of the Great War*, London: Bantam Press, 2014.

Klein, Daryl, *With the Chinks, In the Chinese Labour Corps*, London: John Lane, 1919.

Lee, Janet, *War Girls, The First Aid Nursing Yeomanry in the First World War*, Manchester: Manchester University Press, 2005.

Marcosson, Issac F, *The Business of War*, London: John Lane, The Bodley Head, 1918.

Nicholson, W N, Colonel, CMG DSO, *Behind the Lines, An Account of Administrative Staff-work in the British Army, 1914-1918*, London: Jonathan Cape, 1939.

Ronald, David and Christensen, Mike, OBE *The Longmoor Military Railway, A New History*, Volume One: *1903-1939*, Lydney: Lightmoor Press, 2012.

Saint Paul's Cathedral Service in Memory of Railwaymen, 1919, reprinted by Naval & Military Press and the Imperial War Museum, nd.
Special War Transportation Number, London: The Railway Gazette, 21 September 1920.
Starling, John and Ivor, Lee, *No Labour, No Battle, Military Labour During the First World War*, Stroud: Spellmount, 2009.

Taylorson, Keith, *Narrow Gauge at War*, Brighton: Plateway Press, 1987.
Taylorson, Keith, *Narrow Gauge at War*, Volume 2, Brighton: Plateway Press, 1987.

Weeks, Alan, *Tea, Rum & Fags, Sustaining Tommy, 1914-1918*, Stroud: The History Press, 2009.
Winton, Graham, *Theirs Not to Reason Why, Horsing the British Army*, 1875-1925, Wolverhampton Military Studies, Solihull: Helion, 2013.

Young, Michael, *Army Service Corps, 1902-1918*, Institute of the Royal Army Service Corps and Royal Corps of Transport, London: Leo Cooper, 2000.

Zimmerman, Phyllis A, *The Neck of the Bottle, George W Goethals and the Reorganization of the US Army Supply System*, 1917-1918, College Station: Texas A & M University Press, 1992.

Books: General Logistics

Bowditch, M R and Hayward, L, *A Pictorial Record of the Royal Naval Cordite Factory, Holton Heath*, M R and L Hayward, Caversham: Finial Publishing, 1996.

Cocroft, Wayne D, *Dangerous Energy, The Archaeology of Gunpowder and Military Explosives Manufacture*, Swindon: English Heritage, 2000.

Evans, David, *Arming The Fleet, The Development of the Royal Ordnance Yards, 1770-1945*, Gosport: English Heritage, 2006.

Foxton, P D, *Powering War: Modern Land Force Logistics*, London: Brassey's, 1994.

Gropman, Alan, (Ed.) *The Big L, American Logistics in World War II*, Washington DC: National Defense University Press, 1997.

Levinson, Marc, *The Box: How the Shipping Container Made the World Smaller and the World Economy Bigger*, Princeton New Jersey: Princeton University Press, 2006.
Lynn, John A, *Feeding Mars, Logistics in Western Warfare from the Middle Ages to the Present*, Colorado: Westview Press, 1993.

Macksey, Kenneth, *For Want of a Nail, The Impact of Logistics and Communications*, London: Brassey's (UK) 1989.

Shaw G C, Brevet Lieutenant Colonel, *Supply in Modern War*, G C Shaw RAOC, London: Faber & Faber, nd but 1938.
Sinclair, Joseph, *Arteries of War, A History of Military Transportation, Military Transportation from Alexander the Great to the Falklands - and beyond*, Joseph Sinclair, Shrewsbury: Airlife, 1992.

Thompson, Julian, Major General (Retired) *The Lifeblood of War, Logistics in Armed Conflict*, London & Washington: Brassey's, 1991.
Tuttle, William G T, Jnr, *Defense Logistics for the 21st Century*, Annapolis: Naval Institute Press, 2005.

Van Creveld, Martin, *Logistics from Wallenstein to Patton*, Cambridge: Cambridge University Press, 1977.
Ventham, Philip and Fletcher, David, *Moving the Guns, The Mechanization of the Royal Artillery 1854-1939*, London: HMSO, 1990.

White, M S (Ed.) *Gulf Logistics*, Blackadder's War, London: Brassey's, 1995.
White, B T, *British Tanks and Fighting Vehicles, 1914-1945*, London: Ian Allan, 1970.

Books: Railways & Economics

Allen, Cecil, J, *The North Eastern Railway*, London: Ian Allan, 1964.

Bagwell, Philip, *The Railway Clearing House in the British Economy 1842-1922*, London: George Allen & Unwin, 1968.
Bagwell, Philip, *The Transport Revolution from 1770*, London: B T Batsford, 1974.
Barclay-Harvey KCMG, Sir Malcolm, *A History of the Great North of Scotland Railway*, 2nd Edition, London: The Locomotive Publishing Company, 1949.
Bartholomew, David, *The Midland & South Western Junction Railway*, Volume I, Upper Bucklebury: Wild Swan Publications, 1982.
British Railways Board, *The Reshaping of British Railways*, London: HMSO, 1963.

Casserley, H C (Ed.) *The Observer's Book of Railway Locomotives of Britain*, London: Frederick Warne & Co, 1955.
Christiansen, Rex, & Miller, R W, *The Cambrian Railways*, Volumes 1 & 2, Newton Abbot: David & Charles, 1967 & nd but 1968.
Conolly, W, Philip (Introduction) *Pre-Grouping Atlas and RCH Junction Diagrams*, Hersham: Ian Allan, 2014.
Coppin, Alan, *Oil on the Rails, The Story of an Industry and its Influence on Britain's Railways and its Rail Tank Wagons*, The Historical Model Railway Society, 1999.

Daniels, G and Dench, L, *Passengers No More*, Shepperton: Ian Allan, 1964.
Dow, George, *Great Central*, Volume Three, *Fay Sets The Pace*, 1900-1922, London: Ian Allan, 1965.

Earnshaw, Alan, *Britain's Railways at War*, Penryn: Atlantic, 1995.
Essery, R J, Rowland, D P, and Steel, W O, *British Goods Wagons, From 1887 to the Present Day*, Newton Abbot: David & Charles, 1970.
Essery, R J, *Illustrated History of Midland Wagons*, Sparkford: Oxford Publishing, 1980.

Fairman, J R, *Netley Hospital and its Railways*, Southampton: Kingfisher Railway Productions, 1984.

Gourvish, Terry and Anson, Mike, *The Official History of the Channel Tunnel*, London & New York: Routledge, 2006.

Gray, Adrian, MA, *South Eastern and Chatham Railways, A Marriage of Convenience*, Midhurst: Middleton Press, 1998.

Harman, Richard and Nichols, Gerry, *Atlas of the Southern Railway*, Addlestone: Ian Allan, 2016.

Irving, R J, *The North Eastern Railway Company, 1870-1914*, Leicester: Leicester University Press, 1976.

Klapper, Charles, *London's Lost Railways*, London: Routledge & Kegan Paul, 1976.

Kidner, R W, *The Mid-Wales Railway*, Oakwood Library of Railway History No 79, 2nd Edition, Usk: The Oakwood Press, 2003.

Mulley, A J, *Railway Ships at War, For the King's Service*, Easingwold: Pendragon, 2008.

Nock, O S, *The South Eastern & Chatham Railway*, London: Ian Allan, 1961.

Nock, O S, *British Locomotives of the 20th Century*, Volume I, 1900-1930, Wellingborough: Patrick Stephens, 1983.

Norris, John, Beale, Gerry and Lewis, John, *Edwardian Enterprise, GWR 1900-1910*, Didcot: Wild Swan Publications, 1987,

Plumridge, John, H, *Hospital Ships and Ambulance Trains*, London: Seeley Service, 1975.

Pratt, Edwin A, *The Rise of Rail-power in War and Conquest, 1833-1914*, London: P S King & Son, 1915.

Railway Gazette, *The Railway Year Book for 1913, The Whitaker of the Railway Service*, London: The Railway Publishing Company, 1913.

Ronald, D W & Carter, R J, *The Longmoor Military Railway*, Newton Abbot: David & Charles, 1974.

Ronald, David & Christensen, Mike, OBE, *The Longmoor Military Railway, A New History*, Volume One: *1903-1939*, Lydney: Lightmoor Press, 2012.

Rowland, *British Railway Wagons*, Newton Abbot: David & Charles, 1985.

Simmons, Jack, and Biddle Gordon (Eds.) *Oxford Companion to British Railway History*, Oxford & New York: Oxford University Press 1997.

Tomlinson, W W, *The North Eastern Railway, Its Rise and Development*, Newcastle-upon-Tyne: Andrew Reid & Co, 1914.

The Clearing House Official Handbook of Railway Stations, London: The Railway Clearing House, 1912.

Vallance, H A, *The Highland Railway, The History of the Railways of the Scottish Highlands*, Volume 2, 4th Edition, Newton Abbot: David & Charles, 1985.

Vallance H A, *The Great North of Scotland Railway, The History of the Railways of the Scottish Highlands*, Volume 3, 2nd Edition, Newton Abbot: David & Charles, 1989.

Wilson, Keith, *Channel Tunnel Visions, 1850-1945, Dreams and Nightmares*, London & Rio Grande, The Hambledon Press, 1994.

Wyatt, H, *The Motor Industry, Its Growth, Its Methods, Its Prospects, Its Products*, London: Sir Issac Pitman & Sons, 1917.

Books: General

Bonham-Carter, Victor, *Soldier True, The Life and Times of Field-Marshal Sir William Robertson*, London: Frederick Muller, 1963.

Chapman–Huston, Desmond, Major and Rutter, Owen, Major, *General Sir John Cowans, GCB GCMB, The Quartermaster–General of the Great War*, Volumes I & II, London: Hutchinson, 1924.

Childers, Erskine, *The Riddle of the Sands, A Record of Secret Service*, London: Smith Elder & Co, 1903.

Christopher, Andrew, *Defence of the Realm, The Authorised History of MI5*, Andrew Christopher, London: Allen Lane, 2009.

Cole, Captain, D H, MBE FRGS, *Imperial Military Geography, Characteristics of the Empire in Relation to Defence*, London: Praed, 1924.

Drummond, Maldwin, *The Riddle*, London: Nautical Books, 1985.

Eden, Philip, Philip Eden, *Great British Weather Disasters*, London: Continuum, 2008.

Fergusson, Thomas, G, *British Military Intelligence, The Development of a Modern Intelligence Organization*, London: Arms & Armour Press, 1989.

French, David, *British Economic and Strategic Planning, 1905-1915*, London: George Allen & Unwin, 1982.

French, David, *Military Identities, The Regimental System, the British Army and the British People c 1870-2000*, Oxford: Oxford University Press, 2005.

Fuller, J F C, Major-General, CB CBE DSO, *Memoirs of an Unconventional Soldier*, London: Nicholson and Watson, 1935.

Georgano, G N, *World War Two Military Vehicles (Transport and Half-Tracks)*, London: Osprey Automotive, 1994.

Hankey, The Lord, *The Supreme Command, 1914-1918*, London: George Allen & Unwin, Volumes One and Two, 1961.

Hobsbawn, E J, *Labouring Men, Studies in the History of Labour*, London: Weidenfeld & Nicolson, 1964.

Hogg, Ian, V, *Coast Defences of England and Wales, 1856-1956*, Newton Abbot: David & Charles, 1974.

Holmes, Richard, *The Little Field-Marshal*, Richard Holmes, London: Jonathan Cape, 1981.

Howard, Michael, *The Continental Commitment, The Dilemma of British Defence Policy in the Era of Two World Wars*, Michael Howard, London: Temple Smith, 1972.

Jeffery, Keith, *Field Marshal Sir Henry Wilson, A Political Soldier*, Keith Jeffery, Oxford: Oxford University Press, 2008.

Jomini, A H, *The Art of War*, Westport Connecticut: Greenwood Press, 1971, translated from the French and published in Brussels in 1838.

Keeble, S P, *The Ability to Manage: A Study of British Management 1890-1990*, Manchester: Manchester University Press, 1992.

Layton, C W T, *Dictionary of Nautical Words and Terms*, Glasgow: Brown, Son & Ferguson, 1955.

Le Queux, William, *The Invasion of 1910*, London: Everett & Company, 1906.

Le Queux, William, *Spies of the Kaiser, Plotting the Downfall of England*, William Le Queux, London: Hurst & Blackett, 1909.

Mason, Francis K, *The British Bomber since 1914*, London: Putnam, 1994.

Nicolson, Juliet, *The Perfect Summer, England 1911*, London: John Murray, 2006.

Parkes, Oscar, Dr, OBE AINA, *British Battleships, A History of Design, Construction and Armament*, London: Seeley Service, 1957.

Otte, T G, *July Crisis, The World's Descent into War, Summer 1914*, T G Otte, Cambridge: Cambridge University Press, 2014.

Perkins, Tuner (Ed.) *Channel Tunnel, Full Details of the Present Scheme* – Military, Engineering, Financial, (Ed.) Channel Tunnel Company Ltd, December 1913.

Reid, Brian Holden, *J F C Fuller: Military Thinker, Brian Holden Reid*, New York: Palgrave Macmillan, 1987.

Robertson, William, Field-Marshal, Sir, GCB GCMG KCVO DSO, *Private to Field-Marshal*, London: Constable, 1932.

Searle, G R, *A New England? Peace and War 1886-1918*, The New Oxford History of England, Oxford: Clarendon Press, 2004.

Steiner, Zara, S, and Neilson, Keith, *Britain and the Origins of the First World War*, 2nd Edition, New York: Palgrave, 2003.

Trythall, Anthony John, *"Boney" Fuller: Soldier, Strategist, and Writer*, New Brunswick: Rutgers University Press, 1977.

Wavell, Archibald, *Generals and Generalship: The Lees Knowles Lectures Delivered at Trinity College Cambridge in 1939*, London: Macmillan, 1941.

Whitaker's Red Book or Who's Who in Business 1914, London: J Whitaker & Sons, 1914.

Articles and Chapters

Anderson, E P, Lieutenant-Colonel DSO RE, 'The Railway Organization of an Army in War', *Journal of the Royal United Service Institution*, Volume LXXII, February - November 1927, pp.509-510.

Aylmer, G, Major, 'Indian Mule Transport in this War', *Journal of the United Service Institution of India*, Volume XLVI, 1917.

Bate, T R F, Brigadier-General, CMG, 'Horse Mobilisation', *Journal of the Royal United Service Institution*, Volume LXVII (465) February 1922, pp.16-23.

Bateman, Denis, C, 'Goodbye to Boots and Saddles, The Twilight of the British Cavalry', *British Army Review*, No 114, UK Ministry of Defence, December 1996, pp.75-89.

Battersby, Thomas Preston, Brigadier-General, 'The Army Ordnance Department and Corps', *The Army Review*, No 2, Vol. 2, April 1912, pp.428-443.

Beckett, Ian F W, 'Henry Rawlinson', Ian F W Beckett & Steven J Corvi (Eds.) *Haig's Generals*, Barnsley: Pen & Sword Military, 2006, pp.164-182.

Bonham-Smith, R, Captain, 'Railway Transport Arrangements in France', *Journal of the Royal United Service Institution*, Volume LXI, February 1916, pp.47-62.

Bourne, J M, 'Major-General Sir Archibald Murray, Chief of Staff, GHQ', in Spencer Jones (Ed.) *Stemming The Tide, Officers and Leadership in the British Expeditionary Force 1914*, Wolverhampton Military Studies (Solihull: Helion, 2013), pp.51-69.

Buchanan-Dunlop, C N, Brevet Major, RA, 'Ammunition Supply', *Journal of the Royal United Service Institution*, Volume LVII, January 1913, pp.87-92.

Burnett-Stuart, J, 'The Progress of Mechanisation', J, *Army Quarterly*, Volume XVI, April 1928, pp.30-51.

Burtchaell, C H, Lieutenant-Colonel, 'The Wounded in War'. *The Army Review*, Vol. II, No 2, War Office, April 1912, pp.417-427.

Butler, R P, Captain, 'Reminiscences of Salvage Work', *The Royal Tank Corps Journal*, 1932.

Carter, E E Lieutenant-Colonel, CMG MVO psc ASC, 'The New Transport System: its Principles and their Application', *Journal of the Army Service Corps*, May 1912, pp.671-707.

Carter, E E, Colonel, CMG MVO psc, 'The Services of Maintenance in the Field: Some Object Lessons from the Army Exercise 1913', *The Army Review*, Volume VI, No 2, April 1914, War Office, pp.471-489.

Connelly, Mark, 'Lieutenant-General Sir James Grierson', in *Stemming The Tide, Officers and Leadership in the British Expeditionary Force 1914*, Spencer Jones (Ed.) Wolverhampton Military Studies (Solihull: Helion, 2013), pp.133-150.

"Contact", Yorkshire Waggoners with the ASC, *Journal of the Royal Army Service Corps*, November 1935, pp.497-508.

Cooper, H, 'An Outline of the French System of Mechanical Transport', *Royal Army Service Corps Quarterly*, Volume 10, January 1922, pp.16-30.

Cuninghame, T A A M, Captain, Sir, Bart, DSO, Rifle Brigade, 'The Supply of a Division in the Field with Special Reference to the use of Mechanical Transport', *Journal of the Royal United Service Institution*, Volume LVI, January 1912, pp.9-36.

Crawshaw, Michael, 'The High Tide and the Turn', *British Army Review* No 145, UK Ministry of Defence, Autumn 2008, pp.67-78.

De Pree, Major H, RFA, 'The Supply of Ammunition and Motor Transport', *Journal of the Royal United Service Institution*, Volume LVI (414), August 1912, pp.1149-1164.

De Tarle, A, Captaine d'Artilleri, Brevete d'Etat Major, 'The British Army and a Continental War' (translated by Colonel H Wylly CB) *Journal of the Royal United Service Institution*, Volume LVII,

March 1913, pp.384-401.

Dockrill, M L, 'British Policy during the Agadir Crisis' in F H Hinsley (Ed.) *British Foreign Policy under Sir Edward Grey*, Cambridge: Cambridge University Press, 1977, pp.271-287.

Dye, Peter, 'The Contribution of Aviation Logistics', in Gary Sheffield and Peter Gray (Eds.) *Changing War, The British Army, The Hundred Days Campaign and the Birth of the Royal Air Force, 1918*, Birmingham War Studies, London: Bloomsbury, 2013, pp.171-190.

Findlay, G, Lieutenant Colonel, Sir, 'On the Use of Railways in the United Kingdom for the Conveyance of Troops', *United Service Magazine*, Volume CXXVII, April 1892, pp.37-49.

Fuller, J F C, Captain, 'Notes on the Entrainment of Troops To and From Manoeuvres', *The Army Review*, Volume VII, No 1, War Office, July 1914, pp.184-213.

Grieves, Keith, 'The Transportation Mission to GHQ', 1916, in *Look to Your Front, Studies in the First World War* by the British Commission for Military History, Staplehurst: Spellmount, 1999, pp.63-78.

Hamilton-Gordon, Major-General A, CB, 'Share of General Staff in Preparation for War at Army Headquarters in India', *The Army Review*, Volume VI, No 2, War Office, April 1914, pp.323-332.

Henniker, A M, Major, RE, 'Troop Movements by Rail in the United Kingdom', *The Army Review*, Volume VI, No 2, War Office, April 1914, pp.490-497.

Heys, Steven D, 'Abdominal wounds: Evolution of management and establishment of surgical treatments', *War Surgery, 1914-1918*, Thomas Scotland and Steven Heys (Eds.) Solihull: Helion, 2012, pp.178-211.

Heys, Steven D, 'Penetrating chest wounds and their management', *War Surgery, 1914-1918*, Thomas Scotland and Steven Heys (Eds.) Solihull: Helion, 2012, pp.212-233.

Holland, Robert, 'The British Empire and the Great War', 1914-1918, *The Oxford History of the British Empire*, Volume IV, *The Twentieth Century*, Judith M Brown PhD and Wm Roger Louis CBE D Litt FBA, (Eds.) Oxford & New York: Oxford University Press, 1999, pp.114-137.

Hussey, John, 'Without an Army, and Without any Preparation to Equip One, The Financial and Industrial Background to 1914', *British Army Review*, No 109, UK Ministry of Defence, April 1995, pp.76-84.

Hussey, John, 'Appointing the Staff College Commandant, A Case of Trickery, Negligence or Due Consideration', John Hussey, *British Army Review*, No 114, UK Ministry of Defence, December 1996, pp.99-105.

Keene, A, Colonel, DSO, 'Our Requirements for Home Defence', *The Army Review*, Volume III, No 1, War Office, July 1912, pp.1-18.

Kelly, R M B F, Brigadier-General, CB DSO, 'Coast Defence', *The Army Review*, Volume VI, No 2, War Office, April 1914, pp.508-531.

Kennedy, P M, 'The Development of German Naval Operational Plans against England', 1896-1914, *English Historical Review*, Volume 89, 1974, pp.51-55.

Lindsell, W G, Major (Temporary Lieutenant-Colonel) DSO OBE MC psc RA, 'Administrative Lessons of the Great War', *Journal of the Royal United Service Institution*, Volume LXXI, February 1926, pp.712-719.

Maginniss, C H, Lieutenant Colonel, 'Everybody's Trucking, The Expansion of the British Army's Logistic Vehicle Task Fleet 1938-1940', *Royal Logistic Corps Review*, Regimental Association of the Royal Logistic Corps, 1998, pp.64-71.

Maginniss, C H, Lieutenant Colonel, 'To the Garden of Eden, Lessons from the application of Logistic Support for Force D', October-December 1914, *Royal Logistic Corps Review*, Regimental Association of the Royal Logistic Corps, 1999, pp.77-86.

Maginniss, C H, Lieutenant Colonel, 'Tracks Across France, The role of railway operations in supporting the British Expeditionary Force in France in 1939-1940', *Royal Logistic Corps Review*, Regimental Association of the Royal Logistic Corps, 2013, pp.66-71.

Miller, Roger, G, 'The Logistics of the British Expeditionary Force, 4 August to 5 September 1914', *Journal of Military Affairs*, XLIII (3) October 1979, pp.133-138.

na, Lt-General Sir R Maxwell (QMG, BEF, France, Jan 1915 - Dec 1917), *Royal Army Service Corps Quarterly*, Volume 13, December 1924, pp.536-542.

na, *Movement Control Historical Society, MCHS 0076*, 'The Railway Transport Establishment of the Original Expeditionary Force, World War One', Movement Control Association, 2005.

Neilson, Keith, 'Great Britain', in Richard F Hamilton and Holger H Herwig (Eds.), *War Planning 1914*, Cambridge: Cambridge University Press, 2010, pp.175-197.

Parker, W M, Brevet Colonel, CMG DSO, 'Supply Services in Mesopotamia', *Royal Army Service Corps Quarterly*, April 1921, p.431.

Paul, G R C, Colonel, 'Notes on Recent Developments in Road Transport', *Army Service Corps Quarterly*, Volume 4, 1911, pp.535-551.

Phillips, Christopher, Logistics and the BEF: The Development of Waterborne Transport on the Western Front, 1914-1916, *British Journal of Military History*, Volume 2, No 2, 2016, pp.42-58.

Prytherch, H J, 'The Great Eastern Railway and the Army Manoeuvres in East Anglia - 1912', *Great Eastern Railway Magazine*, November 1912, pp.356-359.

Radcliffe, Percy, General Sir, KCB KCMG CB DSO, 'The WF Plan and the Genesis of the Western Front, A Previously Unpublished Account', *Stand To! The Journal of the Western Front Association*, No 10, Spring 1984, pp.6-13.

RHB, 'Sir John Cowans, The Greatest Quartermaster General', *Royal Army Service Corps Quarterly*, Vol. 13, April 1925, pp.189-197.

Rothwell, J S, Colonel, 'The Conveyance of Troops by Railway', *Royal United Service Magazine*, Volume CXXVII, December 1891, pp.215-221.

Schimdt, Stefan, 'French Plan XVII' in *The Schlieffen Plan, International Perspectives on the German Strategy for World War I*, Hans Ehlert, Michael Epkenhans & Gerhard P Cross (Eds.) (Kentucky: University Press of Kentucky, 2014), pp.209-246.

Sewell, J W S, Lieutenant-Colonel, 'The Supply of Bulk Stores in War', The *RE Journal*, 35 (1922).

Shaw, Diana, 'The Forgotten Army of Women: The Overseas Service of Queen Mary's Army Auxiliary Corps with the British Forces', 1917-1921, *Facing Armageddon, The First World War Experienced*, Hugh Cecil and Peter H Liddle (Eds.) London: Leo Cooper, 1996, pp.365-379.

Sparking Plug, 'A Divisional Train of the Future', *Royal Army Service Corps Quarterly*, Volume 8, April 1920.

Strachan, Hew 'The British Army, Its General Staff, and the Continental Commitment, 1904-1914', *The Schlieffen Plan, International Perspectives on the German Strategy for World War I*, Hans Ehlert, Michael Epkenhans & Gerhard P Cross (Eds.) (Kentucky: University Press of Kentucky, 2014), pp.293-317.

Spencer, John, 'The Big Brain in the Army', Sir William Robertson as Quartermaster-General, *Stemming The Tide, Officers and Leadership in the British Expeditionary Force 1914*, Spencer Jones (Ed.) Solihull: Helion, 2013, pp 89-107.

Taylor, M G, Colonel, CMG, DSO, 'Land Transportation in the Late War', *Journal of the Royal United Service Institution*, Volume LXVI, November 1921, pp.699-720.

Thompson, Rob, 'Delivering the Goods, Operation Landovery Castle: A Logistical and Administrative Analysis of Canadian Corps Preparations for the Battle of Amiens 8-11 August 1918', in Gary Sheffield and Peter Gray (Eds.), *Changing War, The British Army, The Hundred Days Campaign and the Birth of the Royal Air Force, 1918*, Birmingham War Studies, London: Bloomsbury, 2013, pp.37-54.

Todd, Major A G, Army Veterinary Corps 'The Management of Horses on Board Ship', *The Army Review*, Volume VII, No 4, War Office, October 1914, pp.413-425.

Todman, Dan, 'The Grand Lamasery revisited: General Headquarters on the Western Front', *Command and Control on the Western Front, The British Army's Experience 1914-18*, Gary Sheffield and Dan Todman (Eds.) Staplehurst: Spellmount, 2004, pp.39-70.

'Transport of an Army', *Great Western Railway Magazine*, Volume XXI, November 1909, p.257.

Turner, J, 'Experts and interests; David Lloyd George and the dilemmas of the expanding state, 1906-1919' in *Government and Expertise: Specialists, Administrators and Professionals, 1860-1919*, R MacLeod, Cambridge: Cambridge University Press, 1988.

Van Creveld, Martin, 'World War I and the Revolution in Logistics', in Roger Chickering and Stig Forster (Editors), *Great War, Total War, Combat and Mobilization on the Western Front, 1914-1918*, German Historical Institute, Washington DC: Cambridge University Press, 2000, pp.57-72.

Van Vleck, Va Nee, L, 'Delivering Coal by Road and Rail in Britain: The Efficiency of the "Silly Little Bobtailed" Coal Wagons', *The Journal of Economic History*, Volume 57, March 1997, pp.139-160.

White, O W, Brevet Major, Major, DSO, Dorsetshire Regiment, 'The Abolition of Horse Transport in the Administrative Services', *Journal of the Royal United Service Institute*, Volume LXVI (461) February 1921, pp.553-582.

Theses and Dissertations

Clarke, Geoff, 'Supplying The Battlefront: British Frontline Transport in Mobile Warfare 1918', Unpublished MA dissertation, Birmingham: University of Birmingham, 2006.

Phillips, Christopher, 'A Modern Industrial Organization: A Case Study of Fourth Army during the battles of the Hundred Days', Unpublished MA dissertation, Birmingham: University of Birmingham, 2009.

Index

Note: some terms, for example, GHQ, spares, dumps and labour, which appear frequently throughout the text have been omitted from the index unless they are linked to a specific reference.

People

Places

Formations & Units

Expeditionary Force:

Armies:

Corps:

Divisions:

Brigades:

Cavalry & Yeomanry Regiments:

British Infantry Battalions:

Indian Infantry Battalions:

Other Combat and Combat Support units:

Logistic & Engineer units:

Military & Air

Naval

Logistics

Government & Commercial

Commercial Railways

Wars & Battles